A BROKEN REGIMENT

D1714840

Conflicting Worlds: New Dimensions of the American Civil War

T. MICHAEL PARRISH, *Series Editor*

A BROKEN REGIMENT

THE 16TH CONNECTICUT'S
CIVIL WAR

LESLEY J. GORDON

LOUISIANA STATE UNIVERSITY PRESS)|(BATON ROUGE

Published with the assistance of the V. Ray Cardozier Fund

Published by Louisiana State University Press
Copyright © 2014 by Louisiana State University Press
All rights reserved
Manufactured in the United States of America
Louisiana Paperback Edition, 2018

All maps by Mary Lee Eggart

DESIGNER: *Mandy McDonald Scallan*
TYPEFACE: *Whitman*

Library of Congress Cataloging-in-Publication Data
Gordon, Lesley J. (Lesley Jill)
  A broken regiment : the 16th Connecticut's Civil War /
Lesley J. Gordon.
     pages cm. — (Conflicting words: new dimensions of the
American Civil War)
  Includes bibliographical references and index.
   ISBN 978-0-8071-5730-5 (cloth : alk. paper) — ISBN 978-
0-8071-5731-2 (pdf) — ISBN 978-0-8071-5732-9 (epub) 1.
United States. Army. Connecticut Infantry Regiment, 16th
(1862–1865) 2. United States—History—Civil War, 1861–
1865—Regimental histories. 3. Connecticut—History—Civil
War, 1861–1865—Regimental histories. 4. Soldiers—Con-
necticut—Biography. I. Title.
  E499.516th .G66 2015
  973.7'446—dc23

                                              2014011004

  ISBN 978-0-8071-6924-7 (pbk. : alk. paper)

The paper in this book meets the guidelines for permanence
and durability of the Committee on Production Guidelines
for Book Longevity of the Council on Library Resources.♾

For my children,
Colin and Caitlyn

CONTENTS

ILLUSTRATIONS

ACKNOWLEDGMENTS

I first began this project in December 1996, thinking it would be a short article. Since that time, I have accumulated a considerable debt of gratitude to the many archivists and librarians who aided me with my research. I owe a special thank you to the outstanding past and present staff at the Connecticut State Library and Connecticut Historical Society, including Mark Jones, Bruce Stark, Mel Smith, Richard Roberts, Dean Nelson, Bonnie Linck, Christine Pittsley, Paul Baran, and Kelly Nolin. Nora Howard of the Avon Historical Society, Carol Laun of the Salmon Brook Historical Society, Betty Guinan from the East Granby Historical Society, Lawrence S. Carleton from the Canton Historical Society, and Stephen E. Simon of the Simsbury Historical Society helped me immensely with town and local histories. Harry L. Thompson, curator of Port O' Plymouth Museum in Plymouth, North Carolina, was equally generous with his time and expertise. Michael T. Meier, formerly at the National Archives, was a valuable ally and friend in Washington, D.C. The staff of the library and archives at the Military History Institute at the Army War College in Harrisburg, Pennsylvania, and the Friends of Andersonville National Historic Site in Georgia also provided me with important materials. Ted Alexander at the Antietam National Battlefield Park in Maryland opened up a treasure trove of files to me during an unannounced visit several years ago. And I thank the patient staff at the University of Akron's Bierce Library, Ohio, particularly those in the interlibrary loan office, who diligently hunted down numerous articles, books, and newspapers for me.

A number of individuals kindly shared their private collections, personal knowledge, and valuable research related to the 16th Connecticut: Pat Holland, Edward Reller, Cliff Alderman, Shirley McLellan, Alice Collins, Thomas Lowry, and James Burton. Scott Holmes did yeomen work accumulating information on the 16th Connecticut and assisting me with my every request. George Deutsch introduced me to Deac Manross, who generously shipped to me an entire folder of materials full of information on Captain Newton Manross and the 16th Connecticut.

Several fellow historians read, critiqued, and contributed ideas to this manuscript. These include Gary Gallagher, Glenn Robins, George Rable, Richard McMurry, Paul Cimbala, William Blair, Scott Nelson, J. Matthew Gallman, Peter Carmichael, Dana Shoaf, James Marten, Steve Berry, and Matthew Warshauer. Kevin Adams and Brian Miller, my editorial teammates at *Civil War History,* graciously agreed to read a draft of the manuscript when I urgently needed outside advice. A special thanks to Susannah Ural, Anne Sarah Rubin, and Dan Sutherland for their willingness to read portions of the manuscript as well. I also thank John Inscoe for his mentoring, friendship, and support of me over many years. Michael Fellman died just as I was finishing this manuscript. I wish he could have seen the final product.

T. Michael Parrish, series editor at LSU Press, was enthused from the start about this book. He read several drafts, offered advice, and suggested important works that I incorporate. I thank him for his amazing patience and can only hope that this book was worth the wait. Sylvia Frank Rodrigue, formerly at LSU Press, was also one of my early advocates. She has moved on to a different press but remains a good friend, and I thank her too for her faith in me when this project was merely an idea. As the manuscript moved to final publication, I've been pleased to work with Rand Dodson, Lee Campbell Sioles, Neal Novak, and Jennifer Keegan at LSU Press, and copyeditor Julia Smith.

Graduate students at Murray State University, the University of Akron, the University of Georgia, and Central Connecticut State University hunted down sources, scanned newspapers, and previewed maps. These include Carolyn Starr Stephen, Steve Nash, Jennifer Harrold, Angela Zombek, Steve Noble, Barbara Wittman, and Angela Riotto.

I also appreciated the opportunity to share my research and ideas with students and faculty at Beloit College, the College of William and Mary, Columbus State University, Gettysburg College, Marquette University, Pennsylvania State University, SUNY-Oswego, Texas Christian University, the University of Georgia, West Virginia University, and Youngstown State University, and at Civil War Roundtables in Ohio, Pennsylvania, and Arizona, as well as Civil War conferences at Mount Alto, Pennsylvania, and Middleburg, Virginia.

At the University of Akron, I've had wonderful departmental support. I especially thank Stephen Harp, Constance Bouchard, Martin Wainwright, Janet Klein, Martha Santos, and Shelley Baranowski. I gained greatly from two faculty research grants from the University of Akron during the summers of 1999 and

2006. I thank Jan Yoder, too, in Akron's Psychology Department, for her early help with this project.

I also thank my family, including my cousins Alan and Linda Skulsky, who provided food and lodging so I could camp out near the Army War College in Carlisle, Pennsylvania. My parents, Bob and Fran Gordon, have always given me unconditional support and love. I thank my husband John for keeping our young children occupied as I stole away precious hours to work. He is a talented editor, and he read drafts of the manuscript that improved my writing considerably.

Our children Colin and Caitlyn were born in the midst of my researching and writing this book. They are now old enough to ask thoughtful questions about my work and act as two of my greatest supporters. I can only hope that one day they will forgive me for the time it has taken me away from them to complete it.

A BROKEN REGIMENT

INTRODUCTION

———— ∙◈∙ ————

"Clear My Name"

With both "pleasure and pain," William B. Turner reflected on the fateful day in July 1862 when he enlisted as a private in the 16th Regiment Connecticut Volunteer Infantry. "I was among the first to enroll my name in Co. A under Capt. Pasco," Turner wrote comrade George Q. Whitney in 1900, "and I venture to say there was not a prouder man in the regiment than I when the grand old 16th Conn. Volunteers of long ago, the flower of the City all equipped for war, marched through the streets of Hartford to the strains of martial music." Turner added, "I think I am safe in asserting that there was not a regiment that entered the service in those troublous times that was rushed into action with greater haste than the 16th Conn."[1]

Indeed, the 16th Connecticut was heralded as the "flower of the City" in the summer of 1862 when Turner, a twenty-year-old, white, native-born, unmarried gunsmith, enlisted in Hartford. More than three weeks later, the 16th Connecticut while facing their baptism of fire at the Battle of Antietam, panicked and fled from the field. A Rhode Island commander described his own unit faltering in the wake of the 16th's dramatic collapse: "That they finally broke, under such a severe fire, and the pressure of a broken regiment is not surprising, although much to be regretted."[2] Turner, caught in the frenzied retreat, was captured and paroled. He admitted to Whitney, however, that he then deserted: "I became homesick and despondent and was easily influenced into committing the act which I have regretted all of my after life. In company with two comrades, after receiving our pay (which was the first for me since entering the Service) we started for home without leave." Turner made his way to his sister's home in New Jersey and from there to England, where he remained until the war ended.[3]

Decades later, many members of the unit would recall those seemingly innocent weeks of the regiment's founding and dwell on the great promise the 16th had held for the state. After Antietam, the "broken" 16th C.V. spent months languishing in garrison duty and participating in scattered skirmishing. In April 1864, nearly the entire regiment was captured and sent to Andersonville. More than one-third of their members perished in prison. Scores more came home physically and emotionally broken and scarred from the trials of war and imprisonment.

Turner was writing Whitney, the secretary of the regiment's veterans, asking for help in obtaining an "honorable discharge from the army." "I do not desire it for any pecuniary aid," he affirmed, "or benefit of any kind, but to clear my name that it may not be handed down to my posterity with the stigma of 'deserter' attached to it."[4] Survivors like Turner sought to "clear the name" individually and as a group in order to ensure that their service—though often ambiguous and failing to fit within a conventional narrative of white middle-class masculine heroism—would still be celebrated and commemorated. They wanted an unambiguous story told and remembered about themselves and their regiment that would be free of anything embarrassing, unmanly, or dishonorable and that would endure for generations. They wanted to be whole again.

THE REGIMENTAL HISTORY

Celebrating their regiment was something familiar and comfortable for most Civil War veterans to do. Regimental histories, some of the very first recorded histories of the war, were often intended for a specific and small audience: members of the regiment. Veterans sought to share their experiences with each other, aware that what had happened to them was worth remembering. Since these men wrote their own accounts, most were either unable or unwilling to turn a critical eye on their past. Both Confederate and Union soldiers filled volumes, noting the particular role their unit played in the war, downplaying failures and dissension, and highlighting sacrifice and camaraderie, while paying little attention to the war's larger context. The higher the casualties, the more proudly heroic the regiment's claim.[5]

Later authors of regimental histories generally followed the veterans' lead. Composing thick condensed chronicles, authors followed a familiar template: the soldiers settle into camp, engage in combat, become battle-worn veterans, and return to civilian life. Upon coming home, they assimilate, rather inconspicuously, into postwar life. The regiment's home communities and families are largely nonexistent in these accounts, as are the postwar lives of the participants.[6]

These men were doing what historians, novelists, and poets have done for centuries when it comes to writing about war: creating, as Drew Faust has explained, order out of chaos. Soldiers took the most exciting, though also painful and troubling, times in their lives and made them meaningful. War stories, which is what regimental histories inherently are, repeated, refined, mythologized, and sanitized but rarely questioned. First recounted by veterans, then by respectful Americans, they became a central tenet of the historical record.[7]

Yet, most academic historians have been reluctant to write or even consult regimental histories, dismissing them as simple chronicles of past service or embellished anecdotes. The regimental history is perhaps the last genre of Civil War military history that has not undergone any sort of resurgence or reinvention. Historian William Blair once referred to regimental histories as "unmitigated trash—the worst example of municipal chauvinism; used more often for self-promotion or [the] glorification of ancestors." He complained that regimentals were "locked into standard battle narratives that tell [us] nothing new."[8]

It is my contention, though, that regimental histories remain important for the study of the Civil War if only because the infantry regiment was a basic "building block" of the armies and an essential source of identity for most Civil War soldiers. Enlisted men on both sides frequently felt strong affiliation to their nation and state, but most importantly, they felt a deep bond to their specific regiment that reflected communal ties and personal relationships. Most volunteers served alongside friends, family, and local leaders. In battle, on marches, and in camp, the regiment gave men a consistent sense of place, purpose, and "martial masculine" identity, despite the afflictions and dangers of war.[9]

The regimental history as a genre or as a form of storytelling can be an especially fruitful way of thinking about and exploring war and its lasting impact. The familiar narrative *is* there, just as it is there for biographers, so that readers know the basic plot line. Yet, there are unique twists and turns to each particular regiment's story, and perhaps it is time for a new look at this type of history writing. And writing a regimental history about a unit that failed and faltered, rather than succeeded and triumphed, allows us to do what Edward Ayers challenged historians to do some fifteen years ago: offer an alternative to the still dominant celebratory narrative.[10]

A MICROHISTORY

This book, then, is not meant to be a traditional regimental history or an exhaustive chronicle of the 16th Connecticut. It is more a "microhistory" of a group of nineteenth-century individuals thrown together by war and crisis, grappling over questions of military service, manhood, emancipation, race, cowardice, heroism, and the war's larger meaning.[11] Traditional regimental histories usually have a "top-down" approach, focusing on the unit's leaders and celebrating the regiment's best-known battles or campaigns. Here, I examine history from the perspective of the enlisted and commissioned ranks. Certainly, the question of leadership was a significant one for the 16th Connecticut, especially after their first battle at Antietam, where the regiment lost a considerable number of its commissioned (particularly junior) officers due to death, wounds, illness, and resignations.[12] Yet, the full panorama of experience as chronicled from top to bottom reveals a depth and diversity of perspective and opinion.

In any event, this study attempts to be a biography of a whole unit. Chapters one through eight seek to lay out for the reader the regiment's history—its birth, maturation, challenges, and end of service. The last chapter examines the memorialized and celebratory postwar account that the veterans sought to promote but that became mostly forgotten. There are tensions between my narrative and the individual stories told, publically and privately, by the soldiers themselves. I freely use the rich, expressive words of common soldiers as a way of describing the broader attitudes within the regiment. It should be noted, though, that within an organization that at one time counted more than one thousand soldiers, there were always conflicting attitudes and reactions on any given day. Historians routinely use a handful of sources to explicate ideas about broader events from a relatively small sampling. In the case of the 16th Connecticut, the men believed that their regiment had a recognizable personality and reputation, and the conviction that they were an unlucky and unfairly maligned regiment was established early in their war experience. As veterans, they believed that their own identities could be defined as unique because they had been members of the 16th Connecticut. In many ways their experiences were not unusual at all; most Civil War regiments endured difficult times. Still, because these Connecticut soldiers believed that they suffered more than most and because they strove to make their unconventional experiences fit a preconceived notion of what that service *should* be like, they clung to a specific narrative about themselves, which was often only loosely based on their actual military service.[13]

A central theme of their experience is their movement toward self-awareness. A well-worn idea among military historians is that Civil War volunteers were "citizen-soldiers" who struggled but ultimately made the transition from their peacetime identities as free and independent citizens to something different and new due to the experience of war. Scholars such as Gerald Linderman, James Marten, and Frances Clarke describe in varying ways how veterans sought to adapt to the challenges of readjustment. But by probing veterans' expressed attitudes and words, we see a less linear transition. These Connecticut men clung stubbornly to their prewar attitudes and behaviors; they bristled at military codes of conduct, discipline, and drill. They resented their officers and threatened mutiny on more than one occasion when they believed they had been treated unfairly. In January 1864, when ordered to leave comfortable (and relatively safe) quarters in Portsmouth, Virginia, they balked and burned it to the ground. It would take the jarring and stark experience of imprisonment to finally convince the regiment that, indeed, they were stripped of their individual will and entirely at the mercy of the enemy. Then they yearned to return to the battlefield.

THE SOLDIER VERSUS THE REGIMENT

While this book focuses on a handful of specific individuals in the unit, I have tried to avoid making this a set of shared biographies of men who happened to serve together. Thus, instead of tracing an individual's experience during the war, I explore the common experience of the regiment from start to end, blending in a variety of voices at each point of this shared narrative. Throughout, I seek to present not just the individual experiences but also the shared ones, in order that this study demonstrates something broader about the lives of everyday Civil War soldiers. Recent scholarship has enabled us to understand the diverse experiences of Confederate soldiers. I hope this book adds to an appreciation of the varied experiences northern soldiers underwent as well.[14]

With that said, this study does pursue the stories of specific individuals as far as the existing historical record leads. To be clear, this is not meant to be a study of every soldier who served in the unit, nor is it meant to follow their lives from birth to death. My main concern has been to portray how the war shaped them and their postwar lives. Occasionally, an individual makes only a brief appearance and disappears from the narrative, but, by and large, I've chosen a limited but representative group of men to tell the story of how the regiment fared during the war and afterward.[15]

By tracking a group of soldiers affiliated with a single regiment, especially one that did not gain attention as a "fighting" unit, we can gain a fresh look at soldier motivation. Some never wavered in their core belief that the war was honorable and right; others became cynical and disillusioned. Still others were shaken by the violence and become anxious and overly concerned with order and authority. The war robbed several of their health and vitality, even if they were not thrown directly into battle. Much of the recent scholarship on soldiers has centered on men motivated by a mixture of ideology and pragmatism who experienced hard and active combat.[16]

The book may seem on the surface to be solely the soldiers' story, but it also seeks to tell a broader tale that includes civilian spouses, parents, and friends, bridging the gap between home front and battlefront. It tries to see how the regiment's poor performance in battle and long incarceration affected their Connecticut communities. Additionally, in what sense did soldiers such as these align the hard reality of their hapless wartime service with the lofty ideals and high expectations of Victorian America? Over the past twenty years, historians have largely removed the artificial barrier that once separated soldiers from civilians in scholarly studies of the war.[17] Much of the correspondence utilized here was addressed to family members, often females, and it is important to acknowledge that fact. Women played an important role, even if at times they appeared to be away from the spotlight. They visited camps and hospitals, wrote letters to the local newspapers and to military and political officials, including the governor, and were active in postwar commemorative events. There existed a nearly constant dialogue between civilians and soldiers, with each side desperate for information from the other and grappling with the way this bloody war unfolded. Civilians felt cut off and frustrated; they wrote not only their soldiers and the local press but also government and military officials for answers, frequently without success. Soldiers chided their families and friends at home, but they also wrote poignant letters that spoke not purely of disillusion and alienation, as some historians have suggested; these soldiers worried that they were being forgotten by those at home and somehow taken for granted by those in power. This fear would fester throughout their service and into the postwar years.[18]

THE METHODOLOGY

I am interested in the construction of stories and histories, especially how and why soldiers tell them to each other and why some endure while others vanish. In seeking to bridge the gap between the home front and the battlefront, I relied heavily on the three local partisan newspapers: the Democratic *Hartford Daily Times,* the conservative Republican *Hartford Daily Courant,* and the Radical Republican *Hartford Evening Press.* Editors selected soldiers' letters to promote their own positions on various issues, and thus these newspapers also provide a window into the contested political landscape of the state. Wartime governor William Buckingham was a Republican, but the Democrats had a strong presence, and the regiment expressed sympathies with both parties. Buckingham's papers are also an important source for understanding the home front and revealing political tensions, particularly during the regiment's long internment at Andersonville, when desperate family and friends turned to the governor for help.

One of the most significant sources for this book is the George Q. Whitney Collection at the Connecticut State Library. Whitney, who served as a private in the 16th C.V., collected a massive amount of materials on the unit and tried to write individual biographies of every single member. Assisted by Ira Forbes, Whitney never completed his project, but his laborious efforts to record and commemorate every member of the 16th Connecticut's service were remarkable.

A scattering of diaries, especially prison diaries, helps illuminate the experience of incarceration. In a few cases, such as that of Robert H. Kellogg, both wartime letters and diaries survived. Diaries usually served different purposes than letters, and their inclusion allows the historian an added means of exploration into soldiers' thoughts. It is not always clear who the diary's intended reader was. In the case of Robert Kellogg, he wrote regularly to his parents and apparently assumed that they might eventually read his diary too. He wrote his father in early November 1862, "I keep a diary and keep it regularly and if I live it will be of some interest to you when I come back."[19] Oliver Gates had a few reasons for keeping his prison diary. The final entry in his first volume stated, "Now I have almost used up my ink and also this little Book but I have yet another and I shall try to get some ink for I mean to have something to remember this place by."[20] Midway through his second volume, as he endured his extended captivity, he wrote, "Here we can get nothing to counteract the Scurvy or cure the Diarrhea but I am complaining as though I was talking to myself. Well it is about the same for I do not intend this for a journal or for any one else to see unless my wife should wish to read it over if I should be so fortunate to get home." If any Confederate "should get it," Gates continued ruefully, "and should happen to be intelligent enough to read it (although there requires some skill to do that I must admit) he may find some facts registered and thoughts expressed that will reflect anything but honor upon the cause for which they fight or upon the leaders of the so called government."[21] Years later, Gates dismissed his diaries as having no "literary value." His only son valued them "as something that his mother prized." Gates explained in retrospect, "My only object in writing them was with the hope that she might somehow get them if I should *stay* South indefinitely."[22] Ira Forbes, who also dutifully kept a diary while imprisoned, reflected on its significance. For Forbes, his diary's value, at least originally, was extremely personal: "Today I have been reading my diary. I value that little book very highly, and though its intrinsic worth may be small, yet it is quite refreshing to read it."[23] Later, after the war, Forbes appreciated its value to others, and he donated it, in transcribed form, to his alma mater, Yale University.

Letters are also important to this study, both those from the war and after. I tried to be sensitive to the author, audience, and intent of these letters, realizing that such texts are to be carefully interpreted and placed within their proper context. Government and military documents round out my primary sources. Secondary sources help to test, contextualize, and bolster my conclusions.

I am acutely aware of the differences among diaries, letters, unpublished memoirs, and published accounts. But one of the purposes of this study is to reconstruct the story of a regiment and, at the same time, reflect on how the members of that regiment sought to create their own version of that story. As such, I incorporated *all* kinds of narratives, published and unpublished, wartime and postwar. Together, they provide varying versions and fragments of the soldiers' experience and varying ways of telling their story, even some sources that appear fabricated or less than factual to modern eyes.

Memory also plays a central role in this book. I became fascinated not just in the postwar memory of these New England veterans—a separate topic not yet fully explored by historians who have delved broadly into Civil War memory—but also in their individual private and collective public memories during the war itself.[24] Historian Gerald Linderman once theorized that there was a postwar "incubation" period during which veterans, saturated with war and death and alienated from civilians expecting to hear sanitized tales of glamorous combat, refused at first to discuss the war. When they finally did, they selectively chose what they remembered. "Survival," Linderman writes, "became a source of pride."[25]

However, the war experience of the 16th Connecticut shows a complex and even convoluted process of memory, with the "true" narrative of what happened and how it was remembered complicated both during the war and in the decades after. There was ebb and flow but no real "incubation" period. Instead, in the aftermath of the war and Union victory, survivors of the 16th Connecticut struggled privately and publicly to come to terms with the suffering that had deep emotional consequences for them well into the postwar period. Specific stories about their individual experiences were repeated; variations or challenges to this collective memory of the unit were smoothed over or largely silenced. An oversimplified, more heroic, and in many ways more conventional account was left in its place. Still, some aspects of their original war story remained, including a distinctive identity forged during the conflict itself.[26] It was not simply a matter of sifting and separating their individual or collective "memory" from the "true" history of the conflict. Instead, there is often tension between the verifiable lived historical events and the sometimes largely fabricated versions of the same occurrence. I am interested in both manifestations but especially in uncovering the reasons why these soldiers chose to commemorate a different past than the one they experienced.[27]

By focusing on the war experience of a single northern regiment, we can track change over time, whether it was in motivations to fight, attitudes toward emancipation, regimental identity, and, especially, the process of collective memory making. It is a fascinating progression and infrequently undertaken by historians, who often cherry-pick quotes from individual soldier's sources in order to support their theses.[28] Here, the sustained focus is upon a small group of men from the same state who enlisted together and endured a life-changing and, in many cases, life-ending experience. While their postwar narrative accentuated mostly the positive, little of their war record showed much unity or self-sacrifice. There are multiple examples of men in the regiment faltering, disappointing, and failing, although certainly a few excelled and succeeded. Many more simply survived. Throughout, members self-consciously honed, through words, monuments, commemorative activities, and careful record keeping, a portrait of themselves, a portrait they hoped would survive beyond their own lives. Ultimately, even that portrayal faded into the past.

1

Camp Williams
"The Best Class of Volunteers"

When the 16th Connecticut formed during the summer of 1862, hometown expectations soared. Its members, many of them more boys than men, more citizens than soldiers, began to learn the rudiments of military life. The arrival of their colonel, the harsh and humorless West Pointer Frank Beach, was a harbinger of the stark realities that would soon await them when they were hurriedly rushed to the front just three weeks after their formal mustering into the U.S. Army.

"AROUSE THE BRAVE"

By midsummer of 1862, Abraham Lincoln's war for the Union was more than a year old, and he desperately needed more troops. George McClellan's Peninsula Campaign in Virginia had ended in a relative stalemate, and in the west, although significant strategic gains had been made, the Confederates showed no sign of abandoning their quest for independence. On July 1, 1862, Lincoln issued a call for 300,000 volunteers, and two days later Connecticut's governor William Buckingham added his own exhortation: "Close your manufactories and work shops, turn aside from your farms and homes, meet face to face the enemies of your liberties."[1] Likewise, affirmed the state senate, "the state of Connecticut . . . will stand by the Old Flag, and will furnish all the men and money required of her to put down this infamous rebellion."[2] The state had raised 15,000 soldiers to fight in the war when the conflict began over a year earlier, but many of these men had joined three-month regiments and their enlistments had already expired.[3] Now, more than 7,000 additional men were required to fill the state's quota, and there were worries that the number could not be met. Governor Buckingham ordered the formation of six new regiments, including the creation of the 16th Regiment Connecticut Volunteers, one of two raised in Hartford County.[4]

The war had proven divisive for Connecticut. During the antebellum era, the state had endured a brief stint of "Know Nothing" control but had returned to a two-party system by 1860, with Republicans holding onto the governor's seat throughout the conflict.[5] By 1862, there remained powerful Democratic elements, including the outspoken *Hartford Daily Times*, which openly challenged the Republicans and Lincoln's war, particularly with the announcement of the Emancipation Proclamation, not long after Lincoln's call for more troops. To be sure, Connecticut had easily met its military quotas in 1861, filling three separate three-month regiments, but now, with six new regiments, it seemed harder to draw men from their farms and businesses to a war that clearly was not going to end in a few months or even, perhaps, years.[6] Nor was the city of Hartford dominated by Republican voters. Politically, Hartford and New Haven, the state's two capitals, remained decidedly Democratic cities throughout the conflict.[7]

Yet, by that summer of 1862, it would be difficult to go anywhere in Hartford County and avoid the excited talk of volunteering. The cities and towns of Hartford County held "war meetings," with rousing speakers and pleas for volunteers.[8] One Hartford resident, observing the martial fervor, remarked on August 6, 1862, "For the first time since the war commenced has there been anything like excitement in this usually quiet place. Now it seems as if the very devil is let loose."[9] Recruitment posters appeared throughout the city and county exhorting men to join. "Attention Patriots!" one recruitment ad for Company A declared, "Your country calls on you to come forward and deal a final blow to this foul rebellion. The possibility of foreign interference, in order to crush our free institutions should fire every heart and arouse the brave to one more overwhelming rally to our standard at this trying hour."[10]

If nothing else "aroused the brave" to enlist, there were bounties. Men "shopped around" from town to town to find the best bounty offer before enlisting.[11] By late July, the towns of Simsbury, Farmington, East Granby, and Windsor Locks were each offering $100 per enlistment. Avon offered $50 if the enlistment was before September and $30 for those who waited until September. Windsor offered bounties of $180, drawing the money from town funds and private donations. In August, Bloomfield paid $100 to anyone who enlisted for nine months and $150 for the duration of the war. The Democratic *Hartford Daily Times* angrily chided soldiers who fought more for profit than patriotism: "We want men to set the example of volunteering who do not need and will not accept bounties."[12] The editors of the Radical Republican *Hartford Evening Press* were equally dismayed. On July 14, the paper urged men not to enlist purely for the money. Nevertheless, the editors worried that, given the uneven bounties from town to town, a "sprit of speculation" had already been born, with men "going from one recruiting station to another to ascertain who will pay most." "This," the paper declared, "seems to us wrong."[13]

"EXCELLENT MATERIAL"

In the midst of this heightened martialism, the 16th Connecticut Regiment was born. More than one thousand men filled the unit's muster rolls by the time the unit left Hartford on August 29, 1862, for the front. It is not possible to know exactly *why* every one of these men decided to enlist; certainly, historians have offered increasingly varied explanations for Civil War soldiers' motivations to volunteer and to fight.[14] However, by piecing together letters sent home, diary entries, postwar memories, and basic biographical information entered in government military records, we can discern a variety of reasons why volunteers in the 16th Connecticut enlisted that summer.

First, expectations were soaring, and many assumed the regiment would be successful and represent the county proudly. Bernard Blakeslee, who enlisted as a corporal in Company A on July 15 (and who eventually authored the only published regimental history), described his fellow volunteers as "excellent material," stating that "some of the oldest and best families were represented in its ranks; and comprised many of the finest young men whom the commonwealth ever sent to uphold its honor in the field."[15] Throughout the war and years later, the 16th Connecticut would routinely be referred to as *the* "Hartford County Regiment," by the local press, even though the 14th Connecticut drew from the same locales and began enlisting men at the same time. The *Hartford Daily Times* applauded the "best class of volunteers" who enlisted in the 16th, and indeed the regimental rolls were filled with some of the best-known and oldest family names in the state, including Hooker, Hitchcock, Bushnell, Phelps, Holcomb, Hale, Griswold, and even Buckingham.[16]

It is not surprising that the 16th Connecticut received such high praise from hometown newspapers. Many members had direct ties to the local press. Sgt. Charles L. Clark (Co. A), was the son of Abel N. Clark, outspoken editor of the "conservative Republican" *Hartford Daily Courant*.[17] Twenty-three-year-old Pvt. George S. Howe (Co. C) had been employed at the influential *Hartford*

Evening Press,[18] where thirty-three-year-old Pvt. Joseph Flowers, Jr. (Co. C), was a compositor.[19] William Goodrich Hooker, just sixteen when he enlisted in Company A, had been employed by one of the local presses.[20] First Lt. Joseph Barnum (Co. B) had already served in the 1st Connecticut as a private when he returned home to work for the *Hartford Daily Post* but reenlisted when given the opportunity for a commission.[21]

Pure patriotism stirred many, including sixteen-year-old George N. Lamphere, who also had affiliations with a newspaper, the *Hartford Daily Post,* where he worked for his uncle, John Scholfield. Lamphere later recalled that he did not "fully comprehend the meaning of the war or understand the principles involved," but he lived in a "patriotic community," and the "roll of the drum and the whistling of the fife when the first troops were enrolled for the three months of service stirred the fires of patriotism within me and I desired to enlist, but as I was too young for acceptance was obliged to wait." On July 19, 1862, Lamphere enlisted in Company B, not yet seventeen years old. "I was guilty," he later wrote, "of telling a white lie in giving my age as 18, but as I was 5 feet 8 1/2 inches tall and weighed 145 pounds, the statement was not questioned."[22]

Other teens, boys really, were moved by lofty ideals to enlist.[23] Ira Emory Forbes was a nineteen-year-old laborer working on a farm to earn money to attend college.[24] But with the war raging, the call to volunteer was just too powerful to resist. On the evening of July 21, 1862, Forbes enlisted as a private in Company A. His schooling would just have to wait.[25] A few weeks later, eighteen-year-old Robert H. Kellogg, a druggist from the town of Wethersfield, enlisted in the same company as Forbes.[26] Later in the war, Kellogg's aunt would state that her nephew was the "principal support of invalid parents," but he did not, it seems, join merely for money; at least that is not what he told his parents, Silas and Lucy Kellogg, a month after he joined.[27] "God, we must free the blacks or perish as a nation," Kellogg declared in a letter home, stating that he had "long held this view and have been sneered at & called an abolitionist, but I am content to wait. I think I am right." Kellogg firmly believed the United States had been suffering for the sin of slavery: "We've not let the enslaved blacks go free when we had the power."[28] Joel Leander Chapin was a student at the Connecticut Literary Institute in Suffield in the summer of 1862 and had dreams of becoming a missionary to Africa or, at the very least, entering the ministry. However, the excitement of military service caught his imagination, too, and as early as April 1861, before he had turned eighteen, Leander had pleaded with his mother for permission to enlist. His mother, Amelia, was not so sure. "You say I am foolish," Leander wrote her, "Mother, I ask wherein am I foolish? Am I foolish in desiring to perpetuate the free institutions and many other blessings which have descended from God and our forefathers?" Chapin failed to change his mother's mind, but he remained unmoved in his determination to become a soldier.[29] By July 1862, he was old enough to join without his mother's consent, and he eagerly did so. Family friend Roselle Grover wrote Amelia a few weeks after Leander entered the service to try to calm her fears. While Grover sympathized with a mother worrying about the "hardships of a Soldier's life," she was convinced of young Leander's "moral heroism" and thought that he would survive the war to return home safely. "Cheer up!" Grover admonished Amelia, "and be a *proud Mother* that you have such a son to devote to his and our country's service and do encourage him by approving of his course."[30]

Indeed, family and friends, especially mothers and wives, were expected to support these eager volunteers. A July 22 editorial in the *Courant* entreated the "Ladies of Connecticut" to "encourage and even urge the necessity upon our husbands, brothers, and friends, give them our blessing, buckle on their armor and bid them God-Speed."[31] The mother of Lauren C. Mills tried to discourage her seventeen-year-old son from enlisting, but when Capt. Charles Babcock (Co. E) and another officer came to their home in Canton, she relented. Still, she recalled feeling as if she had signed a "Death Warrant."[32] George Robbins lacked the support of not only his mother but also his father. In the summer of 1862, he was working as a machinist's apprentice in Hartford.[33] "The war," Robbins later remembered, "was the consuming topic in the shop." Too young to serve, he did not feel it was his time to volunteer until one evening in July 1862, when he attended a "mass meeting" in the city to "accommodate the working men." It was not the stirring speeches or their patriotic words that affected Robbins. His memory, decades later, was that he was moved by the soprano soloist singing the "Star Spangled Banner": "It gripped me and I knew my hour had struck, that I must respond to my country's call and join the ranks of her defenders." George immediately rushed home to announce his intention to his parents, who were shocked by his decision and refused to support his enlistment. His older brother Lewis "wouldn't be outdone by his younger Brother," and announced that he too would join. In Robbins's words, "Then ensued a battle of will between Father and myself." An emotional meeting with Capt. Newton Manross (Co. K), whose company the brothers wanted to join, broke the impasse.[34] Other parents were ambivalent regarding their sons' enlistment. When John B. Cuzner, an eighteen-year-old Hartford mechanic, told his parents Henry and Jane that he wanted to serve, "they did not believe it." Cuzner joined Company B on Friday, August 15, and, as he told his sweetheart Ellen Van Dorn, "My folks did not know it until Sunday."[35]

The call to war attracted older men, too. Rollin C. Crane, listed as forty-five on the adjutant general rolls, was actually ten years older, according to his concerned son-in-law, Coast Guard lieutenant Alvin A. Fengar, who described Crane leaving his "business & family" "in order to influence others to volunteer." More than six months later, Crane was reported as "being already an old man"; the war had "worn upon his constitution nearly destroying his eyesight and filling his bones with Rheumatism until he is no longer able to perform his duties."[36] Charles S. Granger gave his age as forty-three when he enlisted as a private on July 26, 1862, but census records indicate that he was at least ten years older.[37] Baptist minister Sidney S. Carter, Sr., who enlisted with his son Sidney S. Carter, Jr., listed his age as forty-five when he became a sergeant in Company H, but other records, including the U.S. Census, indicate that Carter was fifty-three years old in 1862.[38]

The lure of an officer's commission further motivated men, particularly Hartford's successful businessmen, to join the 16th C.V. Henry L. Pasco had been a clerk at Day, Owen and Company, a wholesale and dry goods business, since the age of sixteen. He showed little inclination to serve until a captain's commission enticed him to volunteer. Pasco's boss E. H. Owen offered to pay Thomas F. Burke, a frame maker, to serve in the regiment until a commission became available, and one soon did. It is not clear what motivated Owen, or Burke for that matter, although Owen claimed that "Burke enlisted because I paid him $10 per month till he should get a commission."[39]

Newton Manross and Samuel Brown initially seem not to have intended to join at all. A Yale-educated geology professor, Manross had traveled to Latin America, including the Isthmus of Panama, as a mining engineer. When the war began, he was a professor at Amherst College in Massachusetts, filling in for his close friend, chemistry professor William S. Clark, who had left his chair position to become an officer in the 21st Massachusetts. It may have been one of Clark's rousing letters from the front or the pull from home; either way, on the night of a war rally in his hometown of Bristol, Connecticut, in July, Manross abruptly went from being a professor to a soldier.[40] After the speeches and some patriotic music, the call came for enlistments. Within thirty minutes, eighty-two men stepped forward, including Manross. He justified his decision to his stunned wife Charlotte: "You can better afford to have a country without a husband than a husband without a country."[41] His wife allegedly "kissed him and let him go."[42] Described by the *Hartford Evening Press* as "a man of sterling character and ability, strong and sturdy, just the man to head a Bristol company," he was quickly elected captain of Company K.[43]

Twenty-six-year-old teacher Samuel Brown, a graduate of Bowdoin College and Massachusetts native, found the "high fever of patriotism" too distracting. Brown helped to enroll some fifty men from Enfield and, along with another group of volunteers from Suffield, headed to Hartford to sign them into service. He was soon elected captain of the newly formed Company D.[44] For Frank W. Cheney from Manchester, the timing also seemed right. Prior to the war, he had briefly attended Brown University before becoming director of his family's prominent silk business, the Cheney Brothers Manufacturing Company, and spending two years abroad assisting in purchasing goods and inspecting suppliers in China and Japan. He had just returned from China when he gained his commission as lieutenant colonel in the 16th C.V.[45]

Reflecting the state's mixed political divisions, the regiment drew Democrats to its ranks as well as Republicans. Sidney H. Hayden was a twenty-three-year-old unmarried farmer from the small town of East Granby who received a $100 bounty when he enlisted in Company B on July 14, 1862. His many letters to his family reveal a strong Christian faith and conservative Democratic political beliefs. Lacking the formal education of some of his comrades, he was no less thoughtful about the war, its causes, and future consequences. Hayden, who became a corporal, explained to his cousin in March 1863 that he "did not come to free the 'Niggers,' but to stand by the Constitution."[46] He wrote to his younger sister, "I hope that more democrats will attend church and when this war is over there will be no more trouble about slavery for I hope that that institution will be out of existence to make no more fuss in the country."[47] Another avowed Democrat was Martin VanBuren Culver, a twenty-nine-year-old unmarried carpenter from Rocky Hill who enlisted in Company A on August 18. Born the year his Democratic namesake ran for president, the poorly educated Culver wrote expressive, colorful letters to his older brother Jonathan. He offered a different and often irreverent opinion of soldier life, the regiment, and the war itself from the moment he enlisted.[48]

For others, it was less a political or even emotional decision to enter the military than it was a question of duty. Oliver W. Gates traced his roots back to the American Revolution; his father and grandfather had served in the Connecticut militia. Unlike most men in the 16th Connecticut, who had barely ventured out of their local communities before the war, Gates had traveled "around the world as a seaman" before the age of twenty-one. He eventually had settled down as a mason for prominent Hartford builder Henry R. Tryon and married Emariah H. Fox; the couple had a young daughter, Allie. When Gates reflected on his reasons for joining the army and leaving behind his family and job, he stated, "My Country needed my services."[49] To Jacob C. Bauer, "my country," was his newly adopted nation, for he was one of 144 immigrants who served in the 16th C.V.[50] Bauer, a twenty-four-year-old German-born box maker from the town of Berlin, enlisted as a private in Company G on August 11, leaving behind his wife Emily Moore Bauer and a young daughter, Allison.[51] He did not enlist alone; he joined with his eighteen-year-old nephew, Edward Moore, and another young man, George Chamberlain, who were both employed by Bauer's father-in-law, Oliver Moore.[52]

Jacob Bauer's family ties within the regiment were not unusual. Family members often enlisted together. Brothers, cousins, fathers and sons, uncles and nephews, and in-laws, served side by side, frequently in the same company.[53] The Bragg brothers, Syril, Frank, and John, farmers from East Windsor, South Windsor, and Bolton, joined Company H.[54] Ariel and Alonzo Case from the town of Simsbury enlisted in Company E, while their brother Oliver served in the 8th Connecticut.[55] Samuel E. Grosvenor, a native of Staffordshire, England, enlisted on July 23 in Company B. His younger brother Joseph joined the same company five days later.[56] The Himes brothers, James, twenty-one, and Stephen, twenty, also enlisted the same day in the same company (Co. I) from Union, Connecticut.[57] Rufus Monroe Chamberlin and his brother-in-law George S. Faulkner enlisted together on July 22, 1862. Two weeks later, Chamberlin's father, Rufus Chamberlin, became sergeant in the same company.[58] In addition, four cousins—Lewis, Gavett, and Asher Holcomb, and Richard Henry Lee, all farmers from Granby—served together in Company E. Lewis, twenty-one and a former teacher, enlisted on July 28; his first cousin Henry Lee, also twenty-one, joined the very next day and was made sergeant.[59] Gavett was only seventeen when he joined on August 9; Asher Holcomb was the eldest of the group, twenty-five, and he was the first of the cousins to enlist on July 19, 1862.[60]

John L. Griggs convinced his younger cousin Theodore R. Stearns, a native of Massachusetts and recent graduate of the University of Albany, to come to Hartford County and enlist in the 16th Connecticut. The two enlisted on the same July day, and soon Stearns was hoping to persuade another friend to join them: "Now John if your going to war[,] Don't you go off to any of the old Regts," Stearns wrote on August 4, 1862. "But come in with us, you cant find a better company anywhere, and we are going into the 16th Regt which will be the best one that has left the State since the war broke out." Stearns maintained, "This last call has brought out a better class of men than has ever been before. I don't think you will regret it if you should join us. I wish you would think seriously of it." He also wrote approvingly of the regiment's recruiting officers: "They are composed of nice young men from Hartford mostly. Bank Clerks, Dry Goods and Store Clerks."[61]

These familial and communal connections within the regiment would prove important. They created an atmosphere of familiarity and intimacy, especially at the company level, that made it easier for the volunteers to leave behind civilian life for the battlefront. Yet, so many family members enlisting together, often on the same day, made the men's transition difficult. Surrounded by family, friends, and people they had known for years in their close-knit communities, the men found it harder to assimilate into their new military roles.[62]

Before becoming soldiers, about one-third of those who enlisted were farmers; others worked as druggists, carpenters, clerks, joiners, teachers, students, machinists, shoemakers, blacksmiths, bookbinders, teamsters, gunsmiths, and cigar makers.[63] Alexander Austin, a Hartford tobacconist, joined Samuel Brown, the teacher, to raise two squads of men, all cigar makers, from the towns of Suffield and Enfield. Initially, these men had intended to join the 14th Connecticut. William H. Relyea remembered passing their camp, but "seeing several men being punished we concluded to enter the adjoining field where the 16th Regiment was being formed."[64] This decision, seemingly made on a whim, to bypass the 14th Connecticut and instead enlist in the 16th and select their "own" to lead, would have unforeseen repercussions.[65]

While the majority of the 16th C.V.'s volunteers had no prior military experience, a small number did. Some had joined three-month regiments during the early weeks of the war and now sought to reenlist in a three-year unit. These included men who had seen action at First Bull Run. Some had received discharges for various reasons or now sought a commission in the new regiment.[66] One member of the unit who had military experience before joining the 16th C.V. was John Burnham, the regimental adjutant. Twenty-five years old and a former bookkeeper and salesman, Burnham hailed from a prosperous Hartford family that had made its money in tobacco and silk. He had set out with his older brother Albert for the Iowa frontier, where he worked for a time as a store clerk, but returned to Hartford to become a partner in his family's business just before the war erupted, no doubt a more prosperous endeavor. In July 1861, John joined the Hartford City Guard, in which he served as secretary and earned the rank of second lieutenant. When the new regiments formed in the summer of 1862, Maj. George A. Washburn appointed Burnham adjutant of the 16th Connecticut. Newspapers warmly applauded Burnham as "well adapted to the position" and his appointment as "one of the best yet made in any regiment."[67]

"A COMPLETE REVOLUTION IN THEIR METHOD OF LIFE"

All of these individuals, with their varied motivations for joining the 16th Connecticut, assembled at a campground laid out along the well-traveled New Haven Turnpike about two miles from the city.[68] On July 25, Captain Pasco arrived with his company, and soon they were "flying around, busy as bees," setting up their tents.[69] The camp was soon christened "Camp Williams" after the state's adjutant general Joseph D. Williams.[70] On July 29, the *Hartford Evening Press* reported "48 tents up, and about 200 men in camp." Additional volunteers were arriving daily, but there were "no drills yet, and the companies are not yet permanently organized."[71]

The 16th Connecticut encamped "side by side" with the 14th Connecticut's "Camp Foote," "separated by an open space of only a few rods."[72] The mood in both camps was "lively and cheerful." The *Hartford Daily Times* described the environment, "The tents are furnished with board floors, set on wooden pins and separated some three inches from the ground. An appearance of neatness is observed throughout the grounds. New companies arrive every day, and are put upon drill as fast as possible. Various accessories of comfort and convenience are noticeable among them the long camp stoves for cooking which combines the advantages for stove and range." The paper also noted that the men sang in camp, mainly "the John Brown order of melody."[73]

During those early weeks of its existence, the regiment showed little resemblance to a recognizable military organization. Men lacked uniforms and rifles, and the 16th C.V. had no colonel. Visitors were a constant at all hours of the day and night, bringing homemade food, clothing, even bouquets of flowers and other personal gifts from family and friends. There were occasional attempts at drills, but the men, giddy with anticipation, often sang and cheered as they practiced their formations.[74] Rain abruptly stopped drills, sending the new soldiers scurrying for cover, and in the evening, Pvt. Elizur Belden (Co. C) wrote, "They have a gay time, music and dancing."[75] One evening in August, the crowd of visitors was so thick, Belden could barely see the "blue coats of the boys."[76]

On August 9, 1862, the *Hartford Evening Press* noted that the 14th Connecticut had eight hundred men in camp, "most of them in uniform and under drill." "It is well officered," the paper pronounced, "and will doubtless do good service." The 16th Connecticut, however, did not seem to be faring as well. Its ranks were still only about half full by the first week of August, only one or two companies had been formally organized, and no drill had yet commenced. The paper stated, "We hope Colonel Beach will soon be on the field, that the regiment may be organized, put under regular drill and qualified for soldiers. If all the men reported to be enlisted for this regiment were in camp, it would doubtless be full."[77]

On August 14, 1862, Colonel Francis Beach arrived at Camp Williams, and everything began to change.[78] The regiment was, according to the *Evening Press*, getting into "soldierly shape generally as fast as possible" and "on a war footing." Enlistments totaled 1,103, and "regulations for passes are more strict, the soldiers are in uniform, and the men are drilled in squads and companies."[79] Colonel Beach had an impressive resume. He was an 1857 West Point graduate and the son of prominent Hartford banker George Beach. He had served on the Utah frontier and taught at the United States Military Academy, and when civil war broke out, he was an officer in the 4th U.S. Artillery. As aide de camp to Brig. Gen. Philip St. George Cooke, Beach accompanied the Army of the Potomac through the Peninsula Campaign, earning commendation for his performance during the battle of Williamsburg.[80] The twenty-seven year old no doubt relished the opportunity to command his own regiment of volunteers from his native state in the summer of 1862. Many in Hartford had high expectations for young Beach. Charles Cheney, a member of the city's "War Committee," wrote Governor Buckingham that there was "no better selection" than Beach for the post, and Charles Dudley Warner's Republican newspaper, the *Hartford Evening Press*, pronounced Beach's colonelcy "a good appointment!"[81]

Beach's men would soon find him a stern disciplinarian, apparently too recently removed from West Point to realize that troop formations always moved more crisply in textbooks than in battle.[82] When he ordered a review and inspection of his new regiment, Beach angrily blasted the troops for their shortcomings and vowed that such sloppy soldiering would not continue under his command. He issued polish to brighten brass and blacken shoes and instituted strict new restrictions on travel and visitations. No longer could men go and come as they pleased. Frustrated and furious with the raw volunteers, the exasperated colonel seemed unable to give orders without swearing.[83] George Robbins wrote of Beach, "He instituted the discipline of the Regular army which, as results proved, licked us eventually into a high state of efficiency, but was pure punishment for men who until now had known no restraint other than that imposed by the rules of society, many lacking even that, and loud were the curses when out of hearing of the officers."[84] Resentment between officers and men would only continue throughout the regiment's service.

Although the men soon had uniforms and the basic military accouterments, guns were conspicuously missing. "One Who Knows" had written the editor of the *Hartford Courant* on July 31, "Give every soldier if possible," the letter writer stated, "the day he is mustered into camp, a good accurately-sighted rifle, with a supply of blank cartridges, and let special attention be given to target shooting every day, and create a spirit of rivalry by awarding premiums to the best marksmen." He bemoaned the number of "men and boys" rushing to enlist who were "so weak that they could not hold a musket at arms length for five seconds!"[85]

Even without arms, for some the change from civilian to soldier was proving too much to bear. Colonel Beach's regulations and brusque manner seemed unnecessarily unfair. Bernard F. Blakeslee later recalled these early days in camp as a "shock to most of the men" and a "complete revolution in their method of life."[86] William Relyea remembered that for men who had known great personal autonomy in their daily lives, "each day brought some restraint on our freedom."[87] Sidney Hayden wrote his sister Catherine that he had "expected to go home every Saturday night" when he first joined the regiment but was surprised to learn that he could only once "get off 48 hours" before the unit headed for the front.[88] Some felt depressed and surprised, and a few even threatened the "unfeeling" Beach, boasting that once they were in battle, they would "fill his back full of bead."[89]

One woman grew so concerned that she wrote directly to Governor Buckingham in late August about her "many friends in the 16th Connecticut." Mrs. Welles Hawes stated, "They are disgusted with the *profanity* and *brutality* of their Col." "They told me at the Camp yesterday," she affirmed, "that he would never go into but one engagement [and] they were determined to shoot him." Her friends in the regiment had enlisted "for love of country & only ask for leaders that they can respect," and this sort of behavior, she explained, only increased the suffering of the soldiers' families and threatened to discourage volunteers.[90] Buckingham's response (if he did respond) does not survive. However, not everyone was displeased. The same day Mrs. Hawes sent her desperate plea to the governor for a new commander, Democratic state senator and former U.S. congressman James T. Pratt expressed his satisfaction with Beach: "I saw Col. Beach last evening at the encampment of the 16th Ct. and was pleased with his appearance."[91]

Still, it had been a difficult adjustment for the men, and things were only going to get worse. Blakeslee, who unabashedly admired Beach and later defended him in his published regimental history, contended, "In his first connection with the Sixteenth Connecticut Regiment under unfortunate circumstances, many misunderstandings between him and the men gained ground." Blakeslee believed this situation was largely due to the "the jealousy, with which the volunteer soldiers, fresh from home, regarded regular army officers." Eventually, though, "there was not a man of the regiment who was not warmly attached to the Colonel, admired him, was proud of his bravery, his military knowledge, bearing and his standing in the army."[92]

The summer of 1862 was exceptionally hot, and volunteers unaccustomed to outdoor living succumbed to heat exhaustion and sun poisoning.[93] It was difficult to wear the heavy wool uniform and the "flannel underwear." George Robbins recalled the underwear as particularly "intolerable," "never having worn any during the summer and only an undershirt in winter."[94] Blakeslee later claimed, "The outdoor life, though not as hard as yet, was too great for those who led the quiet and easy life of a citizen, and a few of our noble men who had offered themselves to the government were unable to endure the hardships, and died before the regiment left Hartford."[95] However, there is no proof that anyone died due to the "hardships" of Camp Williams.[96] There was at least one death in camp: Pvt. Jason Wright (Co. G), a forty-year-old married farm laborer who enlisted from Enfield. His death on August 25, at least according to one source, was not because of heat exhaustion or sickness. Robert Kellogg wrote in his diary that Wright "committed suicide by taking opium."[97]

As the men bristled under Beach's harsh style of command, rumors circulated that the regiment was going to the front. On Sunday, August 24, 1862, the 16th Regiment Connecticut Volunteers, numbering 1,010 men, was formally mustered into three years of service for the United States.[98] Five days later, they left for the front.

Before the regiment left Hartford, though, there were resolutions offered, and officers received ceremonial gifts—sword, sashes, revolvers, and belts, all certainly valuable, even practical, but also representative of the responsibilities entrusted to them by soldiers' families, friends, and employers. These items symbolizing war, often inscribed and presented with moving tributes, further underscored the high expectations civilians had of their soldiers: that they would fight and fight well.[99] When residents from Suffield presented Lt. Richard Green, Jr. (Co. D), with a sword, sash, belt, and a large Smith and Wesson revolver, Green was moved to publish his thanks in one of the Hartford newspapers: "May I add the hope that no act of mine will ever destroy the confidence reposed in me with the assurance that it shall always be my aim and purpose to serve faithfully the cause of my country."[100] Company H similarly drafted a resolution expressing its gratitude to Lt. Col. Frank Cheney and "other citizens of Manchester" for their "patriotism" and generosity." The soldiers resolved, "That it will be our constant and earnest endeavor by faithfully performing every duty, and by manly deportment to become true soldiers and to merit the confidence so kindly reposed in us." And "That we solicit their continued interest in us and their prayerful remember that in whatever danger we may be placed, we may prove ourselves men and do credit to the towns which we represent."[101] Succeeding in battle meant proving one's manhood. Company H and all the members of the 16th C.V. were determined to do just that.

Perhaps the most significant martial symbol of all was the regiment's state flag. However, the emblem, designed by Tiffany and Company in New York and paid for by the employees of the Sharps Rifle Factory, did not arrive in time to be presented to the men before they left for the front. For a few days, the flag was prominently displayed in a Hartford storefront.[102] The *Harford Courant* praised the flag as "very elegant and reflect[ing] great credit upon the designer and artist." The *Courant* further declared, "It is the handsomest flag that has yet left the State and we hope the 16th will cherish it and bring it home again with honor."[103] The flag would not be formally presented to the unit until late October.[104]

On Thursday, August 28, there was a grand inspection, with Adjutant Burnham "very particular in having the men present a neat and orderly appearance."[105] Several members fainted, though, from the excessive heat and the strain of their overloaded knapsacks. The next day, the regiment left Hartford for Washington, D.C. As the soldiers marched to the city wharf, cheering crowds lined the streets and Governor Buckingham fell in step in front of the regiment. Elizur D. Belden described the memorable scene in his diary: "On we marched, up through the city, the sidewalks covered with people, doors and windows were full of bright eyes, handkerchiefs, and flags were waved, cheers given, through Main street, down State Street."[106]

The unit boarded two steamers, the *City of Hartford* and the *George C. Collins*, and traveled down the Connecticut River, greeted by people lining the riverside. It was an emotional and exciting send-off.[107] Relyea remembered, "Hartford County had given to this regiment a large portion of its very best citizens. Expectations ran high as to its regimental career, and frequent 'God Bless you's' mingled with goodbyes."[108] Blakeslee called the city's response a "perfect ovation."[109] Twenty-one-year-old Pvt. Austin D. Thompson (Co. K) wrote his sweetheart, eighteen-year-old Electra Churchill, that he believed he saw "more people that day than I ever saw in one day in my life."[110] Hartford's local press bid the 16th C.V. farewell, predicting great things: "A better regiment of men never left the State than the 16th Conn," and "The Sixteenth carries off many brave Hartford boys, and we hope to hear a good account of the regiment."[111]

Yet, already the regiment had its first deserters: privates Michael H. Leech, a twenty-year-old, single stonecutter, and Walden E. Dutcher, a nineteen-year-old married farmer, from Company A; twenty-eight-year-old Pvt. John Carroll (Co. G); Pvt. Thomas Walsh (Co. E); and twenty-eight-year-old farmer Charles Pettice (Co. G). The day the regiment left Connecticut, August 29, 1862, the men made their escape. Pvt. Conrad Kistler (Co. E), a twenty-six-year-old mason and possibly a German immigrant, also vanished from the ranks, although the recorded date of his desertion is unclear.[112]

Meantime, the 16th Connecticut made its way south toward the capital. On board the steamers, there was yet another startling reminder to the enlistees of their new military identity. When a few of the wealthier privates tried to pay for cabin berths and staterooms, orders were issued that only officers were allowed above deck. The gulf between officers and men had further widened.[113]

Still, the men appeared to be in relatively high spirits, and even Colonel Beach seemed satisfied with his new command. In New York on Saturday, August 30, the 16th C.V. was served a breakfast "of coffee and dissected vegetables and soup, but minus the soup plates and spoons, so necessary."[114] A newspaper reporter described the scene: "It was a delightful morning, and the men were in good condition and excellent spirits." "Col. Beach," the journalist noted, "had an eye on everything, and if officers of companies were prompt in performance of their duties, or if any of them were remiss, the Colonel's vigilant eye saw it. He was highly pleased with the general conduct of the men, and so expressed himself."[115] In Elizabethport, New Jersey, the regiment shifted from boats to cramped, dirty train cars. They finally arrived in Washington, D.C., on August 31.[116] No crowds greeted them in the nation's capital, and the men spent the night sleeping in the open on a "thin slush of mud."[117]

In less than two months, the 16th Connecticut had come into existence. Drawing men from across Hartford County, the regiment was in many ways a typical northern regiment. It consisted of a boisterous mixture of idealistic teenagers, recent immigrants, ambitious office seekers, hard-nosed artisans and machinists, and independent farmers, all led by a determined and profane West Point–trained colonel.[118] Expectations were high that the soldiers of the "Hartford Regiment" would perform nobly on the battlefield, demonstrate their martial manhood, and make their state proud. How could they not?

2

Antietam
"Soldiering with a Vengeance"

Just three weeks after leaving home, the 16th Connecticut underwent one of its most profound transformations, their baptism of fire. In fact, its first battle, Antietam, would prove to be its only large-scale engagement of the war. Survivors, no longer "earnest Connecticut boys," emerged bloodied and shaken by combat, and some left the regiment, never to return. Antietam forever defined the regiment, and it provided a crucial if not entirely truthful plotline for their later history, which celebrated green troops tested yet bolstered by battle, rather than men broken and fractured, as they actually had been, by its chaos and horrors.

In late August, just outside Washington, D.C., the men were exposed to casualties for the first time, when they encountered ambulances returning from Second Manassas piled high with dead and wounded. The sight sobered and shocked the new volunteers. "This is indeed *war*," Pvt. Robert H. Kellogg wrote in his diary on August 29.[1] Pvt. William Relyea recalled that their previously "exuberant spirits" were "completely subdued." Some of the wounded called out to the green recruits: "God speed you," and "You are wanted bad at the front."[2] Jacob Bauer remembered that seeing the wounded "unnerved some. It did me."[3]

On September 1, the 16th Connecticut made camp near Fort Ward, Virginia, less than ten miles outside of Washington.[4] As Kellogg explained to his father, Fort Ward was "one of the many forts which crown the hills around and beyond Washington, and about 9 or 10 miles from the capitol which is in plain view in the distance."[5] Their first night in camp, the men still lacked tents and slept on the ground with only their blankets to cover them in a drenching rain; they had no fuel for fires.[6] "We were compelled," Bernard Blakeslee wrote, "to sit in the rain all night: this we thought soldiering with a vengeance."[7]

Diaries and letters home reveal that many soldiers were becoming aware of a profound transformation within the regiment with each day that passed. Nineteen-year-old Pvt. Harrison Woodford (Co. I) wrote his sister Mattie that he and his comrades were beginning to look "hard." Unshaven and dirty, Woodford had changed his clothes only once since leaving Hartford. "A soldier's life is a hard old life to lead," he declared on September 10, "but I think I can ride it through. No one knows any thing of the hardships of a soldier's life until they know it by experience."[8] "It was," Bauer reflected years later, "a rough breaking-in."[9]

Adj. John Burnham, however, would claim, at least publicly, that the regiment was in excellent condition. In a letter to the editor of the *Hartford Daily Courant*, Burnham proclaimed that their camp was excellent and the spirit of the unit "cheerful and healthy" with no complaints. "We know as little and perhaps less, [about] what is going on about us than you do at home," but, he added, "as far as I am concerned I do not feel as anxious here and eager for news as I did at home."[10]

Guns finally arrived, Whitney rifles or "*made over* Belgian muskets, which were nasty and dirty." Relyea recalled, "With those guns we had graduated into full-fledged soldiers."[11] In actuality, the men of the 16th Connecticut remained more civilian than soldier, receiving little formal drill in how to use those guns or their bayonets in combat.[12] Instead, they spent the next several days conducting "fatigue duty," helping to build breastworks at the fort, cleaning their weapons, and practicing their aim, but learning next to nothing about battle commands or military movements.[13] Blakeslee affirmed that, while the unit was encamped near Fort Ward, "we had little or no drill, and but few instructions in marching."[14] Bauer wrote his wife on September 5, "We have our guns now rubber blankets and everything necessary to go into battle but we are not drilled enough with the guns to do any mischief." He perceived "a kind of despondency and fear of being led into battle before we are fit which can not be overcome."[15] These feelings of anxiety would only grow over the next week.

On Saturday, September 6, the 16th Connecticut received orders to break camp and prepare for "light marching order," leaving behind knapsacks and extra clothing.[16] The next day, the regiment set out to join the IX Corps of the Army of the Potomac. The 16th Connecticut was to become part of Col. Edward Harland's brigade, which also included the 8th and 11th Connecticut and the 4th Rhode Island. The regiment had been away from Hartford one week, and, as one local history later noted, "it had received no drill, no discipline, and few instructions even in marching. It was little more than a crowd of earnest young Connecticut boys."[17] But the notion that the men would see action any time soon still seemed remote. Cpl. Sidney Hayden wrote his uncle from Leesboro, Maryland, on September 10, "As near as I can learn we are to be kept as a reserve at present until better drilled."[18]

After a difficult seven-mile march back through and out of Washington, the regiment turned toward Frederick, Maryland.[19] "We marched," a soldier described, "more like a mob, because we did not know any better."[20] For men still unused to the rigors of soldiering, the physical strain was exhausting. George Q. Whitney (Co. A) later recalled the start of the march: "very hot and dusty, some 6 to 8 miles north halting for the night in a grove of small pine trees, and had about the toughest night of our three years' service, suffering greatly from the damp penetrating cold, and still no shelter."[21] Tents finally arrived three days later, but the unit continued moving at a hurried rate, with little clear idea of where they were going.[22]

Kept marching at such a vigorous pace, there were numerous stragglers, and morale plummeted.[23] A soldier's letter to the *Hartford Courant* stated, "The march was the toughest I ever experienced; it was hot, and very dusty, and quite a number fell out, but not I."[24] Austin D. Thompson put it simply in a letter home on September 14: "I am most dreadful tired." Thompson fell out of the ranks during the march, but, he told Electra, "I had plenty of company."[25] Indeed, the *Hartford Evening Press* reported: "We have a private letter from a member of the 16th regiment, written at Frederick City, Md., on Sunday the 14th. The march from Leesborough to Frederick he represents as a hard one, and many of the men fell out of the ranks and have not yet reported themselves."[26] A "special correspondent" to the same paper, a soldier in the 11th Connecticut, related encountering the "brand new" 16th Connecticut at Leesboro. Here, the correspondent claimed, the new soldiers "unburdened their woes, told tales of a three-days' horror, and threatened to resign (every ninety-ninth private) if soft bread and fresh meat were not forthcoming soon."[27]

Rations during the march were sometimes of poor quality and limited quantity. Men scoured nearby fields, orchards, and farmhouses for food. They bought items, too, such as apples, onions, grapes, and even a duck.[28] Officers, though, seemed to be eating just fine. One soldier claimed that the officers "steal everything they want to eat," even if it was from some lowly private. Pvt. J. Edward Shipman (Co. C) accused Colonel Beach of hitting a soldier with his sword, "a favorite game with him," and taking a chicken away from a man who bought it.

Afterward, Beach offered to pay for the bird, but, Shipman wrote, "Many of the men swear they will shoot him if he ever goes into action with us."[29]

Although resentment toward Colonel Beach had not abated within the ranks since leaving Hartford, other officers were rising in stature among the soldiers. Lt. Col. Frank Cheney had quickly earned the respect and affection of his men. His future sister-in-law, Frances Louise Bushnell, described Cheney as a "thunder and lightning individual." "Every one," she complained in a letter to her sister Mary upon learning that she and Frank were engaged, "gives up to him. Every one bows before him."[30] But Frances Bushnell was one of the few people whom Frank Cheney did not win over quickly. The men of the 16th Connecticut adored him and would remain loyal to him for decades, long after the war ceased. Capt. Newton Manross of Company K, the former college professor, also stood out for his concern for his men during the march. He constantly encouraged his company, helping them forget their physical pain and discomfort. For those who faltered, he offered to carry their guns until they felt strong enough to bear the weight again.[31] Two more officers who made a good impression were Capt. Samuel Brown and Chaplain Peter Finch,[32] whom one soldier praised as a "very nice man" who spent time with the soldiers.[33]

Others, however, were struggling with their new positions of leadership. Lt. Richard Green, Jr., the Suffield man so handsomely outfitted by his friends with a sash, belt, sword, and large revolver, thought it was a good idea to drill his company as they marched. Relyea mused that Green "wanted to impress upon our minds that he was our superior and that he knew a good deal about military tactics, for as we were marching along in good step and time to the music of the drum corps, we were startled by the command, 'Attention, Company. Change step march.'"[34]

The sights and sounds of war also made a lasting impression. At Frederick, Maryland, the Connecticut men were stunned to encounter a group of ragged, emaciated Confederate prisoners who stared hollow-eyed and silent at the un-tried bluecoats. Near the South Mountain battlefield, dead bodies littered the roadside, and the wounded filled churches and private homes. Robbins caught a glimpse of surgeons amputating limbs and dressing wounds in a nearby barn. He wrote that it "was a horrible sight and I was sick physically and mentally at the horrors of the aftermath of battle, which is conceded by all who have experienced both to be worse than actual participation in conflict, terrible as that is."[35] "You in Hartford," a member of the regiment wrote to the Hartford Daily Courant, "have no idea of what war is, or of the life of a soldier."[36]

On September 16, the regiment passed through Boonsboro, Maryland, where the sounds of battle boomed in the distance.[37] "The men," Kellogg wrote, "were nearly ready to fall with exhaustion."[38] However, the prospect of immediate combat remained remote, at least to most of the men in the ranks. Hayden wrote his uncle from Leesboro on September 10, "As near as I can learn we are to be kepted [sic] as a reserve at present until better drilled."[39] Pvt. Martin V. Culver was unsure if a battle was imminent, but he was fairly confident that he and his comrades would stay on the sidelines: "i do not know wether we are agoing to have fight or not but i think not at present. Not the 16th." The grueling march had convinced Culver of one thing: "I shant stay here three years though if I am well."[40] When orders came confirming that, in fact, the regiment was heading into action, Cpl. Blakeslee remembered: "This took us a little by surprise as we did not expect to go into battle so soon."[41]

By dusk on September 16, the Connecticut unit had marched to a line of battle behind the Rohrbach farm, "in a small meadow between two hills," on the Army of the Potomac's far left line of battle.[42] Hungry and tired, and now without ration wagons to feed them, the men devoured corn and green fruit from nearby orchards and fields. Blakeslee later maintained that it was on this night that the men loaded their muskets for the very first time.[43] Officers prohibited fires and ordered quiet in the camp. There was a light drizzle, and the men slept fitfully on their arms, awakened throughout the night by false alarms from nervous sentries.[44]

"OUR MEN FELL ON EVERY SIDE"

On September 17, Gen. George B. McClellan confronted Robert E. Lee's Army of Northern Virginia, which had invaded Maryland with hopes of replenishing his troops as well as turning the tide of the war. The resulting battle was the bloodiest single day of the entire Civil War. Early that morning, privates Ira Forbes and Robert Kellogg awoke to read the Bible and pray.[45] Orders swiftly came to "fall in," and fighting began at dawn. Confederate batteries began shelling their position.[46] Cpl. Samuel B. Mettler (Co. C) described: "we were lying under a hill, but their shot came so fast and so sure that we were obliged to run to the woods for protection—many falling from the enemy's shots as they ran." To Pvt. Marx Neisener (Co. G) the artillery fire "came like rain—round shot, shells, shrapnel, grape and all. The regiment fell flat and the shot went over them." At least an hour went by, and then the regiment moved to a cornfield to wait for two more hours.[47]

The Battle of Antietam had commenced, and the noise of the shot and shell had grown so loud, men had to shout to talk. "We had," George Robbins recalled, "a magnificent view of the long battlefield stretching away to our right along the undulating country as far as the eye could see, with masses of blue clad soldiers showing for a few moments, then out of sight as the hills hid them from view."[48] The early morning shock of being fired upon by enemy artillery had made it abundantly clear that the regiment was about to go into battle. Exactly when and where they would engage, however, remained a mystery. The waiting only seemed to make things worse. As the hours slipped away, a few restless souls wondered off to pick peaches.[49] Others had already been directly touched by fire. Kellogg's arm had been slightly wounded, a shell fragment had cut out Chaplain Finch's coat pocket, and Surgeon Warner's horse had been shot out from under him.[50]

The battle's frightening sounds and sights made some feel faint and weak, and when noon sick call came, they vanished to the rear. George N. Lamphere explained, "The fact is well known to all soldiers that one of the most trying positions troops can be put into is to be lying around inactive and yet be under fire. It requires courage and it is a great consumer of nerve power."[51] William Relyea scornfully recalled that many of those suddenly "sick" just before battle were the loudest braggarts who had vowed they would kill Colonel Beach. "Rid of regimental rubbish," Relyea alleged, the 16th was then "free from everything that would or could tarnish our good name clear of all weakening influences now ready for the ordeal that awaited us."[52]

Few in the 16th Connecticut, however, were ready for what they would soon face. By the late afternoon of September 17, the 16th was sent to try to outflank the Confederates and find a crossable ford, south on Antietam Creek. The men crossed the creek about a mile below Burnside's Bridge, holding their guns and cartridge boxes high over their heads. Some later contended that the water was shoulder deep. After hurrying up the side of a hill to support a Union battery, officers ordered the men to hit the ground immediately. Rebel cannon took deadly aim on their position, pounding them with grape, canister, and railroad iron. The hill's crest protected most of the unit, but about a dozen suffered injury from the artillery fire. A few privates joked nervously, seeking to break the thickening tension. Colonel Beach barked impatiently at the jokesters, silencing any attempts at levity.[53]

Between 3:30 and 4:00 p.m., Col. Edward Harland was waiting impatiently for the 16th Connecticut and the 4th Rhode Island to advance. The 8th Con-

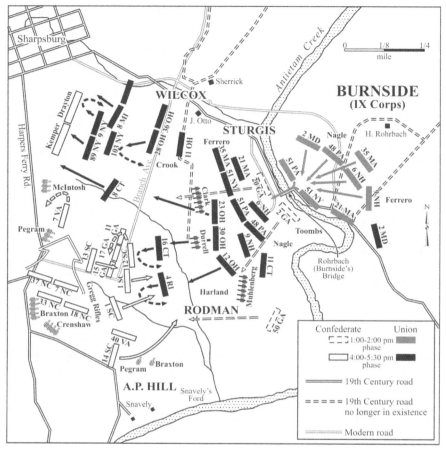

The Battle of Antietam. Late in the afternoon on September 17, the green 16th Connecticut entered the battle. This map illustrates the fateful moments when the regiment collided with charging Confederates, and its ranks (along with those of the 4th Rhode Island)
broke in panicked retreat.

necticut had already moved forward some distance to the right of the regiments,
creating a gap between units. Colonel Harland sent an aide to push the remainder
of his brigade forward, and Brigadier General Rodman went personally to hasten
the men along. Rodman discovered the 16th Connecticut still on the ground, near
the edge of a cornfield. As he conversed intently with Beach, he suddenly spotted
enemy movement to the left of the cornfield. Rodman rushed back to find the 4th

Rhode Island while Colonel Beach quickly ordered the regiment into formation. Because the color bearer forgot to take the flag out of its dark glazed bag, the regiment entered its first battle essentially waving a black flag. It was an eerie premonition of what was to come.[54]

"Attention," Colonel Beach bellowed from atop his white horse, riding up and down the lines, trying frantically to shift half of the regiment to refuse its left and protect its exposed flank. Suddenly, a wave of bullets whizzed through the ranks. In Kellogg's words, it was "one of the most terrific volleys of musketry that I think was ever poured into a Regt." "Our men," he wrote, "fell on every side."[55] Maneuvering soldiers under fire is difficult for any officer to complete, but directing an undrilled and undisciplined regiment such as the 16th Connecticut was nearly impossible. Line officers were just as green and confused as the privates. One officer cried out in desperation, "Tell us what you want us to do and we'll try to obey you." Beach replied, "I want my men to face the enemy."[56] The tall, uneven corn stalks compounded the chaos; men could only see a small portion of their line at a time. A few fell out of formation, losing track of their companies. Nearing a wooden fence, officers issued conflicting orders: "tear the fence down," and "never mind the fence."[57]

Only a few minutes had passed, but it seemed like an eternity. As officers struggled to find some order and direction, Confederate troops unleashed a deadly crossfire into the regiment. "So dense was the corn," wrote South Carolinian James F. J. Caldwell, "that the lines sometimes approached within thirty to forty yards of each other before opening [fire]."[58] Another South Carolinian, Berry Benson, recalled running through the corn, shooting a "galling fire into the fleeing foe." Benson saw bunches of frightened bluecoats crowded into a small hollow at the bottom of the hill, afraid to cross the open slope behind them. "Grouped here in a crouching disorderly line," Benson remembered, "we poured into them volley after volley, doubtless with terrible execution." Other federals huddled behind a stone fence, sporadically breaking away from the fence, in small groups and individually, to flee to the rear.[59] Some members of the regiment recalled firing only one round, and others alleged an actual charge was made. At least one soldier later recounted hearing the "hideous rebel yell." Others remembered hearing orders to "fall back," but it is unclear whether there was ever any official call to retreat.[60] Either way, the 16th Connecticut broke and fled in wild panic. The 4th Rhode Island, which had come up on the 16th's left, held out a little longer before they too retreated in confusion.[61]

Caught up in the swarm of panicked soldiers, Colonel Beach stubbornly fought to regain control. He desperately tried to rally a small remnant of the 16th Connecticut with parts of the 11th Connecticut and redraw a battle line.[62] However, there was little that could be done. Most of the 16th Connecticut were dead, wounded, or gone from the field. Dropping from mental and physical exhaustion, stragglers slept the night of September 17 under fences, on rocks, and in thickets. Many wounded remained on the field all night into the next day, moaning and crying for water.[63]

The Battle of Antietam proved a tactical draw. On September 18, both sides tended to their wounds and buried what dead they could. That night, Lee and his army slipped across the Potomac River and returned to Virginia.

The battle's shattering impact on the regiment was soon apparent. On the morning of September 18, less than one-third of the regiment answered roll call. Throughout the day, two hundred more men stumbled into camp, groggy, disoriented, and fatigued. Over the next two weeks, one soldier recalled, only a few hundred could be mustered for service. The difficult and abrupt transition from civilian life, the hurried and strenuous march, together with the trauma and stress of combat was too much for many. Days after the battle, the straggling continued. On September 23, Cpl. Leland Barlow (Co. E) wrote his sister Jane that there remained "roughs" in the regiment who would "skedaddle if they had a chance." Barlow counted sixty guards "around our little camp," where everyone was being treated as a potential deserter.[64] The October 1862 regimental returns list twenty-six men as deserters, most leaving the day of battle, four disappearing before September 17, and one deserting after Antietam.[65] Two soldiers, Henry Rhodes and F. Dixon Tucker, both from Company A, fled not only the 16th Connecticut but the United States, escaping to Great Britain for the duration of the war.[66]

Soldiers continued to slip away in the days and weeks following the battle.[67] In addition, there were men who had been wounded in the fray, and they seized opportunities to escape from military hospitals. Citing just a few examples from Company D, the company that lost the largest number of men to desertions illustrates the point. William H. Getman and Nathaniel Waters, both nineteen-year-old cigar makers from Suffield, disappeared sometime after the battle.[68] Pvt. John Riley, a nineteen-year-old Irish immigrant, was wounded, but he deserted from the hospital after the battle and fled to Canada.[69] Erastus Bottum was wounded, captured, and subsequently paroled. But in December 1862, not long after entering the hospital due to his ailing wound, he deserted. He was eventually arrested in October 1863 in Boston, Massachusetts.[70] The company also lost men before the battle even started. William Webster vanished prior to Antietam, and so did the Fries brothers, Frederick and Adolph, who left the ranks on September 12 while foraging near Johnstown.[71]

Some desertions were not reported officially, but soldiers discussed them in their private letters. Austin Thompson wrote Electra Churchill a few weeks after the battle about his comrade Pvt. Henry Merriman: "it seems [he] has got over being crazy, and has returned to the Regt." Merriman apparently came back to camp with Pvt. George Nettleton, both in Company K. "The night before the battle," Thompson explained, Merriman "made tracks for Frederick City, and no one here herd [sic] from him until he came back. I suppose that he was pretty badly frightened. I presume that he was disgusted because the rebels made so much noise, and left for a more quiet place." There was another shirker from the regiment, Thompson claimed, who was "so frightened that he went home to Collinsville and has got back without even a scar." Thompson joked, "What a wonderful escape it was." Despite Thompson's light tone about his comrades' cowardice, he assured Electra that he was looking forward to more combat, even though he too ran from the front at Antietam: "I hope that I have the pleasure of killing at least one rebel, if I should be fortunate enough to get into an other [sic] battle."[72]

On September 19, the regiment helped bury the dead. This was "a very unpleasant duty," wrote regimental historian Blakeslee, "and made many soldiers sick."[73] They hastily placed forty of the regiment's dead, privates wrapped in blankets and officers encased in "rude rough boxes," into a mass grave near the cornfield.[74] Chaplain Finch and Adjutant Burnham made certain that "the men of each company [were] laid side by side, and each grave marked so that the bodies could be recovered if desired."[75] Burnham, writing the *Daily Courant*, was "confident none [of the regimental dead] were left on the ground."[76]

Meanwhile, officers and men began to try to make sense of what had happened to them in that awful battle. Official military reports, many submitted just a few days after the battle, offered little insight into what had gone so terribly wrong for the 16th Connecticut. Col. Frank Beach described his men enduring enemy artillery fire all day "until about 5 o'clock when we were brought against the extreme right of the rebel infantry." He made no mention of his exasperated efforts to turn his flank, nor the embarrassing retreat. On September 19, Beach simply stated: "I transmit the casualties. There were probably about twenty taken prisoner. The missing are constantly coming in and it is impossible to give a correct list of them."[77]

Lt. Col. Joseph B. Curtis of the 4th Rhode Island stated in his report dated five days after the battle that the 16th Connecticut's collapse shattered his regiment's ranks. Curtis explained that when the Rhode Islanders moved forward in support of the Connecticut unit, he "found the Sixteenth Ct giving way and crowding upon its right compelling" his men "to move to left, rendering it almost impossible to dress the line." When he tried to rally his troops for an attack, he was unable to find any officer of the 16th to support a charge uphill. Curtis cried to his colonel, "We must depend upon ourselves." A few moments later, the 16th Connecticut completely crumbled, and his regiment soon followed. Curtis defended his Rhode Islanders for fighting well throughout the day. "That they finally broke, under such a severe fire, and the pressure of a broken regiment is not surprising," he concluded, "although much to be regretted."[78]

Colonel Edward Harland also attempted to explain the debacle. On September 22, 1862, he reported his frustration that the Connecticut regiment failed to advance, and he recalled sending an aide to rally both the 16th Connecticut and the 4th Rhode Island. Harland confirmed that Gen. Rodman himself went to hasten the two regiments forward, but he did praise Beach for his attempts to turn the regiment's front and meet the enemy attack. Harland's report stressed the difficult terrain, poor visibility, and the deadly effectiveness of enemy fire. In the end, the men of the 16th who were under fire for the first time "could not be held," and their rout hastened the disintegration of the 4th Rhode Island, and eventually the 8th Connecticut.[79]

"STAND LIKE HEROES"

At home, news of the regiment came in a slow trickle. On September 25, 1862, more than one week after the battle, the *Hartford Evening Press* complained, "Not a line had been received officially from either of the four Connecticut regiments engaged."[80] Soldier letters and lists of the killed and wounded had been shared with the paper. However, information was still fragmentary. Civilians home in Hartford County waited and worried to learn the fate of their loved ones.

Initially, accounts of the regiment's performance at Antietam, especially those in the press, appeared markedly upbeat and positive. The conservative Republican *Hartford Daily Courant* had repeatedly reported that the 16th Connecticut

The Papers praise the regiment (36-37)

was in fine condition and high spirits during the days leading up to the battle. On September 18, just before news of Antietam first reached Connecticut, the paper described the regiment as withstanding the march to the front "bravely, very few giving out." After Beach's initial doubts about the regiment's preparedness, the paper reported, "they were thoroughly drilled, and now the Colonel feels safe in taking them into battle." "Connecticut troops always have fought well," the *Courant* assured readers, "and we have no fears of the brave Sixteenth."[81]

The Radical Republican *Evening Press* provided one of the earliest (and recurring) descriptions of the 16th Connecticut's action at Antietam on September 22 based on a private letter from soldier Aretas Culver (Co. K): "The 16th were posted on the extreme left of Burnside's column, with the 4th R.I. immediately behind them, the 11th Connecticut, and the 17th Michigan in the rear. The enemy commenced a flanking movement, which they were nearly successful in accomplishing, having treacherously displayed the U.S. colors until ready to grapple with the foe." Culver then recounted how Confederates, the "wretches," were calling out to the federals not to fire on their own men: "At that point of attack, they lowered their standards and hoisted the rebel ensign in its place; then it was the Acting Brig. Gen. Harland [who] ordered Col. Beach to change position to escape their deadly cross-fire; Col B. attempted it, but in vain, and he was obliged to report to his superior that his regiment had never had a battalion drill, but one dress parade and scarcely knew how to form in a line-of-battle."[82] Culver further praised Surgeon Warner for being "everywhere he was needed" and spoke "enthusiastically of Col. Beach's gallantry and courage. Lieut. Col. Cheney was the soul of energy and daring." The paper added, "The 16th sustained unbroken ranks under the most destructive fire for an hour, when they fell back, having suffered severely."[83]

On September 27, the *Hartford Evening Press* summed up the performance of all four regiments at Antietam and judged that each of them came out with "unsullied honor." "No where since the war began," the paper maintained, "on any battlefield, in any post of danger, has a Connecticut regiment been panic struck or unfaithful." The 11th and 8th were experienced and battle tried, and the paper praised them for going into combat as "jolly veterans and true as steel," "steady and destructive and compact." The newly raised 14th and 16th Connecticut, "without drill or previous discipline, fresh from their peaceful pursuits, also went in without fear or flinching. It was a cruel necessity that put such green regiments in the front, but how well they bore the test. There may have been a little unavoidable disorganization under the terrible fire and lack of drill, but there was not a symptom of panic. The Sixteenth was for a long time forced to stand and take it without leave to reply, and they did stand like heroes." After recounting the 14th Connecticut's action in holding a stonewall, the paper closed, "We wish to make not invidious comparisons, when all did so well, but if any new troops behaved more handsomely than the Fourteenth and Sixteenth Connecticut we have yet to learn it."[84]

The Democratic *Hartford Daily Times* declared, "The regiment behaved nobly. It was in the thickest of the fight, and though never drilled, and scarcely one month in existence as a regiment, the officers and men fought like veterans, and won high honors, and lavish praises from the old officers." The paper went on to herald them as "The Valiant Conn. 16th—The Hero Regiment of Antietam!" It went on to say, "all accounts show that this new regiment, the Connecticut 16th, performed the part of heroes in the great battle of Antietam."[85]

Indeed, few letters from Connecticut soldiers initially published in the Hartford newspapers questioned these glowing assessments. Burnham proudly reported, "The Sixteenth sustained unbroken ranks under the most destructive fire for an hour, when they fell back, having suffered severely."[86] Lt. Henry Beach from Company G, whose letter to his father appeared in the *Hartford Daily Times* on September 23, recounted that the 16th Connecticut was "badly used" and that his company in particular suffered "the worst of any company in the regiment." Still, Lt. Beach affirmed, "General Burnside says the 16th fought better than any regiment in the field—but they are mostly gone now."[87] Both officers' emphasis on their losses is perhaps to be expected. But at the same time as they celebrated the men's bravery, they began to acknowledge the cost of their sacrifice. A soldier in the ranks agreed with this latter point but was able to place the experience in a broader context. Eighteen-year-old Pvt. Marx Neisener's letter, published in the *Hartford Daily Times,* underscored not just the permanent impact the battle had already made on the regiment's survivors but its lasting historical significance. Promising to send his bullet-ridden coat home to friends, the Polish-born Neisener declared, "It was the greatest battle ever fought in America."[88]

More soldiers' letters and excerpts of letters subsequently appeared in the Hartford papers, some hinting at what went wrong. A letter published in the *Hartford Evening Press* from Pvt. Rollin N. Turnbull (Co. G) to his father Robert Turnbull, minister of Hartford's First Baptist Church, mentioned that he had been dispatched to hospital duty before the battle and thus missed the action. But Rollin Turnbull also reported that fifty soldiers had already fallen out of the ranks due to the "hard fare, hard marching, etc. and were temporarily in hospital. Others were detached for special duty," so that according to Turnbull, "the 16th went into the fight with only about 400 privates."[89] Orderly sergeant Henry Johnson (Co. B), in a letter to his wife Julia that appeared in the *Evening Press*, stated: "I have had one day's experience on the battle field and such a day, as it was, I hope never to experience again. Old soldiers say that it was the hardest fought battle they ever saw. The rebels got dreadfully whipped, but it cost us many lives to do it. We have five men killed in our company. Wm. P. Safford is missing. The 16th is badly cut up. It is enough to make one's heart sick to think of it."[90]

One of the starkest accounts of the battle came from eighteen-year-old corporal Samuel B. Mettler. Describing the chaotic fight in the cornfield, Mettler wrote: "We saw them advancing and supposed they were our men, as they were dressed just like us, but we soon found out the truth. Before we could form, they were upon us, and though they encountered a heavy fire, yet they being nearly 5,000 to 800 of us, drove us back behind our batteries. The slaughter was great on both sides of that encounter, and our retreat was made in great confusion." Grazed by a bullet as he ran, Mettler commented that "the men were so scared, they fled in all directions." The next day, he walked the ground and viewed sights "I never want to see again!" The piles of bullet-ridden corpses were "hard to see" and too "horrid" for him to describe, but Mettler found the "worst sight was [that of] the poor wounded men." "I went to several hospitals and saw heaps of arms and legs cut off. Oh, such groaning—it is enough to make me cry to think of it."[91]

Private, unpublished letters home supported Cpl. Mettler's account, conceding the regiment's poor performance and affirming the battle's startling results. Many confessed openly, as Mettler did, to running in fear. Martin V. Culver wrote his brother Jonathan on September 21, 1862, "We have had a rather hard time since we came out." "We had one hard battle, a very hard one." He estimated that "42 were killed and 145 wounded in the 16th, we have not but 4 or 5 hundred in now." "Some," he noted, "have skedaddled."[92] Relyea wrote his family that he did not consider running until he looked around and "saw only dead men." At that moment, he confessed, "I very quickly decided it was no place for me."[93] Relyea tried to find some humor in his admission to his wife Celia. "It is over now," he mused, "and we laugh at our fears, that is human, so am I."[94] Pvt. William Drake (Co. B) was just as blunt when he told his cousin, "There was some pretty tall running in the 16th and I guess that I made myself scarce rather fast."[95] George Robbins described being taken "into a cornfield where we could not see anything." He did not run, he assured his sister Lydia, "until the rest did."[96] Austin D. Thompson provided few details in a letter home to Electra Churchill. He simply wrote of "marching on," after the loss of their "brave Captain Manross, the father of his company." But, Thompson, wrote, "the bullets flew so thick that the Reg. was all confused and after one or two rallys [sic], were forced to retreat."[97] Elizur D. Belden's diary described the fight in the cornfield as a "scene of terror, every man for himself." Belden "turned with the rest and made for the fence" but was struck in the thigh. He "crawled along through the shower of bullets to a small gutter where I lay down, several others lay down with me, the bullets & shells flew over me thick and fast. There I lay not daring to stir until dark when the firing ceased." When darkness came, Belden was one of the men who helped the severely injured Captain Barber off the field to a hospital. He returned to camp in the morning.[98]

The honesty of these private accounts is noteworthy. John B. Cuzner explained to his sweetheart Ellen that there were members of the regiment who "did not frighten," but he was not one of them. "As for myself," he confessed, "I am a big coward." He claimed that he only "ran when they gave the order to retreat" and then hid behind a stone wall. The regiment, Cuzner wrote, was "cut to pieces most shockingly," and he described men falling all around him. He credited Capt. Mix as the only one who "knows his business." The seriousness of the regiment's loss did not sink in until roll call, when Cuzner realized how many of his comrades were gone. Still, he was not tired of a soldier's life, he promised Ellen. He had a good rifle and knew "how to use it."[99] In a letter written ten days later, Cuzner vowed to write no more about Antietam. "I could fill sheets about it all," he told Ellen, "but you wouldn't like to read about the horrible sights I saw after the Battle." He did have something more to say, though, about the Confederates he had encountered. They were "shirtless and almost shoeless" foes who desperately stripped slain Union soldiers of their clothes, rings, and watches, "and everything worth carrying off leaving their pockets turned inside out." He accused Southern soldiers of burning their own dead, claiming that this "accounts for the few or small number of enemy dead found on the field of Battle." Still, in spite of these disquieting statements, Cuzner tried to reassure Ellen that army life suited him, and if he survived, "it will be the making of me."[100]

Others struggled to put the battle in broader context. Cpl. Leland O. Barlow was dismayed by the "awful sight" of the mangled wounded and dead, surprised he or any of his comrades survived at all. "It was," he summed up, "a hard day for the 16th Reg.”[101] He advised Jane that he did not believe their brother Ed should enlist. “Not that I am sorry that I am a Soldier,” Barlow explained, “but I don’t believe he would fancy the business.” The battle’s carnage had also made Barlow acutely aware of his and his comrades’ mortality. “If we live to ever get home,” he assured his sister, “we can tell some big stories.”[102] Jacob Bauer informed his wife Emily three days after the battle that he too was surprised that he was still alive. Reflecting on that “dreadful hour” in the cornfield, Bauer recalled forgetting everything, even his wife and his own safety. Instead, his “only thought and word was forward, forward, forward, which I could think of and sing out.” But after he fired one shot, he ran with the rest of the regiment in “Bull Run Fashion.”[103] After a few weeks, Bauer changed his mind about the regiment’s failed performance at Antietam and the war as a whole. By October 2, he was “feeling first rate and glad that I can do my duty,” attesting that he “really love[d]” soldiering. The same man who unabashedly stated that he and the rest of the 16th had fled the field “in Bull Run Fashion” started thinking dramatically differently about the rout. If he survived the war, he assured his wife, he would return to Antietam and show her where “the heros [sic] rest side by side.” The 16th had its share of cowards, Bauer wrote, but he was not one of them. Cowards were the ones who cursed the most, he maintained, “and they were the ones who stayed back in the hour of trial.”[104]

Some blasted the enemy, accusing the Confederates of trickery by wearing blue uniforms and waving the U.S. flag.[105] Cpl. Sidney Hayden wrote to his father, “We were ordered into a cornfield to support a battery and the Rebels got close on to us by dressing in our clothes and carrying our flag firing volley after volley on us while we supposed [they] were our friends and tried to stop them without firing a shot ourselves until they were discovered.”[106] When his father asked how many rounds he actually fired at Antietam, Hayden responded, “Strange as it may seem I never fired a shot.”[107]

Two members, Robert Kellogg and John Burnham, penned some of the most searing accounts of regiment’s experience. Kellogg wrote his father a long missive three days after Antietam. In great detail and using much of the same wording from his diary, he recounted the 16th Connecticut’s movements on the field and their subsequent retreat. After withstanding the awful fire and “our men breaking and retreating,” Kellogg “finally retreated out of the cornfield and over the hill again, amidst a shower of bullets.” A soldier fell at his feet, but he kept running until he found safety behind a fence at the top of a hill. He rejoined the remnant of his broken regiment when attempts were made to reenter the fray but was soon ordered off the field and into camp. "We were murdered," he angrily charged, reasoning that a green regiment such as the 16th should not have been left "unsupported in a cornfield in the immediate vicinity of a cunning foe—and as it were, left to take care of itself." He closed his diary entry for September 17: "Thus ended our first day of battle and a fearful one it was."[108] In his letters and diary, Kellogg refused to label anyone in the 16th a coward but admitted to his father that he had felt a sort of "quailing" himself when the shells began to burst. He recalled praying to God throughout that terrible day that "His will be done," and he believed that "God gave me courage & strength to bear up through the fearful scenes of that terrible day." It was the rebels, Kellogg insisted in his letter home, who "skedaddled early Friday morning," fearing another confrontation with the federals.[109]

Adj. John H. Burnham also reflected on his own behavior and that of his comrades in a lengthy letter to his family a few weeks after the battle. Burnham had publicly praised his regiment's performance in the newspapers, but he was more frank in this letter home. His sister Lottie asked him to describe his "personal feelings in the fight." Burnham admitted, "I could sit down and talk to you and tell you all about it easily but I find it more difficult to write how I felt." He remembered little leading up to the attack, as he had been busy issuing orders and preparing the men for battle. He had no time to think of personal danger until he spotted the enemy on his left forming with calm intrepidity, methodically planting a battery in close range to the regiment. At that moment, Burnham wrote, "I am frank to confess that although I had no idea of running away—I trembled. You may call the feeling fear or anything you choose for I don't deny that I trembled and wished we were well out of it." Although he was afraid, he did not act on it, instead assisting Col. Beach in attempting to round up the shattered remnants of the 16th and the 11th Connecticut in some kind of orderly fashion through "as hot a fire as I saw any time during the day." He concluded, "I tried to do my duty and am satisfied." Nonetheless, the experience left the young officer with deeply mixed feelings. On one hand, he "should not be sorry to see the war ended tomorrow without firing another shot," but at the same time, he acknowledged, "I am a little eager to see one more battle. Not from any reckless desire for the excitement but I have a little practical knowledge now and I should be more at home next time and perhaps do better. I should be considerable [sic] cooler I have no doubt." He assured his mother that he hoped to survive the war, but there was something he wanted much more: to prove his manhood. "I hope as I always have," Burnham explained, "that I may have the courage to do my duty well, not recklessly but with simple bravery and fidelity, so that if I fall you may have the consolation of knowing that I not only lose [sic] my life in a good cause but did it like a man." Although, Burnham had "no idea how a fight would affect me," he had "tried it now pretty thoroughly and although I believe I 'stood firm,' I am no more inclined to brag than before." As an officer in a regiment that had performed poorly, Burnham appeared to believe that he had to maintain a careful balance between what one historian has called "martial" and "restrained" manhood: he could not give in to his fears, of course, but nor did he want to aggressively flaunt his battle "courage." Burnham added one final observation on the subject of bravery. "I wish to say particularly this romance about men being shot in the back is all a humbug. A mounted officer is as likely to be hit in the back, and more likely to be hit in the side than in the front and don't ever do any injustice to think ill of him."[110]

Burnham had other concerns besides his personal valor and sense of masculinity. Soon after the battle, in a short note home, he asked his family to "save all newspapers publishing anything about the 16th regiment." He vowed to keep his own "historical record of the regt. on my own private account." After this single battle, with painful questions and troubling accusations already brewing, Burnham wanted to "compare notes and see if they tell the truth about us." The young officer already sensed that there would be angry allegations, even from within the regiment, about what really happened in that cornfield on the afternoon of September 17. "Please take notice," he instructed, "of what our wounded men of the 16th say about the Col & I when they come home, some of them will be there soon."[111] In early October, Burnham learned of the *New York Tribune*'s account and judged it to be the most fair and "correct statement of our operations." "One thing is certain," Burnham wrote, "it was a 'big fight' as the sixteenth found to their severe cost, and although we got the best of it on the whole I am unable to key myself up to a high pitch of exultation over the days work." Still, Burnham, like many of his comrades, could "imagine no earthly reason why we did not go at them the next day with a vengeance."[112]

Members of other regiments commented on the 16th's performance. Dr. Nathan Mayer, then surgeon with the 11th Connecticut, in a letter written to his younger brother Louis at home in Hartford on September 29, 1862, witnessed the "Sixteenth at our side in the thick fire of the enemy, repulsed, rallying, breaking, rallying again and finally thronged and forced back." The doctor labored at dressing wounds and amputations until his head ached. "The carnage," Mayer stated simply, "was frightful." "Still on went the brave regiments, rallying as often as they were broken." When the bullets were whistling by, the cornstalks were crashing down around him, the young doctor confessed to his brother, "one feels like lying down and hugging the ground as closely as possible."[113] Sgt. Henry C. Hall from the 8th C.V., who wrote his sister on October 5, 1862, also recounted the fate of the 16th Connecticut. Hall related how the regiment advanced "but a short distance into the corn when they became engaged with the enemys [sic] skirmishers and in a few moments their lines were in utter confusion and it is thought that they killed each other more than they killed the enemy." "The 16th Conn has received a great deal of praise at home," Hall reflected, "& I think myself they did as well as any green troops would have done but if they had been old troops their conduct would have been shameful, but the time is coming when they will be a splendid regiment if nothing happens [to] them as they have a good Colonel and the regt is composed of good men to make soldiers of."[114] Hall's prediction could not have been more wrong. The regiment may have had "good men," and Beach was a decent, capable commander, but circumstances were already conspiring against them so that the regiment, despite high expectations, would always fall short.

"WE LOST ALMOST HALF OF OUR REGIMENT"

In Connecticut, casualty reports came slowly and were not always reliable. Nine days after the battle, Colonel Beach's official report appeared in the *Hartford Evening Press*.[115] But by then, details about their loved ones had begun to trickle home, and family and friends were absorbing the news of the losses.[116] Regimental chaplain Peter V. Finch furnished one of the first casualty lists to local newspapers. It was generally accurate in number killed (41), although off by more than twenty in the number wounded, and it contained some misspelled names.[117] On September 21, Finch wrote his fiancé Harriet Bronson as he waited with the body of Captain Barber to ensure that it was "properly cared for and sent on to Hartford." "We have had," he explained, "a very severe fight," with the regiment "sadly cut up." In this letter, Finch counted 42 killed and 146 wounded, and he named soldiers by company, as he did in the letter sent to the Hartford papers. "Those poor fellows with the exception of the Officers, I buried at midnight last Thursday on the field of battle. They were all laid in one long grave. Poor fellows their labors are all through with. Our Adjt with whom I sat up the whole night after the battle has written a full account for the papers, and a description of the grave, so that friends can get the bodies of their relatives if they want them."[118]

The final tally would show a casualty rate of over 25 percent. Out of an estimated 940 soldiers engaged, the 16th Connecticut lost 43 killed, 164 wounded (18 mortally), 20 captured, and 19 deserted.[119] The loss in officers was especially acute. One lieutenant and three captains were dead, including Capt. Newton Manross, whose last words reportedly were "O my poor wife, my poor wife!"[120] Lt. Col. Frank Cheney, Maj. George Washburn, two captains, and one lieutenant were seriously wounded. In total, of the regiment's officers, commissioned and noncommissioned, 56 were killed or wounded at Antietam.[121] "We lost," Jacob Bauer later reflected, "almost half of our regiment and the best men in officers and privates."[122]

Among those killed and wounded were some of the unit's best-known members. The *Hartford Daily Courant* editor's son Charles L. Clark was shot in the right thigh. The young sergeant would lose his leg and eventually be discharged from service.[123] Lt. Col. Frank Cheney, who had quickly won the love and admiration of his men in those three short weeks of service, had his left arm severely injured. He wrote his father from a makeshift hospital in Boonsboro, Maryland, surrounded by wounded and dying officers. "Major Washburn is here with me, badly wounded in the hip. Fred Barber has his thigh bone shattered by a ball, too high up the Sergeant says for amputation, I am afraid it is all over with him." Cheney had already seen Captain Manross "by my side dead" in the same hospital. He felt useless: "I wish I was able to help do something for our poor fellows all around me. Every house and barn is a hospital for miles about the battlefield."[124]

The loss of captains was particularly severe. Captain Barber, who had worked for Frank Cheney at his Manchester silk factory, died from his wounds on September 20. Captains Newton Manross (Co. K) and John L. Drake (Co. I) perished on the field, and Charles Babcock (Co. E) and Nathaniel Hayden (G) were both injured and would eventually resign from the unit.[125] Samuel Brown (Co. D), leading his company into the cornfield, was heard urging his men to "keep down." William Relyea later remembered Brown being "anxious that his company would give as good an account of themselves as any in the regiment—he was cool but somewhat angry at us for not forming a line as we had begun to be taught to do on dress parade and scolded at us some a few minutes after we had formed a little more to his satisfaction."[126] A flurry of bullets hit Brown, and he went down, still screaming orders to his men.[127] His body was found on the battlefield two days later, stripped of all his clothing, including his shoes.[128]

Captain Manross's death was a tremendous loss for the regiment. The *Hartford Evening Press* heralded the professor turned soldier as a "gentleman of fine attainments, an accomplished scholar, a pleasant speaker, and though but a few weeks in the service, a brave and efficient officer."[129] Manross's Company K was profoundly shaken by their captain's death. The captain's brother Eli, a sergeant in the 5th Connecticut, whose unit saw no action at Antietam, visited the field soon after the battle ended to view the very ground where his brother fell. "My feelings while standing upon that fatal spot," he wrote his family, "I will not trust myself to describe." Sergeant Manross described the scene: "Trees and fences are splintered by balls, dead horses are strewn over the field together with caps, knapsacks, coats, shells exploded and unexploded, pools of blood where our brave boys fell, broken guns, etc."[130] Captain Manross was buried in Forestville less than a week after the battle.[131] In an obituary by Rev. Leverette Griggs, the minister mused, "How mysterious that such a man should be cut down in the midst of his days—that one so much loved, so much needed, and so well qualified for distinguished usefulness here, should be taken away at the age of 37 years." Griggs, who had mourned the loss of his own nineteen-year-old son John, continued: "God has done it; there is not a sparrow that falleth to the ground without our Father's knowledge. Let Him do as seemeth good in His sight."[132]

Colonel Beach was one of the few officers who emerged from the battle unscathed, although Cheney claimed that Beach's coat took some shots.[133] The *Courant* contended, "Colonel Beach, by his bearing in this battle, has completely won the affections of his men."[134] Despite the fact that his performance on the day of battle earned Beach praise from his superiors, and soon a brevet to brigadier general, he had not won over all of his men. In the days that followed the battle, Beach commanded the brigade and thus was absent from his battered regiment. "I don't know or care much where Colonel Beach is," Cpl. Sidney Hayden wrote home, "but in the division somewhere."[135]

Other soldiers spoke fondly of Beach. Corporal Barlow wrote his father that the colonel looked out for the regiment and wanted his men "up to the mark every time." When Beach returned to the regiment in early October, Barlow was pleased, and despite Beach's stringent standards, claimed, "We were all glad to see him again." Barlow told his father that when some soldiers complained about doing duty, Beach responded that he "did not want any such chaps in the Reg."

He further gave their sutler a "walking ticket" for selling whiskey to the men.[136] Bernard Blakeslee later praised their commander's "personal bravery and heroism" that fateful day and remembered how "sad and full of woe was his heart on the night after the struggle, when the broken remnants of the Sixteenth gathered around him in the rear of the battle ground." Blakeslee contended that Beach "made personal inquiry after each of the wounded, and visited a number of them on that evening and the following days, doing for them all that was possible."[137] But for several weeks Colonel Beach and Adjutant Burnham were both on detached duty, and with so many commissioned officers wounded or dead, Captain Mix was assigned to command the regiment. On October 1, the 16th C.V. counted "less than six hundred men on duty."[138]

Although many soldiers were gone from the ranks, the camp was far from empty, as an increasing number of civilians appeared there after the battle. Family members wanted to bring their loved ones' bodies home; others came to visit the wounded in hospitals, as well as report on the soldiers in camp. Hartford businessmen W. H. D. Callender, Ebenezer N. Kellogg, and J. M. B. McNary arrived on the battlefield to "relieve the anxiety of friends at home and render such assistance as they might be able."[139] Hartford undertaker William A. Roberts was commissioned by several families to travel to Maryland and bring bodies home for burial.[140] "There are many persons from Connecticut here every day," Sidney Hayden wrote his father on October 5, to look "after the bodies of the deceased friends and to care for the wounded."[141] As late as November 6, the *Hartford Evening Press* reported that a "Mr. H. N. Prout of Suffield" had visited the "late Maryland battles" and discovered the "graves of 42 members of the 8th and 16th Connecticut regiments and has a list of their names and places of burials." The paper instructed friends and family to contact Mr. Prout "in reference to the location of the graves of their friends and the expense of exhuming and transporting bodies." Although startling, this discovery was perhaps also comforting to those wondering and worrying about their loved ones from whom no word had been heard.[142]

As the funerals for the dead multiplied at home, ministers strove publicly to paint the unit's stunning losses in commendable terms and to find ways to reaffirm soldiers and civilians' faith in the regiment and the war. Reverend A. W. Ide assured the grieving friends and family of slain first lieutenant William Horton that the young husband and father had "proved himself a true and brave man" and a "kind" commander. Ide quoted letters from members of Horton's company who last saw their lieutenant "surrounded by rebels, defending himself most valiantly" with his sword. Ide asked Connecticut soldiers attending the funeral to relay a message from home to men at the front: "Go, on your return, and tell your dear friends that, whether in life or death they shall not be forgotten. Tell them that from the steps of the house of God, we give praise and honor to the brave of the 11th and 16th Conn. Regiments—both to the living and the dead." Much of Ide's sermon interwove religion and politics, exhorting his congregants that they must "mourn" for their slain "in view of the fact, that the cause of patriotism is a holy cause." He further avowed, "I will not tell you what *I* think God means by this baptism of blood, filling the font of streams flowing from the veins of almost every household; but only say that if we do not understand and obey His instructions and warnings, *His destructions* will comprehend us."[143]

It is significant that Reverend Ide publicly stressed Horton's bravery. William Horton had served as first lieutenant in Company B of the 11th Connecticut from November 1861 to March 1862 but resigned after less than four months to return home. Reverend Ide stated that Horton had volunteered for the 11th Connecticut "without a bounty to allure, or a draft to threaten." "In the month of August of the present year," Ide maintained, "he enlisted again as a private; having, as we are informed, no assurance that he would ever be promoted. He entered with an uncommon degree of determination to wipe out the rebellion."[144] According to Pvt. Ezra Burgess (Co. I), Horton, facing accusations of cowardice, had reenlisted in the 16th C.V., vowing, "I'll show you whether I am a coward or not." Horton bled to death on the field, a death that Burgess believed could have been prevented had he been tended to in time. Burgess concluded, "He was a brave man, although he had to enlist the second time to prove it."[145]

These sermons also offered civilians a way to express deepening concerns and disillusionment with the war itself. At the funeral of seventeen-year-old Granby soldier Roswell Morgan Allen (Co. E), Rev. W. H. Gilbert censured regimental officers for abuse of duty and lack of sensitivity to the men in the ranks. "You all know," Gilbert told his Granby Congregational Church, "how, at the very outset of their career as soldiers, [t]his regiment worn by exhaustive marches, was thrust into the very heat of the awful battle of Antietam."[146] Allen had fallen ill immediately after the battle. He was discharged from service on December 19, and he died nine days later in a Washington hospital. Gilbert read from a letter written by members of Allen's company who praised their dead comrade, and he comforted mourners that Pvt. Allen "ever remained as pure and noble as when he left home."[147]

Many of the regimental wounded from Antietam never returned to the field but languished in hospitals, waiting months, even years, for a discharge to return home. Of no use to the army, they existed in a sort of limbo, caught by the military's bureaucracy and the unclear status of their physical condition. On April 14, 1864, some nineteen months after the battle, Cpl. Charles T. Collins (Co. C) was still in a hospital suffering from wounds sustained at Antietam. The married gunsmith, described as a man "who enlisted from purely patriotic motives" and "who would be the last to quit the service but from a consciousness that he can be of no use to the government," sought a discharge so that "he should have an opportunity to provide for" the support of his family. Collins's discharge came on Feb. 8, 1865.[148]

Cpl. Samuel Baker (Co. F) and Pvts. Van Buren Randall (Co. F) and Newton Willey (Co. A) were all, in Baker's words, "wounded in such a manner [that they] will be unfit for service for months." They similarly remained in a Maryland hospital in the days, weeks, and months following the battle. The soldiers had been granted furloughs from the regimental surgeon, but hospital officials refused to allow them to leave. Baker and Randall were married with families, and the corporal contended that it was "both policy and charity on the part of government" to transfer them to a Hartford hospital. Baker sought help from the governor. An appeal on his behalf came from Hartford printer Alexander Calhoun, echoing similar words William Buckingham used in enticing men to enlist: "I now entreat you, as Governor of the State, to whose call he responded and left, not only his workshop, where he had fitted a situation for ten years, but his wife and family, to take his case in hand." He begged Buckingham to intervene.[149]

It is not clear how much influence the governor or any state official actually had in helping friends and families of the 16th Connecticut to bring their soldiers home, but the governor's office became a sounding board for many grieving and worried people desperate for answers.[150] There is evidence that Buckingham inquired about specific soldiers, and at some point, he dispatched state agents to help relieve the dire conditions of the unit.[151] Another soldier who came to the governor's attention that fall was Pvt. George S. Howe, a printer who had worked for the Radical Republican *Hartford Evening Press* before enlisting in the 16th Connecticut. Howe had been "sick and disabled since the battle of Antietam," like so many of his comrades, but instead of being discharged, he had remained hospitalized in the service as autumn turned to winter and the new year of war commenced. On January 15, 1863, state senator Ammi Giddings, nephew of famed abolitionist Joshua R. Giddings, wrote an urgent letter to the governor describing Howe's fate, claiming, "He seems without friends." Giddings encouraged Buckingham to write to the hospital surgeon and obtain Howe a furlough or discharge. "You will undoubtedly confer a favor on a very worthy & patriotic man." Howe received his discharge two weeks later and arrived home in early February.[152]

Even without battle wounds, some men remained in hospitals for months or were otherwise deemed unfit for duty.[153] Pvt. Theodore R. Stearns, for example, who had joined the regiment at the behest of his cousin John Griggs, wrote that he had been "spared," and "did not get a scratch."[154] Six months later, however, on detached service as a clerk to Gen. Henry W. Halleck in Washington, D.C., he explained: "I find I cant stand soldiering in the field—I have the Rheumatism every now and then contracted while in the field. I had got down pretty low after I went in a hospital, soon after the battle of Antietam."[155] That single combat experience had also quenched the young man's desire to fight: "I have seen all I wish. Distance lends enchantment to the view."[156] Alfred Avery (Co. H) fell "seriously ill" soon after Antietam, although there was no clear answer as to what ailed him. But that single battle permanently changed the twenty-one-year-old unmarried farmer. He was discharged in early December and returned home to live with his parents, where he remained until his death in 1913. "It is supposed," one of his comrades later wrote, "that [a] concussion of shells or something of that nature affected his head as after recovering bodily health, he was more or less irrational as long as he lived."[157]

In the immediate weeks following the battle, Chaplain Finch tried to assure worried family and friends at home that the regiment was healing. In a letter dated October 6 and published soon after in the *Hartford Daily Times,* Finch wrote optimistically: "The health of the regiment is good. We have no more sick in proportion to our numbers than other regiments, and no cases of serious sickness." Still, Finch reported four more dying in hospitals from battle wounds, and that number would only grow in the coming weeks.[158]

Another minister, Rev. J. Morgan Smith from Unionville, spent two weeks with the regiment after Antietam, visiting the wounded and sick, interviewing field officers, and talking to soldiers still in the ranks. He was stunned by their reduced state and by the stories of mistreatment and suffering, describing, "They were beaten over the head by sabers when exhausted on the march, they were struck with fists at slight derelictions from duty and they were sworn at with intense profanity by the Colonel, Lieut. Colonel and Major." Quoting one of the regiment's sergeants, Reverend Smith wrote to Governor Buckingham, "They are a wreck." Smith estimated that, of the nearly 1,000 men who had left the state in late August, perhaps as few as 230 were "ready to march" in early November.[159]

Indeed, the regiment was a shell of its former self. George Robbins later recalled: "It may seem incredible but for two weeks the regiment could not muster but a few hundred out of the one thousand that left the State only one month previous. Many were prostrated by the arduous march, the abrupt changes from civilian life, and the food which if confined to army rations would have sufficed, but which was rejected for all sorts of stuff bought when possible, brought on, with the change in drinking water, bowel troubles which rendered the men unfit for duty."[160] Alonzo G. Case professed that after those few hours of battle, the regiment, which had had 1,000 men, would "never after that" ever "get 500 together."[161] One morning in mid-October, the men heard the sound of distant cannon and were unsure if they were heading into another battle. "Some of the boys," Pvt. Austin Thompson observed, "seem to be a little afraid when they hear the canons roar. I don't know as I blame them much for they are dangerous things to have around, especially when they are loaded and fired at any one."[162]

On Tuesday, October 14, the *Hartford Evening Press* stated that the 16th Connecticut was encamped at Pleasant Valley, Maryland, with 550 men "reported for duty" and Colonel Beach in command.[163] Here the unit remained for two weeks, and as regimental historian Blakeslee recounted, "The regiment suffered severely from sickness, and when the army again took up the line of march they could muster but few effective men."[164] The regiment, bloodied and nearly reduced in half, broke camp on the morning of October 28, 1862, and turned south toward Virginia.

— It was not uncommon during the Civil War that a freshly recruited regiment was heralded with high expectations, rushed into combat, and performed badly. Yet, for many in the 16th Connecticut, a troubling anxiety started to take root, eating away at their early idealism and optimism, convincing them that somehow, someway, they had been singled out and maligned as an unlucky regiment.

3

Fredericksburg and Winter Camp
"Sick of the War"

The regiment continued to reel from the aftereffects of Antietam, witnessing a drain of men from the ranks, a stream of officer resignations and difficult conditions on the march and in camp. Left as mere observers at the Battle of Fredericksburg, the Connecticut soldiers reflected darkly on the Union's prospects for success. They named their winter quarters "Camp Starvation" that winter of 1862–63; this was one of the lowest points of their service.

"MARCHED HARD"

Antietam was a harsh introduction to the realities of war for the 16th Connecticut. They emerged from their first campaign battered and severely reduced in numbers. There were lingering questions about their combat performance and concerns about regimental leadership. Now after weeks of inaction, the Army of the Potomac was on the move again. During the first two weeks of November, federals marched for successive days, with intermittent halts, leaving Maryland, entering Virginia, and finally coming to a stop opposite the town of Fredericksburg. For the 16th, already weakened and hobbled by combat, illness, poor rations, and its initial march to the front, this second march was even more strenuous. Robert Kellogg noted that when the regiment started out, provisions were plentiful and of good quality, and men were holding up against the strain. However, this quickly began to change after a few days. On November 2, Kellogg wrote in his diary, "This has been one of the hardest marches we have seen, going about 15 miles."[1] Then provisions began to give out. On November 11, Kellogg described being "half fed" and having been "marched hard," in a letter to his father. Kellogg blamed a "miserable set of Quarter Masters & Commissaries in the Brigade and we suffer accordingly—Our Quarter Master was overhauled this morning by the officers, but he declared he is not to blame." Kellogg echoed the view of men in the ranks: "I sincerely hope something will be done to remedy these evils. We soldiers are willing to fight, but we must eat & be clothed comfortably."[2] Soon, the foraging began, some of it apparently very destructive. As the regiment marched near Lovettsville, Virginia, Pvt. Elizur Belden (Co. C) was disturbed by the "ransacking" of civilian property by "a lot of soldiers." Belden thought it was "a shame to treat people so [when] there seem to be no men at home." Belden reasoned that much of the country they traveled through was loyal, but his hungry comrades cared little. They stole "chickens, turkeys and every thing they can lay their hands on to."[3]

For some, the march and poor rations was proving too much to bear. Pvt. Belden fell behind after several days, his feet too sore to keep up the double-quick pace. He saw "any quantity of stragglers on the road."[4] Pvt. Edwin C. Bement (Co. D) took sick early in the march and dropped out of the ranks near Wheatland, Virginia. Neither his comrades nor his family ever heard from him again. His family assumed that he died somewhere on the roadside.[5] Still, Belden believed that the 16th Connecticut was better treated than some: "They are not as hard on us as on other regts. Some of them have roll call every hour, drill and dress parade."[6]

The regiment travelled a total of 175 miles in about two weeks. "The men," Bernard Blakeslee wrote, "were completely exhausted from scanty rations and footsore from long marches."[7] When the weary soldiers finally halted at Falmouth, cold, steady rain poured down, preventing them from lighting fires or building their tents. Pvt. Martin V. Culver wrote his older brother Jonathan from what he dubbed "Camp Hungry" on November 16: "i dont like this life i have got sick of it." He was desperate for some tobacco to chew and buckskin gloves to warm his hands. He was thinking about ways to get out: "if I can get home any way i shall do it I shall come if i get a chance without deserting."[8]

The march did not demoralize everyone. Pvt. Lewis M. Holcomb, Jr., wrote his cousin Addie on November 1, 1862, from Loudon County that the troops were "in fine spirits and are confident of victory, although before you receive this another tale may be told." He perceived that the men were anxious for a fight; if only the generals "would give us a chance we would do it." Holcomb had settled into soldier life well: "Ever since the battle which took place some two months ago, I have enjoyed a season of almost uninterrupted happiness. This is owing to the fact that I have been perfectly healthy, more so than at home, which was not the case with me for the first few weeks." Holcomb reported that there was enough to eat, and even though many "of the boys grumble," he refused to give in to despair: "When I think of the Noble cause for which we are fighting, come what may I never will and never can repent that I joined this Army." He reflected that he had risked his life "once" and expected more hardships and risks in the future. "If I ever come home," he wrote his cousin, repeating common patriotic idioms, "I shall be proud of my course. If I die I ask no better death than to die in defense of my country, no better grave than a victorious battlefield."[9] Like Holcomb, Adj. John Burnham found active campaigning invigorating. Burnham wrote his family in early November that he was "remarkably healthy and hearty" and had not been ill one day since the regiment left Hartford. Despite the exposure, hard marching, cold, wet weather, and rampant sickness, Burnham never felt better: "I feel splendid all the time and should be in the best of spirits were it not for the condition of the regiment."[10]

Holcombe and Burnham, though, appeared to be the exception. Colonel Beach, for example, was faring poorly. Chronic diarrhea afflicted him in the early fall, and it continued to plague him for months. But because he was a colonel, he had many advantages. Too weak to ride his horse, he instead rode in an ambulance. Eventually, Beach was too incapacitated to command.[11] Pvt. Culver sourly observed that their colonel had "gone home sick and most all the rest ought to go home for about all of them are most dead." He claimed that the regiment was decimated by illness: "half of them barefoot and have got hard coalds that they will never get over."[12] Although Culver and others believed the 16th was unique in its suffering, the regiment experienced what most all Civil War soldiers did: the harsh weariness of everyday soldiering.[13]

Glum letters began appearing in Hartford newspapers, painting a bleak picture of the soldiers' plight and spreading the news to friends and family at home. In early November, "a lady reader" of the *Hartford Daily Times* sent her brother's letter to the paper. Estimating the regiment's strength to be no more than "180 men at drill," the soldier dolefully predicted that number to grow "less daily." He stated, "We have to sleep on the bare ground without any straw and the ill effects are painfully abundant. It is as frosty here as at the North."[14]

Accusations of cruel mistreatment also appeared in letters and in the press. Bristol insurance agent Josiah Peck complained to Gov. William Buckingham of the "excessively overbearing and brutal" Colonel Beach, drunk and profane surgeons, and generally incompetent and immoral officers who mistreated the enlisted soldiers. "These men are our noblest citizens," Peck contended, "none that have gone from here before could have compared with them for worth & moral character, they went impelled, I believe, solely by a love for their Country to help her in her hour of need & must they receive such treatment at her hands[?]"[15] Another worried resident wrote to Governor Buckingham, concerned about the 14th and 16th Connecticut so recently rushed into battle "in a condition every way unfit for service, the wounded & sick are dying every day for want of care and comforts." A woman identified as "Mrs. E.L.H." warned that these troops in particular were in "such a starving & filthy condition that all patriotism & enthusiasm is withering out of their hearts." The woman closed, "Hardy and brave fellows who have waited patiently & resolutely are despairing of relief & send letters home which stir our souls to exasperation." She exhorted, "Can we help them? Can you sir, help them[?]"[16]

The Republican *Hartford Evening Press* published another disturbing letter from a 16th Connecticut soldier who had recently spent two weeks recovering in a Maryland hospital. He described conditions where there were no nurses and not enough doctors. Instead, "soldier assistants" tried to care for the hundreds of desperately ill men. The food was meager, little medicine was available, and the rooms were unheated. "I do not state these facts," the letter writer explained, "which after all can give but a faint impression of the actual misery which went on in those hospitals—in order to cast blame upon the doctors there, for most of them did what they could." Still, something had to be done: "Many soldiers of the 16th and other Connecticut regiments are today lying in the cold, without blankets, without change of shirts, and without underclothes, while stacks of these articles are heaped up in Washington and elsewhere." He warned that there was a widening gulf between "the benevolence at home and the suffering in the army not yet bridged over, which ought to be and must be or you will soon have no army."[17]

"SADLY DEMORALIZED"

A soldier's letter published in the *Daily Courant* reflected on the unit's prospects for battle given its reduced condition. The soldier estimated, "The regiment has something less than five hundred in camp, a good many being sick and wounded." Hoping that the 16th Connecticut would again be "called into action, I trust we shall do our duty." After the debacle of Antietam, this soldier seemed hesitant to make any optimistic predictions about his regiment's future: "If we do well the credit will be quite as great, and if we do ill, the stigma much less if we make no vain boasts before hand."[18] It had been just three months since the regiment's mustering in, and yet there were real doubts about its future success.

The unit was still reeling from the aftermath of its first battle. One of the Case brothers later reflected on the men's state of mind at this time: "The Regiment to use an army phrase was 'sadly demoralized' first coming from home with high hopes and going into battle without so much as ever being formed in line of battle. They had reason to feel sad."[19] The losses from Antietam were difficult enough to absorb; now there were a high number of men in hospitals, some entirely incapacitated for service. In fact, many would never see active service again. Officers, too, wanted out, worn down by hard marches, exposure to weather, illness, the brutality of battle, and the army's excruciating bureaucracy. Just a few weeks of military service convinced several that they were ready to return to civilian life. Some were angry over promotions, believing they were unfairly overlooked. By late November, Cpl. Leland Barlow in Company E. observed a "good many resignations in this Regt."[20]

There was a steady stream of officer resignations and honorable discharges in the weeks and months following Antietam.[21] The sudden and continued loss of leadership would take its toll on the men in the ranks.[22] Leadership had been a point of contention for the regiment from its beginnings at Camp Williams. Now, many of its commissioned officers were leaving, disillusioned by war's realities. Their actions would only exacerbate tensions between officers and men.[23]

The drain of officers left Capt. Edward Mix temporarily in command of the regiment. Mix, who was one of the few line officers with actual battle experience, earned varied reviews from the men. John B. Cuzner later recalled, "When he first came out he was pretty strict with us but after we all became acquainted we liked him better every day."[24] Ariel Case in his postwar memoir portrayed Mix as arbitrary and arrogant, describing him smoking a "$50 Meerschaum pipe" one day with a look that "he commanded the whole army." He also accused Mix of being "always a little nervous under fire."[25] "Mix don't give very good satisfaction and all the boys are down on him," Sidney Hayden claimed. "Curious chap[.] Swearing one day and praying the next."[26]

Colonel Beach remained a controversial figure in the unit, though Burnham was a steadfast supporter. Captain Mix was "first rate," Burnham opined, but he "is not Col. Beach." "You must not," Burnham urged his mother, "believe the bug bear stories you hear bout the Col." It was "all in your eye," Burnham wrote, suggesting that the angry accusations were relative. Beach, he continued, was "severe, dreadfully severe upon any man who disobeys orders but he is a fine hearted man and any one who is faithful and tries to do his duty will be well treated." Burnham himself had grown "very much attached to him" in the short time he had known the colonel and vowed that he would "sell my shirt to day to serve him and will defend his character to the utmost of my ability against anyone."[27] There were others in the ranks who agreed. Robert Kellogg declared, "Col. B is a splendid officer & the men have great confidence in him."[28]

Meanwhile hospitalized men continued to die from wounds sustained in the battle as well as from illness.[29] Others who had an opportunity to leave were happy to depart. In late November, Kellogg, who was trained as an apothecary, was selected to be a hospital steward on detached service in the hospital department in Gen. Burnside's headquarters. He was clearly pleased with the change, writing his father three days later of better quarters, food, and pay: "I have now no more marching to do, no more sleeping in the mud etc, but shall be well clothed & fed." Confident that he could stay in the position "permanently," following Burnside "wherever he and his staff go," Kellogg showed little regret about leaving his regiment.[30]

Desertion further sapped the regiment of its strength. Sgt. Collins Pratt (Co. D) deserted on November 2, 1862, while marching through Liberty, Virginia.[31] Cpl. Timothy Mayher, an Irish immigrant in Company D who had been wounded at the battle of Antietam, deserted from a hospital in Harrisburg, Pennsylvania, on December 12, 1862.[32] Pvt. John Roberts (Co. E) deserted from the regimental camp in February, 1863.[33] Pvt. Clark Statton (Co. E) also disappeared after he was ordered to return to the regiment from the hospital in February.[34]

By mid-November, a rumor, started by the Democratic-leaning *Hartford Daily Times,* circulated that the regiment's numbers had dwindled to less than 150 men present for duty. On November 17, the *Hartford Evening Press* published a stern correction: "The 16th regiment was at Snicker's Gap last week Monday. It has 500 or 600 men on duty, besides many men absent on furlough. The statement originating in the *Times,* and extensively copied that the 16th had been reduced from the 1040 men to 140 is not true."[35] Less than two weeks later, the newspaper announced the results of the state's adjutant general's monthly reports. The 16th had "only 406" men "reported—some are sick and others are detached for special service."[36]

"SO SADLY NEGLECTED"

By the first week of December, the 16th C.V. had moved to camp opposite the city of Fredericksburg along the banks of the Rappahannock River. Conditions were still dire. One soldier identifying himself only as "M.H." wrote the Democratic *Hartford Daily Times* that the regiment had been encamped across from the city for nearly two weeks. "Since then," he stated, "we have done nothing but drill and *starve;* for we have not had food enough to satisfy the demands of hunger." Judging the regiment's health "very poor," he estimated "not more than 200 being fit for duty." Recounting negligent treatment by "the Surgeon" of Pvt. Arthur De Newfville Talcott (Co. A), who died shortly after returning to the regiment, and claiming that quinine pills were mistakenly handed out for any and all ailments, M.H. asserted that the "sick in this regiment get very little attention." He concluded bitterly: "The poor condition of our regiment is easily accounted for when you consider that it has been marched, starved, and doctored to death."[37]

Yet another letter published in the *Hartford Daily Times* on December 9 from "One Who Knows" demanded help from the state. To the paper's editor, the author, who appeared to be a civilian, wrote, "Can you inform the people of this enlightened community why it is that our brave Connecticut soldiers are so sadly neglected?" Asking who was at fault and why, the letter continued, "I allude more particularly to the 16th, being more familiar with the facts in that regiment than the others, though I understand there are others in a much worse condition than the 16th." Recounting the regiment's short history, the letter writer repeated the increasingly familiar refrain that, despite its woeful beginnings at Antietam, the soldiers, although "ignorant of the use of a musket," fought "side by side with old veterans, those 1,000 brave boys (so Antietam tells)" and "did their full share toward turning the tide of battle, and winning the reputation that every Connecticut boy may well be proud of." The letter went on to claim that the 16th still lacked their knapsacks—leaving many with no change of clothes since departing Washington. Officers were absent, and the men in the ranks were mistreated and forgotten. The letter closed with a plea that the governor "or somebody else" dispatch state agents to the front to provide some relief to the "brave Yankee boys from Old Connecticut who are now suffering on the banks of the Rappahannock."[38]

Another soldier's letter published in early December described difficult conditions in camp. Food was adequate again, but clothing was lacking, and the men had been without their knapsacks since before Antietam. To make matters worse, their shoes were wearing out. The *Hartford Evening Press* complained, "There is rascally incompetency somewhere about the quartermaster's department, which ought to be looked up and punished." The paper summed up the unit's condition: "The regiment has had hard marches, hard fare, hard weather, and a hard time generally, and the severe exposure accounts for the large number on the sick list."[39] Private letters home only affirmed these sentiments. John B. Cuzner wrote Ellen Van Dorn of the difficult conditions in camp, describing "our shoes being worn out," and "some of the boys almost barefooted" as they tried to shovel six inches of snow.[40] In response to these disquieting accounts, the state dispatched agents to report on conditions directly to the governor.[41] Soldier morale was terrible for much of the Army of the Potomac during the winter of 1862–63, and most northern volunteers shared the 16th Connecticut's plight with regards to camp conditions, defection, and absenteeism.[42] Yet, a conviction persisted that military and government authorities were ignoring and unfairly treating the "Hartford Regiment."

"WE WERE HELD, AS IT WERE, IN LEASH"

Meanwhile, Gen. Burnside pressed forward with a planned attack on Robert E. Lee's army, seeking to dislodge him from his position high above the Rappahannock River. On December 11, the regiment awoke, according to Sgt. Henry Lee, to the sound of "cannons thundering over the Rappahannock, and all day stood in readiness to march in that direction." The men trekked through muddy roads for about a mile, but with so many other troops ahead of them, they stopped and returned to camp where their tents remained. The next day, December 12, the regiment again left their camp, this time loaded only with their blankets, haversacks, and three days rations. Sgt. Lee wrote, "Considerable many troops had already crossed the river. We lay this side until night and then entered the old town of Fredericksburg." He was shocked by the sight: "I expected to see some shattered houses, but was not prepared to witness such general ruin as Fredericksburg presented. Almost every house had been struck by shot and shell. Chimneys were gone, windows smashed in, and the sides of houses completely riddled. This should be no matter of surprise, however, when we consider that the city had taken the fire of both forces."[43] Pvt. Belden also took note of the damage done to the town: "The houses in this part are nearly all riddled by shot and shell, many of them burnt, all ransacked by our troops." He remarked that the Union troops who came through town "first had the best chance" at looting. But the 16th Connecticut, who arrived later, "found little of any value, except flour." "Large quantities of tobacco" were salvaged from the river by soldiers desperate for a smoke or chew.[44]

During the futile federal bloodbath that occurred on December 13, the 16th Connecticut remained in reserve. "Our Reg," Cpl. Leland O. Barlow explained to his sister Jane a few days after the battle, "have not been in any real fight, but we have been where the balls flew pretty thick, but not badly hurt."[45] William Relyea recalled: "We were now close to the stonewall at the foot of Mayre's Hill, but we were held, as it were, in leash."[46] A handful of soldiers suffered wounds from stray artillery shells.[47] The regiment remained "in the city all night," sleeping, as one soldier described, "in the mud in the street."[48] With shots flying all around them, the Connecticut soldiers were little more than spectators to the carnage. "Many lives were lost," Belden observed, as he soberly (and accurately) took stock of the federal situation: "The rebels are strongly fortified on the hill beyond the rifle pits and a high stone wall with the natural strength of the position. No efforts of ours can drive them out."[49]

The next day, on Sunday, December 14, Gen. Burnside planned to lead his beloved IX Corps in a final frontal assault on the enemy position. Sgt. Richard Lee related hearing the news just after breakfast, when Lt. Charles Morse took him aside and told him of the general's plan. Morse instructed Lee to ensure that none of the guns were primed. And, with a stark reminder of Antietam, Morse explained to Lee: "We were to move forward in three columns, if the first column broke, the others were to charge on them and bring them to the work again. If any man broke in the ranks, the field closers were to knock him down." Lee believed, "Very few in the ranks knew of the contemplated movement, but those who did, stood in groups speculating upon the results of the movement."[50] Leland Barlow recounted the episode to his father a few days later: "We had orders to make one desperate charge of the Ninth army Corps, it was to be made at ten o'clock Sunday morning, but that hour came and went without any movement."[51] Harrison Woodford was convinced that the Confederate position was "very strong" and would prove "a deathly job to take as it has already proved to be in the attempt." As the regiment waited anxiously, Harrison "committed myself to the Lord before I went under fire. I felt that I could trust myself in his hands."[52] Finally, it was clear that the charge was not going to occur. Lee, though, believed he and the IX Corps could have succeeded. He could only speculate that Burnside did not want to sacrifice the IX Corps, but he was sure some would have made it to the Confederate lines, although many would have died trying. "They had a splendid position," he stated, "1st a line of rifle pits, then light batteries, then heavy guns. I had no desire to make a charge on those works, but if Burnside had said go, would have done it with good cheer, saying farewell Old Granby."[53]

Barlow was not so sure, supposing that there would have been "an awful slaughter if we had gone up there, as it was, we lost ten thousand or more men."[54] The regiment's total casualties from the battle were one wounded and one missing, both enlisted men.[55]

Kept out of the fray, members of the 16th C.V. were philosophical about the battle, watching from afar and assessing the cause of Burnside's defeat. Most were harsh in their criticism of the Union high command, although protective of their former IX Corps commander. Corporal Barlow defended Burnside, arguing, "some body is to blame," though apparently not Burnside. He cited the delay in laying the pontoon bridge, which allowed the Confederates to strengthen "their works so strong that it is almost impossible to drive them out."[56] Had Burnside "had [the] means for crossing the river when he first got here the place might have been taken with one third the men and held."[57] Sidney H. Hayden, however, considered "the retreat from Fredericksburg humiliating," only giving "confidence to our Enemies."[58] Cuzner candidly described the scene: "Our men charged on batteries where they were mown down like grass, those remaining were obliged to fall back while others took their places to be mown down."[59] Kellogg, who remained on detached service with Burnside and his staff during the battle, wrote, "The slaughter has been immense, but it is said that it is not as large as Antietam."[60] Two weeks later, Kellogg still refused to criticize the army's commander: "I have more confidence in Gen. Burnside now than ever, and although he has met with a severe repulse here, he is not the man to be disheartened." He viewed Burnside as "one of the noblest looking men I ever saw," claiming that even after the defeat, his "troops have the most implicit confidence in him and almost idolize him."[61] A scathing letter published in the Democratic *Hartford Daily Times* in late December by an unnamed member of the IX Corps to his mother may well have come from a member of the regiment, perhaps even an officer. Viewing Antietam as a "skirmish," the soldier defended Burnside and castigated his superiors in Washington, especially Halleck. Witnessing the battle from the hill opposite the city, he concluded: "I think it is about time the war was closed. I am ready to come home any time."[62]

Otherwise, there was a notable silence in Hartford papers regarding regimental news. Even though the 16th Connecticut did not see direct action, friends and family at home worried and waited. On December 30, "A Daily Reader of the Times" from Windsor Locks observed, "I think it strange you have made no mention of that Regt since the fight at Fredericksburg, what their loss was and their names." The letter writer added, "If you can give any information of tha[t] Regt.

you will much relieve the minds of many a reader of your independent paper here."[63] In response, the next day the *Times* published a letter from an unnamed soldier in the 16th summarizing their battle experience: "We were ordered at one time to storm the battery, but the order was afterwards countermanded, as the chances were we should lose one half our men and not accomplish much and so we skedaddled." The soldier further complained about the lack of pay, although mail had resumed and Colonel Beach had returned, and so "the boys hope for better things."[64]

"I HAVE LOST ALL MY PATRIOTISM"

"Better things" were not coming anytime soon. As 1862 waned, the Army of the Potomac faced some of its darkest days, and so did the 16th Connecticut. Corporal Barlow warned his father: "When you read about the 'Soldiers being in good spirits and eager for a fight,' you may know that it is a lie. What has our fighting amounted to lately? This war will never be closed by fighting."[65] A few days later, he wrote his sister, "The boys are getting sick of the war." "I have heard," he maintained, "lots of soldiers say they would never go into another fight."[66]

Austin D. Thompson's letters to his sweetheart Electra Churchill reveal heightened tensions between officers and men that winter of 1862–63. Thompson had enlisted, he told Electra, to do his "duty." But "to be treated as we have been it is no wonder that I have lost all patriotism." He was not alone: "You go through the whole Regt. and if you find one that says he is not sick of living in the way that we do, you may have my head for a football." Thompson complained that the officers continued to hoard the best meat, while the men in the ranks did all the work.[67] He insisted that his "principles" were "the same that they always were" and that he was "willing to leave my bones in Old Virginia before I will ever give up my principles." Thompson could not shake the feeling that he and his fellow soldiers in the 16th C.V. had been "shamefully abused." "I am not a democrat yet," he told Electra, "no not yet."[68]

On Christmas morning, 1862, Pvt. Kellogg visited his comrades, pleased to see his friends but sorry to find them so poorly situated. They "didn't look so merry," he wrote his father.[69] Martin V. Culver's letters remained bleak. Referring to the Battle of Fredericksburg as "nothing but a slaughter," he believed that "the troops dont fight as they did a[w]hile ago for they begin to see this war is a humbug and they are cared for so poorly that they dont care[;]they all want to get home[.]" Culver was even more determined to end his enlistment: "If we go into winter quarters and have anothers [sic] summers campane they wont have me to go with them." If Culver could "play sick enough," he would "get away" if there was not "a pretty good sign of peace."[70] He was convinced that if anyone who wanted to "see the war carried on was out here to see it for 6 months they would sing a different song." It certainly had made him even more convinced of its folly.[71]

Other soldiers revealed the regiment's grim mood. Harrison Woodford wrote home on Christmas day, "It is hard work to get the men into a fight." He also observed waning patriotism in the army, wondering what all these deaths were for: "We may fight forever and then another way will have to be devised to settle it." The Emancipation Proclamation was due to take effect within days, and Woodford sensed resentment toward abolitionists and African Americans. "The soldier do dam the abolishnists & niggers the worst kind." Woodford, too, showed a marked resentment toward the contrabands in camp. "The niggers," he wrote home, "are riding around on horses and have their baggage carried and we poor fellows can trudge along with our loads on our backs & it is all well enough but I hope and pray that the time will soon come when we shall be released from these cares and burdens & return to you once more in health & strength."[72] Edwin Merritt, a joiner from Hartford, visited his ill son George in Company G not long after Fredericksburg and affirmed these sentiments. His letter published in the Democratic *Hartford Daily Times* on the day the Emancipation Proclamation became law recounted soldiers demoralized by the "idea of fighting for negro emancipation." The paper quoted Merritt's reaction after spending a few days in camp with men afflicted by continued exposure and hunger: "It was awful." He estimated the regiment's strength to be no more than 271.[73]

Ira Forbes tried to offer a slightly different perspective. On January 15, 1863, the young private wrote a letter from "Camp Hartford" that appeared in the *Hartford Daily Times* a few weeks later. Forbes, described by the *Times* as an "ultra Republican," loyally defended Burnside, whom he claimed had "out-generaled Lee, Jackson and Longstreet; and had the pontoon bridges been on hand, as they should have been, Fredericksburg, with its invincible hills, would have been ours." Like Barlow and Harrison, Forbes had begun to question the idea that killing Confederates was the solution: "I almost believe that this war cannot be ended by fighting. *We must meet as brethren,* and come to good and honorable terms." Believing that profit had corrupted Washington, he desperately wanted the Union restored, though he added, "I am still opposed to slavery, and if in the course of events emancipation shall come, most heartily I welcome it, and bid it God speed; but I cannot willingly aid in making this war an 'Abolition Crusade.'"[74]

In mid-January, Gen. Burnside commenced what would become known as his "Mud March," an attempt to resume an active campaign against Robert E. Lee's Army of Northern Virginia by crossing the Rappahannock River at Banks Ford. However, drenching, springlike rains turned unpaved roads to sludge, immobilizing soldiers, animals, and wagons in the thick mud. After two days, the hapless general ordered his troops back to camp at Fredericksburg, and on January 26, 1863, Gen. Joseph Hooker replaced Burnside as commander of the Army of the Potomac. The 16th Connecticut, "snugly encamped," just missed having to venture out into the mud and the wet weather.[75] Belden watched: "This morning the troops that past the other day were seen returning not as they went but covered in mud and straggling squads from two to hundreds every man for himself all for his old camp." Belden was sure that the 16th Connecticut would have had to participate if the storm had held off twenty-four hours.[76]

Dissension in the ranks was palpable. Corporal Barlow contended that "all the best officers resign; they get disgusted at the way things go and resign. One of the best Capts. in the Reg. and one Lieut. have been dishonorably discharged, they don't care how they are discharged they are bound to leave and when they go it leaves a place for some green fellow which he is not fit for." Barlow mused that it would be a "great favor" if a family member was able to get him a "different position," but it would be a "far greater one if he would get me out of the scrape altogether." The continued loss of officers was an obvious blow to the regiment's morale. Barlow, echoing Austin Thompson, wrote, "I have lost all my patriotism and energy if I ever had any and I did have some for I know I have lost some."[77] Kellogg, who again visited their camp, shared his comrades' discontent. "Little do the ones at home know," he wrote his father on January 20, 1863, "the suffering and misery caused by a 'forward movement,' and I wish some of the newspaper Generals would but carry out in the field, what is so easy to be printed at home."[78] Pvt. Holcomb later reflected on the depressing state of camp to his aunt: "We did suffer much and eventually complaints were many and loud, and I do not blame the soldiers for them." Even once conditions improved, Holcomb believed he would never forget how difficult that winter had been.[79]

"SOME UGLINESS TO DEAL WITH"

Commissioned officers were still resigning and returning home at an alarming rate. The privates perceived the officer resignations as abandonment of them, the war, and the Union cause. John B. Cuzner expressed his frustration: "They [the officers] don't let a private know much if they can help it. I think this will not last long[.] I understand they are all resigning."[80] Rumors spread that Capt. Henry L. Pasco and Colonel Beach were both leaving the regiment, although Beach had been on extended leave due to his poor health.[81] In early January 1863, the *Hartford Daily Times* dolefully predicted, "It is said all the commissioned officers will resign."[82] The Democratic *Times* took great satisfaction in the flood of resignations from the "Hartford County regiment," especially when the officer was an "ardent war Republican." The paper claimed that Capt. Heber Seaver from Company F, who had resigned in late December 1862, had "seen enough of the elephant to cure him of any desire to waste his own life for the nigger."[83] However, the Republican *Hartford Daily Courant* was quick to point out what it deemed to be the *Times*'s "errors" and "omissions" in its coverage of the regiment's resignations. "Capt. Pasco has not resigned," the *Courant*'s editors stated, "and we are confident has no intention of doing so." They then listed seven officers who had submitted resignations, but, the editors pointed out, "we are not aware that any of them have been accepted."[84]

Burnham, who found army life exhilarating, had no thoughts of leaving. He earned a promotion that dark winter of 1862, becoming lieutenant colonel of the regiment on December 26 and thus filling the vacancy left open since the severe wounding of Frank Cheney at Antietam. Burnham wrote his family a few days after his promotion: "I should be very much elated if it were Col. Beach here to take command of the regiment but he is sick again and of course that devolves the command upon me." Capt. Charles L. Upham from the 8th Connecticut was in temporary command, but Colonel Beach apparently wanted Burnham to take the helm immediately. However, Burnham "begged off a few days" to settle into his new position. "I hope," he wrote, "I shall be as successful as I have been in the old position but I confess I accept it with a good deal of misgiving."[85]

The regiment's new lieutenant colonel seems to have had a tin ear when it came to understanding how deeply disaffected his soldiers were. "I intend to treat every man well and see that he gets everything possible for his comfort," but, sounding like Beach, he continued, "and in return I intend that every man shall do his duty and his whole duty." He declared, "There are always shirks, sneaks, and some ugliness to deal with and if you hear about some body getting severely punished don't think I am getting hard-hearted. I hope because I have 'shot up like a rocket' I shan't have to 'come down a stick.' But the future must tell that." With the more experienced Beach absent and so many other officers incapacitated, discharged, or resigning, Burnham struggled to adapt to his new position. Knowing that he still had a lot to learn about leadership and handling a regiment like the 16th Connecticut, he asked his brother to buy him a copy of "DeHart's Military Law" on his way to the front, "never mind the cost of it."[86]

Before Lt. Col. Burnham had time to read his new manual on military law, fresh challenges arose. A number of guns and other military items were disappearing, and Burnham was convinced that it was no accident. On January 17, 1863, he sought to assess the "exact numbers of arms and each article of equipment, in possession of the men, in order that Ordnance returns may be made immediately." "The large number of some parts of the equipments missing from the regiment," the order read, "leads the Lieut. Col. commanding to the conclusion that they are willfully lost or destroyed to avoid keeping them in proper order." Soldiers without the correct equipment would be docked pay. Repeating this offense would lead to "summary punishment."[87]

Burnham believed that destroying guns and other military accouterments was a way for unruly men to avoid duty. It seems more likely that such behavior expressed growing discontent. The men may have been protesting the lack of pay and the unending sufferings they had endured in winter camp. The pay issue was an especially sore point, as many men had joined for financial reasons and had families reliant on them at home in Connecticut. The threat of losing more money because of their protest could only have increased their dissatisfaction. It is not clear how this order was received, but given the continued strain between officers and men, one can assume that the men were not pleased with it, nor its inherent accusations, even if they were true. Burnham assured his family that his promotion was "pretty generally satisfactory both in and out of the regiment."[88] At least publicly, this estimation appeared accurate. Musician Augustus W. Mills, who had been discharged from the regiment in January, attested to the *Hartford Daily Courant* that the "16th are delighted with their new Lieut. Col. Burnham, in fact they almost worship him."[89]

Popular or not, Burnham faced the brewing crisis over lack of pay. The men in his regiment had not been paid since they left Hartford in late August.[90] By year's end, Belden complained, "We have now due us four months pay. I have just 10 cts left of what money I brought with me from Hartford."[91] Six weeks later, Austin D. Thompson wrote Electra Churchill that he and his comrades had "not received any pay from the Government since we came out, and don't know as we ever shall."[92] A story circulated that because of their rushed march to the front their mustering in was somehow improperly administered, and thus the regiment was not formally part of the U.S. Army. John B. Cuzner explained to Ellen Van Dorn, "Our Regiment is in a peck of trouble. They have been paying the [other] troops, they had payed all the rest of the Brigade and cleared out." When an officer asked the paymaster if he had money for the 16th Connecticut, "the Pay Master said he knew of no such Regiment as the 16th Connecticut." Cuzner figured that something would be done to force the men to stay in the service, but he vowed, "They can't get this chick to swear any more, that is if I'm not sworn into the United States Service I never will be." He claimed that a soldier in another unit offered fifty dollars to transfer to the 16th Connecticut.[93] As Leander Chapin explained to his mother, "According to all accounts we have never been mustered into the U.S. service and there is a good deal of talk about it in the whole brigade."[94]

As the weeks turned to months and still no money came, frustration turned to anger. Martin Culver, the same private who was looking to "play sick" so that he could go home, wrote his brother that he was done with soldiering: "i have seen enough of war and so have all the rest of the soldiers." Culver contended, "i think the reason they don't pay us off is they know that half of the soldiers will run away."[95] The lack of regimental pay had repercussions at home, too, where many soldiers' families, in the words of one Hartford resident, "rely almost entirely upon what they receive from the soldiers for support, except the pittance they receive from the state & town, & most towns, I suppose, make no provisions for families."[96]

"THE MAKING OF THE REGT"

Still, by the end of January 1863, there were signs of optimism. When Hooker replaced Burnside, he quickly got to work reorganizing the army and making significant reforms. Rations improved and proper dress coats arrived, as well as shelter tents and regular mail delivery.[97] The 16th, brigaded along with the 8th, 11th, and 15th Connecticut, started to seem to one member of the regiment, "a little like home having remain[ed] in this place so long."[98] Civilian O. P. Case described good conditions when he visited the regiment in late January: "I have inspected many of the soldiers' tents and find most of them quite comfortable and neatly kept." "Camp Hartford" was laid out in streets, and Case believed everything was in "much better order than before the late battle." Officers, in particular, had "nice wall tents." He was impressed with Burnham, too: "Lieut.

Col. Burnham makes one of the best officers from Connecticut, and is highly respected by the entire regiment. There are many officers under him that I might name who are faithful, kind and popular, but I forbear."[99] In early February, Lewis Holcomb declared, "The Regt never looked better than at this time. The number of men for active service has increased, and as we have been newly clothed, we make a good appearance at Dress Parade."[100]

Another bright spot for the unit during those dark winter months was the arrival of Dr. Nathan Mayer, who had emigrated from Germany with his family to the United States at the age of ten. His father Isaac Mayer was a prominent rabbi at Hartford's first Synagogue Congregation Beth Israel. Nathan graduated from medical school in Cincinnati, and, in his own words, "gathered experience in Military surgery in the Austrian Hospitals at Verona after the campaign of '59" and "devoted 2 years of diligent study at the most renowned universities of Germany and France." Mayer had already served as 1st assistant surgeon to the 11th Regular Connecticut Volunteers before joining the 16th Connecticut. With the resignation of Dr. Abner Warner in early January, Mayer became the regiment's new surgeon, and he had an almost immediate positive effect.[101] Ariel Case would later look back at the winter of 1862–1863 as a turning point: "This seemed to be the making of the Regt and from this time we began to improve." Lt. Case especially marked the arrival of Mayer: "He looked after the food and quarters and we began to see what it was to have some one that looked out for our welfare."[102]

Since leaving Hartford nearly six months earlier, the regiment had undergone considerable hardship and change. They had endured their first bloody baptism of fire, which resulted in a panicked rout, several difficult marches, and terrible camp conditions. A large number of its original volunteers were gone due to death, desertion, illness, and resignations. All of this with no pay. The 16th regiment was increasingly convinced that they were suffering more than most, even though their experiences were not necessarily any harder than those of other northern regiments that bleak winter of 1862–63. By the first week of February 1863, Chaplain Peter Finch reported that the "whole number on the roll of the regiment is 754."[103] Finch himself resigned from the regiment in late January, leaving the 16th without a chaplain for months.

For those who remained, the next chapter in their wartime career was about to commence. On the morning of February 6, 1863, the 16th Regiment Connecticut Infantry, along with the rest of the IX Corps, detached from the Army of the

Potomac and headed south.[104] After huddling onto train cars in a cold rainstorm, the regiment boarded the steamer *John S. Brooks* and set out for Newport News, Virginia. It was not clear where the regiment was headed. An anonymous soldier's letter to the *Hartford Courant* expressed hope and optimism about the move: "The men like the idea of a change, and more particularly they are of the opinion that it is the advance of an expedition with the gallant Burnside as their leader."[105]

4

Newport News and Suffolk
"Regeneration"

The winter and spring of 1862–63 brought what one member called the regiment's "regeneration." Morale was still fragile, their ranks were thin, and the crisis over pay almost caused a mutiny. Rumors remained that they had never been properly mustered into U.S. service. Soldiers intently monitored their state elections, bitterly lashing out at Copperheadism as an enemy as serious as the Confederacy. The Connecticut men, in encounters with more African Americans, expressed sharp racism, and many held deep disdain for emancipation. Yet the move south seemed to cheer the unit, and when they fought in Suffolk, in limited, skirmish-like actions, the regiment performed reasonably well. The men appeared to believe that they were transforming as citizen-soldiers, no longer the same hapless regiment that bolted in panic from the field at Antietam. Yet signs of their stubborn, bold defiance remained.

"GOOD TIMES NOW"

"Soldier life," Pvt. Leander Chapin wrote his mother as the 16th Connecticut left the Rappahannock for Newport News, "is very changeable. Sometimes [it] is very hard indeed and then again it not so bad." Chapin, who had joined the army filled with idealistic exuberance in July 1862, had begun to grapple with the realities of soldiering. "I am," he had asserted, "where I have tried for a long while to be and if I don't like the business I can blame myself."[1] Now he mused that the "chance to see the country and [have] our fare all paid too" was worth it. He only wished his anxious mother would not worry about him. Chapin was confident that his fate was in God's hands: "He can care for me here as well as at home."[2]

There seemed to be signs of positive change as soon as the regiment arrived at Newport News on February 8, 1863.[3] There were oysters, clams, apples, and soft bread to eat and sturdy "A" tents to protect them. Even the weather seemed more pleasant.[4] "I wish," John B. Cuzner proclaimed, "they would keep us here until the war is over."[5] Samuel E. Derby agreed, "This is a very pleasant place more so than any we have been in and I hope we will stop some time to come."[6] Elizur Belden wrote that even on rainy days there were "plenty of amusements" including gambling and "playing bluff."[7] Pvt. Lewis M. Holcomb also described the regiment "enjoying ourselves finely" at Newport News during the five-week stay.[8] He told his cousin Addie that he could not believe how "old Granby possibly keeps awake" compared to the exciting times of a soldier. "We are having good times now," Holcomb observed, "and we can console ourselves with the reflection that we cant [sic] never see anything worse than we have seen."[9] Officers were faring even better than the men in the ranks. Lt. Col. Burnham, who continued to enjoy good health, described the amiable conditions to his mother: "It is pleasant here, the place is easy of access and I am comfortably situated, mess all by myself and live like a lord." One meal he had enjoyed included roast turkey, fried oysters, mashed potatoes, applesauce, nuts, coffee, and chocolate.[10]

The men of the 16th were also pleased to be far removed from the main Army of the Potomac as it prepared for active campaigning that spring. Cpl. Leland Barlow wrote his sister: "We are glad to get out of the Army of the Potomac. Some how never liked the way things went. You could see any quantity of horses and fancy dressed officers running races and having good times. They don't care any thing about the war."[11] Harrison Woodford shared Barlow's sentiments when he told his father that he did not mind where the regiment ended up next, "only keep me out of the Army of the Potomac."[12]

Regimental historian Bernard Blakeslee traced the 16th Connecticut's "regeneration" as beginning in its final weeks at Fredericksburg and continuing while stationed at Newport News.[13] The next four months would represent a significant turning point in the life of the regiment. Separated from the Army of Potomac, the men appeared to be gaining strength and self-confidence. The 16th C.V. was no longer the broken, demoralized group of green volunteers who had fled from the field at Antietam. Tensions between officers and men continued, and demoralization within the ranks ebbed and flowed. However, many in the regiment hoped sometime soon they would have a fresh chance to prove themselves in combat and silence any lingering doubts about their manhood and courage.

Efforts were afoot to make the regiment better prepared for its next battle. Soon after their arrival at Newport News, Lt. Col. John Burnham kept the soldiers hard at drill, in the words of one private, "to make a crack regiment of us."[14] It was not just training the men lacked but soldierly comportment. Corporal

Barlow complained in his diary that Burnham "made us unbutton our coats to see if our shirts were clean."[15] There were separate drills for the men and noncommissioned officers, tighter inspections, and Barlow observed that it was "getting strict with the guard."[16] There is evidence that Burnham's efforts were paying off. While stationed at Newport News, Lt. Col. George Bowers from the 13th New Hampshire conducted an inspection of the regiment's muster roll and the field and staff, judging them in "good" condition, including their discipline, instruction, military appearance, arms, accouterments, and clothing.[17]

"WHERE HIS PATRIOTISM ENDED"

Still, the 16th Connecticut's number of active men remained low. Sidney Hayden estimated in early March that the 16th "was reduced to nearly 3/4 since leaving Hartford."[18] Leander Chapin wrote his mother that the 16th C.V. was the "2nd smallest regt. Conn. has in the service. The 11th I think is smallest." He counted some 250 active men on the roster out of a total of 630 in mid-March.[19]

The problem was not just the losses from Antietam. There was the occasional deserter, and medical discharges weakened the ranks.[20] Chapin was one of the soldiers whose health took a turn for the worse when a bad cold turned to bronchitis. He tried to assure his mother that, despite a cough and loss of his voice, he was fine: "It doesn't alarm me any and I see no reason (when you learn the particulars) why you should be troubled by it."[21] He dismissed her anxiety about him as "useless" and promised her that when he was truly sick, he would let her know. In the meantime, Chapin was focused on the fight at hand: "I am bound to see the end of the cursed rebellion if possible before I go home. I came out here to fight and I'm going to fight." He then went on to make a startling disclosure: "I came near dying at home at any rate, I cared so little for my life that I was tempted time and time again to make way with myself. It is true as the Bible though it grieves me greatly to be able to say it. If I had not enlisted I have but little doubt but that I would by this time have been in another world. I am here and want to stay here till the war is over." His life now had a higher purpose, and he wanted to die in the service of his country. His only regret was that he had not joined sooner.[22] But ten days later, Chapin's illness had worsened enough for Surgeon Nathan Mayer to authorize him to leave the regiment for a twenty-day furlough, describing Chapin's condition as "chronic Bronchitis." The earnest young Chapin would be absent from his beloved regiment until August.[23]

Officer resignations had not abated either. Pvt. Sidney Hayden noted in a letter to his father that the same individuals who had helped enlist volunteers and create companies were now abandoning them to return to the comforts of home, "where they enjoy themselves the best." Hayden thought that this "kind of patriotism don't amount to much."[24] He later bitingly added in another letter home, "Officers keep resigning and leaving the regiment and if they keep on unless the regiment is recruited, we shall all get to be officers[,] resign and go home."[25] But this was no laughing matter. The drain of officers countered many of the positive effects the move to Newport News brought. Hayden himself began to wish that he had only enlisted for nine months rather than three years.[26]

Even the rumor of an officer leaving stirred angry reactions from the men. Pvt. Austin D. Thompson was openly disdainful of Lt. Julian Pomeroy (Co. K), who Thompson mistakenly believed had received a discharge in February 1863. Thompson claimed that although Pomeroy "tried to do the best he knew how, the fact is he is no military man, and I never saw a coward that is." "When he left home," Thompson alleged, "he was full of patriotism because he thought that he was going to get a commission. I guess that was where his patriotism ended."[27]

Capt. Joseph Barnum (Co. H) was one of the officers who did tender his resignation in February 1863, citing "reasons of a private nature" that required his immediate attention.[28] Lt. Col. Burnham wrote on the back of Barnum's request the real reason why Barnum wanted to leave the service: "Capt Barnum states that the regiment having been six months in service and having rec'd no pay his family at home are suffering and he feels it his duty to go home and provide for them." Burnham supported the captain and asked that he be allowed to go home. Brig. Gen. George W. Getty, commanding the 3rd Division, deemed Barnum's reasons insufficient, but Maj. Gen. William F. Smith, commanding the IX Corps, approved Barnum's request, and the captain duly resigned.[29] Less than a week later, one day after Barnum officially resigned, Lt. Col. Burnham wrote Gov. William Buckingham asking that Barnum be recommissioned. Calling Barnum a "good officer," Burnham wanted to "retain him in the regiment if at all possible." He added, "If he can arrange his affairs satisfactorily he will call upon you with a note from me requesting a commission."[30] Indeed, Joseph Barnum, unlike so many of his fellow officers who left the regiment for good, returned several weeks later and was commissioned again as captain in Company H.[31]

Captain Barnum was not the only one distressed by the lack of pay. The men in the ranks were unhappy, too, but unlike Barnum, they could not resign. "I don't know as we shall ever get any pay," Samuel E. Derby wrote his wife Elizabeth on February 11, 1863. "We have the promise of it yet but I guess we shall before the first of March for then they will owe me 78 dollars and I want the money to send you it is so long since I saw any money I have almost forgot how it looks." He urged Elizabeth, "Don't you starve as long as there is any money to be had for when I come home I want to see you so fat you can't see out of your eyes."[32]

Hartford newspapers printed a story blaming a drunken paymaster for the oversight. The *Courant* explained, "The reason that the 16th Connecticut and other regiments in the army of the Potomac were not paid for weeks was because the Paymaster whose duty it was to make the payment was on a drunken spree in Philadelphia." The paper further claimed that as "soon as the matter was reported at headquarters another paymaster was assigned to the duty, and we shall soon expect to hear that the troops have received their long neglected dues."[33] The next day, a correspondent to the *Courant* reported that a "special paymaster has been sent down to Newport News to pay off the 16th regiment. He was appointed at the earnest solicitation of Col. Almy. It is a shame they have not been paid before." "The men," the paper noted, "have been quite discontented."[34]

According to the *Hartford Courant,* the crisis was finally resolved by Governor Buckingham and Col. J. H. Almy, the state's assistant quartermaster. "The 16th Regiment was paid off on the 20th, to the 1st of January," the paper stated, "being the first pay they have received since leaving Hartford. The boys of the 16th are indebted to Col. J. H. Almy, Assistant Quartermaster of Connecticut for this. While on a recent visit to Washington, he was apprised of the fact that this regiment had not received their pay, and immediately repaired to the Paymaster General's office to know the reason why. He there ascertained that a paymaster had been assigned for the 16th, but that all the other regiments were to be serviced first, as the 16th was by itself, and the only regiment from Connecticut on the list." Colonel Almy requested a special paymaster to proceed to the 16th C.V.'s camp and promptly settle the matter.[35] Three days later, the *Courant* followed up with a clarification that Colonel Almy was merely acting under the instructions of the governor, who "called Col. Almy's attention to the fact that the 16th had not been paid, and requested him to use every effort to secure their immediate payment."[36]

William Relyea later told a different story. He recounted members of the unit selecting a committee to draft a pointed letter to the governor. "We were willing to serve our term of enlistment," Relyea recalled, "but we wanted our pay and unless that was forthcoming or some proper reason was given why we did not receive it, we should consider our contract with the government null and void."

Their letter affirmed that they did not "wish to shirk our duty in any way," but that "if we were an unknown quantity and have not been properly mustered into the service of the United States we should request the Governor to recall us as we had been out of the state longer than the law allowed them to keep us." If, in fact, they were not really soldiers, they would willingly go home and resume their civilian lives. According to Relyea, Governor Buckingham's response was swift and unsympathetic to the soldiers' complaints. He accused them of mutiny and threatened to have the entire regiment remustered with no pay for the time already served. Relyea claimed that lawyers were retained, and it looked like the 16th Connecticut's next real combat experience was going to be a legal one rather than on the battlefield. He credited Burnham for quelling the regiment's discontent by making a personal visit to Washington; pay was issued, and "the boys were made happy."[37] Relyea gave no credit to Buckingham or Almy. Instead, it was the regiment's bold assertiveness that finally led to action. Parts of Relyea's story are probably true; no doubt the men groused and threatened to go home and refuse to serve if they were not compensated. Leander Chapin related in his diary that there was talk of stacking arms and refusing to follow orders once they were moved from the Rappahannock. Soldiers of the 16th viewed their service as a sort of contractual relationship. If they believed something to be unfair and unjust, they were quick to cry foul and act accordingly. Still, it was probably wrong of Relyea not to recognize Buckingham's efforts. The governor knew he could not allow his "Hartford Regiment" to remain in the field indefinitely without pay.[38]

By the first week of March, the men had received their pay.[39] According to John B. Cuzner, the regiment was in "good spirits living like fighting cocks."[40] Robert H. Kellogg, who would soon rejoin his regiment from detached service, wrote his father that he had heard from Adj. John Clapp: "They are at Newport News Va. Camped in a beautiful spot, near to fish, oysters, clams, etc. they have been paid off, and I should judge from John's letter, are in excellent spirits."[41] One soldier wrote home, "Talk of stacking arms now to any man you would see him swell with indignation as he exclaims, 'Stack arms no sir we fight or die in the Old Ninth.'"[42]

Even though the pay crisis had passed, there remained signs of discontent. A brief mention of the unit in the *Hartford Evening Press* stated that at last account the 16th regiment was in Newport News "in good health and comfortably situated." The paper observed, "The regiment has not lost a man since removing from Falmouth." However, the *Press* added that their guns had been inspected and were in such poor shape that they would be "condemned." The paper then quoted a private letter: "One poor fellow, in the 16th Conn., cut his throat a few days ago." There was no other mention of the incident, nor was there any explanation for such an act. Surely, this would have been disconcerting for anyone at home to read in the evening papers.[43]

Capt. Henry Beach (Co. I), home on a furlough in early March, insisted that the regiment was doing extremely well. "He gives glowing accounts," the paper attested, "of the soldier's life." The *Courant* declared, "His words and looks give the lie direct to the many letters which have been published with accounts of the great privations and hard treatment of the soldiers." Indeed, Beach vowed that men who wrote such letters should be punished and that the "army would be better without them."[44] Ten days later the *Daily Courant*'s correspondent insisted that all was well with the 16th. "I have just come in from one of their dress parades," he wrote, and "the regiment presents a fine appearance, and is not all demoralized, as we often hear reported in Hartford. It now numbers 450 men." The correspondent continued: "The first sound of church bells was heard by them with delight this morning; all religiously inclined were permitted to attend, and the minister made the remark that it was the most attentive audience he ever preached to."[45]

"SOLDIERS ARE ANXIOUSLY WATCHING THE ELECTION"

Meantime, as winter turned to spring in 1863, a gubernatorial election was fast approaching, and Gov. Buckingham could use every vote. The election keenly interested members of the regiment, as it did other Connecticut soldiers. The incumbent Republican Buckingham vowed to support Lincoln and the war, while his Democratic opponent Thomas H. Seymour challenged the war's human and monetary cost. Several members of the regiment sent letters to the papers expressing their individual opinions, believing, it seems, that their voices meant something to the people at home. The pro-Democrat *Hartford Daily Times* published accounts and letters attesting to soldiers' demoralization and discontent with the war; the pro-Republican *Daily Courant* and *Evening Press* countered with letters and descriptions affirming soldiers' unwavering support of Lincoln and the war.[46]

An article called "Patriotic Appeal," published in the Hartford papers on March 20 and 21, included the signatures of Lt. Col. John H. Burnham and eighteen other commissioned officers in the unit, as well as seventy-seven officers from the 8th, 11th, 17th, and 21st Connecticut. "We learn," the appeal stated, "with sorrow, that in our noble State of Connecticut, within whose borders so many homes have been made desolate by traitors' hands, an effort has been made to sow the seeds of dissension in the North, and to excite the people to acts of hostility against the federal Government." As men in uniform, they felt a "soldier's regard for our foes on the James and the Rappahannock on account of their skill and courage; but towards the enemies of the Republic on the Thames, the Connecticut and the Housatonic, we can have no other feelings than those of the most unmitigated scorn and contempt."[47] These officers distinguished between legitimate enemy combatants who fought valiantly with "shot and shell" and dissident civilians, whom they deemed disgraceful traitors. Implied in these words was a distinction between a brave enemy and a cowardly citizenry.[48]

A member of the 16th with apparent Democratic leanings wrote, "You cannot imagine how indignant the soldiers are about the nomination of Seymour. It is true that two-thirds of the voters in the army are Democrats, and have been since they came out; but Seymour for Governor could not command *one vote in ten among them*." He steadfastly supported Buckingham, adding, "I was in hopes the North would not adopt the means the South has done to raise men, but as they have got to do it, I want to see it carried out—and that's what's the matter."[49] Indeed, Harrison Woodford predicted that the Union army would be triumphant if "the copperheads in the North don't get the impish Tom Seymour in governor."[50]

It was one thing to harbor Democratic sentiments but quite another to be accused of Copperheadism. When the charge was made against a member of the 16th Connecticut, the soldier's mother refused to stand by silently. Nancy M. Bowen wrote the *Hartford Courant* to defend her son, Pvt. Charles F. Bowen, of Company H., Mrs. Bowen declared, "He has not become a copperhead (as has been scandalously reported), but is as fully as ever resolved to stand or fall with his country, and has no idea of being associated with those who are enemies to her liberties, her constitution, and laws." She was quick to note that her son was "particularly anxious that a few of the croakers at the North be sent down and compelled to 'shoulder arms,' and participate in the struggles which good and loyal men are maintaining (at the hazard of life and limb) for the love they bear to their country." Her son predicted that if such Democrats were forced to serve, he and his fellow veterans would "see some of the tallest skedaddling they had ever witnessed."[51] Even soldiers who had previously expressed despair over the war could not stomach the Democrats' position, at least not openly. Leland Barlow was confident that the 16th would vote Republican. Writing to his sister, who apparently asked him if he agreed with the Copperheads, he said, "We want to see the Rebelion [*sic*] put down and are willing to help do it."[52] Austin D. Thompson tried to "calm" himself that he was "fighting in a good cause" despite the hardships he had to endure. Thompson, who months earlier had said all his patriotism was gone, now affirmed, "I know if I ever live to get home that I shall never be sorry that I came to war." Thompson had no respect for the Copperheads, judging them "brave cowards," who were "afraid to acknowledge what they honestly believe, because they are such cowards."[53]

Select soldiers, it seems, were furloughed by the War Department to go home to vote Republican in the state's election. George Robbins described Connecticut soldiers from Camp Distribution in Alexandria, Virginia, being provided with passes "by order of the Secretary of War" to go home to Connecticut on a twenty-day furlough. "They are," he stated bluntly, "to vote the Republican ticket." Robbins hoped his own father, who had just been to visit him at the camp, would return "home in time to vote, so that Seymour will be defeated. If I had been here 4 days ago I suppose I could have gone too, for there are two of them [*sic*] men here that are going that are not twenty-one."[54] Governor Buckingham won reelection by a slim majority.[55]

For some, the gubernatorial election bridged the gap, at least temporarily, between battlefront and families on the home front. Soldiers wrote excitedly about the election, and politicians spoke emotionally about the war and its consequences. But for other families, the distance between the war and home life only widened. Northern women, separated from their husbands, sons, brothers and fathers, sought ways to be part of the masculine, military world.[56] Teenaged Ellen Van Dorn, who regularly corresponded with her beau John Cuzner through the winter and spring of 1863, scribbled sentimental rhymes of longing and desire on the back of his letters. In one, she mused,

> When you are on the battlefield
> wearing the brass and blue
> Cast a long and lingering thought
> on her, who ever thinks of you.
> Remember, my love,
> I'm always with thee,
> No matter how great,
> Your distance from me.[57]

Widow Charlotte Manross, whose husband had told her upon enlisting that she would be in "better condition," with him dead than "without a country," faced dark days after his death. She only had memories and their two-year-old daughter Lottie to comfort her in her grief. One day in early April, she penned a poem, "The Widow's Tear," to express her pain and attempts to find solace. The first stanzas read:

> The husband of my youth is dead,
> My bosom friend a half score year
> Tho' mourners tears I oft have shed,
> I ne'er before shed widow's tears.
>
> Around my home and through each room
> How sad and vacant all appear;
> I think of husband and tomb,
> And shed profusely widow's tears.[58]

The sense of loss that Charlotte Manross described in her poem was shared by countless grieving widows. The war made many women feel hopeless and disillusioned, shaken by the mounting casualties.[59]

"GREAT CONFIDENCE IN THEMSELVES"

As Charlotte Manross struggled to move past her husband's death, the 16th Connecticut changed positions yet again. On March 15, the regiment shifted from Newport News to Suffolk and was placed under the direct command of John J. Peck as part of George W. Getty's 3rd Division.[60] Robert E. Lee dispatched James Longstreet's corps that spring to lay siege to the town, seeking to push back the occupiers but also to gather necessary provisions for his hungry army. The siege of Suffolk would prove a failed endeavor for the Confederates, but for the 16th Connecticut, it would offer a renewed opportunity for battle. Just the anticipation of combat cheered the men. Martin Culver betrayed signs of confidence when he wrote his brother Jonathan: "I may be rong but if they want to fight let them come[.] they will have a sweet time to get in hear for we have got rifle pits and breast works around the place and 10 or 15 forts mounted with heavey guns."[61]

Samuel E. Derby, however, offered a more sober view of the regiment's situation. He wrote his wife Elizabeth on April 9, 1863, from Suffolk that he hoped the regiment would "stay here until the war is over," adding, "I wont complain as long as we are kept as well as we are now and no fighting or marching to be done but if they go to marching as we have done I don't believe I would stand it as good as I did last fall." He also observed some fighting within the ranks: "We first arrest them and put them under guard and make them do the Nigger work around the camp for a few days and then send them to their companies all right." One man was that day under guard for being "so dirty on inspection so you see we have to go very straight in the army." Despite his vow not to complain, Derby struggled to adjust to army life: "I don't like it much[;] it aint the life for me and I live in hopes it will not last long but still we cant tell how long it will last."[62]

A few familiar faces returned to the regiment at Suffolk. Colonel Beach was back after nearly six months to retake command. Due to illness, Beach had not been with the 16th since Antietam, except for a few days while they were stationed at Pleasant Valley.[63] The reaction of the men varied. "He looks as savage as ever," Elizur Belden wrote, and "all the men actually hate him."[64] Austin D. Thompson was also displeased: "Our old Colonel has returned to the Reg. once more to our sorrow." He told Electra Churchill, "I wish his furlow [sic] had been three years long."[65] Corporal Barlow preferred Beach and even Burnham over the lieutenants who "don't know anything." Of Beach, Barlow declared, "We like him better than we did. He won't see his men abused by any one; he wants to do it himself if any one."[66]

Pvt. George Robbins and Sgt. Robert Kellogg also returned to the regiment at Suffolk. Falling ill soon after Antietam, Robbins was now exhilarated to be with his comrades. "I was glad to be back," he later remembered. "I had been absent from the regiment four and one half months, spent in hospitals and various camps, and felt that now I was really a soldier and ready and willing to share whatever might fall to our lot."[67] Kellogg initially was ambivalent about returning; he assured his father, "I am a soldier and must obey orders, and as I've got to go, why I shall try to be as cheerful as I can and do my duty wherever I am."[68] He found his regiment "greatly improved" and said that it was now "looked upon as a 'crack regt.'" The 16th Connecticut was armed with Enfield rifles, "a very superior weapon," food was plentiful, and everyone seemed in "good spirits and health." His comrades greeted him warmly, and he was hopeful for his own future, even though he recognized that he was in greater danger than he had been while serving as a hospital steward. The pious Kellogg placed his faith in God, but he also revealed some obvious ambition. "I intend to remain in the regiment hereafter," he wrote, "as there is a great chance for promotion. Many who were my equals when I left are now commissioned officers." After some scattered skirmishing, he was thrilled to fire his rifle at the "vile traitors." He also knew things would be different than they had been at Antietam: "Suffolk is very strongly fortified and our troops are eager and willing to fight. We are behind the fortifications this time, and are anxious to give them a touch of Fredericksburg."[69]

Suffolk was no Fredericksburg; nor was it anything like Antietam. The siege represented an opportunity for the unit to redeem itself, at least among its own ranks, and to quiet any lingering doubts about its abilities on the battlefield. As Confederates tried to break the Union stronghold, the unit participated in several armed clashes with the enemy. These skirmishes tested the regiment's abilities, and this time the men performed well. Although casualties were low, the losses were painful and had long-lasting effects on a regiment still rattled by Antietam and its aftermath.

The first skirmish occurred on April 24, 1863, at the Edenton Road. Kellogg described how the regiment encountered advancing rebels, who were "pretty thick and saucy, but we followed them up closely and peppered them so that they had to retreat to their rifle pits." The 16th Connecticut continued "to make a stand," giving a cheer and charging forward. "This," Kellogg recounted, "produced panic among them [the Confederates] and they fled like sheep, leaving many things behind them in their haste, including several of their men, whom we took prisoners." Kellogg admitted, "It was an exciting sort of fight, but it was not a battle really."[70] George Robbins wrote that once they got to the edge of the swamp it was "each man for himself for it was so swampy that we could keep no line." Soldiers walked on "fallen trees and sticks and bogs, then we had to wade through the mud, which was just like the muck in the old form only thinner and of course there was more."[71] Confederates quickly abandoned their position, leaving "their coffee boiling over the fires."[72] Before falling back, the soldiers set fire to two large houses.[73] The regiment's casualties were light—one killed and seven wounded, all enlisted men—and apparently, there were no stragglers. The one man killed on the day of the battle was Pvt. Robert Scott (Co. C), who was "killed instantly by a rifle ball to the left temple."[74]

Bernard F. Blakeslee recalled, "This was a very successful skirmish and gave the men great confidence in themselves."[75] Robbins, who had rejoined his comrades days before the skirmish, noticed a marked difference since he had last been with them in the fall of 1862: "The line was formed very quick, for our Regt has improved wonderfully since I left them." He assessed, "I suppose the object of the expedition was accomplished, which appeared to be a reconnaissance to see where and how strong the enemy were."[76]

Just over a week later, the 16th C.V. faced enemy guns again. On Saturday, May 2, the men received orders to march at 3 a.m. with "two days rations and in light marching orders." The devout Kellogg was "sorry we must break God's holy day by marching hard[,] perhaps fighting."[77] The next morning, Sunday, May 3, the 16th Connecticut again went into action, this time along the aptly named Providence Church Road. The unit quickly found itself charging across a "broad, plowed field" flanked by woods filled with rebel soldiers. The fighting was intense, and the 16th came, according to Kellogg, "within a few rods of the rebels."[78] Sgt. Richard Henry Lee preferred this type of combat. "Skirmishing," he wrote his cousin, "is the best way of fighting if you want fun, because you can then, to a certain extent, choose your own ground."[79] Robbins noted, "It was a long way across and the bullets flew fast and thick before we got half way across they opened fire on us from a battery throwing a few shell[s] which did no damage, but they did not fire long, for one of our batteries came up and pitched the shot and shell into them so fast and near to them that they had to shut up." Robbins and his comrades moved into a ravine and were ordered to take cover under the bank. Soon, the regiment moved to relieve the "right wing" under a "high bank." "Col. Beach was with us all the time," Robbins added, "and he told us not to fire unless we saw something to fire at."[80] Kellogg's rifle became too hot to hold, so he snatched another one from the ground. In the chaos of combat, he "accidently shot away the ramrod of this piece. The rebs must have thought we were getting desperate when they saw that ramrod coming." The regiment held their position until they were relieved by the 15th Connecticut and "part of our reserve." Kellogg estimated that he fired "76 rounds at short range during the fight." When he and his comrades returned to camp that evening, they were "all tired out, but feeling that we had done our duty."[81]

Official reports of the skirmish were generally favorable. Col. Robert S. Foster, from the 13th Indiana, who commanded the 2nd Brigade, praised all the participating regiments "on my front" including the 16th C.V.: "All the commands exerted themselves to the discharge of their duties in an acceptable and praiseworthy manner, at all times meeting every detail with promptness and in every way discharging their duties in a soldierlike manner."[82] Brig. Gen. Edward Harland described the regiment's successful support of the 103rd New York. After relieving the New Yorkers, Harland stated, the 16th "engaged the enemy and moved forward a short distance until the right of the regiment rested on the bank of the river. This position was held by the regiment until night, when the troops were withdrawn to the other side of the river."[83]

The regiment's casualties were relatively slight: two killed and eight men wounded.[84] Lt. Colonel Burnham "had his leg greased by a musket ball."[85] Sgt. Bernard Blakeslee was hit in the back of the head by a rebel sharpshooter who might have been aiming at Colonel Beach.[86] Blakeslee survived, and the colonel was not injured at all. "Old Beach was there," Pvt. Hayden observed ruefully, "but there is no danger of his ever getting hurt."[87]

Jacob Bauer would later credit Colonel Beach for the regiment's success that day. In 1915, he recalled, "Our Col. Frank Beach had been a captain of a battery in the regular army and knew how to take care of us and not expose us to needless slaughter." Beach ordered the men to double-quick march, and the soldiers successfully got to the ravine "without losing a man." The aged Bauer, his memories softened with time, reasoned, "Other officers, not familiar with artillery practices would have led us across and probably our losses would have been severe."[88] Cpl. Harrison Woodford was impressed with Beach and Burnham's performance that day on Providence Church Road. He wrote his sister that the 16th C.V. had "two of the best Cols to lead us into a fight, I believe that there is in the service (the coolest)." "They were," he affirmed, "right along with the men leading them on."[89]

Lost in the fight, though, was another talented officer, twenty-three-year-old captain Charles A. Tennant. He was shot just below the thigh, as the regiment had, according to one report, "been ordered to lie upon the ground in order to avoid a battery of the enemy."[90] Captain Tennant was removed to Fort Monroe to recover; his leg wound was healing when lockjaw set in, and he died on May 24.[91] Blakeslee later praised Captain Tennant as "greatly beloved," "a brave young officer and one of the best in the service."[92] Lewis Holcomb told his aunt that Tennant was "considered by the regiment to be a gentleman, as well as a superior officer, which is not always the case."[93]

The death of this one officer from the "Hartford Regiment" apparently struck a chord. Even though a more significant campaign with heavier casualties had just occurred at Chancellorsville, the *Hartford Daily Courant* declared, "There has not been a burial in this city since the war began of one of its heroes, which called out a larger number of people than were in attendance on this occasion."[94] A newspaper account stressed Tennant's final hours and his "good death" in the presence of an uncle: "It is a source of great satisfaction to his relatives and friends, to know that he honored his profession in life, and that he died as only the good die, trusting in the merits of his Redeemer, resting all his hopes on Him."[95] The regiment would later name their camps at Suffolk and Portsmouth after the slain captain.[96]

Burnham, who was shot in the left shin during the same skirmish and sent home to Hartford to recover, also was present at Tennant's funeral.[97] In a letter to his mother, he described his injury as "exposing the bone a little" and "considerably bruised," but it did not seem serious. Initially, Dr. Mayer had directed the lieutenant colonel to keep his "leg propped up on a chair & talks about my staying in my tent and keeping it in that position at present, but I don't know as I can exactly see that."[98] Ten days later, however, with the abrasion festering and inflamed, Burnham obtained a month-long furlough to return to Hartford and try to heal properly.[99] It was during this convalescence that his family began to observe a disturbing transformation: once cheerful, optimistic, and easygoing, John Burnham was now nervous, excitable, and prone to long periods of depressed silence. He also complained of excruciating headaches.[100] When he rejoined the regiment in June 1863, Sergeant Blakeslee noted something different about the colonel. Burnham had always been concerned with discipline, but after Suffolk, it became his obsession. Blakeslee recalled, "I first noticed the change in the actions of Col. Burnham in the latter part of 1863 when he suddenly became unnecessarily punctilious, continually worrying without adequate reason over unimportant points; [and] approached each review or inspection with great and unreasonable anxiety," displaying what Blakeslee deemed to be an "unaccountable change from his former manner."[101] The *Hartford Daily Courant*, nonetheless, pronounced Burnham "one of the best officers in the service."[102]

Another loss to the regiment was nineteen year-old Pvt. Henry W. Barber. Regimental historian Blakeslee later maintained, "Young Barber's last words were 'Tell Mother that I never was a coward.'"[103] Barber's death left an impression on several of his comrades. Kellogg recorded in his diary, "Poor Barber was shot here and died soon after."[104] George Q. Whitney later wrote, "Barber was shot through the forehead and instantly killed, Sergeant John Gemmill of his company being very near him and taking his rifle, his own not working to his satisfaction." Whitney added, "Barber was quite a favorite, and his death was deeply regretted."[105]

Most members of the 16th Connecticut would insist that as a unit they performed bravely at Suffolk on May 3. Ira Forbes later recounted the courage of Cpl. Daniel Gibson (Co. A) when it was discovered his company had run out of ammunition. Gibson was ordered "to secure a new supply" under fire, exhibiting "nerve and courage."[106] The skirmishes reminded Pvt. Hayden how little he relished combat, but that did not mean he would not fight. "I wish that somebody that said our division ought to take Richmond," he wrote home, "would come down an[d] help take it, [for] it [is] easier to talk than to act." He quickly added, "I am willing to do my part towards helping put down the Rebellion but don't want to get into all the engagements." But Hayden proudly stated, without any hint of irony (or memory of Antietam), "Old Burnside says that his 3 divisions has never skedaddled and I suppose this is the reason they wanted to get us into all the fights."[107]

Official reports from these two engagements indicate little straggling, although after the battle, William H. Relyea remembered Capt. Henry Beach from Company I being "placed under arrest and we saw him going through camp, doing no duty at all, and soon after he resigned and went home, thus severing his connection with the regiment."[108] Pvt. Henry A. White (Co. C) made a candid admission in a letter to Governor Buckingham when he described how fatigued he had been feeling just before the fighting at Providence Church. "I kept up with the Regt," White explained, "until they came to an open field when they started to run and I started with them [and] fell in range of their cannon where shell was bursting around me. I went as far as my strength would carry me and for doing this I was arrested and my name recorded as a coward." White demanded that the governor ask the people from his hometown of Griswold about his "worthyness" [sic], clearly convinced that it was the trying circumstances of military life that caused him to falter, not anything in his moral character.[109] Sgt. Henry Lee told his cousin Adelaide that "one of our Lieuts was reduced" to the ranks "for cowardice" on May 7. "All of the men," Lee asserted, "who showed the white feather in the Skirmish were reported. This is right, for it is much the duty of one man as another to go forward in the face of danger." Lee was pleased, though, that "none enlisting from Granby were among those whom I reported from our Co."[110]

Overall, the skirmishing at Suffolk offered tangible evidence to the 16th C.V. that the regiment could fight, and fight well. Although the action they experienced was considerably less dangerous (and less significant) than what armies at Chancellorsville or those in the environs of Vicksburg experienced, the 16th believed that they were proving to themselves, their families, friends, and the outside world that they were capable, worthy soldiers. Broken and battered at Antietam, passive observers at Fredericksburg, Suffolk was their regeneration.

"WE SOLDIERS HANDLE THE THORNS"

For the rest of their time at Suffolk, the men were generally in good spirits. Even though they shifted camp several times and often found themselves sleeping in the open with shoddy rations, the men appeared to take their situation in stride.[111] The 16th eventually settled on the banks of the Nansemond River. With company streets neatly arranged and trees providing shade, they made, in the words of Robert Kellogg, "a beautiful camp."[112] The men swam, bathed, and fished in the river.[113] The Hartford Soldiers' Aid Association helped, too, by providing the men with much needed items including flannel shirts, drawers, woolen socks, magazines, newspapers, and Bibles.[114] Frequent visits to town allowed the men to indulge in a variety of pleasures not provided by the Soldiers' Aid societies, including ice cream and lemonade.[115] Cpl. Leland Barlow wrote his sister Jane in early May, "I think it agrees with me to live outdoors and I would like Soldiering well if it wasn't for marching and fighting. I don't like to fight, that is so! But we have got a lot of it to do before we subdue the Rebs."[116] By the end of May, Austin Thompson confessed to Electra Churchill that when he had enlisted, he had thought he would be home by spring. Still, he declared, "we must whip them if it takes fifty years to do it."[117] John B. Cuzner pronounced on June 1, "I am not sorry yet that I enlisted."[118] Sgt. Henry Lee also refused to waver in his belief in the war effort, explaining to his Democratic-leaning cousin, "You at home are taking the roses of life while we Soldiers handle the thorns and we will do it cheerfully if you will only give up your support.[119]

The regiment's numbers were stabilizing. By the first week of June, the *Hartford Daily Courant* reported the 16th Connecticut's "numbers in aggregate" to be 638–428 present with the regiment, "of which three hundred and sixty are fit for duty."[120] The unit's health showed signs of improvement, too. In a letter to the Hartford Soldiers' Aid Association, Dr. Mayer pronounced the physical condition of the regiment "very good of late," although he knew the soldiers could not "hope to escape wholly the disease of this clime and season." Mayer insisted that he could ward off illness with "good sanitary precaution."[121]

Conditions seemed safe enough for soldiers' wives and children to visit the camp at Suffolk. Sidney Hayden, who judged it not "quite the place for ladies," recalled that Colonel Beach's wife Julia was "there most of the time."[122] Jacob Bauer's wife, Emily, also came to visit Suffolk for two weeks. Bauer remembered, "My tent had been fitted up and decorated with flowers and the entrance embellished with green bushes and a flag. She enjoyed it very much, attended roll call, saw us drill and witnessed evening dress parade calls." His wife's presence in camp left him with "lasting and pleasurable memories." Bauer claimed that the officers and the men were "very courteous to all the ladies" during these visits.[123]

To be sure, restlessness and war weariness lingered among some members. "I think," Harrison Woodford wrote his father on June 10, "we have suffered long enough, the way the war is conducted." Woodford was disgusted by the number of soldier deaths, believing that it would have been better had there been no war at all, saving "thousands of valueable [sic] lives." He reflected bitterly, "It is very easy for men at home to talk large and patriotic, but it is another thing for them to come out here and show it by fighting."[124] Time "hung heavy on our hands," George Robbins remembered, and "quite naturally we spent quite a large part of the time during the day playing cards, Euchre being the favorite game."[125] Robbins also complained about the continual movement of the 16th C.V.: "Indeed it seems to be the fate of the 16th to keep moving as often as possible, or at least as often as we get a good camp and begin to enjoy it a little."[126] Hostility toward immigrants and officers remained. Hayden got along with most of his company mates, except for the Irish; he judged everyone else "all tip top chaps."[127] It was the officers who drew most of Hayden's ire. He wrote his mother that the general policy for advancement was, "Don't promote anybody in our Regiment unless he can swear and get drunk. If they come from Hartford they are all right."[128]

While at Suffolk, there were many men intent on enhancing their spiritual health. The regiment had "open air prayer meetings" every Sunday. Lacking its own regimental chaplain since the resignation of Peter Finch, the unit was visited by civilian clergy and other chaplains.[129] Sgt. Richard Henry Lee told his cousin that he attended church "every Sunday, half a day," although he said the only ones in attendance were "lads, but no 'lasses.'"[130] Robbins also went to prayer meetings "two or three times a week."[131] Kellogg and Forbes obtained passes to go into Suffolk to attend church. "It was very good," Kellogg wrote, "for us to be there."[132]

As the regiment traveled further South, the Connecticut soldiers encountered more African Americans, both enslaved and free. As historians have recently noted, Union soldiers displayed complicated and often conflicting attitudes about race and emancipation.[133] In February, soon after their arrival at Newport News,

Pvt. Cuzner thanked Ellen Van Dorn for her picture: "It is the first woman's face I have seen in a month except a black face." Six weeks after the official issuance of the Emancipation Proclamation, he stated coldly, "That is what we are fighting about, the negro. A negro here can ride a horse, a private soldier can walk if he is able if not he can lie down."[134] Arriving in Suffolk, Cuzner described a large African American presence. "Here," he wrote Ellen disapprovingly, "they think a white man is as good as a negro if he but behaves himself." He accused African Americans of stealing clothes and even firing a shot at a soldier for peering into their home. The soldier was unhurt, but Cuzner angrily proclaimed, "That shanty must come down."[135] Martin V. Culver observed from Suffolk that "there are plenty of nigs here," but he was much more intent on noting that he could buy "blackstrap" or black coffee for only ten cents and there was "plenty of it at that."[136]

Sidney Hayden remained unmoved in his conservative views. He had enlisted "to support the Constitution of the U.S. so far as I could and not to free the Nigger although I should not stop him if he started to run." He was bitterly disdainful toward African Americans, whom he judged "did not come to Suffolk to work but come to be free." He complained that the "Negro idea of freedom is [being] free from labor."[137] Leander Chapin wrote his mother, that the "darkies are plenty" and "thicker than toads after a shower." He found them an amusing distraction: "The sight of the little nigs is enough to tickle the bushes," he said.[138] Lewis M. Holcomb attended an African American church in the town of Suffolk and was "perfectly delighted with the order of exercises that I wished that I was a 'cullered individual' myself." While somewhat sympathetic and pleased to find African Americans attending church and interested in education, Holcomb still exhibited an ingrained racism and condescension. He described the church service to his cousin: "Pen cannot describe the scene so I will not attempt; Only try to imagine a large room full of black faces, the owners of which were swaying to and fro in their seats making hideous faces and groaning as though they were attacked by the 'Cholera Infantum' and had it bad." Nonetheless, upon meeting contraband coming into camp from North Carolina, he observed, "I never saw any who did not rejoice in their freedom, and was very gratefull [sic] to Northern soldiers for whatever they had done to procure their Freedom. If anything would make me an abolitionist, it would be to hear these people talk."[139]

George Robbins recounted an exchange with a local "old negro" about the nearness of a building they spotted from picket duty. He used decidedly racist dialect to recount the alleged conversation, concluding, "We remained [as] ignorant of the distance from our post to Norfolk, as when I began to question the darky."[140] In a letter home, Robbins was more direct. He recounted passing through Suffolk, "a very dirty place like all the rest of southern cities, with the everlasting nigger staring and grinning from every corner and alley."[141] Harrison Woodford, who had been resentful toward the African Americans he observed at Fredericksburg, supported the raising of a black unit from the contrabands at Suffolk. "I think," he wrote his mother, "it is time they were doing something for their own selves."[142] One historian finds that these everyday encounters with African Americans "eroded and modified" New England soldiers' racial attitudes.[143] Their bigotry, a product of prewar New England society, is obvious. Nevertheless, there were subtle shifts in those attitudes as they pondered the meanings of emancipation. The war's military goals had changed, and these soldiers would increasingly face the implications of that change the longer the war lasted.

Another festering concern was whether the regiment had been legitimately mustered into the U.S. service when it departed Hartford in August 1862. The rumor persisted despite the fact that the regiment had been paid twice, once in March and again in June.[144] Sergeant Blakeslee, supported by ten fellow noncommissioned officers representing each company, wrote directly to the governor's office in early June: "As there has been, and is at present a very general feeling of doubt existing in this Regiment, with regard to the legality of our being mustered into the service of the United States, and in consequence thereof not entitled to the Bounties and Pensions guaranteed thereby, we the undersigned would respectfully request your Excellency to transmit such information to us as will permanently settle the case in question, satisfactorily both to yourself and us." Blakeslee added that there were "facts of almost daily occurrence" that had led him to write the governor, "and while we are ready, as we ever have been to maintain the honor and integrity of the good old Commonwealth on the field of battle, we are anxious to know whether we are entitled to, and may receive the full benefits guaranteed to those who may be legally mustered into the service of the United States."[145] Cuzner vowed that he and his comrades were again ready for "more fuss and muss" if they did not receive "a satisfactory answer" from Governor Buckingham. He reasoned, "If we are not sworn into the United States service legally, we cannot claim protection from that Government if we lose a limb or are disabled in any way, it is all d[one] with us and no pension for us."[146] William Relyea firmly believed, "We were mustered all right but had not been registered in Washington. In the score, we were forgotten."[147] Volunteering was one thing, but having the sustaining motivation to stay in the field and feel supported by those at home was another, and it was vitally important to them. If they believed that they were forgotten, mistreated, or neglected by their government, their communities, and their families (all intertwined to northern volunteers), then it was a struggle for them to support the Union cause and remain obedient soldiers.[148]

Yet another wave of agitation hit the regiment when word spread that the position of major, vacant since the death of George Washburn at Antietam, was to be filled by a lieutenant from the 15th Connecticut. Edward H. Mix, one of the two original captains who had been with the regiment since leaving Hartford in August 1862, voiced his displeasure in a letter to the governor in late May 1863. "The 16th Regt. have now been in the service about nine months," Mix recounted, "and during that time have seen hard service as you know reducing our numbers by the bullet and by disease until only seven of the line officers that left Hartford with us are with us now." Pointing out his own experience leading and helping to drill the regiment for some three months as well as an entire week between the battles of Antietam and Fredericksburg, Mix was quick to add that fellow captain Henry L. Pasco "is a Gentleman and a soldier, a man that is always at his post and [in] every way worthy of promotion." Captain Mix demanded to know why the lieutenant of a regiment that has "*never been in action* should be promoted over our heads?" Mix described the officers as "all feeling badly" and unappreciated; the noncommissioned officers and privates were "indignant."[149] There were other signs that Mix knew he had no chance of promotion and instead grew defiant. On June 1, 1863, he found himself charged with neglect and disobedience for failing to do morning or battalion drill, leaving camp, and failing to report at Suffolk. The captain received a reprimand and lost two months pay for his insubordinate behavior.[150] It is not clear if he was openly protesting the treatment of the regiment or if this behavior was personal.

In the end, Pasco won the promotion that June, rather than Mix, but the captain's words provide a telling insight into the regiment's state of mind that late spring of 1863. There is pride and a hint of defensiveness in Mix's words regarding the regiment's "hard service" as compared to that of the 15th Connecticut. The only real difference between these two units was Antietam. The 15th formed in the summer of 1862, a "distinctively New Haven county regiment," but remained defending Washington while the troops clashed at Antietam in September.[151] Although the 16th Connecticut's performance there was less than stellar, that difficult combat experience—deliberately and publicly spun in a positive way by one of its captains and others—helped to shape the unit's evolving sense of identity.

Defiant yet straining for confidence, still believing they had been overlooked, even disrespected, as citizen-soldiers, the regiment readied to move to yet another position. On June 13, 1863, the 16th Connecticut loaded onto railroad cars to travel to Portsmouth.[152]

5

Portsmouth

"A Perfect Village"

Moved from Suffolk, Virginia, to a camp near Portsmouth during the summer of 1863, the 16th Connecticut Volunteers settled into relatively pleasant quarters. They were further removed from major campaigns including Gettysburg, Vicksburg, Chickamauga, and Chattanooga and, except for the infamous "Blackberry Raid," spent most of their time in garrison duty. Men built winter cabins, a church, and a hospital. Military discipline was lax, and the men enjoyed poker games, theatrical productions, and plentiful liquor. Mail was steady, and civilian visitors common. When ordered to leave their agreeable camp for yet another new destination, the soldiers demonstrated that they would not so easily surrender what they believed to be "their" property to the U.S. government.

"DO ALL THE DAMAGE POSSIBLE"

The regiment arrived near Portsmouth, Virginia, on June 16, 1863, and settled into what appeared to be very comfortable quarters. One soldier wrote the *Daily Courant* just days after their arrival to report that their camp was about three miles from town, a spot previously occupied by the 22nd Georgia. "There are many farm houses in this vicinity," he explained, "and we can purchase almost anything we like, such as milk, poultry, vegetables, etc."[1] Other soldiers commented on this bounty, too. Harrison Woodford (Co. I) wrote his mother, "We can get almost anything we want here from peddlers. We can get ice cream, lemonade, pies & cakes, cherries, onions, fried fish, beer & almost anything else."[2] George Robbins reported that nearby farmers sold "cucumbers and ripe tomatoes and now potatoes and beets," and "milk is brought into camp every day." He also told his parents of the great "quantity of cakes and pies and ice creme [sic], enough to make a man sick to see all the stuff."[3] Lewis M. Holcomb (Co. B) was particularly pleased with the fresh bay water: "We enjoy the bathing very much, and think it very kind of Uncle Samuel to take us to this exceedingly pleasant place to spend the summer."[4] During the heat of summer, a "refreshing sea breeze" cooled the men, and the nearby salty Elizabeth River, was a "splendid bathing place."[5] Even cantankerous Martin Culver recognized how favorable their location was. "I dont kno how long we shall stay hear," he observed, "but I hope it will be for as long as I have to stay in the armey for we shall never get a better place than this."[6]

Less than a week after their arrival at Portsmouth, the regiment embarked on a diversionary expedition up the York River toward Richmond. This raid, undertaken while Robert E. Lee and his Army of Northern Virginia began their move northward, was meant to cut Confederate communication lines, destroy railroads and bridges, and, in the words, of General-in-Chief Henry Halleck, "do all the damage possible."[7] The 16th C.V. boarded steamers in the early morning hours of June 21, 1863, with little idea of what awaited them. Arriving on the Virginia Peninsula, it was clear that a large operation was about to commence. Robert Kellogg wrote his father from Yorktown, "I don't know what is up, but propose that we are going to attack Richmond under General Keys or Dix."[8] Robbins also expected that they were headed to the Confederate capital. "If you hear of our Division going into Richmond," he informed his father, "you must not be surprised, for I think it will be tried in earnest this time."[9]

This operation lasted nearly three weeks and led the men into what Kellogg called "a perfect garden" of wheat fields and fruit orchards: "We got all the cherries and blackberries that we could possibly eat and then left enough for an army of a hundred thousand men."[10] Robbins wrote his parents that the "country through which we are traveling is, as you have probably heard or read, the richest section in Virginia having never been traversed by any large army."[11] The men of the 16th also saw the remnants of slavery. "Nearly every plantation we passed," Kellogg observed, "is now stripped of its slaves." At White House Landing, Virginia, an elderly female slave greeted the Union troops, explaining that she had been hiding in the woods, "supplied with food by her daughter who remained with her master." Kellogg, who had spoken passionately against slavery in previous letters to his parents, was appalled by her appearance: "The old woman's hands were horribly broken & twisted, caused by a blow from a club in the hands of her cruel master. This shows the felicity of the 'peculiar institution.'"[12] Years later, Robbins vividly remembered the "swarm of young and old negroes that lined the roads in the vicinity of the plantations, beseeching us to take them with us." The sight of these slaves, so desperate, some of them on their hands and knees, pleading for help, was "pathetic" for Robbins to hear. But, he reasoned, "it was not possible to be hampered with them when we had to march at such a rapid pace."[13] Kellogg later believed that the 16th C.V. at least had helped distract the Confederates in Richmond, preventing them from sending reinforcements to Robert E. Lee's army in Pennsylvania.[14] Bernard Blakeslee alleged that he and his comrades "did a great deal of good" in convincing Lee to retreat once he found "his communications cut in the rear."[15]

Dubbed the "Blackberry Raid" because of the great amount of the fruit found along the soldiers' route, the operation, however, was essentially ineffective.[16] George N. Lamphere later remembered that, "after tedious marching in the heat of mid summer and through the miasmatic swamps, the advance reaching as far as Hanover Court House, we returned to our several posts, having accomplished nothing."[17] Sgt. Jacob Bauer declared the experience a "failure."[18]

The raid took a harsh toll on its participants. Marching in extreme heat, some of the men barefoot, and pursued by enemy cavalry, the regiment came back to Portsmouth exhausted. "We saw no fighting," Lt. Col. John Burnham wrote his mother Sarah a day after returning to camp, "but had a very hard time in other respects." He stated, "I have had several men ruined for life by the heat. They will be unable to go into the sun as long as they live."[19] Kellogg claimed that at one point the regiment marched thirty-one miles in nineteen hours. It was too much for many in the 16th Connecticut, including Kellogg. His shoes gave out, and his feet became severely bruised and sore. Surgeon Mayer insisted that Kellogg ride his horse, while the doctor marched on foot. Kellogg soon switched to an ambulance and then steamer, "not the only barefooted one."[20] Cpl. Leland Barlow wrote on July 3, "Marched 20 miles. Lots fell out. About a dozen fell dead. Outrageous." Barlow would end up so weakened and ill that he was hospitalized.[21] Lt. Ariel Case, in charge of Company E due to the illness of Captain Cone, was stunned by the raid's effect on his men. July 3 was the worst day. He had forty men in his company that morning, but only ten were still with him by day's end. "Two or three men of the Regt.," Case stated, "never did any duty after that day's march."[22]

Cpl. William H. Jackson (Co. B) disappeared from the ranks during the raid. This seemed quite out of character for the corporal, a well-respected man who had become one of the unofficial religious leaders in the regiment. When he returned, Jackson explained that he "had been compelled to fall out of the ranks on the march to Portsmouth by an acute attack of diarrhea that resulted in his complete prostration. He rejoined the regiment as soon as he was able. Jackson's reduction to the ranks was not unexpected, but the men found it excessively harsh and unnecessary when Lt. Col. Burnham decided to have Jackson's corporal insignia "removed in the presence of the Regiment at dress parade." On August 11, 1863, Jackson stood before his comrades as Pvt. Charles F. Campbell (Co. B) cut off the chevrons from his sleeve. Forbes later recalled, "The severity of this punishment inflicted was the cause of regret through the ranks."[23]

There were no accolades to gain from this failed, futile raid. While their comrades fought and died on the battlefields of Gettysburg and Vicksburg, the 16th C.V. limped back to Portsmouth to lick its wounds.

"I SHALL SOON FORGET THAT I AM A SOLDIER"

At the end of August 1863, the regiment moved from the west branch of the Elizabeth River to yet another location. They shifted one mile west, near Fort Griswold, positioned, in the words of one soldier, "toward Suffolk, near our line of defense that we are to help protect." Soon the regiment settled into its new home and began to recover from the Blackberry Raid. "We have our camp nicely laid out," a soldier wrote in a letter to the *Hartford Daily Courant*: "The tents are raised four feet and stockaded. Most of them have good board floors and bunks, which makes it pleasant and comfortable for a soldier. We have plenty to eat, and that which is good. The health of the regiment is good. But few, compared with other regiments, are in the hospital."[24] Surgeon Nathan Mayer later remembered their site as a "perfect village." He recalled, "The most perfect order, the most civilized condition prevailed. The tents were neatly and prettily furnished, as our Connecticut homes are, and the ground was always in beautiful condition."[25] George Robbins also described Portsmouth as "beautiful" and "warm and snug," so much so that it caused the "envy and admiration" of all other regiments in the division.[26]

Discipline had grown remarkably lax at Portsmouth, but Lt. Col. Burnham began to institute changes in August, earning the men's ire. "They make us come out to roll call," Robbins complained to his mother, "with our dress coats on and buttoned up caps and shoes all on. Before the boys used to come out barefooted and bareheaded without coats on or anyway they was a mind to."[27] Their new daily routine consisted of drills, fatigue, and picket duty. Mostly this was tedious manual labor, which many resented doing; it was certainly not the type of soldiering they had anticipated when they volunteered one year earlier. Some would have preferred active campaigning to such an easy service. "There is nothing going on but the usual daily duty," Lewis M. Holcomb wrote his aunt in August, "like a tread mill it is the same thing over [and over]." Holcomb claimed that the brigade was nearly sent to Charleston but was too small, with its number of effective men counting "only 800 for duty." Despite the regiment's pleasant and safe quarters at Portsmouth, he was disappointed: "I almost wish we had gone." The twenty-two-year-old Holcomb, who had been a Granby farmer and teacher before the war, sensed a marked change in himself: "The army has taken what little poetry and imaginative power I did have completely out of me, and left nothing but hard dry facts. I have seen too much of the *Real* to leave any room for the *Ideal*."[28] A few days before he penned this letter to his aunt, Holcomb wrote his cousin Addie, "Camp life is dull with us, nothing to do or write about. I am having altogether to[o] easy a time, am very fat, and in perfect health, but feel that this War is very Cruel (That was writ sarcastical [sic]) (A. Ward)."[29]

Camp life was dull, and soldiers looked for diversions. They read newspapers, books, and the Bible.[30] They also played games like chess and baseball, sang, and formed debate clubs.[31] Less wholesome diversions included gambling, drinking, and consorting with prostitutes.[32] The regimental band entertained the troops, and a theater was built where soldiers performed plays. Austin Thompson described the theater, "carried on by a New York Battery," as large enough to hold three or four hundred spectators. "If we are surrounded by all these things," Thompson told Electra Churchill, "I shall forget that I am a soldier."[33]

The regiment's devout Christians sought ways to nurture and spread their faith despite the regiment's idleness and constant temptation. They were not unique. Civil War soldiers North and South were increasingly turning to religion and seeking new converts by the end of 1863.[34] Pvt. Sidney Hayden described his comrades attending prayer "meetings," which he hoped would make "better soldiers of the men as well as better soldiers of the cross."[35] Pvt. George N. Champlin was pleased with the weekly Saturday prayer meetings attended by forty to fifty men. Champlin described the new chaplain, Dixon, as a "a real Methodist," and "tip top," explaining to a friend, "He don't preach nothing but the gospel and he is a good Christian man." He also claimed that in late November 1863 there had been a "little revival" in the regiment and twenty-five to thirty men had "returned to the 'Fold of God.'"[36] Ira Forbes maintained that there was a high level of religiosity in the regiment at Portsmouth. He attended services at the chapel of the 11th

Pennsylvania Cavalry before the 16th Connecticut dedicated its own "regimental chapel."[37] Forbes also regularly read devotions and perused sermons on his own.[38]

On January 3, 1864, the regiment dedicated its chapel at Portsmouth. George Champlin described the pews filled "to overflow long before the services commenced." Soldiers and "twenty ladies" attended.[39] Forbes wrote of the occasion: "The services were delightfully interesting. Chaplain [Moses] Smith of the 8th C.V. preached an excellent sermon."[40] Robbins described a number of chaplains present from regiments stationed nearby. "Many came," Robbins stated, "that could not gain admittance and were obliged to go home." He judged the sermon "interesting" and the music "excellent," sung by a choir from the Regt assisted by several of the Ladies who are on a visit to their husbands in the Regt."[41] "Horse John" described the chapel in a letter to the editors of the *Connecticut War Record* in January 1864: "A nice tight house, floored and warmed with benches and a real pulpit." Although it had no proper choir, it had kneeling stools. The soldier mused, "I have bowed in every grand church, from incense cloud altars of St. Peter's to the music reverberating aisles of St. Paul's, and I vow, I can worship in this homely little chapel, with as much reverence as in any of these."[42]

Even though there was a regimental chapel, at least two chaplains in camp, and two separate services on the Sabbath, some Christians in the regiment sought more. Surrounded by so much temptation, a small group of soldiers broke away on January 9 to form a separate organization called the "Christian Association of the 16th Regiment of Connecticut Volunteers." Twenty-one men joined immediately, including Alfred Dickerson, Charles G. Lee, James M. Keith, George Keith, Champlin, and Forbes. Members vowed to be more devout and end their sinful ways.[43] Forbes was "happy to belong to such a regiment of noble men. We have many Christians here and a good chaplain and all are willing to do their duty. Oh that the holy spirit might be poured out and our hearts thoroughly enlisted in the work."[44]

Although soldiers also successfully created a Temperance Society, urging men to sign a pledge not to indulge, alcohol was readily available to those who sought it. On some occasions, like Thanksgiving, men drank to excess; Holcomb described his comrades celebrating "in a high old manner." Kellogg took special note in his diary on January 1, 1864: "There is I'm sorry to say a great deal of intoxication in the Reg. today both among officers and men."[45] Robbins noted that "a great many of the companies have had liquor furnished them by their Officers and are of course fairly happy tonight." As for his own company (Co. K), Robbins stated, "Our Capt has given the boys some liquor but they are not very drunk."[46]

Overall, the 16th C.V.'s time at Portsmouth would prove to be an odd hybrid of military and civil life. With no active campaigning, the regiment existed on the margins of war. Increasingly, wives, parents, and children began to appear in camp, making Portsmouth seem even less like a combat zone. As one historian has noted, "these visits tended to bring the war very close to the home folks."[47] Indeed, the opposite was also true; they brought home to the soldiers. In September 1863, Oliver Hayden paid his son Sidney a surprise visit at Portsmouth. It was short but memorable, leaving his son thinking it was "like a dream his having been here coming so unexpectedly and leaving so soon."[48] It cost considerable money for family and friends to travel to camp, and for some it was too expensive. Martin Culver noted to his brother Jonathan that he "should like to have you come out hear but it costs quite a sum for a citizen to come on" while "it costs a soldier about $8 to go and come."[49] Samuel E. Derby expressed similar views when he wrote his wife Elizabeth in September 1863 that he had heard of his friend Hiram Clark's wife Ellen deciding not to visit. "I think she acted very wisely in not coming down here," Derby explained, "for what good could come of it for he is well and she could not be of any benefit to him whatever it would be money foolishly spent." If Hiram were sick, then Derby could understand Ellen making the trip. Speaking for his friend and no doubt as much for himself, Derby continued, "but as long as he is well it is better for both not to meet until he comes home it would be very hard to part again harder, than it was the first time for now we know how to appreciate the comforts of a good home more than we used to, you see we did not know how to appreciate it until we were deprived of them."[50]

Wives, sisters, and mothers who did manage the journey often remained for weeks, and their presence had a noticeable effect on the camp. Austin Thompson counted "about a dozen women" visiting in mid-December. "They are coming," he judged, "and going almost every week, if not quite."[51] At the end of 1863, Harrison Woodford observed ladies helping to provide seasonal trimmings and celebrate Christmas Eve with a festive dance. He wrote that there were "a dozen men that have their wives here & with the officers were the ones that done the dancing."[52] Kellogg recalled a "number of ladies" visiting their husbands at the time the regiment erected its chapel at Portsmouth, the women adding to its "comfort and neatness."[53] The Case brothers, Ariel and Alonzo, brought their wives and sister to camp at Portsmouth.[54] "There were many misgivings among officers and men," Alonzo later admitted, "about having their wives come at first for fear that the men would be rough and ungentlemanly but nothing was farther from the truth."

"It seemed," he wrote, "as though every man tried to see how well he could be-have in the presence of ladies."[55] However, when John Cuzner's mother Jane and sweetheart Ellen expressed interest in coming for a visit, he strongly opposed the idea. Military Camp, he stated, "is no place for women[;] there is too much vulgar talk." "I had become toughened to it," he added, "but last night one of the boys got tight and his swearing made my hair stand straight up."[56] Neither was Cuzner sure about children. He described seeing "two or three other women with infants around, but I should think they would not like camp life."[57]

One of the notable women who came to camp was Lt. Col. Burnham's mother, Sarah. Mrs. Burnham arrived in late August and departed in mid-October, hav-ing spent considerable time caring for patients in the hospital.[58] To most, Mrs. Burnham made a positive impression. One soldier maintained, "She is a mother to every soldier that she meets, no matter what his rank is. She makes us all think of our dear mothers that we left at home one year ago."[59] "Lieut. Robins" confirmed the deep affection soldiers held toward Mrs. Burnham in a letter to his father quoted in the *Daily Courant* a few weeks later: "That most excellent of women, Mrs. Burnham mother of our lieutenant colonel, has been with us for some time to see her son. From morning till night she is engaged in visiting the sick in camp and hospital, and ministering to them comfort in the way of gruels and appetizing food, and you may be assured is followed by the blessing of many who are languishing on beds of pain."[60] Corporal Woodford called Mrs. Burnham a "perfect angel compared to her son." Woodford, who himself had been very ill, appreciated that she brought "good things to the sickest ones every day almost."[61] Dr. Mayer also commented on Sarah Burnham's presence. "We have of late had quite a number of ladies visiting us," he wrote in a letter from Portsmouth,

and the effect on our men has been very good. Whereas you formerly could hear an oath now and then from an aggravated individual, now no such imprecations sully the air. Let me here mention the incalculable ser-vices rendered to our sick by Mrs. Burnham, mother of Lieut.-Col. John H. Burnham, now commanding the regiment. Almost seventy years old, this grand old lady displays a vigor and tenderness, a discrimination and practical kindness, in her attentions to the sick, that have gone far to help us through a dreadful epidemic of diphtheria and of remittent fever, with the loss of only three men. She is constantly engaged in preparing those nice home tit-bits so dear to the sick soldiers. Not satisfied with preparing them, she administers them, talking all the time to the delighted men as only a great, good woman of that age and such motherly feelings can talk.[62]

Ariel Case later remembered Sarah Burnham going "through the regiment and if she saw any one not feeling well she would get them some little delicacies for them until they called her the 'Mother of the Regt.'"[63]

"A POOR PLACE"

Just as it had at Suffolk, the presence of African American troops in and around the camp drew varying reactions from the white soldiers. Sidney Hayden claimed to speak for many of his comrades when he wrote his mother Jane in mid-September: "One thing that is humiliating to the boys and one they declare they won't do is to salute nigger officers." He described "a regiment of colored individuals" at Portsmouth with "negro commissioned officers and they (the officers) give the guards a scolding for not saluting them." Hayden, who frequently and angrily blamed African Americans for the war and routinely expressed racist views in his letters home, declared, "The nig feels big when he gets on the shoulder straps. That's a leetle [sic] to[o] much for me."[64] Leland Barlow also remarked on the presence of black troops at Portsmouth. "The old Secesh don't like them at all," he observed, "they are afraid of them." Local whites warned that the black troops would run as soon as they "hear the first bullet near them." But Barlow thought otherwise: "I think they will fight."[65]

Contrabands were also present in camp. Even Robert Kellogg, a devoted abolitionist, revealed the racism so prevalent among Union troops when he wrote on January 16, "Great deal of fun in the Reg. today, throwing niggers in blankets, etc. etc."[66] Lewis Holcomb explained what this meant in a letter to his cousin, recounting visiting a house on the border of the Dismal Swamp where he and fellow soldiers had a "good time generally." "Our principal amusement there," Holcomb continued, "was catching all the little niggars that we could lay our hands on, turning them into a room together and making them dance to the infinite delight of all lookers on." If any blacks tried to escape, the soldiers gave "them a tossing up in a blanket. It always produced the desired result."[67] George Robbins described the African American population of Portsmouth in markedly racialized language to friends in Plainville. He explained, "There are any quantity of all colors and sizes from there that are so black that Charcoal would smoke a white mark on them to those nearly white."[68]

Soldiers also coped with disease in Portsmouth, especially during the summer months.[69] In late August, Pvt. Culver wrote his brother that although he was "well and as tough as a brick so far thare is a great deal of sickness hear now it is a kind of soar throat and they call it the dipthera." He added, "We muster 180 men for duty."[70] By mid-September, Pvt. Cuzner estimated that two hospitals were completely filled and the regiment had a mere ninety men in camp.[71] Ira Forbes later wrote of a "plague" of diphtheria striking the Union encampment at Portsmouth that September, crediting Dr. Mayer and Sarah Burnham with helping to prevent more deaths. "There were a large number of deaths in neighboring regiments," Forbes wrote. But the "noble" Mrs. Burnham "was in camp while the epidemic was at its highest and left nothing undone for the comfort of the Sixteenth men, who were stricken by the disease. She was well advanced in life and had a motherly care of the sick."[72] Robbins, who was sick, well recalled her trying to soothe him in his despair.[73] He eventually recovered due to the ministrations of Dr. Mayer and hospitalization. In one particularly heartbreaking case, illness ravaged a soldier's family. "We have had a funeral today," Robbins informed his parents in September. "One of the ladies that came in brought two children with her & one of them a girl of two years died last night of Dysentry [sic] and was buried today in Portsmouth." Apparently, the child had accompanied her mother to visit her father, Martin Hull in Company E, who was "sick with fever." Robbins observed, "It is a hard blow for him to have his children come on to see him and to lose one out here."[74] "It is," Leland Barlow observed, "a poor place for children out here."[75]

Malaria also swept through camp, and Lt. Col. Burnham became extremely sick, suffering, as Dr. Mayer later described it, from "severe malarial attacks and from neuralgias of the head and neck" while at Portsmouth. These malarial outbreaks would plague Burnham the rest of his life.[76] It was not until November that the cold weather and the first hard frost brought relief to their camp.[77]

A "SORT OF HOLIDAY"

Antietam still cast a long shadow on the regiment. In July 1863, the Democratic *Hartford Daily Times* printed a story about "Lieut. J——u, late of the 16th Connecticut," who encountered an Irish-accented, "half soldier, half beggar" on Main Street in Hartford who greeted the officer and blessed him excitedly. The lieutenant did not recognize the man and asked him how they were acquainted. "'It is how do I know your honor?' responded the Pat. 'Good right, sure, I have to know the man who saved my life in battle.'" The officer gave the man money, "highly gratified at this tribute to his valor." The Irishman then added, "Sure it was at Antietam, when seeing your honor run away as fast as your legs would carry you from the Rebels, I followed your lead and ran after you out of the way; whereby, under God, I saved my life. Oh! Good luck to your honor, I will never forget it to you."[78]

This anecdote underscores several significant points about the regiment, especially the deep shame of running off the battlefield, not just for the soldiers but for their families and supporters. This soldier, represented as a poor Irishman, no less, would not let the regiment forget. His challenging an ex-officer in the streets of Hartford juxtaposed the contradiction of heroism and death, as well as the differences between the poor soldiers in the ranks and the moneyed officer class. Both men survived the horrific battle, but their behavior that day, perhaps understandable and justifiable given their greenness and ill-preparedness for combat, was, by many definitions, dishonorable. Readers would have found neither the Irishman nor the ex-officer to be characters worth emulating.

The soldiers of the 16th C.V. were deeply mindful of Antietam, and they struggled with mixed emotions as its one-year anniversary approached. In August, Leland Barlow mused to his sister Jane that he did not "consider the battle ground of Antietam a very sacred place." He was not bothered by the idea of farming the lands again where he and his comrades had fought, as long as the graves were left undisturbed: "O! It was a desolate place around Sharpsburg. I think the sooner any such place as the battle field can be blotted out the better. I would not disturb the grave of our poor soldier, and I think our Reg's each buried their own dead together so they wont be disturbed."[79] In another reminder of Antietam, members of Company K raised money to send back to the town of Bristol, Connecticut, to raise a monument to their slain captain Manross, killed in action. Robbins estimated in mid-August that already $120 had been collected among his company mates.[80]

On the actual anniversary of the battle, September 17, 1863, John Cuzner wrote Ellen Van Dorn that the regiment had planned a "sort of holiday" and wanted "to have a good time; it being the anniversary of our first battle, Antietam." However, the successive deaths from diphtheria of Sgt. William Hubbard (Co. B) on September 16 and Sgt. Samuel Woodruff (Co. G) on September 17 quashed their plans.[81] The loss of Hubbard, in the words of one member of the regiment, "cast a gloom over us all."[82] Corporal Barlow simply wrote in his diary: "One year Battle of Antietam."[83] The next day he continued, "Year ago today we were on the field of Antietam getting our dead and wounded buried forty in one grave."[84] Robbins shared the same memory with his parents on September 19: "I received your letter on the 17th, one year from the date of the battle of Antietam which we all remember so well. How different is our situation today from what it was at that time, one year ago today we were burying the fallen of both sides without regard to rank or position and now we are lying quietly in camp with the exception of the five companies at South Mills who will return in a day or two."[85] Gavett B. Holcomb also took note of the one year anniversary of Antietam: "We are raising a flag to day and well we might for one year agoe [sic] was the day that we received a warm reception from those grea [sic] backs, such a one as, I never shall forget, that day was the 17 Sept 1862. That day many of our brave Soldiers die[d]." But then he wondered if this date meant as much to his parents as it did to him.[86]

In December 1863, a soldier calling himself "Adelphi" wrote a public letter for the *Connecticut War Record,* using Antietam as a point of comparison for the regiment's improvement in drill and performance. "Our experience at Antietam," he reflected, "where we were brought in deadly conflict with a subtle foe, without any preparation, demonstrates this fact quite clearly, at least to our own minds." The soldier concluded, "It was a dear lesson to us, and I am glad to say that we have applied ourselves so diligently to perfecting our drill that we compare favorably with other regiments, especially in the manual of arms."[87] Notwithstanding the soldiers' complaining, Lt. Col. Burnham's efforts were apparently paying off.

"THIS KIND OF LIFE"

Soldier letters and diary entries during this time reveal their continued reflection on the war's larger causes and their personal reasons for enlisting. Soon after returning to Portsmouth from the raid, Austin Thompson assured Electra Churchill that he and his comrades were still fighting for a noble cause. Battle was a "horrid thing," Thompson admitted. But he urged her to "remember that I am fighting in a most glorious cause, a cause that neither of us will ever be ashamed of as long as we live."[88] In July 1863, Pvt. Cuzner wrote a revealing letter to Ellen Van Dorn: "I had not heard from you for many weeks, it was a long time to wait for a letter from one of whom I'm constantly thinking." Ellen had apparently scolded John about the "tone" of his letters, and he was quick to confirm that he tried to be careful, not wanting to "write all my thoughts, feelings, expectations, etc." But, he stated, "It is hard to be out here doing the best we can and not hearing from our friends." Cuzner continued, "You said you would give me up for Our Country's sake if you knew I fell fighting bravely. I admire you for your spirit. I wish the people of the North all felt as you do, but it is not so. They will write discouraging letters to their friends in the Army." Cuzner, who had openly admitted to being a "coward" in a letter to Ellen right after Antietam, now sought to pronounce his courage: "When I enlisted I expected to fight, four times have I been under fire and had my tent mates shot down, but no one can say, truthfully, that I was one foot, out of my place."[89]

By August, Lewis Holcomb insisted that he and his fellow soldiers "never felt so confident that the Rebellion would be crushed as now. They do not expect sudden peace, but feel willing to bide the time when Peace will again visit the country. We have always expected that the war would end sooner than was reasonable." Holcomb predicted that "another year will end it." Holcomb was willing to keep fighting: "I'm for a war with England, France or any one else who wishes to mind our affairs."[90] Harrison Woodford was equally confident about the Union army's prospects and despite hot weather attested to having "jolly times here for the army."[91] When Sgt. Henry Lee heard that a relative had died in the army, he expressed sadness mixed with pride that his family member "had been fighting for constitutional liberty." Lee envisioned, "When the history of this War shall be written there will be found many a parallel case. The music of the gentle breeze that rustles the leaves around many a cottage, and the old homestead, will be like a requiem for the slain, but all men must die, and what better death could we ask for than that of a brave Soldier who fights for Sacred Liberty and a nation's honor?" Lee, differing from his cousin Lewis Holcomb, admitted that he had witnessed many a comrade who grumbled "over hardships and wish[ed] he was out of the army who could not be induced to give up the consciousness that he was doing all that he could for his country."[92]

Cpl. Leland Barlow admitted in a letter to his uncle that there were many things to discourage northern soldiers like himself, including those who would take "advantage of the soldier to fill his own pockets and to make a political thing of the war." But Barlow, who had waivered in his commitment to the war at times, had grown more resolute: "Give me good health and I will willingly stay to see the Union restored again. I should feel it is my duty; we get used to the hardships of camp life and enjoying it. The fighting is not so pleasant but thank God we don't have to go into Battle everyday."[93]

Pvt. Leander Chapin had returned to the 16th Connecticut in August 1863 after an extended hospital stay and a short stint in the Veterans Reserve Corps. He was happy to be back. As one of his friends, a fellow soldier in another unit, stated, "A man with any pluck had much rather be with his regt. than in the 'invalid corps.'"[94] Chapin wrote his younger brother in late November that he had "never been sorry I enlisted, though I have been in many tight and bad places and I hope to return again when the war is over to a peaceful occupation but while my country needs me I want to stay."[95]

George Champlin was also pleased with his lot—so much so that he encouraged his hometown friend Samuel Bartlett, formerly a member of the 25th Connecticut, to consider joining the 16th. "Well, Samuel," he wrote in late November 1863, "I don't feel like asking a *returned soldier* to enlist again, but I should like to have you enlist in my Co. I don't think you would regret it." Portsmouth was pleasant, he pointed out, and there seemed little chance of active campaigning with winter approaching. Champlin also said that he never once regretted enlisting, despite the death of his brother who served with him in the 16th: "I thought it was my duty & think so now." He proudly declared, "We have got a good Co. and one of the best Regts. in the army."[96]

There were, of course, the grumblers in the regiment, and they would grow more vocal as the weather grew colder. They complained about bad food, unfair officers, and continual sickness. They did not like picket duty or building breastworks, and going on sporadic raids was rarely exciting. Lewis Holcomb expounded one day to his cousin Addie after a stint constructing fortifications: "We don't work hard, you may believe that Add, but yet it is tedious to go about and stay 5 hours at a time."[97] Even the regimental band, which was meant to cheer the men with lively musical performances, grew tiresome for some. Listening to them one day, Martin Culver wrote his brother, "We have got a band in the regt that has just commenced to play and they get along nicely if anybody likes to hear it. i have heard it so mutch that i have got tired of it."[98]

Yet deeper issues were troubling the men. "I don't think," Sidney Hayden wrote, "we should have had a nigger war if it had not been for the nigger but might have on something else." He added in the same letter, "Tell Father that I consider it the duty of every man to put down treason but money is considered above *patriotism* by the world." Hayden's words reveal a common resentment toward those men who refused to serve, especially those who were gaining financial profit from the war. Nevertheless, Hayden insisted that he felt compelled to "shoulder the musket when the Government needed help," though he could not help looking forward to the end of military service: "Well, the old 16th Boys are going to have those privileges of driving on the roads, going to meeting, getting our regular sleep [at] night, going to cattel [sic] and hog shows and such like." "Well," he then added, "If we live to get home we shall know how to appreciate them better."[99] Several weeks later, Hayden continued to hope to survive the war, serve out his term, return home and "stick to farming like leech." He worried about the detrimental effects of military service: "I have thought that this kind of life if followed 3 years would spoil a man for any thing but I hope not."[100]

Soldiers like Hayden believed that their fellow northerners failed to appreciate all that they had sacrificed, even if they were not fighting on the front lines. "I tell you," Robbins wrote, "the people at the north have no idea of what the Soldiers are silently enduring for them and the country's sake, if they *could* know there would be more done *by them* to prosecute the war with renewed *vigor* and a fixed determination to bring it to an honorable but speedy end."[101]

"MILITARY DISCIPLINE"

There also remained tensions among officers and men. Some of the problems stemmed from Burnham's style of leadership, which had grown stricter since his return from convalescence after Suffolk. Harrison Woodford complained to his parents in August that if men "commit offenses," he "makes spread eagles of them" or has them "carry a log on their shoulders." "He made one man carry a log upon his shoulder to-day till he dropped down under it. The laws of the army are very rigid," Woodford determined, "but the best way is to obey them."[102] Leland Barlow complained bitterly of his captain: "Capt Morse is under arrest; he is a good for nothing drunken fellow. I hope he will be dismissed from the service. The Co. are worthy of a better man to command them."[103] Barlow was only slightly more impressed with Captain Cone: "He understands military tactics decently well and can show off well, and as far as that goes he is a good Capt I suppose; there is no principles about him; he is ignorant, a hard chap is no name for him."[104]

Men in the ranks also remained fixated on the idea that they had never been properly mustered into the U.S. Army.[105] In June, Sgt. Bernard Blakeslee notified the governor that there existed "a general feeling of doubt" among the men in the regiment "with regards to the legality" of their muster. This rumor had festered since February 1863, when the regiment failed to receive any pay, but why these rumors persisted now is not clear. Pay, both the various bounties and monthly wages, had been appropriately allotted. Governor Buckingham told Blakeslee, "I know of no grounds whatsoever for the doubts to which you refer." However, if an illegal muster had been made, all payments would be "recovered & all future payments stopped." He added, "If you have not been legally mustered you are not released from service but may be mustered now" and essentially reprocessed "to serve three years from this time." Buckingham urged Blakeslee to "dismiss it from your mind." "I know you are honorable, patriotic & true" [and] that you wanted neither [to] dishonor yourself or the state."[106] A few days later, Burnham wrote the governor, "I have learned with much surprise and pain that you have been addressed upon the subject of the muster of this regiment." "I imagine," Burnham stated, "the difficulty arose more from a disposition to breed trouble than from any apprehension about the muster." Not knowing that it was Sergeant Blakeslee who had written the governor, Burnham asked the governor to identify who the "agitators" were. Apparently, Buckingham did not oblige. The two men seem to have known each other personally, as the governor closed the letter by assuring Blakeslee, "You know I love you too well and am too much bound up with your honor and your interest to deceive you."[107]

By the fall, these tensions spilled into the pages of the Hartford press. It began in early September 1863 when Pvt. Horace B. Steele of Company F sent a letter to the editors of the *Hartford Daily Times,* angrily accusing regimental officers, in particular Burnham, of abuse. Steele claimed, "In this regiment men have been ordered to the guard house for some trivial offence and abused most shamefully." He described a recent incident in which a man was made to "carry a log that weighed from 50 to 60 pounds on his back, when the thermometer marked 102 in the shade." He then bitterly narrated his recent attempt at obtaining a furlough he considered himself "entitled to by the regulations of this army." One of his children was seriously ill, and Steele desperately wanted to be home with his wife and sick child. Burnham turned down his request. Steele closed his letter by asserting that the committee appointed by the governor to investigate the regiment's condition had been "feasted by the officers and not allowed to go into the privates' tents for fear they will tell the truth and expose the practices on the privates."[108]

Lt. Col. Burnham responded a few weeks later with his own letter to the paper. He was clearly rattled by Steele's decision to air his grievances openly. "The publication by an officer or soldier of such a letter as that of Steele's," Burnham maintained, "even if its statements were true, would be one of the grossest violations of military discipline, and the falsity of this one certainly aggravates the offense." He vowed not to punish Steele but instead offered to send him before a court-martial where he could properly air his grievances and "where he cannot fail to be treated with strict impartiality." It turned out that the "trivial offense" committed by Pvt. Patrick O'Brien from Company H was going AWOL from camp and being spotted "drunk in Portsmouth" days after his one-day pass expired, "thereby rendering himself liable to a charge for desertion." The regimental surgeon attested that O'Brien's exhaustion was not due to the punishment but to sunstroke intensified by his days of "dissipation."[109]

Another private from the 16th was quick to disagree, sending an angry letter to the paper in early October accusing Burnham of making up facts out "of whole cloth." "We have been most shamefully abused by our commissioned staff," reaffirmed the unnamed soldier, "pretty much since we left Hartford, being kept upon half rations, &tc, &tc, while other regiments close by us have had enough and to spare." Sick men, too, this man asserted, were also suffering: "For I have known men to lie in their tents for days and then died from the neglect, because the doctor did not pay them proper attention." When commissioners came to investigate the regiment's conditions, Burnham wined and dined them, "telling them such stories as he pleased, and they not going around to see how the privates lived!" Why did officers and doctors treat the 16th Connecticut so shabbily? These two soldiers insisted that it was incompetence, selfishness, and fear. Burnham "was afraid to have things exposed, and to have it known how such a gentleman as he professes to be, treats his fellow beings."[110]

There are several revealing aspects to this brief but heated flurry of accusations. As an officer, Lt. Col. Burnham clearly viewed his treatment of the offender wholly warranted to ensure, as he had told his mother in January 1863, that men like O'Brien "do his duty and his whole duty." Burnham could have meted out a more serious punishment than carrying a log. Steele, desperately seeking a furlough himself so he could be home with his family, could only sympathize with O'Brien. He and his comrade viewed O'Brien's actions—usually thought cowardly and dishonorable—as inconsequential, even understandable, and his punishment entirely unjustifiable. They bitterly resented Burnham's demand for discipline and proper behavior. The "coward" in this case was not their fellow soldier but their lieutenant colonel, who abused his power and position.[111]

Perhaps to calm tempers, news came a few weeks later that each member of the regiment would receive a ten-day furlough. The men were thrilled. One soldier wrote the *Hartford Daily Times*, "They all *do* so want to visit home."[112]

The furlough was intended to allow every man to go home. On October 19, the *Hartford Daily Courant* explained, "A few at a time in each company are to be let off, till the boys have all visited their homes—and they don't feel angry about it either."[113] Upon hearing the news, John Cuzner imagined what it would be like to see his sweetheart Ellen after so long an absence. "Ten days is a short time to be at home after being gone a year," he wrote her, "but it is better than none." Still, he worried that after such a short visit he would not want to return to the regiment.[114] But the furloughs came slowly, with only a few soldiers allowed to leave at a time. When a month went by and his furlough had not come, Cuzner's spirits fell. Even though he declared the regiment's camp at Portsmouth "splendid," the promise of a furlough had cast a cloud over the young private. "I should have felt perfectly satisfied if there had been nothing said about furloughs, but they promised me one and I should not be satisfied now until I have been home." Cuzner finally obtained his in early December 1863.[115]

Even though the regiment had become "almost a second home" to the soldiers, the emotional pull from far away was very strong and could take many forms.[116] For some, it was a basic yearning to return to their prewar lives as farmers, students, or workers. Sidney Hayden, for example, dwelled continually on returning to his beloved farm: "I hope by next summer," he wrote a family member in late July, "to have exchanged the uniform of a soldier to the garb of a farmer."[117] To see their friends and families again was always a powerful desire for lonely soldiers, but there were other things for which they yearned. Lewis Holcomb told his cousin Addie, "You can not imagine how much good it would do me to ride through New England, even if I did not speak to a single individual. To see her hills and valleys would be happiness." Since leaving the peninsula, the regiment had experienced seemingly the "same dead level and the scenery of the same spiritless character."[118]

Furlough or not, there were men who sought a way out any way they could. Musician Wilmer H. Johnson, wrote Governor Buckingham in October 1863, explaining, "I have been wounded at Antietam three times and am unfit to do duty." Johnson admitted that he had passed the division surgeon's test and no doubt would suffer the same fate with the regimental surgeon Dr. Mayer. Nonetheless, Johnson tried to sway the governor by using the power of the press and politics. "I am an old reporter, I was on the N. Y. Eve[ning] Express two years and have been on the Hartford Post, in fact am at present a correspondent for that paper." Johnson added, "In the course of Business, I have often had the pleasure of mentioning your name ever since the Republican Party was first started, I have been with them heart and soul, but I claim no extra privileges on that account." "What I ask now," he wrote, "is what I am entitled to and that is an immediate discharge." There is no evidence of Buckingham responding, and Johnson stayed in the ranks until the war ended, dying within three weeks of his return home. The cause of death is unclear.[119] Pvt. Franklin Peck, worried about his widowed mother and two young children, unsuccessfully sought a discharge, reasoning that his family was dependent on him but he "did not earn enough as a private to properly support them."[120] Austin Thompson also wanted to come home. "But," he wrote his fiancé, "if I can stand it through to the end, I had much rather do it, than go home with a name that some of the boys have."[121] When two soldiers of the 8th Connecticut were executed for desertion, the sight made an impression on Thompson: "I went down to see them shot, and although it was not a pleasant sight yet I think I should not hesitate to see more shot for the same thing. Because if we are [to be] successful we must have some discipline." He avowed to Electra, "I enlisted for three years or during [sic] the war, and if I desert before the expiration of that time, of course I must expect to suffer the consequences."[122] These soldiers' commitment to the North's war to save the Union and end slavery seems to have diminished. They stayed because they had to, not because they were motivated by the war's larger ideals.

There were those who absconded anyway. Deserters from the 16th C.V. included Pvt. James Gillen (Co. I), who deserted the regiment in July;[123] and Cpl. George W. Green, who deserted in August, apparently from Washington, D.C. (It is not clear why he was in the capital.)[124] Pvt. Henry M. Stratton (Co. G), a New York–born cigar maker, had been granted a twenty-day furlough after a stay in the hospital. He never returned to the regiment and was listed as a deserter in early September.[125] The regiment also continued to lose men to discharges, mainly due to illness.[126]

The 16th C.V. clearly needed men. In July, a rumor began to circulate that the regiment would soon be "filled up with drafted men." "Some of the boys do not like it very much," Austin Thompson remarked, but he "did not see as they can help themselves."[127] George Robbins informed his parents, "This regt and the 8th and probably the 11th are to be filled with conscripts and two or three officers and thirteen men are going home to bring those for our regt in."[128] Leland Barlow was pleased with the news, "We will have a 'bully 16th' again as the boys used to sing in the John Brown tune; now three rousing cheers for the bully 16th and we will hang Jeff Davis on a crab apple tree. Before the Antietam fight they used to sing it after that our troops are successful all the way around."[129] Barlow told his sister, "The boys like the notion of having the conscripts come into the Reg. because they say they can rough it on them; make them do more than their share of duty."[130] "I reckon," Harrison Woodford predicted, "we will have a great time drilling them."[131] In September, Barlow wrote of "three hundred conscripts" arriving at Portsmouth for the 8th Connecticut. "They were guarded more like Prisoners than anything else. A good many of them old soldiers from New York." He judged them to be "hard boys; went hollering through the place, but they will get tamed down and be good soldiers most of them. I pity the good honest boys that are with them."[132] On September 15, Sidney Hayden expected "160 conscripts to join us mostly foreigners next week."[133] But by late October when no conscripts had arrived, George Robbins was pleased. He wrote his parents, "We have not had any conscripts yet and I hope we shall not for they are very troublesome." The 8th Connecticut, Robbins noted, had lost sixty of their drafted men to desertion. He judged them "mostly subs" who had "been in the army before and enlist for the bounties."[134] Hayden bluntly declared, "We don't want substitutes but volunteers."[135]

In mid-July 1863, Robert H. Kellogg had left Portsmouth, along with several other commissioned and noncommissioned officers and men, for Connecticut to "bring conscripts to the regiment."[136] Kellogg remained at "Camp Conscript" in Fair Haven until the fall, doing what he described as "arduous, arduous" duties, "drilling them and watching them." He mainly referred to the men as "substitutes," rather than conscripts, and labeled them "a tough set of human beings."[137] At one point, the men set the recruitment building on fire, apparently hoping to escape service. "We were all commanded," Kellogg told his mother, "to load our guns and were then placed outside of the building so that not a man could escape without being shot."[138] Unlike his previous detached service as a hospital steward, this time Kellogg was unhappy to be away from the 16th C.V. He wrote, "We have more duty to do here than we ever had in the regt. and unpleasant duty too."[139]

By the end of the year, the 16th C.V. turned to recruiting soldiers rather than drafting them, a significant difference. Officers and men from each company were sent on detached service home to Hartford to stir enlistments.[140] One soldier who welcomed the recruits wrote to the *Hartford Courant*. "It is true," he admitted, "that the first flush of enthusiasm is over, and that now he who responds to his country's urgent call for more men encounters a sober reality, and not a rose-colored picture of ease and pleasure." He urged "any true hearted man" to show his patriotism. "Don't wait to be drafted, but act like men and join our number; share with us the glory of Antietam, of Fredericksburg and of the engagements of the Nansemond." He added, "To those about to enlist, I would favorably notice our regiment—the 16th—than which a better is not in the service. Well disciplined, well clad and fed, and quartered for the winter near Portsmouth, Va, and being composed mostly of Hartford county men, you will find yourself in the midst of friends if you join us. Don't wait any longer then, but come and help fill up our ranks. You cannot spend New Year's Day in a more pleasant manner than with the boys of the 16th Conn. Vols."[141] Another soldier reporting for the *Connecticut War Record* noted the regiment's dire need for more recruits: "Instead of the long line which we used to make, we can bring out for parade hardly enough for two good companies." He declared, "We greatly need an increase in numbers."[142] By the first week of January 1864, Austin Thompson calculated a dozen recruits arriving in camp.[143] In total, the 16th C.V. would count seventy-five recruits in its ranks by war's end.[144]

"A UNIVERSAL CONFLAGRATION"

As the weather turned colder, the regiment began preparations for winter camp. Soldiers first put brick floors in their tents and then built sturdy log cabins and new wooden houses for officers, a church, and a hospital.[145] The hospital, one member declared, was the "finest Regiment Hospital in this Department." Built of pine, with fourteen beds, white beddings, and oysters, chocolate, butter, and milk, the hospital was, at least to "Horse John," the "next thing to Paradise."[146] "Ever since we have been in this camp," Austin Thompson wrote home, "some of the boys have been constantly at work fixing comfortable quarters for the coming winter. And I believe that it is the prettiest and neatest camp in the whole department."[147]

As the New Year loomed, most were convinced that they would remain in Portsmouth "for some [time] to come."[148] Compared to the unit's situation one year earlier, Portsmouth was a prime location indeed. Lewis Holcomb noted to his cousin, "Not like last winter is our present life, burrowing in our holes in the ground covered by a shelter tent no bigger than a respectable table cloth, but right royal is our quarters, large A tents raised four feet from the ground and stockaded." He added, "I hardly ever lie down at night without feeling thankful that we are so pleasantly situated."[149] Austin Thompson was also aware of the changes that had come to the regiment in one year. On January 4, he wrote Electra Churchill, "One year ago we lay in Falmouth with a heavy heart, with nothing but mud and sleep for consolation, and many already to give up in despair. Many of [our] hopes were like a man standing on the scaffold ready to be plunged into eternity." But now, Thompson noted, "We are in good winter quarters, and I for one appreciate it with all my heart."[150] They had little desire to exchange their camp for the bloody battlefront, arduous marches, or exhausting raids. The 16th C.V. was content to be more civilian than soldier in their "perfect village."

In December 1863, Colonel Beach finally returned to the regiment after an absence of several months, and some in the ranks welcomed him back. Resentment toward Burnham had only grown, and Beach's arrival was cause for celebration.[151] "We are all glad to see him," wrote Leander Chapin to his mother Amelia, "and went up to his house and gave him three rousing cheers." Chapin predicted, "Things will be different now since he has returned [and there will be] not quite so many drunken officers around I guess he will just veto that business and Col. Burnham will have to haul down his colors a little also Adj. J. B. Clapp." Chapin declared, "We all like Col Beach and as heartily hate Col. Burnham."[152] Pvt. Elizur Belden, who in March had claimed "all the men actually hate him," now said of Beach, "All are very glad that he has returned."[153] "Horse John" wrote to the editors of the *Connecticut War Record* that the "boys" greeted Beach with "three cheers." "Everything is spontaneous," he added, "and all previous feelings turned into one gush of affectionate recognition."[154]

On Sunday, January 17, 1864, the 16th Connecticut was ordered to pack their belongings with three days rations and prepare to march at any time. The order, as George N. Champlin described in his diary, "created a great deal of excitement all day. We do not wish to leave our good winter quarters."[155] The next day, as a steady rain developed, the regiment remained at their post. Rumors circulated that they were headed to North Carolina, leaving Portsmouth for good. Men were annoyed and bored; with idle time on their hands, some turned to liquor. Champlin and Ira Forbes instead attended a Temperance meeting.[156] Austin Thompson used his free time to write home to Electra Churchill: "We feel bad to be oblige[d] to leave our excellent winter quarters. But such is the life of a soldier. It has always been our luck just as soon as we get our quarters fixed up in good style we have to leave for the unknown."[157]

On Wednesday, January 20, the regiment was paid and expected to leave the next morning. By then annoyance had turned to anger and, as Champlin wrote, "Several of the boys have burnt a part of their houses and one of the guard's tents. A number of the boys were drunk and have destroyed a part of the cook house."[158] "This evening," Forbes recorded in his diary, "there is general destruction about Camp. Our magnificent flag-staff has been cut down, and ther[e] is considerable prospect of a universal conflagration before daylight to morrow morning."[159]

In the early morning hours of January 21, the men awoke to a stern warning to get up or "be burned."[160] They quickly discovered the entire camp, in Champlin's words, "all on fire and by daylight it was all consumed." He maintained, "The boys were all in good spirits, but did not seem to care to leave the camp standing for Gen. Heckman to put his 'pets' in."[161] Sgt. Henry E. Savage (Co. G) wrote in his diary that "it was all we could do to save our things."[162] Samuel Derby described the scene to his wife Elizabeth: "I was got out of bed a little quicker than I like to be [and] the camp was all on fire and the tent next to mine all in a blaze but I happened to have almost all my thing[s] packed up the night before but I had to scratch pretty fast to get them out."[163] Forbes attributed the destruction to some "reckless fellows" who had "set fire to their tents & the flames spread rapidly, and soon nearly the whole encampment of the enlisted men was wrapped in a blaze making one of the grandest spectacles imaginable. In an hour or two nearly the whole camp, except the officers' quarters and hospital was burned down."[164]

Leander Chapin explained to his mother, "Gen. Heckman (successor to Gen. Getty) acted too aristocratically to suit us and we thought we would show him that we were not to be roughed on too much." Chapin claimed that Heckman wanted the camp for his own former regiment, the 9th New Jersey, but "we couldn't see it, nor saving the beautiful flag staff for him so we destroyed the whole though he ordered Col Beach to save it." Chapin even attested that Beach "was of the same mind as us and encouraged us." The 13th New Hampshire was ordered to guard the camp and try to stop the violence, and the scene from nearly a year before seemed about to replay when the regiment threatened munity over its lack of pay.[165] Kellogg asserted that the New Hampshire soldiers were "ordered off by Maj. Pasco." But shortly after that, "Capt. Gardner A.A.G. rode up in a passion, put Maj. P. under arrest and sent for a section of battery to 'subdue' us. The boys groaned & hooted him out of camp. At 11 a.m. we left our old camp amid the hearty cheers of the 13th N.H. & others."[166]

This was not wanton destruction; the men were deliberate in their actions, and more than one credited Beach with instigating their behavior. Robbins provided his parents with a detailed description of the episode. He explained (and seemed to excuse) his comrades' violence as being a result of their anger that a "Regt lying idle at Newport News" would inherit "such good quarters" from them. Robbins recalled that when orders first came that the regiment would be abandoning its camp, Beach, who was then in command of the brigade, sought to give their flagstaff—a particularly high one, well over ninety feet—to another officer. When Gen. Heckman "ordered that everything be left standing in the camp," Beach promptly cut down the flagstaff and had it burned. This, Robbins argued, gave the soldiers of the 16th C.V. license to do the same: "About three o'clock the next morning everything was burned but the tents which were taken off and the Officers homes." As they awaited orders the next day to board cars for Portsmouth, the men set to work destroying the officer's quarters. This action led to Heckman arresting nearly all of the regiment's commissioned officers and threatening to turn an artillery battery on the regiment. At this point, some "of the boldest of the regiment stepped out of ranks," Robbins stated, "and declared that if the men stood firm and refused to go without our officers they would be released." "This," he later remembered, "was mutiny but we were in an ugly mood." The 1st Delaware Battery was in position to fire on the regiment, but "reason prevailed," and the men marched onto the waiting cars to leave their camp for good. Robbins added that once the men finally got to Portsmouth to board boats, they again grew restless: "We had got our pay before leaving camp and a great many of the men got dead drunk, and were left when the Regt went away." Robbins guessed that some were still "there now probably."[167] "The boys," he wrote in his diary, "were determined that nothing be left for the troops that were ordered here."[168]

Harrison Woodford gave a slightly different version of the burning. He also traced the cause of the trouble to Gen. Heckman's order to leave their camp untouched, including the flagpole, "which," Woodford emphasized, "was the nicest one in the department." "Well the night before we started," Woodford explained, "Col. Beach wanted some firewood so he ordered the men cut it down. He stayed out there seeing them cut. Says he, it is ridiculous but D—— them, D—— Them. I want some fire wood. This was Wednesday night & we was to go the next morning. At three o'clock the camp was a burning & before light it was in ashes & before we left the officers houses were torn down, the chimney pushed over & we had a terrible smash up—I tell you." Woodford repeated the assertion that it was not "military necessity" that caused their move, but Gen. Heckman's personal preference. He added, "The houses that we built didn't belong to the government. We bought them & paid for them & we wont a going to leave them for any one else."[169]

This was a common sentiment among the soldiers. Sergeant Lee wrote his cousin Adelaide that their "splendid and commodious camp" at Portsmouth was the regiment's "pride," but "like all things earthly, it has passed away." He blamed Heckman for judging the 16th to be "terrible fellows."[170] Austin Thompson wrote Electra Churchill, "I must tell you about how we burned up our Camp. Just as soon as we found out that we were going to leave, we made preparations to burn it up. We had orders from the General to leave everything and [he] would not even allow us to sell our own property. But we thought we knew our own business best, and just before we left we set fire to the whole conserve. And it made the most beautiful fire I ever saw. But I did feel very bad about leaving."[171]

Nearly all the regiment's commissioned officers were arrested for allowing the camp to be destroyed and doing little to prevent it. Lt. Col. Burnham was notably absent, having left for home just a week earlier to take care of family business.[172] Captain Mix and Maj. Pasco were both "relieved from duty."[173] Captain Barnum, who had just received word that his wife had given birth to a baby girl, vanished from camp to go to Norfolk in order to express money home. Barnum was charged with "neglect of duty to the prejudice of good order and military discipline" for his actions on January 21 and found guilty by a general court-martial. His sentence was to be "reprimanded by the commanding officer in the presence of his regiment."[174] Colonel Beach apparently emerged unscathed.[175]

The local press was generally sympathetic to the regiment. The *Hartford Daily Courant* published a letter from a soldier in the 16th describing the incident but further defending the regiment's actions. This soldier admitted that a "spirit of insubordination" had arisen "among both officers and men" as soon as they learned they had to vacate their camp. The men intentionally set it afire, the flames spreading so quickly that "in an hour the handsomest and most comfortable camp in the department was in ashes. Some of the men barely escaped with their lives, the flames reaching their beds while they were asleep." "The rumor is," the soldier defiantly stated, "that the regiment is to be disgraced for insubordination. If so, let it be so. Let the generals fight for rank, and we will fight for houses that we built and paid for out of our own pockets. Gen. Heckman, or any other general cannot have camps that cost us from $2000 to $3000." He summed up the entire episode: "The cause of the trouble was owing to the fact that the boys had, at great expense, built a fine camp, and they believed that the object Gen. Heckman had in view in removing them was solely to give the camp to some of his pet troops; and they broke up the plan as stated." The soldier refused to accept that their behavior was in any way inappropriate for soldiers, especially during wartime.[176] The March issue of the *Connecticut War Record* included "Horse John's" version of the burning of Portsmouth. He noted the soldiers' dread and resentment when they realized that they would have to vacate their prized encampment, adding that the soldiers had left "some trash in camp" which "caught fire." "By a like unaccountable accident, the officers were out of wood in the evening, and no other being at hand, the lofty flagstaff was hewed down to supply them." Winds blew, and in no time the entire camp was enflamed. The next morning, when the sun arose, "the camp of the Sixteenth Conn. Vols. was a desert, as flat as my grandfather's bald pate."[177] It took a newspaper outside of Hartford, the *New Haven Daily Palladium,* to be openly critical of the unit's actions. Under the headline "Insubordination in the Sixteenth Connecticut Regiment," the paper reported learning from a letter sent to the *Hartford Courant* that the regiment was guilty of "mutinous and disorderly conduct."[178]

That these soldiers believed that their camp was their property—that they had built and paid for it and thus it "belonged" to them—is quite telling. These men had been in uniform for just over a year and had fought in one major campaign. Otherwise, they had spent their time in garrison and raid duty, shifting from place to place, further and further removed from the seat of war. They openly balked at their commanders, complained loudly about lack of pay, and claimed that they had never been properly mustered into service. They told civilians at home how to vote, castigating those who refused to serve, and yet they rarely expressed open support for the war's high ideals. Instead, they complained of the slightest discomfort, even though their sufferings paled in comparison with those of their sister regiment, the 14th Connecticut, which had endured the battles of Fredericksburg, Chancellorsville, and Gettysburg. The burning of their camp at Portsmouth, which they deemed their own property, was an act of bravado and defiance by men refusing to accept their lot as restricted soldiers rather than autonomous citizens.

About 10 a.m. on January 21, 1864, the 16th Regiment Connecticut Volunteers marched out of camp, climbed onto railroad cars, and eventually boarded steamers and headed south. Their route took them directly to Portsmouth, then they went by boat to Fort Monroe and Morehead City, where they got back onto trains to New Bern. There they boarded another steamer for Plymouth, North Carolina. "And now if you have followed the route," a soldier wrote in a letter to the editors of the *Hartford Daily Courant*, "how far do you think we are from Portsmouth after traveling six hundred miles? Just sixty miles!"[179] Cpl. Ira Forbes described "an alarming amount of drunkenness" on the journey from Portsmouth.[180] There was a good deal of seasickness too. "The next morning," Pvt. Chapin wrote, "found many of us customers at the rail (not the bar) casting up our accounts with Jonah but we got over it by night."[181] Seasickness was an ominous portent of the regiment's next chapter of war service.

Jacob and Emily Bauer, 1863. Emily Bauer visited her husband Jacob in camp at Suffolk, Virginia, where the couple posed for this photograph. Record Group 069:023, George Q. Whitney Civil War Collection, 1861–1925, Connecticut State Library, State Archives, Hartford, CT.

Col. Frank Beach [ca. 1863–65]. The regiment's controversial colonel stirred his men's ire; they resented his harsh discipline and penchant for profanity. When he died in 1873 at the age of thirty-eight, though, he was heralded for his bravery. Picture Group 570, Connecticut Military Portraits, circa 1860–1959, Connecticut State Library, State Archives, Hartford, CT.

Second Lt. Bernard Blakeslee [ca. 1863–64]. The author of the unit's only published regimental history, Blakeslee died at the age of fifty-one in the Hartford Retreat for the Insane. Record Group 069:023, George Q. Whitney Civil War Collection, 1861–1925, Connecticut State Library, State Archives, Hartford, CT.

Lt. Col. John Burnham [ca. 1863–1864]. Burnham, who also died in the Hartford Retreat for the Insane, displayed great devotion to the 16th, despite struggles with discipline and bitter resentment from the men. Picture Group 570, Connecticut Military Portraits, circa 1860–1959, Connecticut State Library, State Archives, Hartford, CT.

Lt. Col. Frank Cheney, 1862. Perhaps the most beloved of all the commissioned officers in the regiment, Cheney deeply cared for the regiment long after he was forced to resign due to his wounding at Antietam. Picture Group 570, Connecticut Military Portraits, circa 1860–1959, Connecticut State Library, State Archives, Hartford, CT.

Color Cpl. Ira E. Forbes, 1902. Forbes worked tirelessly to celebrate the regiment's wartime record, yet near the end of his life, just before his admittance to the Hartford Retreat for the Insane, he found himself at odds with his closest comrades. Forbes died nine years after this photograph was made. Ira E. Forbes Collection, Connecticut State Library, State Archives, Hartford, CT.

Pvt. Norman L. Hope [ca. 1862]. Only seventeen years old when he enlisted, Hope survived until 1924, penning a history of Andersonville Prison and serving on Connecticut's Andersonville Monument Commission. Picture Group 570, Connecticut Military Portraits, circa 1860–1959, Connecticut State Library, State Archives, Hartford, CT.

Sgt. Maj. Robert H. Kellogg [ca. 1864–65]. Along with George Whitney and Ira Forbes, Kellogg actively promoted the unit's postwar memory and published a harrowing firsthand account of Andersonville soon after his release. Picture Group 570, Connecticut Military Portraits, circa 1860–1959, Connecticut State Library, State Archives, Hartford, CT.

Surgeon Nathan Mayer, 1863. Jewish and German-born, Dr. Mayer was a popular member of the 16th C.V., providing medical expertise and unquestioning devotion. Record Group 069:023, George Q. Whitney Civil War Collection, 1861–1925, Connecticut State Library, State Archives, Hartford, CT.

Sgt. William F. Relyea [ca. 1863–64]. A cigar maker by trade, Relyea enlisted at the age of twenty-nine and later served as the official "historian" of the regiment's veteran's association. He wrote his own complete history of the regiment, labeling them "nomads," due to their constant movement from place to place. Picture Group 570, Connecticut Military Portraits, circa 1860–1959, Connecticut State Library, State Archives, Hartford, CT.

Pvt. George Robbins, 1863. A machinist-apprentice, seventeen-year-old Robbins enlisted in the 16th C.V. against the wishes of his parents. He later claimed that hearing a woman's stirring rendition of the "Star Spangled Banner" had spurred him to join. Picture Group 570, Connecticut Military Portraits, circa 1860–1959, Connecticut State Library, State Archives, Hartford, CT.

Pvt. George Q. Whitney, 1887. After the war, Whitney, with the help of Forbes, Cheney, and Kellogg, amassed a tremendous amount of biographical material on the regiment but never published any of it. Picture Group 570, Connecticut Military Portraits, circa 1860–1959, Connecticut State Library, State Archives, Hartford, CT.

Granby soldiers, Company E, 16th Regiment, Connecticut Volunteers. This photograph was probably taken just before the regiment left for the front in the summer of 1862. Included are seventeen-year-old Pvt. Roswell Allen, Cpl. Leland Barlow, Sgt. Richard Henry Lee, and Pvt. Justus Porter Griffin. Allen perished in December 1862 due to illness. Barlow, Lee, and Griffin were all imprisoned at Andersonville; Barlow died there in early October 1864. Photograph courtesy of the Salmon Brook Historical Society, Granby, CT.

"Andersonville Boy," Hartford, CT. The duplicate of Connecticut's Andersonville monument includes the inscription, "In Memory of the Men of Connecticut Who Suffered in Southern Military Prisons, 1861–1865." Photograph by author.

Plymouth
"The 'Rebs' Took Us All"

*Moved to the destitute town of Plymouth, North Carolina, the 16th declared themselves "nomads,"
resigned to the idea that they would never remain anywhere for long. Serving in Plymouth alongside
units that had endured hard combat, they felt even more cut off from the front. Limited to garrison
duty and occasional guerrilla skirmishes, this different kind of war was not what the 16th had
expected to experience. Although hampered by disease, disaffection, and one brutal large-scale battle,
the unit had escaped the harshest violence of the war. That changed dramatically one April day.*

"A LITTLE WORTHLESS PLACE"

After three days of travel, the 16th Connecticut arrived at their new camp in
Plymouth, North Carolina, around midnight on January 24, 1864. By the next
morning, the soldiers began to take stock of their new post. Leander Chapin
described it to his brother Gilbert: "It is a kind of barbarian place here, about 9
miles from nowhere, as the boys say."[1] Plymouth *was* isolated and far removed
from the active battlefront; nonetheless, it was strategically significant to both
sides. Located on the south bank of the Roanoke River, Plymouth anchored the
northernmost point of federal occupation on the North Carolina coastline, serving as a supply depot for Union troops stationed there.

Now part of the XVIII Army Corps, District of North Carolina, Sub-district of
the Albemarle, the 16th Connecticut was stationed just outside the town, along
with the 101st and 103rd Pennsylvania and 85th New York Volunteer Infantry,
portions of the 2nd Massachusetts Heavy Artillery, the 24th New York Independent Battery, a squad of the 12th New York Cavalry, and two companies of the
2nd North Carolina (Union) Infantry. There were also "a few negro recruits,"
although the exact number is unclear.[2] Four gunboats patrolled the river, pro-

tecting the small garrison from enemy attack. All told, there were about 2,800 men at Plymouth under command of Brig. Gen. Henry W. Wessell. Most troops were veterans, and except for the 16th, the units had endured hard fighting. "All of these regiments," William Relyea observed, "were but the remnants of noble regiments that had been decimated by battle and disease."[3] "The 16th," Relyea wrote, "became a wandering body of nomads and so remained until the end."[4]

By late January 1864, Plymouth was a town ravaged by war and damaged by Confederate raids and Union occupation. Most white residents had fled, and many houses and business were burned-out ruins.[5] "Plymouth," George N. Champlin noted, "was a very pretty little city before the war. It is now nearly destroyed."[6] Samuel E. Grosvenor was pleased by signs of Unionism: "Looks like dismal country to me but manifestations of Loyalty are quite hearty."[7] "Horse John," writing for the *Connecticut War Record,* depicted Plymouth as "a quiet little town" which had "been burnt down to some extent by the rebs." However, he was happy to report that the regiment's location possessed "excellent fortifications; well guarded," and that Gen. Wessell was in command: "a Connecticut man; belongs to the regular army, in which he is a Lieut. Colonel; good, kind old gentleman with high military knowledge."[8] A soldier referring to himself as "Dixie" wrote to the editors of the *Daily Courant* and described Plymouth as "flat—and you can use the term in any acceptation you please." The weather was hot, with heavy nighttime dews. Mosquitoes, fleas, and snakes were plentiful. So too was illness ("fever and ague").[9]

Life in Plymouth differed greatly from that in Portsmouth. "We are comfortably situated," Leander Chapin observed, "but [it is] quite different from what we have been but it seems rather lonely here in the wide wilderness. We hardly know where we are."[10] He later told his mother, "This place is so far out of the world that mails are few and far between, at Portsmouth we use to get them every day. I have come to the conclusion that I am quite forgotten."[11] Champlin had reflected on the first full day of their arrival: "This is just about out of the civilized world, and we do not get mail but once or twise [*sic*] a week." It was, in one word, "dull."[12]

Although most of Plymouth's residents had long gone, a steady stream of slaves, Unionist civilians, and Confederate deserters came over the lines to seek refuge in the federal garrison.[13] Robert H. Kellogg observed one day in February, "A large number of refugees have come into our lines today, and it is said that *several hundred* more are awaiting an opportunity to come in."[14] Massachusetts soldier Warren Lee Goss described Plymouth as a "general rendezvous for fugitive negroes, who came into our lines by families, while escaping conscription or persecution, and for rebel deserters, who had become mean, hungry, ragged, and dissatisfied with fighting against the Union."[15] Harrison Woodford was more blunt in a letter to his mother Alma: "This is a great place for deserters & refugees & niggers to come in. The way they manage it, our fellows will go up the rivers in boats & they will come down to the shore & come aboard. They enlist in our army nearly as fast as they come in." Woodford counted "40 white men & as many niggers came in yesterday & said there was a great many more lying around in the swamps that wanted to come in. They are generally ragged & rough looking set & they look very destitute."[16] Still, Leander Chapin claimed that the residents of at least one nearby town preferred the 16th C.V. to other northern units. He wrote his mother, "A regiment is to go to E[denton] and efforts are being made by the Mayor and people to get the 16th there. They like our regt. very well. We have been there three times and they are much pleased by our appearance and good behavior. Wherever we go we are well spoken of."[17]

As at Suffolk and Portsmouth, refugees at Plymouth, black and white, stirred varying, often negative, responses from the men. Leland Barlow commented to his sister in April that "a few refugees of the poorer class" came into camp one day when he was on picket duty. The family included a husband, wife, and their three children, accompanied by a cart and a cow and carrying, it seemed, everything they owned. "I presume," Barlow mused, "they were obliged to come in, or suffer for the want of the necessaries of life." The Connecticut soldier generalized, "The poor whites of the south are poor enough, and they look low lived and mean . . . they are about a hundred years behind the times." Still, Barlow, like many of his comrades, had a grudging respect for the Confederate soldiers' tenacity in battle: "The south are going to fight desperately, their bravery is worthy of a better cause."[18] Cpl. Ira Forbes pitied the poor southern whites he encountered at Plymouth, worrying that the children lacked formal schooling and that the civilian mortality rate was so high. He gave some his own money to a handful of residents but implored, "Would to God that I could do more to alleviate this misery."[19] These patronizing attitudes were common among northern soldiers, especially among New England troops.[20] Kellogg, though, was more impressed with what he described as "a large, increasing and *genuine* Union element here which operates boldly upon the rebs." "There are quite a number of loyal North Carolinian soldiers here in P[lymouth]," he wrote his father in late February, "and they do good service in scouting, acting as guides, and fighting. They are brave fellows." Kellogg further described the African Americans who came into camp: "Darkies are made to don the Yankee uniform almost as soon as they set foot within our lines and thus it is [how] Ben Butler raises his negro troops."[21]

A contraband Sunday school, run by Massachusetts women Sarah Freeman and her daughter Kate, also attracted the curiosity of the Connecticut soldiers.[22] Forbes mentioned visiting the "Negro School" as early as January 26, and he offered to help teach the contraband students, but he also expressed a desire to open a "School for white Children," apparently meaning the children of Unionist whites in the area.[23] Forbes took great satisfaction from his teaching, commenting frequently in his diary on his visits to the school.[24] Champlin volunteered to teach a class of "colored girls."[25] Kellogg also taught at the school, visiting for the first time on February 21: "In the afternoon I went to the 'Contraband Sabbath School' and took charge of a class and I think I will continue to do so after this."[26] Grosvenor went to the Sunday School for "colored people" and "tried to teach a class." He was "delighted with the attention of the scholars."[27] George Robbins described visiting the Sabbath school one Sunday in March and was markedly impressed with the African American boys he encountered: "They were very attentive to their lesson and to what I had to say to them."[28]

There were some similarities to their situation at Portsmouth; there was time and opportunity to read, play games, and attend church.[29] Prostitutes were available, too.[30] Lt. Ariel Case described their service at Plymouth as consisting of "drilling, camp and picket and every few days some would go out into the surrounding country and pick up cotton and bacon, corn or any such thing as was of value." They burned whatever they could not carry back to ensure they were not helping "to feed the enemy, for Plymouth was an outpost and everything outside was rebeldom."[31] The Temperance Society continued sponsoring formal debates on varying resolutions, such as whether "intemperance is a greater evil than war," or "the present war will be productive of more good than evil," and whether "woman exerts a greater influence in society than man."[32] They again built comfortable quarters, putting floors into their tents and building brick fireplaces.[33] To celebrate George Washington's birthday on February 22, the regimental band performed, the glee club sang, there was a "splendid parade," and in the evening, Chaplain Dixon delivered an address before a "large audience" entitled "The American Republic."[34] Soldiers' wives continued to visit. Robbins counted "nine Ladies, four of whom have their husbands here with them."[35] The Case brothers' wives remained with their husbands at Plymouth, at least for a few weeks after the regiment's arrival.[36] Barlow remarked that Lt. Alonzo Case's wife had been in camp "a long time." She "probably thinks she knows all about soldiering."[37]

Generally, though, the Connecticut soldiers were unsure of what to "expect in this place." Sergeant Grosvenor predicted, "We'll have picket duty enough to do." Either way, he wrote in his diary, "We feel ready for most anything."[38] Sidney Hayden wrote his sister Catherine that he thought their new duty would "consist of going on expeditions on gun boats often up the river and cruis[ing] around to see what we can find and picket duty."[39] Any chance for actual combat seemed even more remote. Lewis M. Holcomb, who had been anxious for battle at Portsmouth, was still frustrated: "I had so much rather be where there is active service." He wrote his aunt from Plymouth, "The service here is *active* enough, but not of the kind I like, being principally confined to guerrilla hunting and skirmishes."[40] Leander Chapin informed his mother, "I do not think we will have any fighting to do, nothing more than a little skirmish occasionally. There is not force enough here to do any amount of fighting. We are simply [a] garrison."[41] Martin V. Culver judged their position "very well fortified," and Austin Thompson thought that only if the Rebels attacked "with a very heavy force" would there be "a chance" for the 16th C.V. "to lodge in Libby prison. But I am quite shure [sic] they will never find us."[42] Robbins assured his parents that they should not worry, despite rumors of an attack. "But there has been no real alarm as yet," he wrote on February 7, predicting, "its not probable the Johnnys will trouble us here[.] it would cost them too much to attempt it and they would run a great risk of being cut of[f] from their friends if they should happen to try it."[43] In late February, Leland Barlow wrote his sister, who was equally anxious about his safety: "We are not liable to have any very large battles here, unless we are attacked. Raids are common here but don't amount to much."[44]

The Confederates did not attack Plymouth, at least not initially. Meanwhile, the regiment spent its time manning forts, posting sentries, and mounting guard duty. There were frequent detachments sent out on scouting expeditions and raids, targeting Confederate positions all along the coastal waterways. But even these raids hardly seemed like "real" warfare, at least to Chapin, who liked the "fun" but thought the raids were "tiresome." He complained, "There is but little danger for they [the Confederates] do not stand for fight at all."[45] One raid into Bertie County included three commissioned officers and seventy-five noncommissioned officers and privates, along with men from the 15th Connecticut and other regiments under command of Lt. Col. Wilson C. Maxwell of the 103rd Pennsylvania. They embarked at midnight and traveled upriver by boat, targeting a storehouse guarded by rebel cavalry. They had already abandoned the location, and the raid resulted in the destruction of large quantities of bacon and cotton. Only one man was lost, from the 103rd Pennsylvania. In another raid up the Chowan River, the men skirmished with enemy cavalry and destroyed tobacco and food.[46] They also stole brass band instruments from the 62nd Georgia.[47] It is not clear how it was determined who would go on these raids, but Ira Forbes provided some insight on February 29: "This evening a small force leaves here. Men 'who would'nt [sic] run' were called for."[48]

Soon rumors circulated that the regiment was heading for New Bern to re-inforce troops there in the aftermath of Confederate major general George E. Pickett's failed attempt to retake the town. In a letter to the editor of the *Hartford Daily Courant,* "Dixie" assured family and friends: "Gen. Wessell, however, thinks this place needs all the troops here, and refuses to send us." The regiment at the time was "encamped close along the breastworks, four companies form the left wing at the west end of the town, and the six remaining companies on the south side." There was picket duty from three in the morning until sunrise, but "Dixie" assured readers that there was little chance of an early morning attack.[49]

Confidential correspondence between Gen. Wessell and Gen. John J. Peck's assistant adjutant general Benjamin Foster indicate that Peck believed another Confederate attack was in fact coming toward New Bern, with a possible feint at Washington. "It may be necessary," Foster informed Wessell, "to call upon you for one of your smallest regiments, say the Sixteenth Connecticut, and you will therefore have them in readiness to move either to Washington or New Bern at the shortest notice." Foster tried to assure Wessell that it was not Peck's intention to "call away any troops if it can be avoided, and this direction is given you only as preparatory to a contingency that may arise."[50] At least for the time being, the regiment remained in Plymouth.

The idleness was beginning to weigh on the men. On March 2, "Dixie" wrote another letter to the *Daily Courant,* clearly bored: "Our course of duty still consists of camp-guard, and picket with an occasional drill when the weather and other circumstances permit." Supplies were plentiful, and the men had been paid with money to spend on luxuries if they so desired, including fresh shad. He added, "Something has occurred to prevent the frequent raids which used to form the only relief to the tedium of our inactivity; whatever it is, whether the temporary illness of the commanding General, the moonlight night, or some other cause we all hope it may speedily be removed."[51]

"TOO MUCH RESTRAINT"

Just days after "Dixie" penned this letter, the regiment left Plymouth for New Bern. Kellogg was thrilled: "I am right glad that we have left Plymouth for a more out-of-the way place is hard to be described. I think we will never go back there again." He hoped that the regiment would continue to travel "around the country free of expense" until their enlistment or the war had ended.[52] Forbes felt differently: "It is also reported that we are to remain here only a few days, and then return to Plymouth. Think I should be pleased to go back."[53] A March 7 letter to the editor of the *Daily Courant* from a member of the regiment reported the 16th's arrival in New Bern after a twenty-hour voyage aboard the *John Farron*. "We found everything quiet here," he stated, "though it was rumored before we left Plymouth that Newbern was attacked. The regiment is enjoying quite good quarters in barracks, for the present." The soldier, calling himself "Alvah," added, "The health of the regiment is good."[54] A few days after their arrival, "Dixie" reported that the regiment was "now camped on the old fair ground, the men in barracks, and the officers in new wall tents; now nothing is lacking but a visit from the paymaster to put us in the best of circumstances." The soldiers performed camp-guard, picket duty, and work on the neighboring fortifications. The regiment remained at New Bern building fortifications until they returned to Plymouth on March 21.[55]

While in New Bern, Forbes complained that a tightening of discipline was having a negative effect on the men: "I am not much pleased with this place. Too much restraint; All unnecessary. Not so in other regiments,—bad effects; men disobey and act in a manner prejudicial to military discipline."[56] He also noted a growing "discontent" on "account of the scarcity of rations." "Someone," he wrote, "is greatly at fault."[57] Harrison Woodford also commented on this problem in a letter to his father, stating that the men "were kicking up a good deal of fuss about it lately." Woodford blamed the commissioned officers: "I believe we have got the slackest set of officers in our Regt that the Lord ever let live."[58] Clearly, the men in the 16th Connecticut were still struggling to adapt to military life, continuing to believe that they were somehow worse off than other soldiers anywhere else in the war.

While they were stationed at New Bern, a "negro riot" occurred near the Trent River on Sunday, March 20, 1864, which somehow involved African American troops and slaves. Capt. Thomas F. Burke (Co. A) was dispatched with 100 men from the regiment to bring order. According to Bernard Blakeslee, Captain Burke "soon quelled it, bringing with him between two and three hundred prisoners, whom he turned over to the Provost Marshal."[59] Robbins and Kellogg were both returning from church services when they heard about the commotion across the Trent River. Robbins explained that "a disturbance" had arisen between "two camps of Negroes who got fighting about some thing or other."[60] Kellogg quickly joined the detachment: "The boys had a great time with the darkies and marched two or three hundred of them into New Berne to the Provost Marshall's office and returned to camp about 2 PM."[61]

On March 7, 1864, the 16th Connecticut lost its last original captain to a tragic accident at sea. Capt. Edward H. Mix, en route to New Bern after an extended absence following his arrest at Portsmouth, was, in Blakeslee's words, "accidently thrown overboard by a blow from the boom and drown[ed] ere assistance could reach him." Even though Mix was a good swimmer, he was apparently weighed down by a heavy coat and boots. His death, Blakeslee wrote, "snatched [him] from the bloody glory of dying in his country's cause, to perish alone and un-cheered—no banner above him but the silent clouds—no sounds around him but the rush of waters." It profoundly shook the regiment, particularly the officers, who were "sadly moved by their inability to give his remains the last honor due to the soldier—to shroud it in his country's flag and fire the volley over his grave." Blakeslee added, "He was well versed in tactics and military discipline, and was the last of the original captains of the Sixteenth."[62] The regiment's commissioned officers issued a special resolution bowing "submissively to the Almighty," yet offering their profound sympathy to Mix's family and vowing that his "memory will be cherished while the regiment has a history."[63] On April 21, the *Hartford Daily Courant* published a poem entitled "Drowned" by "Euclid" in memory of the captain's death. The second stanza read: "'Tis well that we should weep for him / Whose patriot heart no wave can dim— / 'Twere criminal to check the tear / For those who fight to shield us here."[64] Sgt. William Relyea later remembered Captain Mix as "a capable and brave man. A loss of this kind was felt more perhaps at this time as the regiment had been growing steadily less."[65]

Around midnight on March 21, the 16th Connecticut left New Bern to return to Plymouth.[66] The trip back was arduous. Kellogg described their journey as

"some interesting though rather perilous adventures." The regiment first embarked on an aging steamer, the *Thomas Collier,* traveling in hurricane force winds
and a cold driving rain before running aground. Food and fuel were scarce, and
Kellogg thought "the 16th stood a poor chance of re-enlisting or indeed ever getting home again. But He who rules the waves took care of us."[67] While aboard the
ship, Kellogg wrote in his diary: "Pretty rough seas and a few of the boys sea sick.
As is usual on board of transport, there has been a great deal of boisterous sport
going on, and as one result of it, I have received a slight 'wound' in the forehead
from a 'hard tack' thrown from somebody."[68] The next day he observed, "Aground
all day and no prospect of getting off. The sea ran high all day and in the night the
wind blew a perfect gale. The steamer triumphed upon the bottom the timbers
groaned and creaked and it rather looked as if we would be wrecked but being
a new steamer and well built she stood the test nobly. Amused myself as well as
possible by reading, talking, and watching the fun going on all around me. *Who
wouldn't be a soldier?*"[69] Once the *General Berry* rescued the men, the regimental
band "regaled us with some of their finest airs." But rations were running low,
and it was another rough night on the water. Forbes summed it up: "We have had
a very unpleasant voyage, and our quarters to night are by no means agreeable."[70]

On March 23, 1864, the 16th Connecticut finally got to Plymouth. George
N. Champlin wrote, "We found a large number of soldiers and citizens on the
shore ready to welcome us." He claimed that he and his comrades were "all in
good spirits," yet roll call was held several times that afternoon to "keep the men
from going straggling."[71] By the next day the regiment had settled back into its old
campground alongside the 103rd and 101st Pennsylvania.[72]

Meanwhile, Connecticut's gubernatorial race was nearing in the spring of
1864, and some members of the regiment were allowed to go home on furlough
so they could vote. Champlin was one of the lucky ones—about ninety by his
estimation—selected to leave in late March to make it home in time for the April
election. The weather was so stormy, however, that the men were forced to return
to Plymouth after "living on the water six days and six nights."[73] Champlin wrote,
"We are not in very good spirits on account of our disappointment. I believe Gen.
Peck is to blame for our not going home."[74] Forbes had also been tapped to join this
group, unaware of the reason for their "mysterious movement."[75] They returned
to Plymouth late on April 6, in the words of Martin Culver, "hungry as hell." "We
gave them a hearty reception and they were mad as the devel," Culver wrote.[76]
Barlow wrote his sister that the men were told they were going home to "enforce

the draft," but he seemed to sense there was more to it than that. "I did think it was something of importance to call troops ways from the front and where they are expecting an attack too, but it was nothing but a little political speculation." "Can we," he asked, "ever be prospered [*sic*] and successful in putting down the rebellion as long as there is so much corruption and wickedness in the country."[77]

John B. Cuzner was suspicious, writing Ellen Van Dorn, "Between ninety and one hundred men with eighty officers started for Connecticut, they were all Republicans, which leads us that remain to infer they may have gone to vote."[78] Ezra Burgess later remembered, "[When] we landed how the Boys hooted at us on our return, 'Only Democrats have stood by the Flag while you have been gone.' *We were going home to vote.* And it was a fizzle."[79]

Democrat Samuel E. Derby could only watch in anger: "If I ever was to come home now I will never cast a vote for William a. Buckingham for governor of my native state if they [Republican comrades] have gone home I hope the polls will just be closed so they wont get a chance to vote." He looked forward to ending his service when he was "free again" to vote, and "the black republican abolishionst [*sic*] party cant have me any more." Derby was disgusted enough with politics that he vowed, if the "good old democratic party cant get up a nominee good enough for me to vote for I will not vote at all." "This war has altered a good deal since we left the state then it looked more like a war for the union but now it looks like a war for political capital and money for some are making . . . fortunes out of this war." He concluded, "All I look for is the 24 of august A.D. 1865 to be free to live so long."[80]

This episode again revealed men in the regiment disheartened by the war, notably with the Union's conduct of it. Kellogg, himself an avowed Republican, was deeply disturbed by it. In his diary, he wrote, "Rather lonely in camp today so many being gone and there is a great deal of dissatisfaction among the men in regard to so many going home to vote & I think it is very wrong."[81] In a letter to his father the same day, he recounted how a "large list of names sent from the *War Department* came to the Regiment, and orders were given for these individuals to get ready *immediately* to go on board the transport which was in readiness at the dock, and in a very short time the Lieu. Colonel, Major, Adjutant, three Captains & several Lieutenants with 94 enlisted men, left Plymouth on the steamer "Col. Rucker" for where?—*Connecticut,* and *to vote for Gov. Buckingham.*" All of these men, Kellogg attested were Republicans. "Now Father," Kellogg asked, "is this right?" He admired and respected the Republican war governor, but he also observed that his party would not always be in power, and surely Republicans would not want Democrats following such a "bad precedent."[82] Kellogg had even darker concerns: "Another noticeable fact is that our men went *fully armed and equipped.* I fear that our Nation is rapidly drifting toward a military despotism. This abuse of arbitrary power in a free land & people will work incalculable mischief. When I view the corruption and wickedness in the country I tremble for our future. It is not the South alone that has sinned, but the whole Nation and we ought to thank God that he has not destroyed us but blessed us with victory after victory."[83]

Robbins shared Kellogg's outrage. In a letter to his mother on April 3, he declared, "If I were to explain my candid opinion on the subject I should say that it is a *disgrace* to any party and *especially* to the Republicans who claim to do things *fairly* and are supposed to be *above* such *meanness!*" He was confident that the Republicans could have won the election "without sending men home from the fire of the enemy." However, what galled him was that several of the men selected to go home had only recently been on furlough. "Now if a man were sick or even *dying* or his *family* at *home* was *sick* and *needed* his *presence* and *assistance*," Robbins reasoned, that soldier might somehow "procure a *short* furlough to *save his life*" or possibly make it home to "what is *dearer* the *comfort* of his *loved family.*" He was furious at the injustice that soldiers would "be sent *home* to procure the election of a *Republican candidate* for *Governor.*"[84] In his diary, Robbins added some important details: "An order came last night soon after roll call for men to go to Connecticut to vote or at least it was supposed that was the object of their leaving. Lt. Col. Burnham and the Major, and Adj. and some of the line officers with about 100 men left last night with their equipment with them[,] even taking their guns." "The Democrats left behind," Robbins emphasized, "do not like the announcement as all that were sent home were Black Republicans."[85]

By early April, the 16th C.V. had resettled into its position at Plymouth. "Our duty at present," Sidney Hayden wrote his mother in mid-April, "is tolerable easy."[86] Rumors continued, though, that the regiment would move again, perhaps to rejoin its old command, Ambrose Burnside's IX Corps. Barlow ruefully predicted that their easy living would end if they left Plymouth. "We are having many comforts now," he wrote his sister on April 11, "which I fear we will be deprived of ere long; there is no telling what our lot will be, one thing is almost certain there is to be some desperate fighting done, and that before many months, fighting more desperate and bloody than Antietam, Fredericksburg or Gettysburg." Still he hoped active campaigning would end the desertions, "rascality," and "all kinds of wickedness" that had been eating away at the regiment for months.[87] Barlow was appalled by the increasing number of recruits who had joined the 16th C.V. Convinced that "good Union men" had gone to great lengths "to contrive every way to keep out of it themselves," he maintained, they instead "send such poor miserable good for nothing fellows to do the fighting." He was brutal in his assessment: "They are not half of them that will ever do anything, some are natural farm fools, some with one hand gone, some blind [in] one eye, and old men that will hardly hold together, if a man commits any crime except murder, it pardons him to go into the Army."[88]

While the 16th Connecticut languished indefinitely in garrison duty, its sister regiment, the 14th Connecticut, which had originated from the same county at the same time, was accumulating a dramatically different military service record. The 14th had remained with the Army of the Potomac, earning accolades and battle honors, most notably at the Battle of Gettysburg when they were positioned along Cemetery Ridge and met the onslaught of Pickett's ill-fated charge. On April 15, 1864, a member of the 14th wrote to the *Daily Courant* to complain about what he perceived to be unfair press attention given to the "more or less heroic deeds done" by the 16th and the 21st Connecticut as they performed "their duty as provost-guards at Norfolk, Suffolk and Portsmouth." From its inception, the 16th Connecticut had a remarkably high number of members connected to the Hartford press. "That nice, white gloved duty," the soldier wrote, with obvious disdain, "no doubt, told their fortune, while we, that have been in the front of the Army of the Potomac ever since we came into the service, have been in the front of the battles of Antietam, Fredericksburg, Chancellorsville, Gettysburg, Auburn, Bristoe Station, Mine Run, and Morton's Ford; have borne aloft, waving side by side, with the emblem of our country, the banner of Connecticut, having in one battle captured five of the enemy's battle flags." The soldier, calling himself "Union," had had enough: "Surely this much that we have done for the honor of the State we so dearly love, ought to be appreciated." Even so, he insisted, it was not "newspaper reputations," he and his comrades in the 14th wanted; they sought "simple justice and shall be satisfied."[89] Whether they were aware of it or not, the 14th Connecticut was enduring a more heroic and costly Civil War experience: one that would become the conventional model that all units strove to emulate.

Private soldiers letters from the 16th's time at Plymouth reveal men still struggling with conflicting attitudes toward the war and nagging worries about their families and life at home. In late February, Sidney Hayden was "more encouraged than I was a year ago at Newport News," and although he was anxious to be done with the army, he assured his mother, "I had much rather come home after the Rebelion is throuroughly [sic] crushed."[90] A few weeks later Hayden admitted to his sister that he was feeling "pretty blue some times" for not saving any money. The unmarried twenty-five-year-old farmer lamented that "the best part of my life" had been "thrown away" instead of spent tending to his land.[91]

Despite expressions of discontent and demoralization in the ranks, there is also evidence that others were ready to do their duty without question. In February, Lewis Holcomb wrote his aunt, "I am hopeful for the future which to me looks glorious." He candidly admitted, "Although in our dark hours, my faith has wavered, as whose has not? Yet I never entirely doubted the end." "But Aunt," he insisted, "I am more than ever wedded to the cause in which I am engaged; it is one in which I would make any sacrifice and although I hope to see home again, yet if it is my fate to die, it shall be my best endeavor to meet death with a smile, as a soldier should."[92] Leander Chapin wrote his brother Gilbert in March 1864: "Your advice in begging me to keep out of danger sounds harsh coming from a friend of his country. I know how you feel and highly appreciate your motive but I beg of you not to write in such a way. It is productive of no good, rather harm. Shall I not do my duty wherever I am called to go? It is much safer to go right along even though the enemy's balls are dealing death on all sides than it is to seek a better place. Experience proves this. Let me die a hero rather than live a coward." Chapin would not go home to face his friends and family "with the approval of conscience when I had shirked my duty." He had enlisted to fight, and fight he would until the rebellion had been quelled. Chapin had revealed one year earlier that the army had saved him from certain suicide, and his personal wartime letters show a consistent commitment to ending the rebellion, an earnest loyalty to his regiment, and an unshakable faith in God. In this last surviving wartime letter he sent home to Connecticut, he chided his family for hoping the regiment would be sent to a safer place—the 16th Connecticut already was far removed from the action and at a well-fortified spot.

To be sure, the type of soldiering the 16th Connecticut had so far endured had failed to match their initial expectations of martial glory; nor did it match the experiences of many other units close to the front. Yet for young Leander Chapin, the 16th Connecticut gave him something his predictable prewar life in a small Connecticut town could not: comradeship, adventure, and a sense of identity and purpose larger than himself. Chapin proudly stated, "Where my regiment goes[,] there I go."[93] George Robbins had similar feelings about the 16th C.V. when he found himself left behind, ill, at Plymouth when the regiment went to New Bern. "I don't want to be away from the Regt any longer than is necessary. I want to go everywhere the Regt. does be it into action or wherever it may be sent."[94]

"BRAVE HEARTS"

There were constant rumors of an attack on Plymouth, and by early April, reports of large numbers of approaching rebels circulated almost daily.[95] There was also talk of the Union planning its own offensive. Most of the men in the 16th Connecticut, though, remained skeptical. Sergeant Kellogg wrote his father in early April that that if there was no attack on Plymouth that spring, he believed it would "not happen at all." He expected the regiment to resume raiding "on an enlarged scale," which he claimed not to mind; however, he added, "[It] is very hard work for the men." He maintained that the soldiers had changed their view of their district commander, Gen. John J. Peck, whom he judged as overly cautious, although he took care of his troops: "I think a great deal better of him than we did a year ago at Suffolk, though it cannot be denied that he was pretty well panic stricken when the 'rebs' made their appearance there." Kellogg described reading New York papers full of reports of "the desperate things anticipated every moment by Gen. P. while we were having good times, and everything was as quiet as a New England village." "We had to laugh in our sleeves," Kellogg mused, "just a little to think of the awful dangers which were so near us. But we were in a far different place from N.B. now for we know that the 'rebs' are not far from us here."[96] On April 11, George Robbins recorded in his diary a rumor that Gen. James Longstreet was close with fifteen thousand men. Robbins, however, did not believe it: "He has other work to do."[97] By April 15, Robbins described what he supposed would be their continued state for the near future: "Everything is going on in the same dull routine with no news from the outside world except an occasional rumor."[98] The next day, Harrison Woodford told his father that the "Gen. is still expecting an attack here" and that there was a "great deal of talk about a RAM the Rebs have got up the river." Woodford saw no signs of the ram but fully expected that the federal gunboats could handle it. "I am not frightened," he assured his father, "but I don't know but I shall be when it comes."[99]

Confederates were in fact very close and preparing their attack, and Gen. Peck was readying for their advance, although there was some dispute over how immediate the threat to Plymouth truly was. Correspondence between generals Peck and Butler reveals Union officials monitoring enemy movements. On April 14, 1864, Peck forwarded to Butler a letter from Wessell predicting an attack on Plymouth "by land and water."[100] A dispute then ensued over Wessell's request for reinforcement, which he clearly did in his letter to Peck's assistant adjutant on April 13: "At all events, I do not feel disposed to neglect their [his informants'] warnings, and in view of their importance, I request a temporary re-enforcement of 5,000 men."[101] Peck defensively stated that he received a telegram on April 18 from Wessell claiming that he "did not apprehend any attack, and did not think there was a very large force on his front."[102] In the meantime, Confederates had already converged on Plymouth.

It was a "beautiful Sabbath morning," Sunday, April 17, 1864, remembered musician Robert Holmes, and the men went through their regular routine without any indication of what they soon would face.[103] Sgt. Oliver Gates recalled how, that morning, "our regiment lay in camp at Plymouth, N.C. and none of us expected an Attack, but ere the day closed we were surrounded by twelve thousand Confederate Soldiers and Gen. Hoke."[104] At noon, Union cavalry reported the enemy just a few miles away.[105] George Robbins similarly wrote in his diary that it had been a "bright pleasant day, but the Sabbath has been desecrated by the Rebels." By 5 p.m. the 16th Connecticut had just marched onto the parade ground for dress parade when a courier rushed into camp reporting an enemy attack.[106] George N. Lamphere (Co. B) was among the skirmishers ordered into reconnaissance action. "We went out," Lamphere remembered, "in a front, across the esplanade to the edge of the timber, and a little beyond came upon the enemy in force. They pressed upon us and compelled us to fall back. We held out stubbornly, dodging behind stumps and logs and firing at the enemy all the way to our line of works." Within a few hours, all the skirmishers had returned to camp, and the rebel attack was in full force.[107] Confederate brigadier general Robert Hoke was at the head of a large combined land and naval operation that outnumbered the federals nearly four to one.[108]

The 16th Connecticut totaling about four hundred manned Fort Williams, which was at the center of the Union breastworks.[109] "Our position," Robbins described, "was on the west bank of the Roanoke river about eight miles from its mouth, protected by log breast-works from the attack of the enemy, running from the river in a circular form and encompassing the small town to a point some two-thirds of a semi-circle, leaving the space to the river on the south protected by

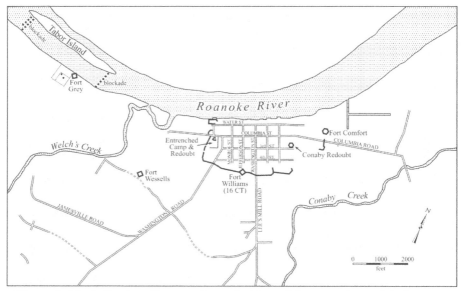

Plymouth, North Carolina. This map shows the Union defenses at Plymouth before Confederates attacked on April 17, 1864. The 16th Connecticut was stationed at Fort Williams.

light gunboats of which three were anchored abreast the town."[110] Kellogg wrote a short letter to his father at 8 p.m., a few hours after the initial assault began: "We are having an interesting time of it." He urged his father to be firm in their Christian faith: "Don't be anxious on my account—God will keep me. Trust him."[111] Leland Barlow also scribbled a quick note to his sister on Sunday evening: "The Rebs showed themselves about 5 PM and we are having a right smart artillery fight." "Never fear," he hastily closed.[112] Lamphere remembered that he and his comrades were at first quite confident of success. They were on the high ground, and their works were defended by "good 12 pound brass howitzers" and an "abundance of ammunition." "The troops," he wrote, "were in good spirits; in fact we were in a state of the highest enthusiasm, as we were to fight behind breastworks, and we felt that we could whip four or five times our number, and we could and did for two days." In front of them lay a swamp "about 900 yards wide" and felled logs "sprawling in all directions over the miry and boggy ground."[113]

The Confederate assault, however, was unrelenting. By 11 p.m. Company H was ordered to escort "all loyal" women, children, and other noncombatants aboard the steamer *Massasoit,* which was headed for Roanoke Island. Forbes bitterly complained in his diary that the Confederates attacked without first allowing "the non-combatants to leave, and have thereby violated one of the principles of civilized warfare."[114] Meanwhile, the Confederate cannon fire continued until near midnight.[115]

On Monday, April 18, Confederate guns resumed their fire just before sunrise. Rebel soldiers poured out of the woods, overpowered the Union skirmish lines, and forced the federals to retreat inside their forts. After a "sharp engagement" in the morning between a rebel battery and Fort Wessell on the Union right, there was a short respite. Then around 3 p.m., Forbes wrote, "the enemy moved forward in line of battle on the Washington Road." After this movement was checked, Confederates advanced again, driving "our pickets and skirmishers, and opened on us from a battery which they had succeeded in planting in a fine position." For some three hours, the Confederate guns blasted away at the Union position at Fort Williams until they finally "were silenced, and our picket line was again established." Forbes judged that there was "splendid shooting on both sides," with the federals taking relatively "slight" casualties.[116] Confederate gunboats and artillery cannon unleashed a withering fire, which did not stop until 10 p.m. At one point, an artillery battery was planted directly in front of the regiment's position, which, according to Kellogg, "blazed away with the greatest rapidity upon our camp and Fort Williams."[117] To Samuel Grosvenor, it was "one of the most furious cannonades" he had ever witnessed.[118]

Under this blizzard of fire, some men began to falter and struggled to keep their composure. Lt. Col. John Burnham tried to soothe the regiment's nerves by ordering the band to play "*National airs.*"[119] At first, this seemed to work. Kellogg later remembered, "Brave hearts became braver, and if the patriotism of any waxed cold, and the courage of any faltered, they here grew warmer and stronger until the pride of country had touched the will, and an indomitable principle had been kindled that virtually declared the man a hero until death." But before long, Confederate artillery took aim at the musicians, and shells began to drop over their heads. At this moment, Kellogg recalled, "the musicians retired precipitately, the bass drummer throwing his sticks in one direction and his drum in another, leaving the defense of the breastworks to the boys with the rifles."[120] As enemy fire persisted into the darkness of night, Kellogg sought solace in his faith: "God has given me courage and calmness. I try to trust in Jesus *Christ.* May His will be done."[121] Years later, Forbes recalled Burnham's cool conduct during the siege: "He was a man of unquestioning bravery and held his men in perfect discipline awaiting the charge."[122]

As the siege continued into its third day, the situation began to look bleak for the federals. "It was evident to us," Blakeslee later wrote, "that we must either be killed or go to 'Libby.'"[123] On Tuesday, April 19, Kellogg declared, "This morning finds us in a rather bad plight."[124] During the early morning hours, the Confederate ram *Albemarle* slipped past federal guns to sink the USS *Southfield*, driving off other Union gunboats and cutting off the position from outside communication.[125] "We are," George Champlin wrote in his diary, "surrounded."[126] By midafternoon, Forbes too realized what might be coming: "It indeed looks dark for us, but the traitors must yet fight and that right hard, before they can take this place." He read his Bible and felt "very pacified."[127] At some point on April 19, Maj. Henry L. Pasco ordered Lt. Alonzo Case to select a group of men and hold them "in readiness to charge over the works in case the rebels came up to them in our front." Case deemed this extremely dangerous and was convinced that few would return from such a mission. But he made the offer to his own Company E, about forty men, and every one of them volunteered. "I was proud of that Company at that time," Case recalled. "They were," he stated, "more brave than I. I was ordered to go, they volunteered."[128] Fort Wessell fell, and the *CSS Albemarle* began shelling the town. "We went to work," Lamphere wrote, "throwing up earthworks to defend us from the riverside and soon had some protection."[129] Soldiers were ordered to begin digging "for our lives, building traverses, bombproofs, etc."[130] There seemed no question among the men or their commanders that such defensive behavior was unheroic or cowardly. It was simple survival.[131] Firing continued into the darkness, and the men had another sleepless night, anxious about what awaited them the next day. Samuel Grosvenor predicted bleakly, "The 'rebs' evidently intend to take us."[132]

On Wednesday morning, a portion of the 16th Connecticut received orders to provide reinforcements to the left.[133] "In doing so," Lamphere recalled, "we had to pass through the village, and as we reached a point a little past Fort Williams, we discerned, not clearly, as it was not yet light, a black line within our defenses. We were formed in a line of battle and we marched cautiously toward it, and being sufficiently near discharged a broadside into their ranks, getting the first shot. The order was to fall back and to reload while so marching with face toward the enemy. This order was executed promptly." Pvt. Lamphere was in the process of loading his gun when "murderous musketry fire from the enemy who had advanced on the run" tore through the ranks. A minié ball hit his left arm, and Lamphere's rifle fell to the ground. He was ordered to fall back to a hospital tent. "I did reach the tent," he remembered, "and it did not seem to me more than ten minutes until the whole place swarmed with the enemy who came pell mell, tearing and swearing and firing without much regard to the sanctity of the hospital flag, and the tent was riddled with bullets." Lamphere and a few other wounded members were separated from the regiment. He never saw his regiment again and was moved first to Raleigh, then to Salisbury, and then to Libby Prison in Richmond. His left arm was amputated on May 22.[134]

Meantime, Confederates charged to take the town and pounded Fort Williams from every direction.[135] There was another flurry of fighting, and the cannon fire was "perfectly awful."[136] As the day unfolded, Confederates demanded surrender, according to Lt. Bernard Blakeslee, three separate times in order "to save further sacrifice of life." But each time the Confederates were rebuffed. After the last time, General Hoke defiantly declared, "I will fill your citadel full of iron; I will compel your surrender, if I have to fight until the last man."[137] Wessell later reported, "I was now completely enveloped on every side, Fort Williams an inclosed work in the center of the line, being my only hope. This was well understood by the enemy, and in less than an hour a cannonade of shot and shell was opened upon it from four different directions. This terrible fire had to be endured without reply, as no man could live at the guns." Wessell decided that he had no more options. "This condition of affairs could not be long endured, and in compliance with the earnest desire of every officer I consented to hoist a white flag, and at 10 a.m. of April 20 I had the mortification of surrendering my post to the enemy with all it contained."[138] "General this is the saddest day of my life," Wessell reportedly observed to Hoke. Hoke responded, "General Wessell, this is the proudest day of mine."[139] Sergeant Bauer later asserted that after the surrender, a member of his Company G still had his gun and aimed to fire it at a Confederate general who was on horseback. Another soldier stopped him. "It was good luck," Bauer maintained, "because had a Reb been killed after surrender, they would have killed us all."[140]

Instead, the "'rebs' took us all," Sergeant Grosvenor scrawled in his diary on April 20. Indeed, nearly the entire regiment was captured except for Company H and a scattering of men on detached service.[141] The regiment's casualties (except for those captured) were relatively light: one killed and twelve wounded.[142] Years after the war, Kellogg reasoned, "The comparatively small loss of the Sixteenth at Plymouth was by reason of its fighting behind defenses for the first time in its history. The attacking Confederate forces, fighting in the open, sustained losses so heavy that they were never reported in detail."[143]

Even before he agreed to terms, Gen. Wessell worried about the fate of African Americans as well as white North Carolinians in Union uniforms. Wessell allegedly told Gen. Hoke that "he would surrender if the negroes and North Carolina soldiers would be treated as 'prisoners of war.' This was refused."[144] The *Charleston Daily Courier* reported that between "three and four hundred women and children, who had been taken from their legal owners, were recaptured at Plymouth. The men were either killed in battle, or made their way to the swamps and forests. Many of the latter will no doubt be taken."[145] In fact, Confederate troops shot a large number of African American men, women, and children at Plymouth rather than taking them prisoner. Some estimates run as high as three or four hundred dead. Soldiers of the 16th Connecticut remarked on the slaughter; others recorded the information without commentary. Sgt. Oliver Gates described in his diary, "They showed the Negroes no mercy but shot some down in cold blood."[146] Champlin wrote dispassionately, "The Rebels killed several negro troops after they had surrendered."[147] Warren Lee Goss, who served alongside the 16th Connecticut in the 2nd Massachusetts Heavy Artillery, recalled, "There were about twenty negro soldiers at Plymouth, who fled to the swamps when the capture of the place became certain; these soldiers were hunted down and killed, while those who surrendered in good faith were drawn up in line and shot down also like dogs."[148]

George Robbins recounted in his 1918 unpublished reminiscences that the day after their capture, while he was tending to the wounded, "I saw some thirty negroes under guard, drawn up in open rank, while their former masters picked out their property. Having learned of the capture of the town they hastened to recover their slaves who had run away and come in to our lines. I did not see that any proof of ownership was required to substantiate a claim of ownership." The blacks were soon "disposed of and were marched off by their old (or new) masters," Robbins wrote, "seeming quickly reconciled to this change of condition by the laughing and joking as they separated to go back into bondage after a short taste of freedom." But Robbins also commented on the killing of armed African Americans, what he estimated to be a "company of Negroes." He recalled, "A day or two after the incident referred to I heard volley firing in the town and asking a nearby guard the reason was told, 'They lined up them d——d niggers you all enlisted and are shooting 'em off'n the docks.'" Robbins added, "I had no doubt of the truth of his statement."[149] Although Robbins made no mention of this incident in either his wartime letters or diary, he did observe in his diary: "All the Reb Soldiers that I have talked with seem to be very much worked up on account of our Govt employing Negro Soldiers. They say a white man ought to be killed that will do it."[150]

"THE HEROES OF PLYMOUTH"

Gen. Benjamin Butler, commanding the Department of Virginia and North Carolina, first notified Lt. Gen. U.S. Grant on April 19 that the Confederates were attacking Plymouth. But Butler, who was headquartered at Fort Monroe, received incomplete reports over the next few days. By April 24 he confirmed that Plymouth had surrendered. Still, Butler concluded, "If the reports are correct, it has cost the enemy in men all it has gained."[151] On April 21, Peck's assistant adjutant general J. A. Judson officially notified Adj. Gen. Lorenzo Thomas of Plymouth's fall: "This result, however, did not obtain until after the most gallant and determined resistance had been made." Judson added, "For their noble defense the gallant Gen. Wessell and his brave band deserve the warmest thanks of the whole country, while all will sympathize with them in their misfortune."[152]

Unlike their accounts of Antietam, soldier descriptions of Plymouth were free of any sense of indignity or embarrassment. On the day of his capture, Robert H. Kellogg was shaken but refused to admit any wrongdoing: "A flag of truce now came from the 'rebs' demanding surrender," Kellogg recorded, "but Gen. Wessell refused the offer and the fight went on. Soon they advanced upon us in force and we threw up the white rag and *gave up to them*."[153] He later maintained in his published reminiscences, penned in early 1865, that they surrendered "with no willing grace, yet it could not but be attended with the consciousness that we had tried the virtue of resistance to the utmost."[154] Gates similarly explained, "We could not do much against such odds so we were obliged to surrender."[155] Champlin wrote on April 20, "About eleven o'clock we were compelled to surrender."[156] Forbes stressed the stern courage of the Union defenders at Plymouth, despite worsening conditions. On the morning of April 20, he recorded, "Our men fought with the utmost bravery, against overwhelming odds." A few hours later, after continued combat, Forbes wrote, "Gen. W. Wessell with several of his Commanding Officers have had a parley with the rebel Gen. in reference to surrendering his forces. Gen. W. would not surrender. The engagement resumed. At length about 11 A.M. the enemy gained possession of the breastworks, and the troops surrendered themselves after having struggled with the utmost gallantry to maintain their position."[157]

It was one thing to have an entire regiment captured, but to have one's colors seized was especially dishonorable. The exact details vary, but several accounts agree that just before their surrender, Lt. Col. Burnham ordered the regimental flags destroyed and the poles buried. He then commanded Color Cpl. Ira Forbes (Co. A) and Color Sgt. Frank Latimer (Co. C) to tear the flags into shreds and distribute them to the men.[158] The rest were most likely burned, although where and when is not clear. Mary Livermore, the famed women's rights activist and journalist who helped lead the Sanitary Commission efforts during the war, provides an especially stirring account of the flags' rescue.

> At this juncture, with every hope of escape destroyed, surrounded by nearly ten times their number, Lieutenant-Colonel Burnham shouted to the color-guard: 'Strip the flags from their staffs and bring them here.' To tear each flag from its staff was the work of a moment; but who should carry them across a field five hundred feet, through that merciless hail of grape and canister? It required brave men, and they were not wanting. Color-Sergeant Francis Latimer took the national color, Color-Corporal Ira L. Forbes the state flag, and, crossing the most exposed part of the field, safely delivered them to Colonel Burnham. Corporal Forbes then returned and brought back the flag of the 101st Pennsylvania Regiment. The only thought now was to save the colors from capture. An attempt was made to burn them, and was partially successful. What was left was torn into small pieces and distributed among members of the regiment near at hand, who at once concealed them on their persons.[159]

Color Cpl. Ira Forbes made no mention of saving the colors in his diary, although this may be because he worried about Confederates discovering the hidden scraps. He did, however, write about receiving a "small piece of the 101st battle flag" while imprisoned at Andersonville by one of that unit's sergeants.[160] The normally loquacious Kellogg failed to say anything about flag saving in his wartime diary either, although he did talk in April 1865 of returning to Plymouth to find the buried flagstaffs.[161] The flag fragments would remain dispersed, yet many were preserved, as the men faced their certain imprisonment. This heroic tale of saving their colors would become central to the regiment's postwar reconfigured narrative of redemption. But that was still in the future.

Soon after their surrender, commissioned officers were separated from the rest of the men and transported north to Richmond. Colonel Frank Beach and surgeon Nathan Mayer were both quickly paroled and returned home. On May 1, Beach wrote from the James River awaiting exchange, "I am out of jail, after only five days of confinement. I hope to get to Hartford in a week or two." "The 16th" he added, "is somewhere in Georgia."[162]

After being marched several miles inland, the regiment was unsure of their final destination. But after having been kept awake with little sleep and little food for three days under nearly constant artillery fire by the enemy, the end of the battle perhaps came as a relief.[163] Cpl. Joseph Flower, Jr. (Co. C), wrote in his diary on April 21, "We left Plymouth about noon and had a hard march. We did not go into camp until dark[.] marched about fifteen miles and entirely played out." The next morning, Flower added to this entry: "Slept soundly and felt better in the morning."[164] On April 22, Kellogg recorded the regiment marching early in the morning until 1:30 p.m. "with very little rest." They did stop for about forty-five minutes, then resumed marching. He closed his entry, "We have been treated *splendidly* by our captors today."[165]

The 35th North Carolina Infantry apparently treated their captives surprisingly well. Confederates did not search their prisoners too closely, and men were allowed to keep their personal valuables such as jewelry and their money.[166] Kellogg contended, "We couldn't be better treated than by them."[167] "I must admit," Gates stated, "that on our march they used us well [and] allowed us more privileges than our own officers would on the same march, we halted often and got water at every opportunity.[168] Forbes agreed, declaring the North Carolinians to be "very courteous, gentlemanly fellows" who "have treated us kindly." Forbes noted that there were "some Va. troops with us. They are less generous and kind to those whom the fortunes of war have placed in their power."[169] Some of the Connecticut soldiers freely talked and traded with the rebel troops.[170]

Others were not so pleased with their captors. Jacob Bauer recalled "Some Rebs" as "saucy and ugly" who "took away from the boys canteens, a good pair of shoes, boots and blankets, especially rubber blankets—all necessary articles for either party."[171] They also pillaged for morphine and arms.[172] Some soldiers had retrieved their clothing during the flag of truce, but Gates was one of many who had "saved nothing."[173] Marched onto a road and put under guard, Gates resentfully watched Confederate "officers riding our horses and driving our teams past, carrying our knapsacks and haversacks and canteens and wearing our clothes and every such thing." The rebels, Gates alleged, "were allowed to plunder the town and they done it completely."[174] Grosvenor perceived nothing positive about their sudden confinement. He complained about the high prices Confederates charged for food, and he was unhappy that he could not freely take a "stroll through the fields and admire the beauties of nature unmolested by men." When he sold his overcoat to the rebels, he instantly regretted it. Bored and stricken by diarrhea, he had thoughts of escape but doubted his chances of success. "One week of Captivity," Grosvenor wrote in his diary, filled with shame: "One week of disgrace!"[175]

The sudden change in circumstances was dramatic. Kellogg later remembered, "Instead of the calls to which we had been wont to listen and the labor we had been accustomed to perform, we were but passive beings, subject to the will of the conqueror."[176] Soldiers in the 16th Connecticut hurriedly wrote letters home, assuring loved ones that they were safe and predicting a quick exchange. Kellogg sent his father a short note and again told him not to worry. He was dirty but "all safe and sound." "The rebs treat us *very kindly*," he assured his father, "[and] are as a whole a fine set of men & good soldiers." He was stunned by his sudden change of fortune: "I can but laugh at the ridiculous plight we are in."[177] Robbins, who, along with a handful of other men from the regiment had been left behind at Plymouth to care for the wounded, also sought to calm his parents: "I write this short note to inform you that I am well and though a prisoner tending our wounded in this town, don't worry about me, I am all right!!"[178]

Hartford newspapers began to report on Plymouth a few days after the surrender, but accounts were scanty and specific information regarding the plight of the 16th Connecticut limited. On April 21, the *Hartford Evening Press* included a firsthand account describing the Confederates' initial attack. This story, authored by an unidentified soldier, stressed that Gen. Wessell "was not taken by surprise" and that noncombatants had been evacuated but that even if Union gunboats were successfully driven off by the Confederates, "our naval force in guns is superior to the enemy's." Another account by a "refugee" from Plymouth, published in the same day's paper, affirmed that Wessell had "Plymouth well fortified and pronounces it impregnable."[179] In the days that followed, more information began to trickle out. By April 24, a headline in the *Press* read "Gloom and Dependency" and "Danger to Plymouth," but the article included no real details.[180] On April

26, the *Hartford Evening Press* announced the surrender of Gen. Wessell "after a desperate resistance of overpowering numbers, because he was out of ammunition and cut off from any supply."[181]

Worried family and friends waited to hear exactly what fate awaited the 16th Connecticut C.V.[182] On April 23, Lewis Holcomb and Richard Henry Lee's cousin Adelaide Holcomb heard "by the papers that the rebel ram has been smashing up the boats at Plymouth and the town is in rebel hands. All are anxious to hear who survives, but of course we cannot expect to know as they are prisoners. All must endure this terrible suspense."[183] On May 2, Holcomb reported, "No news from the 16th."[184] Decades after the war ended, the widow of Sgt. William Smith (Co. F) remembered following the papers closely, anxious for word of her husband's fate: "That news was full of assurance of conquest. Such faith as our Conn. boys had in each other, the expectation of being able to overcome all obstacles."[185]

Bits of information came from individuals, mainly officers, publishing letters in the local press. On May 5, a "private letter" from Capt. Mark C. Turner (Co. D) was cited in the *Daily Courant*: "I am well, but a prisoner." Turner noted only that the entire regiment had been captured.[186] The next day, another detail was revealed, when Adj. John Clapp wrote that the regiment was "being taken to Americus Georgia" and that he "had been treated well."[187] The *Hartford Daily Times* published a letter from musician George H. Bryant (Co. I), who, like Robert Kellogg, assured his father that the men had been treated well by their captors and expected a quick parole.[188] Dr. Mayer, who was captured but quickly paroled, supplied a more complete list of the regiment's casualties to the *Hartford Daily Courant,* which published it on May 6.[189] Mayer, too, stressed the bravery and determination of his Connecticut comrades, both in the ranks and among its leaders.[190]

There clearly remained a need to soothe publicly any doubts about the regiment's gallantry. On April 26, the *Hartford Evening Press* reported rumors of the capture, attesting, "The 16th was there and bravely stood their position; the state may justly be proud of them." "In fact," the paper added, "the Connecticut regiments are all much thought of here and there is no such thing as run attached to their names."[191] By the first week of May, certain tenets of the story of Plymouth began to be repeated: The Confederates had successfully captured the garrison, but Gen. Wessell fought courageously until he had no choice but to surrender to a numerically superior foe. An April 24 letter from New Bern, published in the *Hartford Daily Courant,* confirmed these "facts": "From all accounts General Wessell and his little band of fifteen hundred veterans, fought like heroes for four days and nights, leaving the rebel dead in heaps in every street, which they admit will number seventeen hundred."[192] A *New York Tribune* correspondent clarified details of the fight on May 7, again affirming Gen. Wessell's bravery and his refusal to surrender until he was without other options.[193]

Hartford newspapers also informed readers about Confederates killing African Americans at Plymouth. One of the first accounts appeared in the *Hartford Daily Courant* on April 26, 1864. After heralding the "heroic defense" of the Union troops," the paper added, "the rebels, with fiendish brutality, after the surrender, repeated the Fort Pillow massacre, by murdering the white Union soldiers of a North Carolina regiment, and all the negroes found in uniform."[194] These allegations were repeated and broadened, with more details, the next day: "It is stated that all the negroes found after the surrender were stripped of their clothing and brutally murdered in cold blood. They were formed into line, in a nude state, and fired at by the brutal soldiery, purporting to represent Southern chivalry."[195] On April 28, a report appeared in the *Evening Press* claiming that "all Union and loyal North Carolinians as well as the negroes were shot after the surrender."[196] Again on May 2, the *Courant* reprinted an account from the *North Carolina (New Berne) Times*: "On the surrender of the place the colored soldiers and Second Loyal North Carolina stampeded for the swamps. Most of the negroes, we regret to hear, are said to have been massacred. It is reported that the rebel loss was between six hundred and two thousand killed and wounded, while our loss was comparatively small. All honor to the heroes of Plymouth."[197] A correspondent for the *New York Tribune* estimated that the "rebels killed between one and two hundred blacks, after the surrender."[198]

As the bloody details of the events at Plymouth emerged, the 16th Connecticut continued marching deeper into the Confederacy, boarding trains, a ferry, and more trains. Jacob Bauer remembered the jarring train rides as extremely cramped, with the soldiers packed tightly together and guards riding atop the cars and at each door. There was no fresh air and nowhere to sit. "It was," he recalled, "an awful journey."[199]

7

Andersonville, Florence, and Charleston
"Oh Horrors of Horrors!"

Nearly four hundred members of the 16th Connecticut Volunteers entered Andersonville Prison in early May 1864. About one-third of them would die in prison; all of them would be forever changed by the brutal internment. Imprisonment transformed the regiment's sense of identity. It further fed inmates' conviction that their own government, as well as the Confederacy, had treated them poorly. Imprisonment also tested their expectations of achieving manly glory on the battlefield. How could they prove themselves patriotic heroes if they were left helpless, weak, and emasculated in a southern prison?

"THE MOST OFFENSIVE PLACE I EVER SAW"

On May 3 and 4, 1864, the men of the 16th Connecticut arrived at Andersonville prison. Robert Kellogg recorded the moment in his diary: "As we entered the place a spectacle met our gaze which almost froze our blood—our hearts failed us as we saw what *used to be* men now nothing but mere *skeletons* covered with filth & vermin. God protect us! He alone can bring us out of this awful mess."[1] "Oh horrors of horrors!" Sgt. Samuel E. Grosvenor declared, "I only got so as to look into the stockade where I am likely to stay quite a while when my heart goes sick and my blood curdles in my veins."[2] Cpl. Ira Forbes wrote, "Of all places of distress and misery and suffering which I have ever seen this is the worst."[3] George N. Champlin knew immediately that death stalked close: "It is a dirty filthy place. A large number die here daily. Twenty one died today."[4] Sgt. Oliver W. Gates noted in his diary that he and his comrades had heard many stories about the prison but had assumed they would be provided with some sort of shelter. Instead, they were shocked to discover an open enclosure swarming with twelve thousand starving, half-naked prisoners, "just like so many cattle not a tree or shelter of any kind to protect them from the sun or rain or cold." Gates was already sure "it was the hardest trial in my life although I have faced Death in many forms."[5] Sgt. Henry Savage (Co. G) stated plainly, "Its [sic] the most offensive place I ever saw."[6]

The Confederacy erected Andersonville near the town of Anderson, deep in Georgia, eleven miles northwest of Americus. After two years of war and the federal policy of refusing prison exchanges, the Confederates desperately needed a new location to handle the growing number of Union captives overwhelming Richmond's prisons. Andersonville, first opened on February 24, 1864, initially measured about sixteen and one-half acres. Later it was enlarged by ten more acres. About the time the 16th arrived, in early May 1864, just over twelve thousand inmates crowded into the open-air stockade. By the time Andersonville closed its gates for good, forty-one thousand men had been imprisoned there, and close to 13,000 of them had died within its confines.[7]

At first glance, the experiences of this single regiment may not seem unique. Like their fellow inmates, they suffered from exposure, contagious disease, lack of adequate sanitary facilities, tainted water, improper diet, and insufficient medical care. Diarrhea, dysentery, and scurvy tormented the inmates. Relatively healthy when they entered the prison, the men of the 16th soon grew weak and severely ill. Nearly one-third of the estimated four hundred members of the regiment who were imprisoned at Andersonville died there.[8]

Like other prisoners, these Connecticut men relied on their comrades to sustain them during their incarceration. Relationships that had developed over eighteen months of service helped many to survive the horrific conditions in the pen.[9] Organized into groups of ninety, the 16th Connecticut soldiers continued to share their living quarters, often sticking to the company affiliations they had from the start of their enlistment. Diaries attest to the dire necessity for friends to help weaker prisoners persevere despite the horrific conditions.[10] Examples of Connecticut comrades aiding comrades during their long imprisonment are many. Oliver Gates made special mention of Sgt. Henry A. Viberts ("Vib"), who cooked for Gates when his health failed and was "very kind to me and taken good care of me."[11] In another instance, Gates described his tent mate Pvt. Hiram D. Williams (Co. F), sickened with dysentery "for a long time." Gates attested, "We have managed to keep him alive by furnishing him a light diet." Gates used some of his own money to buy better rations for Williams, but he died on September 15, 1864.[12] Samuel Grosvenor recorded helping comrades from the 16th Connecticut, as well as others admitted to the prison hospital.[13] Jacob Bauer was able to buy a pea-jacket from a sailor in the prison and used it to cover comrade William Bidwell, whom Bauer described as "almost naked." Bidwell claimed that this act of kindness saved his life.[14] Ira Forbes recounted selling his "beautiful gold pen and holder for the purpose of assisting a sick friend." For a prolific writer like Forbes, this indeed was a meaningful action.[15]

Relying on one another was crucial because the Connecticut men entered prison with little cash in hand. Other regiments, including the two Pennsylvania units captured with them at Plymouth, had been paid recently. Sergeant Gates noted that some of these other units had reenlisted and thus received "large bounties" just before capture, so they had "money plenty" when they entered the prison. Gates, however, did not see this as an advantage: "Those that had money even in this place could supply themselves with many things that were pleasant to the taste but I think very bad for the health considering the fare we got in this place to mix up with them. I am satisfied that many of them would have lived much longer if they had less money but had they kept their money until now they may have saved themselves with it."[16] Forbes agreed that the money did the Pennsylvania regiments little good, explaining that "mortality in these two commands, however, was not much under that in the Sixteenth, the 'greenbacks' of the government not being able to buy exemption from the great destroyer's harvest."[17]

Like most first arrivals, soldiers were optimistic that their time in this horrendous place would not be long. Champlin noted that during their early weeks at Andersonville, patriotic songs helped to lift the men's spirits.[18] A short letter Kellogg mailed home a few weeks after capture indicated that he was still hopeful, "in tip top spirits," telling his father that "prison life & fare agrees with me very well." Kellogg urged him not to worry. "We hope to get out of this scrape before many weeks & then I guess the Regt will be allowed to go home to recruit."[19] Pvt. Horace B. Steele (Co. F) wrote his wife Julia, knowing how anxious she would feel for his safety when she learned that he was in prison. "I am feeling first rate," he assured her, "and take everything in good spirits hoping the time will come soon when there will be an exchange." He closed by instructing her not to write him "unless there is something the matter."[20]

There were constant rumors of exchanges and victorious Union advances, few of them accurate. On the first full day of their incarceration, rumors circulated that the regiment's exchange was imminent.[21] John B. Cuzner explained that he and his fellow prisoners "hoped and expected everyday that an army would come to liberate us or that we would be exchanged prisoners of war." "It was that hope," he remembered, "which kept some of us alive, from day to day."[22] Some soldiers were more guarded when they heard rumors of release and dramatic news of Union victories and Confederate defeats. Grosvenor believed it "strange" that there should be so many "conflicting reports."[23] Gates found it "nearly amusing to hear the many Rumors that get into this pen every day about exchange, about [what] our Armys [sic] are doing etc." Yet he thought it hard to believe that the thousands of men in the stockade would not be released, "as our Government have many more of their men and so [could] stop this horrid suffering."[24] By June, when the whole camp was abuzz with a story that the exchange would commence on July 7, Gates wanted to believe it, but after so many false alarms, "I can hardly get it down."[25] Cpl. Joseph Flower, Jr., was also cautiously optimistic in June: "There are all sorts of rumors afloat in camp, one is that we are to be paroled. I hope it is so but I can't see it yet."[26] Rumors could cause fear, alarm, and deepening depression when they proved untrue. On May 11, only one week into their imprisonment, Kellogg was already becoming discouraged with all the false reports: "The rumors of immediate exchange are stronger than ever today, but I've heard so many that I'm tired of them." He vowed, "When I see the army leaving I'll believe we are going."[27] There were also frightening rumors like the one Champlin described on June 11: "I heard last night that one thousand prisoners [are] to be taken [out] of this prison next week to be shot or hung in retaliation." However, Champlin added, "I do not believe it."[28]

The longer the regiment remained in the filthy, putrid stockade, the greater the risk of death. When the month of June turned stormy, Gates braced for the onslaught: "It has rained ever day this month so far and thousands in here have caught the seeds of Death that will soon hurry them from their present misery."[29] "Men," Champlin reflected on June 13, "die here very fast."[30] Just over a week later, Champlin likened the constant death to falling leaves "in autumn."[31] On July 20, Gates counted eleven dead from the 16th Connecticut since they arrived at Andersonville in early May: "More than ever died in camp since we left home and while in our own lines but here we get nothing to eat and no care."[32] Prisoners were dying in tents, in the open sun, anywhere and everywhere. With little to do except focus on the suffering, the effect of so much death—especially this kind of unheroic, helpless death—was profound for those who did survive. Just two weeks into his incarceration, Corporal Flower grimly reflected, "I wish I was almost anywhere else but in this miserable hog pen but I will try and have patience to endure it as there is no help for it." Flower "endured" until early August, when chronic diarrhea ended his life.[33] By mid-August, Grosvenor "scarcely knew what to write" in his diary anymore. The "mortality" rate was "terrible in camp, the weather is unbearable & men's hearts are sinking."[34] Sgt. Henry Savage observed, "Almost every day Some one of our Reg dies. We are certainly warned to be prepared. Some days one looks forward and wonders whose turn will come next."[35]

Like other prisoners, the men of the 16th filled their prison diaries with daily descriptions of the weather, the amount of time they had spent imprisoned, the increasing numbers of inmates, the rampant rumors of exchanges and escape schemes, the scanty and rancid rations, and their personal struggles with their health and trying to stay alive. With so little to do, time nearly became an obsession.[36] On May 8, Flower wrote, "The fifth day. It is dreadful hot dull business, but there is no help for it."[37] John B. Cuzner recounted, "Outside in the Army there was so much to do; now we had nothing to do."[38] Indeed, there was little to do, and no one to help them, except each other, in their daily struggle to stay alive.[39] On June 17, Champlin reflected on the short but troubled past that had brought the regiment to this awful locale: "Two months ago to-day the Rebels attacked us at Plymouth, N.C. and twenty-one months ago to-day we fought the battle of Antietam." Now, the regiment was in a "dirty filthy place."[40]

July 4 stirred deeper reflection on their service and the war's meaning. Cpl. Charles Lee wrote on that day, "This is the anniversary of our national independence and instead of celebrating it in Connecticut as I have done every year of my life except last year, I am a prisoner of war shut up in this nasty bull-pen with no immediate prospect of getting out. Yet I am perfectly willing to suffer it all, if it does anything towards saving the union."[41] Grosvenor had a starkly different reaction: "Independence day in the Confederacy is one of the meanest things imaginable."[42] Forbes contrasted July 4 inside and outside the prison: "A great day in the States. Ushered in amidst the boom of cannon and the Shouts of excited music & expressions of praise and jubilees. Enthusiasm rules the day. Orators rehearse to attentive audiences the glorious achievements of our honored forefathers in their historic struggle for Independence." "Not thus," Forbes wrote, "in Camp Sumpter." It was merely "the same dull, monotonous, manner of living—almost a blank."[43]

Prisoners reflected on their time in the army. Kellogg mused, "Two years ago today I entered Uncle Sam's service and I can honestly say now that I am not sorry that I enlisted, even if I am 'in durance vile.'"[44] Pvt. Henry H. Adams stated simply on August 24, "Our Regt has been two years in service."[45] Champlin further recalled, "Two years ago to-day the 16th Conn. left Hartford for the seat of war. Now we are in the Rebels prison and are treated worst than brutes."[46] On the eve of his thirty-first birthday, Gates looked back a year to when the 16th was comfortably situated in Portsmouth: "We were in a pleasant camp where we could get everything we wished for to eat or drink. We all enjoyed good health. I think that no soldier ever had better times in active service. But now we are in Camp Sumpter where there is nothing but suffering, no food fit for human beings to exist on, no medicine to alleviate the suffering."[47] Like others in the unit, Gates had already begun to resent men at home whom he believed were profiting from the war.[48] As he reflected on the second anniversary of his enlistment, he confessed to having regrets about leaving his wife and young daughter behind to do "a Soldier's Duty faithfully." He despaired, "No human suffering can exceed what we witness here. When I came in here three months ago, I was a strong healthy man and could endure almost anything as I thought but now I am but the wreck of my former self almost a Cripple."[49]

Some yearned to return to the battlefield. Barely two weeks into his captivity, Forbes wrote, "It would be the source of unspeakable happiness to me to return to our army and again fight beneath our glorious banner. I hope this career in prison will be brief."[50] On the anniversary of Antietam, George Robbins mused, "It was just two years ago today since the Battle of Antietam . . . I would rather be there than to be situated as I am at the present time."[51] The soldiers felt their helplessness to be unmanly. As Kellogg later explained, "They do not ask to be free from all participation in the strife, but they do long to walk forth from their *cankerous* dens, even though it may be to meet the sulphurous smoke of the cannon, in the fiercely contested battle, for there, at least would be *glorious action*."[52]

Imprisonment was like nothing the men in the 16th Connecticut had ever experienced, and it would haunt them, underscoring their sense of helplessness and humiliation. On the second day of his incarceration, Forbes visited one of the prison hospitals and was deeply shaken by what he saw: "I have seen many slain on the battlefield. I have seen them at the execution but have never seen them in a condition so heartrendering [sic] at this. Their situation is indescribable."[53]

As the weeks turned to months and no exchange came, it was astonishing how much physical suffering the prisoners witnessed and endured. Forbes was convinced no other place could possibly compare to the "misery and destitution" of Andersonville. "Perhaps I am rash in thinking so," he wrote in August, "but it does seem that men can not suffer much more than they do in here."[54] A few days later, Forbes reassessed his statement, thinking that "the loss of health, exposure to privation and physical suffering consequent on the manner of life we are compelled to live, are not the saddest effects of our present captivity." Instead, it was the mental toll: "It is with the greatest difficulty that one can fix his mind studiously and intently upon a subject for a period extending a few minutes at farthest. And again, the finer feelings, that which makes a man lovly [sic] as a social being—love, affection, friendship, kindness, Sympathy, Courtesy are being constantly deadened, rooted out from the heart & leaving the poor victim in what is truly a woful [sic] condition."[55]

"I CAN STAND THE SUFFERING"

Ira Forbes and many others found solace in faith and religion during their long confinement. They pored over scripture, prayed, and looked for signs of God's intervention. They yearned to be home, attending church with friends. "But," Forbes wrote, "God is not confined to places, and He is here as well as in more favored localities."[56] One rainy, cold, gloomy June morning, Forbes, Robert Kellogg, and two other prisoners sat bemoaning their condition. When one of the men opened the Bible and turned to "this remark of St. Paul: 'I have learned in whatsoever state I am therewith to be content.' We all felt it was for us."[57] George Champlin strove to view his prison ordeal as affirming his faith: "If God spares my life and permits me to return home I will serve him and consecrate myself anew to his service for time and eternity."[58] Henry E. Savage struck a defiant note after attending a prayer meeting one Sunday evening: "Although they can take nearly all our privileges from us that they can not."[59] As Joseph Flower grew gravely ill, he looked to his personal relationship with Jesus: "I feel about as usual this morning, very weak, no ambition but my trust is in Christ the Savior of the world. He alone can save me."[60] On August 5, with his mouth covered in sores and diarrhea ravaging his body, Flower awoke just after sunrise to scribble a short entry into his diary: "My bones ached so I could not lay any longer and so got up and am sitting on a log. I have got so weak that I can't get my coat on without help. Have bad cough." Still he noted, "A lovely morning. My only trust is in Christ." This was Flower's final entry; he died four days later.[61] Kellogg visited the prison hospital and sought to comfort the patients there by reading them scripture. As his comrades began to die in increasing numbers, he still saw God's presence: "Truly God is speaking to us all & bidding us prepare for death, bidding us to purify our hearts & lives & let the Master find us ready & waiting when He calleth for us."[62]

Some revealed their religious faith more subtly in their prison diaries. Oliver Gates, for example, seldom mentioned religion but did state that he was "very grateful to God for mercy he has shown me at all times and especially in this imprisonment."[63] As a family man and one of the older members in the regiment, he tried to take the long view: "I am glad that I have seen adversity enough already to school me and to show me that I have only to have patience and trust in God and in His own time he will Liberate us. If I have my health I can stand the suffering here for many months to come."[64] Gates continued to cling to his faith as he watched more sicken and die and his own health weakened: "*God* has been merciful to me and has spared my life thus far and I will *trust* in *Him* although I am weak and sick I will trust in *him* and have no fear of anything."[65] Sgt. Samuel Grosvenor, whose diary entries are short but often starkly poignant, occasionally made reference to his faith. On September 6, he recorded the deaths of Burton Hubbard and Charles Richardson, remarking that an exchange seemed to be on the horizon: "Although the day has been marked by the death of two of our men still it is one of the days to be remembered. Glory to God the day has dawned at length when we can see deliverance."[66] Two days later, when another comrade perished, he reflected, "Newton J. Evans died today in the hope of a glorious immortality."[67]

As the death toll mounted, members of the regiment kept tabs on each other. Although the prison's system of organization divided the unit, word traveled fast about new arrivals, those who entered the hospital, and those who died. Some were more meticulous than others in noting the names, dates, and apparent cause of death.[68] On June 20, Charles Lee described the loss of Cpl. Alonzo N. Bosworth (Co. D): "This is the first death which has occurred in our regiment since we came here and we have none at all in the hospital. But we are all liable to be taken down and die in a few days."[69]

Like most Civil War soldiers and their families, members of the 16th C.V. were concerned that they die a "good death" and have some sort of appropriate Christian service, despite the horrific conditions that surrounded them.[70] Forbes opined, "Generally in camp there are no religious services held at the death of the men—and none outside—a fact that reflects great disgrace upon the authorities in charge of the prisoners."[71] Gates was confounded to observe, "When a man dies here he is carried out on a stretcher just as he dies and put in the dead house and when they are ready to bring them into a wagon just as a man would load a cord [of] wood and they cart them to the burying ground and dig a hole for each man and throw him in as he would a dog and cover him up without any ceremony except some one to curse him for dying so soon."[72] One evening Gates happened upon a dying prisoner who had collapsed on the ground near the brook: "Who knows but what this man had a loving family at home who may never know his sad end. They may hear that he died in Prison down in Georgia and that will be all, but no one outside of this den will ever realise [sic] one half of the suffering that occurs here but it is better I suppose."[73] As members of the 16th began to succumb, however, Gates noted that "appropriate" prayers and funeral services were conducted over comrades' remains before they were taken to the dead house.[74]

Years after the war, it was a point of pride among survivors that no member of the 16th Connecticut "lacked reverent burial."[75] Forbes later explained,

The question of Christian burial was raised by members of the Sixteenth Regiment in the prison at the first death that occurred in that command. It was impossible for members of the deceased comrades' company to take the body outside of the stockade. A detail of bearers could not be arranged. Even religious ceremonies of any kind was not to be thought of at the trenches. It was decided that there should be scriptural readings and prayers over the body of each man of the regiment that should die inside the stockade. This service was carried out without regard to the creed or nationality of the deceased. Catholics and Protestants alike were given the simple but tender service in the midst of scenes and surroundings that cannot be described by men or speech at the present time.

Forbes credited himself and Pvt. William H. Jackson with conducting most of the services, ensuring that no one from the regiment who died at Andersonville "was deprived of the last tribute of Christian comradeship." He further maintained, "Death was witnessed daily in the most revolting form in the prison, but it was met calmly."[76]

Death was taking a heavy toll on the 16th C.V., but not every member met it "calmly." Often, it was awful and agonizing to witness, and some prisoners' deaths appeared to make a greater impression on their comrades than others. Kellogg vividly remembered the "good death" of his friend John Damery on July 18: "At about five, PM I went to see him, and found him in a dying state, unconscious, and breathing very hard. I spoke to him, but there came no response. He had spoken his last words upon earth." Kellogg emphasized the sense of peace and solemnness. After reciting a short Bible verse, Kellogg and some others brought Damery's body to the prison's gate.[77] Gates also was shaken by Damery's death: "He tented next to me," he wrote, "and when he came in here he was a strong well man but he could not stand the fare we get here." Damery had a bit of money when he entered the prison, but when he became sick, rather than "buying rice and flower [sic] and such things to nourish him, he bought eggs, ginger bread and such things and in my opinion, hastened his death by doing so." It was tough to lose comrades: "It makes one feel as though life was more and more uncertain each day that we have to stay in here." When he learned that two more members of the regiment had died, Gates wrote with dismay, "The Rebels seem to be quite insensible to our sufferings."[78] Forbes made special note of John Damery's death in his diary: "My heart is deeply pained when I think of his poor wife and children, and the heart rending anguish they will experience when they learn that he is dead." "But," Forbes added, "God moves in a mysterious way his wonders to perform."[79]

Two days later, on the morning of July 20, Pvt. J. Leander Chapin also died. A few weeks after entering Andersonville, he had written his mother a letter that she would not receive until six months after his death. He had tried yet again to reassure her: "I am well and in good spirits and pray that you may be the same." His poignant words were prophetic: "I am contented to work out my destiny as I am if it be God's will. Doubt not the ability or will of my Protector, who is my strength and fortress. In his care I rest secure, to whom I commend all the dear ones at home."[80] Forbes, who shared a tent with Chapin, watched as his friend died "easily," although he had been "out of his head for quite a while before he died" and left "no word for his friends at home." Chapin had told Forbes just a few days earlier that "he had strong hopes of returning home."[81]

Men tried to imagine the lives and homes they had left behind hundreds of miles away. They contrasted their awful plight with that of their friends and families, whom they hoped had plenty to eat, warm beds, and clean clothes. On Sundays and holidays, especially, prisoners' thoughts drifted northward. On the first Sunday the regiment spent at Andersonville, Grosvenor explained, "Sunday in such a place as this is one of the worst days in the week because one spends the time mostly thinking & when he contemplates the misery all around & contemplates it with the comforts of home, the heart grows sick."[82] "It is very little like *Sunday* today," Kellogg observed a few weeks later. "Oh how I would like to be at *home* today."[83] He later explained to readers in his published book, "We awoke Sunday morning to find our thoughts *'homeward bound,'* as usual. We wondered what they were doing, thinking and saying there, and it really seemed to do us good to think and dream of home."[84] He tried to imagine how his parents would feel seeing their "only son seated on the ground, selling beans by the pint and loudly extolling their excellent qualities."[85] Husband and father of four young children, Joseph Flower, Jr., missed his family: "I would like to be home today very much."[86] On the "fifty first day" of his imprisonment, he longed "to be at home," wishing "now I could take a little break just with my wife."[87] As his body became wracked by deadly dysentery, his thoughts remained fixed: "I am anxious to see my wife and children."[88] Some prisoners wished they could go to church; the devout Forbes wrote in his diary that he would "greatly rejoice to be at home with my dear friends, and enjoy with them the sacred ordinances of the Sanctuary."[89]

With so little news from home, it was easy for prisoners to give in to fears that their friends and families might forget them. On June 2, Forbes reflected, "To night I am feeling well, and am thinking of home and dear ones far away. Surely they remember me. Thank God for such amiable friends as I have."[90] Dying so far from home was tormenting. As one sickly prisoner told Kellogg, "If I could only live just to see my wife and mother, I could die happy; but to die *here*, far away from home and be buried here,—I tell you Robert it is tough."[91]

"THE EXPEDIENCY OF MEASURES"

Gnawing questions for the men of the 16th, as for most Andersonville captives, were: Why? Why did they remain so long incarcerated? Why was their suffering so horrific? And who was to blame?[92] Certainly, their southern foe took much of the blame. Oliver Gates referred to the rebel guards at Andersonville as "cowardly," "Brutes," and "ignorant half civilized Slave driving Dupes of an Aristocratic band of Traitors." He accused them of committing "crimes against all humanity."[93] Rebel "crimes" included their failure to provide adequate food or shelter and shooting men near the "deadline,"—a line around the prison yard across which prisoners could not cross without drawing deadly fire from the guards. On July 27, Gates described witnessing a guard kill a man at the deadline "as calmly as though he had only shot a Turkey Buzzard." "No man with any of the cultivated refinement of a greasy Northern mechanic could stand and deliberately murder an innocent unarmed prisoner without one word of warning but these high bred chivalric Southerners like no better sport than to torture and murder their fellow men," Gates blasted.[94]

However, the prisoners' rage was not just against the hated foe; there was also a deepening disdain toward the federal government for not doing more to free them. Gates wondered if Union officials were aware of their hardships. "It seems cruel for Uncle Samuel to allow his Boys to stay here and suffer as they do while he takes such good care of our inhuman Enemy but I think he hardly realises [sic] our situation. I hear that Frank Leslie has caricatured the camp in his paper. He cannot possible exagerate [sic] the Picture."[95] He returned to this conviction again in July: "How long must *United States Soldiers* suffer such inhuman usage?" He refused to believe that northern leaders were fully aware of their misery.[96] He also struggled with the idea that somehow the use of black soldiers had something to do with his continued imprisonment. Before his capture, he had been supportive of the federal policy toward arming blacks, but after more than three months at Andersonville, Gates bitterly wrote, "For my part I am sorry that she [the Union] ever armed a nigger as a Soldier for I think if she had not, prisoners would have received proper care and the exchange would have been continued." He confessed, "The idea that the prisoner is patriotic enough to say that he is willing to stay here a Prisoner until the nigger is recognized as a Soldier as subject of exchange equal with the white man is entirely false." He stated that all white prisoners had a "perfect hatred" toward African Americans and "that the government would be the gainer by giving three for one in exchange if she accounts human life in the proper scale." Getting out of prison alive was his only concern.[97]

It was difficult for the prisoners to believe that political and military leaders were not doing all they could to free them. Forbes observed that "not a few of the men" were "much inclined to think that the Govt is forgetting us, if not forgetting us, neglecting us." He did not distinguish whether the men he described included members of the 16th, but he recorded that he and Sgt. Richard Henry Lee believed that it was a wrong impression. He and Lee had discussed this question, and Lee argued "very wise and patriotic reasons for the long delay on the part of the Government to exchange." Forbes maintained that making soldiers "of negroes is a wrong feeling, yet I deem it our duty, since they have been made soldiers, to protect them as such."[98] Kellogg, though, worried that the Confederates helped to stir this "cruel suspicion" that "we were abandoned by our government and our friends." This doubt, he maintained, was more difficult to accept than the actual "sickness, hunger and exposure and the thousand petition ills which beset us."[99]

In July 1864, a petition circulated among the Andersonville prisoners pleading for the government to do more to obtain their release. Kellogg, Forbes, and Richard Henry Lee sought to convince fellow members of the 16th not to sign it. Forbes was "disgusted with the entire affair." "Should it be carried through," he predicted, "I cannot see how it can fail to produce discord among our people and involve our Administration in some considerable difficulty, which would be highly pleasing to the rebels." Believing it would only disgrace the prisoners who signed it, he concluded, "It can do no good but will do much harm."[100] Forbes also wrote that he and Kellogg consulted with Sergeant Lee "concerning the expediency of measures which are being taken for the purpose of effecting our release from imprisonment. It is proposed that a petition shall be sent to the Governors of the loyal States requesting them to urge the General Government to exchange prisoners immediately." "I am opposed to such a measure," Forbes wrote, as was "Robert, Sergt. Lee," and "all the best men of our regt." He added that the idea of the petition was first suggested by the rebels themselves.[101] It was the "older prisoners" who were most in favor of it, he claimed. "They have become discouraged," he wrote, "and seem to lose confidence in the Administration. They are placed in peculiar circumstances, dragging out a miserable existence, death every hour staring them in the face, and but little seemingly to cheer and encourage them."[102] Forbes stayed firm in his conviction that it was a mistake, and on July 26, he reported that the petition was read to his "mess" and was "voted down."[103]

To Kellogg, the petition seemed an acknowledgement that Union military and political officials *could* release them but for some reason chose not do so. This was an assumption about the northern people and government he refused to make.[104] Kellogg would later claim that the majority of prisoners were in favor of the petition, but he managed to persuade at least everyone in his "ninety" not to sign it.[105] He recollected talking to Sergeant Lee and both agreed "that it was a *foolish affair,* and one not calculated to effect anything in getting us out, while, at the same time, it would materially lower our standing as *soldiers* and *men,* both with the government and the people."[106] Forbes credited Lee with giving a moving speech to convince his comrades to refuse the petition. Years after the war in a Memorial Day speech, William C. Case, former speaker of the Connecticut House, embellished the story of Lee's plea to his fellow soldiers, calling the petition "an unworthy thing—unworthy of themselves—unworthy of their government. Case further claimed that a vote was taken "by every ragged starving hero" and there was not a single vote in the affirmative.[107] However, at least one member of the 16th Connecticut, George Robbins, appeared to show some support for the petition in his wartime diary. He wrote of the petition "being read to the men as fast as possible." He thought that "if they give their vote to have it go," then the sergeants of the detachments would sign it. "The thing," he judged, "is well worded & if it goes North, will rouse the people."[108] The petition was sent north, but it is unclear how much direct effect it had on changing the United States government's position on political exchange.[109]

Loved ones at home had hardly forgotten their soldiers, but it did take time for them to understand the dire straits in which their men were placed. The Hartford press took weeks to report the regiment's captivity, and when it did, most papers simply stated that the men had been transferred to Georgia and were being treated well. The June issue of the *Connecticut War Record* explained that the regiment was "somewhat scattered. The line officers, adjutant, chaplain and the majority of the men are at Tarboro, N.C.—the field officers in Libby, except the colonel—the colonel and surgeons are released on parole—Co. H. with individuals absent on special duty, on Roanoke Island—Lieut. Case with two men on recruiting service at the U.S. Rendezvous."[110] A few weeks later, the *Daily Courant* announced, "It is known that nearly all the members of the 16th Conn. regiment are prisoners in rebel hands."[111] For months, however, most prisoners' families had little specific information about their soldiers' plight.[112] "We had no knowledge," Elizabeth Smith later recalled, "of the fate of our loved ones." She was home in Connecticut anxious for news of her husband, Sgt. William Smith (Co. F). "We heard [that the] Government was preparing for [the] Exchange of prisoners, and made ready for their home coming. Waited and watched."[113]

Other family members gleaned what they could from those fortunate enough to come home, notably, regimental officers. Surgeon Nathan Mayer, who was in Hartford briefly after his exchange in June, provided what information he could. Leander Chapin's worried mother, Amelia, learned from her friend Nancy Phelps that her son was "well & did not get wounded at all" at Plymouth. Phelps's husband Daniel had seen Dr. Mayer in Hartford and asked about Pvt. Chapin and was assured that "he is a prisoner with the rest but they are treated well." Mrs. Phelps did not know if Amelia had heard anything from Leander but hoped this news would ease her "mind somewhat."[114]

Officers still incarcerated had more freedom than enlisted men to write letters home, and it was from them that families began to learn what had happened to their soldiers. Lt. Edgar E. Strong (Co. F) wrote his father several letters, which

were excerpted in Hartford papers, attesting to the health and safety of the captured officers, even when moved from Richmond to Macon. Strong described
their Georgia location as "healthy, well supplied with water, occupied by nearly
1,000 of us, as comfortable as can be for officers."[115] Learning that his regiment had
gone to Andersonville and knowing the horrid conditions there, Lt. Strong wrote
in June, "I fear the men will suffer."[116] In September, another letter from Strong
to his father was printed in the newspaper, this one passed along from surgeon J.
M. G. Robinson of the 104th Pennsylvania, who had been imprisoned with Strong
at Savannah. Strong repeated that he was "hearty, and quite comfortable."[117]

Lt. Col. John Burnham's letters to family began to appear in Hartford newspapers in late July. In a letter dated May 22, Burnham, imprisoned in Macon, stated
that his health was "good," but he and the other incarcerated officers had no idea
how long they would be kept prisoners, perhaps all summer. "We are in the open
air here," Burnham stated, "which will be more conducive to health than being
shut up indoors. All the Plymouth officers are here together." He added an important piece of information: "The men are at Andersonville, near Americus."[118] This
may have been one of the first public confirmations of where the soldiers of the
16th Connecticut had been sent, although news of the regiment's fate probably
had begun to seep back in private letters. The paper excerpted another letter from
Burnham, dated June 5: "I hope our government will wake up to the necessity
of effecting an exchange of prisoners before long. The health of our officers here
is good, but the mortality among the enlisted men is large. The 16th have as yet
lost none by disease, and I hear that they are all in good health." Burnham urged
friends and family to write the prisoners, hoping some missives might get through
the lines, because the "greatest trial of captivity is having nothing from home."[119]

High-ranking officers, including Colonel Frank Beach and Dr. Mayer, were
quickly released after spending only a short time at Richmond's Libby Prison.
Others had to wait much longer. Asst. Surg. Nehemiah Nickerson and Chaplain
Charles Dixon were not released until September 1864 and were formally paroled
in late November.[120] Lt. Col. Burnham remained incarcerated for several months.
In a letter composed soon after his release, Dr. Mayer assured Burnham's family
that Burnham was "well and hearty" and "full of hope." Still, he encouraged them
to use their political influence to get the colonel released. "For Libby is a dreadful
place," Mayer wrote, "and will be more so in summer."[121] Burnham's family and
friends sprang into action. Prominent businessman and outspoken Republican
Calvin Day, characterized as "one of the richest men in Hartford," wrote directly

to the governor, hoping that his influence might bring an "early exchange" for the colonel. One of Burnham's brothers also visited the governor's office to make a personal plea.[122]

However, Burnham and several other commissioned officers from the 16th remained imprisoned. They were moved from Richmond to Macon and eventually Charleston, South Carolina, as spring turned to summer. The *Charleston Tri-Weekly Mercury* published Burnham's name along with those of several other Union officers who were imprisoned there. The officers might soon "share the pleasures of the bombardment" from federal guns turned on the port city. "These prisoners we understand," the paper pronounced, "will be furnished with comfortable quarters in that portion of the city most exposed to the enemy's fire."[123] "We have learned," a letter writer to the *Charleston Daily Courier* stated, "with much pleasure that the fifteen hundred Plymouth prisoners have been quartered in the lower part of the city, directly under the enemy's fire. That is as it should be." The letter writer went on to say, "If these fiends have no mercy upon our women and children, who from various causes, are obliged to live under the enemy's fire, why should we hesitate to quarter their prisoners under that same fire."[124] Years later, former officers John B. Clapp, Bernard Blakeslee, and Henry Wessell would agree that, for Burnham, the prison ordeal after Plymouth was particularly harsh. Clapp, who was imprisoned along with Burnham at Macon, described the colonel suffering "greatly from exposure, starvation and brutal treatment—his clothing was insufficient, he had little or no shelter," and the "rations were raw, and maggot-ridden."[125] When the Confederates moved the captured officers at Charleston close to the fire of the Union guns, it took a toll on Burnham's already weakened constitution. Wessell later judged, "This prison fare and exposure might have a tendency to injure the physical and nervous system of a sensitive organization."[126] Joseph Burnham remembered the damaging effect of this experience on his brother's "nervous system." It was hard enough for him "to be shut up in a prison," but it was even worse "that he was shut up in the jail at Charleston with the worst kind of criminals."[127]

John Burnham was not released from prison until August, when he returned home for a month-long furlough. Despite his ordeal, he sought to console anxious families that both Union and Confederate authorities would ensure that their letters and packages got safely through enemy lines to their imprisoned soldiers. "The rebel authorities in Charleston assured us," he wrote in a letter published in the *Courant,* "that they would faithfully forward and deliver whatever was brought to them by Gen. Foster, and judging from my intercourse with them during the latter part of my stay in Charleston, I believe they will do it." Regarding the hundreds of men still incarcerated in Georgia, Burnham was hopeful, hearing in mid-July that only one member had died and the rest "were just beginning to show the effects of their confinement."[128] Burnham wrote another letter to the *Courant* during his month-long furlough, sharing his conviction that the rebellion was nearing collapse. It was not money that the Union cause needed to crush the Confederacy but sheer manpower. Supporting the opinion of Brig. Gen. T. Seymour, with whom Burnham had been imprisoned at Charleston, he wrote: "What we want is men. Give us a little less of your money, if necessary, and more of yourselves! Come out and join us! All we want is an overwhelming force to crush their armies and end the war. Make but half the sacrifices for a few months that the rebels have made for three years, and the bright day of glorious peace will draw upon the country almost before the most sanguine among you expect it."[129]

In September, Lt. Col. Burnham began his journey to rejoin the remnants of the 16th Connecticut at Roanoke Island, North Carolina, but he was recaptured on September 9, when the mail steamer he was traveling on was attacked by Confederates.[130] Writing from prison in Goldsboro, North Carolina, on September 19, Burnham observed, "I am very unfortunate but am quite well and much better provided than when I was captured before so I shall try and weather through it." Asking his mother not to worry about him, he did instruct his brothers "to try and get a special exchange for me if they can—perhaps Col. Beach could do it through Major Mulford."[131] He was paroled on October 17, briefly reported to Camp Parole, Maryland, and then he was allowed to return to Hartford for another leave of absence to await his official exchange.[132] "Lieut. Col. John H. Burnham, 16th C.V., of this city," reported the *Daily Courant*, "seems to be peculiarly unfortunate."[133]

When Chaplain Dixon arrived home to Wallingford, Connecticut, in September, he provided a detailed list of the regiment's sixty-six Andersonville dead to the local papers. The names, with the death dates included, appeared in the Hartford papers the first week of October.[134] Dixon's list began to convey to civilians the imprisoned regiment's devastating losses. One former unit member, John T. Porter, was shocked to see Leander Chapin's name on the list. That very day Porter, then serving with the 1st Connecticut Heavy Artillery, penned a letter to the grieving soldier's mother to express his sympathy. Porter had known Chapin in school in Suffield and served with him. The two had been hospitalized together in December 1862, forming what Porter characterized as an "intimate friendship." He now wanted to assure Amelia Chapin that her son was not only a "faithful soldier" but a devout Christian. "I feel certain," Porter wrote, "of his preparation to meet his God in peace."[135] Roselle Grover also wrote Amelia Chapin soon after she saw Leander's name on the list of the dead. Grover, who had urged Amelia to be proud of her son's decision to enlist and assured her that he would survive the war, now sought to comfort her. "I know," Grover admitted, "I should be unequal to that task, but I can recommend you to look to our kind heavenly Father for consolation who has assured us He does not afflict willingly but for our profit and though we cannot see it all clearly we have his promise that it *shall* all be made plain." Grover, who confessed to worrying that Leander could not have survived "through all the exposures & privations to which they were subjected," now stressed that his suffering was over. "My heart aches," she closed, "for those who are left."[136]

Distraught family members sought help from Connecticut governor William Buckingham, asking him to intervene. Sometimes they sought information, other times a soldier's release from prison; they also begged for financial assistance since their husbands' or sons' imprisonment meant that no money was coming home to support them. Family members waited in anguish as weeks turned to months with little word of their loved ones' fates.[137] Kellogg's aunt Caroline D. Hale implored the governor in August 1864 to use his power to release her "beloved nephew," who was the "principal support of invalid parents, the father for four years past a cripple and the mother for years in feeble health." "All this summer," Hale wrote, Kellogg's parents had been in "constant anxiety about him, their only son. Col. Burnham, says their suffering, the prisoners, can't be told."[138]

By Christmas Day, 1864, Adj. John Clapp's mother, Elizabeth, had begun to hear from her son "occasionally and find that he is not well." Clapp had been moved to Columbia, but he urged his mother to write the governor, thinking that Buckingham could affect an exchange. "I am extremely anxious," Elizabeth added, "that something should be done for his *immediate* exchange. If you can help me any your kindness will never be forgotten an anxious mother will always be grateful to you."[139] Governor Buckingham promptly wrote to Lt. Col. John E. Milford, Assistant Agent for Exchange at Fort Monroe, and requested the exchange of Adjutant Clapp. Replying to Clapp's mother the same day he wrote to Fort Monroe, Buckingham admitted that he had "no confidence" that his efforts would help. "Yet it gives me pleasure to do what I can," he wrote, closing his letter, "with much sympathy."[140]

Elizabeth Derby also wrote Governor Buckingham, describing her hands trembling as she put pen to paper to recount her family's plight. Her husband Samuel remained imprisoned, and she was destitute at home with their two boys, "one four years old and my baby a year and ten months." Elizabeth, who also had two brothers in the army, described her children growing "delicate every day because I cant give them what is fit for such little fellows to eat." The last time she had received money from Samuel had been in December, and now, six months later, she had little left to pay rent or buy food, firewood, and clothing for herself and her children. Lizzie had already sought assistance from local authorities but had been apparently rebuffed. "We say oh how cruel the rebels is [for] they starve our Husbands and Brothers [and] they are wretches but they cant do it more perfect than the select men here." Derby apologized for bothering the governor but explained "you have been our Governer [sic] for many years."[141]

Cpl. Charles G. Lee's sister also beseeched the governor to make special efforts to help free her brother, a member of the "unfortunate 16th C.V. captured at Plymouth." "Could you not, Sir, make a special application to our commission for his *exchange*," Mary E. Lee asked, believing that the exchange of prisoners was still continuing "more or less," and "perhaps by so doing be the means of relieving the distressing anxiety of an aged & infirm father who mourns for his son as one dead." Mary Lee closed, "Hoping that the voice of 'one in *Authority*' might have an effectual hearing in this matter of a 'special application,' & that our worthy governor will grant us the favor of making the applications."[142] But, as tragic as the situation was, there was nothing unique at that time about a sister distressed about her twenty-year-old brother wasting away in a far-off prison. And there was little that a man in authority, such as Governor Buckingham, could do for any of these families except wait.[143]

The letters preserved in the governor's correspondence at the Connecticut State Library indicate that Buckingham responded occasionally to civilians' letters, including to wives and mothers of soldiers. He wrote more often to those asking for help for soldiers in hospitals and in prison but was less inclined to respond to a request for a discharge. This pattern of response had more to do with what he could do than what he wanted to do. In a letter typical of his reaction to pleas for discharge, Buckingham coolly explained to one worried mother in early February 1864: "In reply I would say that I have no power whatever over soldiers in the field and no authority in procuring their discharge. If the condition of your son warrants his discharge from the service, the approval of the Surgeon will undoubtedly obtain for an application, regularly made, a favorable consideration by the proper authorities."[144] To Susan Greene, the mother of Pvt. John Deming in Company F, who had just entered Andersonville, Buckingham similarly explained, "I have no authority over him & can give you but little encouragement that the War Department will discharge him just now yet I shall be happy to do for you [that] which I can properly."[145] Such cold comfort did not stop families from continuing to make their pleas.

Governor Buckingham did, however, formally urge the War Department to resume prisoner exchanges. Individual letters from family members may have prompted him, or perhaps he did it because so many Connecticut soldiers were in peril in southern prisons. On May 5, 1864, just weeks after the fall of Plymouth, the governor wrote Maj. Gen. Benjamin Butler asking him to "aid in securing an exchange as early as is permitted."[146] The governor also tried to free the two sutlers captured with the regiment, Joseph Albert Doane and E. G. Johnson, making a special request directly to Maj. Gen. J. G. Foster, who commanded the Department of the South: "As they are non combatants cannot some measures be taken for their release upon a parole or a special exchange be made[?]"[147]

"RELIEF FROM THEIR SUFFERINGS"

As weeks turned to months, existence in Andersonville prison took its toll on regimental unity and numbers. The filth, medical neglect, disease, and hunger weakened even the healthiest soldier, and the 16th Connecticut continued to see its ranks dwindle. For some, basic human instincts of self-preservation began to take over. Confederates eagerly offered prisoners their freedom if they took an oath of allegiance to the South, and hundreds did, no doubt out of utter desperation. Robert Kellogg described a Confederate officer asking for volunteers to help work on "fortifications & said if they'd not volunteer he would force them." "He had not need to use force," Kellogg wrote, "for several hundred cowardly traitors offered their services & were accepted. I regret that 4 were from the 16th Reg."[148] Pvt. Augustus Moesner, a German immigrant and new recruit from Company G who later admitted that he was "not well acquainted with the English language," volunteered for a parole on May 24. He became a clerk in Captain Wirz's office, making copies, writing in a roll book, and carrying returns and reports between the commandant's headquarters and the stockade, as well as the commissary.[149] Quartermaster sergeant Hiram Buckingham and Pvt. Andrew Spring (Co. E) also accepted paroles to work outside the stockade. Spring left on May 27, just three weeks after the regiment first entered the prison.[150] Sidney Hayden heard that Pvt. James Odie, a skilled shoemaker, had "come into the pen at Florence fat and hearty saying he lived with an old chap 50 miles from Florence and was making shoes for him and having a good time generally and sticks to that and he did not take the oath to the Confed[eracy]." Hayden observed, "But all say he took the oath for I know no one who could go out" without it.[151] Other members of the regiment looked on this behavior with disdain. "Some of the Plymouth men have been foolish enough to go outside today," Kellogg complained on May 23, "taking a parole & going to work on the stockade."[152] George Champlin reacted angrily to the news that eight members of the 7th Connecticut had accepted the Confederate oath to receive a parole: "They have disgraced themselves. I will die in prison before I will aid the Rebels one iota."[153]

Sometimes it was a specific skill that enabled prisoners the opportunity for relief. The Confederates especially needed shoemakers, and some prisoners, including members of the 16th Connecticut, tried to take advantage of this need.[154] Native German Jacob Bauer was selected by Captain Wirz to "write out the Register of Deaths." The first time he was asked in August, Bauer declined but was fed a dinner of roast beef and Irish potatoes. "The guard marched me back into the stockade," Bauer wrote, "and let me shoulder a big stick of wood. When my boys saw me coming back, they really shouted for joy to get the wood—a precious article." A few weeks later, the offer came again to "have a better living." This time Bauer accepted. In his recollections, he reasoned, "It did not last long, for an exchange took place—or rather removal—as Gen. Sherman's army was at Atlanta and was likely to pay a visit and free us."[155] It was also alleged that when native German corporal Casper Young (Co. A) died, passes from Captain Wirz were found in his wallet "allowing him complete freedom in going in and out of the stockade."[156] Nonetheless, George Q. Whitney would insist after the war that "very few accepted" the Confederate oath.[157]

The question of accepting Confederate parole, and thus taking the oath, was not so black and white for every member of the regiment. At first, Sgt. Oliver Gates criticized any Union prisoner who accepted a parole to work outside "strengthening the Stockade," saying they ought to "have to stay in this pen as long as they live."[158] When he learned about men in his own regiment, specifically, Hiram Buckingham and Spring, accepting paroles at Andersonville, Gates bitterly hoped, "The Government will not recognize them for exchange."[159] Yet, when he was moved to Florence in September, he vowed, "When I get well I am going to try to get paroled to do some kind of work to save my life." Gates took the parole to become a hospital steward, gaining extra rations and "a little more liberty."[160] On October 15, Gates "at last" had his parole, and he swore "not to attempt to escape or aid others to do so." His rations improved, and he had a pass to go "even to the brook to wash," and stay out of the prison camp.[161] Gates's responsibilities consisted of calling the hospital rolls, identifying the dead, making reports, and administering medicine. He found the work "just what I need and [it] keeps me alive for in my opinion I should not live a month in the *pen* with the other boys."[162] In the final pages of his wartime diary, Gates candidly admitted how his feelings had changed toward those he had originally condemned: "Terrible we looked upon them [those who accepted paroles] then as the next thing to traitor but afterward we were glad to accept the same condition ourselves and we have learned to be more Charitable to others while we are ignorant of the nature under which they act." Gates was convinced that staying out of the pen saved his life, and even though he considered his diaries private and "written expressly for my darling wife," he believed he needed to explain his actions, since he "finally took a part in just the same business that I was so bitter against in others."[163]

John Cuzner also offered a different perspective on these paroles, albeit years after the war had ended. In recounting his difficult prison experiences to his daughter, he credited his company mate Pvt. Maurice H. Shields for keeping him alive by accepting a Confederate parole. Cuzner later recalled that he had been "quite sick during my captivity" and "would never have lived to come out if it had not been for my friend M. S. who was large, strong and older and could work, he would carry out the dead, traded inside and out and worked for the Rebs outside, he made money and I've see him have a roll of bills as large as a fist, often." Shields obtained extra food, even a small turkey on Thanksgiving, by "working for the officers outside for which he received extra and better rations which helped to keep him well and strong." Cuzner refused to condemn him: "His trading inside and out was a great advantage as he was able to buy such things as he wanted and needed. He was wonderfully good to me getting me nutritious food that I was able to eat when sick." Cuzner was convinced, "I would not have lived to be liberated if it had not been for him."[164]

Kept in close confinement, stripped of their traditional sense of order and authority, weakened, exhausted, and increasingly disheartened, some men also turned on each other. Robert Kellogg described two members of the regiment "who got into a dispute & resorted to blows to settle a question." "They ought to have come to some conclusion," Kellogg remarked, "after bloody noses, black eyes, etc which both received."[165] The next day, Kellogg counted *"five* coming off before roll call."[166] He repeated this incident in *Life and Death in Rebel Prisons,* reasoning that the change in weather somehow played a role: "On the return of a pleasant morning, they had five distinct fights before roll-call, which was in the early part of the day; but one must remember we had no laws but those of our own making, and these could not be enforced with authority they thought binding."[167] In another instance, Ira Forbes and one of the Woodfords in Company I came to blows over a "misunderstanding about the water pail." Kellogg observed, "Both parties got a good wetting in the mud puddle and there was a vast amount of talk about 'Christians fight' etc. I'm sorry that Ira gave way to his temper."[168] Forbes himself described the incident in his diary: "I have done very wickedly this morning in becoming involved in a quarrel about the wash pail with a young man of our Regt." "My conduct," he wrote, "was wretched, and such as a true Christian ought never to be guilty of. It causes me stinging regret and sadness & makes me appear contemptible even to myself." He prayed that God would forgive him, and he was determined not to have it happen again.[169] Leland Barlow and Oliver Gates also commented on the fighting among prisoners. Barlow described prisoners beaten by fellow inmates for disclosing tunnels or over money and other valuables. One day in June, he counted three fights before breakfast: "No restraint against fighting or gambling."[170] "Amid all the horrors of this place," Gates observed, "one would think the men would get along without quarreling, but not a day passes but that we have to witness some brutal fight. There is no law here and no punishment. Men act more like savages than anything else."[171]

The first week of September 1864, Confederates began moving prisoners out of Andersonville. It appeared that, finally, the long-awaited prison exchange had come. Instead, Confederates were simply shifting inmates to new locations in the face of Union general William Sherman's advance through Georgia, leaving weak and lame prisoners behind.[172] Kellogg suspected something was afoot when Andrew Spring, who had left the prison by accepting a Confederate parole, returned one day "for a short time," loaning "$200.00 to the boys to be repaid in our lines at the rate of 2 to 1." Kellogg mused, "It must be that he has good reason for believing in our approaching exchange."[173] Spring later recalled being shocked that day by the appearance of his comrades: "A great many of the boys were very poor; they were some of my best friends whom I could not recognize until they came up and shook hands with me and made themselves known, and even then I could hardly believe they were the same men."[174] The next day, Kellogg learned from other members of the regiment who "worked outside" that they would be moved to a new prison: "Our Reg. is getting sadly thinned and God only knows how many of us will ever return home again." "Well," Kellogg declared, "almost any change will be agreeable—even a change of prison."[175]

The general reaction to the move was elation; finally, they were leaving Andersonville, and many assumed freedom would soon follow. "Cheer after cheer rent the air this evening," Champlin wrote on September 6, "when the order came to be ready to leave."[176] Forbes was thrilled: "At last I believe the happy day of deliverance is upon us. Thank God. This morning ten Detachments have moved out of camp."[177] Grosvenor was "very anxious to get the orders to leave" and exited "without any regrets except for those we leave behind." He thanked God that he was "out."[178]

As Confederates hurried prisoners out in groups of ninety, those too weak or sick were left behind. Kellogg left on September 10, as part of one of the first ninety to exit Andersonville. Among those left behind was Ira Forbes. Kellogg wrote, "It was hard to leave them but it was the only alternative."[179] He described Forbes "lying on the ground, too sick to be moved."[180] Oliver Gates was another who stayed behind, feeling he could not "walk a step" when his detachment left on September 10, but he departed for Florence five days later.[181] For those who remained, conditions only worsened. Confederates halted regular food rations, and dead bodies rotted unattended in the open air. Leland Barlow, also too sick to leave, wrote in despair: "An awful place! Men dying groaning praying, cursing! Crazy men." The next day: "Very bad smell near us. Dead man by my head." On October 9, Barlow died.[182] The "Second Andersonville" turned out to be even more deadly and horrific than the first.

Most Andersonville prisoners first went to Charleston, South Carolina, where they were kept a few miles northwest of the city in an open field once used as a racecourse. George Robbins remembered that the ground was very low, "with no drainage so that the frequent thunder showers not only wet us to the skin but left the ground wet for days."[183] Initially, there were better and more rations, as well as soap and salt. Henry Savage judged the conditions in Charleston "more reasonable than at Sumpter[;] here you can buy a loaf of bread for ten cts." Other items, including sweet potatoes and biscuits, were also available if a prisoner had the cash to spend.[184] "This day has been a most beautiful day," Kellogg wrote upon his arrival in Charleston, "& I feel more like a free man than I have for a long while."[185]

Other prisoners went directly to the Confederate prison at Florence, South Carolina. Those at Charleston would join them in early October. Gates left Andersonville on September 15 and boarded an overcrowded boxcar, packed with "happy cripples and sick men."[186] Relieved to leave Georgia, Gates wrote, "Although we have no shelter but the broad blue sky above us we feel better and breathe easier." Even the guards and locals seemed to take pity on them. Dr. Strothers, the medical director initially in charge at Florence, whom Gates described as a "fine man," told the northerners "that it is all the fault of our Government that we are not exchanged and I begin to believe it is. So far I know that they are anxious to get rid of us."[187] Their Confederate captors provided no shelter, although some of the men from the 16th were fortunate enough to still possess tents. By this time, however, many of the men's uniforms were reduced to rags, and they were barefoot. Prisoners began to receive items from the U.S. Sanitary Commission, including tomatoes, sweet potatoes, milk, crackers, coffee, blankets, and new clothes.[188] Still, hundreds of sick and weak men lay on an "old corn field," exposed to the rain and cooling weather.[189] "It is enough," Gates wrote, "to break one's heart to see men suffer and die here as they do now for the want of propper [sic] shelter and clothing."[190]

At Florence, rebels continued to press prisoners to take the oath of allegiance to the Confederacy. "Persistent efforts were made by the Commandant to induce our men," Robbins explained, "to forsake their allegiance to the Federal Government and enlist in the Confederate army, promising good food and clothing and immunity from service at the fronts, and I am forced with shame to record that hundreds accepted the base offer." Robbins added, "In strict justice I must also say that no doubt a large number, starved, nearly naked without blankets and with no shelter from the cold and rain were driven to take the step making a mental reservation that they did so only as a refuge from death from exposure, and resolving to escape at the first opportunity."[191] Savage observed a number of fellow inmates taking the enemy's oath of allegiance but was unmoved: "I think I prefer Starving to any such arrangement."[192]

Meanwhile, as officers and a few soldiers from the ranks of the 16th Connecticut arrived home, stories continued to circulate about the horrendous conditions in southern prisons, particularly Andersonville. Public anger and frustration grew over the administration's failure to resume the exchange system. The Democratic

Hartford Daily Times was only too happy to be an outlet for such discontent. On August 15, 1864, the paper referred to a "returned soldier of the Sixteenth C.V.," who confirmed that thousands of Union men were "suffering severely" at Andersonville. "This soldier," the paper professed, "expends his indignation less upon the Rebels than upon Secretary Stanton and the President, who act together in this matter, and who persist month after month, in refusing to abandon their insane hobby of an equal exchange of negroes for white men!"[193] Upon hearing of the death of Pvt. John W. Ensworth (Co. C) in Andersonville, the paper pronounced, "The sufferings of these poor fellows have only been equaled by the horrors of the old Jersey Prison Ship. Lincoln refuses to release them unless an equal exchange of negroes is made." "Several hundred," the paper proclaimed, "have found relief from their sufferings in death."[194]

The Republican *Courant* also published prisoners' accounts, but it used them to stress the desperation of the Confederates. In a graphic account of the conditions at Columbus, Georgia, where several officers of the 16th Connecticut were held, the *Courant* concluded, "Our government should not delay any longer the exchange of prisoners. Exchange man for man and settle differences afterward."[195] On November 29, the *Courant,* under the headline "Barbarism of Slavery: Jeff Davis a Murderer. Our Prisoners. Horrible Barbarities of the Rebels," reprinted an extended description of Andersonville's horrors for its readers, provided by the Port Royal correspondent for the *New York Times.* This journalist, after interviewing several exchanged prisoners at Savannah, wrote, "It is a distressing fact, but one which I have found abundant proof in many conversations with the men so far brought back, that the prisoners very generally believe that they have been abandoned by our government."[196]

Hartford papers persisted in printing a series of "eyewitness accounts" of the prison's miseries, starting in November 1864 and continuing into the New Year, and debates over what to do (if anything) in retaliation.[197] On February 9, 1865, the *Courant* called for a general exchange. "The northern people know full well," the editorial stated, "what their sons, and brothers, and friends endure in rebel dungeons, the tale has been told too often and too eloquently to need repetition." The *Courant* added, "The motives attributed to the war department for discontinuing the exchange are extremely discreditable." The paper urged Lincoln's administration to take responsibility for the prisoners and their suffering: "It rests immediately upon the secretary of war, and ultimately upon the President, as commander-in-chief."[198]

Some prisoners refused to wait for a formal exchange and sought any way out. Capts. Thomas F. Burke, Alfred A. Dickerson, and Timothy B. Robinson fled the Confederate prison at Columbus, Georgia, on November 3, 1864, and crossed into federal lines. The three officers slipped away when paroled to collect wood, then fled into the countryside, aided by local blacks. After just over a week, the captains were safe aboard U.S. vessels and soon en route for Connecticut.[199] Their arrival home was reported in the *Hartford Daily Courant* on November 19, 1864. The Republican paper was pleased to announce to its readers: "The testimony furnished by Captains Burke and Dickerson relative to the condition of the rebels, fully endorses the statements of other reliable witnesses. The rebellion is fast failing, and the re-election of Abraham Lincoln has thrown despondency upon the Southern leaders." The captains claimed that the other officers they had left behind in Columbus were fine, "but the privates of the regiment were not in such position as to be reported." The paper described to worried prisoners' families and friends: "They are scattered over considerable territory, with other prisoners, to prevent recapture."[200] Maj. Henry Pasco and Capts. Mark Turner and Charles W. Morse also escaped from Columbia, South Carolina, in February 1865.[201]

Andrew Spring, one of the soldiers who accepted Confederate parole, managed to escape Andersonville in September and make it all the way through the lines to New England. The *Courant* initially described Spring escaping as the prisoners were being transferred from Andersonville to Savannah, reporting that he "jumped from the train" and "managed to reach Sherman's line without detection."[202] The next day, the *Courant* dramatically embellished this account: "Mr. Spring did not escape from the cars, as stated by us yesterday, but fell out of the line in the night, whole on the march, and in the company with a Western soldier, took to the woods, where they remained many days, working their way North." Then, according to the paper, the escaped prisoners "made out their course by moss upon trees, which grows upon the north side. After many trials they reached Atlanta, and had an interview with Gen. Sherman, who shed tears at that story of the grave sufferings of their comrades they had left behind."[203] However, Bernard Blakeslee wrote that Spring "in some manner" obtained enough money to bribe a guard and break free with two comrades, then successfully travelled across rebel lines.[204]

Spring's escape and his account of the terrible conditions in Andersonville stunned people waiting anxiously for news of their loved ones' release. The *Courant* reported that Spring "gives a terrible account of the sufferings of our soldiers who are held as prisoners by the rebels. He more than corroborates the published statements concerning their hardships. They die by scores, being absolutely starved to death. One dollar has been paid for a single onion to keep off scurvy. To prevent their escaping the rebels had guns planted at Andersonville, bearing upon the camp."[205] When the father of another prisoner visited Spring and heard his "sorrowful tale of the sufferings of our brave boys from the lack of proper food, clothing and care," he wrote an impassioned letter to the *Hartford Daily Times* demanding an immediate resumption of prisoner exchange. He blamed Lincoln and the "authorities in Washington" who refused, "for the reason that they cannot make an arrangement to suit them for the exchange of a few hundred negro soldiers." The father was convinced that Lincoln in particular was responsible: "They *can* be released—a word from President Lincoln will do it. Only let him say 'exchange,' and 20,000 of our sons are relieved from horrible sufferings and lingering death!"[206]

For the families of prisoners who remained incarcerated, it was alarming to learn firsthand of their sufferings. James Whitney, whose only son George remained in Florence, recounted that he had heard from returning soldiers that his son and his fellow prisoners "are barefoot and without shirts their boots & pants most worn off without any shelter at this inclement season of the year." Whitney implored, "You cannot know how we feel who have sons there in such condition unless you have one in the same. These sons enlisted and went out to fight for the Union and haven't they a right to expect some protection from the state or general government? Are they to be left there to suffer on and die?"[207]

The prison ordeal for most of the regiment lasted until December, when exchanges finally resumed and survivors were transferred to Camp Parole in Annapolis, Maryland. The feeling of joy and relief is palpable in the existing sources. George Champlin recorded in his diary: "I am a free man and feeling good."[208] Ira Forbes, on board a ship headed north, gazed up at the U.S. flag: "It never appeared more beautiful than it does today."[209] Robert H. Kellogg wrote his parents from the U.S. transport ship the *General Lyon*: "Thanks to a kind Heavenly Father I am once more in a civilized country alive & well. We leave shortly for Annapolis and probably I will be with you by Christmas."[210] Oliver W. Gates was equally thrilled: "Many hearts were gladdened by the sight of the stars and stripes." But he was saddened by "a large number of boys that lived to get almost in sight of home after all their suffering [that they had] endured" but "gave out and died" en route. He lashed out bitterly at the Rebel government, wondering: "Are such men worthy ever to become national brother[s] entitled to the protection of a Nation that they have risked their lives to destroy?"[211] In 1915, Jacob Bauer vividly remembered his emotions when he finally saw the U.S. flag again: "How beautiful the flag looked. A sight never to be forgotten. We shouted, we cried, we thanked God for the sight of friends. What an inspiration the flag carried—a guiding star, an emblem of power and freedom." For Bauer, the flag had added meaning: "While I was not born under it, I have never loved any other. I followed it through fire and smoke of battle and no one can realize just what the flag means and stands for unless he has gone through the experiences of a prisoner of war."[212]

The core of the regiment had undergone at least six months of horrific imprisonment in the South's worst prisons. A third of them perished, and most of the survivors never fully recovered their physical or mental health. Now, with formal exchange restored, survivors still had time due to the U.S. military. Neither the war, nor their military service, was over quite yet.

8

Roanoke, Camp Parole, and New Bern
"Another Day Gone and One Day Nearer Home"

Some members of the regiment, mainly Company H, never experienced imprisonment at all, and they continued in active service under the official name "the 16th C.V." Eventually, their comrades who survived incarceration were released, and many returned to the unit. However, going home and staying there was almost everyone's prime goal. The war and its larger purposes seemed of little concern to them. Sick, exhausted, disillusioned, with many close to death, the soldiers yearned to end their military service. Yet even in those closing days of the regiment's existence, some members and the public strove to promote the image of the regiment's heroism and self-sacrifice.

"A COMPACT AND TANGIBLE FORCE"

While most of their comrades endured imprisonment, Company H remained at Roanoke Island. This single company, ordered to leave Plymouth in the midst of the fight to ferry civilians away from the forts, stayed in active service until the war ended. The greatly reduced 16th Connecticut was now part of the District of North Carolina, led by Brig. Gen. Innis Palmer, and the Sub-District of the Albemarle, under the command of Colonel David W. Wadrop.[1] In the months following the attack, as Bernard Blakeslee explained, their numbers were reinforced "now and then by men who had previously been detached for special service, or were absent sick, also by a few who were exchanged from time to time, representing every company, and thus composed the 16th regiment in actual service."[2]

With most of its senior officers in prison, the regiment had a new leader, Company H's captain, Joseph Barnum. A man who had spent time gambling and visiting prostitutes and had been charged with "neglect of duty" now commanded the condensed unit. Blakeslee later defended him: "Captain Barnum labored with much zeal under many difficulties to preserve the former prestige of the regiment."[3] And

Ira Forbes credited the captain for important service in "keeping Co. H and the members of the Regiment outside of that Company, as they reported at Roanoke, in a compact and tangible force."[4] Barnum, however, was miserable. He complained bitterly about his crippled command and incompetent subordinates, and, in May 1864, he requested that the remnants of the regiment be returned to Connecticut to recruit until the rest of the unit was released from prisons. Gov. William Buckingham referred the request to the War Department, which refused it.[5]

Capt. Barnum was also distracted by continued worries about his family's finances. In June 1864, he asked permission to leave the island to go to Norfolk "for the purpose of expressing money to the North for myself and command." He said that he and his men lacked confidence in the Adams Express Company at New Bern and would rather transact business in person in Norfolk.[6] This request was also denied. The captain was free to visit Norfolk "for the purpose of pleasure or otherwise a leave of absence can be granted," but Gen. Innis N. Palmer would not allow him to visit the city for the purposes of conveying money for his men.[7] There was also tension between Captain Barnum and his officers. In August 1864, Barnum threatened Capt. Julian Pomeroy with a charge of "Disobedience of Orders" for failing to fill out a detail for the guard in what the captain judged to be a timely manner.[8] A few months later, Barnum chided Lt. Ariel J. Case for not understanding the "usual and proper form of making details from companies." The captain sharply instructed Case that if he again deemed it necessary to question the "authority of this Hd Qrs," then any such "communication will be addressed to my superior or superiors."[9] Case was detailed to the Conscript Camp in New Haven, but Barnum soon requested his return to Roanoke, "there being no commissioned office in command of my company and only one commissioned officer with me in the regiment."[10] In early April 1865, Captain Barnum was still dissatisfied, this time because he had lost his clerk, Pvt. Lay, and had no adjutant or any other clerk to assist him with his regimental duties.[11]

As Barnum struggled with his reduced staff, the men settled into their new encampment at Roanoke Island. On July 4, 1864, a soldier wrote the *Courant*, using the pen name "Veteran," to describe conditions. The men were thankful for the ocean breeze, which occasionally broke through the sweltering heat. Soldiers were set to celebrate Independence Day with lemonade, speeches, and fresh tobacco. Officers were starting to return to the depleted unit, including Dr. Mayer, whom "Veteran" described as "looking as finely as though he had just come out of a band-box instead of Libby prison." There were a growing number of African

Americans coming to reside on the island, occupying "shanties" aligned along streets and avenues. They set up small patches of gardens, "where the occupants can raise a few potatoes (and they will be few I should judge from the poor soil here) if he is disposed, or can sun himself, which is much more congenial with his feelings, to great advantage." There were also religious meetings and Sunday school classes, "most of them taught by soldiers of the 16th." He assured readers, "The worthy clergyman, by the way, speaks highly of the men of our regiment, and has repeatedly told me that he hoped, they would stop here all summer, for they were good men." Even so, this soldier spoke disparagingly of the "'nigger' meeting," as loud and overly emotional.[12]

Another letter from a "Veteran" later in July described the "monotony of camp life," occasionally "relieved by a raid to some little town, within a few hours steaming." The regiment's health was good and supplies plentiful; most notably, they had fresh bread. The 16th also performed provost guard duty at the island, something it had done only rarely since leaving Hartford in the summer of 1862. "Veteran" commented, "The small number of men that we have brings it their turn for guard duty every other day, which considering that there is a drill of an hour's length for every man on the day that he comes off guard with a dress parade every night, give him about all the duty he can attend to." Heat and fleas were a constant, but the men sought relief from the sun by building "arbors of pine boughs in front of our tents."[13]

Indeed, with little prospect of large-scale battle, the reduced 16th Connecticut embarked on raiding missions to Columbia, Edenton, and the nearby country-side.[14] In an expedition to Foster's Mill, the men destroyed large quantities of grain and, in the words of Lt. Blakeslee, returned "with various spoils."[15] In a raid to Hertford, North Carolina, the men "captured large quantities of cotton, tobacco, finished carriages, and buggies, several feet of lumber, several mules and forty contrabands."[16] "Veteran" described a raid in which thirty men from the 16th Connecticut participated, along with soldiers from other regiments. Their task was to sail up the "Scuppernong river to destroy a bridge over the river at Columbia, Tyrell County, over which the rebs were carting large supplies for their army." The raid was successful, and all "returned to camp without loss and in good spirits." The men were pleased with the sutler stores on the island, "at which most everything can be purchased." However, "Veteran" reported, "there is much complaint among the men of the 16th, about the non-receipt of newspapers sent from home."[17]

It was not very dangerous service, but the steamy weather took its toll on the men nonetheless. In September, "Roanoke" informed the *Connecticut War Record* that nearly one-third of the men were "sick either in camp or in hospital."[18] Pvt. Cornelius Doty, who described himself as not doing "any duty" for four months due to "the fever and ague," attested in early November 1864 that two of his five children were sick and his wife was struggling to care for them. He requested the governor to procure him a furlough so he could regain his health and help his family.[19]

Desertion continued to eat away at the regiment, especially among recent recruits. One deserter was twenty-six-year-old Irish native Patrick McSullie, a recruit in Company A who had enrolled on December 21, 1863. According to Forbes, McSullie "accidently shot himself," inflicting "a severe wound in the wrist" in March 1864.[20] Another soldier writing to the *Daily Courant* also described the shooting as an accident: "He had laid down his gun, and in picking it up caught it by the muzzle, when the charge was exploded and the ball driven through his wrist; his coolness in calling the corporal, demanding the countersign, and being regularly relieved, was worthy of a veteran."[21] However, by the summer of 1864, McSullie deserted the regiment entirely.[22] Another new recruit, English-born Richard Collins, a member of Company I, had only been with the 16th Connecticut since April 2, 1864. But on June 9, the twenty-three-year-old private deserted, allegedly "to the enemy."[23] One day in February 1865, seven privates from Company I, all recruits, were put under arrest for a variety of charges, including "disrespect," "disobedience" and "conduct prejudicial."[24]

Cut off from most of their officers and comrades, the regiment could ill afford to lose more men. When, on May 11, 1864, Pvt. Albert S. Harris died, the men in the ranks organized a "meeting of Co. H., 16th Conn. Vols." at their camp on Roanoke Island to vote on a set of formal resolutions similar to those issued in honor of Capt. Edward H. Mix. Resolving that Harris, who died from pneumonia, "will ever be remembered and lamented by the company," the members of Company H further added, "That the example of bravery and readiness to discharge the duties devolving upon him at any and all times is worthy of imitation by all good soldiers." The men offered their sympathies to Harris's widowed mother and only sister. These resolutions were then sent North with the request that they be published in all the major Hartford newspapers and forwarded to Harris's family.[25]

Despite these losses, some insisted that the unit was doing just fine. "Roanoke," another soldier from the 16th writing for the *Connecticut War Record* in June 1864, praised their performance in dress parades, claiming that the sight of them impressed onlookers. He believed that all the regiment really needed was "a few competent men to act as privates."[26] In December 1864, Capt. Barnum filed a positive inspection report, stating that the field and staff were in "good" condition in the categories of discipline, instruction, arms, accouterments, and clothing. For the category of "Military Appearance," he judged them "excellent."[27] And the December 1864 issue of the *Connecticut War Record* stated that the unit was "quietly doing duty and building winter quarters."[28]

An expedition to retake Plymouth in the fall broke the monotony. In October 1864, Company H provided infantry support to naval lieutenant William B. Cushing's ambitious plan to attack the port town and destroy the Confederate ram *Albemarle*.[29] The 16th C.V. "took [a] credible part" in the expedition.[30] Finally, on March 4, 1865, after nearly a year at Roanoke Island, the 16th Connecticut was ordered to New Bern. "The news spread quickly over the little island." "Roanoke" wrote to the *Connecticut War Record* that "the camp was soon filled with men, women and children, white, cream colored and copper colored, and from that to genuine, right-up-and-down black." The men found themselves in New Bern doing provost duty, "all comfortably housed, and (I grieve to say), shabbily fed."[31] Two weeks later, Captain Barnum reported, "In the Regt. there are (9) enlisted in daily duty, four musicians, four sick, an orderly for Regimental Hd. Qrs. A total of (18) and an aggregate of (82) men leaving seven enlisted men and their line officers for duty the next 24 hours." Some thirty-one enlisted men were detailed for "Patrol Duty" in New Bern, "assigned to each district whose instructions are to patrol their respective district once every two hours, also to arrest all enlisted men without passes and all unemployed negroes, and report them to the Provost Marshall the next day at 10 A.M."[32]

By the spring of 1865, the depleted 16th Connecticut had begun to greet into its ranks its comrades from prison. Released prisoners first went to Camp Parole in Annapolis, Maryland. There they found themselves in a sort of "limbo," waiting to be formally exchanged so they could commence their furloughs they were to have before returning to service.[33] Cpl. Harrison Woodford notified his family that he was safe and alive: "I feel very thankful to my heavenly Father that he has snatched me as I have reason to think from the jaws of death." He was convinced that in just a few more weeks he would have perished. Crippled but able to move around with crutches, Woodford was anxious to return to Avon and give "a full account of my trials."[34]

Meanwhile, the men bided their time, visiting members of the regiment at the College Green Barracks and going into the town of Annapolis for meals and other indulgences. Robert Kellogg and Forbes recounted seeing "our much loved" Lt. Col. Burnham at Camp Parole.[35] Pvt. Martin V. Culver resumed his trade as a carpenter.[36] One of the first things released prisoners did was bathe and obtain clean clothes, and John Cuzner and Sidney Hayden assisted with cleaning and clothing the men before they entered camp.[37] There was a "reading room," allowing soldiers like Forbes to return to their voracious reading habits. Forbes also resumed writing for the *Religious Herald*.[38] When Kellogg arrived at the Naval School Hospital at Annapolis on December 5, he was pleasantly surprised to be greeted by fellow members of the 16th Connecticut, including Forbes and John Lapaugh, who were detailed as nurses. "Here," Kellogg wrote, "I got a good wash & a clean suit of under clothes which made me feel & look more respectable."[39] The next day at Annapolis, he set down a "roll of the dead in the Regt. & also of the men who came through with me on the 'Gen Lyon' which will be published in the Hfd papers."[40] He also met with an investigative commission from Washington and was "closely questioned as to my prison life." He felt the interview went well: "Rec'd some flattering compliments from them & a promised copy of the printed report."[41]

Existence at Camp Parole, though vastly better than prison life, proved tedious. "This is a lazy life now, nothing to do but draw our grub and eat it," Cuzner decided.[42] A week later, he wrote Ellen Van Dorn: "Time passes very slowly here," and "I have nothing to do now but write."[43] Forbes was anxious to give up nursing and go home. "I greatly dislike my present employment," he pronounced. "It is too confining, and what is worse one is made a sort of slave for Tom, Dick and Harry."[44]

Members of the regiment knew that they would have to return to service, but they reveled in the brief time they had with family and friends. The kindnesses extended to them made an impression: "It almost pays," Kellogg remarked candidly in his diary, "to be a prisoner of war."[45] Still, there could be awkward moments in the civilian world. Kellogg described socializing with female friends in New Haven when one of the women offered a toast: "Success to the Southern Confederacy." The recently returned prisoner of war refused to raise his glass. If there had not been women present, Kellogg reasoned, "I would have raised a small row immediately. This is a 'free country,' though & treason like this can be uttered here in our midst."[46]

"CHANGED MEN"

The journey northward was not easy, whether one was traveling directly from prison or from Camp Parole. One soldier from the 16th recounted leaving Florence, South Carolina, for home after his exchange. He was crowded onto train cars with other released prisoners for days without any food, no room to sit, and barely space to stand. Men died, and bodies were simply buried on the side of the railroad track. When the soldier finally arrived in Hartford, after an additional mishap where he banged his head, he was already in a "wandering state." "There were no cheering crowds waiting to greet him when he reached the Hartford depot. Weak and disoriented, he fell to the platform and lay there, with no idea where to go or what to do. In his frenzied state, he tossed away his wallet full of greenbacks. A stranger came by and helped him, and he finally made his way to a nearby business and eventually home to recover. This unnamed soldier was sixteen when he enlisted, described as "a young man of strictly temperate habits, and connected with a very respectable family, which has sent four sons into the army, one never to return."[47] George Robbins's journey to his family in Plainville was also exceedingly difficult. When he was notified of his thirty-day furlough, he tried to plead with the surgeon that he was far too weak to make the long trip home to Connecticut. The train he boarded was full of furloughed or discharged soldiers, many of them drunk. Seated in the back of a rail car, unable to sleep and worried about being robbed, Robbins endured "the climax of my sufferings."[48] When he reached his parents' home, enfeebled by the combined effects of scurvy and dysentery, he was placed under the care of the family doctor, Dr. Moody. The physician soon requested an extension to Robbins's furlough to allow him to remain home to recover. Instead, Robbins was ordered to report to the Knight General Hospital in New Haven or risk, he alleged, being listed as a deserter. Robbins did as he was told but "after examination [was] sent to bed inwardly raging at such treatment." He then determined that he would rather be with his comrades, and he demanded that he rejoin them at Roanoke. Instead, he was readmitted to the hospital and finally mustered out on June 1, 1865.[49]

For others, the imprisonment had been too long. Pvt. Lewis M. Holcomb was paroled in December 1864.[50] He came home "a wreck," according to his aunt, and "so weak and starved that he could hardly turn in the bed," according to local doctor Frederick Williams, a boyhood chum.[51] Holcomb's cousin Addie went to visit him soon after his arrival and found him "miserable," "thin," and complaining of a sore throat.[52] But his health seemed to improve, and by April, he returned to the regiment, determined to be formally mustered out with his comrades.[53] However, he was not fully recovered, and on May 19, 1865, he entered a military hospital in Fairfax, Virginia. He died four days later at the age of twenty-four.[54] Wallace Woodford, cousin to Harrison Woodford, successfully reached his home in Avon, but his body was so broken by imprisonment that he died on January 10, within a week after his arrival. The *Courant* reported, "When asleep he would throw his arms about, thinking he was in Andersonville (he said when he awoke) endeavoring to obtain food. He was so much exhausted that he could not inform his friends in detail of the treatment he received by the rebels, but he told them 'words could not describe the horrors he had witnessed.'" His gravestone reads: "8 months a sufferer in Rebel prisons; he came home to die." Woodford was twenty-two years old.[55] Sidney H. Hayden, released on December 16, first went directly to East Granby on his furlough and then dutifully reported to Camp Parole. Awaiting a formal exchange to rejoin the 16th at Roanoke, Hayden and fellow company mate Robert Holmes reminisced about "old familiar scenes" from their hometown, confident that their "sojourn out here is done." Seeking to "work for my self individually and let the public go to pot," the prison experience had left Hayden, still a devout Christian, jaded about any sort of higher purpose behind his military service. "*Honor,*" he mused, "*is a poor thing to live on.*"[56] Granted a second furlough on March 18, he died at home from typhoid fever on April 4, 1865.[57]

Oliver Gates almost suffered the same fate as Sidney Hayden. In December 1865, Gates finally arrived on a "stormy wintery morning" to his "little cottage door." Weak and barely able to stand due to the "accumulated disease that coursed through my blood and brain," he was met by his wife with a pained expression and finger to her lip. His young daughter Allie, whom he had waited so anxiously to see, was ill. Three days later, Allie died. A severe bout of typhoid took hold of Gates himself in January, and he too nearly died. Aided by an "excellent physician," "kind nurses," and his "devoted wife," Gates was well enough to rejoin the 16th Connecticut in April.[58]

Coming back to soldier life was challenging. After his month-long furlough, Sgt. Jacob Bauer's 1865 diary reveals his inner struggle as he returned to service. Bauer described himself as "somewhat blue" about having to leave his wife Emily and their young daughter Allison, and he grew disgruntled as he waited to rejoin the regiment still stationed at Roanoke Island.[59] On board a steamer for Norfolk, Bauer had to report to the provost guard and, as he described, endure being "shut up in a nasty stinking room with a nigger guard placed over" him. Bauer bitterly wrote: "Such is the treatment . . . of a U.S. soldier returning from captivity." He could only take comfort in the fact that "my time is soon out."[60]

After John Cuzner returned to Camp Parole in late January 1865 from his month-long furlough, he was amazed to discover how quickly his body began rebounding from the prison ordeal. He admitted to Ellen Van Dorn that when he had been home everyone "said I was sick and I thought what they all said must be so, so I played sick." Yet, back in the service, he began to feel remarkably better, "I was surprised I had so much strength after what I went through." He wrote Van Dorn, "I feel as well as I ever did."[61] However, his homesickness grew after he returned to Camp Parole, and he was convinced that the furlough had only made him feel worse about remaining in the army. "I never since I enlisted longed so much for next August," Cuzner confessed to Van Dorn, "as I have since I came home. When my time is out[,] I shall not be thinking well, I have to report at such and such a time but will go and come when I please."[62] He went to work at the College Green Barracks, a sort of way station for recently returned prisoners before they entered Camp Parole. Responsible for cleaning and clothing the men, Cuzner wrote in early March 1865, "Just at present they are coming in so fast we have to work night and day." He did this voluntarily: "I am not compelled to work but when I see men in the condition our returned prisoners are I want to be doing something to help them."[63] Just a few weeks later, after being granted another thirty-day furlough home, Cuzner fell gravely ill with typhoid.[64] As he bided his time in the Camp Parole hospital, the question of marriage hung heavy over the couple. Van Dorn wanted to wait five years; Cuzner, after his months in prison and serious illness, understandably wanted to speed up the date.[65]

During his first furlough home, Robert Kellogg made two significant changes that had profound effects on his future. On Sunday, January 1, 1865, Kellogg wrote in his diary that he had taken "one of the most important steps of my life," by formally joining the Congregational Church and thus "uniting with the Cong. Church by profession my faith in Jesus Christ." He spent the day praying that he would stay true to his vows, and he visited his "dear old Sabbath School class."[66] It was also during his first furlough home that Kellogg began converting his wartime and prison diaries into a book manuscript for publication. He started in mid-January 1865, soon after he returned home, and continued writing almost daily, mailing manuscript pages to his Hartford publisher, L. Stebbins who promised Kellogg "$1000 to $500 for my labors."[67] Kellogg returned to Camp Parole on January 16 but kept writing at a steady clip, despite discomfort to his right hand, which he had injured in prison. "I shall be glad when my work is done," he stated in his diary on January 27, 1865, "so that I can have leisure to read and improve my mind. The book will be out soon and I have great curiosity to see it."[68] The next day he completed the manuscript and mailed the final installment to Hartford: "I am glad it is over with," he wrote.[69] By mid-February, Kellogg began receiving proofs, and the book was published in March 1865. Ira Forbes later professed that Kellogg's book was the "first work that was issued in the North concerning the stockade and edition after edition was exhausted in a few weeks."[70]

Kellogg's memoir had a very long title: *Life and Death in Rebel Prisons: Giving a Complete History of the Inhuman and Barbarous Treatment of our Brave Soldiers by Rebel Authorities, Inflicting Terrible Suffering and Frightful Mortality, Principally at Andersonville, Ga., and Florence, S.C., Describing Plans of Escape, Arrival of Prisoners, with Numerous and Varied Incidents and Anecdotes of Prison Life.* Its dedication was equally lengthy: "To The Widows, Children, Fathers, Brothers, And Sisters, Of The Thousands Of Brave Men Who Have Left Their Homes In The Morning Of Life; Sundered Family And Social Ties; Abandoned Cherished Enterprises And Business Schemes, For The Purpose Of Maintaining The Laws Of Freedom Inviolate, And In The Faithful Performance Of Their Duty, Have Been Captured By The Enemy, And Gone Down To Untimely Graves Through Unparalleled Sufferings, Is This Volume Most Respectfully Dedicated."[71] On Saturday, March 11, Kellogg received the first shipment of 189 copies of his book and they sold out in three hours. Kellogg was confident that he could "have sold twice as many if I only had them."[72]

Individually and in groups, released prisoners began to rejoin the regiment after their stay at Camp Parole and various furloughs. On January 2, 1865, 2nd Lt. Bernard Blakeslee (Co. G) returned to duty; Cpl. Ira Forbes and Pvt. George Q. Whitney (Co. A) returned to duty on May 4, 1865.[73] Two weeks later, however, Forbes had to obtain another furlough and leave the regiment.[74] Sgt. Oliver Gates (Co. F) returned to duty on April 16, 1865.[75] Soon after their return to the regiment, several of the men obtained an additional leave of absence.[76]

Bauer came back to the regiment on January 18, 1865. He enjoyed a "good welcome" and was happy to see his old comrades again.[77] However, he quickly discovered army life to be tedious and "dull" and recorded repeated accounts of men "drunk and disorderly."[78] He was kept busy preparing muster and pay rolls, and the regiment shifted camp in early March 1865 from Roanoke Island to New Bern, North Carolina.[79] Occasionally the routine was broken by rumors that the unit was headed to active campaigning or expecting the arrival of someone famous like Gen. William T. Sherman, who visited their camp at New Bern for two hours in late March.[80] But sickness continued to take its toll, and morale was low. Bauer was lonesome for home and worried about his wife and daughter.[81] After the shock of combat, the drudgery of garrison duty, and the long brutality of imprisonment, Bauer's resilience was giving way. He found his worries about his family almost too much to bear. Many of his fellow soldiers had turned to alcohol, no doubt to numb some of their nagging anxieties. Instead, Bauer turned to Christianity, openly declaring his faith in Jesus Christ at a prayer meeting on February 5.[82] Religion appeared to give him some measure of comfort as he counted the days until his three-year enlistment was up, or the war ended, whichever came sooner. "I felt it was good for me to be there," he wrote in his diary one night after returning from an evening prayer meeting where he had spoken out "in favor of our Savior." That night he "went to bed quite happy and contented."[83] Five weeks later Bauer wrote, "Another day gone and one day nearer home."[84]

Another soldier who returned to the regiment was Kellogg. He was headed back to the 16th in April 1865 after his third furlough (this one to vote in the state election), when he stopped in Philadelphia: "There were but a few of us soldiers present, and we rec'd every kind of attention—Old ladies, young ladies, children and all had a kind word for us. A soldier is treated as well as a citizen in Phila. If not much better."[85] On the evening of April 9, Kellogg had retired to bed early in the "lodging house" where he and a comrade, Charles Higgins from Company C., were staying for the night, only to be awakened by loud cheers and shouts in the streets below. Robert E. Lee had surrendered at Appomattox Courthouse, and excitement was spreading through the city: "That was too much for our equanimity so we began turning summersets [sic] on our bed, then we cheered, sang songs, and ended by dressing and going out into the streets and joining in the jubilee which was in progress." The next morning, Kellogg joined other members of the 16th Connecticut in a "grand war dance in the backyard of the Hotel in honor of the grand event."[86] A few days later, he heard the dreadful news of President Lincoln's assassination: "The feeling is very intense."[87]

Kellogg arrived at New Bern on April 20, exactly one year to the day after his capture at Plymouth. Capt. Thomas Burke had command of the regiment, with Colonel Frank Beach in charge of the defenses of New Bern. All told, Kellogg estimated the regiment's strength to be some 126 men. He resumed his role as sergeant major, although it was an "awkward" feeling to be in this position again after so long and after so much had happened.[88] He described the regiment at New Bern "pleasantly camped in the city." A few weeks later, Kellogg counted only eighty men, including noncommissioned officers, reporting for duty in the 16th Connecticut. That was a stunning drop from the 1,010 men in the ranks who had left Hartford that long-ago August day in 1862. "The duty is pretty hard," Kellogg wrote to his parents on May 11, "and consists principally in guarding the Depot & large repair shop connected with it, seeing to transportation passes etc. on all trains going and coming from Sherman's Army, etc. We also furnish a guard for the Comdg General's resident, and one for Col. Beach's house." He added, "Whenever any extra smart & good looking men are wanted, the 16th is usually called upon." Despite his humor, Kellogg knew that their long imprisonment had left deep, perhaps permanent scars. Scurvy reappeared in camp, and Kellogg's weakened hand was causing him great discomfort: "The men can stand but little fatigue now, the effects of rebel treatment now will follow most of us to our graves."[89] Due to his injured hand, Kellogg returned to Connecticut in May on another extended furlough, was hospitalized in Knight Hospital in New Haven, and never again rejoined the regiment.[90]

Kellogg mustered out on June 1, writing his mother the day before of his prospects as a civilian; he was considering a position as an agent for the Berkshire Life Insurance Company. In the meantime, his book was selling briskly. He wrote his mother: "I mean to get $200 or $300 more out of Mr. Stebbins if I can." The publisher had predicted selling "40 or 50,000 copies. I'll get quite a little fortune together soon for *a boy*."[91] He visited Stebbins in Hartford, seeking "final settlement of our account." Stebbins "rather demurred but finally drew off a check for $200 & I gave him a receipt in full."[92]

Yet another tragedy afflicted the unit when the steamer *Massachusetts*, carrying several recently released prisoners back to the regiment, collided with the *Black Diamond* at the mouth of the Potomac River in late April 1865. A soldier from the 101st Pennsylvania, also aboard the *Massachusetts*, recalled, "We glided down the river very nicely until after dark when a strong wind began to flow and the river became very rough, and as our boat was an old one and unfit to carry more than half the number she had on board, the outlook was not very encouraging." By 10 p.m. there was an "awful crash" and a "sudden jar," and the men realized they had collided with the *Black Diamond*. Both boats were sinking. It was very dark and, according to Ira Forbes, "There was a general rush from the Steamer by the men on board to the 'Diamond,' which was carried down."[93] Survivor George Hollands wrote, "We clung to our positions all night and could hear the cries for help in all directions from the boys who had jumped overboard." Holland estimated that some sixty-five men died.[94]

The 16th Connecticut lost seven of its own.[95] Among the victims was twenty-three-year-old Pvt. George N. Champlin, who had gone home on a furlough to Stafford, where he was greeted warmly by friends and family. According to his younger brother Oliver, Champlin "was getting to be a something of a politician," having returned from prison an avid Republican, no longer a conservative Democrat. He wrote Oliver, "Some of the Copperheads curse me for taking stands with the union men. I have taken my stand, and on the platform I now stand I will sink or swim."[96] Champlin left to rejoin the 16th Connecticut soon after composing those ominous words.[97] Sgt. Samuel E. Grosvenor (Co. B) also perished in the *Black Diamond* accident. He too had come home to Guilford on furlough before resuming his military service. His final diary entry for December 1864 read: "I have suffered much & doing little. Still I find myself enjoying every blessing."[98] Pvt. Martin V. Culver, who had returned home on extended furlough after suffering from "bilious pneumonia," was on the *Massachusetts* that fateful day. The tough carpenter survived, writing his brother a few days after the accident: "We arrived at New Bern last Saturday after a long and hard passage[.]" "[W]e had," Culver added, "bad luck as usual."[99] Forbes later reflected, "The whole event was of a pathetic character and sent sorrow into home after home in Connecticut."[100]

On April 12, 1865, the regiment received news that Lee had surrendered to Grant and the war was nearing its end. "Flags, music, shouting, and rejoicing was the order of the day," Bauer recorded in his diary. "A great many got drunk," he added, "and of course rows occurred."[101] The shocking news of Lincoln's assassination soon followed, and the regiment participated in a special service to mourn their dead president.[102] On April 24, U. S. Grant traveled through New Bern, trekking after Joe Johnston, who was nearing surrender. Members of Company H served as Grant's escort, an obvious honor for a regiment that had endured questions about its courage, discipline, and trustworthiness throughout the war.[103] This was, according to Forbes, "one of the highest episodes in the Company's career."[104] Officers of the unit, acutely aware of its uneven public reputation, used this opportunity to defend the 16th. They wrote to the *Hartford Courant*, stressing their dependability and explaining their various duties, despite their reduced numbers: "Our men stand high in the opinion of the military authorities as *reliable* soldiers. They are mostly away at present. Twenty have gone as an escort to Gen. Grant, who went through here for Raleigh last night; fifteen more have gone to guard some men to Wilmington; sixteen have gone to Fortress Monroe, guarding the lot of rebels. We also guard the depot and see to the transportation, passes, & on the trains. We expect to go home soon."[105]

"MUSTERED OUT"

Few of the commissioned officers were still with the unit by the end of April 1865. Colonel Beach, who had spent limited time with the men since Antietam, briefly returned to the regiment sometime in late 1864 or early 1865.[106] Surgeon Nathan Mayer, who had been released from prison shortly after capture in May

1864, did not rejoin the regiment either. Instead, Dr. Mayer took charge of four hospital wards in New Bern and gained prominent notice for the role he took in managing a devastating outbreak of yellow fever. A few members of the 16th Connecticut detailed as clerks or nurses at Mayer's request, joined him at the hospital.[107] Mayer, who also suffered from the illness, won high praise for his management of the epidemic at New Bern, gaining appointment as medical purveyor of the district in December 1864 and thus severing "his connection with the 16th."[108] It was a significant loss to the shrunken regiment.

Lt. Col. John Burnham spent little time with the regiment at Roanoke Island and New Bern. After his second imprisonment, extended furlough, and exchange, he received orders to return to the 16th Connecticut after a short stay at Camp Parole, Maryland. However, by February 1865, perhaps due to the reduced state of the unit, Burnham instead received appointment as chief provost marshal at New Bern, and then in March he joined the staff of Brig. Gen. Edward Harland as acting assistant inspector general.[109]

Although separated from the 16th Connecticut, Burnham remained staunchly loyal to his men, even when offered promotion to colonelcy in the 11th Connecticut in January 1865. Burnham declined without hesitation. Explaining his decision to his mother, he characterized the 11th Connecticut as a unit he could feel no pride in commanding: "The regiment is not only demoralized, but has been taken from the front and scattered about," mainly on "detached duty." "They were taken from the front," he added, "because they deserted so freely to the enemy." And it was not merely a question of poor discipline or mismanagement, something that perhaps could be corrected. It was, Burnham contended, that "the material composing the regiment is evidently of the worst character." After more than two years defending the 16th's name, striving to instill discipline and lead by example, Burnham saw little he could do to salvage the "evil reputation" of another Connecticut regiment. He refused to command a regiment "that cannot be trusted in [the] face of the enemy."[110] Instead, he preferred to "take his chances" with the 16th Connecticut, even if it meant remaining in "service longer than my present term." Hearing that more members of the unit were being exchanged, he wrote, "I would like to see them all together again for a better set of boys were never got together in a regiment."[111] Indeed, the *Hartford Daily Times* reported that Lt. Col. Burnham "declined to accept the colonelcy of the 11th regiment—one account says because he prefers to stay with the boys he helped recruit; another that the 11th is too full of bounty-jumpers to please him."[112]

Later, in March 1865, while still at New Bern, Burnham had the opportunity to judge another Connecticut regiment in combat at the Battle of Wyse Fork near Kinston. Temporarily assigned to the staff of Gen. Harland, Burnham witnessed the sad fate of the 15th Connecticut during the fight. "Col. Upham's regiment suffered a very serious disaster," he wrote his mother, "much worse than the 16th at Antietam."[113] In fact, the regiment endured a fate eerily similar to the 16th at Plymouth when hit hard by attacking Confederates, surrounded, and forced to surrender.[114] Harland, who commanded the First Brigade (the Second included the 15th Connecticut), praised Burnham in his official report of the battle: "To Lieutenant-Colonel Burnham of the Sixteenth Connecticut Volunteers, who was acting assistant inspector-general, I am under especial obligations. During the whole of Tuesday, the 7th instant, he was the only staff officer present, and his services were invaluable."[115] When combat resumed a second day, Burnham wrote of many soldiers performing "nobly" but added "that a few cursed cowards who are sneaking to the rear are spreading all sorts of hobgoblin stories about our being cut to pieces and that."[116]

The war had taken a toll on Burnham's mind and body. Existing private letters reveal a man who was introspective, optimistic and cheerful when the conflict commenced; now he was deeply disheartened. He had demonstrated unquestioned bravery in combat, suffering a wounding and two separate captures. His imprisonment at Macon was harsh, and exposure to malaria at Portsmouth had weakened his robust constitution. The change in him is apparent when he castigated the 11th Connecticut and the federal soldiers at Kinston as "cursed cowards." To be sure, cowardly behavior was heinous to most nineteenth-century Americans, especially volunteers and veterans such as Burnham who had endured the hardships of war. However, his experiences with the 16th at Antietam and Plymouth, where he had witnessed his own men fail and falter, did not allow him to be more charitable in assessing the 11th's performance. He seemed less introspective and more bitterly judgmental than he had been early in the war when he wrote his mother grappling with questions of courage and masculinity. Like the regiment that he defended so fiercely, Burnham had become a shell of himself during those final months of war.

Even after Gen. Joe Johnston's surrender, with the Confederacy no more, the 16th Connecticut was still waiting for orders to go home. Released prisoners continued to return to camp, weakened and susceptible to disease. These survivors were "looking," in the words of Burnham, "very well, but alas, they are but a drop in the bucket to the great number of those whose bones are lying under the sand in dixie." He spoke for many of his comrades, although he could have been speaking of his own prison ordeal, in vowing: "Some body must have a terrible punishment in store for themselves for treating our men with such horrid brutality."[117] Military discipline was nearly nonexistent, the drinking only continued, and the days seemed endless. Bauer was "disgusted with the company" that he had "been obliged to be in, who should set a better example."[118] On May 11, he wrote, "It is too bad to keep us here. The boys are getting very careless; no discipline is thought of not even a roll call."[119] "We look daily," Burnham wrote his mother in May, "for some formal announcement by President Johnson that the war is ended." It was also galling to watch Confederates return freely to their homes in New Bern. Jacob Bauer recorded in his diary one day in May, "Secesh inhabitants arriving daily looking up their deserted houses and property." "The rascals," he added bitterly.[120] By the first week of June, Lt. Col. Burnham was so anxious that he requested permission to go to Raleigh "for the purpose of explaining to the commanding general the condition of the records of this regiment with a view to asking that it may be ordered to Conn. to be mustered out."[121]

Finally, the 16th Connecticut Volunteer Regiment received orders to go home in June 1865. On June 6, the *Courant* predicted, "The 16th C.V. are expected home in about a week or ten days, and the past members of the regiment propose to give them a reception. It is believed that a larger number can be got together to receive the regiment than are now in it. The boys at home want to turn out in uniform and carry guns, if the State authorities will loan them the latter."[122] It did not quite work out that way.

First, it took much longer than a week to ten days for the regiment to arrive home. Lt. Blakeslee later explained, "On June 19th Major Pasco returned from Connecticut, with the necessary muster rolls and papers to enable us to complete the muster out rolls. Then both day and night did the officers work on discharge papers and muster-out rolls."[123] On June 23, 1865, the unit pulled down its camp, turned in its tents and equipment, and prepared to board ships to travel back to Connecticut. Bauer recorded, "Every body is in excellent sprits."[124] On June 24, 1865, at 5 p.m., the remaining members of the unit were formally mustered out of U.S. military service by a captain from the 2nd Massachusetts Heavy Artillery. Blakeslee wrote that a few men remarked, "while standing in line, waiting patiently 'that while it did not take long to enlist, it took a long time to get mustered out.' It proved quite true; for while we enlisted for three years, it was not supposed that it should be out more than three or six months at most; and many of the men enlisted expect to return in a short time, not one of us realizing the hardships and sufferings we must pass through."[125] Finally, on Monday, June 26, 1865, the 16th Connecticut left Morehead City, North Carolina, for New York City. They were due to arrive in Hartford on June 29, 1865.[126] That very same day, Maj. Samuel M. Letcher reported to Governor Buckingham that the 16th Connecticut Infantry "comprising twenty-six (26) commissioned officers and three hundred and fifty (350) enlisted men mustered out of service yesterday and ordered to rendezvous at Hartford."[127] Yet, by the time, the regiment arrived in Hartford, its numbers had been reduced to a mere 130 men.[128]

As family and friends waited in anticipation, the Hartford press encouraged its readers to greet the 16th C. V. and thank them for their "patriotic services."[129] On June 29, the *Courant* announced that the regiment was due to "come up on the half-past nine train this morning" from New York City. Flags should be displayed and "an earnest welcome given the brave boys."[130] However, the regiment arrived early, and the official welcoming ceremony was hastily arranged. The sight of the survivors was a shock: "Many who had seen the regiment leave for the war three years before, and now witnessed the decimated ranks were effected to tears," Blakeslee later recalled. He remembered family members who "watched us eagerly and looked strangely into the ranks, hardly believing that any could be missing. One lady, the wife of an officer, was told for the first time of her husband's death. So great was her grief that friends who accompanied her could hardly get her into a carriage to convey her home."[131] The Governor's Guard, City Guard, and Colt's band duly received them and escorted the soldiers down several city streets to the front of the United States Hotel. There Governor Buckingham greeted and thanked them for their service to the state. State senator Ezra Hall gave a longer, prepared address heralding the 16th Connecticut as "Heroes of many a hard-fought battle and worthy veterans of a redeemed country!" Hall recalled the summer day in 1862 when the 16th Regiment Connecticut Volunteers first left for war: "It was hard to leave your situations, your homes, and those you loved. And a sharper pang would steal along your feelings as you thought the step might take you forever from the dear New England hills and all you held dear." But love of country superseded love of home and family, Hall contended, and "manfully . . . you went out from your homes to camp." He proclaimed, "No braver regiment ever went out from our city or state." Hall also made special mention of the regiment's officers: "You have been led by the honored Col. Beach; and the name of your Lieutenant Colonel, he who would not leave his regiment for the colonelcy of another, he who has been with you in the camp, in the battle, in the prison, on the march until now, than whom there is none better, or braver on all the veteran roll, his name, John H. Burnham, has long been with us a household word." After recounting the "sad day" at Antietam, their unforgettable capture at Plymouth, and their "martyred dead" at Andersonville, Hall declared, "Go bear your honors and your trophies to your homes, and, around your own hearths be as great and good as you have been in war." Hall assured them that the regiment's honored dead would never be forgotten: "History will keep fresh their memories and write their names on more than granite shaft or marble column." And if there were any remaining doubts about the regiment's courage, Hall responded, "Your thinned ranks, your torn colors, give convincing proof of your deeds of bravery."[132]

After breakfast at the Trumbull House and United States Hotel, the regiment marched in another short parade to the armory, again escorted by the City Guard and Colt's band, and stacked arms. Lt. Col. John Burnham rose to bid farewell to his soldiers for the last time. It was an emotional moment for Burnham, who had remained loyal to the regiment despite petty accusations, chaotic combat, humiliating imprisonments, and extended separation from his beloved unit. He made no mention of the failures or frustrations; nor did he spin tales of hero- ism. Instead, he honestly assessed the regiment's war record: "Although a less amount of glory in the field has fallen on our lot than to some others, no regiment from the State has been subjected to so much suffering." At that moment in June, nearly three full years after the regiment's creation, Burnham felt only pride: "Whenever in the future I am asked of what in all my life I am proudest, I shall always answer 'that I belonged to the 16th Connecticut in the Union army.'"[133] Burnham's words were prophetic for nearly all of the regiment's veterans. Indeed, for most Civil War veterans, pride would replace any lingering disillusionment, bitterness, or war weariness. Eventually, all talk of cowards abated, and instead, a celebration of heroes remained.

Themes of martial heroism and self-sacrifice were readily apparent in the newspaper coverage of the regiment's return. The *Courant's* headline read: "Our Brave Veterans," announcing the reception of the 16th and 18th regiment's arrival. The paper stated, "We all—that is all who have put hope and faith in the nation's defenders during the war against treason—rejoice to see our brave veterans come home from the war, delight to do them honor."[134] The paper could only praise the regiment, despite the shockingly low number who marched in the return parade: "Their tidy and soldierly appearance was the subject of general comment."[135] The

Courant closed its story about the regiment's return by recounting its service: "The record of the 16th is a credit to the State and an honor to every man who has shared its fortunes." It faced "hot fire" at Antietam, continued to Fredericksburg, Suffolk, and Plymouth, where many were captured and taken to Andersonville. "Here," the paper concluded, "two hundred men died, the victims of rebel cruelty!"[136]

Ten years after the war ended, in 1875, when Bernard Blakeslee published the only official regimental history of the unit, he had no regrets: "How many around us today do we see who blush and say the greatest mistake they ever made was that they did not go to the war. How many would say as did a prominent man to me the day we returned home; 'I would give fifty thousand dollars to have seen and been through what you have.'"[137]

9

· · ·

Postwar

"They Were Heroes"

The Civil War had ended, and soldiers became civilians once more. Most came home to Hartford County to try to resume their prewar lives and occupations. Even though they clung to many of their prewar ideals, their families and hometown communities had changed, and they had, too. By the turn of the century, veterans were actively commemorating their military service, stressing themes of self-sacrifice, honor, and courage. Because former members of the 16th Connecticut could not claim the conventional mantle of the gallant combat soldier, they sought to construct a different public image— that of the suffering, yet no less heroic, manly volunteer. They wanted to ensure that their military past would be remembered in the best possible light despite the complex reality of that service.

"NOT FORGOTTEN"

In the late summer and early fall of 1865, four members of the 16th C.V., Robert Kellogg, Andrew Spring, Augustus Moesner, and Hiram Buckingham, served as witnesses in the trial of the former commandant of Andersonville, Capt. Henry Wirz.[1] Learning that the besieged captain was imprisoned in the Old Capitol Prison, Kellogg had thoughts of trying to see him. "How the tables have turned in one short year!" Kellogg mused, "*There* he was in his glory, gloating over our sufferings, now he is in a cell, and *we* are 'after him with a sharp stick.'" He predicted, "I guess there is but little doubt that his neck will become intimately acquainted with a piece of rope about six feet long."[2] A few days later, still waiting to give his testimony, he caught a glimpse of Wirz, escorted by guards, entering the courtroom: "All of his bravado gone—no gleam of malicious triumph in his cruel eyes. There he stood between the guard, his knees knocking together, and his whole appearance indicative of the greatest cowardice."[3] Kellogg, apparently a credible witness, provided testimony for both sides. Judge Advocate Norton P.

Chipman later described Kellogg in his published account of the trial as "among the more intelligent witnesses called by the prosecution. His veracity is conceded by the prisoner, who called him for the defense."[4] Kellogg's testimony was mostly descriptive, with little personal commentary. His strongest statement came early in his testimony: "When my regiment went there the men were healthy; after that they gradually sickened, until I remember one morning at roll-call out of my ninety men, there were thirty-two who were not able to stand up when the rebel sergeant came to call the roll." He further related that he saw Captain Wirz frequently, yet "never heard him give any orders" nor "ever saw him perpetuate any acts of cruelty on the men—not to my personal observation."[5]

In October, Kellogg was subpoenaed to return to Washington and provide additional testimony for the defense.[6] He stated that he did not "remember any special case of ill-treatment." "I speak of nothing of that kind in my book," Kellogg contended, "that I recollect now, not of my own personal observation." When pushed about whether he "heard" of any acts of cruelty, he again denied remembering anything in particular. Even so, Kellogg said, Wirz's "character was cruel and brutal, and we all understood that perfectly well. We understood that from hearing his language, which was insulting and profane; and from the general treatment there in the prison. We saw that we were badly treated and miserably provided for; and we naturally supposed that he, as commandant of the prison was, in great degree at least responsible for it; we supposed of course that somebody was responsible for it."[7]

Other soldiers from the 16th who accepted paroles to work outside the prison testified, seemingly without emotion or guilt, about the terrible conditions they witnessed. Spring, who worked in the cookhouse, testified that even though he left soon after the regiment's arrival, "I have seen idiots in the stockade; I have seen men acquaintances of mine, who would go around there not knowing anything at all, and hardly noticing any thing; I have seen men there who were crippled up so that they had scarcely any life in them at all." He insisted that the one day he reentered the prison to see his comrades, he "was intending to help some of them, but after I helped one, I was called from one place to another, and I found that I had more than I could attend to, so I had to leave them entirely." Spring, at least as evidenced by this testimony, showed little remorse for his actions.[8]

German-born Moesner, who was paroled to work as a clerk for Wirz, maintained that he was "only a short time inside the stockade" and testified on behalf of the defense. Moesner was asked about "little boys" being removed from the stockade, and he confirmed that Capt. Wirz ordered forty to fifty boys out of the pen to work as nurses or cooks rather than letting them remain in the prison where they would most likely "get sick and die inside the stockade or they would get spoilt there." Moesner added that Wirz believed "if it was in his power, he would send them to our lines, because it was no use to take boys as prisoners of war." Moesner denied anyone dying of dog bites at Wirz's headquarters, and he described boxes safely arriving at the prison from the North. He pronounced, "I never saw, knew or heard about Captain Wirz shooting, beating, or killing men in any way while I was there; I never saw, knew or heard in any way of Captain Wirz carrying a whip while I was there. He never did."[9] Moesner refuted the contention that rations were ever stopped for the entire camp but did concede that Wirz would occasionally halt rations for a "squad" when someone from that squad had been reported missing. He explained receiving an extra ration for his work, which he sold to Wirz for 80 cents worth of Confederate money. Moesner, like Spring, revealed no regret for his actions at Andersonville. The tone of his testimony seemed unemotional. And despite his statement that he was "not well acquainted with the English language," his statements are clear and easily understood.[10] The testimony of the former 16th soldiers mattered little; a vengeful North had found in the former prison commandant a target for its anger. Wirz was found guilty, sentenced to death, and hanged on November 10, 1865.[11]

Like other Civil War veterans, the members of the 16th returned home to try to begin again. They focused on family and work, many resuming their lives as farmers, artisans, mechanics, and businessmen. Most remained in Connecticut; others sought a fresh start in new states. Jacob Bauer recorded his first day as a full-fledged civilian: "At home once more and free feeling happy."[12] However, happiness could be fleeting, and the postwar years proved anything but free of pain or suffering for the survivors of the regiment.[13] Bauer took a job in Middletown, too far from his home in Kensington to see his family every night. Staying in a boarding house seemed unbearable after the years of forced separation from his wife and daughter. After one week, Bauer determined, "Shall make arrangements to go home every night."[14] It is not clear what he did about his work, but he eventually found employment "selling paper" closer to Kensington, where he resided until his death. Bauer noted his continued attendance at prayer meetings the first few weeks after he returned home, but his diary entries become less informative and less frequent by September 1865, merely recording money paid and owed.[15]

Robert Kellogg briefly worked in the adjutant general's office and the state's pension bureau, but he eventually returned to his prewar employment as a drug store clerk in Norwich. The first day of his new job in early October, he wrote of feeling "so much out of practice and not knowing the prices of the different things."[16] A few weeks passed, interrupted by his return to Washington, D.C., to testify in the Wirz trial. Kellogg began to feel more and more isolated and alone in the new city: "I haven't a single 'chum' in Norwich—they're all scattered—some in one place & some in another all fight their way through the world—as we all must."[17] When a local deacon died, Kellogg was numb, unable to feel the "solemnity of the occasion. Death seems to have lost its solemnity in me since 'Andersonville.'"[18] He bemoaned the lack of letters from home or friends, worrying that he had been forgotten: "Well, if my friends at home forget me, I must make new friends here—but pshaw! I know I am not forgotten!"[19] Kellogg did receive "papers" from comrade and close friend Johnny Clapp, "my dearest & truest friend on earth whom I love more than I would a brother."[20] Soon, he met Amelia Clark Gallup in Norwich, and the two married on October 6, 1868, and began a family. The Kelloggs moved briefly to New Hampshire but then returned to Connecticut to reside in Manchester, where Robert was employed in the office of the Cheney Brothers and served as a member of the Connecticut legislature. He was also active in the Republican Town Committee. By 1881, the Kelloggs had left Connecticut for Ohio, settling in Delaware County, where Robert sold life insurance.[21] Kellogg kept in close correspondence with his comrades from the 16th Connecticut, including Ira Forbes and George Q. Whitney. Forbes once described Kellogg as "one of the most respected members of the Sixteenth Regiment and universally popular in the Command."[22]

Oliver Gates remained in New London, working as a grocer before resuming his prewar occupation as a mason. In 1867, he and his wife Emariah had another child, Charles Robert. But in December 1874, tragedy struck again when typhoid claimed Emariah's life.[23] Gates married Abbie J. Fowler (age twenty-six) on April 26, 1876. In 1897, while at work at a construction site erecting a building for the New London Gas & Electric Company, Gates almost severed his left arm when his clothes became entangled in a piece of machinery. Unable to do manual labor, he lived for the next ten years mainly off his modest veteran's pension provided by the U.S. government for the lingering effects of rheumatism and the "disease of the eyes" he contracted while imprisoned at Andersonville.[24] When Gates died, his widow Abbie, with no children of her own, would claim that he left her with nothing to support her, just the interest from a small savings account.[25]

John B. Cuzner married Ellen Van Dorn three weeks after he returned home to Connecticut on July 8, 1865.[26] The couple's marriage lasted forty-seven years; Ellen died in 1912 at the age of sixty-six, and John lived until just one month shy of his 83rd birthday. Cuzner returned to work as a machinist, employed at the Colt's factory in Hartford and the Wheeler and Wilson's factory in Bridgeport, as well as creating his own "light metallic articles," including a nutcracker and a pocket lamp.[27]

Ira Forbes graduated Yale University in 1870, then spent a year at the Yale Theological Seminary. Rather than pursuing a life in the cloth, he turned to teaching and, later, journalism. It is not entirely clear why; his obituary states simply that his "mind took a fancy to newspaper work."[28] He married Sarah Rhodes Short on July 18, 1872, and they settled in Hartford. Forbes worked as a reporter at the *Springfield Union* from 1872 to 1874 and was telegraph editor for the *Hartford Evening Post* until October 1890. He assumed for several years the post of Hartford correspondent for the *New York Times,* and he wrote for the *Aetna,* a publication issued by Aetna Life Insurance Company. By the turn of the century, Forbes was a staff writer for the *Hartford Daily Times.*[29]

Richard Henry Lee resettled in Granby, married Mary Elizabeth Holcomb in 1866, and had two daughters. His health broken from the war, he set out westward to start afresh. His wife recalled, "I went to Minnesota because of my husband's poor health. We were entire strangers when we went to St. Paul. My own health was feeble, consequently we remained strangers."[30] The Lees were residing in Lansing, Iowa, in 1876, when Henry, only thirty-five years old, succumbed to his multiple ailments. The official cause of death was "Consumption."[31] He was buried in Granby, and although a public plea was made that his name be added to the Civil War monument, "as he had been a faithful soldier, contracted disease in rebel prisons and had recently died from its effects," it never was.[32]

George Robbins married and resided with his parents in Plainville, finding employment as a bookkeeper. The Robbins eventually moved to Waterbury, where George worked in a "clock shop" and later dabbled in real estate and insurance.[33] Robbins's wartime experiences remained heavy on his mind, and he wrote an unpublished memoir in 1918. He died one year later at the age of seventy-four.

Frank W. Cheney, the regiment's beloved first lieutenant colonel, remained closely affiliated with the 16th Connecticut until his death in 1909. After his discharge in December 1862, he returned home to Manchester, continued in his family's lucrative silk business, and expanded into the state's burgeoning insurance industry after the war. In November 1863, he married Mary Bushnell, the daughter of famed Congregational minister and theologian Horace Bushnell, and the couple had twelve children. An active Republican, Cheney was a leading figure in the state's veteran commemoration activities, serving as life president of the Sixteen Regiment Association, as well as president of the Army and Navy Club of Connecticut. He was a prominent member of the state's Andersonville Commission, which constructed the monument there. He stood as perhaps the most popular of all the members of the unit, despite that his time with the regiment was so short. Forbes's biographical sketch of Cheney, written for Whitney's history of the regiment, praised him for his "heroism and leadership" at Antietam and his postwar "example of citizenship and patriotism."[34] When the Spanish American War erupted in 1898, Cheney's son Ward, a twenty-three-year-old Yale graduate, had "the war fever on" and sought to follow two of his brothers who had enlisted as volunteers in local companies. Cheney wrote Gen. Joseph R. Hawley, "I hesitate about putting so many valuable eggs in one basket. Can you suggest any better way of his going into the service of his country than as a common soldier? This is a straightforward and honorable way I know." Cheney added, "I know all about the trials of a young officer without previous training being forced to assume too heavy responsibilities all at once."[35] Like most members of the 16th, Cheney's military service changed him. He regularly attended postwar regimental reunions, and the men rewarded him on his 76th birthday with a Tiffany silver cup etched with the image of Burnside's bridge. When he died on May 26, 1909, the remaining few survivors of the regiment came to pay their last respects to their most admired leader. One of Cheney's grandchildren recounted, "On the day of my grandfather's funeral, one of his comrades who had previously been reluctant to give up his piece of the flag cut his piece in half and pinned one-half to grandfather's coat and that was buried with him."[36]

Frank Beach, the regiment's controversial colonel, continued in the military until 1871, when he retired from active service "for disability contracted in the line of duty."[37] He died in February 1873 at the age of thirty-eight in New York City. His pallbearers included John Burnham, Dr. Nathan Meyer, and Frank Cheney. His body was moved to Arlington National Cemetery in 1903.[38] By 1908, Ira Forbes could only commend Beach: "The name of Colonel Francis Beach, who was second in command at Plymouth is held in the most loyal regard by the old members of the Sixteenth Connecticut."[39] In an unpublished manuscript about the battle of Plymouth, Forbes added that Beach was a "man of polished intellect, acute judgment, and unfailing heroism" yet "a strict disciplinarian."[40]

There was a marked coolness between Joseph Barnum and his former comrades. In January 1866, Barnum initially sought an appointment in the regular army, but he later settled for a position in the Buckingham Rifles and Hartford Light Guard.[41] Ira Forbes praised him for infusing a "military spirit" into the Washington Commandory Knights-Templar. Barnum also founded and edited the *Hartford Sunday Journal,* but he seemed to keep his wartime memories separate from his journalism career.[42] A small clue concerning Barnum's lasting estrangement from his comrades can be found in a letter Cheney sent to Whitney upon hearing the news of Barnum's death in 1902. "It must be a happy relief," Cheney wrote, "to Joe Barnum and his family to have him get to the end of his troubles and safely buried. There can be no regrets for the present, though many for the past." Cheney planned to attend the funeral and encouraged Whitney to send flowers "as usual, that it may be done decently and in order." "I am sorry," Cheney added, "that I can't shed any tears or express more feelings upon this occasion."[43]

Others pursued their separate lives but kept their ties to the regiment until their deaths. Austin Thompson settled back in Bristol, where he and Electra married and had two children. Electra died in 1880, but Austin never remarried. He worked as carriage maker and, as noted by Whitney, "never held political office attending to business closely." Thompson was commander of the local Grand Army of the Republic post named after his younger brother, Gilbert, who also served in the regiment. Harrison Woodford married twice, had three children, and served as the state legislator from his hometown of Avon. Soon after the war, William Relyea and his wife Celia moved with their three children to New Britain, where he continued working in the tobacco business. He became "Historian of the regiment" and a familiar presence at regimental reunions. He was an "influential citizen" as New Britain's Water and Street commissioner and member of the Board of Relief. He died in 1918.[44]

"NOT BE UNMINDFUL"

George Whitney, who had been an "expert machinist" before the war, came back to his native Hartford to work as a contractor at Pratt and Whitney. Whitney would outlive nearly all of his comrades in the 16th C.V., and he would spend considerable time tracking those comrades down. Assisted by Ira Forbes, Whitney set out sometime in the postwar years to make a record of every single member of the regiment and to create an individual biography of each, no matter how short or insignificant his term of service was. Whitney never finished, but he left behind a treasure trove of materials on his beloved regiment. He worked on it continually, updating files as he discovered new information and comrades moved or, increasingly, died. As he explained in a letter to the secretary of war: "I am doing what I can in my limited time to get as good a record of every man as possible, and enclose a blank that will give some idea of the work being done."[45] Most members of the unit have at least one page devoted to them, which includes the basic biographical information found in the Adjutant General Office records, although there are many gaps. Some pages contain only a soldier's name and no other information. In a 1906 newspaper article in the *Connecticut Courant*, Forbes commented, "Major Whitney is the secretary of the regiment and has performed valuable work in the accumulation and preservation of records relating to the members." Ignoring the already published history of the 16th by Bernard Blakeslee, and neglecting to mention his own role in Whitney's efforts, Forbes added, "These records will be of much importance when the history of the regiment is written."[46]

Mixed in the Whitney papers are the individual stories of soldiers otherwise lost to history. Most of these men did not do anything particularly noteworthy or historic. The veterans, old men by the time Whitney tracked them down, often reflected candidly and without romanticizing the war and their service. Walter E. Smith, who had enlisted as a nineteen year old in Company G, wrote Whitney in 1905: "It was a couple of years or so after my discharge before I was good for much." Smith was released from prison suffering from scurvy, dropsy, and varicose veins in both legs; he was not yet twenty-three. His service had also included a wounding at Antietam where he lost several teeth, a bout with typhoid fever, and an accident with an ambulance.[47]

Whitney was especially intent on establishing his comrades' vital records, the kind of information that genealogists track today. Sometimes he found that his subjects did not know the most basic information about themselves. William Wakefield, former sergeant in Company I, was not sure of his own age and was eager to find it out because he might increase his pension if he could prove that he had reached the age of seventy-five. He asked Whitney for help to confirm his actual birth date. "It seems," he wrote Whitney, "that I must have forgotten my age, for I thought my correct age does not tally with my age in my enlistment papers."[48]

Frank Cheney also assisted Whitney in tracing sick and dead comrades, even covering funeral costs as well as helping obtain pensions. It was important to both men to attend funerals as representatives of the regiment.[49] Cheney wrote Whitney, "We must keep on and not be unmindful of our old comrades when they pass away and go when we can to any funeral."[50] He praised Whitney, "You are very good in keeping track of the old fellows, and I always want to know about them when they are in trouble."[51] Cheney even sought ways to supplement government pensions with money out of his own pocket. "I wish," he wrote Whitney, "they could all be cared for by the Government, but if they cannot be, we must try to do for them what we can ourselves."[52]

Family members also sought help directly from Whitney and Cheney. William B. Hancock's sister wrote Whitney explaining that her brother had come home from the war "more dead than alive, a living skeleton, could not read or write, did not know his own name. Oh! Such wicked treatment! He went away a strong young man. He came home a perfect [w]reck broken in body and mind." She sought Whitney's help to gain an increase in his monthly pension.[53] In one case, soldier James Bannon's widow contacted Cheney's widow, asking for help to find a job: "I need the work very much. I go out by day, I wish you would ask some of your friends I have very good references. If you wish me to call on you I would be pleasend [sic], because I need the work very much."[54] Mary Bushnell Cheney asked Whitney about the woman, saying she did not see how she could help Mrs. Bannon since she lived in Hartford, "but if she is deserving and the wife of a Sixteenth Regiment man there is every reason why I should do what I can for her."[55]

Many veterans, North and South, were intent on preserving the history of their unit's military service. However, one wonders what drove Whitney to accumulate such a massive amount of material, since he never published anything. His own service with the regiment seems to have been unremarkable, although he did survive imprisonment. In September 1906, he wrote Cheney after a recent reunion to tell him about attendance and the association's finances. He thanked Cheney for all he did for him and his comrades, adding, "I get also many good words from the members in many ways that make me think they are more than satisfied with what is done for them by both and either of us and becoming united as ever before." Whitney—who often wrote the pensions office for his comrades, made personal visits, attended funerals, and sent flowers—told Cheney he did not expect the men to "know all that I do." "The main thing to me," he wrote, "is that they should be satisfied and pleased with what they know is done."[56] In 1906, the *Courant* praised him: "Major George Q. Whitney, the regimental secretary of the Sixteenth, has been indefatigable in keeping the records of the regiment and has rendered much service in making up the roll of the present Andersonville survivors in the command."[57]

Whitney clearly never intended his work to be a typical regimental history. He included personal details of a kind rarely found in unit histories, especially those penned by participants. Whitney, who had been active in commemorating and celebrating the 16th C.V., also seemed to want to hear and tell the "truth," even when it was painful, contradictory, or unpleasant. In describing Alvin P. Cole, for instance, he wrote, "He inherited a taste for liquor from his Father (who was Alvin Cole) and struggled against it all his life, but it many times got the best of him." Whitney added, "He was well liked by his neighbors and townsmen and was a fine workman at anything he undertook."[58] Even when dealing with the difficult topic of desertion, Whitney appeared to be sympathetic. He occasionally used humor, too. For comrade William Perry Amadon, a sergeant in Company I, next to the word "Deserted," Whitney wrote, "Not much."[59] For Alpheus Alanson Rockwell, formerly a private in Company B, Whitney prepared two separate records. In one, on a line next to word "Deserted," Whitney also wrote, "not much." However, Rockwell actually was discharged for disability in March 1863 after suffering severely frozen feet at Falmouth while guarding a quartermaster tent during a snow storm.[60] Afflicted with rheumatism, Rockwell was unable to walk properly and was in dire financial straits by the time Whitney communicated with him. After Whitney found out what had actually happened to him, he made a second record explaining Rockwell's fate. (Even so, he kept both records in his files.)[61] Rockwell's daughter thanked Whitney for the interest he took in her father, which included trying to help him increase his modest pension. She also recalled attending a recent regimental reunion where many attendees "seemed to be quite feeble but could use their feet and hands to get around easily which I thought was something they ought to be very thankfull [sic] for." Her father was sometimes reduced to crawling.[62] Rockwell wrote Whitney in 1905, thanking his comrade for all he had done for him, and confessing, "If I could have my legs back [the way] they were before the war they could have the pension."[63]

Whitney was not shy about openly challenging what he deemed to be obvious fabrications about individual soldiers. John L. Hart had moved to Minnesota after the war, and upon his death was hailed as a "Pioneer" and "Civil War Veteran" who "had some very thrilling experiences serving in the Army of the Potomac." His obituary recounted, "On one occasion he escaped from his captors, disrobed, swam the Roanoke river and wandered through the woods and underbrush the rest of the night in his negligee till rescued by comrades from a friendly boat of the Sixth Connecticut Co."[64] Indeed, Hart's widow Mary proudly informed Whitney, "I heard him tell of his capture and escape when he first came home from the army and many times since, and always the same that he was captured and started with the rest for Andersonville prison from Plymouth, N.C. but managed to drop out between the guards and lay in hiding until all had passed by then took to the woods and river as stated in the paper." She added that her husband had "always been a member of the G.A.R. and was very devoted to the cause. For many years he received notice of the annual reunion of the 16th Conn. and often expressed a wish that he might be with them on these occasions."[65] Whitney wanted to set the record straight. According to him, Hart was detached from his company, E, as a brigade blacksmith in November 1862 and later was a teamster with the ammunition train until mustered out with the regiment in 1865. Hart was not with the regiment at Plymouth; nor was he with Company H at Roanoke Island. "This is verified by members of his company," Whitney judged, "his story" "of capture and escape being a myth."[66]

Whitney also solved lingering mysteries for families who had long wondered and worried what had happened to their beloved soldiers. Lewis M. Holcomb's relatives heard nothing about where he died after he returned to the regiment in May 1865 or where he was buried. In 1919, a cousin, Florence J. Tryon, wrote Whitney asking if he had any information on Holcomb. She did know he had died as a "result of the hardships endured in Andersonville." "I am anxious to place a memorial to his memory," she explained, "for it seems a dreadful thing for him to lie in an unmarked grave." She was also "anxious to place a monument to his sacrifice."[67] Born in 1860, she never knew her cousin but had heard stories about Lewis from her mother, and she was touched by Whitney's efforts to help her and memorialize the regiment. When Whitney sent her a copy of the booklet commemorating the dedication of the monument known as "Andersonville Boy," Tryon wrote, "I feel honored to receive it, and to have had a correspondence with one who has borne such a share in the war, and in paying tribute to those who fully deserved the name of martyr."[68] She eventually learned that Holcomb was buried in the National Cemetery in Alexandria, Virginia, "under a large maple tree, not far from the main entrance." She was thrilled to have the knowledge and told Whitney that if not for him, "I might never had received it." She decided that it was "best to let Lewis rest where he is, in the care of the government for which he gave his life."[69] Tryon contacted several of Holcomb's comrades and searched records, seeking to discover how her cousin spent his final months and how he actually died. "It really seems as if everything," she once wrote, "had conspired to consign him to oblivion." She was, though, "so thankful" to Whitney for his "share in helping to find his records."[70] Tryon also encouraged Whitney to write his own history of the 16th: "A worthy history of the regiment would be a noble tribute to the story of Connecticut in the Civil War. Personally, I feel as if I should like to follow them every step of the way from their enlistment to their mustering out."[71]

Not everyone, though, wanted reminders of their service. Pvt. Jasper H. Bidwell, who had enlisted at the age of nineteen in Company E, was hurt slightly in the shoulder at Antietam. He apparently suffered more while assisting the wounded off the field, including his own captain Charles Babcock, to a makeshift hospital during the battle. His back severely strained, he stayed with a Virginia family to recover and eventually transferred to a convalescent camp in Alexandria. This camp, described as "ill kept" and "very lousy," was in stark contrast to the comfortable conditions he had found at the Confederate private home. Bidwell soon received his discharge from service, but, according to George Q. Whitney, "the treatment at this camp so embittered him that for years (forty years or more) he would have nothing to do with his regiment or anything military." In 1907, attempts were made to reestablish contact with Bidwell and invite him to a regimental reunion, but Bidwell had an accident and never attended. He died in 1915.[72] James R. Bradley, who had been a private in Company C, claimed to have endured imprisonment longer than most, remaining at Andersonville more than a year due to illness. He was not formally released until May 28, 1865. When he finally returned to Connecticut, he married twice, had three children, and became a sewing machine salesman. But in the last few years of his life, he suffered from "nervous prostration being confined to his room." Bradley died at the age of sixty-three. Whitney had trouble tracking him down and eventually gained information from Bradley's wife, perhaps after his death. He explained, "Bradley's identity with the Regiment was lost until a short time before his death, having never attended a reunion or meeting with the Ex-Prisoners association being very reticent and retiring in his ways."[73]

Forbes was essential in assisting Whitney in his endeavors, writing some seven hundred lengthy narratives to adjoin forms Whitney created and adding his own detective work in uncovering family information, stories from the war, and postwar details.[74] He contacted family members and others directly, usually by mail. Sometimes, he came up empty.[75] Forbes also offered his own commentary

regarding an individual's worthiness as a soldier, often making sweeping statements about his character. Sometimes he provided anecdotes to support these
claims; other times, he simply stated his assessments as known fact.[76]

Forbes, who had been the color bearer, was now a prolific journalist, and he
clearly wanted to ensure that neither he nor his comrades would ever be forgotten. And he wanted "his" version of their story remembered. He highlighted
amusing stories or significant accomplishments, but sometimes he struggled to
find something noteworthy to say. For one entry, he wrote, "Horace H. Forbes
had an uneventful career through the war." This Forbes, apparently no relation,
had headed west after the war, and Ira Forbes lost track of him. "Much time has
been spent in ascertaining the time and place of his death but without success."[77]

Forbes's work for Whitney was exceptionally time consuming. However, he
clearly took great satisfaction in it.[78] He determined, "The information that has
been secured is of much importance, and will give the future historian of the
Sixteenth facts of boundless interest for use."[79] At one point, he claimed to have
authored "more than 175 personal sketches of Field, Staff and line officers and
of the men" and said that he had "written a long ways beyond what allowance
he [Whitney] had in hand for the work, $35, making it a labor of love in its way."
Forbes wanted to continue with the sketches, for he believed "it is a splendid idea
of Whitney's." And if he had the time to do it, he would do it "credibly."[80] However, as he continued to compose more and more sketches for Whitney, Forbes
began to worry about whether all of his hard work was being appreciated. He
was no less pleased with his results: "Some of the stories" he declared, "giving
the Experiences in prison, and the Escapes, have been more exciting than fiction."[81] When he delivered a batch of papers to Whitney one day in July 1906, he
sensed Whitney's reception of him was rather cool.[82] Forbes met personally with
Cheney about a week later, and afterward, he seemed momentarily mollified that
at least his former colonel recognized his accomplishments: "The sketches of
Sixteenth Regiment men, which I have been preparing for a number of months
met with his approval and the work will be taken up again as I have opportunity.
My visit was extremely satisfactory."[83] However, Whitney was becoming more
and more concerned with Forbes's version of their prison experience. While he
praised Forbes for "faithfully" doing "a lot of work," in a letter to Cheney, Whitney
declared, "I am perfectly satisfied that he prefers to tell an imaginary story than
to telling the truth."[84] Forbes grew anxious that his comrades did not appropriately appreciate his efforts in collecting biographical information and writing

historical sketches, and he continued to feel that he had not been sufficiently compensated monetarily.

Even many years after the war had ended, the experience remained the defining event of their lives for most members of the regiment, as for the majority of Civil War veterans. Still, they did not remember everything. Former 1st Sgt. Samuel Fenn (Co. C), when asked to provide his biographical information in 1906, admitted to Forbes that he had no memory of him: "The name Ira E. Forbes in connection with the Sixteenth Connecticut volunteers sounds quite familiar & still I am unable to recall your identity. The sixty-seven year old Fenn quickly added, "However, reference to my regimental history assures me you were O.K."[85]

"THESE RELICS"

Memories of the regiment's history had already begun to shift and alter within its members' lifetime. George Whitney, Ira Forbes, Bernard Blakeslee, and Robert Kellogg, among others, deliberately set out to configure their painful and troublesome past as something more positive and worth preserving. Some, like Forbes and Kellogg, emphasized their regiment's bravery and unity; Whitney and Blakeslee's version were more qualified. Yet, each of these survivors sought to maintain their regimental identity and kept close correspondence with each other, recalling their three-year service. Like other Civil War veterans, members of the 16th took increasing pride in simply surviving the war. They spoke rarely about race or the end of slavery. But these Connecticut men, haunted by the helpless suffering they endured and the many dead they left buried in Georgia, still wanted to give deeper meaning to their torment and leave no doubt that their difficult ordeal had been for a larger moral purpose: saving the Union.[86]

This postwar recasting of the regiment's "bad luck" took several forms. Antietam, Plymouth, and Andersonville were merged in public memory to create a new redemption narrative that emphasized the 16th Connecticut's courageous suffering and underplayed or entirely silenced any questions regarding their battlefield performance, failed leadership, commitment to the war, racial attitudes, or other unsettling concerns about their service. Former corporal Bernard Blakeslee began the process by authoring the only complete published history of the unit in 1875. He sought to create a "permanent record" of his regiment and offer a "sad memorial" to those who had died in battle and prison.[87] He was not exempt from seeking to defend the unit's reputation. Recounting the unit's August 1862 mustering in, for example, he stated, "It was almost entirely made up of men in the County, and of excellent material, some of the oldest and best families were represented in its ranks; and comprised many of the finest young men whom the commonwealth ever sent to uphold its honor in the field." Blakeslee added, "Many of the men were accustomed to all the refinements of wealth and all of them had been reared in abundance."[88] Yet the actual rosters, listing modest farmers, mechanics, and artisans, failed to support this statement.[89] He also wrote bluntly about the wanton killing of African Americans at Plymouth.

It would be Plymouth and the story of the regiment's colors that took on new and dramatic meaning in the postwar period. As described above, just before their capture, Lt. Col. Burnham ordered the unit's color guards to tear the flags into shreds and distribute the pieces to members. Hastily burying the flagstaffs in the ground, men hid pieces of flag in their clothes.[90] Robert Kellogg later claimed that it was he who decreed that the colors had to be saved, but it was Burnham who ordered the flags torn and distributed among the men.

> Seeing no hope of escape and believing that the next charge would be the last, the Sergeant Major directed that in order to save our colors from capture they should be stripped from their staffs, which was immediately done. Shouting to Col. Burnham, who, with Adjutant Clapp, was standing in a somewhat sheltered position some rods to the right, "What shall we do with the colors?" he replied "Send them to me." With great bravery, Color Corporal Ira A. Forbes of Co. A. volunteered to carry the colors to Colonel Burnham, which he safely accomplished under heavy fire. The staffs were rammed down a hole under the breast works.[91]

"The history of the Sixteenth's colors," Kellogg continued, "is well known in Connecticut. Torn into shreds, the pieces of the flag were distributed among our men, carefully secreted by them, and sacredly preserved by them through all the hardships of imprisonment." Norman L. Hope counted "285 sacred pieces" of the original flag "gathered together" after the war to create a new banner, designed by Tiffany Company of New York.[92]

Unfurled on Battle Flag Day on September 17, 1879, according to Kellogg, "no color received such a greeting as this restored flag of the old Sixteenth."[93] Hartford public schools were cancelled on Battle Flag Day to allow children to "see the celebration and enjoy the day." The Cheney brothers were among the private donors who contributed $100 to help defray the costs for the celebration.[94] Burnham was chosen as the assistant marshal representing the 16th Connecticut. A specially selected committee of women assisted in preparing the flags and reported on the condition of all the colors for each regiment.[95] Civil War veterans from across the state congregated in Hartford to unfurl their old banners and march in a parade to celebrate their military service. The *Hartford Courant* reported that the "city looked handsome, the day was perfection." An estimated ten thousand veterans, "boys" again for that single day, marched by a large crowd of onlookers, bearing their old flags, some torn and faded, some in rags.[96] The flag's complete inscription reads:

> The device of this flag is composed entirely from remnants of old colors of the 16th Regiment Connecticut Volunteers. The colors were torn into shreds by the officers and men and concealed upon their person in order to save them from the enemy at the Battle of Plymouth, N.C. April 20th, 1864, where together with the whole Union force at the post, after three days of fighting, the regiment was compelled to surrender. Many of the men bearing these relics were taken to southern prisons where, under untold privations, they still sacredly watched over and kept their trusts, successfully returning them to their native state.[97]

Today the flag remains on display behind glass in the Connecticut State House. "We old boys still love to look at it and revere it," Jacob Bauer wrote in 1915.[98]

Ira Forbes noted that even after the new flag was complete, "a few pieces of the old colors" remained. Frank Cheney took some of these scraps, put them into lockets, and presented them to George Q. Whitney, George E. Denison, Norman L. Hope, Robert H. Kellogg, William H. Lockwood and Timothy B. Robinson and Forbes. "They are valued," Forbes wrote, "as the most precious tokens."[99] Whitney thanked Cheney for the "gift that I prize more as coming from you, than from any other person living."[100]

This inspiring flag-saving story helped to sustain and spread the heroic image of the unit, despite their uneven service. The tale would be repeated by veterans and appear in many postwar publications.[101] Mary Livermore's detailed version of the story appeared in her memoir, included her stating, "All through the terrible days of their imprisonment the little patches of the old flag were carefully guarded and preserved by those to whom they were intrusted."[102] In an 1894 biography of war governor William A. Buckingham, Samuel G. Buckingham described how the 16th Connecticut was "hurried into the field of Antietam almost as soon as they received their arms, where they maintained their position and behaved themselves like veterans." Buckingham continued, "This was the most unfortunate regiment that left the State, being taken prisoners within a year after (all but one company), in North Carolina, and sent to Andersonville, where they patiently endured for another year more than the hardships of scores of ordinary campaigns, and were subjected to tortures which only fiends could inflict." "A touching sequel," Buckingham wrote, "to their story was, that when captured they tore their blue State flag into scraps to be distributed among the men and concealed about their persons." Years later these scraps were collected to form a "blue shield, not bigger than your hand, made up of the bits of the State flag distributed when they were captured, and preserved like holy relics through humiliation, torture and *all but the anguish of crucifixion*." Rev. Samuel Buckingham, brother of the war governor and a doctor of divinity, made the metaphor plain in recounting the alleged reaction of onlookers: "And when these veterans came marching by, the shouts that greeted them, expressive of mingled pity and praise, as this strange symbol of heroism and suffering came to be understood, were enough to make a hero of anybody, and a martyr too!"[103] Survivors were being compared to Christ and celebrated as martyrs for the Union, a cause many of them questioned when they were actually in uniform.

An account published by a southerner in the 1890s added yet another dimension, and a decidedly reconciliatory tone, to the dramatic story. Frank P. O'Brien, an Alabama artilleryman who fought at Plymouth, stated in an 1893 *Blue and Gray* article that one of his comrades snatched a flag from the hands of the color corporal. O'Brien recalled, "The brave fellow begged for possession of his colors. It proved to be the battle-flag of the 16th Connecticut, and when this was denied him, he asked that a piece be given him as a memento." The captor, Pvt. G. M. "Mortie" Williams, cut out a corner from the bottom of the flag and gave it to the color bearer. Years later, O'Brien claimed to have met John Burnham (whom he called "major,") in July 1884 in New York City's Union Square Hotel, but this was four years after Burnham had entered the Hartford Asylum for the Insane and one year after his death. In this alleged meeting, Burnham learned the identity of O'Brien and exclaimed, "O'Brien, where is my flag? I would give a thousand dollars to get it back. Do you know what was done with it?" O'Brien informed Burnham that the flag was in still in the possession of Mortie Williams, and after several more meetings between the two men, O'Brien promised to recover the lost flag. In 1888, O'Brien claimed that the flag was discovered and returned to the state of Connecticut. He included an excerpt from the *Hartford Times*, asserting that this was not, however, the regiment's battle flag, but instead one of its guidons, probably presented by the Hartford City Guards. The paper concluded, "Although this is not a battle-flag, the good feeling of the Alabama veterans in returning it is as greatly appreciated by the 16th as if it were a flag which had been torn by shot and shell in the rage of battle. It is the fraternal feeling, not the flag alone, which is appreciated." O'Brien ended the piece by praising "old soldiers who have braved the dangers of the battlefield" and who reunited to "talk calmly and dispassionately of the great Lost Cause; regretfully, too, maybe, but laying aside all resentment, knowing themselves brothers of a common nation, and uniting in the belief that 'whatever is, is right.'"[104] The *New York Times* reported the story on September 17, 1887, acknowledging that even though the returned flag was merely an "extra guidon," "that does not effect the value of the gift or the lofty feeling with which it has been made. It is an acknowledgment of the worth of the soldier fighting his battle bravely and of the man fighting for his country and as such the regiment gratefully accepts it." The spirit of reconciliation was strong among the survivors in 1887. They thanked the Alabamians for their "high-hearted action, and for the good and generous feeling which dictated it." The statement went further: "We do not seek to obliterate or forget the memory of the civil war, for they teach us to estimate the valor and devotion of our Southern brethren, even as the present peace exhibits their acceptance of the issue, the generosity of their impulses, and the courtesy of their action."[105] The emphasis, at least at this juncture, was on remembering the "valor and devotion" of their former enemy rather than the war's brutality or the divisiveness of slavery.[106]

The 16th Connecticut's flag story was sacrosanct. In 1906, former Pvt. Wallace Fowler wrote Whitney, claiming that it was he, not Sgt. Francis Latimer, who saved the national colors at Plymouth. Whitney wrote Kellogg, "The statement seems to me outrageous and I want to drive a nail in it right now, so I shall bring the matter up at Reunion if possible." Whitney mentioned that he went to see Forbes to ask him about it but that Forbes "gets so nervous in talking about it, that I am afraid of serious results if I try to discuss it with him."[107]

The unfurling of the newly constructed flag also allowed for acknowledgment of the regiment's battle honors. Since the 16th Connecticut's only major combat experience occurred at Antietam, that battle became the focal point for their postwar commemorative activities. Benjamin C. Ray, a former member, published a collection of sketches on every Connecticut regiment during the war to commemorate "Flag Day." When he came to his own regiment, he recounted the increasingly familiar story of Antietam: "Without having time allowed to learn even the rudiments of military science (many of its members having never loaded a gun), it was hurled forward, and took an active part in the battle of Antietam." Ray, who was injured and captured at Antietam, was quick to add, "The men preserved a coolness and displayed a courage highly creditable as was sufficiently well attested by the severe loss sustained." Ray quoted Beach's official report from Antietam—"Col. Beach, in his report dated Sept 19, 1862, remarks that 'the enemy commenced shelling us at daylight, and we were kept under a heavy artillery fire at intervals during the day, until about five o'clock, when we were brought against the extreme right of the Rebel infantry"—but Ray added the phrase, "*where the battle raged with great fury.*" Ray further appended to Beach's succinct summary of the facts: "That the Sixteenth did nobly is the verdict of all who witnessed its heroism on the battlefield on Antietam."[108]

In June 1891, regimental survivors returned to Antietam for another commemorative service. They went not to the fields of battle but instead to a church where so many of them had suffered and some had died. The German Reformed Church had served as a makeshift hospital to hundreds of the wounded in the days and weeks after the bloody battle. Whitney, who had been wounded at Antietam, was one of those who vividly remembered the church, and he wanted to mark the spot permanently by presenting the church with specially designed stained glass windows. Created in Utica, New York, and costing some $400, the windows together measure twenty-five feet high and ten feet wide. Whitney helped to design the images, which featured the regiment's famed reconstructed flag, the badge of the IX Corps, and the words "Peace on Earth, Good Will to Men," as well as "In Memory of the Sixteenth Regiment, Connecticut Volunteers." Merged in one physical space were the themes of Christian sacrifice, martial valor, and postwar reunion. The windows were presented in a special ceremony on Sunday, June 14, 1891. Today, they remain in the church, now the Christ Reformed Church of the United Church of Christ, and they were recently restored and rededicated.[109]

The reconfigured postwar tale of the inexperienced but ultimately courageous 16th Connecticut at Antietam appeared repeatedly in printed histories, personal reminiscences, newspapers, and public addresses. In 1869, the *Catalogue of Con-*

necticut Volunteer Organizations used familiar language to describe the regiment's first battle experience: "Without having time allowed to learn even the rudiments of military science, it was hurried forward and was in regimental line for the first time on the battlefield of Antietam." The *Catalogue* declared, "That the Sixteenth did nobly, is the verdict of all who witnessed its heroism on the battlefield of Antietam."[110] In 1900, W. J. Shafer, the historian of the U.S. Army and Navy Historical Association, stated as "facts" that the 16th Connecticut was "hurried to the front without having time allowed to learn even the rudiments of military science and was in regimental line for the first time in the battle of Antietam, Maryland, September 17, 1862, where it displayed wonderful courage, losing no less than 185 officers and men in killed, wounded and missing."[111] George Robbins wrote in his 1918 unpublished recollections: "As a green regiment, deficient of all but the rudiments of military training, freshly arrived after an almost constant journey since leaving Connecticut on the 29th of August, we had no idea what we would be called upon to participate in this fearful struggle, so we lay around, idle spectators, but watching intently the progress of the conflict as it surged back and forth." He stressed, "I do not undervalue the courage and willingness of the men of the 16th. Connecticut Infantry under these most trying conditions." Robbins was convinced, like many of his comrades, that someone had "blundered" in forcing untrained troops into such precarious circumstances.[112] Decades after the war had ended, the heroic yet tragic narrative of the "Brave Sixteenth" at Antietam had been carefully fashioned and publicly accepted. Few people, inside or outside the regiment, were willing to question or even consider challenging that celebratory image.[113]

As Civil War veteran activities grew more popular during the 1880s and 1890s, surviving members of the regiment were eager to participate. Some members of the 16th even wanted to reclaim the military identity that they had resisted during their actual service. Now old, graying civilians in peacetime, the veterans seemed to find that martial past increasingly appealing. The 16th Connecticut selected the anniversary of their first and only large-scale battle experience in the war, September 17, as the date of their annual reunion. Like the reunions of other Civil War veterans, North and South, these events were not meant to dwell on past humiliations or failings; instead, they were opportunities to visit with old comrades, mourn the dead, and take pride in their military service. Wives, children, and grandchildren attended, enjoying rousing speeches, music, and bountiful food. Hartford newspapers began referring to the regiment as the "Famous,"

"Fighting," "Brave," and "Gallant 16th," and they made special note of each year's reunion.[114] In 1908, a Hartford paper reported, "The battle of Antietam, one of the fiercest of the Civil War, was fought forty-six years ago today, and one of the Connecticut regiments which took an important part in the great contest was the famous Sixteenth." Some two hundred people attended this particular reunion, one hundred of them veterans, including Whitney, Frank Cheney, and John B. Cuzner.[115]

On the fiftieth anniversary of the battle, one Hartford newspaper explained,

Despite the efforts of the officers and the bravery of the men, the regiment was literally cut to pieces by the first few minutes' fire and before it could return anything but a feeble fire, fell back demoralized, through the Eighth Connecticut, taking up a position in the rear. It was here that the regiment felt its lack of experience. Without anything like proper drilling, barely able to form a line of battle the troops had been thrown into the thickest of the fight and when they fell back demoralized, it was nearly impossible to reorganize. It was said that the next morning hardly 300 answered roll call.[116]

In 1894, the 16th Connecticut joined other state units to raise funds and place a monument at the Antietam battlefield.[117] Erecting the monument near where the unit broke and ran, veterans made no public mention of their disappointing performance under fire. Rev. Charles Dixon, who had not been at Antietam with them, described the 16th Connecticut as full of "noble men whose hearts glowed and burned with patriotic fire."[118]

"A LESSON IN PATRIOTISM"

If their unheroic performance at Antietam could be recast as heroic, so too could their dehumanizing captivity at Andersonville. Members intent on recounting their individual and shared stories of imprisonment sought to emphasize not merely the horror but also a new brand of manly bravery. Robert Kellogg had published *Life and Death in Rebel Prisons* in 1865, dedicating it to the "Brave Men" who perished "through unparalleled suffering" in prison. Others felt compelled to provide personal testimonies to ensure that the horrors would not be forgotten. Norman Hope presented his own "Story of Andersonville" in a public forum in

Manchester, Connecticut. He heralded all the prisoners as brave, "demonstrating their valor" and "their superior patriotism," which he considered on par with that of all courageous Civil War soldiers. He denied that any of his comrades accepted the "the safety and comfort proffered them by their enemy" and declared that they "remained faithful to their colors until death." Hope emphasized the unique valor of prisoners of war. "We hear the prisoners of Andersonville described as heroes. *They were heroes.* Any man who enlisted and did service for his country was more or less a hero. But what of those poor unfortunates? In the midst of all the sufferings, temptations were put before the prisoners to induce them to desert their flag. But they remained *firm and true.*" Hope, like most of his other comrades, refused to acknowledge publicly that any Andersonville prisoners, let alone men in his own regiment, accepted Confederate paroles to work outside the pen or in the prison hospital to allay their condition.[119]

Members also refused to endorse southern apologists seeking to tone down the conditions they faced at Andersonville. George Robbins, who recorded his reminiscences in 1918, maintained, "A number of books have been written and published by men recounting not only their individual experiences but the conditions existing in this so-called Southern Military Prison, commonly known as the 'Bullpen.' None that I have read, and I have read most of them, exaggerate in the least degree the horrible conditions existing in the stockade."[120] George Whitney attacked the South's reclamation of Andersonville in a lengthy public address entitled "Prisons of the Confederacy." He observed that "history is being taught in the schools of the south, making Traitors Patriots and Treason commendable which should I hope be counteracted." "There are," he proclaimed, "many mistaken ideas about Andersonville." Whitney viewed not just Henry Wirz but other Confederate officials, such as John Winder, James Seddon, and Jefferson Davis, as guilty of cold-blooded murder. As a survivor of Andersonville, Whitney reflected that it was "humiliating to humanity to know that men claiming to be civilized, boasting of chivalry and refinement beyond all the rest of the world" could "upon American soil be guilty of a barbarism such as has been sketched."[121]

Telling their stories was important, but survivors wanted something more permanent to commemorate their terrible suffering at Andersonville. Encouraged by the success of other northern states in winning public support and funds to build monuments, veteran leaders of the 16th Connecticut sought to erect their own. In 1905, Kellogg and Whitney began to persuade other veterans and state leaders to create a monument. Although it was to honor all Connecticut soldiers who suffered in any southern prisons, members of the 16th led the effort. In an address to the military committee of the state legislature, one of the veterans explained the need to build the monument immediately: "There are many aged fathers, mothers and other near relatives of those who suffered and died there whose declining years would be in a measure smoothed to know that their State had given some little show of appreciation of the much that those who were personally dear to them had done to her honor and credit."[122]

In 1905, the state appropriated $6,000 to build the monument and appointed a commission to oversee the project. Four of the five men chosen for the state commission were veterans of the 16th Connecticut: Frank Cheney, George Whitney, Norma Hope, and George Denison.[123] Ira Forbes explained, "It was fitting that so many of the Sixteenth should be selected, that regiment having suffered most disastrously in the Confederate prisons at Andersonville, Charlestown and Florence, S.C."[124]

On May 3, 1906, some forty-two years after the captured soldiers of the 16th Connecticut entered the prison, commission members Hope, Denison, and Whitney, along with Frank Wakefield and Theron Upson traveled to Andersonville to survey the grounds and select an appropriate spot for the Connecticut monument. Kellogg was invited as a special guest of the commission. Hope's wife Lillian, who accompanied the group, described the experience in a speech to the Women's Relief Corps in Hartford soon after her return home. The veterans were especially struck when they found the famed "Providence Spring," which had emerged seemingly as a gift from God one particularly brutal day in August. "Oh what memories," she exclaimed, "that stream of water brought back to those four men who were once prisoners there." Whitney, Kellogg, Hope, and Denison also searched out the very spot where they had first made their camp upon entering the "Hell Hole as the Boys called it. But they have no regrets today. And they would have suffered 'Death before dishonor.' I can not tell you how long we staid there for the Hours were like minutes and the stories and reminiscences of those days filled our Hearts with sobs and our eyes with tears." To Mrs. Hope, all of this was evidence of "'Man's inhumanity to man.'" She quoted from a letter she had received from Mary Cheney: "Beautiful as the spot is there, it was a spot of the most pathetic associations. Never shall I forget it all. Even if I never go there again. And also the picture of those former prisoners standing shoulder to shoulder on the rough field, their faces full of earnestness and love and sadness will stay with me as long as life lasts a vivid picture."[125] Hope ended her talk by assuring her listeners: "The Commission will soon select an appropriate design for the Connecticut Monument and it will then be placed upon the Beautiful Site selected for it. To you who are interested in Andersonville and who had loved ones who suffered there, I advise you to visit it when the monument is dedicated, no matter what the cost may be."[126]

The commission carefully selected the memorial's design, seeking, in the words of Mary Cheney, "a figure which should represent a very young man, in Civil War uniform to the smallest details, and whose expressions should be that of courage and heroism that are developed in suffering,—strong, modest, hopeful." They wanted to portray "a typical soldier-boy of the northern people, and his bearing that of one who has learned poise by endurance."[127] Bela Lyon Pratt, a student of Augustus Saint-Gaudens, was named the sculptor, and the man chosen as the model for "Andersonville Boy" was supposedly the 16th Connecticut's former sergeant major, Robert Kellogg. The bronze figure depicts a young, beardless private, stripped of his gun and equipment, standing with his left foot forward and his kepi in one hand by his side. More civilian than soldier, only his uniform marks him as a warrior. At the base of the statue are the words, "In Memory of the Men of Connecticut Who Suffered in Southern Military Prisons, 1861–1865."[128] The *Boston Transcript* characterized the statue as "a simple figure of a private infantry soldier, disarmed and helpless, standing with a sober foreknowledge of the very probable fate before him." He seemed "a mere boy, a typical New England lad," fresh from school and the New England town in which he resided. The paper described him: "Manly and modest, he is one of the kind who take things as they come, without bravado and without posing. But there is something in the genuineness, the simplicity, the rugged naturalness of the boy's bearing which makes it seem safe to predict that he will be constant and faithful to the end."[129] A recent historian has noted that the statue has "little that identifies his terrible ordeal as a prisoner at Andersonville."[130] Indeed, this statue appears to convey ideals of an antebellum restrained manhood rather than the more "primitive manhood" of late nineteenth and early twentieth century America. The figure further highlights the youthful innocence of males untouched by the hard realities of either war or captivity.[131]

The Connecticut state legislature appropriated another $7,500 in 1907 to complete the monument and fund transportation of any living ex-prisoners interested in attending the dedication ceremony. However, space was limited, and the cost of travel made it necessary for the commission to restrict invitations to one hundred soldiers, their family members, and a handful of state dignitaries. Cheney stressed that only those veterans in "good health" should be "encouraged to take the trip for it is a rather hard one for old men who are not pretty strong and tough."[132] He was worried: "We must spread out our fund so as to make it go as far as we can. I hope there will not be more applicants than we can provide for. It will be embarrassing to discriminate and decide upon who shall go and who shall stay at home."[133] There was discussion over limiting invitations to ex-prisoners who had served in Connecticut units, rather than including those who had moved to the state after the war. Whitney also wanted to be sure that everyone who went on the trip behaved properly: "We think it better to not have to send any home or to put them where they can injure the reputation of the State."[134] Forbes was alarmed to learn that certain veterans were not allowed to attend. He personally lobbied commission president Frank Cheney to include any current Connecticut resident who had been an inmate of Andersonville.[135]

Eighty-three men accepted the offer to return to Georgia, and on October 21, 1907, these veterans, along with twenty other guests, including family members and some state officials, boarded trains bound for the South. At least forty-three of the veterans were members of the 16th C.V.; others came from the 5th, 6th, 7th, 11th, 17th, 18th, and 20th Connecticut Volunteer Infantry Regiments, the Connecticut 1st Cavalry, and the 14th U.S. Regulars.[136] Two days later, on October 23, 1907, three daughters of men from the 16th unveiled "Andersonville Boy." It was an emotional moment. Men wept as they remembered their terrible ordeal in the stockade and the deaths of so many comrades. Jacob Bauer spoke for many when he recalled how very different the return journey to Andersonville was for him and the other veterans; this time they rode in comfortable parlor cars, rather than cattle cars, and arrived to find the filthy stockade gone, replaced by blooming flowers, trees, and shrubs, and chirping birds among the graves of thousands. "We had," he wrote, "a splendid time."[137]

Successive speakers affirmed the dead and living prisoners' great sacrifice and courage. State comptroller Thomas D. Bradstreet, who accepted the monument officially on behalf of Connecticut, thanked the commission. "It is by such deeds," he declared, "that the works, sentiments, and love of the passing generations give knowledge to the generations to come." He further likened the statue to a young Nathan Hale: "Hardly more than a mere boy, but with manliness in every line of the strong face, which looks you right in the eye. The figure is erect and the young man who is made to typify the Connecticut soldier confined in the place of unspeakable horrors, shows in his bearing true courage and at the same time the serious thoughtful expression which indicates a full appreciation of the odds against him." Overall, Bradstreet saw in the figure a stirring appeal to patriotism.[138] Former lieutenant colonel Frank Cheney, who himself was not imprisoned at Andersonville, thanked the state of Connecticut for "having so generously provided the ways and means for carrying out our sacred duty." He described the "Soldier Boy of Andersonville" as "the ideal young soldier, as he stood for all that is noble and loyal and enduring, when he offered himself and his life, if need be, for our loved country." "We leave him here," Cheney stated, "feeling that he is a son or brother, loved and lost in the service of his country, and that he is now with our comrades at rest."[139]

Kellogg also spoke. Standing beside the bronze likeness of his younger self, the sixty-three-year-old veteran addressed the small crowd. Forty years was a long time, and he was not there to dwell on the disquieting memories of that distant time. Nor did he feel, as he had in 1865, that he needed to focus on spreading "storms of indignation" among his listeners. Instead, he pronounced his and his comrades' imprisonment at Andersonville "a lesson in patriotism. To this retired and beautiful spot will thousands resort in the long years to come, to learn again and again lessons of heroic sacrifice made by those who so quietly sleep in those long rows of graves." Kellogg referred to the prewar lives he and his comrades left to "voluntarily" enter military service, stressed the "passive part" the prisoners played in winning the war, and reaffirmed his regiment's unity during its long trial. The former abolitionist refrained from expressing any bitterness toward the Confederates or mentioning the demise of slavery, instead praising his Connecticut comrades as self-restrained, honorable, disciplined, unselfish, and loyal—he and his comrades' ideal of northern males. Prisoners died "not in the heat and excitement of the battle" but "in the loneliness of a multitude, with a comrade only by their side, within an enemy's lines and under a hostile flag." Kellogg proudly reported later that a white southerner who stood nearby listening to his speech judged his words entirely true. Kellogg's only regret was that more people from Connecticut did not share in the ceremony.[140]

Plans were already in the works for a replica of "Andersonville Boy" to be erected on the grounds of the Connecticut state capitol. Not long after the ceremony in Georgia, Whitney gave a formal address to dedicate the second monument. Whitney declared that many of his listeners "know nothing of the Men whom I represent, so it seems to be the proper time and place to speak of them." He recounted the story of their recruitment, harsh exposure to military life, shocking baptism of fire at Antietam, capture, and long imprisonment. "We did," he concluded, "the best we could, learning as fast as possible, and were soon in shape to stand up with the best." Whitney unabashedly proclaimed, "No one has ever disputed that our record was a credit to the state and an honor to every man who has shared its fortunes." He ended his speech by assuring the crowd, "You need never be ashamed that you have in this way helped to honor those who honored their country in peril."[141] It was yet another chance to recast the regiment's story and ensure that it would be remembered in the most positive manner. Kellogg wrote Whitney that having the duplicate in Hartford finally brought the regiment's prison experience, as well as those of other Connecticut soldiers, home: "A duplicate Monument on the Capitol grounds at Hfd will round out the whole memorial plan in a noble way. With *that* there, the one in the Cemetery at Andersonville will never be forgotten."[142] He later added, "The thought of our 'Andersonville Boy' standing in Connecticut soil, where it may be seen by Conn. People fills my heart with rejoicing." Kellogg also hoped that the duplicate monument would serve as a lesson for future generations and a meeting place where "children would play, and lovers meet, and old soldiers rest and think."[143]

Forbes, who by this time was a journalist for the *Hartford Daily Times,* had been writing his own history of Andersonville, entitled *Andersonville: Connecticut Men in the Old Connecticut Stockade, Roll of Present Survivors; Long List of Men, who Died in the Prison.* He dedicated it to Lt. Col. Frank Cheney, "with genuine affection and loyalty."[144] Back in 1865, not long after he was freed from Confederate prison, Forbes had published a short history of the place, including his own personal experiences. This article, "At Andersonville," appeared in Allen O. Abbott's *Prison Life in the South.* Forbes quoted from his own prison diary, recounting the scenes still fresh in his mind.[145] Only months removed from the horrors of prison, he refused to be vindictive: "So far as I am concerned personally, I can forgive our bitter foes the cruelties which they have inflicted upon me. I do not desire revenge. That is the farthest thing from my heart. God will punish them for their evil deeds. They have already suffered terribly. I feel that all should now try to do whatever they can to narrow the breach which exists between them and ourselves. I have always been glad our government so nobly declined to resort to retaliation. We can not afford to be cruel. It is our highest honor to reward good for evil."[146]

More than forty years later, Forbes was still remembering and writing about Andersonville and his Civil War experiences. He had grown even more intent on forgiving his former foe, and while his Christian faith, at least as revealed in his postwar diary, appears to have been as strong as ever, his relationship with his former comrades in arms was becoming markedly strained.[147] He had been working on his own complete history of Andersonville prison for years, and in the summer of 1907, with the dedication pending for the monument and the commission active and receiving state funding, the time seemed right for publication. Forbes approached Whitney, Cheney, and his close friend Kellogg, who remained intimately tied to the other veterans of the regiment, and tried to convince them of the worthiness of his study. Kellogg, who had published his own forceful and furious account of Andersonville in 1865, tried now to stay neutral and support his friend. He read the manuscript "carefully several times." "It strikes me," he wrote Cheney, "as being of much present interest, and of great future value. Forbes has put a [good] deal of careful, intelligent, painstaking work into the compilation of these statistics, and in the preparation of the narrative portions." Kellogg praised the manuscript's accuracy and recommended the commission publish it, predicting that the book would "not only serve to arouse a deep and general interest in the work it has in hand, but that it will be accepted as authoritative in regard to matters involved."[148] He further encouraged Forbes in May 1907: "You are doing a grand good work in a thorough and careful way, and it makes mighty interesting reading. There's a new generation on the stage that is beginning to take a keen interest in the details of the great conflict, and you are giving them just what they want. Keep it up."[149]

Whitney, however, was not so sure. He wrote Cheney during the summer of 1907 that Forbes wrote "from his own point of view, instead of from authorities." Whitney found Forbes's dismissal of the Wirz trial troublesome, too. "In writing history," Whitney reasoned, "I believe in putting things as they were, not as you wish they had been."[150] Cheney had other reasons to reject the manuscript; he considered it not in "good form to be published as part of the Andersonville trip. It is too voluminous and carelessly put together." As far as its historical accuracy, he refused to pass judgment since he had not been at Andersonville.[151] They decided not to publish Forbes's work, and he felt rebuffed.

"UNFORTUNATE COMRADES"

Like many Civil War veterans, regimental survivors found themselves needing assistance from the federal government in the form of pensions or residence in soldier homes and often both. They applied for a pension, frequently citing their lengthy imprisonment as the cause of their physical debility. Martin Culver, who had complained incessantly about soldiering and his desire to escape service, applied for a pension. Culver was an aging widower, childless, and stricken by severe rheumatism, hernia, and near blindness. He cited the scurvy and rheumatism he contracted at Andersonville, some thirty years prior, as exacerbating his failing health. He had returned to his trade as a house carpenter after the war, but his health increasingly impeded his ability to support himself, and he received a federal pension from 1891 until his death in 1907.[152]

Many veterans entered soldiers' homes, including Fitch's Home for Soldiers in Noroton Heights, Connecticut.[153] Most entered these institutions voluntarily, some staying for months and years, others for days or weeks. Sometimes family members admitted veterans, believing they could receive better care at the home.[154] Augustus Vanderman, a resident of the Soldier's Home in Dayton, Ohio, wrote Ira Forbes in December 1906: "Church is full 3 times on Sunday, Tues and Friday Evening." There was also a Beer Hall, which Vanderman believed was a "curse, and some will [say] it is [a] good thing."[155]

There are also tragic postwar stories. Wells Anderson Bingham was barely sixteen years old when he joined the 16th Connecticut, Company H, on August 7, 1862. His older brother John was killed at Antietam, and his two half-brothers, Waldo J. Gates and Herbert M. Gates, served in the same company with him. Despite his young age, Bingham attained the rank of full corporal by November 1863 and served with the regiment until his formal discharge in July 1865. After graduating Dartmouth College, Bingham married, began a family, and settled in Bloomfield, New Jersey, engaging in the wallpaper manufacturing business. One day in August 1904, while his family was away from home for the summer, Bingham took his own life by "inhaling illuminating gas at his home." He left behind a suicide note explaining that his business worries had prevented him from sleeping and warning his two sons to never follow his path in the paper business.[156] There is, of course, no way to know if Bingham's Civil War experience had anything to do with his depression and suicide, but given that his life had been shaped by his Civil War service, it is easy to wonder. His obituary mentions his membership in the Grand Army of the Republic, and his family wanted to remember to highlight his Civil War service most of all. A special headstone mentioning his service was placed on his grave in New Jersey.[157]

Hubbard Hollister, Jr., also committed suicide after the war. According to one newspaper account, he had "never recovered mentally from the effects of a long imprisonment at Andersonville." Hollister was fifty-seven years old.[158] Richard Hale Smith committed suicide on May 12, 1908, in Springfield, Massachusetts. His brother had written Whitney after the war to explain that his brother was only seventeen when he enlisted and was not "rugged" for his age. He suffered from sunstroke and developed an abscess under an arm; his service with Company H was very short, and he was discharged for disability on November 28, 1862.[159] George McNall took his life in July of 1886 because, according to Ira Forbes, he "became despondent, fearing that he could not retain his property." McNall left behind his wife and children.[160]

A notable number of the unit's veterans were identified as "insane" and consigned to state institutions. These included men in the ranks, as well as prominent officers.[161] Theodore R. Stearns, whose service had ended abruptly after Antietam, was formally discharged in September 1863. Widowed and separated from his surviving family, his health wracked by rheumatism, varicose veins, diarrhea, and a broken limb that never fully healed, he contended that he could no longer work as an insurance agent. Stearns won his veteran's pension, but in 1916, at nearly seventy-five years old, he entered the Illinois Soldiers and Sailors Home in Quincy, where he remained for two weeks. One month later, he became a "volunteer inmate" at the state hospital, where he was "judged insane." Stearns died at there on June 6, 1918.[162] Austin M. Tuller, who had suffered an injury to his head at the Battle of Antietam, was, in the words of Whitney, "never able to use his mind."[163] When Tuller's wife died in 1871, their nine children "were scattered." His son Edgar explained, "We could not trust him to do any work. Tried to have him apply himself to several things but always found he failed to remember and make good." Tuller died in 1896.[164] Former private Thomas Bidwell, who had only been with the 16th Connecticut for four months, received a discharge from the regiment due to a "rupture" in December 1862, and served briefly in the 2nd Connecticut Artillery. After the war, he settled in Massachusetts with his family and was engaged as a "Wire Worker." According to Whitney, "For the last few years of his life he was failing slowly and became insane, being violent at night for the last few weeks."[165] The regiment's hospital steward, Ithamar W. Butler, a former druggist, ended up dying in Connecticut's Insane Asylum in Middletown in 1893.[166] Other members labeled as insane after the war included W. Chester Case, Horace Smith, Hiram Winchell Hart, George Washington Hill, Joseph Irish, and Hiram Buckingham.[167]

Regimental historian Bernard Blakeslee, who survived two gunshots to the head as well as his lengthy imprisonment, returned to Hartford and became active in veteran affairs. He was employed as a stockbroker and then a "special agent" at the U.S. Stamped Envelope Works until, as Forbes explained, "his mental facilities broke down."[168] In December 1891, at age forty-eight, Blakeslee entered Hartford's Retreat for the Insane. He died there on April 25, 1895.[169]

John Burnham had returned to Hartford to begin again. In 1866, he married the daughter of a prosperous seed grower, Helena Estelle Ferre, whom he had courted during the war, and he returned to his family's lucrative tobacco business.[170] His wife died in 1876, leaving him a widower with no children. He served as deputy and then full postmaster from 1872 to 1880.[171] However, the disturbing behaviors that he had exhibited during the war worsened. He was prone to long, sullen periods of sitting with a blank stare, nervously twisting his mustache, seemingly unaware of his surroundings. His work became his refuge, but he often went days without sleep and with little food. He complained of searing head pain and frequently exploded in angry outbursts. Close friends remembered seeing him on the streets of Hartford, where the agitated Burnham appeared not to recognize them.[172] Dwight H. Buell, who had known the former colonel for many years, recounted Burnham once asking "if I ever felt like putting a pistol to my head and blowing out my brains."[173] Burnham even grew estranged from his aging mother, to whom he had always been so devoted and with whom he had corresponded so faithfully during the war.[174] His brother-in-law, Edward Williams, described him as "irritable," "cold," "easily excited," and "so entirely different from his old self as to occasion universal comment." Burnham, Williams affirmed, descended into "hopeless insanity." His family and friends were convinced the cause was the war, particularly his imprisonment.[175] In September 1880, Burnham's family committed him to the Hartford Retreat for the Insane. The asylum's superintendent, Dr. H. P. Stearns, described him as restless, babbling incoherently, and occasionally violent.[176]

In the meantime, Burnham's brother Joseph filed an application for a federal disability pension on his behalf, contending that John's insanity had developed gradually from the time of his wounding at Suffolk and was exacerbated by his imprisonment.[177] His surviving pension file includes sworn statements from friends and his brothers John and Albert as well as his brother-in-law Edward. In addition, several doctors gave their assessments of his mental and physical state. They agreed that John Burnham was incurably insane but debated the cause.[178] Dr. Nathan Mayer, who had become Burnham's family physician after the war, recounted his patient's affliction with malaria during the war, stating, "It is my opinion that this present disability results from the impairment of health acquired in the army, the action of the malarial poison, to which he was very sensitive, and the pressure of responsibility, which kept his nervous system on the strain, with the added detriment of prison fare and treatment leading to the present results of mental disability."[179] But no clear consensus emerged.[180] After weeks of depositions, physicians' examinations, and another round of testimony, John's older brother Joseph became so frustrated with the process that he abandoned the claim.[181] Special examiner Homer Riggs voiced his obvious skepticism in his final report: "While it is a remote possibility that the claimant's disability may, in some unexplainable manner, have been connected with his military life, yet I believe, as Mr. Burnham says . . . that the evidence does not exist that will satisfactorily show the fact, besides there is nothing in the testimony that would tend to show that he was in any manner inclined towards insanity until a short time before he entered the Retreat."[182] Burnham's pension application was ultimately rejected, with the word "Insane," scrawled across the file.[183]

By December 1881, Burnham's condition had so deteriorated that he was moved to the state hospital in Middletown. He died there on April 10, 1883, at the age of forty-six. Obituaries praised him as "gallant" and a "born soldier." "He was," one newspaper stated, "utterly unconscious of fear, and possessed the ability of communicating his own daring and fortitude to others." His pallbearers included Gen. Edward Harland, Colonel Frank Cheney, and Colonel Charles L. Upham.[184]

Neglecting to mention the tensions between Burnham and his men, Whitney wrote of him in his postwar regimental biographical files, "He was remarkably well liked by all." Forbes agreed, "Lieutenant Colonel Burnham was a man of chivalric instincts and personality and was a universal favorite in the Sixteenth."[185] In an account of Plymouth published in 1908, Forbes declared, "He was a man of unquestioning bravery and held his men in perfect discipline, while awaiting the charge."[186] The year that Burnham died, Dr. Mayer offered a motion at the 16th Connecticut's annual reunion, praising their former lieutenant colonel's gallantry and loyalty: "He contributed much to make the regiment a superior military organization, and while he did this for his command he made himself a superior military officer." At a banquet that same year, Bernard Blakeslee similarly remarked, "He did much to bring his regiment to a high state of discipline and to make the men soldiers in spirit, appearance and action."[187]

Ira Forbes, perhaps one of the regiment's true heroes, also spent his final years in an insane asylum. In 1911, he was committed by George Whitney and John Gemmill. The previously pious Forbes had grown "profane, abusive and obscene," "abusive and threatening to [his] wife," and denunciatory toward his friends and relatives. Forbes died nine months later at the age of sixty-eight.[188] He had warred bitterly and publicly with his comrades over differing versions of the regiment's service, notably challenging Blakeslee's account of the mass killings of blacks at Plymouth, and was conspicuously absent from the reunion trip to Andersonville. Yet, his obituaries mentioned none of this, only celebrated his courage and modesty. *The Hartford Daily Times* stated, "His exploit at Plymouth, N.C. when the Sixteenth Connecticut was under such galling fire and when that gallant command suffered hardship of the kind that tried the souls of men showed a bravery that stood out prominently even in a time when brave deeds and gallant action were the rule." The paper attested, "He was a modest man, his bearing was unassuming and he was the last to recount the deeds of war time unless the telling of the story involved the action of others. Of the bravery of his comrades he was always eloquent; of his own exploits he was strangely reticent."[189] The *Courant* also noted this "signal act of bravery" in helping to save the colors at Plymouth. This paper further noted his extensive career in journalism: "Ten years ago he was one of the most widely known newspaper men in Hartford and the older ones now at work well recall his politeness and pertinacity which characterized him."[190]

◆

In 1907, Robert Kellogg sent a short note to George Q. Whitney as he was amassing materials for his detailed history of the regiment. "Were we really ever *in* Andersonville?" Kellogg scribbled on the back of a business card.[191] There must have been moments when the raw realities of that place seemed like a horrible dream, as did their entire odd and uneven Civil War experience. Kellogg, Whitney, Forbes, and others were determined to transform their "broken" regiment's history into something whole, heroic, and meaningful. Most of all, they were determined to remember, even if their individual experiences were painful. And yet, as members died—Whitney was one of the last in 1925—so, too, did the history of the 16th Connecticut.

CONCLUSION

"Only Remembered by What I Have Done"

By September 1931, sixty-nine years after the regiment fought at Antietam in 1862, a mere five men attended the 16th Connecticut's annual reunion. The year before, ten veterans had made it, including Jacob Bauer, but now only five of the twelve members still living were well enough to be present.[1] The old soldiers regretfully agreed that this would be their last reunion and voted to disband. "Furtively several hands brushed their owners' cheeks," a newspaper account recorded, "as they decided that their failing strength would no longer permit the strain of their yearly gathering." The men and the guests of the "old Fighting Sixteenth Connecticut" "recounted incidents of more than a half century ago, re-fought a few battles, told stories, laughed and apparently forgot that they had just decided to take leave of one another this year; perhaps for ever." They decided to turn over their records to the state library, along with what remained in their regimental treasury ($19.99), and adjourned to dinner.[2]

Their descendants strove to keep the memory of the regiment alive. They naturally took pride in their family members' service in the Civil War. Ida Foster's grandfather George Creighton had enlisted as a private from Glastonbury. At the time, he was a thirty-four year-old married weaver. Creighton was shot through his side at Antietam but returned to the regiment, only to be captured at Plymouth. Existing military records list him as paroled from Andersonville on December 11, 1864. However, Foster claimed that he was "kept until the close of the war where he died of starvation" and that "his body was never found." She erected a stone in memory of her "Dear grandfather who suffered so much for his Country" and arranged that it was "decorated once a year by old remaining Soldiers & children." "I don't believe," she told the Connecticut Historical Society's librarian in 1907, "any woman living is prouder of the fact than I."[3] Descendants like Foster emphasized their family members' resilience. Shirley McLellan summed up her great-uncle Martin VanBuren Culver's life and war experience: "He never lived to be an old man, never rich, never famous, just a country boy who went to war and survived." Even though Culver and his wife Julia had no children, everyone in his hometown knew him as the "'old soldier,' who knew so many stories about the War Between the States."[4]

John Cuzner's daughter Laura Jane "Jennie" Cuzner Sperry saved her father's letters to her mother, written during their wartime courtship. She edited and transcribed them, planning to publish them along with her own annotations and personal recollections of his stories, but never completed the project. The letters were donated to the Connecticut Historical Society soon after her death in 1939. In her preface, Sperry wrote, "The main object of this little book and labor of love is to be a link in the endless chain of Peace. If every one could realize all the hardships and suffering and trials connected with war; just what war is, was and always will be; Peace would encircle the world." She declared in 1933 that there were no "Rebs and Yanks, prison pens and battle fields, but a grand United Country, with the motto 'United we stand, divided we fall' imbedded to last forever." Sperry echoed the prevalent nationalism and isolationism of her time, but she also seemed profoundly affected by her father's experiences of war and captivity.[5] In a poem, "When the Sixteenth Marched Away," Sperry imagined her father as a young man in the 16th Connecticut, the "Flower of the City," leaving Hartford with crowds cheering and the sun shining. The last stanzas of the poem read:

> Some fell on Southern battlefields, to keep our Nation free;
> In Prison pens they suffered, and they died for you and me.
> They gave their best—youth and health and strength, and few are here today
> Of those brave men who did their part.
> When the Sixteenth marched away.[6]

Sperry closed the collection of her father's papers by observing that his favorite hymn was, "'Only Remembered by What I Have Done,' so if he knew of this little book he would know [that] he is remembered."[7]

Except for family members and occasional historians researching Antietam or Andersonville, not many people knew or cared about the 16th Connecticut. The monument at Antietam was until recently difficult to reach and largely overlooked by visitors to the battlefield. The stained-glass windows in the Dutch

Reform Church in Antietam survive, but as the years passed, churchgoers forgot their origin. "Andersonville Boy" still stands in Andersonville and Hartford, but without any mention on the statues' signage of the regiment, few learned about the specific efforts of the 16th Connecticut to erect him. Despite its efforts to be remembered, the 16th Connecticut has been largely overshadowed by the dramatic escapades of other regiments.[8]

In the end, the history of the 16th Connecticut was not conventionally heroic, and that no doubt helps to explain their obscurity. Yet, as found in these pages, their service included moments of courage and painful sacrifice. There were also extended periods of failure, discontent, and demoralization. Nevertheless, in their uneven service, we can see men seeking to fit in, deeply concerned with societal expectations. In their driving desire to create a positive permanent history, veterans of the 16th C. V. tried to reshape their shared and individual identity. Survivors took their unique wartime experiences and attempted to reconfigure them into something to be revered. Stressing the ordeals that they endured, particularly in captivity, members were intent on demonstrating that they too were courageous. The hegemonic narrative that demanded that all Civil War soldiers be perceived as heroic combat veterans led these white, middle- and working-class males to justify their wartime experience in terms that would publically commemorate their trauma in an acceptable context.[9]

Members of the 16th Connecticut also felt a compelling personal need to tell their stories, individually and collectively, in order to justify their adversity. They sought to prove their significance as men and as soldiers, even when it was difficult to quantify their accomplishments by standard measures of martial heroism. However, because their wartime service did not follow the standard and expected heroic trajectory, they were largely ignored. Telling their story was a way to redeem themselves and their regiment's history; yet in doing so, they created a series of partial, individual truths that lacked coherence at a larger regimental level. In uncovering the historical account of their wartime ordeal, as well as their efforts to control it, this book has sought to synthesize these various accounts into the shared memory of a collective experience, one that demonstrates not just the Civil War's far-reaching and dehumanizing effects but the power of narrative to shape an often obscure, though illuminating human past.[10] We see experiences lived and partially hidden, memories shaped and sometimes rejected, and sacrifices endured, as well as humiliations and indignities. The 16th Connecticut's war of suffering and soldiering included it all.

APPENDIX
Cast of Main Characters

While this study is not meant to be a comprehensive unit history of a regiment, it does try to provide a sense of the 16th Connecticut's regimental "personality" by highlighting several specific members' lives and attitudes as the war progressed and in the years after. I selected these men for a number of reasons, not the least of which was that each left behind enough personal papers to allow me to delve into their service, families, and in some cases, postwar experiences, and enable me to tell the story of the 16th through their words and differing perspectives. I relied extensively on these individuals' words and thus their memory of the war to recreate a cohesive narrative of the 16th Connecticut Volunteers. This list includes most of the major figures the reader encounters in the book.

CPL. LELAND ORRIN BARLOW, CO. E (1837-1864): Barlow was a twenty-six-year-old Massachusetts native and an unmarried farmer when he enlisted from Granby. He was close to his family and wrote them regularly, especially his sister Jane, candidly describing camp life and the hapless experiences of the regiment. After the battle of Antietam, he reassured his father, "If I did get hit in the back, I was with the Regiment and in my place and kept there."[1] Barlow perished at Andersonville in October 1864.

CAPT. JOSEPH H. BARNUM, CO. H (1838-1902): A man thrust into the spotlight when his company was detached to escort noncombatants away from Plymouth during the siege, Barnum escaped capture and imprisonment at Andersonville. The captain's diaries, letters, and public papers reveal a complex man, devoted to his wife Mary and daughter, yet repeatedly indulging in late-night vices such as gambling, drinking, and possibly visiting prostitutes. He was found guilty of dereliction of duty at one point for leaving his post to wire money home upon hearing that his wife had just given birth to their daughter. After Plymouth, Barnum's Company H essentially became the regiment, much to Barnum's ire. He complained that a single company could not perform as well as an entire regiment. After the war, he commanded a state guard unit and enjoyed a successful career as a publisher, but he did not participate actively in regimental activities.

SGT. JACOB BAUER, CO. G (1838–193?): A German immigrant, Bauer left behind few papers, but the ones that have survived are especially poignant. Letters to his wife Emily record in stark terms how humiliated he felt after Antietam but how eventually his memories of cowardice and failure were replaced with ones of heroism and triumph. Bauer's 1865 diary is particularly valuable in showing the grind and despair of those last months, when exchanged prisoners returned to their demoralized and depleted regiment to await their final mustering out. Finally home, Bauer became active in postwar veteran activities. He outlived nearly all of his comrades.

COLONEL FRANK BEACH (1835–1873): The regiment's enigmatic colonel, Beach was intermittently hated and tolerated by the men. Suffering from physical ailments (their exact nature is unclear) throughout much of the war, he was absent from the unit for extended periods of time. His role during the early months of the 16th Connecticut's service, particularly in the weeks leading up to Antietam and during the battle itself, would prove extremely significant to the regiment's downtrodden sense of itself. Beach set an unpleasant tone and created tension between the men and officers that never entirely dissipated. He died from an unspecified "disease contracted in the service" at the age of thirty-seven.[2]

2ND LT. BERNARD BLAKESLEE, CO. A, G (1844–1895): Blakeslee enlisted as an eighteen-year-old corporal in July 1862 and gained commission as a second lieutenant by December 1863. He was injured twice in battle, both wounds to the head. After the war, Blakeslee authored the only published history of the regiment, basing his account on "diaries written by me at a young age, the importance of which was not yet comprehended."[3] His book drew controversy by insisting that there was a "massacre" of African American Union soldiers and civilians at Plymouth. Several members of the 16th Connecticut supported Blakeslee's claims, but some, including Ira Forbes, angrily rejected his account. Blakeslee was found to be insane and was admitted to the Hartford Retreat for the Insane, where he died in 1895 at the age of fifty-one.

LT. COL. JOHN H. BURNHAM (1836–1883): Burnham, the embattled successor to Lt. Col. Frank Cheney, struggled to earn the respect of the 16th Connecticut, a unit he labeled "an unfortunate" regiment, declaring that no other unit had undergone "so much suffering."[4] Articulate and reflective, Burnham's letters to his mother Sarah provide important insight into the inner workings of the regiment. Burnham had bitter detractors as well as faithful admirers, and he himself seemed deeply conflicted about the war and forever changed by its brutalities. Yet Burnham's loyalty toward the 16th was unflappable. In 1880, Burnham was committed to the Hartford Retreat for the Insane, where he died at the age of forty-six. His family and friends were convinced that the hardships of military service caused his mental illness.

PVT. JOEL LEANDER CHAPIN, CO. A (1843-1864): Chapin stayed true to the high ideals of "cause and comrades" to the end. He was one of the regiment's most idealistic members and died tragically at Andersonville. Chapin, a close friend of Ira Forbes, was a thoughtful, devout Christian who had plans to enter the ministry before the war. He defied his worried mother's wishes and enlisted, but his time with the regiment was limited due to illness. Still, he seems to have left a lasting impression on many who knew him during his short life.

LT. COL. FRANK CHENEY (1832-1909): The beloved original lieutenant colonel of the unit received a severe wound to his left arm at Antietam, forcing him to leave the service permanently soon after the battle. His affiliation with, and affection for, the 16th Connecticut continued until his death. He and his wife Mary Bushnell Cheney and their many children used their wealth and political connections to contribute to the regiment's extensive, celebratory commemoration activities.

PVT. JOHN B. CUZNER, CO. B. (1843-1926): Cuzner was an eighteen-year-old machinist from Hartford courting his future wife, Ellen Van Dorn, when he joined the 16th Connecticut. He maintained a lively correspondence with his fiancé, revealing his thoughts and fears about combat, soldier life, and their budding relationship. John survived prison to return home and marry Ellen the very day the regiment was discharged in Hartford. Cuzner was one of the last survivors of the regiment, dying just a month shy of his eighty-third birthday.

COLOR CPL. IRA E. FORBES, CO. A (1843-1911): The 16th Connecticut's color corporal was a pious, idealistic nineteen year old, preparing for college when he enlisted. Just before capture at the Battle of Plymouth, Forbes heroically helped save the regimental colors. During the regiment's imprisonment, Forbes kept a detailed diary, recording his hopes, fears, and despair. After the war, he returned to school, graduated from Yale University, and became a prolific newspaper journalist. In a surprising twist, Forbes became bitterly embattled with his former comrades, most notably, George Whitney and Robert Kellogg, over the "true" history of the 16th Connecticut. When Forbes began to recount their capture and imprisonment in dramatically different terms than other members did, he found himself branded a southern apologist and cut off from his closest friends. His mental health suffered, and like many of his comrades from the 16th Connecticut, he apparently suffered a complete mental breakdown and died in an insane asylum.

SGT. OLIVER GATES, CO. F (1833-1907): Older and less idealistic than Forbes and Kellogg, and more pragmatic about his service, Gates's lengthy prison diary offers a sobering perspective on the regiment's service and long incarceration. His diary contains graphic descriptions of the brutal suffering he witnessed, which he deemed "crimes against all humanity," and his growing rage toward his captors. Gates candidly questioned why he had ever enlisted and left his wife and little girl far behind in Connecticut.[5]

CPL. SIDNEY H. HAYDEN, CO. B (1838-1865): An unmarried and pious farmer from the small town of East Granby, Hayden wrote faithfully to his family throughout his service. Conservative politically and openly hostile to emancipation, Hayden increasingly pined for his farm, where he would be beholden to no one but himself. Yet he never openly doubted, at least in his surviving letters, that it was his duty to "shoulder the musket when the Government needed help."[6] Hayden endured imprisonment only to succumb to typhoid fever and die a few days before the war ended.

PVT. LEWIS M. HOLCOMB, JR., CO. E (1841-1865): Left an orphan as a boy and raised by his aunt, Holcomb was very close to his extended family in Granby, including his cousins, Richard Henry Lee and Addie Holcomb. Holcomb was a farmer and teacher before the war, clearly well read and bright. His letters include references to Lord Byron, Alfred Waud, and Shakespeare, among other writers. Apparently, he struck some of his comrades as elitist. Cpl. Leland Barlow once praised Lewis as "a smart fellow and no mistake! And if he had his just dues he would have been Lieut. now; he has been hopped over three times, and once by a Corpl; it may be some of his superfluous airs have kept him back perhaps."[7] Although he did not explain his reasons for enlisting, in a letter home, he wrote that the Virginia scenery was "positively delightful," but "under a system of free labor," it would be "more delightful still."[8] Holcomb returned home after his parole from prison but insisted on returning to service, only to die in May 1865 in a Virginia hospital.

SGT. MAJ. ROBERT H. KELLOGG, CO. A (1844-1922): Thoughtful, ardent, and a dedicated abolitionist, Kellogg was just eighteen when he enlisted. He would become one of the 16th Connecticut's most respected members, even though he spent months away from the regiment on detached service, initially believing (and desiring) that he would not return and seeking appointment to West Point. However, he shared the two most significant experiences, Antietam and Andersonville, with his comrades. After the war, he worked tirelessly to ensure that the regiment's public reputation would be both positive and enduring. Kellogg left behind published and unpublished papers and is allegedly the model for "Andersonville Boy," the statue built to commemorate Connecticut soldiers who suffered in all southern prisons during the war. Kellogg belonged to what one historian has called a "network of professional Andersonville survivors who all seemed to know each other," many of whom had "connections to journalism."[9]

PVT. GEORGE N. LAMPHERE, CO. B (1845-1918): A native of Mystic, Lamphere was working in Hartford as an apprentice for his uncle, James M. Schofield, editor of the *Hartford Daily Post,* when the war began. Not quite seventeen in the summer of 1862, he eagerly enlisted in the 16th Connecticut and became severely wounded during the siege of Plymouth. He lost an arm and was briefly imprisoned in North Carolina and Virginia. After the war, Lamphere moved far from his native Connecticut to Minnesota to start a family, resume his newspaper work, dabble in insurance and real estate, and become active in local politics. He also served as secretary of Minnesota's Soldiers' Home. Late in life, he moved to Washington state and became mayor of the town of Palouse. Despite his abrupt separation from his comrades and subsequent long years away from Connecticut, Lamphere wrote movingly of his regimental experience in an unpublished memoir.

1ST SGT. RICHARD HENRY LEE, CO. E. (1841-1876): Lee was a twenty-one-year-old unmarried farmer who, like Lewis Holcomb, maintained a steady correspondence with their cousin Addie Holcomb. He would become one of the most respected members of the unit, credited with urging the prisoners at Andersonville not to sign a petition to request the federal government to restart paroles. In May 1863, Lee wrote Addie, "Soldiers are taught to anticipate nothing, but act in the capacity of a machine. They cannot act their own will, and being aware of the fact, hardly care to think of themselves."[10] Lee died of tuberculosis at the age of thirty-five.

SURGEON NATHAN MAYER (1838-1912): German-born and Jewish, Mayer received his medical training in Europe and America and saw hard service with the 11th Connecticut before becoming the 16th Connecticut's regimental surgeon in 1863. He quickly won the affection and loyalty of his men for his diligent efforts tending to the unit's sick, wounded, and dying. After the war, Mayer remained steadfast in seeking to commemorate the unit and affirm a public portrait of regimental sacrifice and heroism.

SGT. WILLIAM H. RELYEA, CO. D (1833-1918): The 16th Connecticut veteran association's official "historian," Relyea penned his own account of the unit in 1909; it was edited and published in 2002. Relyea was no objective observer, however, and he literally "named names," identifying deserters at Antietam and bitterly denouncing men whom he believed stained the regiment's reputation on that fateful day. Relyea's memoir provides yet another fascinating window into wartime memory and the regiment's postwar efforts to come to terms with its disconcerting experiences. Relyea further claimed to have served as a drummer boy in the Mexican War and as part of William Walker's filibustering expedition to Nicaragua and Costa Rica.

PVT. GEORGE ROBBINS, CO. K (1844-1919): A seventeen-year-old machinist apprentice, George Robbins enlisted with his older brother Lewis on the same day. George hailed from a prominent Farmington family; his father is listed as a "gentleman" in the 1860 U.S. census, although George would later claim that his family was poor and utterly dependent on him. What is clear is his deep devotion to his parents, as evidenced by his letters home, which began soon after his enlistment and continued until his imprisonment. He also kept a prison diary and wrote an extended postwar memoir.[11]

SGT. AUSTIN D. THOMPSON, CO. K (1842-1918): The Vermont-born Thompson joined the regiment and was in the same company with his younger brother Gilbert, who became a corporal. He wrote his sweetheart Electra Churchill back home in Bristol as often as he could. His long letters were filled with blunt assessments of soldier morale, politics, and his concerns about their courtship. Thompson survived imprisonment and the war to return to Electra, marry, and raise a family. They had two children, but Electra died in 1880, leaving Austin a widower the remainder of his life.

PVT. GEORGE Q. WHITNEY, CO. A (1843-1925): Whitney was a young private in 1862 whose own service appears to have been unremarkable, but he emerged from the war determined to track the service of every single member of the 16th Connecticut. Aided by Kellogg, Forbes, and Cheney, he spent the rest of his life amassing a huge amount of biographical material, fascinated not just by what his comrades did in the war but also by what happened to his fellow survivors after they returned home. George's older brother Amos helped found the venerable Pratt and Whitney Company for which George also worked after the war.

CPL. HARRISON WOODFORD, CO. I (1841-1903): Harrison was one of four Woodford cousins who joined Company I from Avon. He wrote his family often, including his sister Mattie, whom he teased about feeling lonely with "all of the young men going away."[12] As the war dragged on, he began to question its terrible violence and cost. He survived imprisonment to return to Avon to farm, marry, and raise a family. He also served in the Connecticut state legislature, in the words of one of his comrades, as an "honored and influential citizen held in high regard by his fellow townsmen."[13]

NOTES

When quoting diaries and letters, I corrected obvious punctuation and spelling errors. I occasionally used [*sic*] to indicate to the reader original spellings.

INTRODUCTION

1. William B. Turner to George Q. Whitney, 1900, George Q. Whitney Civil War Collection, 1861–1925, Connecticut State Library, Hartford (hereafter cited as CSL).

2. "Report of Lieut. Col. Joseph B. Curtis, Fourth Rhode Island Infantry, of the battle of Antietam," *The War of the Rebellion: A Compilation of the Official Records of the Union and Confederate Armies*, 128 vols. (Washington, DC: Government Printing Office, 1880–1901), ser. 1, vol. 19, pt. 1, 455–58 (hereafter cited as *OR*).

3. William B. Turner to George Q. Whitney, 1900.

4. William B. Turner to George Q. Whitney, 1900. Turner further admitted that while in Newark he had read in the newspapers of an amnesty to all soldiers who had deserted Camp Parole: "I made the most grievous mistake, the one most regretted by me for instead of returning as I should and would have done if I had been properly advised, I accepted an invitation to visit some relatives in England not returning to the United States until the war had come to an end." Turner joined on July 16, 1862, and according to the 1869 Adjutant General's Office Report, he "deserted" from Camp Parole. However, the 1889 AGO states that there is no further record of him after his parole. See *Record of Service of Connecticut Men in the Army and Navy of the United States During the War of the Rebellion, Compiled By Authority of the General Assembly Under Direction of the Adjutants-General* (Hartford: Press of the Case, Lockwood & Brainard Co., 1889), 621 (hereafter cited as AGO 1889); *Catalogue of Connecticut Volunteer Organizations (infantry, cavalry, and artillery,) in the Service of the United States, 1861–1865: with Additional Enlistments, Casualties, &c., &c., and Brief summaries, Showing the Operations and service of the Several Regiments and Batteries. Prepared from the Records of the Adjutant-General's Office* (Hartford: Brown and Gross, 1869), 645 (hereafter cited as AGO 1869). Whitney explained that after his capture at Antietam, Turner was paroled "11 days afterward." Whitney provided no indication that Turner deserted or anything else about his subsequent service in his biography of him. Turner was a native of New York City and lived in Springfield, Massachusetts, in 1860; after the war he resided in Newark, New Jersey, where, according to Whitney, he "engaged in the butter and egg business." See "William B. Turner," Whitney Collection, CSL; also 8th Census of the United States, 1860: Population Schedule, Springfield, Hampden, MA, at ancestry.com, accessed Mar. 10, 2010. Turner was one of the earliest, but Marshall D. House was reportedly the very first man to enlist in the unit and to be formally sworn into the regiment on July 11, 1862, as a private in Company E. There were also several other men who enlisted that day. See "Marshall Dallas House," in Whitney Collection, CSL.

5. This fact is perhaps best argued by Lt. Col. William F. Fox in his famous *Regimental Losses*. He

states plainly, "Wars and battles are considered great in proportion to the loss of life resulting from them. Bloodless battles excite no interest. A campaign of maneuvers is accorded but a small place in history." Fox goes on to argue the significance of regiments in understanding combat loss: "The regiment is the unit of organization. It is to the army what a family is to the city. It has a well-known limit of size, and its losses are intelligible; just as a loss in a family can be understood, while the greater figures of the city's mortuary statistics leave no impression on the mind." See William F. Fox, *Regimental Losses in the American Civil War, 1861–1865: A Treatise On The Extent And Nature Of The Mortuary Losses In The Union Regiments, With Full And Exhaustive Statistics Compiled From The Official Records On File In The State Military Bureaus And At Washington* (Albany: Albany Publishing Co., 1889), 1. I am also indebted to William Blair for stressing this point at a meeting of the Society of Military Historians at Pennsylvania State University in Apr. 1999. It should be noted that of Fox's "300 Fighting Regiments," the 14th Connecticut was included (the 16th Connecticut was not); it formed and left Hartford at the same time as the 16th Connecticut. The 14th remained in active service, performing well, most notably in the battles of Antietam and Gettysburg. Fox writes, "The Fourteenth sustained the largest percentage of loss of any regiment from the State." He calculates 727 total killed and wounded. The 16th, in comparison, lost 82 killed or died of wounds; 243 died of disease, accident, or imprisonment, for an overall total of 325 dead from the regiment, including officers. Fox further states, "The deaths in the 16th Regiment include 154 deaths in Confederate prisons, over 400 of this regiment having been captured at Plymouth, N.C." See Fox, *Regimental Losses*, 182, 473, 467.

6. Edward Hagerty includes an informative discussion on the evolution of regimental histories in his study of the 114th Pennsylvania. See his *Collis' Zouaves: The 114th Pennsylvania Volunteers in the Civil War* (Baton Rouge: Louisiana State University Press, 2005), xii–xiii. Another solid study is Richard F. Miller, *Harvard's Civil War: The History of the Twentieth Massachusetts Volunteer Infantry* (Boston: University Press of New England, 2005). Warren Wilkinson's *Mother May You Never See the Sights I Have Seen: The Fifty-Seventh Massachusetts Veteran Volunteers in the Last Year of the Civil War* (New York: William Morrow and Co., 1990) remains one of the best regimental histories published to date. It is superbly written and exhaustively researched. The author is not afraid to delve into the 57th Massachusetts' darker side, discussing ethnic tensions within the unit, leadership problems, and the soldiers' deep disillusionment with war. Most regimental histories, however, are disappointingly narrow, and unit histories like Alan Nolan's *The Iron Brigade; a Military History* (1961; reprint, Bloomington: University of Indiana Press, 1994), James I. Robertson's *The Stonewall Brigade* (Baton Rouge: Louisiana State University Press, 1963), and John J. Pullen's *The Twentieth Maine; a Volunteer Regiment in the Civil War* (Philadelphia: Lippincott, 1957), seek simply to narrate the soldiers' laudatory history without offering any penetrating critique of the war experience as a whole. Earl J. Hess describes unit histories as a "unique part of Civil War historiography," maintaining that an "ideal" unit history should "be complete and definitive, covering all aspects of its subject." See Hess, *Lee's Tar Heels: The Pettigrew-Kirkland-MacRae Brigade* (Chapel Hill: University of North Carolina Press, 2001), xv. T. Harry Williams, in an introduction to the second edition of Nolan's *Iron Brigade*, praised the value of unit histories: "In short, in reciting the story of a brigade he also tells the story of a democracy at war, and thereby demonstrates the validity of unit history" (xiv).

7. Drew Faust, "'We Should Grow Too Fond of It': Why We Love the Civil War," *Civil War History*

50, no. 4 (Dec. 2004): 368–83. See also Edward Ayers, "Worrying about the Civil War," in Edward Ayers, ed., *What Caused the Civil War: Reflections on the South and Southern History* (New York: W. W. Norton, 2005), 103–30.

8. Comments by William Blair, Pennsylvania State University Workshop, "The 16th Connecticut in Captivity," Sept. 24, 1999. Aaron Sheehan-Dean calls regimental histories "antiquarian and heroic," serving "more a memorial purpose than a historical one." See "The Blue and the Gray in Black and White," in Aaron Sheehan-Dean, ed., *The View From the Ground: Experiences of Civil War Soldiers* (Lexington: University Press of Kentucky, 2007), 10. In contrast, Peter Luebke explores the underappreciated significance of regimental histories in the introduction to Albion W. Tourgée, *The Story of a Thousand* (Kent, OH: Kent State University Press, 2011). Gary Gallagher also addresses the overlooked value of regimental histories in *The Union War* (Cambridge: Harvard University Press, 2011), 65–66.

9. Michael Musick explains, "In truth, the regiment was the primary object of identification for the men who fought the war." See "The Little Regiment," *Prologue Magazine* 27, no. 2 (Summer 1995), www.archives.gov/publications/prologue/1995/summer/little-regiment-1.html. Some 80 percent of all Civil War soldiers served in the infantry. See James I. Robertson, *Soldiers Blue and Gray* (Columbia: University of South Carolina Press, 1988), 19. Peter J. Morrone, Jr., explores concepts of "martial masculinity" and "theatrical militarism" ("theatrics of martial masculinity"), as well as the role of gender expectations in enforcing "martial idealism," in his essay on Ambrose Bierce's writings. Much of this had to do with open, public affirmation of what was perceived to be militarily courageous. See Peter J. Morrone, Jr., "Disciplinary Conditioning and Self-Surveillance in Ambrose Bierce's War Fiction," *Midwest Quarterly* 54 (Spring 2013): 310–25. Members of the 16th Connecticut appeared desirous that their service be publicly acknowledged, but it was frequently overlooked.

10. Ayers, "Worrying about the Civil War," 129–30. For more on national narratives as well as national biographies, see Benedict Anderson's *Imagined Communities: Reflections on the Origin and Spread of Nationalism* (London: Verso, 1983). Triumphant narratives of the American Civil War include James McPherson's *Battle Cry of Freedom* (New York: Oxford, 1988), which argues that the war had an overall positive purpose despite the high cost in human life. Ken Burns's influential 1991 documentary "The Civil War" has an equally celebratory message. Frances Clarke adds to this discussion by seeking to understand the purpose of the sentimental stories that not only soldiers but also civilians constructed about themselves and their war. Her work has helped me with my own conclusions about the soldiers considered here, especially their continual emphasis on "suffering." See Frances M. Clarke, *War Stories: Suffering and Sacrifice in the Civil War North* (Chicago: University of Chicago Press, 2011). See below for more on the 16th C.V.'s efforts to reconfigure their seemingly unique experience with suffering and make it meaningful.

11. On microhistory, see Jill Lepore, "Historians Who Love Too Much: Reflections on MicroHistory and Biography," *Journal of American History* 88, no. 1 (June 2001): 129–44; Richard Brown, "Microhistory and the Post-Modern Challenge," *Journal of the Early Republic* 23, no. 1 (Spring 2003): 1–20.

12. An important look at just how important junior officers were to Civil War armies is Andrew Scott Bledsoe, "Citizen-Officers: The Union and Confederate Volunteer Junior Officer Corps in the American Civil War, 1861–1865" (PhD diss., Rice University, 2012).

13. Ellis Spear recounted the experience of the famed 20th Maine, which followed a similar path from rushed recruitment in the summer of 1862 to fighting at Antietam three short weeks later. But, he concluded, "That line, so awkward, raw, and unprepared at first, in all the subsequent campaigns, from Antietam to Appomattox Court House, in fights as stiff, and under fire as searching and deadly as any, was never broken. Never!" See Spear, "The Story of the Raising and Organization of a Regiment of Volunteers in 1862," *Loyal Legion, District of Columbia Commanding, War Papers, No. 46* (Washington, DC, 1903), accessed at www.gutenberg.org/files/32604/32604-h/32604-h.htm.

14. There is a growing body of work on Union soldiers, including Reid Mitchell, *The Vacant Chair: The Northern Soldier Leaves Home* (New York: Oxford University Press, 1993); Earl Hess, *The Union Soldier in Battle: Enduring the Ordeal of Combat* (Lawrence: University Press of Kansas, 1997); Lorien Foote, *The Gentlemen and the Roughs: Manhood, Honor, and Violence in the Union Army* (New York: New York University Press, 2010); and Steven J. Ramold, *Across the Divide: Union Soldiers View the Northern Home Front* (New York: New York University Press, 2013). Studies on Confederate soldiers are far more numerous and stress differences between regions, states, and even armies. Among them are Joseph Glatthaar, *General Lee's Army: From Victory to Collapse* (New York: Free Press, 2008); Aaron Sheehan-Dean, *Why Confederates Fought: Family and Nation in Civil War Virginia* (Chapel Hill: University of North Carolina Press, 2007); Thomas L. Connelly, *Army of the Heartland: The Army of Tennessee, 1861–1862* (Baton Rouge: Louisiana State University Press, 1967), and *Autumn of Glory: The Army of Tennessee, 1862–1865* (Baton Rouge: Louisiana State University Press, 1971); Bell Irvin Wiley, *The Life of Johnny Reb: The Common Soldier of the Civil War* (Baton Rouge: Louisiana State University Press, 1943).

15. See appendix, "Cast of Main Characters."

16. Some of the best and most nuanced work has been done on Confederate soldiers in the eastern theater. Glatthaar's recent *General Lee's Army* stresses the hard and constant campaigning of the Army of Northern Virginia; Sheehan-Dean's *Why Confederates Fought* insists that ultimately a core group of Virginia soldiers fought defiantly and bravely until the very end. Motivators for Confederate enlistment included honor, defense of home and kin, defense of slavery (or fear of emancipation), and Confederate nationalism. Some of these more pragmatic factors mattered more than the idealistic ones, as Kenneth Noe has argued persuasively in his recent study of late volunteers to the CSA. See his *Reluctant Confederates: The Confederates Who Joined the Army after 1861* (Chapel Hill: University of North Carolina Press, 2010). There has also been increased attention to the emotional and psychological costs of war. See Eric T. Dean, Jr., *Shook Over Hell: Post-Traumatic Stress, Vietnam, and the Civil War* (Cambridge, MA: Harvard University Press, 1997); R. Gregory Lande, *Madness, Malingering, and Malfeasance: Transformation of Psychiatry and the Law in the Civil War Era* (Washington, DC: Brassey's, 2003).

17. Examples include Mitchell, *The Vacant Chair*, and Sheehan-Dean, *Why Confederates Fought*. Studies on guerrilla warfare reject any sort of outright separation between soldiers and civilians, home front and battlefront, outright. See, e.g., Michael Fellman, *Inside War: The Guerrilla Conflict in Missouri during the Civil War* (New York: Oxford University Press, 1989); Daniel E. Sutherland, *A Savage Conflict: The Decisive Role of Guerrillas in the Civil War* (Chapel Hill: University of North Carolina Press, 2009).

18. Gerald F. Linderman, *Embattled Courage: The Experience of Combat in the American Civil*

War (New York: Free Press, 1987), best addresses the alleged disillusionment between soldiers and civilians, but others have recently revisited this topic. See, e.g., Lisa Laskin, "'The Army Is Not Near So Much Demoralized as the Country Is': Soldiers in the Army of Northern Virginia and the Confederate Home Front," in Aaron Sheehan-Dean, ed., *The View from the Ground: Experiences of Civil War Soldiers* (Lexington: University Press of Kentucky, 2006), 91–120; Leonard Bussanich, "'To Reach Sweet Home Again': The Impact of Soldiering on New Jersey's Troops during the Civil War," *New Jersey History* 125, no. 2 (2010): 37–60; and Ramold, *Across the Divide*.

19. Robert H. Kellogg to Silas Kellogg, Nov. 1, 1862, Robert H. Kellogg Papers Connecticut Historical Society, Hartford (hereafter cited as CHS).

20. Oliver W. Gates Diary, July 8, 1864, CHS.

21. Gates Diary, Aug. 14, 1864, CHS. Gates's three-volume diary is extremely insightful, but as he admitted in his diary's "Explanation," he made "errors in spelling or composition" too "numerous to mention." Gates wrote cogently, but his punctuation was erratic, and while he only occasionally made spelling errors, his capitalization could be inconsistent. I corrected the most glaring errors to punctuation and capitalization throughout so as not to distract the reader.

22. Gates Diary, undated note, CHS. This note is addressed to a "Mr. Yates." Gates's first wife Emariah, who was the mother of his son Charles Robert, probably had died by the time these words were written.

23. Ira Forbes Diary, Aug. 3, 1864, Sterling Memorial Library, Yale University, New Haven, CT (hereafter cited as YU).

24. David Blight's *Race and Reunion: The Civil War in American Memory* (Cambridge, MA: Belknap Press, 2002) is the current seminal book on American Civil War memory, but there is a growing body of scholarship that expands beyond Blight's conclusions, especially recent works on northern memory. These include John Neff, *Honoring the Civil War Dead: Commemoration and the Problem of Reconstruction* (Lawrence: University Press of Kansas, 2005); Barbara Gannon, *The Won Cause: Black and White Comradeship in the Grand Army of the Republic* (Chapel Hill: University of North Carolina Press, 2011); Brian Matthew Jordan, "'Living Monuments': Union Veteran Amputees and the Embodied Memory of the Civil War," *Civil War History* 57, no. 2 (June 2011): 121–52. See also Caroline E. Janney, *Remembering the Civil War: Reunion and the Limits of Reconciliation* (Chapel Hill: University of North Carolina, 2013).

25. Linderman, *Embattled Courage*, 277, also 266–68.

26. On the broad concept of "collective memory," see Maurice Halbwach, *On Collective Memory,* trans. and ed. Lewis A. Coser (Chicago: University of Chicago Press, 1992). Michael Kammen explores collective memory, myth making, and American nationalism in *Mystic Chords of Memory: The Transformation of Tradition in American Culture* (New York: Vintage, 1993).

27. Carol Reardon, "Writing Battle History: The Challenge of Memory," *Civil War History* 53, no. 3 (Sept. 2007): 252–63. As she does in her book-length study of Pickett's Charge, Reardon in this essay seeks to separate soldiers' conflicting memories from actual battle history, concerned with how "veterans of the war generation compromised and confused the historical record they handed down to the present" (263). I do not see such a binary distinction between the two. See also Reardon, *Pickett's Charge in History and Memory* (Chapel Hill: University of North Carolina Press, 1997). For an exploration of "disputed memories" and the historian's task, see Robert E. McGlone, "Deciphering

Memory: John Adams and the Authorship of the Declaration of Independence," *Journal of American History* 85, no. 2 (Sept. 1998): 411–38. David Paul Nord states that the "subjective, idiosyncratic, truncated, mistaken, even willfully false memories need not be the enemy of history; they can be an entrée into history." See Nord, "The Uses of Memory: An Introduction," *Journal of American History* 85, no. 2 (Sept. 1998): 410.

28. Jason Phillips discusses this tendency in his article "Battling Stereotypes: A Taxonomy of Common Soldiers in Civil War History," *History Compass* 6 (Nov. 2008): 1407–25. Phillips notes that Civil War historians frequently adopt stereotypical portraits of common soldiers. My work seeks to challenge those stereotypes by showing soldiers changing over time rather than portraying them unrealistically as static, one-dimensional "heroes" or "cowards."

CHAPTER ONE

1. Quoted in John Niven, *Connecticut for the Union: The Role of the State in the Civil War* (New Haven: Yale University Press, 1965), 78.

2. *Hartford Courant*, July 11, 1862, quoted in Jarlath Robert Lane, *A Political History of Connecticut During the War* (Washington, DC: Catholic University Press, 1941), 204.

3. Niven estimates this to be 6 percent of the male population in *Connecticut for the Union*, 78.

4. The 14th Regiment Connecticut Infantry was the other one from Hartford County. Other regiments raised and mustered into service that summer included the 15th Regiment Connecticut Infantry from New Haven County, the 19th Regiment Connecticut Infantry from Litchfield County, the 18th Regiment Connecticut Infantry from New London County, and the 17th Regiment Connecticut Infantry from Fairfield County. The 20th Regiment Connecticut Infantry from New Haven County was mustered into service in September. See *Hartford Daily Times,* July 28, 1862, and Aug. 6, 1862.

5. William Buckingham handily won reelection to governor in April 1862, even in "traditional Democratic strongholds such as New Haven and Hartford Counties," which, as Lane writes, "registered almost complete reversals of their usual anti-Republican majorities." He reasons that Democrats simply did not go to the polls in 1862 but returned to vote in later elections. See Lane, *Political History of Conn*, 168, 198, 200.

6. See, e.g., the *Hartford Daily Times,* July 31, 1862, for discontent over the threat of a draft should the state's quota for volunteers not be met. After the 16th Connecticut left the state, a draft was enacted in some towns, which was wildly unpopular. The Democratic *Times* alleged that most draftees were "poor, dependent upon their labor for support" (Sept. 12, 1862).

7. A still useful and comprehensive study of Connecticut wartime politics is Lane's *Political History of Connecticut.* See also Matthew Warshauer's *Civil War Connecticut: From Slavery to Commemoration* (Middletown: Wesleyan University Press, 2011). Connecticut had two separate state capitals at this time, with the legislature rotating between the two.

8. These meetings occurred in towns large and small throughout Hartford County. For a planned meeting in Suffield, the *Hartford Evening Press* urged its readers, "Citizens of all parties should turn out to hear them" (July 14, 1862). An estimated five thousand people attended a meeting held at Hartford's Allyn Hall on July 11, 1862, including the mayor William J. Hamersley and other

prominent city residents. See William Augustus Croffutt and John M. Morris, *The Military and Civil History of Connecticut During the War of 1861–1865: Compromising A Detailed Account of The Various Regiments and Batteries, Through March, Encampment, Bivouac, And Battle; Also Instances of Distinguished Personal Gallantry, And Biographical Sketches of Many Heroic Soldiers: Together With a Record of the Patriotic Action of Citizens At Home, and of the Liberal Support Furnished by the State in Its Executive And Legislative Departments* (New York: Ledyard Bill, 1869), 227.

9. Sydney Stanley quoted in Lane, *Political History of Connecticut*, 206. Stanley was clerk in the Connecticut legislature, although it is not clear if he served in this position during the war.

10. *Hartford Evening Press*, July 14, 1862.

11. Lane, *Political History of Connecticut*, 204.

12. Quote and bounty amounts from *Hartford Daily Times*, July 23, 1862; see also July 28, 1862, for Windsor bounty and Aug. 14, 1862 for Bloomfield. Local historians Mary Jane Springman and Betty Guinan note that towns raised their bounties when Governor Buckingham threatened to institute the draft if town quotas were not met. See their *East Granby: The Evolution of a Connecticut Town* (Canaan, NH: Phoenix, 1983), 211–12.

13. *Hartford Evening Press*, July 14, 1862.

14. James McPherson's *For Cause and Comrades: Why Men Fought in the Civil War* (New York: Oxford University Press, 1997) remains the seminal work on the question of Civil War soldier motivation. Other important works include Rand Jimerson, *The Private Civil War: Popular Thought During the Sectional Conflict* (Baton Rouge: Louisiana State University Press, 1994); Earl Hess, *Liberty, Virtue, and Progress: Northerners and Their War for Union* (Brooklyn: Fordham University Press, 1997); and more recently Chandra Manning, *What This Cruel War Was Over: Soilders, Slavery, and the Civil War* (New York: Random House, 2008); Aaron Sheehan-Dean, ed., *The View from the Ground: Experiences of Civil War Soldiers* (Lexington: University Press of Kentucky, 2007).

15. Bernard Blakeslee, *History of the Sixteenth Connecticut Volunteers* (Hartford: Case, Lockwood, and Brainard Co., Printers, 1875), 5.

16. Quote from *Hartford Daily Times*, July 19, 1862. There were four Griswolds who enlisted in the summer of 1862, Samuel, Ellis, Daniel, and Moses. Twenty-two-year-old Nathan Hale, no doubt a direct relation of *the* Nathan Hale, enlisted in company A. See Blakeslee, *History of the Sixteenth Connecticut Volunteers*, 5. Charles D. Page, the regimental historian of the 14th C.V. stated, "No Connecticut regiment ever took to the front a more noble representation of the best elements of the state than did the Fourteenth." See his *History of the Fourteenth Regiment, Connecticut Volunteer Infantry* (Meriden, CT: Horton Printing Co., 1906), 17.

17. Lane, *Political History of Connecticut*, 209. For information on Charles L. Clark, see A. N. Clark to William A. Buckingham, July 31, 1862, Governors' Correspondence, CSL, in which Clark informs the governor that his son "is a private in that regiment." Charles L. Clark was sergeant in Company A. Abel Clark urged Buckingham to commission George A. Washburn as colonel. See also *Hartford Daily Times*, Sept. 27, 1862, and Abel N. Clark's obituary, *New York Times*, Mar. 26, 1867. See also "Charles Le Roy Clark," Whitney Collection, CSL.

18. Ammi Giddings to Gov. William Buckingham, Jan. 15, 1863, Governors' Correspondence, CSL.

19. Flower's affiliation with the press is mentioned in the *Hartford Evening Press*, Apr. 28, 1863.

20. See "William Goodrich Hooker," Whitney Collection, CSL. It is not clear for which

paper Hooker worked. Hooker was a direct descendent of Rev. Thomas Hooker, the founder of Connecticut.

21. *Hartford Evening Press,* July 14, 1862; Aug. 22, 1862; see also Joseph H. Barnum, Compiled Service Record, RG 94, National Archives, Washington, DC (hereafter cited as CSR, NA).

22. George N. Lamphere, "Experiences and Observations of a Private Soldier," George N. Lamphere Papers, Minnesota Historical Society, St. Paul (hereafter cited as MHS). The *Hartford Evening Press* took note of Lamphere's enlistment on July 14, although his official date of enlistment was July 19. See *Hartford Evening Press,* July 14, 1862. One year earlier, Lamphere had been employed as a farm laborer in Groton, not far from his family home in Mystic.

23. Croffutt and Morris, *Military and Civil History of Connecticut,* 227–29; Blakeslee, *History of the Sixteenth Connecticut Volunteers,* 5; *Catalogue of the 14th, 15th, 16th, 17th, 18th, 19th, 20th and 21st Regiments and the Second Light Battery Connecticut Volunteers; and the 22d, 23d, 24th, 25th, 26th, 27th and 28th Regiments Connecticut Volunteers for Nine Months. Compiled from Records in the Adjutant-Generals Office 1862* (Hartford: Press of Case, Lockwood and Co., 1862), 47–67 (hereafter cited to as AGO 1862); "Muster and Descriptive Rolls, 16th Regiment Connecticut Volunteers," Records of the Military Department, Connecticut Adjutant General's Office, RG 13, CSL. Other members who were under eighteen include Theodore Glasson, George W. Frisbie, Theodore W. Goodwin, and Samuel W. Allen. See Ira Forbes's biographies of each of these men in Whitney Collection, CSL.

24. "Ira Forbes," J. A. Spalding, *Illustrated Popular Biography of Connecticut* (Hartford: Press of the Case, Lockwood, and Brainard Co., 1891), 187. See also Ira Forbes, "Wethersfield Men in Company A" in Forbes Collection, CSL.

25. Ira was the eldest son of six children born to Henry and Adelia Forbes. According to the 1850 U.S. Census, Henry Forbes was a thirty-one-year-old blacksmith, then residing with his family in East Hartford. He died when Ira was very young, leaving Adelia to raise their five children. (Forbes also referred to his "adopted Sister Mary" in his diary, as well as a sister who died in infancy; see Forbes Diary, Feb. 11 and June 11, 1864, YU.) By the time of the 1860 census, Forbes was residing in East Hartford, but his enlistment papers give Wethersfield as his residence. See 8th Census of the United States, 1860: Population Schedule, East Hartford, Hartford County, CT, at ancestry.com, accessed Oct. 14, 2008. See also Ira Forbes, CSR, NA.

26. Kellogg was the son of Dr. Silas Root Kellogg and Lucy Church Hale Kellogg of Sheffield, Massachusetts. His father had become too ill to practice medicine, though it is unclear what ailed him. Robert resided with his maternal grandmother Lucy Hale in Wethersfield, Connecticut, from an early age due to his mother's extended illness. (She lived until May 9, 1895.) See "Robert Hale Kellogg," Whitney Collection, CSL; and 8th Census of the United States, 1860: Population Schedule, Sheffield, Berkshire, MA, and Wethersfield, Hartford, CT, at ancestry.com, accessed Nov. 19, 2008. According to the 1850 census, Lucy Hale was a wealthy landowner. See 7th Census of the United States, 1850: Population Schedule, Wethersfield, Hartford, CT, at ancestry.com, accessed Nov. 19, 2008. On August 11, 1862, Robert Kellogg enlisted in Company A, receiving only a small bounty of $25. See Robert H. Kellogg, CSR, NA; Robert H. Kellogg Enlistment Papers, Kellogg Papers, CHS; and "Robert Hale Kellogg," Whitney Collection, CSL.

27. Quote from Caroline D. Hale to William A. Buckingham, Aug. 12, 1864, Governors' Correspondence, CSL.

28. Robert H. Kellogg to Silas and Lucy Kellogg, Sept. 10, 1862, Kellogg Papers, CHS.

29. J. Leander Chapin to Amelia Chapin, no date, quoted in "J. Leander Chapin," Whitney Collection, CSL. According to Whitney, Chapin's father Joel was Yale educated and a Congregational minister who died in 1852. But the 1850 census lists Leander's father as a "schoolteacher" living in Bridgeport. See 7th Census of the United States, 1850: Population Schedule, Bridgeport Ward 3, Fairfield, CT, at ancestry.com, accessed July 29, 2008. Biographical information also from "Joel Leander Chapin," Whitney Collection, CSL. The Connecticut Literary Institute later became Suffield Academy. George Q. Whitney referred to Chapin as a "Theological Student" upon enlistment, although officially his occupation was listed on the roster as a "farmer." See AGO 1862. In 1905, Ira Forbes wrote that Chapin "was studying for the ministry in the Congregational Church" before his enlistment. See "Sixteenth C. V. at Andersonville," *Connecticut Courant,* Mar. 15, 1906, newspaper clipping in Forbes Collection, CSL.

30. Roselle Grover to Amelia Chapin, Aug. 14, 1862, Chapin Family Papers, Hargrett Rare Book and Manuscript Library, University of Georgia, Athens (hereafter cited as UGA); also see 8th Census of the United States, 1860: Population Schedule, Enfield, Hartford County, CT, at ancestry.com, accessed July 10, 2008; AGO 1862.

31. *Hartford Daily Courant,* July 22, 1862.

32. Lydia Adams Mills Humphrey to Ira E. Forbes, Feb. 5, 1906, Whitney Collection, CSL. Mills, who became color corporal, died from wounds received at the battle of Plymouth on April 28, 1864. For more on the topic of northern women, see Elizabeth Leonard, *Yankee Women: Gender Battles and the Civil War* (New York: W. W. Norton, 1995); Nina Silber, *Daughters of the Union: Northern Women Fight the Civil War* (Cambridge: Harvard University Press, 2005); and Judith Giesberg, *Army at Home: Women and the Civil War on the Northern Home Front* (Chapel Hill: University of North Carolina Press, 2009).

33. George and his brother Lewis Robbins were the sons of Jehiel and Dorothy Robbins, prominent residents of Farmington; Jehiel is listed as a "gentleman" in the 1860 census. See 8th Census of the United States, 1860: Population Schedule, Farmington, Hartford, CT, at ancestry.com, accessed July 16, 2010. Robbins claimed that by 1862 his father had sold his farm and moved to the village of Plainville, and Robbins was set to learn the trade of a machinist. He also stated that at least by the summer of 1862, his father was "poor." Robbins, who had been educated at local public schools, was working as an apprentice machinist in Hartford when the war began. See Robbins, "Some Recollections," CHS. Although Robbins's recollections date from fifty years after the war's end, they are consistent with his wartime letters.

34. Robbins, "Some Recollections," 7–8, CHS. I have not found any corroborating evidence that Robbins's father was poor as George suggests; he is referred to as a "deacon" in Henry Allen Castle, *The History of Plainville, Connecticut, 1640–1918* (1967; reprint, Chester, CT: Pequot Press, 1972), 132. In September 1863, after seeing a photograph of his mother, Robbins wrote that he was "pained to see how thin" she appeared and worried that she was working too hard bringing in "the wood and water, now that Father is away at work." If then seventy-year-old Jehiel Robbins had to seek employment outside of their home, this would indicate financial need on the part of the family, even though there were other grown children and George was mailing home his army pay. He also encouraged them to take reimbursement for any items they sent him from home "and

use any or all of it, if you want it." See George Robbins to Jehiel and Dorothy Robbins, Sept. 5, 1863, Robbins Papers, CHS. Note that these are copies of the original letters located at the CHS. Robbins's wartime letters and diary reveal a thoughtful young man who struggled to stay resolute in his devotion to the Union. He would repeat well-worn maxims about the war, but he showed doubts about emancipation and what he deemed the selfishness of northerners unwilling to sacrifice as he and his comrades did. His religious faith gave him comfort, and he often used it to reassure his worried parents. As he awaited to return to the regiment after an extended illness, he wrote his mother: "I wish for your sakes that I could be with you today, where all is quietness and peace on this Sabbath day and go once more to Sabbath School and hear the voice of our loved pastor addressing the children under his charge, but the wish is in vain and I must be content to stay and suffer if need be for our cause, which has cost so much in treasure and in the lives of those dearest and best loved at home, and then my lot is no harder nor as hard as that of the thousands who have suffered and are suffering for the cause we know to be right and which God helping us we will maintain." See George Robbins to Dorothy Robbins, Apr. 12, 1863, Robbins Papers, CHS.

35. John B. Cuzner to Ellen Van Dorn, Aug. 27, 1862, Cuzner Letters and Papers, CHS. Cuzner is listed in the 1860 census as a sixteen-year-old weaver residing with his parents in Middletown. See 8th Census of the United States, 1860: Population Schedule, Middletown, Middlesex County, CT, at ancestry.com, accessed Sept. 3, 2008. Cuzner's parents were both English natives. His father Henry enlisted in the 21st Connecticut Infantry on Sept. 5, 1862, and was discharged for disability on Aug. 17, 1863. See *The Story Of The Twenty-First Regiment, Connecticut Volunteer Infantry The Civil War. 1861–1865, By Members Of The Regiment* (Middletown, CT: Press Of The Stewart Printing Co., 1900), appendix, 13. While stationed at Falmouth, John was able to see his father daily. See John B. Cuzner to Ellen Van Dorn, Nov. 22, 1862, Cuzner Letters and Papers, CHS. See also John B. Cuzner, CSR, NA.

36. Alvan A. Fengar to William A. Buckingham, Mar. 10, 1863, Governors' Correspondence, CSL. Crane was discharged for disability on March 13, 1863. See AGO 1889. A Rollin C. Crane appears in the 1850 U.S. census as thirty-eight years old and living in East Windsor. His name is not found in the 1860 or 1870 Connecticut census. See 7th Census of the United States, 1850: Population Schedule, East Windsor, Hartford County, CT, at ancestry.com, accessed May 15, 2008. However, George Q. Whitney gave Crane's birthday as May 8, 1811, and stated that he was "51 years old at enlistment." There is also a family tree on ancestry.com which lists Rollin C. Crane with the same birthdate (accessed July 28, 2009).

37. The 1860 census lists Granger as fifty, and he was forty-one according to the 1850 census. See 8th Census of the United States, 1860: Population Schedule, Granby, Hartford County, at ancestry.com, accessed May 27, 2009; 7th Census of the United States, 1850: Population Schedule, Simsbury, Hartford County, at ancestry.com, accessed May 27, 2009. See also AGO 1862 and "Charles S. Granger," Whitney Collection, CSL. Granger was discharged for disability in May 1863.

38. Carter served just one year in the regiment and was discharged for disability on August 13, 1863, but he was transferred to the Veterans Reserve Corps and remained with them until the war's end. He lived until 1895. See "Sidney S. Carter, Sr.," Whitney Collection, CSL.

39. See E. H. Owen to William Buckingham, Jan. 24, 1863, Governors' Correspondence, CSL; *Geer's Hartford City Directory, 1861–1862*, 95, http://distantcousin.com/Directories/CT/Hartford/1861_62/Pages.asp?Pages=095, accessed Apr. 10, 2008. Owen also was part of a group

of prominent citizens who attended a special town meeting in Hartford in July 1862 to appropriate money to stir enlistments and provide for soldiers' families. Owen partnered with well-known businessmen Calvin Day to found their successful wholesale company sometime prior to the war. See Calvin Day obituary, *New York Times*, June 12, 1884; and John C. Kinney, "The War of the Rebellion," 1:95–96, and Mary K. Talcott, "Prominent Business Men," 1:670–71, in James Hammond Trumbull, ed., *The Memorial History of Hartford County Connecticut, 1633–1884*, 2 vols. (Boston: Edward L. Osgood, 1886).

40. Manross's close friend and colleague William S. Clark was an officer in the 21st Massachusetts; Manross occupied Clark's chair at Amherst College until he decided to enlist. See William S. Clark to Newton S. Manross, Sept. 10, 1861, William Smith Clark Papers, W. E. B. Dubois Library, University of Massachusetts, Amherst (hereafter cited as UMA). Clark wrote Manross from New Bern that he "came to fight and suffer and die if need be, in a good cause and it is not for me to complain or be disheartened. I must go forward so long as my life is spared and if I am slain by traitors I will die as a soldier should." These words, and others in letters not preserved, may have weighed heavily on Manross as he contemplated his decision. See Clark to Manross, Mar. 30, 1862, William Smith Clark Papers, UMA.

41. Manross quoted in Croffutt and Morris, *Military and Civil History of Connecticut*, 276. Manross earned his Ph.D. in 1851. His family were prosperous clockmakers from Bristol. Additional biographical details from Newton S. Manross Collection, private collection, copies in author's possession, used by permission. See also 7th Census of the United States, 1850: Population Schedule, Bristol, Hartford County, ancestry.com, accessed June 29, 2008. Newton had two younger brothers who also joined the army; Eli was a member of the 5th Connecticut, and John joined the 2nd Connecticut Heavy Artillery.

42. Quote from Rev. Leverette Griggs, obituary of "Captain Manross," undated newspaper clipping, William Smith Clark Papers, UMA. Griggs was a Congregational minister from Bristol and father of Cpl. John Griggs, who died Sept. 1, 1862.

43. *Hartford Evening Press*, July 22, 1862.

44. "High fever of patriotism" from William Relyea, "Obituary of Samuel Brown," and Whitney Collection, CSL; see also "Samuel Brown," Whitney Collection. Also *Hartford Evening Press*, Sept. 30, 1862.

45. Cheney had been expelled (or resigned under protest when threatened with expulsion) from Brown University for attending a Jenny Lind concert on a Sunday, which was against school regulations. See Eileen R. Learned, ed., "The Letters of Mary Bushnell Cheney and Frank Woodbridge Cheney," unpublished typescript, Sophia Smith Collection, William Allan Neilson Library, Smith College, Northampton, MA, 7–9 (hereafter cited as SC).

46. Sidney H. Hayden to "Cousin Sam," Mar. 7, 1863, Hayden Papers, East Granby Public Library, East Granby, CT (EGP). See also Springman and Guinan, *East Granby*, 211.

47. Sidney H. Hayden to Abby Hayden, Nov. 14, 1863, Hayden Papers, EGPL.

48. Martin V. Culver Letters, private collection, copies in author's possession, used by permission. See also 8th Census of the United States, 1860: Population Schedule, Rocky Hill, Hartford County, and Middletown, Middlesex County, CT, at ancestry.com, accessed Oct. 31, 2008. Jonathan Culver was a Middletown shoemaker who did not serve in the war. The 1860 census lists

Martin Culver as twenty-seven years old in 1860, and his Compiled Service Records and Pension Records both confirm his enlistment age as twenty-nine; however, George Q. Whitney gave his birth date as Sept. 23, 1834, and age at enlistment as twenty-seven. See "Martin VanBuren Culver," Whitney Collection, CSL. The 1900 census further lists Culver's birthdate as Sept. 1834. See 12th Census of the United States, 1900: Population Schedule, Portland, Middlesex County, CT, at ancestry.com, accessed July 16, 2009.

49. See "Oliver W. Gates," Whitney Collection, CSL. "My Country needed my services," Gates Diary, Aug. 10, 1864, CHS. By the end of August 1862, Oliver's two younger brothers also enlisted: William (born ca. 1844) in the 1st Connecticut Cavalry on August 11 and Benjamin (born ca. 1846) in the 26th Connecticut Volunteer Infantry on August 30. William A. Gates served the entire war and was mustered out June 3, 1865; Benjamin F. Gates was honorably discharged a year later on August 17, 1863. See www.civilwar.nps.gov/cwss/soldiers.cfm and 8th Census of the United States, 1860: Population Schedule, Waterford, New London, CT, at ancestry.com, accessed May 12, 2009. Another Gates brother, Charles, was apparently too young to serve. See also *Catalogue of Connecticut Volunteer Organizations* (1869), 70, 851, at ancestry.com, accessed May 12, 2009. Cpl. Henry Viberts, also in Co. F, was employed as a mason by Tryon, and he resided with him in Hartford according to the 1860 census. Viberts and Gates would mess together at Andersonville. See Gates Diary [May 25, 1864], CHS. Later, Gates's brother-in-law David C. Fox enlisted in Co. D of the 18th Connecticut in Jan. 1864 and was wounded and captured on June 5, 1864. See Gates Diary, July 31, 1864, CHS; *Catalogue of Connecticut Volunteer Organizations* (1869), 675, at ancestry.com, accessed May 19, 2009. It is not clear if, in fact, Fox ended up at Andersonville.

50. The largest group of immigrants in the regiment was the Irish (71), followed by English and German natives (30). The remaining immigrants included a smattering of Scottish, Canadian, Austrian, Polish and French-born soldiers. Company D had the largest number of immigrants (39) and the most Irish (15) and English (13) natives, as well as eleven German-born soldiers. Numbers for immigrants are approximate and aggregated from AGO 1869 and 1889, and census records, as well as biographical material included in the Whitney Collection, CSL. For more on immigrants and the Union army, see Susannah Ural Bruce, *The Harp and the Eagle: Irish-American Volunteers and the Union Army, 1861–1865* (New York: New York University Press, 2006); Susannah Ural, ed., *Civil War Citizens: Race, Ethnicity, and Identity in America's Bloodiest Conflict* (New York: New York University Press, 2010); and William Burton, *Melting Pot Soldiers: The Union Ethnic Regiments* (New York: Fordham University Press, 1998). The *Hartford Daily Courant* on July 30, 1862, referred to "hundreds of young strong Irish and Germans about the city" available for service. The paper urged their enlistment, but "don't let their number outstrip that of the Americans."

51. Bauer was born in 1838 in Alsfeld, Germany, but it is not clear when he came to the United States, nor when he married Emily Hart Moore from Kensington, Connecticut. See "Jacob Bauer," Whitney Collection, CSL. It is difficult to find Bauer in the 1860 census. However, he appears in the 1880 census with his four daughters, including then nineteen-year-old "Alice," the eldest. In his 1865 diary, Bauer noted her birthdate as April 2, 1861, and he called her "Allison." See 10th Census of the United States, 1880: Population Schedule, Berlin, Hartford County, at ancestry.com, June 22, 2009. See also Bauer Diary, Apr. 2, 1865, U.S. Army Military History Institute, Carlisle, Pennsylvania (hereafter cited as MHI).

52. Jacob Bauer, "Personal Experiences of the War of the Rebellion Written by J. C. Bauer, ex-Soldier, at the earnest request of his children and grandchildren at Kensington, Conn., during the month of Jan. 1915," 1, typescript copy at Port O'Plymouth Museum, Plymouth, North Carolina (hereafter cited as PPM). There are notable inconsistencies between Bauer's wartime writings and this unpublished memoir that he ostensibly recounted for his family. Bauer mixed up the chronology of the regiment's service and confused Gen. Hood for Gen. Hoke at Plymouth, but there are some revealing insights in the text, nonetheless. Edward Moore was Emily's brother James's son. See Benjamin D. Wright, *History of the Descendants of Elder John Strong of Northampton, Mass,* 2 vols. (Albany, NY: Joel Munsell, 1871), 2:1080–81.

53. Eighty-eight brothers (and four half-brothers) served in the regiment together and eighteen cousins. Also, four fathers served with five sons, three uncles with four nephews, and seventeen in-laws served together.

54. The youngest brother John gave his age to be eighteen, but a family friend would later claim that John was underage when he enlisted. Later in the war, when the brothers' father died in February 1864, this family friend, A. M. Tryon, tried to convince Governor Buckingham that John at least should be allowed to come home: "If that poor mother could only have her youngest son now in her bereavement to care for and console her it would be a great comfort to her in her distress." George Q. Whitney explained, "John was discharged at the request of the Selectmen of his town his Father having died leaving a Widow with no one to care for her and the farm and two Brothers (Syril & Frank) in the service." John was "discharged for disability" on June 14, 1864, at Roanoke Island. See "John Bragg," Whitney Collection, CSL. However, John Bragg's grave located in Center Cemetery, South Windsor, affirms the age listed on the roster; as does the birthdate Whitney provides: November 7, 1843. John Bragg's grave found at Findagrave.com, accessed May 5, 2008. A. M. Tryon to William A. Buckingham, Feb. 25, 1864, Governors' Correspondence, CSL. The other two Bragg brothers remained in the regiment until the war's end in 1865. See also AGO 1889, 634.

55. Reference is made to the three brothers in a letter written by family friend Watson L. Wilcox; see Wilcox to Gov. Buckingham, Feb 3, 1865, Governors' Correspondence, CSL; Oliver would die at Antietam while his brothers survived the war. Ariel Case later transferred to Company H when made second lieutenant. See "Ariel Job Case," Whitney Collection, CSL.

56. According to the 1860 census, Joseph was an apprentice carriage maker. See 8th Census of the United States, 1860: Population Schedule, Guilford, New Haven, CT, at ancestry.com, accessed May 26, 2009. Another brother, Daniel W. Grosvenor, served in the 1st Regiment New York Volunteers as a musician but was discharged for disability. See D. W. Grosvenor to Ira Forbes, Aug. 13, 1906, "Samuel E. and Joseph H. Grosvenor," Whitney Collection, CSL.

57. See "James Himes" Whitney Collection, CSL. Stephen had attempted to enlist in 1861 in the 5th Connecticut Infantry, but as Ira Forbes explained, "On account of his age he was discharged the same day." See Forbes, "Stephen Himes," Whitney Collection, CSL; also AGO 1869, 275.

58. See Rufus M. Chamberlin to Whitney, Nov. 1906, "Rufus Monroe Chamberlin," Whitney Collection, CSL.

59. Lewis Monroe Holcomb, Jr., was raised by his grandparents, Ebenezer Seymour and Almira Holcomb, after his father Lewis M. Holcomb, Sr., died in October 1846. Involved in a financial dispute, he shot and killed a man, then turned the gun on himself. The amount in dispute was

allegedly $300. Lewis's mother Mary had died in 1844 of consumption when he was only three. See Carol Laun, *The Holcomb Collection* (Granby, CT: Salmon Brook Historical Society, 1998), 76, 85, 94, 96. Lewis clearly gained a formal education and taught in local schools, but his employment was listed as "farmer" when he joined the 16th Connecticut in July 1862. See AGO 1862. His close relationship with his extended family in Granby is obvious from his letters to his first cousin Adelaide.

60. See AGO 1862; Laun, *The Holcomb Collection,* 85–93, 97. Adelaide Holcomb and her father, to whom the two male cousins wrote, appear to have been Democrats, perhaps even Peace Democrats, given the antiwar sentiments expressed in her wartime diary. Local historian Carol Laun speculates that the outspoken Adelaide Holcomb was a young woman born "ahead of her time"; see *The Holcomb Collection,* 51–61.

61. Theodore R. Stearns to "John," Aug. 4, 1862, Stearns Family Papers, CHS. Stearns and Griggs both enlisted on July 25, 1862, from the town of Bristol. According to George Q. Whitney, Stearns "spent most of his life to 1859 in Springfield, Mass when he was sent to Williston Seminary, Easthampton, and from there to the University of Albany, N.Y. where he graduated in the spring of 1862 with the degree of L.L. B." See "Theodore Randall Stearns," Whitney Collection, CSL. Cpl. John L. Griggs was the son of a Congregational minister, Rev. Leverette Griggs, and lived in Bristol. See 8th Census of the United States, 1860: Population Schedule, Bristol, Hartford County, CT, at ancestry.com, accessed Nov. 20, 2008. Corporal Griggs died of typhoid fever on Sept. 1, 1862; the location of his death was Bristol, according to Whitney. See also "John Laurence Griggs," Whitney Collection, CSL. Stearns wrote to a friend in another regiment, "I suppose you heard that my cousin John Griggs with whom I enlisted was taken sick with typhoid fever and died soon after we left the state. This was a hard blow to me as I did not know hardly any one in the Regiment." See Theodore R. Stearns to "John," Mar. 15, 1863, Stearns Family Papers, CHS.

62. For the best discussion of these connections and how the regiment mimicked and even replaced familial relationships, see Gerald Prokopowicz, *All for the Regiment: The Army of the Ohio, 1861–1862* (Chapel Hill: University of North Carolina Press, 2000.) Reid Mitchell also discusses the significant communal ties among Union soldiers in *The Vacant Chair,* 21–25.

63. I found 296 farmers among some 1,109 men identified as members of the regiment. For some, I have been unable to establish an occupation upon enlistment, especially among recruits from 1863 or 1864. Socioeconomic and demographic information discussed here and below is gathered from biographies found in the Whitney Collection, CSL; Adjutant General Reports (1862, 1869, 1889); "Fitch's Home for Soldiers," located at www.cslib.org/fitchres.asp, accessed June 4, 2005; F. W. Chesson, "Connecticut 16th Regiment Graves," http://pages.cthome.net/fwc/16-CT.HTM, accessed Sept. 5, 2005; findagrave.com; census records; local histories; and Hartford newspapers.

64. Relyea, "Obituary of Samuel Brown," in Whitney Collection, CSL.

65. Not only did both lieutenants leave the regiment under a cloud but also the company had the dubious distinction of counting the highest number of desertions (fourteen) of the entire regiment. Along with Company I, it suffered the highest casualties from Antietam.

66. For example, Frederick Williamson served in the 2nd and 3rd Connecticut before enlisting in the 16th C.V., Hancy Hamilton served in the 12th Connecticut before being discharged in February 1862 to join the 16th C.V., and George Washburn and Edwin Mix had both served previously. See

F. M. Williamson to William A. Buckingham, July 7, 1864, Governors' Correspondence, CSL; AGO; Hancy's name is misspelled as "Hansey" on the 12th Connecticut Roster. See www.itd.nps.gov/ cwss/soldiers.cfm, accessed May 5, 2008. See also AGO 1869, 509; www.itd.nps.gov/cwss/index. html, accessed May 15, 2008; E. H. Mix to William A. Buckingham, July 12, 1862, Governors' Correspondence, CSL. Mix was from Plymouth, also in Litchfield County, but joined the 16th Connecticut even though it drew primarily from Hartford County. For more on Mix, see *Hartford Daily Times,* Mar. 22, 1864; and Civil War Soldiers and Sailors System, www.itd.nps.gov/cwss/, accessed June 1, 2008.

67. *Hartford Daily Times,* Aug. 2, 1862; *Hartford Daily Courant,* July 31, 1862. Biographical information from 8th Census of the United States, 1860: Population Schedule, Cass, Cass, IA, at ancestry.com, accessed May 16, 2008; "Lieutenant Colonel John H. Burnham" http://members.aol. com/SHolmes54/burnham.html, accessed Feb. 8, 2008. *The City Directory of Hartford, CT, 1861–1862* listed "J.D. Burnham & Co. as "tobacconists" at 243 State Street. See *Geer's Hartford City Directory, 1861–1862,* 68, http://distantcousin.com/Directories/CT/Hartford/1861_62/Pages.asp?Pages=068, accessed Apr. 10, 2008. Edward D. Williams was married to John's sister Charlotte. See 8th Census of the United States, 1860: Population Schedule, Hartford Ward 4, Hartford County, CT, ancestry.com, accessed July 3, 2008. See also John H. Burnham Pension file, National Archives (hereafter cited as NA).

68. Page, *History of the Fourteenth Regiment,* 14.

69. *Hartford Daily Courant,* July 25, 1862.

70. *Hartford Daily Courant,* July 26, 30, 1862; *Hartford Daily Times,* July 29, 1862.

71. *Hartford Evening Press,* July 29, 1862.

72. *Hartford Daily Times,* Aug. 13, 1862. The 14th C.V. named their camp after navy commodore Andrew Hull Foote, a New Haven native who had gained national attention for his exploits at Forts Henry and Donelson earlier that year. See Page, *History of the Fourteenth Regiment,* 14.

73. *Hartford Daily Times,* Aug. 13, 1862. A few days later, the *Hartford Daily Courant* "found everything in good order, camp life going on in earnest and the men happy and contented." See *Hartford Daily Courant,* Aug. 18, 1862.

74. *Hartford Daily Times,* Aug. 12, 1862; see also Elizur D. Belden Diary, Aug. 23, 1862, CHS.

75. Belden Diary, Aug. 19, 1862, CHS. See also entry for Aug. 23, 1862.

76. Belden Diary, Aug. 26, 1862, CHS.

77. *Hartford Evening Press,* Aug. 9, 1862. On August 11, the paper reported 1,200 "men enlisted" for the regiment, but clearly not that many were in camp. By August 12, the paper stated that 748 enlistees were present at muster. See *Hartford Evening Press,* Aug. 13, 1862. The 14th Connecticut also received its arms, Whitney rifles, sooner than the 16th Connecticut and more than a week before it left for the front. According to the *Hartford Evening Press,* Aug. 20, 1862, five of the regiment's ten companies had their rifles by August 20, with the rest expected that day. When they received arms would be a point of contention regarding the performance of the 16th Connecticut at Antietam.

78. Beach arrived in Hartford on Wednesday, August 13, and the next morning "entered upon his duties"; see the *Hartford Evening Press,* Aug. 14, 1862. See also *Hartford Daily Courant,* Aug. 15, 1862.

79. *Hartford Evening Press,* Aug. 14, 15, 1862. On August 18, the *Hartford Daily Courant* claimed that the regiment numbered 1,150 men.

80. Cook praised Beach for his bravery, judgment, and military abilities in the field. See *OR*, ser. 1, vol. 11, pt. 1, 427; vol. 11, pt. 2, 42.

81. Charles Cheney to William Buckingham, Aug. 2, 1862, Governors' Correspondence, CSL; *Hartford Evening Press*, Aug. 8, 1862. The *Hartford Daily Courant* reported, "The 16th express much satisfaction at the appointment" (Aug. 9, 1862).

82. William H. Relyea, "History of the 16th Connecticut Volunteer Infantry," 3, William H. Relyea Papers, CHS. The published version of Relyea's memoirs, edited by John Michael Priest, is *16th Connecticut Volunteer Infantry: Sergeant William H. Relyea* (Shippensburg, PA: Burd Street Press, 2002). *Hartford Courant*, Aug. 9, 15, 1862; Kinney, "The War of the Rebellion," in Trumbull, *The Memorial History of Hartford*, 1:98, n. 1. See also "Francis Beach," Whitney Collection, CSL; Blakeslee, *History of the Sixteenth Connecticut Volunteers*, 101–2. Governor Buckingham was asked to consider at least one other prominent Hartford man for the position of colonel, Charles Prentice, Captain of the City Guard. See George P. Bissell to William Buckingham, July 28, 1862, Governors' Correspondence, CSL.

83. Rev. W. H. Gilbert, *Sermon Delivered in Granby, Conn., Jan. 4, 1863, at the Funeral of Roswell Morgan Allen, Private in Co. E., 16th Reg't. C.V. Who Died at the Hospital Near Washington, Sunday, Dec. 28, 1862* (Hartford: Charles Montague, 1863), 12.

84. Robbins, "Some Recollections," 9, CHS. George Q. Whitney recounts a quarrel between 1st Lt. William Lockwood and Colonel Beach in those early weeks of the regiment's formation. Lockwood, the son of prominent Hartford merchant James Lockwood, exclaimed: "Don't ever God Damn me while I am in the service. You have come here from the regulars and you can't expect in a day to make the regulars out of men just out of banks, stores, shops and from farms. They are good men ready to do their fair share of duty, but will not stand abuse and if you ever damn me again, you will be called to account for unmilitary conduct." See "William H. Lockwood," Whitney Collection, CSL.

85. *Hartford Daily Courant*, July 31, 1862. The 14th C.V. also lacked guns in those early weeks of its existence. See Page, *History of the Fourteenth Regiment*, 16–17.

86. Blakeslee, *History of the Sixteenth Connecticut Volunteers*, 5; also *Hartford Daily Times*, July 25, 1862.

87. Relyea, *16th Connecticut Volunteer Infantry*, 4. Kellogg, who "like[d] camp life," wrote his father of awakening at 4:30 a.m., drilling three times a day, and guard mounting. Roll call was at 9:30 p.m., taps at 9:45, "when all lights must be blown out and all noise cease." Robert H. Kellogg to Silas Kellogg, Aug. 19, 1862, Kellogg Papers, CHS. See also Belden Diary, Aug. 19, 1862, CHS. For more on this difficult transition from civilian life, see Foote, *The Gentlemen and the Roughs*, 10.

88. Sidney H. Hayden to Catherine Hayden, Aug. 13, 1862, Hayden Papers, EGPL.

89. "Unfeeling," from Gilbert, *Sermon*, 12; "fill his back full of bead," from Relyea, "History of the 16th Connecticut," 4; See also Croffutt and Morris, *Military and Civil History of Connecticut*, 228–29; Blakeslee, *History of the Sixteenth Connecticut Volunteers*, 6.

90. Mrs. Welles Hawes to William A. Buckingham, Aug. 27, 1862, Governors' Correspondence, CSL. Hawes suggested Lt. Col. Cheney replacing Beach.

91. James T. Pratt to William A. Buckingham, Aug. 27, 1862, Governors' Correspondence, CSL.

92. See Blakeslee, *History of the Sixteenth Connecticut Volunteers*, 103–4.

93. Blakeslee, *History of the Sixteenth Connecticut Volunteers*, 5; George Robbins, "Some Recollections," 9, CHS; Relyea, "History of the 16th Connecticut Volunteer Infantry," 3–4; Robert H. Kellogg to father, Aug. 19, 1862, Kellogg Papers, CHS; Charles Gilbert Lee Diary, Aug. 20–23, 1862, CHS; see also Croffutt and Morris, *Military and Civil History of Connecticut*, 229.

94. Robbins, "Some Recollections," 9, CHS.

95. Blakeslee, *History of the Sixteenth Connecticut Volunteers*, 5.

96. As mentioned above, John Griggs, who had enlisted with his cousin Theodore Stearns, died from typhoid on Sept. 1, 1862, apparently at home in Bristol. But existing records do not record any deaths occurring in Camp Williams except for Wright's death.

97. Robert H. Kellogg Diary, Aug. 25, 1862, CHS. Wright enlisted from Enfield, but in 1860 he was residing in Wethersfield. See 8th Census of the United States, 1860: Population Schedule, Wethersfield, Hartford County, CT, at ancestry.com, accessed Dec. 26, 2008.

98. Blakeslee, *History of the Sixteenth Connecticut Volunteers*, 5–6.

99. See, e.g., *Hartford Daily Times*, Aug. 25, 28, 1862; *Hartford Evening Press*, Aug. 26, 27, 28, 29, 30, and Sept. 1, 1862.

100. *Hartford Daily Times*, Aug. 27, 1862; also *Hartford Evening Press*, Aug. 27, 1862. Green resigned one month later, some two weeks after Antietam on September 30. See AGO 1889, 625.

101. First Lt. Samuel H. Thompson, Sgt. Allyn S. Hale, Cpl. George F. Rich, Cpl. George M. Spencer, and Sgt. Ambrose N. Holmes signed the resolution. *Hartford Evening Press*, Aug. 29, 1862.

102. *Hartford Daily Times*, Sept. 1, 1862.

103. *Hartford Daily Courant*, Sept. 1, 1862. The *Courant* described it in detail: "The flag is composed of the richest blue Italian silk; size 6 by 9 feet; finished with a heavy gold-colored bullion fringe, and it is mounted on an elegant oak staff, which is surmounted with a handsome silver spearhead. . . . In the centre is painted a large gilt-framed *party per fersse* shield, one half of which is occupied by the thirteen stripes and stars, while the other displays the coat of arms of the State. Above this the American eagle and the name of the regiment; below is the state motto, 'Qui transtulit, sustinet.'" The *Courant* further noted, "Every man employed at Sharps' contributed something" toward the $110 cost of the flag, although Samuel H. Green, the Secretary of the Company, "contributed a sufficient sum." The *Hartford Evening Press* described the flag in an article on August 30: "The state flag is a heavy blue silk, with fringe of yellow cord, mounted on a handsome staff, with cord and tassels, and silvered spear head. On each side it bears the name of the regiment and state motto in gilt letters; and a Shield surmounted by an eagle. On one half of the shield is the Connecticut coat of arms; on the other red, white and blue. On one side of the shield is a scene representing a light house, a point of land, one or two houses, and a sea view; on the other a small landscape, in which the Charter Oak is the central object. Both these paintings were finely executed by a New York artist." See the *Hartford Evening Press*, Aug. 30, 1862.

104. Elizur Belden made mention of the flag in late October. See Belden Diary, Oct. 24, 1862, CHS. The regiment did not have their state flag at Antietam. Months later, in April 1863, the unit received additional "Guide Colors," also designed by Tiffany & Co. of New York. "Procured for the officers of the regiment by Lieut. Col. Burnham" at a cost of $60, they were "composed of the richest 'Mexican' blue Italian silk, bordered with a heavy gold colored fringe. In the centre upon a ground of white the coat of arms of the State is worked (by hand) in chenille. Above and below this the name

of the regiment is also worked in letters of gold upon the blue ground. The whole is mounted upon a rich black walnut staff with sliver spear head and tip. These 'guides' are without exception, the richest we have ever seen and reflect great credit upon the officers and the manufacturers, Messrs. Tiffany & Co., of New York." *Hartford Daily Courant,* Apr. 4, 1863.

105. *Hartford Daily Courant,* Aug. 28, 1862. The *Courant* described the camp in "the greatest confusion" as the soldiers prepared to leave the day before (Aug. 27).

106. Belden Diary, Aug. 31, 1862, CHS. Also see Robbins, "Some Recollections," 9, CHS.

107. Relyea, "History of the 16th Connecticut," 4; Croffutt and Morris, *Military and Civil History of Connecticut,* 229; Blakeslee, *History of the Sixteenth Connecticut Volunteers,* 6. Also see the *Hartford Evening Press,* Aug. 29, 1862.

108. Relyea, *16th Connecticut Volunteer Infantry,* 7.

109. Blakeslee, *History of the Sixteenth Connecticut Volunteers,* 6.

110. Austin D. Thompson to Electra M. Churchill, Sept. 3, 1862, Thompson Papers, CHS. Electra's cousin Charles Churchill, Jr., was also a member of Co. K. See "Austin David Thompson," George Q. Whitney, CSL. More descriptions of the crowds that day include Kellogg Diary, Aug. 29, 1862, Kellogg Papers, CHS; Belden Diary, Aug. 31, 1862, CHS; Robbins, "Some Recollections," 9, CHS.

111. *Hartford Daily Courant,* Sept. 12, 1862; *Hartford Evening Press,* Aug. 29, 1862.

112. The AGO 1869 gives Aug. 28, 1862; AGO 1889 gives Aug. 29, 1862, but the Bound Regimental Records lists Aug. 24, 1862, the same day the regiment was officially mustered into service. George Q. Whitney had no additional information on the men in his biographical materials, beyond that they were listed as deserters in a separate list of each company. See Whitney Collection, CSL. With regard to individuals, in one example, Whitney wrote on the biographical sheet for Carroll: "Deserted August 29th 1862, the day we left for the front." See "John Carroll," Whitney Collection, CSL. There are at least three John Carrolls in the 1860 census who were born around 1834 in Connecticut, and all three were Irish immigrants. However, at this point I have found no additional evidence to confirm that any of them were *the* John Carroll who enlisted in the 16th Connecticut. 8th Census of the United States, 1860: Population Schedule, Hartford County, CT, at ancestry.com, accessed Aug. 12, 2009. It is certainly noteworthy that John Carroll gave his enlistment occupation as "soldier." See AGO 1862. In the Bound Regimental Papers for the 16th Connecticut, it is noted that Walden Dutcher was arrested in Brattleboro, Vermont, on Dec. 19, 1863. See Bound Regimental Papers, RG 94, entries 112–15, Bound Records of the Union Volunteers Regiments, vol. 2, NA. Twenty-four-year-old William Brown (Co. H) also deserted on August 29, was arrested in March 1863, and sentenced to six months of hard labor. He eventually returned to the regiment, but deserted again on June 7, 1865. See Bound Regimental Papers, RG 94, entries 112–15, Bound Records of the Union Volunteer Regiments, vol. 2, NA. Muster Rolls, Returns, Regimental Papers, Box 148 [unbound papers], RG 94, NA.

113. Relyea, "History of the 16th Connecticut," 6. Jacob Bauer remembered this, too, in his 1915 unpublished reminiscences. See Bauer, "Personal Experiences of the War," 1, PPM.

114. George Q. Whitney to Augustine Lonergan, Nov. 17, 1913, "William Leaf Carpenter," Whitney Collection, CSL.

115. *Hartford Daily Courant,* Sept. 1, 1862.

116. Blakeslee, *History of the Sixteenth Connecticut Volunteers,* 7.

117. George Q. Whitney to Augustine Lonergan, Nov. 17, 1913, "William Leaf Carpenter," Whitney Collection, CSL.

118. Average age upon enlistment in the unit was twenty-five, and the majority were unmarried (587, or 53 percent). The total number of immigrants was 144, or nearly 13 percent, with most foreign-born soldiers volunteering in the summer of 1862. Some immigrants, though, were recruited in late 1863 and into 1864. According to McPherson, the average age for all Union soldiers upon enlistment was 25.8 years old, and the median age was 23.5, with three-fifths of the men age 21 or younger at the time of enlistment. However, in other ways, the regiment was not reflective of the average: 30 percent of all Union soldiers were married, and 24 percent were foreign born. See McPherson, *For Cause and Comrades*, viii; and *Ordeal by Fire: The Civil War and Reconstruction* (New York: Knopf, 1992), 355. Warshauer notes that 10 percent of Connecticut's overall population served in the military, which amounted to 47 percent of men between the ages of fifteen and fifty. He writes that the state sent "a striking proportion of its male population to war." See Warshauer, *Connecticut in the American Civil War*, 5.

CHAPTER TWO

1. Kellogg Diary, Aug. 29, 1862, CHS. An earlier version of this chapter is Lesley J. Gordon, "All Who Went into that Battle Were Heroes: Remembering the 16th Connecticut at Antietam," *The Antietam Campaign*, ed. Gary W. Gallagher (Chapel Hill: University of North Carolina Press, 1999): 169–91.

2. Relyea, "History of the 16th Connecticut," 10; also Blakeslee, *History of the Sixteenth Connecticut Volunteers*, 7–8.

3. Bauer, "Personal Experiences of the War," 2, PPM.

4. *Hartford Evening Press*, Sept. 1, 1862; *Hartford Daily Courant*, Sept. 10, 1862. The regiment remained at Fort Ward for six days.

5. Robert H. Kellogg to Silas D. Kellogg, Sept. 6, 1862, Kellogg Papers, CHS.

6. John H. Burnham to Sarah B. Burnham, Sept. 3, 1862, Burnham Papers, CSL. See also George Q. Whitney to Augustine Lonergan, Nov. 17, 1913, "William Leaf Carpenter," Whitney Collection, CSL. News of these problems would reach the governor as well as complaints of other shortages. See, e.g., James T. Pratt to William A. Buckingham, Oct. 4, 1862, Governors' Correspondence, CSL.

7. Blakeslee, *History of the Sixteenth Connecticut Volunteers*, 8.

8. Harrison Woodford to Martha Woodford, Sept. 10, 1862, Harrison Woodford Letters, private collection, used by permission.

9. Bauer, "Personal Experiences of the War," 2, PPM. Ramold discusses this "hardening" among northern soldiers and the resentments it created between soldiers and civilians, in *Across the Divide*, 8–12.

10. "J. H. B." letter to the editor, Sept. 4, 1862, *Hartford Daily Courant*, Sept. 10, 1862. J. H. B. is most likely Adj. John Burnham, who was routinely sending letters to the *Courant*. He informed his mother Sarah on September 14, "If I have time tonight I shall drop a line to A. N. Clark." Clark was the editor of the *Hartford Courant*. See John H. Burnham to Sarah B. Burnham, Sept. 14, 1862, CSL.

On September 16, the day before Antietam, a letter appeared in the *Courant* signed "J. H. B," praising Gen. McClellan as "the only man who can bring order out of the present chaos."

11. "Whitney rifle," from Robert H. Kellogg to Silas D. Kellogg, Sept. 6, 1862, Kellogg Papers, CHS; "Belgian muskets" from Relyea, *16th Connecticut Volunteer Infantry*, 13. See also Belden Diary, Sept. 3, 1862, CHS. The question of when the regiment obtained their guns would become a point of contention after the war in emphasizing the regiment's greenness. A Hartford newspaper fifty years after the battle claimed that the 16th C.V. received "rifles and forty rounds of ammunition" while on the march toward South Mountain. See unnamed newspaper clipping [1912], Whitney Collection, CSL. Jacob Bauer claimed in 1915 that the 16th was not issued their "old Springfield rifles" with forty rounds of ammunition until "two days before the battle of Antietam." See Bauer, "Personal Experiences of the War," 2, PPM. Tents arrived while the men were marching. See George Robbins to Jehiel and Dorothy Robbins, Sept. 9, 1862, Robbins Papers, CHS. It is not clear why there was a delay in the issue of arms to the regiment, but it may well have been a breakdown in the quartermaster's department or some other part of the army's bureaucracy. As described below, the men also had difficulty receiving proper food and their pay.

12. Elizur D. Belden noted on September 4, "Drilled to day for the first time with arms." See Belden Diary, Sept. 4, 1862, CHS. See also Bauer, "Personal Experiences of the War," 2, PPM.

13. Relyea further stated that it was not until the regiment reached "Brookeville" on the morning of September 12: "Here our officers thought it best to teach us." See Relyea, "History of the 16th Connecticut," 11–12.

14. Blakeslee, *History of the Sixteenth Connecticut Volunteers*, 8.

15. Jacob Bauer to Emily Bauer, Sept. 5, 1862, typescript copy of original, "16th Regiment Connecticut Volunteers," File Folder, Antietam National Battlefield, Sharpsburg, Maryland (hereinafter referred to as ANB). See also Blakeslee, *History of the Sixteenth Connecticut Volunteers*, 8; Croffutt and Morris, *Military and Civil History of Connecticut*, 237. Bauer's letter to his wife contradicts his 1915 recollection that the regiment did not receive guns until September 15. See Bauer, "Personal Experiences of the War," 2, PPM.

16. Blakeslee, *History of the Sixteenth Connecticut*, 8. See also George Q. Whitney to Augustine Lonergan, Nov. 17, 1913, "William Leaf Carpenter," Whitney Collection, CSL. It would be months before the regiment saw those knapsacks again, by then emptied of their belongings.

17. Croffutt and Morris, *Military and Civil History of Connecticut*, 260, note that the 14th Connecticut was similarly green. Describing inexperienced Civil War soldiers as a "mob" or "crowd" was not unusual. James Robertson describes the first wave of Civil War volunteers in 1861 as "armed mobs" "congregating for war." See Robertson, *Soldiers Blue and Gray*, 17. The problem of untrained volunteer soldiers thrown into battle and the frustrations of their West Point–trained officers is explored most recently in Wayne Wei-Siang Hsieh, *West Pointers and the Civil War: The Old Army in War and Peace* (Chapel Hill: University of North Carolina Press, 2009).

18. Sidney H. Hayden to Uncle, Sept. 10, 1862, Hayden Papers, EGPL.

19. Blakeslee, *History of the Sixteenth Connecticut Volunteers*, 8.

20. Bauer, "Personal Experiences of the War," 2, PPM.

21. George Q. Whitney to Augustine Lonergan, Nov. 17, 1913, "William Leaf Carpenter," Whitney Collection, CSL.

22. Descriptions of the march's difficulties include Theodore R. Stearns to "John," Mar. 20, 1863, CHS; Kellogg Diary, Sept. 11, 13, 15, 1862, CHS.

23. Cpl. John W. Gray (Co. K), e.g., fell away from camp while at Frederick City, Maryland, without permission. He was duly reduced to ranks, although Captain Manross promised to reinstate him. Manross died in the subsequent battle, and Gray was injured in the hand and eventually discharged in March 1863 without ever regaining his rank. George Q. Whitney considered this a "very trivial offense" after the war and also claimed that there were "several others" who suffered the same fate as Gray. See "John W. Gray," Whitney Collection, CSL. Another soldier exhausted by the hurried march to the front was twenty-two-year-old Nathan Hale. Described as "not a man of robust strength," Hale fell prostrated by exposure and exhaustion" by the time the 16th Connecticut reached Frederick City. He was hospitalized and died on October 12, 1862. See "Nathan Hale," in Whitney Collection, CSL. His death was mentioned in the *Hartford Evening Press,* Oct. 18, 1862. His body was returned to Wethersfield where he was buried.

24. This letter was dated September 8 and 9, from Leesboro, Maryland, although the soldier's identity is unknown. See *Hartford Daily Courant,* Sept. 12, 1862.

25. Austin D. Thompson to Electra M. Churchill, Sept. 14, 1862; quote from Thompson to Churchill, Oct. 3, 1862, Thompson Papers, CHS.

26. *Hartford Evening Press,* Sept. 17, 1862.

27. "A Retrospect and a Battle," by "J.H.C." in the *Hartford Evening Press,* Sept. 27, 1862.

28. See, e.g., Kellogg Diary, Sept. 12, 13, 14, 1862, Kellogg Papers, CHS. See also George Q. Whitney to Augustine Lonergan, Nov. 17, 1913, "William Leaf Carpenter," Whitney Collection, CSL.

29. J. Edward Shipman to "Friend Hubbard," Sept. 14, 1862, Lewis Leigh Collection, MHI; see also Croffutt and Morris, *Military and Civil History of Connecticut,* 265. A soldier quoted in the *Evening Press* alleged that during the march Colonel Beach "refused to allow them to accept the invitation" from a "Union man" to "help themselves to fruit in their orchard." See *Hartford Evening Press,* Sept. 18, 1862.

30. Frances Louise Bushnell to Mary Bushnell, Sept. 9 (1863), in Learned, "The Letters of Mary Bushnell Cheney and Frank Woodbridge Cheney," SC, 13. Frances did not explain in this correspondence why she so disliked Cheney.

31. Robbins, "Some Recollections," 16, CHS.

32. William Relyea to George Q. Whitney, Feb. 25, 1909, Whitney Collection, CSL. Relyea described Brown as a "gentleman in every respect."

33. Leland O. Barlow to "Friends," Sept. 14, 1862, Barlow Letters, CSL.

34. Relyea, *16th Connecticut Volunteer Infantry,* 14.

35. Robbins, "Some Recollections," 12, CHS. The Battle of South Mountain occurred on September 14, 1862, along the mountain passes at Crampton's, Turner's, and Fox's Gaps. Federals drove divided Confederate forces back but stalled before the fighting resumed on September 17 at Antietam.

36. *Hartford Daily Courant,* Sept. 12, 1862; Blakeslee, *History of the Sixteenth Connecticut Volunteers,* 9–10; See also Relyea, "History of the 16th Connecticut," 16–20.

37. For more on the march toward Leesboro, see Relyea, "History of the 16th Connecticut," 14–15; Lee Diary, Sept. 7, 1862, CHS. Sources vary on the regiment's march distances. According to the "Monthly Returns, 16th Regiment Connecticut Volunteers, Sept. 1862," Records of the

Military Department, Connecticut Adjutant General's Office, RG 13, CSL, the regiment traveled the furthest on September 7 (13 miles), September 12 and 15 (12 miles), and September 13 (14 miles). But according to the "Record of Events" located in the regimental "Muster Roll Returns," NA, the regiment marched the most on September 11 (14 miles) and September 13 (14 miles), the least on September 8 (four miles). The 14th Connecticut, just as new and untested by military service as the 16th, also endured a severe march to the front. Capt. William Tubbs complained to Governor Buckingham that the "severe marches work upon me severely," requesting a transfer so that he could ride rather than walk; however, the regiment was faring much better. "Our regiment is getting along finely and . . . if they fight as well as they can march all will be well." Tubbs would soon find his prediction true. See William H. Tubbs to William A. Buckingham, Sept. 12, 1862, Governors' Correspondence, CSL.

38. Kellogg Diary, Sept. 16, 1862, Kellogg Papers, CHS. Also, Blakeslee, *History of the Sixteenth Connecticut Volunteers*, 11.

39. Sidney H. Hayden to Uncle, Sept. 10, 1862, Hayden Papers, EGHS.

40. Martin V. Culver to Jonathan Culver, Sept. 12, 1862, Culver Letters, private collection.

41. Blakeslee, *History of the Sixteenth Connecticut Volunteers*, 11. See also Croffutt and Morris, *Military and Civil History of Connecticut*, 265; Relyea, "History of the 16th Connecticut," 21; Robbins, "Some Recollections," 13, CHS. Emphasis on how "surprised" the men were about going into battle appears in both postwar accounts and contemporary sources. Dr. Nathan Mayer, then with the 11th Connecticut, spotted the 16th just before battle and claimed they were "fresh, cheery boys, clean and well uniformed." Mayer quoted in Stanley Weld, *Connecticut Physicians in the Civil War* (Hartford: Connecticut Civil War Centennial Commission, [1965?]), 14.

42. Robert H. Kellogg to Silas Kellogg, Sept. 20, 1862, Kellogg Papers, CHS.

43. Blakeslee, *History of the Sixteenth Connecticut Volunteers*, 11. As already mentioned above, accounts vary as to when the men actually received instructions on how to load and fire their guns. Blakeslee's postwar assertion that they actually loaded their muskets for the first time the night before Antietam may have been made to emphasize their poor preparation and, thus, to avoid blaming the men themselves. Others indicate that the men practiced shooting while encamped near Fort Ward, although perhaps without live ammunition.

44. Niven, *Connecticut for the Union*, 216; Croffutt and Morris, *Military and Civil History of Connecticut*, 265; Bernard Blakeslee, "The Sixteenth at Antietam," in Walter J. Yates, ed., *Souvenir of Excursion to Antietam and Dedication of Monuments of the 8th, 11th, 14th and 16th Regiments of Connecticut Volunteers* (New London, CT: 1894), 13; Robert H. Kellogg to Silas Kellogg, Sept. 20, 1862, Kellogg Papers, CHS.

45. Robert H. Kellogg to Silas Kellogg, Sept. 20, 1862, Kellogg Papers, CHS; also Kellogg Diary, Sept. 17, 1862, CHS.

46. Kellogg described praying to God for "courage and strength" during the battle; he hoped that his life would be spared, "but if not prepare me to die in peace." See Robert H. Kellogg to Silas Kellogg, Kellogg Papers, Sept. 20, 1862, CHS.

47. Samuel B. Mettler's letter was published in the *Hartford Daily Times*, Sept. 27, 1862; Marx Neisener's letter appeared in the *Hartford Daily Times*, Sept. 29, 1862. Neisener's name is misspelled as "Marks Nezemer."

48. Robbins, "Some Recollections," 13, CHS.

49. Robbins, "Some Recollections," 13, CHS. In these unpublished reminiscences written in 1918, Robbins also stressed the surprise of being called into action.

50. Robert H. Kellogg to Silas Kellogg, Sept. 20, 1862, Kellogg Papers, CHS. William A. Bushnell, a private in Co. B, later claimed that Chaplain Finch was the "first man hit that morning while we were going to that piece of the woods, a fragment of shell struck him on the hip, tore his pocket book to pieces and dented a cent in it." See W. A. Bushnell to George Q. Whitney, Oct. 23, 1915, Whitney Collection, CSL. The *Hartford Evening Press* reported that Finch had his "coat and pants torn by a shell" (Sept. 22, 1862).

51. Lamphere, "Experiences and Observations," MHS.

52. Relyea, "History of the 16th Connecticut," 22–24; quote from 24. See also Croffutt and Morris, *Military and Civil History of Connecticut*, 265.

53. Relyea, "History of the 16th Connecticut," 24–26; Blakeslee, *History of the Sixteenth Connecticut Volunteers*, 14–16; Niven, *Connecticut for the Union*, 220. At least one soldier claimed Confederate artillery fired at them with "old pieces of chain, railroad iron, junk bottles, hatchets and stones." See Henry E. Bradley (Co. C), quoted in *Hartford Daily Courant*, Sept. 29, 1862.

54. Relyea, "History of the 16th Connecticut," 42–43; Niven, *Connecticut for the Union*, 220–22; Croffutt and Morris, *Military and Civil History of Connecticut*, 271; Blakeslee, *History of the Sixteenth Connecticut Volunteers*, 16. As explained above, this was not the regiment's state flag but its national flag. Ira Forbes noted that this flag was saved from capture by Cpl. Francis Latimer, who earned promotion to color-sergeant on Oct. 13, 1862, no doubt for this action. See Forbes, "Color Guard, Sixteenth Regiment," Forbes Collection, CSL.

55. Robert H. Kellogg to Silas Kellogg, Sept. 20, 1862, Kellogg Papers, CHS.

56. Relyea, "History of the 16th Connecticut," 26; also Blakeslee, *History of the Sixteenth Connecticut*, 16, 102.

57. Quote from Robbins, "Some Recollections," 14, CHS. See also Relyea, "History of the 16th Connecticut," 26–27; Blakeslee, *History of the Sixteenth Connecticut Volunteers*, 16.

58. James Fitz James Caldwell, *The History of a Brigade of South Carolinians, Known First as "Greggs," and Subsequently as "McGowan's Brigade"* (Philadelphia: King and Baird, Printers, 1866), 46–47.

59. Berry Benson Memoirs, 18, Robert S. Brake Collection, MHI.

60. Henry M. Adams, "brief account of army injuries of hospital care in Maryland," in "Henry M. Adams," Whitney Collection, CSL.

61. Niven, *Connecticut for the Union*, 222; Stephen Sears, *Landscape Turned Red* (New York: Houghton and Mifflin, 1983), 286–89; Blakeslee, *History of the Sixteenth Connecticut Volunteers*, 16; Blakeslee, "The Sixteenth Connecticut at Antietam," 19; Relyea, "History of the 16th Connecticut," 27.

62. Niven, *Connecticut for the Union*, 222.

63. Niven, *Connecticut for the Union*, 223; Blakeslee, *History of the Sixteenth Connecticut Volunteers*, 17. See also John H. Burnham to Sarah B. Burnham and family, Oct. 4, 1862, Burnham Papers, CSL. One soldier, Pvt. Bela L. Burr (Co. G) was wounded and left behind for nearly forty-eight hours. A Georgia soldier heard his groans and gave him water as he lay in the cornfield. Burr's story became the basis of a postwar poem by A. W. Burkhardt, celebrating a moment where "two foes became friends." Burr's service was over; he spent months in the hospital and finally was discharged for

disability on Nov. 20, 1863. See "Bela Lewellyn Burr," Whitney Collection, CSL. See A. W. Burkhardt, "Forty Hours on the Battlefield or the Foeman Friend," MHI.

64. Leland O. Barlow to Jane Barlow, Sept. 23, 1862, Barlow Letters, CSL. In the 1860 and 1850 censuses, Barlow is listed as "Orrin L. Barlow," but he signed his wartime letters home "L.O.B." and "L. O. Barlow." His grave at Andersonville, where he died in October 1864, is also listed as "Leland O. Barlow." Yet in his 1864 diary, he wrote on the inside cover: "O. L. Barlow" and also used the initials "O. L. B." See O. Leland Barlow 1864 Diary, CSL; 8th Census of the United States, 1860: Population Schedule, Granby, Hartford County, and 7th Census of the United States, 1850: Population Schedule Hampden County, Granville, ancestry.com, accessed June 29, 2008. Nationwide graveside locator at http://gravelocator.cem.va.gov/, accessed 29 June 2008. Whitney used the name "Leland O. Barlow" in his records. See "Leland O. Barlow," Whitney Collection, CSL. In a letter to his sister, Barlow stated, "I am better known as O. L. Barlow here; please direct your letters so hereafter." Yet, he continued to sign his letters to her "L.O.B." See Leland O. Barlow to Jane Barlow, Aug. 16, 1863, Barlow Letters, CSL.

65. Company D, commanded by the slain captain Samuel Brown, counted the largest number of deserters: eight. Company A, led by Captain Henry Pasco had six. Company I had four; Company E, three; Company B, two; Company G, two; and Company K, two. See "Monthly Returns, 16th Regiment Connecticut Volunteers, Oct. 1862," Records of the Military Department, Connecticut Adjutant General's Office, CSL. See also Blakeslee, *History of the Sixteenth Connecticut,* 17–19; Lee Diary, Sept. 18, 1862, CHS. See also "F. Dixon Tucker," in "Military and Biographical Data of the 16th Connecticut Volunteers," Whitney Collection, CSL. Of the twenty-six deserters during the Antietam Campaign, seven were immigrants. It is not clear if this was a factor in desertion. Information gathered from "Monthly Returns, 16th Regiment Connecticut Volunteers, Oct. 1862," Records of the Military Department, Connecticut Adjutant General's Office, CSL. Robert H. Kellogg wrote in his diary that Company A had twenty-five men present on the morning of September 18, 1862. Some, like Pvt. John B. Ball (Co. D) deserted after his release from capture after the battle. The AGO 1869 lists him as simply "deserted," with no additional information, but Whitney stated that, after Ball's capture at Antietam and subsequent parole, there was simply no further record on him. See "John B. Ball," Whitney Collection, CSL. According to the 1860 census, Ball, a cigar maker from Suffield, was married with two young children. See 8th Census of the United States, 1860: Population Schedule, Suffield, Hartford, CT, at ancestry.com, accessed June 19, 2009. There appears to be no record of Ball in subsequent census records. It is not clear if Ball is counted in the number of deserters "after Antietam." However, in the Bound Regimental Papers, Ball is simply listed as a deserter from Company D: "wounded and taken prisoner at Battle of Antietam Sept 17, 1862 has since his return deserted while on parole furlough" and "Deserted while on leave of absence from Parole Camp, MD." See Bound Regimental Papers, RG 94, entries 112–15, Bound Records of the Union Volunteer Regiments, vol. 2, NA. John Cooney, an Irish immigrant who deserted at Antietam, was married with three children according to the 1860 census. He reappeared in the 1870 census, residing in Windham County with his wife Hannah, employed as a railroad worker, with eight children. His three eldest, Mary (15), James (12) and Ella (10) were all listed as employed in the local cotton mill. See 9th Census of the United States, 1870: Population Schedule, Windham, Windham County, CT, at ancestry.com, accessed July 29, 2009. A family tree also posted at ancestry.com indicates that

Cooney relocated to Iowa by 1880, but I cannot confirm this with the census records. Pvt. William Waterman (Co. E) was captured during the battle and soon paroled. However, he deserted from Camp Parole on September 28, 1862. See Bound Regimental Papers, RG 94, entries 112–15, Bound Records of the Union Volunteers Regiments, vol. 2, NA.

66. Ira Forbes later wrote of Rhodes that he had been a sea captain and was "familiar with English ports." Fellows Dixon Tucker was the eighteen-year-old son of Rev. Mark Tucker, an elderly Congregational pastor from Wethersfield. Forbes stated, "Subsequently Rhodes returned to Connecticut and died of the Dropsy in New Haven. His last months were attended with great destitution and sufferings. Tucker never returned to this country except secretly." See Forbes, "Wethersfield Men in Company A," Forbes Collection, CSL. Forbes further claimed that Tucker "declined to avail himself of the amnesty after the war, preferring exile." See "F. Dixon Tucker," Whitney Collection, CSL. See also 8th Census of the United States, 1860: Population Schedule, Vernon, Tolland, CT, at ancestry.com, accessed Jan. 23, 2010. Robert H. Kellogg remained in contact with Tucker, who probably had been a prewar friend. He wrote in his diary (without any commentary about Tucker's desertion from the regiment) on February 24, 1864, while stationed at Plymouth that he had received a paper from "Dick Tucker, Liverpool Eng. Also a tip top photograph of him in exchange for the one I sent him." See Kellogg Diary, Feb. 24, 1864, CHS; also see entry for Apr. 12, 1864. This photograph remains in the Kellogg Papers at the CHS. On the final page of his 1864 diary, Kellogg wrote Tucker's address: "F. Dixon Tucker, care Captain John M. Kendall, No. 33, Great Homer St., Liverpool, England."

The *Hartford Daily Times*, Oct. 6, 1862, reported the arrest of "a deserter from one of the last regiments, by the name of Rhodes." The man, who had been hiding out in an abandoned house along a roadside, was arrested and imprisoned in Hartford. There are several Connecticut soldiers with the last name "Rhodes" in the Civil War Soldiers and Sailors System database, including Albert Rhodes in the 22nd Regiment Connecticut Infantry, one of the last regiments raised in the state, but this Rhodes was mustered out July 7, 1863 (www.itd.nps.gov/cwss/soldiers.cfm., accessed May 20, 2008). Henry W. Rhodes, according to Whitney, fled to England with Dixon but eventually returned to the United States, where he lived in poverty. He died of heart disease on July 2, 1868. Whitney believed that Rhodes's widow, who was English, had returned to her native country. See "Henry W. Rhodes," Whitney Collection, CSL.

67. The 16th Connecticut was certainly not alone in losing men to desertion. Confederate desertion was notably high for Lee's Army throughout the Maryland Campaign. See Gary Gallagher, ed., *Antietam: Essays on the 1862 Maryland Campaign* (Kent, OH: Kent State University Press, 1989), 11. Ella Lonn states that within two hours after the battle ended, approximately 30,000 of McClellan's men had deserted. See Ella Lonn, *Desertion During the Civil War* (New York: Century Co., 1928), 144. More recent studies on desertion and its broad effects on the war effort include Jack Lawrence Atkins, "'It is Useless to Conceal the Truth Any Longer': Desertion of Confederate Soldiers from the Confederate Army" (MA thesis, Virginia Polytechnic Institute and State University, 2007), and Mark A. Weitz, "Desertion, Cowardice, and Punishment," Essential Civil War Curriculum, Apr. 2012, www.essential.civilwar.vt.edu/assets/files/ECWC TOPIC Desertion Cowardice and Punishment Essay.pdf. Also Robert Fantina, *Desertion and the American Soldier, 1776–2006* (New York: Algora, 2006).

68. Bound Regimental Papers, RG 94, entries 112–15, Bound Records of the Union Volunteers Regiments, vol. 2, NA.

69. See Bound Regimental Papers, RG 94, entries 112–15, Bound Records of the Union Volunteers Regiments, vol. 2, NA. The AGO 1869 gives the date of Riley's desertion as Dec. 1862, the AGO 1889 lists July 21, 1863, and the Bound Regimental Papers state, "Deserted after the Battle." The muster rolls state that both Riley and William Webster, also from Co. D, "deserted from hospitals [in] Sept & Dec. [and] never [heard] from only in Canada." See Muster Rolls, Returns, Regimental Papers, RG 94, Box 148 [unbound papers], NA.

70. See "Erastus Bottum," Whitney Collection, CSL; see also "Descriptive List of Deserters Arrested & Returned," Nov. 30, 1863, Muster Rolls, Returns, Regimental Papers, RG 94, Box 148 [unbound papers], NA. Relyea later explained, "Seven of those wounded [at Antietam] deserted from hospitals and it is reasonable to suppose that their wounds were slight, for but a few days had elapsed after the battle. When they were reported back to us as deserters the following are the names so reported: Patrick Leavey, Erastus Bottum, John Riley, Robert Grey, James Leach, Bela M. Keith, Levi Stone. Several were captured, two of whom we never heard of afterward. John P. Braman was one of whom it is said was badly wounded. No knowledge of his fate ever reached us and his disappearance remains a mystery until this day (1912). Of the other man, no information could be gathered as to his name or company by the writer of this history." Relyea, *16th Connecticut Volunteer Infantry,* 29. Braman is listed in the 1869 AGO as among the dead at Antietam on Sept. 17, 1862; in 1889 the record was adjusted to read, "Missing in Action, Sep 17, 1862, Antietam, MD; probably killed," with no further record. Whitney, however, claimed that Braman deserted "without doubt." See "John P. Braman," Whitney Collection, CSL; AGO 1869, 648; AGO 1889, 624. Pvt. Bela Keith, the youngest of three Keith brothers who enlisted in the regiment, was believed to have rejoined the army and fought on the frontier before settling in the South after the war. See "Bela M. Keith," Whitney Collection, CSL.

71. Bound Regimental Papers, RG 94, entries 112–15, Bound Records of the Union Volunteers Regiments, vol. 2; AGO, 1889. Pvt. George Long deserted before the battle but, according to Relyea, returned to the regiment "voluntarily." See Relyea, *16th Connecticut Volunteer Infantry,* 14, 42.

72. Austin D. Thompson to Electra M. Churchill, Oct. 8, 1862, Thompson Papers, CHS. Neither Merriman nor Nettleton's names are found on any official list of deserters. It is not clear who the soldier from Collinsville was. Thompson had spent the night after the battle in the woods with George Robbins, returning to the regiment the next morning. See George Robbins, "Some Recollections," CHS, 15.

73. Blakeslee, *History of the Sixteenth Connecticut Volunteers,* 21. Robert H. Kellogg wrote in his diary, "It was a very disagreeable duty and made me almost sick." See Kellogg Diary, Sept. 19, 1862, CHS.

74. Leland O. Barlow to sister, Sept. 23, 1862, Barlow Letters, CSL. Blakeslee described this spot as "under a large tree, near the stonewall, where the hardest of the battle was fought." See Blakeslee, *History of the Sixteenth Connecticut Volunteers,* 21.

75. Finch also personally "prepared the body" of Captain Barber to be sent home to Manchester. Soldiers' remains left in the mass grave were later removed to the Antietam national cemetery or transported north to Connecticut. See *Hartford Daily Times* and *Hartford Daily Courant,* Sept. 25, 1862. See also Blakeslee, *History of the Sixteenth Connecticut Volunteers,* 18; Blakeslee, "The Sixteenth

at Antietam," 21. Drew Faust discusses mass burials and the different treatment afforded to officers and men. See Faust, *The Republic of Suffering: Death and the American Civil War* (New York: Knopf, 2008), 61–101.

76. *Hartford Daily Courant*, Sept. 30, 1862. Burnham described the specific location of the mass grave about midway between the "Stone Bridge" and the town of Sharpsburg: "on a hill on the south side of the road, just back and west of a white house with a high piazza in front, and opposite of which is a brick house and large barn. The bodies lie near a large standing tree alone, and which I blazed on all sides so it can be easily discovered."

77. Francies Beach to Joseph D. Williams, Sept. 19, 1862, copy of original, ANB.

78. "Report of Lieut. Col. Joseph B. Curtis, Fourth Rhode Island Infantry, of the battle of Antietam," *OR*, ser. 1, vol. 19, pt. 1, 455–58.

79. "Report of Col. Edward Harland, Eighth Connecticut Infantry, commanding Second Brigade, Third Division, of the battle of Antietam," *OR*, ser. 1, vol. 19, pt. 1, 452–54.

80. *Hartford Evening Press*, Sept. 25 and 26, 1862. The *Press* shared information with other newspapers, including the *New York Tribune*.

81. *Hartford Daily Courant*, Sept. 18, 1862.

82. *Hartford Evening Press*, Sept. 22, 1862. This version of what happened to the 16th Connecticut would persist postwar. It became the "script" for the unit's collective memory of the battle. See McGlone, "Deciphering Memory," 420–21. See Chapter 9 for more on this topic.

83. *Hartford Evening Press*, Sept. 22, 1862.

84. *Hartford Evening Press*, Sept. 27, 1862. A piece in the *Hartford Daily Courant* on September 26, 1862, noted that "friends of 14th Connecticut regiment wonder why so much is said about the other Connecticut regiments in the Antietam fight, while the 14th is barely alluded to." The paper explained that more information had been reported on the 8th, 11th, and the 16th than on the 14th Connecticut. The irony is, of course, that the 14th performed better than these other units during the battle. The 16th Connecticut, as has been noted earlier, also had close ties to the Hartford newspapers. Antietam proved the costliest battle of the entire war for Connecticut soldiers. Total casualties for all Connecticut regiments engaged were 689, which included 131 killed and 515 wounded. See Blaikie Hines, *Civil War Volunteer Sons of Connecticut* (Thomaston, ME: American Patriotic Press, 2002), xv.

85. *Hartford Daily Times*, Sept. 23, 1862. Also, see *Hartford Daily Courant*, Sept. 23 and 26, 1862.

86. *Hartford Daily Courant*, Sept. 22, 1862.

87. *Hartford Daily Times*, Sept. 23, 1862. Pvt. Henry E. Bradley (Co. C) wrote, "The regiment fought well for a new one, and will sustain the honors already won by Connecticut soldiers." See *Hartford Daily Courant*, Sept. 23, 1862. Bradley further referred to the 16th "falling back," but the *Courant's* editors explained that the tall corn, and the difficulty of maneuvering men in it, caused the regiment to "fall back."

88. *Hartford Daily Times*, Sept. 27, 1862. Information on Neisener found in 10th Census of the United States, 1880: Population Schedule, New Milford, Litchfield, CT, at ancestry.com, accessed May 20, 2008. Although born in Poland, Neisener's parents were both German.

89. *Hartford Evening Press*, Sept. 23, 1862. Whitney Collection. Four hundred privates is an exaggeration. The regiment had at least 800 or even 850 soldiers in its ranks when it went into

action on September 17. See *Hartford Evening Press*, Sept. 25, 1862; also *Hartford Daily Courant*, Sept. 26, 1862. See also Gurdon Robbins letter, dated Sept. 21, 1862, published in the *Hartford Daily Courant*, Oct. 6, 1862.

90. Quoted in the *Hartford Evening Press*, Sept. 24, 1862. The letter was also quoted in the *Hartford Daily Courant* the same day. Corporal Safford was severely injured and died on September 23 from his wounds. See AGO 1889, 622. Johnson was soon promoted to 1st lieutenant after the battle. See *Hartford Evening Press*, Nov. 14, 1862.

91. *Hartford Daily Times*, Sept. 27, 1862; Cpl. Mettler left the regiment in May 9, 1863, with a discharge for disability.

92. Martin V. Culver to Jonathan Culver, Sept. 21, 1862, Culver Letters, private collection.

93. Wartime letter quoted in Relyea, "History of the 16th Connecticut," 43–44.

94. William H. Relyea to wife, Sept. 26, 1862, William H. Relyea Papers, CHS.

95. William H. Drake to Timothy Loomis, Sept. 29, 1862, Civil War Letters Collection, CHS.

96. George Robbins to Lydia Robbins, Sept. 23, 1862, George Robbins Papers, CHS.

97. Austin D. Thompson to Electra Churchill, Sept. 21, 1862, Thompson Papers, CHS.

98. Belden Diary, Sept. 19, 1862, CHS.

99. John B. Cuzner to Ellen Van Dorn, Sept. 21, 1862, Cuzner Letters and Papers, CHS. Cuzner was among the skirmishers caught in a crossfire, pinned down, and ordered to retreat. Cuzner's daughter Jennie relates a story "told in the letter writer's words as near as possible." The story recounts, "I ran behind a tree and looking around saw my Captain running for another tree's protection; thought I'd follow him, after a moment's rest off he went again and took shelter behind a clump of bushes and then an old stump." Cuzner then continued to follow Captain Mix "until we had the shelter of the stone wall between us and the firing." He concluded, "In this retreat, as long as I was following my Captain's flying coat tails I felt I was all right and it would have been laughable had it not been extremely serious." See "The Retreat," Cuzner Letters and Papers, CHS.

100. John B. Cuzner to Ellen Van Doren, Sept. 27, 1862, Cuzner Letters and Papers, CHS.

101. Leland O. Barlow to Jane C. Barlow, Sept. 19, 1862, Barlow Letters, CSL. After the fight, Barlow wrote, "We have been through a hard battle and about half of our Company are missing[.] probably there are some to come yet. We had many narrow escapes. I had a shell strike me on the back; it was so near spent that it did not do much damage to me." Leland O. Barlow to "Friends," [Sept. 1862], CSL.

102. Leland O. Barlow to Jane C. Barlow, Sept. 21, 1862, Barlow Letters, CSL.

103. Jacob Bauer to Emily Bauer, Sept. 20, 1862, ANB. In his 1915 unpublished reminiscences, Bauer claimed that he was slightly wounded during the battle, was "helped across the river," and found himself the next morning "in a pig pen near a farmhouse, stretched on straw." He wrote, "The doctor attended my scratch, gave me bandages and in a couple of weeks I was sound again." However, Bauer's name was not included in the official list of wounded. He said that he rejoined the 16th C.V. at Fredericksburg. See Bauer, "Personal Experiences," 5, PPM.

104. Jacob Bauer to Emily Bauer, Oct. 2, 1862, ANB. For more on fear and cowardice, particularly in battle, see John Keegan, *The Face of Battle* (New York: Viking, 1976), 16; Christopher Walsh, "'Cowardice Weakness or Infirmity, Whichever It May Be Termed': A Shadow History of the Civil War," *Civil War History* 59, no. 4 (Dec. 2013): 492–526.

105. Many repeated the accusation that Confederates deliberately carried a U.S. flag and posed as federals. See, e.g., Leander Chapin quoted in a letter dated Sept. 18, 1862, in "J. Leander Chapin Co. A 16th Regt. C. V.," Whitney Collection, CSL; Kellogg Diary, Sept. 17, 1862, and Robert H. Kellogg to Silas Kellogg, Sept. 20, 1862, Kellogg Papers, CHS. Adj. John Burnham told his family that he did not personally witness the Confederates waving the U.S. flag, but "I can find fifty men and some officers in our regt. and in the 8th Conn. and 4th Rhode Island who would willingly take their oath that they carried our flag and shouted out to us not to fire on our own men." Burnham added, "This cry 'Don't fire on your own men' I heard distinctly in front of us myself and supposing it to be from some regiment of ones who were in advance of us I ordered the men near me to cease firing and they did so." See John H. Burnham to Sarah B. Burnham and family, Oct. 4, 1862, Burnham Papers, CSL. The story of the Confederates "treacherously" displaying the U.S. colors "until ready to grapple with the foe" also appeared in the *Hartford Daily Courant* on Sept. 22, 1862, recounted by a Lieutenant Davis from the 11th Connecticut and Pvt. Artetus Culver (Co. K). See also *Hartford Evening Press*, Sept. 22, 1862. The story was repeated in the *Courant* on September 26, with the added detail that Captain Rankin (Co. C) "shot the rebel standard bearer." Similarly, Robbins wrote his sister, "The Rebels came upon us with the Ohio State flag and National colors, and part of them had on our clothes. They called out to us not to fire on our own flag, and then they fired." George Robbins to Lydia Robbins, Sept. 23, 1862, Robbins Papers, CHS.

106. Sidney H. Hayden to Oliver Hayden, Sept. 20, 1862, Hayden Papers, EGPL. A. P. Hill's men may in fact been wearing blue uniforms captured from Harper's Ferry earlier in the day, and there is a possibility that the blue flag Connecticut men mistook for the federal flag, or the Ohio state flag, was the 2nd South Carolina's banner. After the fight, Burnham described seeing "the bodies of several dead rebels dressed in our blue uniforms which they had taken in the recent fight near Manassas." See John H. Burnham to Sarah B. Burnham, Oct. 4, 1862, John B. Burnham Papers, CSL.

107. Corporal Hayden, who with Company B had been dispatched as skirmishers before the regiment entered the cornfield, hesitated until he "could see something to fire at," but after two bullets from rebel sharpshooters nearly killed him, orders came to pull back. "After that our regiment was ordered in to the cornfield where we were ordered to lie down and not fire on our friends." Hayden attested, "I obeyed all the orders given. Some soldiers scattered but no general order was given. We faced the enemy's batteries and marched in good order untill [sic] ordered to retreat." See Sidney H. Hayden to Oliver Hayden, Dec. 9, 1862, Hayden Papers, EGPL. Hayden was reduced to ranks around the time of this letter and in the next sentence after discussing Antietam, he told his father that Captain Mix had demoted him, "no reasons assigned and no questions asked." It is not clear if his behavior at Antietam had anything to do with this action; he insisted that his demotion was not due to "bad conduct."

108. Kellogg Diary, Sept. 17, 1862, Kellogg Papers, CHS.

109. Robert H. Kellogg to Silas Kellogg, Sept. 20, 1862, Kellogg Papers, CHS. He also prayed, as so many Civil War soldiers did, that if he should die, God would "prepare me to die in peace." See also Robert H. Kellogg to Father, Oct. 17, 1862, Kellogg Papers, CHS. In this letter, Kellogg referred to the Confederates again as having "skedaddled over the river." Cuzner used similar language in describing Lee's retreat from the battlefield in John B. Cuzner to Ellen Van Dorn, Sept. 21, 1862, Cuzner Letters and Papers, CHS.

110. John H. Burnham to Sarah B. Burnham and family, Oct. 4, 1862, Burnham Papers, CSL. Burnham's sister Charlotte, or Lottie, was one year older than he, according to 7th Census of the United States, 1850: Population Schedule, Hartford, Hartford County, CT, at ancestry.com, accessed June 25, 2008. For more on the concepts of "restrained" and "martial" manhood, with which Burnham seems to be grappling, see Amy Greenberg, *Manifest Manhood and the Antebellum American Empire* (Cambridge: Cambridge University Press, 2005), 9–14.

111. John H. Burnham to "Folks," n.d., Burnham Papers, CSL.

112. John H. Burnham to Sarah B. Burnham and family, Oct. 4, 1862, 1862, Burnham Papers, CSL.

113. Nathan Mayer to Louis Mayer, Sept. 29, 1862, published in the *Hartford Daily Courant,* Oct. 7, 1862.

114. Henry C. Hall to "sister," Oct. 5, 1862, Henry C. Hall Papers, Duke University. Hall later won promotion to captain but died on July 11, 1864, during the Petersburg Campaign. See AGO 1869, 388; AGO 1889, 344. Hall praised the 11th and his own 8th: "Upon the bloody battlefield of Antietam the 8th and 11th Conn Vols have won immortal honor and when I say this I do not mean they have gained newspaper notoriety through the silly puffs of hised [sic] blowers, but I mean that by their coolness and unflinching bravery" during "the most terrible fire of the enemy they have won the respect of all the generals and other military men who witnessed their conduct." It is not clear if he meant that the 16th Connecticut had gained "newspaper notoriety," but, as evidenced here, the regiment gained a good deal of positive press from Hartford newspapers, more it seems, than these other two regiments.

115. *Hartford Evening Press,* Sept. 26, 1862; see also *Hartford Daily Times,* Sept. 27, 1862. On September 22, the *Hartford Evening Press* published a preliminary list of the killed and wounded; the *Hartford Daily Courant* followed on September 23.

116. There are numerous examples of inaccurate information about the fate of individual soldiers appearing in Hartford newspapers. A "painful rumor" circulated in the city soon after the battle that Lt. Col. Frank Cheney was dead, when in fact he had been wounded, shot through his left arm. Mary Bushnell, whom he later married, went to pay her condolences to his family only to be greeted by Frank himself. See the *Hartford Daily Times,* Sept. 22, 1862; Learned, "The Letters of Mary Bushnell Cheney and Frank Woodbridge Cheney," SC, 12. See also Faust's discussion on the need for information in *This Republic of Suffering,* 103–7. The *Hartford Daily Courant* reported on September 23, 1862, that Cheney was wounded. Capt. John Drake's death was reported in the *Hartford Daily Times* on September 22, five days after Antietam, with the word "probably" after his name. He was indeed dead. In successive days, the *Hartford Daily Times* gave varying lists of the dead; see, e.g., papers from September 24 and October 3, 1862.

117. For example, "Alfred" should be "Albert"; other misspellings include "Prior" for "Pryor," "Gladden" for "Gladding," "Brigham" for "Bingham," and "McCarty" for Macarty." "Harry Barnett" was repeatedly misreported as "Harry Burnett." See the *Hartford Daily Times,* Sept. 24 and 25, and *Hartford Daily Courant,* Sept. 25, 1862. Pvt. William Relyea also provided a list of casualties in his Company D in a letter home to Suffield, which was published in the *Hartford Daily Times* on September 25. Finch himself later noted that he and Burnham made out the list with "great care" and that he believed it was accurate. See Peter V. Finch to George Q. Whitney, Oct. 1, 1894, Whitney Collection, CSL.

118. Peter V. Finch to Harriet Bronson, Sept. 21, 1862, copy of letter, Whitney Collection, CSL. Finch later provided George Q. Whitney with an ink copy of the list after explaining that his wife had recently found the original in a box but that it was in pencil. This letter appears to indicate that some of the errors of spelling were made by Finch, others by the newspaper.

119. Casualty numbers vary from source to source. These numbers are abstracted from AGO 1889, 619–39. Hines provides slightly different numbers (and categories): 44 killed, 1 missing, 159 wounded, 15 captured, and 4 wounded and captured. The 1894 Antietam monument that stands today on the battlefield lists 779 engaged, 43 killed, and 161 wounded. The *Hartford Daily Courant* stated on September 26, 1862, that 850 reported for duty the morning of the battle and 585 reported for duty the next day. A Hartford newspaper in 1912 stated that the total losses for the 16th C.V. were 13 officers and 289 men, "and so many others were in bad shape from fatigue and improper food that the regiment never mustered 600 men after that." See unnamed newspaper clipping [1912], Whitney Collection, CSL. There were also those with lighter wounds, such as Cpl. John Gemmill, who was "struck on the right side by a piece of shell" that "[cut] his blouse & shirt." He was "sore for a few days" but not listed officially as wounded in the AGO. See "John Gemmill," Whitney Collection, CSL. Fox's *Regimental Losses* lists 42 killed, 143 wounded, and 185 total casualties for the 16th; the 8th Connecticut lost 34 killed, 139 wounded, and 21 missing, with 194 total. Comparatively, Fox cites the 15th Massachusetts as losing the most with 65 killed, 255 wounded, and 24 missing, and 344 total. See Fox, *Regimental Losses*, 432; Hines, *Civil War Volunteer Sons*, 183.

120. Croffutt and Morris, *Military and Civil History of Connecticut*, 276; Blakeslee, *History of the Sixteenth Connecticut Volunteers*, 18.

121. "Casualties of the 16th Regiment Connecticut Volunteers Battle of Antietam Sept. 17, 1862," CSL. Many of those officers wounded at Antietam left the regiment for good in the weeks and months following the battle, either by resigning or obtaining a discharge for disability. See below for more on this. The large loss of officers in battle was not necessarily unusual, but for the 16th C.V. that loss—combined with resignations, desertions, extended absences, lack of pay, and other events—made them believe they were unfortunate.

122. Bauer, "Personal Experiences of the War," 4, PPM.

123. Whitney described the bullet hitting Clark "through the right thigh"; the young sergeant would lose his leg and eventually be discharged for disability on March 12, 1863. See *Hartford Daily Times*, Sept. 27, 1862; "Charles Le Roy Clark," Whitney Collection," CSL; also AGO 1889, 620. Mention of Clark's honorable discharge can be found in the *Hartford Evening Press*, Mar. 13, 1863.

124. Frank W. Cheney to Charles Cheney, Sept. 19, 1862, in Learned, "Letters of Mary Bushnell Cheney and Frank Woodbridge Cheney," SC, 10–11; also Frank Cheney, CSR, NA. Cheney's injury was so serious that he resigned and was formally discharged in December for physical disability; his emotional attachment to the unit would remain until the end of his life. See "Frank Woodbridge Cheney," Whitney Collection, CSL. Maj. George A. Washburn arrived home October 21 and was discharged for disability Jan. 17, 1863. See *Hartford Daily Times*, Oct. 22, 1862; AGO 1889, 619.

125. AGO 1889.

126. William H. Relyea to George Q. Whitney, Feb. 25, 1909, Whitney Collection, CSL.

127. There are varying versions of exactly what the captain last said to his men before he died. See *Hartford Evening Press*, Sept. 30, 1862; Relyea, "Obituary of Samuel Brown," Whitney Collection, CSL.

128. William H. Relyea to George Q. Whitney, Feb. 25, 1909, Whitney Collection, CSL. Relyea and Grohman found their captain's body on September 19 and removed it for burial. Eventually, Brown was reburied in his hometown of Danvers, Massachusetts.

129. *Hartford Evening Press*, Sept. 23, 1862.

130. Eli Manross to Mary Clementine Manross, Oct. 15, 1862, transcript copy, Newton S. Manross Collection, private collection. Eli also sent home a piece of cloth torn from his brother's uniform and a piece of "rebel writing paper" that he collected from the battlefield.

131. See findagrave.com, accessed May 19, 2008. The *Hartford Evening Press* reported Manross's burial on Tuesday, September 23, 1862. See also *Hartford Evening Press*, Sept. 25, 1862.

132. Leverette Griggs, obituary of "Captain Manross," undated newspaper clipping, William Smith Clark Papers, UMA.

133. Frank W. Cheney to Charles Cheney, Sept. 19, 1864, Learned, "Letters of Mary Bushnell Cheney and Frank Woodbridge Cheney," SC, 11. The *Hartford Courant* also reported that Beach "had several bullets through his clothing but escaped the balls aimed at him" (Sept. 26, 1862). Pvt. Aretas Culver (Co. K) complimented Beach's "gallantry and courage": "he sat upon his horse during the trying ordeal, as calm and self-possessed, as if on dress parade" (*Hartford Daily Courant*, Sept. 22, 1862).

134. *Hartford Daily Courant*, Sept. 26, 1862.

135. Sidney Hayden to Jane Hayden, Sept. 26, 1862, Hayden Papers, EGPL. Hayden later praised Captain Upton from the 8th Connecticut and stated that he would rather have him take command and see Beach resign. Upton was not as profane as Beach.

136. Leland O. Barlow to Harvey Barlow, Oct. 10, 1862, Barlow Letters, CSL.

137. Blakeslee, *History of the Sixteenth Connecticut Volunteers*, 102.

138. *Hartford Daily Courant*, Oct. 9, 1862.

139. *Hartford Evening Press*, Sept. 22 and 26, 1862. Callender and McNary returned on Sept. 25; Kellogg on Sept. 26 with the wounded Cheney.

140. Among the forty-three killed from the 16th Connecticut at Antietam, Roberts brought home the bodies of five men from the regiment in early October: Capts. John Drake and Samuel Brown, Sgt. Thomas Macarty, and Pvts. William W. Nichols and Seth Franklin Prior. The *Courant* referred to Roberts as an "Undertaker." See *Hartford Daily Courant*, Sept. 29 and Oct. 11, 1862; *Hartford Daily Times* and *Hartford Evening Press*, Oct. 10, 1862. There is a William W. Roberts listed as a furniture maker in Hartford in *Geer's 1861–1862, Hartford Directory*, 208, and as a "master cabinet maker" in the 1860 census. See 8th Census of the United States, 1860: Population Schedule, Hartford District 2, Hartford, CT, at ancestry.com, accessed May 20, 2010. Apparently, he was also an undertaker. Whitney refers to him as a "Hartford undertaker" in his sketch of Captain Drake. See "John Louis Drake," Whitney Collection, CSL. Roberts brought home the bodies of men from other regiments, too, including Capt. Jervis E. Blinn from the 14th Connecticut and Cpl. John H. Simons from the 8th Connecticut.

141. Sidney H. Hayden to Oliver Hayden, Oct. 5, 1862, Hayden Papers, EGPL. See also Robert H. Kellogg to Silas Kellogg, Oct. 5, 1862, Kellogg Papers, CHS.

142. *Hartford Evening Press*, Nov. 6, 1862; *Hartford Daily Courant*, Nov. 7, 1862. I was unable to match the name H. N. Prout to anyone in the 1860 census.

143. A. W. Ide, *Sermon Preached Oct. 8, 1862 at Stafford Springs, at the Funeral of Lieut. William Horton, of Co. I, 16th Conn. Regt. Volunteers, Who Was Killed at the Battle of Antietam, Sept. 17, 1862* (Holliston, MA: E. G. Plimpton, Printer, 1862), 14, 15, 17, 19–20. Emphasis from original. The location was the Stafford Springs Congregational Church. See also Faust, *This Republic of Suffering,* 164; Harry S. Stout, *Upon the Altar of a Nation: A Moral History of the Civil War* (New York: Viking, 2006), 91–92, and George Rable, *God's Almost Chosen People: A Religious History of the American Civil War* (Chapel Hill: University of North Carolina Press, 2010), 140, regarding such funeral sermons.

144. Ide, *A Sermon,* 14.

145. Ezra Burgess to George Q. Whitney, Mar. 22, 1909, Whitney Collection, CSL. See also AGO 1869, 468.

146. Gilbert, *Sermon,* 12.

147. Gilbert, *Sermon,* 22. Allen's father Dr. Francis Allen, a Granby physician, brought his son's body home from Washington on December 30, 1862. See the *Hartford Daily Times,* Jan. 1, 1863; Carol Laun, "The Valiant Sons of Francis and Eliza Allen," *Southwoods* (May 1989): 4; 8th Census of the United States, 1860: Population Schedule, Granby, Hartford County, CT, at ancestry.com, accessed May 28, 2008. Adelaide R. Holcomb recorded Allen's body arriving home in Granby on December 31. See Adelaide R. Holcomb Diary, Dec. 31, 1862, Holcomb Family Papers, SBHS. Dr. Allen was the family physician for Adelaide's cousin Richard Henry Lee, and Lee recorded Dr. Allen arriving in camp to try to obtain his son's discharge: "Roswell is in quite a bad way, but if he could go home would get better." See Richard Henry Lee to Adelaide R. Holcomb, Dec. 18, 1862, Holcomb Family Papers, SBHS.

148. See Albert Day to William A. Buckingham, Apr. 14, 1864, Governors' Correspondence, CSL. The letter writer is no doubt prominent businessman and former lieutenant governor Albert Day of Albert Day, Sons and Co. See Talcott, "Prominent Business Men," in Trumbull, *The Memorial History of Hartford County,* 1:670. Collins never fully recovered from the festering wound to his left leg, dying in 1893 in Windsor, Connecticut, at the age of fifty-one. Whitney stated, "His death was caused by blood poisoning from a Doctor trying to close up the wound." See "Charles T. Collins," Whitney Collection, CSL. The *Hartford Evening Press,* Oct. 9, 1862, made mention of Collins undergoing an operation the day before, which "extracted a number of bones, some of them measuring some three inches in length." The paper continued, "The unfortunate man suffered intense pain through the night, but is now comfortable as can be expected. He lies at the residence of his mother, No. 49 Park Street." Clearly, Collins' required additional medical care; hence, his extended hospital stay.

149. Alexander Calhoun to William A. Buckingham, Feb. 11, 1863, Governors' Correspondence, CSL. Biographical information on Alexander Calhoun from Charles Moore, *History of Michigan* (Chicago: Lewis Publishing Co., 1915), 2:752. Baker is listed in the AGO 1862 report as a printer. Months later, all three were finally discharged from service due to their Antietam wounds: Baker on May 26, 1863, Randall on Mar. 14, 1863, and Willey on Feb. 6, 1863. Samuel Baker to William A. Buckingham, Oct. 6, 1862, Governors' Correspondence, CSL. Willey later became a lieutenant in the 31st U.S.C.T., dying at home in South Windsor in October of 1864. See www.findagrave.com, accessed Feb. 21, 2008. Baker wrote the governor again in February 1863 from Frederick City, Maryland, complaining that he did "not receive any answers, supposing that at that time nothing could be done for me." He repeated his contention that he would "perhaps never be able to again

do duty in the Regt." See Samuel Baker to Gov. William A. Buckingham, Feb. 11, 1863, Governors' Correspondence, CSL.

150. There are many examples in Governor Buckingham's correspondence of soldiers' family members writing for aid. See, e.g., Mary W. Havens writing about her ill son Edward N. Havens on December 14, 1862, in Governors' Correspondence, CSL. Havens was discharged for disability on December 31, 1862.

151. See Faust, *The Republic of Suffering*, Stout, *Upon the Altar of the Nation*, and Franny Nudleman, *John Brown's Body: Slavery, Violence, and the Culture of War* (Chapel Hill: University of North Carolina Press, 2004), for more on how the war and its unprecedented violence forged a new relationship between northerners (and eventually all Americans) and the "state." Although these historians have stressed how the war changed northerners' relationship with the federal government, these letters underscore the tie between the state government and its citizens, at least in Connecticut. For an example of Buckingham trying but failing to help a specific soldier in the regiment obtain a furlough, see Nathan Mayer to William A. Buckingham, May 22, 1863, Governors' Correspondence, CSL. In this instance, the governor sent a letter to Surgeon Mayer inquiring as to the health of Pvt. Fernando A. Bradley in Co. A, but Mayer responded that although Bradley had been "a little sick some time ago," he had "fully recovered." Mayer judged Bradley "healthy and robust in appearance" and presently "employed in light duty in the kitchen of the officers in the mess." Bradley remained in service the remainder of the war.

152. Ammi Giddings to Gov. William A. Buckingham, Jan. 15, 1863, Governors' Correspondence, CSL. Biographical information on Giddings is from Joseph Anderson, ed., *The Town and City of Waterbury, Connecticut, from the Aboriginal Period to the Year Eighteen Hundred and Ninety-Five*, 3 vols. (New Haven: Price and Lee Company, 1896), 3:821; see also *Hartford Daily Times*, Feb. 7, 1863. Another grieving parent writing Buckingham was Congregational minister Asahel C. Washburn, who lost his son 1st Sgt. Wadsworth A. Washburn (Co. G) at Antietam. See A. C. Washburn to William A. Buckingham, Jan. 29, 1863, Governors' Correspondence, CSL; "Wadsworth A. Washburn," Whitney Collection, CSL.

153. Examples include Frederick A. Crane, who "was taken sick immediately after the battle of Antietam" and subsequently placed in a Frederick City, Maryland, hospital where his condition failed to improve. He transferred to convalescent camps in northern Virginia but, in the words of his brother, was "unable to walk any distance without fatigue." Crane, like so many of his comrades, would eventually be discharged for disability. See L. G. Crane to William A. Buckingham, Mar. 30, 1863, Governors' Correspondence, CSL.

154. Theodore R. Stearns to "John," Mar. 15, 1863, Stearns Family Papers, CHS.

155. Theodore R. Stearns to "John," Mar. 20, 1863, Stearns Family Papers, CHS.

156. Theodore R. Stearns to "John," Mar. 15, 1863, Stearns Family Papers, CHS. See also Theodore R. Stearns Pension File, NA, and Theodore R. Stearns, CSR. Stearns admitted that his desk assignment was gained "through the influence of some of my friends." He wrote, "If I was with my Regiment I should stand a pretty good sight for a Commission as there are but two Non-Commissioned officers in the company," but he was comfortably situated and content to remain an army clerk. See Theodore R. Stearns to "John," Mar. 20, 1863, Stearns Family Papers, CHS. Stearns never returned to the regiment or to active service. His extensive pension file describes a bout

of sunstroke during that grueling march. Stearns also suffered from diarrhea, varicose veins, and rheumatism during the war, all ailments that grew worse with age. See Theodore R. Stearns Pension File, NA; also see "Theodore Randall Stearns," Whitney Collection, CSL.

157. See "Alfred Avery," Whitney Collection, CSL. Avery is listed as insane in the 1880 census. See 10th Census of the United States, 1880: Population Schedule, South Windsor, Hartford, CT, at ancestry.com, accessed June 18, 2009. At this time, Avery resided with his parents and was "Helping at Home." Avery had two older brothers who served in the 25th Connecticut. He died of pneumonia at the age of seventy-two in his hometown of South Windsor.

158. *Hartford Daily Times,* Oct. 10, 1862.

159. J. Morgan Smith to William A. Buckingham, Nov. 14, 1862, Governors' Correspondence, CSL. James I. Robertson observes that Union regiments were rarely able to keep at full strength after their initial mustering in. He cites Livermore's statistics to show that the average federal regiment by April 1862 only numbered 560 men; by July 1863, a mere 375. See Robertson, *Soldiers Blue and Gray,* 21, 22. Still, many in the 16th C. V. believed that they had been uniquely diminished after Antietam.

160. George Robbins, "Some Recollections," CHS.

161. Case added, "I always felt there was some bad mistake made in putting us into so hot a place when we knew nothing about the duties of a soldier" ("Memoirs," Simsbury Historical Society, hereafter cited as SHS).

162. Austin D. Thompson to Electra M. Churchill, Oct. 16, 1862, Thompson Papers, CHS.

163. See *Hartford Evening Press,* Oct. 14, 1862. This number was dated to Sunday, October 12, 1862. The regiment had moved on October 7 to Pleasant Valley, about eight miles from Antietam Creek. See Muster Rolls Returns, Regimental Papers, RG 94, Bound 148 [unbound papers], NA.

164. Blakeslee, *History of the Sixteenth Connecticut Volunteers,* 22.

CHAPTER THREE

1. Kellogg Diary, Nov. 2, 1862, Kellogg Papers, CHS; also Nov. 3, 1862.

2. Robert H. Kellogg to Silas Kellogg, Nov. 11, 1862, Kellogg Papers, CHS.

3. Belden Diary, Oct. 29, 1862, CHS.

4. Belden Diary, Nov. 18, 1862, CHS.

5. Bement is not listed as a deserter; instead, the 1889 AGO simply states, "Fell out on march (sick) near Wheatland, Va., Nov. 1, '62. N.f.r. A.G. O." See AGO 1889, 626. See also "Edwin C. Bement," Whitney Collection, CSL.

6. The 16th had roll call three times a day, and the camp guard had been called off, although there was a "brigade guard" posted in the evening. Passes were also required for soldiers to venture out. Belden complained about the rations during the march. See Belden Diary, Nov. 13 and 1, 1862, CHS.

7. Blakeslee, *History of the Sixteenth Connecticut Volunteers,* 25.

8. Martin V. Culver to Jonathan Culver, Nov. 16, 1862, Culver Letters, private collection.

9. Lewis M. Holcomb to Adelaide R. Holcomb, Nov. 1, 1862, Holcomb Family Papers, SBHS.

10. John H. Burnham to Sarah B. Burnham, Nov. 11, 1862, Burnham Papers, CSL.

11. See John H. Burnham to Sarah B. Burnham, Nov. 11, 1862, Burnham Papers, CSL; Robert

H. Kellogg to Silas Kellogg, Nov. 11, 1862, Kellogg Papers, CHS. The *Hartford Evening Press* reported Beach's illness on November 21, 1862: "Co. Beach is quite sick, says a letter from the regiment, and Capt. Mix is in command." Also see *Hartford Daily Times,* Nov. 20, 1862. Beach's service record documents his illness from November 1862 until at least July 1863 and his various leaves of absence. In the summer of 1863, a doctor determined that Beach had "chronic Dysentery." In November 1863, he also had lumbago and bronchitis. Blakeslee indicates that Beach's maladies dated to his prewar service, although he fails to specify what they were. See Blakeslee, *History of the Sixteenth Connecticut Volunteers,* 102; also Frank Beach, CSR, NA. On January 1, 1863, the *Hartford Evening Press* reported that Beach submitted his resignation but that Gen. Sumner refused to accept it.

12. Culver had remained healthy through November, though still unhappy with soldier life. Later in December he became sick with a cold. See Martin V. Culver to Jonathan Culver, Nov. 29, 1862, Culver Letters, private collection.

13. Other historians have described this phenomenon in common soldiers. Wiley discusses the "ebb and flow" of soldiers' morale depending on a variety of factors. See Bell Irvin Wiley, *The Life of Billy Yank: The Common Soldier of the Union* (1952; reprint, Baton Rouge: Louisiana State University Press, 1971), 76; 275–95; also McPherson, *For Cause and Comrades,* 9; Linderman, *Embattled Courage,* 113–33.

14. *Hartford Daily Times,* Nov. 4, 1862.

15. Josiah T. Peck to William A. Buckingham, Nov. 24, 1862, Governors' Correspondence, CSL.

16. Mrs. E. L. H. to William A. Buckingham, n.d. [Nov. 1862], Governors' Correspondence, CSL.

17. *Hartford Evening Press,* Nov. 29, 1862. The letter writer only gave his initials, "J.M.S." It could have been James M. Steele (Co. F), although he did not reside in Unionville, from where this letter came.

18. *Hartford Daily Courant,* Nov. 21, 1862.

19. Ariel or Alonzo Case, "Simsbury in the Civil War," SHS.

20. Leland O. Barlow to Jane E. Barlow, Nov. 30, 1862, Barlow Letters, CSL.

21. Examples included 1st Lt. Henry Gay (resigned Nov. 1, 1862), 2nd Lt. John M. Waters (Oct. 13, 1862), and 2nd Lt. Joseph Barlow (Co. F, Oct. 29, 1862); see *Hartford Evening Press,* Nov. 12, 1862. Waters was later recommissioned into the unit in May 1863 as a first lieutenant. Second Lt. John Fiske (Co. I) left the unit because another man was promoted over him after Antietam. See "John M. Fiske," Whitney Collection, CSL. Burke replaced the slain lieutenant William Horton. First Lt. Henry O. Goodell (Co. B), 1st Lt. George S. Gouge (Co. C), and 2nd Lt. Henry T. White (Co. H) resigned, too. Second Lt. George W. Cook, II (Co. G), also resigned when he learned that a sergeant "was promoted over him. See *Hartford Evening Press* and *Hartford Daily Courant,* Oct. 20, 1862.

22. Commissioned officers continued to leave the regiment that winter. Capt. Edward Rankin (Co. C) was honorably discharged on Jan. 25, 1863, and Capt. William Lockwood (Co. K) resigned Feb. 4, 1863. See the *Hartford Evening Press,* Jan. 31, 1863. When Rankin left the regiment, he alleged that it was "in better fighting condition than ever before, the men well fed and hearty." See *Hartford Evening Press,* Feb. 18, 1863.

23. Tension between officers and men in the ranks was nothing new within a Civil War regiment or among volunteers in other wars in U.S. history. See Marcus Cunliffe, *Soldiers and Civilians: The Martial Spirit in America, 1775–1865* (Boston: Little, Brown, 1968); Fred Anderson, *A People's Army: Massachusetts Soldiers and Society in the Seven Years' War* (Chapel Hill: University of North Carolina Press, 1984); and Bledsoe, "Citizen-Officers." Lorien Foote further discusses the organized action of

northern privates protesting the "perceived injustice, incompetence or tyranny" of their officers in *The Gentlemen and the Roughs*, 160, 167–69.

24. John B. Cuzner to Ellen Van Dorn, May 15, 1864, Cuzner Letters and Papers, CHS.

25. Case, "Memoirs," SHS.

26. Sidney H. Hayden to Jane Hayden, Jan. 24, 1863, Hayden Papers, EGPL. As noted above Mix reduced Hayden to the ranks, which could have colored Hayden's opinion of the captain. It is not clear exactly when or why Hayden was demoted, but he remained a private until his death in April 1865. See CSR, copies included in Hayden Papers, EGPL.

27. John H. Burnham to Sarah B. Burnham, Nov. 11, 1862, Burnham Papers, CSL.

28. Robert H. Kellogg to Silas Kellogg, Nov. 11, 1862, Kellogg Papers, CHS. Austin Thompson was none too thrilled to see Beach's return. Austin D. Thompson to Electra M. Churchill, Dec. 19, 1862, Thompson Papers, CHS.

29. Ninety men died between August 31 and December 12, 1862. These included sixty-seven from battle wounds, five from illness, and eighteen from unknown causes. Pvts. Miles Shepard (Nov. 13, 1862) and Cpl. Stanford Stoughton (Oct. 28, 1862) died in Maryland hospitals. Number of deaths calculated from AGO 1869, AGO 1889; Muster Rolls, Returns, Regimental Papers, RG 94, Box 148 [unbound papers], NA, among other sources. See also *Hartford Daily Times*, Dec. 1, 1862.

30. Robert H. Kellogg to Silas Kellogg, Nov. 28, 1862, Kellogg Papers, CHS. Kellogg later referred to his "traveling drugstore," which he carried thinking he might be called on to help wounded soldiers from Fredericksburg, but it appears that he mainly administered medicine to officers on Burnside's staff. See Robert H. Kellogg to Silas and Lucy C. Hale Kellogg, Dec. 13, 1862, and Robert H. Kellogg to Silas H. Kellogg, Dec. 25, 1862, Kellogg Papers, CHS. In late January he was not sure if he would "ever be ordered back to the 16th," but he did make frequent visits to camp until the regiment left for Newport News in February 1863. See Robert H. Kellogg to Silas Kellogg, Jan. 28, 1863, and Robert H. Kellogg to Lucy Hale Kellogg, Jan. 20, 1863, Kellogg Papers, CHS. See also Robert H. Kellogg, CSR, NA.

31. Bound Regimental Papers, RG 94, entries 112–15, Bound Records of the Union Volunteer Regiments, vol. 2, NA. The AGO lists the date of Pratt's desertion as November 2, 1862, but the Bound Regimental papers cite October 15, 1862, and January 26, 1863.

32. Bound Regimental Papers, RG 94, entries 112–15, Bound Records of the Union Volunteer Regiments, vol. 2, NA.

33. The date of Roberts's desertion was February 11, 1863, according to AGO 1869 and 1889; however, the Bound Regimental Records claim that Roberts deserted in December 1862 from Fredericksburg. He may have disappeared while the unit was leaving Fredericksburg for Newport News. See Bound Regimental Records, RG 94, entries 112–15, Bound Records of the Union Volunteer Regiments, vol. 2, NA.

34. It was reported that Stratton returned home to Connecticut. See Muster Rolls, Returns, Regimental Papers, Box 148 [unbound papers], RG 94, NA.

35. *Hartford Evening Press*, Nov. 17, 1862.

36. This is compared to 716 soldiers counted in the 11th Connecticut, although of that number 348 were listed as "fit for duty." See *Hartford Evening Press*, Nov. 29, 1862.

37. *Hartford Daily Times*, Dec. 8, 1862. If "M.H." simply stood for a soldier's name, the

possibilities include Marshall House (Co. C), Michael Halery (Co. D), Mathias Heck (Co. I), Martin Hennessey (Co. I), or Michael Holland (Co. E). Records indicate that all five were with the regiment in December 1862.

38. *Hartford Daily Times,* Dec. 9, 1862. There were equally bleak reports in Hartford papers regarding conditions among other units, including the 14th Connecticut. See, e.g., *Hartford Daily Times,* Dec. 10, 1862.

39. Many repeated the story of leaving behind their knapsacks, including George Lamphere, who claimed that they remained in a Washington, D.C., warehouse until late in the war (Lamphere Memoirs, MHS). However, the *Hartford Evening Press* stated that Captain Tennant "sent for them. They came, but many of them had been rifled of their contents" (Dec. 11, 1862).

40. John B. Cuzner to Ellen Van Dorn, Dec. 8, 1862, Cuzner Letters and Papers, CHS.

41. Governor Buckingham became aware of the worsening situation as early as October. See D. H. Chase to William A. Buckingham, Oct. 18, 1862, Governors' Correspondence, CSL; see also Niven, *Connecticut for the Union,* 94–95.

42. Wiley, *Billy Yank,* 277–80. George Rable describes the army's disaffection on the eve of the Fredericksburg campaign as caused by a combination of inactivity after Antietam, cold weather, lack of food, and rampant illness. There were extensive supply problems affecting much of the army while encamped, but these were especially acute when the army marched. See George Rable, *Fredericksburg! Fredericksburg!* (Chapel Hill: University of North Carolina Press, 2002), 12, 20, 56, 68, 100–115.

43. Richard Henry Lee to Starr Holcomb, Dec. 17, 1862, Holcomb Family Papers, SBHS; also Leland O. Barlow to Jane E. Barlow, Dec. 16, 1862, Barlow Letters, CSL.

44. Belden Diary, Dec. 14, 1862, CHS. Megan Kate Nelson explores the larger significance of this type of destruction that Belden encountered in Fredericksburg in *Ruin Nation: Destruction and the American Civil War* (Athens: University of Georgia Press, 2012).

45. Leland O. Barlow to Jane E. Barlow, Dec. 16, 1862, Barlow Letters, CSL.

46. Relyea, *16th Connecticut Volunteer Infantry,* 59.

47. *Hartford Evening Post,* Dec. 17, 1862. Blakeslee counted only one soldier wounded, Isaac Hamilton (Co. I), and one missing, George Creigton (Co. G), in regimental losses from the battle. See Blakeslee, *History of the Sixteenth Connecticut Volunteers,* 29. According to the AGO 1889, 635, Pvt. Isaac Hamilton (Co. I) was wounded at Fredericksburg, but he recovered, was promoted to corporal, and remained with the regiment until mustering out in 1865. Pvt. John Harrigan (Co. F) also suffered wounds during the battle, according to Ira Forbes. See "John Harrigan," Whitney Collection, CSL. There is no mention of George Creighton's disappearance at Fredericksburg in either AGO.

48. See Martin V. Culver to Jonathan Culver, Dec. 20, 1862, Culver Letters, private collection.

49. Belden Diary, Dec. 13, 1862, CHS.

50. Richard Henry Lee to Adelaide R. Holcomb, Dec. 18, 1862, Holcomb Family Papers, SBHS.

51. Leland O. Barlow to father, Dec 24, 1862, Barlow Letters, CSL.

52. Harrison Woodford to "friends at home," Dec. 16, 1862, Harrison Woodford Letters, private collection.

53. Richard Henry Lee to Adelaide R. Holcomb, Dec. 18, 1862, Holcomb Family Papers, SBHS.

54. Leland O. Barlow to father, Dec. 24, 1862, Barlow Letters, CSL.

55. *OR,* ser. 1, vol. 21, 133. Capt. Charles L. Upham from the 8th C.V. formally commanded the regiment. His brief report of the regiment's action is included in *OR,* ser. 1, vol. 21, 351.

56. Leland O. Barlow to father, Dec. 24, 1862, Barlow Letters, CSL.

57. Leland O. Barlow to father, Dec. 24, 1862, Barlow Letters, CSL. Leland Barlow wrote his sister on December 16, 1862: "I think Burnside found the Rebs to[o] strong for him to hold the place." He added, "They have got fortified so it is almost impossible to drive them out. See Leland O. Barlow to Jane E. Barlow, Dec. 16, 1862, Barlow Letters, CSL.

58. Sidney H. Hayden to Oliver Hayden, Dec. 28, 1862, Hayden Papers, EGPL.

59. John B. Cuzner to Ellen Van Dorn, Dec. 22, 1862, John B. Cuzner Letters and Papers, CHS.

60. Robert H. Kellogg to Silas and Lucy C. Hale Kellogg, Dec. 13, 1862. See also Kellogg Diary, Dec. 13, 1862, CHS.

61. Robert H. Kellogg to Silas Kellogg, Dec. 25, 1862, Kellogg Papers, CHS. Kellogg blamed "the authorities in Washington" for delays in building the pontoon bridges and thus, it would seem, Burnside's defeat. The affection members of the 16th had for Burnside would remain long after the debacle of Fredericksburg. In mid-February 1862, Sgt. Richard Henry Lee wrote home to praise Burnside as "the *best Gen,* and the *noblest man* in the army." See Richard Henry Lee to "cousin," Feb. 14, 1862, Holcomb Family Papers, SBHS. Emphasis in original

62. *Hartford Daily Times,* Dec. 30, 1862. It is unclear who the author was, though it is extremely unlikely that Lt. Col. John H. Burnham, a frequent contributor to the *Courant,* would have written such a dispirited letter. The jarring final statement does not mesh with the private letters Burnham composed to his family.

63. *Hartford Daily Times,* Dec. 30, 1862.

64. *Hartford Daily Times,* Dec. 31, 1862.

65. Leland O. Barlow to father, Dec. 24, 1862, Barlow Letters, CSL.

66. Leland O. Barlow to Jane E. Barlow, Dec. 29, 1862, Barlow Letters, CSL.

67. Austin D. Thompson to Electra Churchill, Dec. 27, 1862, Thompson Papers, CHS. Thompson had complained about the men in the ranks doing all the work in October.

68. Austin D. Thompson to Electra Churchill, Jan. 4, 1863, Thompson Papers, CHS.

69. Robert H. Kellogg to Silas Kellogg, Dec. 25, 1862, Kellogg Papers, CHS.

70. Martin V. Culver to Jonathan Culver, Dec. 31, 1862, Culver Letters, private collection. There is no indication from Culver's December letters that he suffered from anything more serious than a cold; in addition, his Compiled Service Records fail to indicate any injury or illness that month. However, in his pension records, there is testimony from Culver (supported by others, including his cousin, but no one from the regiment) that on December 12, 1862, a horse kicked him in his left groin, causing a rupture that never fully healed. See Martin V. Culver Pension Records, NA, and Martin V. Culver, Compiled Service Record, NA. It seems that if such a serious injury occurred in 1862, Culver surely would have complained of it to his brother, but there is no mention. On December 24, 1862, Culver wrote home from "Camp opposite Fredericksburgh": "Seeing that i have a chance to send a fewe lines to Portland I thought that i would write you a fewe lines to let you kno that I am well"[.] See Martin V. Culver to Jonathan Culver, Dec. 24, 1862, Culver Letters, private collection.

71. Martin V. Culver to Jonathan Culver, Dec. 20, 1862, Culver Letters, private collection.

72. Harrison Woodford to "My dear friends at home," Dec. 25, 1862, Harrison Woodford Letters, private collection.

73. *Hartford Daily Times,* Jan. 1, 1863; see also *Geer's Hartford City Directory, 1861–1862,* 178, at Distantcousin.com, accessed May 28, 2008.

74. *Hartford Daily Times,* Jan. 24, 1863, emphasis in original. The letter is signed "I.F.," but the only likely match is Forbes. By January 1863, Hartford papers were routinely publishing soldier letters to score partisan points, particularly in reaction to the Emancipation Proclamation. See Warshauer, *Connecticut in the American Civil War,* 108–12.

75. Quote from Leland O. Barlow to Jane E. Barlow, Jan 20, 1863, Barlow Letters, CSL.

76. Belden Diary, Jan. 23, 1863, CHS.

77. Leland O. Barlow to Jane E. Barlow, Jan. 26, 1863, Barlow Letters, CSL.

78. Robert H. Kellogg to Silas Kellogg, Jan. 20, 1863, Kellogg Papers, CHS.

79. Lewis M. Holcomb to "Aunt," Apr. 2, 1863, included with "Lewis M. Holcomb," Whitney Collection, CSL. These specific letters were transcribed and excerpted by his cousin, Florence J. Tryon, and sent to George Q. Whitney in the fall of 1919. Tryon explained to Whitney: "The parts omitted are personal observations or family matters. The former are interesting but do not, to me, seem to bear on the regiment or the army." See Florence J. Tryon to George Q. Whitney, Nov. 26, 1919, Whitney Collection, CSL.

80. John B. Cuzner to Ellen Van Dorn, Dec. 22, 1862, Cuzner Letters and Papers, CHS.

81. *Hartford Daily Times,* Jan. 2, 1863.

82. *Hartford Daily Times,* Jan. 2, 1863. Captain Upton from the 8th Connecticut remained "acting colonel." See Sidney Hayden to Oliver Hayden, Dec. 28, 1862, Hayden Papers, EGPL.

83. *Hartford Daily Times,* Jan. 10, 1863.

84. These included Captains Tennant, Beach, and Barnum, and Lieutenants Burke, Clapp, Chamberlin, and Hawley. See *Hartford Daily Courant,* Jan. 16, 1863.

85. Burnham was pleased with the increase in pay, which was now $165 per month. John H. Burnham to Sarah B. Burnham, Dec. 30, 1862, Burnham Papers, CSL; see also John H. Burnham, CSR, NA.

86. The full title of Capt. William C. DeHart's book was *Observations on Military Law, and the Constitution and Practice of Courts Martial, With a Summary of the Law of Evidence, as Applicable to Military trials; Adapted to the Laws, Regulations and Customs, of the Army and Navy of the United States* (New York: Wiley and Putnam, 1846). See John H. Burnham to Jane and Lottie Burnham, Jan. 12, 1863, Burnham Papers, CSL.

87. In addition, company commanders were responsible for the "performance of this trust." See General Orders, No. 3, Headquarters 16th Regiment Connecticut Volunteers, By order of Lt. Col. John H. Burnham, Jan. 17, 1863, Burnham Papers, CSL.

88. John H. Burnham to Jane and Lottie Burnham, Jan. 12, 1863, Burnham Papers, CSL.

89. *Hartford Daily Courant,* Jan. 19, 1863.

90. On August 26, the regiment's soldiers each received $13, their first month's advance pay. The next day, Belden recorded receiving $60 more: "fifty of the state bounty, ten the advance of the thirty dollars promised by the state." See Elizur D. Belden, Aug. 26 and 27, 1862, CHS. Wiley notes that pay for northern soldiers was "commonly tardy, sometimes more than six months." Yet what appears to

have happened with the 16th C.V. was that while other regiments serving alongside them received their pay, the 16th did not. Explanations for this oversight, whether accurate or not, only fed their resentments. See Wiley, *Billy Yank*, 49. Hagerty describes similar anger and resentment over lack of pay in the ranks of the 114 Pennsylvania (*Collis' Zouaves*, 102–3).

91. See Belden Diary, Dec. 31, 1862, CHS.

92. Austin D. Thompson to Electra M. Churchill, Feb. 4, 1863, Thompson Papers, CHS.

93. John B. Cuzner to Ellen Van Dorn, Feb. 5, 1863, Cuzner Letters and Papers, CHS.

94. Leander Chapin to Amelia Chapin, Feb. 7, 1863, Chapin Papers, CHS.

95. Martin V. Culver to Jonathan Culver, Jan. 19, 1863, Culver Letters, private collection.

96. E. H. Owen to William A. Buckingham, Feb. 10, 1862, Governors' Correspondence, CSL.

97. For more on the reforms Hooker instituted and their positive impact, see Daniel Sutherland, *Fredericksburg and Chancellorsville: The Dare Mark Campaign* (Lincoln: University of Nebraska Press, 1998), 96–99. For evidence of plentiful food in the regiment's winter camp, see Leland O. Barlow to father, Jan 13, 1863; Leland O. Barlow to Edmund B. Barlow, Jan. 14, 1863. Barlow further described the men receiving dress coats in late December, although many had ragged pants and coats that did not match. See Leland O. Barlow to Jane E. Barlow, Dec. 29, 1862, Barlow Letters, CSL. See also *Hartford Daily Courant*, Jan. 17, 1863.

98. Sidney H. Hayden to Oliver Hayden, Jan. 16, 1863, Hayden Papers, EGPL.

99. Case praised Dr. Mayer for his attention to the sick but noted that several men in the ranks were ill, many gravely. See *Hartford Daily Courant*, Feb. 2, 1863. O. P. Case probably was Orville P. Case, a Hartford grocer. It is not clear if he was related to the many Cases in the regiment. See 8th Census of the United States, 1860: Population Schedule, Hartford District 2, Hartford, Connecticut; ancestry.com, accessed May 21, 2010.

100. Lewis M. Holcomb to Adelaide R. Holcomb, Feb. 2, 1863, Holcomb Family Papers, SBHS.

101. See Nathan Mayer to William A. Buckingham, July 15, 1862, Letters Received, Governors' Correspondence, CSL; Weld, *Connecticut Physicians in the Civil War*, 11. Information on Isaac Mayer from www.jewishvirtuallibrary.org/jsource/judaica/ejud_0002_0008_0_08481.html, accessed on May 21, 2010.

102. Case, "Memoirs," SHS. As noted above, these improvements also coincided with the arrival of Hooker and his important reforms, including improving sanitation and the overall health of the army. See Sutherland, *Fredericksburg and Chancellorsville*, 97–98.

103. Finch further explained, "There are absent on detached service 52; absent, sick and wounded, 246; total officers and men at camp, 456; able to do duty, 382; sick 44; extra and daily duty, 30." See *Hartford Daily Courant*, Feb. 3, 1863.

104. Relyea, *16th Connecticut Volunteer Infantry*, 73. The regiment remained part of the Army of the Potomac until April 1863.

105. *Hartford Daily Courant*, Feb. 10, 1863. See also Relyea, *16th Connecticut Volunteer Infantry*, 73–74.

CHAPTER FOUR

1. Chapin quote from Jan. 1863 letter in "J. Leander Chapin," Whitney Collection, CSL.

2. J. Leander Chapin to Amelia Chapin, Feb. 7, 1863, Chapin Papers, CHS.

3. Barlow Diary, Feb. 8, 1863, CSL; Richard Henry Lee to [Adelaide R. Holcomb], Feb. 14, 1863, Holcomb Family Papers, SBHS. The 16th Connecticut, though moved from the Rappahannock, remained attached to the 2nd Brigade, 3rd Division, IX Army Corps, Army of the Potomac. In April 1863, the regiment would be transferred to the 2nd Brigade, 2nd Division, VII Army Corps, Dept. of Virginia. See Frederick Dyer, *A Compendium of the War of the Rebellion* (1908; reprint, Dayton, OH: Press of Morningside Bookshop, 1978), pt. 3, 1013.

4. Sidney Hayden to Jane Hayden, Feb. 27, 1863; Sidney Hayden to Oliver Hayden, Feb. 28, 1863; Sidney Hayden to Catherine Hayden, Mar. 2, 1863; Hayden Papers, EGPL. Leland Barlow still complained of the cold and wet throughout the month of February, and in March he told his sister that the "air is very bracing here perhaps too much so for some, especially if their Lungs are not sound." However, he reported that he and his comrades were "growing very fleshy" due to their abundance of food. Leland Barlow to Jane Barlow, Mar. 10, 1863, Barlow Letters, CSL. See also Barlow Diary, Feb. 11, 13, 17, 18, 19, 22, 23, 1863, CSL.

5. John B. Cuzner to Ellen Van Dorn, Mar. 8, 1863, John B. Cuzner Letters, CHS.

6. Samuel E. Derby to Elizabeth Derby, Feb. 11, 1863, Derby Letters, CHS. In the same letter, Derby mentions clams and oysters being available in Newport News and states that the regiment had "plenty to eat if we had any money to get them with."

7. See Belden Diary, Mar. 10, 1863, CHS.

8. Lewis M. Holcomb to "Aunt," Apr. 2, 1863, in "Lewis M. Holcomb," Whitney Collection, CSL. Holcomb penned this letter from Suffolk, but he recounted the regiment's time in Newport News.

9. Lewis M. Holcomb to Adelaide R. Holcomb, Feb. 26, 1863, Holcomb Family Papers, SBHS. See also Austin D. Thompson to Electra M. Churchill, Mar. 11, 1863, Thompson Papers, CHS; and Barlow Diary, Feb. 27, 1863, CSL.

10. John H. Burnham to Sarah B. Burnham, Mar. 12, 1863, Burnham Papers, CSL.

11. Leland O. Barlow to Jane Barlow, Feb. 10, 1863, Barlow Letters, CSL.

12. Harrison Woodford to Harvey Woodford, Mar. 28, 1863, Harrison Woodford Letters, private collection. It was not until April 1863 that the unit formally split from the Army of the Potomac and joined the Department of Virginia, but Woodford and Barlow probably meant the larger army rather than the detached service they were later engaged in at Suffolk.

13. Blakeslee, *History of the Sixteenth Connecticut Volunteers,* 30.

14. Sidney H. Hayden to "Cousin Sam," Mar. 7, 1863, Hayden Papers, EGPL.

15. Barlow Diary, Feb. 10, 1863, CSL.

16. Barlow Diary, Feb. 21, 1863, CSL.

17. Muster Rolls, Returns, Regimental Papers, RG 94, Box 148 [unbound papers], NA.

18. Sidney H. Hayden to "Uncle," Mar. 7, 1863, Hayden Papers, EGPL.

19. J. Leander Chapin to Amelia Chapin, Mar. 18, 1863, Chapin Papers, CHS.

20. During the months stationed at Newport News and Suffolk, deserters included Pvt. Emerson P. Snyder (Co. B), who deserted on Mar. 7, 1863. Snyder made his way to Iowa, where Whitney claimed that Snyder was also known by an alias, Emerson R. Preston. See Bound Regimental Papers, RG 94, entries 112–15, Bound Records of the Union Volunteer Regiments, vol. 2, NA. Also "Emerson P. Snyder," Whitney Collection, CSL. However, Snyder can be found in the census for 1870 and 1880 residing in State Center, IA. See 9th Census of the United States, 1870: Population Schedule,

State Center, Marshall, IA; 10th Census of the United States, 1880: Population Schedule State Center, Marshall, at ancestry.com, accessed Aug. 19, 2010. On May 1, 1863, Frank H. Kane (Co. E) vanished from the ranks. See Bound Regimental Papers, RG 94, entries 112–15, Bound Records of the Union Volunteer Regiments, vol. 2, NA. Irish-native Pvt. Michael Quinnen (Co. D) never returned from furlough in early April 1863. See Muster Rolls, Returns, Regimental Papers, RG 94, Box 148 [unbound papers], NA.

21. J. Leander Chapin to Amelia Chapin, Mar. 18, 1863, Chapin Papers, CHS.

22. J. Leander Chapin to Amelia Chapin, Mar. 19 [1863], Chapin Papers, CHS.

23. See Nathan Mayer, Mar. 29, 1863, "Medical Certificate," in J. Leander Chapin, CSR, NA. Chapin went home and spent several weeks recuperating in New Haven's Knight Hospital. He transferred to the 3rd Regiment, Veteran Reserve Corps in July 1863, not well enough to return to the 16th Connecticut until late August. G. Q. Whitney's postwar biography states that Chapin "went over the river at the battle of Fredericksburg practically barefoot, caught a severe cold, loosing [sic] his voice as did many others, and was sent to the hospital." See "J. Leander Chapin," Whitney Collection, CSL. Whitney must have confused the timing of Chapin's illness, as all other evidence, including Chapin's own letters cited above, show him becoming sick at Suffolk in March.

24. Sidney H. Hayden to Oliver Hayden, Feb. 14, 1863, Hayden Papers, EGPL.

25. Sidney H. Hayden to Oliver Hayden, Feb. 25, 1863, Hayden Papers, EGPL.

26. Sidney H. Hayden to Catherine Hayden, Mar. 11, 1863, Hayden Papers, EGPL.

27. Pomeroy was not discharged but instead was promoted to captain of Co. I and remained in the service until January 1865. See Austin D. Thompson to Electra M. Churchill, Feb. 27, 1863, Thompson Papers, CHS.

28. Joseph H. Barnum to John B. Clapp, Feb. 18, 1863, in Joseph H. Barnum, CSR, NA.

29. Joseph H. Barnum, CSR, NA.

30. John H. Burnham to William A. Buckingham, Feb. 24, 1863, Governors' Correspondence, CSL.

31. Barnum was recommissioned on April 7, 1863, as captain by Governor Buckingham. See Joseph H. Barnum, CSR, NA. Barnum's continuing concerns about money and trying to transfer funds home got him into trouble in January 1864.

32. Samuel E. Derby to Elizabeth Derby, Feb. 11, 1863, Derby Letters, CHS.

33. *Hartford Daily Courant*, Feb. 17, 1863.

34. *Hartford Daily Courant*, Feb. 18, 1863.

35. *Hartford Daily Courant*, Feb. 25, 1863.

36. *Hartford Daily Courant*, Feb. 28, 1863.

37. William Relyea, "The History of the 16th Connecticut Volunteers," 92–94, CHS. The 16th Connecticut was not alone in behaving this way. The *Hartford Daily Times* reported in late December 1862 that soldiers stationed on Long Island Sound had not been paid. See *Hartford Daily Times*, Dec. 20, 1862.

38. This attitude is similar to the contractual expectations found among Massachusetts provincial troops in the Seven Years War. Fred Anderson writes that for soldiers and officers, "If the conditions of the contract were violated, the army would cease to exist." See Anderson, *A People's Army*, 172. Foote discusses tensions between Union officers and men in *The Gentleman and the Roughs*, 145–70.

39. Leland Barlow recorded being paid on February 20: "Got paid off to the 1st of Jan. Received 50 Dollars & 25 cents." Barlow Diary, Feb. 20, 1863, CSL.

40. John B. Cuzner to Ellen Van Dorn, Mar. 8, 1863, Cuzner Letters and Papers, CHS. See also Sidney H. Hayden to "Uncle," Mar. 7, 1863, Hayden Papers, EGPL.

41. Robert H. Kellogg to Silas Kellogg, Mar. 3, 1863, Kellogg Papers, CHS.

42. Unnamed soldier's letter quoted in Relyea, *Sixteenth Connecticut Volunteer Infantry,* 78.

43. *Hartford Evening Press,* Mar. 11, 1863.

44. *Hartford Daily Courant,* Mar. 9, 1863. Captain Beach resigned soon after the regiment saw action in Suffolk, when there appeared to be implications of dereliction of duty or, worse, cowardice.

45. *Hartford Daily Courant,* Mar. 19, 1863. The correspondent's initials were "F. C. S."

46. For example, the *Hartford Daily Courant* quoted a letter from a cavalryman: "The soldiers one and all, except a few renegade skulks and deserters, are for Buckingham, and love him like a father; for they know that he had done all that could be done to advance their interests." See *Hartford Daily Courant,* Mar. 7, 1863. Warshauer describes the importance of this election and influence of these soldiers' letters, which frequently appeared in the major Hartford papers, in *Connecticut in the American Civil War,* 107–13.

47. The appeal appeared in the *Hartford Evening Press* on March 20, 1863. The *Hartford Daily Courant* stated the next day, "There is evidence that the men in the ranks were paying attention to the election." Sidney Hayden wrote his sister, "We are waiting anxiously to hear from [the] Connecticut election." Sidney H. Hayden to Catherine Hayden, Apr. 8, 1863, Hayden Papers, EGPL.

48. *Hartford Daily Courant,* Mar. 21, 1863. Timothy Orr finds Pennsylvania soldiers in the Army of the Potomac passing similar resolutions and reacting, he argues, even more angrily toward reports of Copperheadism at home. Orr observes, "Sending letters to family and friends provided a simple means of influencing political sentiment on the homefront." See Timothy J. Orr, "'A Viler Enemy in Our Rear': Pennsylvania Soldiers Confront the North's Antiwar Movement," in Sheehan-Dean, *The View from the Ground,* 179, 183–90.

49. *Hartford Daily Courant,* Mar. 26, 1863. Emphasis in original. This soldier's estimate that "two-thirds of the voters in the army are Democrats" is, no doubt, an exaggeration. For a discussion of Civil War soldiers' heightened interest in politics, see Joseph Allen Frank, *With Ballot and Bayonets: The Political Socialization of American Civil War Soldiers* (Athens: University of Georgia Press, 1998).

50. Harrison Woodford to Harvey Woodford, Mar. 28, 1863, Harrison Woodford Letters, private collection.

51. *Hartford Daily Courant,* Mar. 27, 1863. Nancy Minor Bowen is found in the 7th Census of the United States, 1850: Population Schedule, Manchester, Hartford County, CT, at ancestry.com, accessed June 5, 2008. Charles Bowen, who was thirty-six and widowed when he enlisted, ended up discharged with disability in September 1863. See AGO 1889, 634. McPherson calls Copperheadism the cause of the "greatest estrangement between soldiers and civilians." See McPherson, *For Cause and Comrades,* 143. See also Orr, "A Viler Enemy in Our Rear," 180–81.

52. Barlow opened the letter by writing, "I see by your letter that you are afraid I am not Loyal. You don't think I'll go over to the Rebs do you? Well I haven't any notion of it; if I ever go it will be against my will; as for Patriotism I don't think I have got much of that kind some folks have up your way." See Leland O. Barlow to Jane Barlow, Apr. 4, 1863, Barlow Letters, CSL.

53. Austin D. Thompson to Electra Churchill, Apr. 5, 1863, Thompson Papers, CHS. Richard

Henry Lee wrote his cousin Adelaide, an avowed Democrat, accusing Seymour of having "sympathies with the murderers of my comrades." See Richard Henry Lee to Adelaide R. Holcomb, Apr. 3, 1863, Holcomb Family Papers, SBHS. For more on the divisiveness that Peace Democrats stirred between soldiers and civilians, see Ramold, *Across the Divide*, 115–42.

54. George Robbins to Jehiel and Dorothy Robbins, Mar. 29, 1863, Robbins Papers, CHS. The Democratic *Hartford Times* accused Republicans of furloughing only Republican soldiers to allow them to vote in this election and leaving Democrats in the ranks (Apr. 8 and 10, 1863). See also Warshauer, *Connecticut in the American Civil War*, 113–14. Republicans used these same tactics in the spring of 1864; see Chapter 6. It took until the summer of 1864 for the Connecticut legislature to pass a constitutional amendment and thus allow their state's soldiers to vote in the field. See Josiah Henry Benton, *Voting in the Field: A Forgotten Chapter of the Civil War* (Boston, 1915), 174–81.

55. Croffutt and Morris, *Military and Civil History of Connecticut*, 327.

56. Scholarship on northern women and the war has expanded but still pales in comparison to studies on Confederate women. See Silber, *Daughters of the Union*; Giesberg, *Army at Home*; and Leonard, *Yankee Women*.

57. These lines appear on the back of John B. Cuzner to Ellen Van Dorn, Feb. 15, 1863, Cuzner Letters and Papers, CHS. Her words of mournful longing contrast dramatically with his letters, in which he playfully teased her about other women and her alleged romantic interest in another soldier. In June 1863, he kidded, "You speak of keeping me from the girls when I get home. How can you talk so after I have been out here so long and not seen a girl. You have the wrong idea. I'm right in with the girls every time. That's the calculation!" Cuzner mocked his romantic rival John Hinman, in the 8th Connecticut, "I guess J. H. is playing off as we call it, when our boys shirk their duty, but farmers don't have much time to play so we must make allowances for that." John B. Cuzner to Ellen Van Dorn, June 1, 1863, Cuzner Letters and Papers, CHS. Hinman was listed as a "farm laborer" from Newton in the 1860 census. See 8th Census of the United States, 1860: Population Schedule, Newtown, Fairfield, CT, at ancestry.com, accessed on Sept. 19, 2008.

58. From Charlotte H. Manross, "The Widow's Tear," Apr. 4, 1863, Newton S. Manross Collection, private collection.

59. Drew Faust and Stephanie McCurry, among others, have explored the effect death and loss had on women, North and South, during the war. See Faust, *This Republic of Suffering*; Stephanie McCurry, *Confederate Reckoning: Power and Politics in the Civil War South*. Cambridge (Cambridge: Harvard University Press, 2010). For scholarship specific to widows, see Jennifer Lynn Gross, "'And for the Widow and the Orphan': Confederate Widows, Poverty, and Public Assistance," in *Inside the Confederate Nation: Essays in Honor of Emory M. Thomas*, ed. Lesley J. Gordon and John C. Inscoe (Baton Rouge: Louisiana State University Press, 2005), 209–29; Robert Kenzer, "The Uncertainty of Life: A Profile of Virginia's Civil War Widows," in *The War Was You and Me: Civilians in the American Civil War*, ed. Joan E. Cashin (Princeton: Princeton University Press, 2002), 262–85.

60. The *Hartford Evening Press* reported the 16th Connecticut at Suffolk on March 15. See also *Hartford Evening Press*, Mar. 19, 1863.

61. Martin V. Culver to Jonathan Culver, Apr. 22, 1863, Culver Letters, private collection.

62. Samuel E. Derby to Elizabeth Derby, Apr. 9, 1863, Derby Letters, CHS. According to Derby's CSR he was "sick left behind," during the Mar. in late Oct. 1862. See Samuel E. Derby, CSR, NA.

63. J. Leander Chapin to Amelia Chapin, Mar. 18, 1863, Chapin Papers, CHS. On March 21,

1863, the *Hartford Daily Courant* reported his return to the regiment, stating that he had been absent for forty days. During his six-month absence, Beach had remained mostly in Philadelphia sick with chronic diarrhea. His status was mentioned occasionally in Hartford newspapers. See, e.g., the *Hartford Evening Press*, Feb. 28, 1863.

64. Belden also claimed that Beach first arrived at Newport News just as the 16th Connecticut left for Suffolk. See Belden Diary, Mar. 13, 1863, CHS. A few days later he noted that Beach resumed command of the regiment. See Belden Diary, Mar. 16, 1863, CSL.

65. Austin D. Thompson to Electra M. Churchill, Mar. 15, 1863, Thompson Papers, CHS.

66. Leland O. Barlow to Jane Barlow, Mar. 27, 1863, Barlow Letters, CSL. Barlow also complained to his sister of the "little young lieutenants" who "don't know anything more than the privates and they make hog-ish work drilling us."

67. Robbins, "Some Recollections," 20, CHS.

68. Robert H. Kellogg to Silas Kellogg, Apr. 3, 1863, Kellogg Papers, CHS. In a subsequent letter, Kellogg explained that the medical director's office was vacated and only the regular hospital stewards retained. See Robert H. Kellogg to Silas Kellogg, Apr. 7, 1863, Kellogg Papers, CHS.

69. Robert H. Kellogg to Silas Kellogg, Apr. 18, 1863, Kellogg Papers, CHS.

70. Robert H. Kellogg to Silas Kellogg, Apr. 25, 1863, Kellogg Papers, CHS. In his diary, Kellogg wrote, "After firing a while, we advanced with a cheer and drove them out taking several prisoners. They retreated from their pits in great haste leaving behind a great many things. I captured a good frying pan." Kellogg added, "Thank God my life was spared and I have again learned to perfectly trust in *Him*." See Kellogg Diary, Apr. 24, 1863, CHS. Sidney Hayden wrote of Edenton Road, "Drove the Reb Pickets when they opened on us with a batery [*sic*] and a sharp engagement ensued." Hayden's Company B was deployed as skirmishers through the Dismal Swamp, some of the men wading waist deep through the mud. See Sidney H. Hayden to Catherine Hayden, Apr. 27, 1863, Hayden Papers, EGPL. George N. Lamphere remembered "some of the boys going down in the soft and shiny mud up to their waists. One man near me was in danger of going over his head, and I believe if I had not been able to rescue him, he would have disappeared in that horrible mire." See George N. Lamphere, "Experiences and Observations," 17, MHS.

71. George Robbins to "Parents and friends," Apr. 25, 1863, Robbins Papers, CHS.

72. Lamphere, "Experiences and Observations," 17, MHS.

73. Harrison Woodford to Harvey Woodford, Apr. 25, 1863, Harrison Woodford Letters, private collection. See also John B. Cuzner to Ellen Van Dorn, May 2, 1863, Cuzner Letters and Papers, CHS.

74. Dr. Nathan Mayer provided a detailed list of the casualties in a letter to the editor of the *Daily Courant* dated April 23, 1863, and published one week later. See *Hartford Daily Courant*, Apr. 30, 1863. Another soldier, Pvt. George L. Brookman (Co. H), died, his skull fractured by a rifle ball, on April 29. See *Hartford Evening Press*, May 1, 1863; see also *Hartford Daily Courant*, Apr. 30, 1863. Among the wounded was Cpl. Joseph Flowers (Co. C), who was listed with a "fractured shoulder blade, gun shot wound." See *Hartford Evening Press*, Apr. 28, 1863. The *Hartford Daily Courant* had previously listed Sgt. George Johnson (Co. B), "left hand, third finger amputated"; Sgt. John Taylor (Co. C), "slightly right arm"; Cpl. Joseph Flower (Co. C), "severely, shoulder and back"; Pvts. David W. Deming (Co. C), "slightly in arm"; Mayer described "a slight contusion in the left fore-arm, caused by a shell." See *Hartford Daily Courant*, Apr. 30, 1863. Other wounded included Henry C. Williams (Co. C), "forehead"; George L. Eaton (Co. F), "severely left leg, amputated above the knee"; George

Brookman (Co. H), "mortally, head"; Martin Hennessy (Co. I), "gunshot wound, left foot." See *Hartford Daily Courant,* Apr. 29, 1863. Mayer added, regarding Hennessy, "slightly wounded in 4th toe of left foot by a rifle ball." See *Hartford Daily Courant,* Apr. 30, 1863.

75. Blakeslee, *History of the Sixteenth Connecticut Volunteers,* 36, 107. See also Steven A. Cormier, *The Siege of Suffolk: The Forgotten Campaign, Apr. 11–May 4, 1863* (Lynchburg, VA: H. E. Howard, 1989), 230–33.

76. George Robbins to "Parents and friends," Apr. 25, 1863, Robbins Papers, CHS. Harrison Woodford was less sure of the skirmish's purpose in a letter home. See Harrison Woodford to Harvey Woodford "and friends at home," Apr. 25, 1863, Harrison Woodford Letters, private collection.

77. Kellogg Diary, May 2, 1863, CHS.

78. Robert H. Kellogg to Silas Kellogg, May 6, 1863, Kellogg Papers, CHS.

79. Richard Henry Lee to Adelaide R. Holcomb, May 7, 1863, Holcomb Family Papers, May 7, 1863, SBHS.

80. George Robbins to Jehiel Robbins, May 4, 1863, Robbins Papers, CHS.

81. Robert H. Kellogg to Silas Kellogg, May 6, 1863, Kellogg Papers, CHS.

82. Robert S. Foster to J. J. Blodgett, May 9, 1863, *OR,* ser. 1, vol. 18, 294.

83. Edward Harland to Charles T. Gardner, May 6, 1863, *OR,* ser. 1, vol. 18, 312.

84. On May 7, 1863, the *Hartford Daily Courant* listed nine men wounded and one killed from the skirmish, but the list would grow in the coming days. By May 11, the *Courant* counted one killed and twelve wounded. See also *Hartford Daily Courant,* May 8, 1863.

85. Robert H. Kellogg to Silas Kellogg, May 6, 1863, Kellogg Papers, CHS.

86. Kellogg stated, "The shot was probably intended for our Col. who was just in front of him in full uniform." See Robert H. Kellogg to Silas Kellogg, May 6, 1863, Kellogg Papers, CHS. Lt. Ariel Case claimed that Blakeslee was shot "in the head in the very same place that he was at Antietam, supposed to be fatal, but he soon recovered to be able for duty very soon after." See Case, "Memoirs," SHS. Blakeslee added that he was left for dead on the field after being examined by both Colonel Beach and Maj. Pasco. A New Jersey chaplain saved him, and Dr. Mayer tended to his wounds. See Blakeslee, *History of the Sixteenth Connecticut Volunteers,* 36.

87. Sidney H. Hayden to Catherine Hayden, May 4, 1863, Hayden Papers, EGPL.

88. Bauer, "Personal Experiences of the War," 8, PPM.

89. Harrison Woodford to Martha Woodford, May 4, 1863, Harrison Woodford Letters, private collection.

90. Quote from *Hartford Daily Times,* May 26, 1863; see also May 23, 1863.

91. *Hartford Daily Courant,* May 30, 1863.

92. Blakeslee, *History of the Sixteenth Connecticut Volunteers,* 37.

93. Lewis M. Holcomb to "Aunt," June 19, 1863, in "Lewis M. Holcomb," Whitney Collection, CSL.

94. *Hartford Daily Courant,* May 29, 1863. See also Blakeslee, *History of the Sixteenth Connecticut Volunteers,* 37; *Hartford Daily Times,* May 27, 29, 1863. Many officers listed who participated in the funeral had resigned from (or otherwise left) the regiment in the months prior to Tennant's death.

95. *Hartford Daily Courant,* May 30, 1863. See Faust, *This Republic of Suffering,* 3–31; Neff, *Honoring the Civil War Dead,* 23–24, for more on the significance of ritualized mourning and the "Good Death."

96. Lt. Col. Burnham took credit for naming their camp at Suffolk "after our gallant young

Captain." See John H. Burnham to Sarah B. Burnham, June 14, 1863, John H. Burnham, CSL. The official order was reprinted in the *Hartford Daily Courant*, June 18, 1863.

97. *Hartford Daily Courant*, May 29, 1863.

98. John H. Burnham to Sarah B. Burnham, May 4, 1863, Burnham Papers, CSL.

99. *Hartford Daily Times*, May 13, 1863, and June 8, 1863. On June 8, the *Times* reported Burnham returning to the regiment later that week, although the paper mistakenly claimed that Burnham's wound was from the Battle of Chancellorsville. See also Nathan Mayer, "Medical Certificate," May 13, 1863; and John H. Burnham to John B. Clapp, May 13, 1863, in John H. Burnham, CSR, NA.

100. Nearly twenty years later, family and friends provided sworn statements to federal officials describing this alteration, most of them dating it to his wound at Suffolk. See Affidavit of Edward D. Williams, Nov. 23, 1881; see also "Exhibit A," Testimony of Joseph D. Burnham, Feb. 1, 1882, John H. Burnham Pension File, NA.

101. B. F. Blakeslee to William W. Dudley, Oct. 18, 1881, John H. Burnham Pension File, NA. Blakeslee recounted nothing of this in his published regimental history.

102. *Hartford Daily Courant*, June 8, 1863.

103. See Blakeslee, *History of the Sixteenth Connecticut Volunteers*, 37.

104. Kellogg Diary, May 3, 1863, CHS.

105. See "Henry W. Barber," Whitney Collection, CSL. Barber's grave is located at the Hampton National Cemetery, Hampton, Virginia. See findagrave.com, accessed Dec. 7, 2010. Barber was apparently married, but it is difficult to find any additional biographical information about him. According to the 1860 census, Barber, employed as a "laborer," lived with a family named Buffington in Somers. See 8th Census of the United States, 1860: Population Schedule, Somers, Tolland, CT, at ancestry.com, accessed Dec. 7, 2010.

106. See "Daniel G. Gibson," Whitney Collection, CSL. Gibson was one of the few members of the unit who had served previously in the 3rd Connecticut. He died at Andersonville on September 30, 1864.

107. Sidney H. Hayden to Catherine Hayden, May 13, 1863, Hayden Papers, EGPL.

108. Relyea, *16th Connecticut Volunteer Infantry*, 84. Beach resigned on May 18, 1863. See AGO 1889, 635. His resignation was reported in the *Hartford Courant*, May 23, 1863. George Robbins alleged that Beach was wounded during the Battle of Providence Church, but he was not listed anywhere else as injured during the fight. See George Robbins to Jehiel Robbins, May 4, 1863, Robbins Papers, CHS. Henry Beach's obituary states, "In June 1863, Captain Beach was persuaded by Gideon Welles of this city, then secretary of the navy, to resign his commission and superintend the erection of machinery for three large sloops of war, which duty lasted until 1866." Undated obituary, "Henry L. Beach," Whitney Collection, CSL. Harrison Woodford, however, mentioned Captain Beach's resignation, explaining to his father that Beach "is very hard sick." Woodford had helped carry him to the hospital, and Dr. Mayer had declared he would not recover. See Harrison Woodford to Harvey Woodford, June 10, 1863, Harrison Woodford Letters, private collection.

109. White wrote this letter six months later, when he was feeling especially sick and unfit for service; the doctors refused to discharge him. White wrote that he enlisted "because I loved my country and hated her enemy and not to make money or rob any one and if my health would permit me I should feel it a duty and stay without a murmur." White, like so many of these privates, never received his discharge and remained with the regiment to face imprisonment at Andersonville seven months later. Henry A. White to William A. Buckingham, Oct. 20, 1863, Governors' Correspondence, CSL.

110. Richard Henry Lee to Adelaide R. Holcomb, May 7, 1863, Holcomb Family Papers, SBHS. It is not clear who this lieutenant was. The men reduced to ranks in Co. E on May 7 included Sgt. John H. Good, who had already been reduced to ranks from corporal previously but then had received a promotion to sergeant in January 1863. If desertion can be classified as cowardly, especially desertions just before or after battle, then regimental records indicate very low desertion at this time, too. Seven men deserted the unit between February 11 and April 17, 1863, but only two between May 1 and July 7, 1863. In the middle of June, the regiment moved to Portsmouth, where it remained for several months. From early July until mid-September, there was another wave of deserters; six are recorded in the adjutant general's records. Numbers abstracted from AGO 1869, 619–39. Deserters from the regiment during the Suffolk campaign included Pvts. Franklin H. Kane and Lucien M. Stewart, who both deserted from Co. F on May 1, 1863. See AGO 1889, 630. Pvt. Clark Stratton (Co. E) has two conflicting dates of desertion: February 16, 1863, and May 1, 1863. See AGO 1869, 653, and AGO 1889, 629.

111. While in Suffolk, the regiment moved positions at least four times. See Sidney H. Hayden to Catherine Hayden, June 13, 1863, Hayden Papers, EGPL.

112. Kellogg Diary, May 27, 1863, CHS. See also Sidney H. Hayden to Catherine Hayden, May 13, 1863, Hayden Papers, EGPL.

113. Martin V. Culver to Jonathan Culver, May 6, 1863, Culver Letters, private collection. See also Kellogg Diary, May 2, June 8, 13, 1863, CHS. Robbins described the men catching eels, crabs, and "some other kinds of fish but not many." George Robbins to Dorothy Robbins, June 6, 1863, Robbins Papers, CHS.

114. Pvt. Owen Flanagan (Co. A) wrote from the convalescent camp on April 17, 1863, thanking the Soldiers' Aid Association for their efforts: "We return all of you our sincere thanks for flannel shirts, flannel drawers and also woolen stockings." See *Hartford Daily Courant*, Apr. 25, 1863. Flanagan was discharged on May 22, 1863, for disability. See AGO 1889, 621.

115. Kellogg referred to visiting the town of Suffolk and indulging in "ice cream, lemonade, soda water, etc., etc." See Kellogg Diary, June 15, 1863, CHS.

116. Leland O. Barlow to Jane Barlow, May 9, 1863, Barlow Letters, CSL.

117. Austin D. Thompson to Electra Churchill, May 29, June 6, 1863, Thompson Papers, CHS.

118. John B. Cuzner to Ellen Van Dorn, June 1, 1863, Cuzner Letters and Papers, CHS.

119. Richard Henry Lee to Adelaide R. Holcomb, June 2, 1863, Holcomb Family Papers, SBHS. Leland Barlow told his sister Jane that he would take "soldiering as it is down here and it is a life to be desired." See Leland O. Barlow to Jane Barlow, May 29, 1863, Barlow Letters, CSL.

120. *Hartford Daily Courant*, June 6, 1863.

121. Mayer further informed Mrs. S. J. Cowan, the Secretary of the Aid Association, that the men were in great need of newspapers and "old magazines." He explained, "Without good reading matter supplied from home, the soldier it too apt to purchase trashy novels, which are the sole stock of the book vendor here." See the *Hartford Daily Courant*, June 9, 1863. There still lurked the danger of illness. Cpl. Barlow had noted just prior to Mayer's letter, "Six cases of small pox in Pest House." See Barlow Diary, May 31, 1863, CSL. And on June 5, Kellogg counted "quite a number of cases of diarrhea in the regiment." See Robert H. Kellogg to Silas Kellogg, June 5, 1863, Kellogg Papers, CHS.

122. Sidney H. Hayden to Catherine Hayden, June 24, 1863, Hayden Papers, EGPL. Francis Beach married Julia DeCay Morgan on January 2, 1862. Information from ancestry.com, accessed

June 13, 2008. For more on Julia, see 8th Census of the United States, 1860: Population Schedule, Pittsburgh Ward 4, Allegheny, PA, at ancestry.com, accessed June 13, 2008. Her father, James B. Morgan, is listed as a wealthy coal merchant.

123. Bauer, "Personal Experiences of the War," 6–7, PPM. The couple had their photograph taken during this time; Bauer kept it on his bedroom wall decades after the war ended.

124. Harrison Woodford to Harvey Woodford, June 10, 1863, Harrison Woodford Letters, private collection.

125. Robbins, "Some Recollections," 21, CHS.

126. George Robbins to Dorothy Robbins, May 30, 1863, Robbins Papers, CHS. One week later, Robbins wrote his mother that they had shifted camp yet again, this time "but a short distance, about half a mile and we are pleasantly situated on the banks of the Nansemond, about two miles from Suffolk." George Robbins to Dorothy Robbins, June 6, 1863.

127. Sidney H. Hayden to Catherine Hayden June 8, 1863, Hayden Papers, EGPL. Co. B only had four Irish soldiers, as opposed to Co. D, which, as mentioned above, had the highest number, fifteen.

128. Sidney Hayden to Jane Hayden, June 4, 1863, Hayden Papers, EGPL. Hayden still nursed deep resentment toward Captain Mix: "When the war is over, I shall be equal to him." He was also finding that he lost "any sympathy with the Rebels and the more I see of them the worse I hate them."

129. Quote "open air meetings" from Robert H. Kellogg to Silas Kellogg, May 6, 1863, Kellogg Papers, CHS. Kellogg refers to "Conn. clergymen Rev. Messrs. Eustis & Tiffany" visiting the regiment at Suffolk. Chaplain Peter Finch had resigned January 25, 1863, and their new chaplain, Charles Dixon, a Methodist minister who had been serving as a private in the 8th C.V., did not arrive until June 1863. See also "Charles Dixon," Whitney Collection, CSL.

130. Richard Henry Lee to Adelaide R. Holcomb, Apr. 3, 1863, Holcomb Family Papers, SBHS.

131. George Robbins to Dorothy Robbins, May 30, 1863, Robbins Papers, CHS.

132. Kellogg Diary, May [10], 1863, CHS.

133. For a close analysis of similar attitudes among New England troops, see David A. Cecere, "Carrying the Home Front to War: Soldiers, Race, and New England Culture during the Civil War," in *Union Soldiers and the Northern Home Front: Wartime Experiences, Postwar Adjustments*, ed. Paul A. Cimbala and Randall M. Miller (New York: Fordham University Press, 2002), 293–323. Warshauer discusses the racial attitudes of the state, which shaped these men before they went to war, and Manning describes the shifting attitudes of Union soldiers, generally, as they encountered more African Americans, the war lengthened, and emancipation became the Union military's key objective. See Warshauer, *Connecticut in the American Civil War*; Manning, *What This Cruel War Was Over*.

134. John B. Cuzner to Ellen Van Dorn, Feb. 15, 1863, Cuzner Letters and Papers, CHS. Cuzner also mentioned that at Newport News, "The negroes bring things into camp to sell such as apples, pies, cider and oysters." See John B. Cuzner to Ellen Van Dorn, Mar. 8, 1863, Cuzner Letters and Papers, CHS.

135. John B. Cuzner to Ellen Van Dorn, Mar. 29, 1863, Cuzner Letters and Papers, CHS.

136. Martin V. Culver to Jonathan Culver, Apr. 22, 1863, Culver Letters, private collection. "Blackstrap," defined in Paul Dickson, *War Slang: American Fighting Words and Phrases Since the Civil War* (New York: Pocket, 1994), 128.

137. Sidney H. Hayden to Catherine Hayden, June 13, 1863, Hayden Papers, EGPL.

138. J. Leander Chapin to Amelia Chapin, Mar. 18, 1863, Chapin Papers, CHS.

139. Lewis M. Holcomb to Adelaide R. Holcomb, Mar. 31, 1863, Holcomb Family Papers, SBHS. Emphasis from original.

140. Robbins, "Some Recollections," 21, CHS.

141. George Robbins to Parents, Apr. 30, 1863, Robbins Papers, CHS.

142. Harrison Woodford to Alma Woodford, Mar. 1863, Harrison Woodford Letters, private collection.

143. Cecere, "Carrying the Home Front to War," 323. See also Peter Luebke, "Equal to Any Minstrel Concert I Attended at Home: Antebellum Popular Culture, White Northern Soldiers, and the Limits of the Civil War," paper presented at the Society of Civil War Historians Annual Meeting, June 2010, Richmond, VA.

144. On April 2, 1863, Barlow wrote, "got two months pay"; on April 26, he stated that he received his "bounty check." See Barlow Diary, CSL. John B. Cuzner mentioned receiving regular pay in early March 1863 and again in June. See John B. Cuzner to Ellen Van Dorn, Mar. 8, June 1, 1863, Cuzner Letters and Papers, CHS. Cuzner further stated that the second payment in June only occurred because "the state sent a man to pay us to keep us still."

145. In addition to Blakeslee, the ten NCOs who signed the letter were Hiram T. Simmons, Co. B; William Levaughn, Co. C; Peter Grohman, Co. D; Richard H. Lee, Co. E; Oliver W. Gates, Co. F; Jacob Bauer, Co. G; William H. Robinson, Co. H; Ezra T. Burgess, Co. I; Harmy Bruns, Co. K; and Sgt. Maj. Herbert Landon, Co. B. See Bernard F. Blakeslee to William A. Buckingham, June 8, 1863, Governors' Correspondence, CSL. Relyea includes an excerpt from a letter to him from Lt. Alonzo Case, which claimed that Lt. Col. Burnham threatened to "reduce every one of them to the ranks" for writing the governor. Case refused, arguing that he too had never been formally "mustered in" "until I was commissioned" and that Burnham "let the matter drop there." Relyea added, "This is the only mistake Colonel Burnham ever made in his dealing with the men, and to the end of his days he firmly held the love and respect of every member of the regiment." See Relyea, *16th Connecticut Volunteer Infantry,* 76.

146. John B. Cuzner to Ellen Van Dorn, June 14, 1863, Cuzner Letters and Papers, CHS. Harrison Woodford predicted to his father that the controversy would "all play out." See Harrison Woodford to Harvey Woodford, June 10, 1863, Harrison Woodford Letters, private collection. Leland Barlow wrote his family to see if they had heard anything about it at home. See Leland O. Barlow to Jane Barlow, June 6, 1863, Barlow Letters, CSL. It is noteworthy that on February 28, 1863, Barlow recorded in his diary, "Had an inspection and was sworn into the U.S. service." Then on April 10, he added, "The Reg. mustered into U.S. service." See Barlow Diary, CSL. Clearly, there remained considerable confusion within the ranks regarding this issue.

147. Relyea, *16th Connecticut Volunteer Infantry,* 76.

148. On the question of Civil War volunteers' motivation, as well as further discussion of their identity as civilian-soldiers, see Marvin Cain, "A Face of Battle Needed," *Civil War History* 28, no. 1 (Mar. 1982): 5–27. Reid Mitchell writes about the interconnected web of family, community, and governmental loyalties and their effect on northern volunteers in the *Vacant Chair.*

149. E. H. Mix to Gov. Wm. Buckingham, May 23, 1863, Governors' Correspondence, CSL. The 15th C.V., raised in New Haven at the same time as the 16th, had not fought at Antietam and, like

the 16th C.V., only tangentially at Fredericksburg. By May 23, 1863, it was stationed at Suffolk along with the 16th. 15th C.V. regimental service information from *Dyer's Compendium,* found at www .civilwararchive.com/Unreghst/unctinf3.htm#15thinf, accessed Apr. 25, 2008. See also Sidney H. Hayden to Jane Hayden, June 4, 1863, Hayden Papers, EGPL.

150. Records of the Bureau of Military Justice, RG 153, NA.

151. The 15th Connecticut's regimental historian stressed the morality and education of its members but also, like the 16th Connecticut, its lack of military experience when first mustered. Writing decades after the war, he explained that he and his comrades were "too sensible not to know that they who could scarcely handle a ramrod were ill fitted to go into action, and yet had the blundering order been insisted upon, as in the case of the 16th Conn., they would have done the utmost to uphold the honor of the old commonwealth." The author claimed that, due to the intensive training and drilling his regiment received, it earned the reputation as "the best drilled command within the defenses of Washington, south of the Potomac." See Sheldon B. Thorpe, *History of the 15th Connecticut Volunteers in the War for the Defense of the Union* (New Haven, CT: The Price, Lee and Adkins Co, 1893) 13, 21, 23; also 14. Thorpe was a 3rd sergeant in the 15th C.V.

152. Sidney H. Hayden to Oliver Hayden, June 20, 1863, Hayden Papers, EGPL. Leland Barlow recorded that they started at 2 a.m. for Portsmouth on June 22. See Barlow Diary, June 22, 1863, CSL.

CHAPTER FIVE

1. "A Soldier," letter to the *Courant,* June 20, 1863, *Hartford Daily Courant,* June 24, 1863.

2. Harrison Woodford to Alma Woodford, June 19, 1863, Harrison Woodford Letters, private collection.

3. George Robbins to Jehiel and Dorothy Robbins, July 9, 1863, Robbins Papers, CHS. In another letter, Robbins described peaches and figs. See George Robbins to Jehiel and Dorothy Robbins, July 20, 1863, Robbins Papers, CHS.

4. Lewis M. Holcomb to "Aunt," June 19, 1863, in "Lewis M. Holcomb," Whitney Collection, CSL.

5. "Refreshing sea breeze" from Sidney H. Hayden to "Uncle," July 27, 1863, Hayden Papers, EGPL; "splendid bathing place," from Robert H. Kellogg to Silas and Lucy C. Hale Kellogg, June 19, 1863, Kellogg Papers, CHS.

6. Martin V. Culver to Jonathan Culver, Aug. 9, 1863, Culver Letters, private collection. Culver complained of "boiles," heat as high as 122 degrees, and "blue tailed" flies that bit through his uniform.

7. Henry W. Halleck to John A. Dix, June 14, 1863, *OR,* ser. 1, vol. 27, pt. 3, 111. Halleck mistakenly believed at this time that Lee was heading toward the Shenandoah Valley. Gen. Dix commanded the raid.

8. Robert H. Kellogg to Silas Kellogg, June 21, 1863, Kellogg Papers, CHS.

9. George Robbins to Jehiel Robbins, June 22, 1863, Robbins Papers, CHS.

10. Robert H. Kellogg to Silas Kellogg, July 11, 1863, Kellogg Papers, CHS. Robbins claimed that the regiment returned to camp on July 14. He had returned a few days earlier due to his weakened condition. See George Robbins to Jehiel and Dorothy Robbins, July 20, 1863, Robbins Papers, CHS.

11. George Robbins to Jehiel and Dorothy Robbins, July 2, 1863, Robbins Papers, CHS. See also Leland Barlow to Jane Barlow, July 25, 1863, Barlow Letters, CSL.

12. Robert H. Kellogg to Silas Kellogg, July 11, 1863, Kellogg Papers, CHS.

13. Robbins, "Some Recollections," 22, CHS.

14. Robert H. Kellogg to Silas Kellogg, July 11, 1863, Kellogg Papers, CHS. Kellogg identified the woman as owned by William Smith of King William County.

15. Blakeslee, *History of the Sixteenth Connecticut Volunteers*, 40.

16. "I never saw berries so thick before," Robbins wrote his parents. See George Robbins to Jehiel and Dorothy Robbins, July 9, 1863, Robbins Papers, CHS.

17. Lamphere, "Experiences and Observations," MHS. Dix defended the actions of the "gallant troops under my command"; he resented that he was ordered back prematurely and that Gen. Erasmus D. Keyes hesitated to attack, and he insisted that the expedition successfully threatened Richmond and occupied a "large force of the enemy." Dix only regretted not destroying more railroad bridges before he was ordered to return. But Halleck was clearly disappointed. See Henry W. Halleck to John A. Dix, Dec. 20, 1863, *OR*, ser. 1, vol. 27, pt. 1, 19. See also Report of John A. Dix to Henry Halleck, July 1863, *OR*, ser. 1, vol. 27, pt. 2, 820–24. See Edwin Coddington, *The Gettysburg Campaign: A Study in Command* (New York: Scribner's), 100–102, for more on this raid and the controversy surrounding it.

18. Bauer, "Personal Experiences of the War," 6, PPM.

19. John H. Burnham to Sarah B. Burnham, July 15, 1863, Burnham Papers, CSL. John B. Cuzner told Ellen Van Dorn that he "marched several days including the Fourth of July barefoot." He further stated, "We had quite a hard march, most of the boys had sore feet." Several weeks later, he complained that his feet were still sore from the raid. See John B. Cuzner to Ellen Van Dorn, July 13, Aug. 28, and Sept. 7, 1863, Cuzner Letters and Papers, CHS.

20. Kellogg counted "seventy-one from the 16th including myself" aboard the steamer *Juanita* on the final leg of the trip back to Portsmouth. Robert H. Kellogg to Silas Kellogg, July 11, 1863, Kellogg Papers, CHS. Cpl. Harrison Woodford wrote home, "They marched us night & day & it was awful & hot & a number of the men dropped down almost dead & I believe some of them did die." See Harrison Woodford to Alma Woodford "& dear friends at home," July 11, 1863, Harrison Woodford Letters, private collection. George Robbins was also sickened and exhausted by the march; his feet were severely blistered. When he finally returned to Portsmouth, he announced, "I am very glad to get back and think I had rather dig all summer than go on another such expedition." See George Robbins to Jehiel and Dorothy Robbins, July 9, 1863, Robbins Papers, CHS. Further descriptions of the march's difficulty can be found in Martin V. Culver to Jonathan Culver, June 27, 1863, Culver Letters, private collection; Benjamin C. Ray, comp., *The Old Battle Flags. Veteran Soldiers' Souvenir, Containing A Brief Historical Sketch Of Each Connecticut Regiment, The Various Engagements, Casualties, Etc., During The War Of The Rebellion* (Hartford, 1879), 31.

21. Barlow Diary, July 3, 1863, CSL. See also entry for July 9, 1863. Barlow wrote his sister Jane on July 24, "I was put on a Boat at White House without any pass to go to any Hospital more dead than alive." See Leland O. Barlow to Jane Barlow, July 24, 1863, Barlow Letters, CSL.

22. Case, "Memoirs," SHS.

23. Ira Forbes, "Charles F. Campbell," Whitney Collection, CSL. George Whitney too believed this added humiliation was "one of more regret than satisfaction by his comrades." See George Q. Whitney, "William Henry Jackson," Whitney Collection, CSL. Jackson later played an important

role while the regiment was imprisoned at Andersonville, helping to administer a proper Christian ceremony to dead comrades.

24. *Hartford Daily Courant,* Sept. 5, 1863. The letter dated Sept. 1, 1863, from "Camp Tennant," is signed "B. M. T." It is not clear who this soldier was. He added, "The duty of the regiment is digging on fort, and picket duty once in six days."

25. Nathan Mayer's 1867 recollections quoted in Blakeslee, *History of the Sixteenth Connecticut Volunteers,* 44; see also Sidney H. Hayden to Oliver Hayden, June 20, 1863, Hayden Papers, EGPL. It appears that the regiment moved at least once during its time at Portsmouth. See George Robbins to Jehiel and Dorothy Robbins, Aug. 26, 1863, Robbins Papers, CHS.

26. Robbins, "Some Recollections," CHS. In a letter home, Robbins declared, "This is a splendid camp." He was pleased with the pine trees, plentiful oysters, and the salt water nearby. See George Robbins to Jehiel Robbins, June [21], 1863, Robbins Papers, CHS. Decades later, Robbins still remembered Portsmouth fondly: "Here we enjoyed salt water bathing and fine oysters daily, details being made for picket, and building corduroy roads. This was altogether the best location in our experience." See Robbins, "Some Recollections," 21, CHS.

27. George Robbins to Dorothy Robbins, Aug. 1, 1863, Robbins Papers, CHS. Robbins reasoned that the tightening of discipline was due to the "anticipation of the coming conscripts."

28. Lewis M. Holcomb to "Aunt," Aug. 23, 1863, Whitney Collection, CSL. His aunt could well be Almira Holcomb with whom he resided. See 8th Census of the United States, 1860: Population Schedule Granby, Hartford, CT, at ancestry.com, accessed Aug. 24, 2009.

29. Lewis M. Holcomb to Adelaide R. Holcomb, Aug. 17, 1863, Holcomb Family Papers, SBHS. These reactions fit what scholars such as Lorien Foote and Kevin Adams have uncovered in their studies of soldiers in the wartime and postwar army: class and ethnic (and racial) tensions divided men and officers. Men resented the manual labor, which few officers deigned to perform. See Foote, *The Gentlemen and the Roughs,* 145–70; Kevin Adams, *Class and Race in the Frontier Army: Military Life in the West, 1870–1890* (Norman: University of Oklahoma, 2009), 7–8, 58–72, 132–93.

30. During just the month of January 1864, Ira Forbes consumed portions of the memoirs of Rev. Abner Kingman Nott and the *Complete Duty of Man,* as well as a book on physiology. He also practiced arithmetic. See Forbes Diary, Jan. 5, 7, 8, 12, 13, 14, 1864, YU. The books he read were *Memoirs of Abner Kingman Nott, late pastor of the First Baptist church in the city of New York; with copious extracts from his correspondence,* ed. Richard Means Nott (New York: Sheldon and Co., 1860); Henry Venn, *The Complete Duty of Man: or, A system of doctrinal and practical Christianity: To which are added, forms of prayer and offices of devotion for the various circumstances of life* (London: Printed for S. Crowder, and G. Robinson . . . and Carnan and Newberry . . . , 1779). It is not clear which edition Forbes read; there were various editions available by 1864. This reference found at Library of Congress, www.loc.gov/index.html, accessed June 15, 2009.

31. Ira Forbes also mentioned playing chess, as well as attending prayer meetings and reading devotions. Regarding chess, see Forbes Diary, Jan. 15, 1864, YU.

32. Joseph Barnum's diary appears to indicate visits to prostitutes, as well as games of poker and baseball and drinking. See, e.g., Joseph Barnum Diary, Jan. 1, 2, 5, 1864, CHS. Martin V. Culver recounted to his brother Jonathan: "We have some fun with the wenches that come to camp you can bet[.]" He wrote this just after stating that his sweetheart Julie Wright had sent him a photograph:

"she gets up in good stile and is a very good looking woman." See Martin V. Culver to Jonathan Culver, Aug. 29, 1863, Culver Letters, private collection.

33. Austin D. Thompson to Electra M. Churchill, Nov. 30, 1863, Thompson Papers, CHS. Martin Culver was less impressed with the theater than the music: "thare is a theater clost by hear but the plays are not mutch[.] we have a very good brass band." See Martin V. Culver to Jonathan Culver, Dec. 27, 1863, Culver Letters, private collection.

34. For a broad overview of religion and the war, including soldiers' religious activities and revivalism, see Rable, *God's Almost Chosen People.*

35. Sidney H. Hayden to Jane Hayden, Dec. 6, 1863, Hayden Papers, EGPL. See also J. Leander Chapin to Gilbert Chapin, Nov. 29, 1863, Chapin Papers, CHS.

36. George N. Champlin to Samuel [Bartlett], Nov. 25, 1863, John S. Bartlett Letters, CHS. According to the 1860 census, Champlin was an eighteen-year-old spinner residing in Stafford. See 8th Census of the United States, 1860: Population Schedule, Stafford, Tolland, CT, at ancestry.com, accessed Aug. 13, 2008. George's older brother Andrew was also a member of the 16th Connecticut, but he died in December 1862.

37. Forbes Diary, Jan. 3, 1864, YU; see also his entries on Jan. 9 and 11.

38. See, e.g., Forbes Diary, Jan. 15, 16, 1864, YU.

39. Champlin Diary, Jan. 3, 1864, CSL.

40. Forbes Diary, Jan. 3, 1864, YU.

41. Robbins Diary, Jan. 3, 1864, CHS.

42. "Horse John," Letter to Editors, Jan. 1 [1864], *Connecticut War Record,* Jan. 1864.

43. Champlin Diary, Jan. 9, 1864, CSL. Robert H. Kellogg told his father that Chaplain Dixon planned to "form a Regimental Church, and I intend to join it." See Robert H. Kellogg to Silas Kellogg, Jan. 8, 1864, Kellogg Papers, CHS. George Robbins described morning and evening Sunday services held in the quartermaster's tent in October 1863. See George Robbins to Jehiel and Dorothy Robbins, Oct. 14, 1863, Robbins Papers, CHS.

44. Forbes Diary, Jan. 9, 1864, YU. The next day, Sunday, Forbes wrote, "I am desirous to see Zion prosperous in this regiment." See Forbes Diary, Jan. 10, 1864, YU.

45. Kellogg Diary, Jan. 1, 1864, CHS.

46. Robbins Diary, Jan. 1, 1864, CHS.

47. Quote from Niven, *Connecticut for the Union,* 321. Ramold describes visits by officers' wives as having a "civilizing" effect on the all-male environment of military camp. See *Across the Divide,* 33.

48. Sidney H. Hayden to Jane Hayden, Sept. 28, 1863, Hayden Papers, EGPL. Harrison Woodford's father Harvey visited him sometime in the fall of 1863. See Harrison Woodford to Alma Woodford, Nov. 20, 1863, Harrison Woodford Letters, private collection.

49. Martin V. Culver to Jonathan Culver, Oct. 18, 1863, Culver Letters, private collection.

50. Samuel E. Derby to Elizabeth Derby, Sept. 14, 1863, Derby Letters, CHS. Hiram Clark was married to Ellen M. Bushnell, the sister of Pvt. Huber Bushnell, also in Co. K. Ellen, a former schoolteacher, became a widow when Hiram died in prison in 1864. She remarried George A. Wright, a veteran from the 22nd C.V. See "Hiram A. Clark," Whitney Collection, CSL; and 8th Census of the United States, 1860: Population Schedule, Rocky Hill, Hartford, CT, at ancestry.com, accessed Nov. 10, 2008.

51. Austin D. Thompson to Electra M. Churchill, Dec. 19, 1863, Thompson Papers, CHS.

52. Harrison Woodford to Harvey Woodford, Dec. 29, 1863, Harrison Woodford Letters, private collection. Martin V. Culver noted that Pvt. Franklin Peck (Co. A) returned to camp at Portsmouth in Nov. with his wife Jane. See Martin V. Culver to Jonathan Culver, Nov. 23, 1863, Culver Letters, private collection. Franklin and Jane Peck had two young children. See 8th Census of the United States, 1860: Population Schedule, Rocky Hill, Hartford County, CT, at ancestry.com, accessed Nov. 3, 2008.

53. Robert H. Kellogg, *Life and Death in Rebel Prisons: Giving a Complete History of the Inhuman and Barbarous Treatment of our Brave Soldiers by Rebel Authorities, Inflicting Terrible Suffering and Frightful Mortality, Principally at Andersonville, Ga., and Florence, S.C., Describing Plans of Escape, Arrival of Prisoners, with Numerous and Varied Incidents and Anecdotes of Prison Life* (Hartford: L. Stebbins, 1865), 205.

54. Joseph Barnum described Lt. Ariel Case arriving with his "wife & sister" in early January. See Barnum Diary, Jan. 6, 1864, CHS.

55. Case, "Memoirs," SHS. By 1863, Alonzo and his wife Julia had one daughter, Lillia, born in 1860, and a son, Alonzo Chaffee, born April 1, 1862. The younger Alonzo would die in August 1864. See *Commemorative Biographical Record of Hartford County,* 526; also 9th Census of the United States, 1870: Population Schedule Simsbury, Hartford, Connecticut, at ancestry.com, accessed July 26, 2010. Ariel's wife Mary found the coldness tough to take, though. Lt. Col. Burnham described her as "very frigid," in a letter to his mother on January 10. Ariel and Mary had five children by the time Lt. Case was at Plymouth; the youngest, Oliver, was just over two years old in January 1863. See John H. Burnham to Sarah B. Burnham, Jan. 10, 1864, Burnham Papers, CSL. Information on Mary E. Case from 9th Census of the United States, 1870: Population Schedule, Hartford Ward 4, Hartford County, CT, at ancestry.com, accessed June 30, 2008; see also "Ariel Job Case," Whitney Collection, CSL. Pvt. George N. Champlin also mentioned Mary Case in camp with her husband and attending the meeting of the "Christian Association of the 16th Regiment of Conn. Volunteers" on Jan. 9. See Champlin Diary, Jan. 9, 1864, CSL. The Case women would remain with the regiment when it moved to Plymouth. See Case, "Memoirs," SHS.

56. John B. Cuzner to Ellen Van Dorn, Aug. 28, 1863, Cuzner Letters and Papers, CHS.

57. See John B. Cuzner to Ellen Van Dorn, Sept. 8, 1863, Cuzner Letters and Papers, CHS. On opposition to northern soldiers' wives visiting camp, see Ramold, *Across the Divide,* 48–49.

58. Lt. Col. Burnham had encouraged his sister Lottie to accompany his mother, but she demurred. See John H. Burnham to Sarah B. Burnham, Aug. 21, 1863, Burnham Papers, CSL; also John H. Burnham to H. P. Gates, Oct. 14, 1863, John H. Burnham, CSR, NA.

59. *Hartford Daily Courant,* Sept. 5, 1863.

60. Quoted in the *Hartford Daily Courant,* Sept. 21, 1863. "Lieut. Robins" may have been Quartermaster Gurdon Robins, Jr., but it is more likely that this was Pvt. George Robbins writing to his father. Soldiers praising Mrs. Burnham include Sidney H. Hayden to Jane Hayden, Oct. 8, 1863, Hayden Papers, EGPL; Leland O. Barlow to Jane Barlow, Sept. 16, 1863, Barlow Letters, CSL; John B. Cuzner to Ellen Van Dorn, Sept. 8, 1863, Cuzner Letters and Papers, CHS.

61. Harrison Woodford to Alma Woodford, Nov. 10, 1863, Harrison Woodford Letters, private collection.

62. Quoted in Croffutt and Morris, *Military and Civil History of Connecticut*, 476–77.

63. Case, "Memoirs," SHS.

64. Sidney H. Hayden to Jane Hayden, Sept. 15, 1863, Hayden Papers, EGPL. Commissioned black officers were few; there were more noncommissioned ones. See John David Smith, ed., "Let Us All Be Grateful That We Have Colored Troops That Will Fight," in *Black Soldiers in Blue: African American Troops in the Civil War Era* (Chapel Hill: University of North Carolina Press, 2002), 36; and Joseph Glatthaar, *Forged in Battle: The Civil War Alliance of Black Soldiers and White Officers* (New York: Free Press, 1990), 176–82. The black troops stationed at Portsmouth were most likely the 1st Regiment U.S. Colored Infantry. See Civil War Soldiers and Sailors System, www.nps.gov/civilwar/index.htm, accessed Feb. 27, 2013.

65. Leland O. Barlow to Harvey Barlow, Sept. 10, 1863, Barlow Letters, CSL.

66. Robert H. Kellogg Diary, Jan. 16, 1864, CHS.

67. Lewis M. Holcomb to Adelaide R. Holcomb, Dec. 6, 1863, Holcomb Family Papers, SBHS.

68. He added disparagingly that the "people around here are very ignorant some of them don't know how to write or even to spell their own name." See George Robbins to "Friends," Oct. 29, 1863, Robbins Papers, CHS.

69. See Andrew McIlwaine, *Mosquito Soldiers: Malaria, Yellow Fever and the Course of the American Civil War* (Baton Rouge: Louisiana State University Press, 2010), for more on disease and its devastating effects on soldiers, especially those stationed near coastal cities like Portsmouth. Jim Downs explores the catastrophic impact these diseases had on African Americans, particularly slaves, in *Sick from Freedom: African American Illness and Suffering During the Civil War and Reconstruction* (New York: Oxford University Press, 2012).

70. Martin V. Culver to Jonathan Culver, Aug. 29, 1863, Culver Letters, private collection.

71. John B. Cuzner to Ellen Van Dorn, Sept. 17, 1863, Cuzner Letters and Papers, CHS.

72. Ira Forbes, "William H. Hubbard," Whitney Collection, CSL. The *Hartford Courant* included a statement from a "private letter from one of the members of the 16th regiment" that of the "thousand and forty men who left New Haven a year ago, only some five hundred remain fit for duty. The writer also states that the diphtheria has made its appearance among the men." See *Hartford Daily Courant*, Sept. 5, 1863. It is not clear if the paper mistakenly printed "New Haven" instead of "Hartford" or if the letter writer was from the 15th Connecticut, which drew from New Haven County and was also stationed at Portsmouth.

73. Robbins, "Some Recollections," 23, CHS.

74. George Robbins to Jehiel and Dorothy Robbins, Sept. 13, 1863, Robbins Papers, CHS. Martin Hull, a thirty-four-year-old farmer from New Hartford when he enlisted would die in Andersonville of this same ailment on August 27, 1864. See also William H. Jackson Diary, CSL.

75. Leland O. Barlow to Jane Barlow, Sept. 16, 1863, Barlow Letters, CSL.

76. Nathan Mayer, "Physician's Affidavit," Mar. 15, 1881, John H. Burnham Pension File, NA.

77. Sidney Hayden wrote in early November, "The late frosts have killed the Malaria that pervades the swamps in a measure and many of us who were ailing are now well." See Sidney H. Hayden to Jane Hayden, Nov. 5, 1863, Hayden Papers, EGPL. See Bell, *Mosquito Soldiers*, for more on contemporary attitudes toward and treatments of malaria, esp. 22–24.

78. *Hartford Daily Times*, July 27, 1863. It is not clear who this lieutenant was and whether this

story had any truth at all, but that the *Times* published it is significant. As noted above, a number of lieutenants resigned from the regiment, especially after Antietam; however, 2nd Lt. John Williams (Co. D) was "dismissed" on October 13, 1862. Sgt. William H. Relyea singled him out as one of the "weakening influences" on the eve of Antietam: "Second Lieutenant John Williams of Company D was under arrest for being 'absent without leave,' and did not enter the fight and was soon after dismissed from the service in disgrace." See Relyea, *16th Connecticut Volunteer Infantry*, 24.

79. Leland O. Barlow to Jane Barlow [Aug. 1863], Barlow Letters, CSL.

80. George Robbins to Jehiel and Dorothy Robbins, Aug. 16, 1863, Robbins Papers, CHS.

81. John B. Cuzner to Ellen Van Dorn, Sept. 17, 1863, Cuzner Letters and Papers, CHS.

82. See Sidney H. Hayden to Catherine Hayden, Sept. 17, 1863, Hayden Papers, EGPL; *Hartford Daily Courant*, Sept. 21, 1863. Ira Forbes wrote that Hubbard came from "one of the oldest and most respected families in Guilford" and that his death was "deeply lamented in Guilford." See Ira Forbes, "William H. Hubbard," Whitney Collection, CSL. Croffutt and Morris added a note about Sgt. Hubbard in their history of Connecticut during the war: "He was a well educated young man, moral and circumspect in his life and happy in the hour of his sacrifice" (*Military and Civil History of Connecticut*, 476, note 1).

83. Barlow Diary, Sept. 17, 1863, CSL.

84. Barlow Diary, Sept. 18, 1863, CSL.

85. George Robbins to Jehiel and Dorothy Robbins, Sept. 19, 1863, Robbins Papers, CHS.

86. Holcomb wondered if the presence of black troops and a visit by Massachusetts's Governor Andrews would interest his parents more. See Gavett B. Holcomb to Edmund and Harriet Holcomb, Sept. 17, 1863, Gavett B. Holcomb Papers, SHS.

87. "Adelphi," Letter from Camp of the Sixteenth Connecticut Volunteers, Dec. 7, 1863, for *Connecticut War Record*, Jan. 1864.

88. Austin D. Thompson to Electra Churchill, July 17, 1863, Thompson Papers, CHS.

89. John B. Cuzner to Ellen Van Dorn, July 25, 1863, Cuzner Letters and Papers, CHS.

90. Lewis M. Holcomb to "Aunt," Aug. 23, 1863, from Whitney Collection, CSL.

91. Harrison Woodford to Harvey and Alma Woodford, Aug. 12, 1863, Harrison Woodford Letters, private collection.

92. Richard Henry Lee to [Adelaide R. Holcomb], Aug. 5, 1863, Holcomb Family Papers, SBHS.

93. Leland O. Barlow to S. B. Barlow, Sept. 22, 1863, Barlow Letters, CSL. Barlow also wrote, "Croaker Copperheads are very few in the army."

94. David T. Conklin to J. Leander Chapin, Sept. 18, 1863, Chapin Papers, CHS. Conklin was a sergeant in the 127th New York Infantry.

95. J. Leander Chapin to Gilbert Chapin, Nov. 29, 1863, Chapin Papers, CHS. Chapin's commitment to the war and his regiment, at least as revealed in his personal letters to his family, remained firm.

96. George N. Champlin to [Samuel Bartlett], Nov. 25, 1863, John S. Bartlett Letters, CHS. Samuel Bartlett enlisted instead in the 10th Connecticut. See Civil War Soldiers and Sailors System, www.itd.nps.gov/cwss/soldiers.cfm, accessed Aug. 13, 2008.

97. Lewis M. Holcomb to Adelaide R. Holcomb, Oct. 2, 1863, Holcomb Family Papers, SBHS.

98. Martin V. Culver to Jonathan Culver, Dec. 27, 1863, Nov. 23, 1863, Culver Letters, private collection.

99. Sidney H. Hayden to Jane Hayden, Aug. 22, 1863, Hayden Papers, EGPL.

100. Sidney H. Hayden to Oliver Hayden, Oct. 20, 1863, Hayden Papers, EGPL.

101. George Robbins to Jehiel Robbins, Dec. 14, 1863, Robbins Papers, CHS. The deceased soldier was Fred Bulkley, whose older sister Hattie was a friend of George's. By January, Robbins was considering not reenlisting; however, he would wait until his time had expired in August 1865. Either way, he was done with the infantry and would choose the cavalry next time. See George Robbins to Jehiel and Dorothy Robbins, Jan. 9, 1864, Robbins Papers, CHS.

102. Harrison Woodford to Harvey and Alma Woodford, Aug. 12, 1863, Harrison Woodford Letters, private collection.

103. Leland O. Barlow to Jane Barlow, Nov. 16, 1863, Barlow Letters, CSL.

104. Leland O. Barlow to Jane Barlow, no date, Barlow Letters, CSL. For more on northern officers and their struggles to discipline men in the ranks, see Foote, *The Gentlemen and the Roughs*, 119–44.

105. Sidney Hayden wrote his father, "Most all of the boys think we are not sworn into the United States Service as we were not mustered in as a Regiment at Washington but I think they will hold us 3 years." See Sidney H. Hayden to Oliver Hayden, June 20, 1863, Hayden Papers, EGPL.

106. William A. Buckingham to Bernard Blakeslee, June 12, 1863, Governors' Correspondence, CSL; parts of this letter are illegible, and Blakeslee's original letter to Buckingham is not preserved in the collection.

107. John H. Burnham to William A. Buckingham, June 18, 1863, Governors' Correspondence, CSL; William A. Buckingham to Bernard Blakeslee, June 12, 1863, Governors' Correspondence, CSL. The *Hartford Daily Times* reported on August 27, 1863, that the regiment had "been paid to July 1st."

108. *Hartford Daily Times*, Sept. 10, 1863. Steele had requested a furlough just days before he penned this letter to the *Times*. See Edgar E. Strong to John B. Clapp, Sept. 1, 1863, in Horace B. Steele Papers, CSL. It does seem significant, too, that Horace's brother Nathan, a thirty-five-year-old married gunsmith, deserted the regiment in early March 1863. See AGO 1889, 630. See "Horace Steele," Whitney Collection, CSL. Whitney notes that H. B. Steele was a "valued member of Co. F as was also James M. Steele." According to the 1860 census, Samuel Steele resided with Horace in a boarding house run by Eliza Steele. See 8th Census of the United States, 1860: Population Schedule, Hartford District 2, Hartford, Hartford County, CT, at ancestry.com, accessed July 7, 2011.

109. *Hartford Daily Courant,* Sept. 25, 1863.

110. *Hartford Daily Times,* Oct. 7, 1863.

111. The *Times* refused to publish any more on this subject, stating, "In justice to the soldier who writes this, and much desires us to print it, we give it place, but we prefer not to continue this unpleasant controversy in these columns." See *Hartford Daily Times*, Oct. 7, 1863. Historians have recorded changes in definitions and reactions to desertion among southern soldiers more than they have among northern men. Drew Gilpin Faust has explored the issue of Confederate desertion and how it played against southern familial obligations and Confederate nationalism in *Mothers of Invention: Women of the Slaveholding South in the American Civil War* (Chapel Hill: University of North Carolina Press, 1996). Brian Holden Reid and John White contend that the widespread desertion in both armies was mainly an issue of inconsistent military discipline clashing with Civil War volunteers' natural propensity for autonomy. They, as do most historians, dismiss the "cases of overt cowardice in the face of the enemy" as rare and seemingly inconsequential. See Brian

Holden Reid and John White, "A Mob of Stragglers and Cowards: Desertion from the Confederate and Union Armies, 1861–1865," *Journal of Strategic Studies* 8 (1985): 64, also 75. See also Joan Cashin, "Deserters, Civilians and Draft Resistance in the North," in Joan Cashin, ed., *War Was You And Me: Civilians in the American Civil War* (Princeton, NJ: Princeton University Press, 2002), 262–85. A more localized but no less significant book is Robert Sandow's *Deserter Country: Civil War Opposition in the Pennsylvania Appalachians* (New York: Fordham University Press, 2009). A recent study of cowardice and desertion argues that Union soldiers were statistically most likely to desert if they were foreign born, married, and/or older men. The authors further posit that men with stronger community ties within a regiment were less likely to desert. See Dora Costas and Matthew Kahn, *Heroes and Cowards: The Social Face of War* (Princeton, NJ: Princeton University Press, 2008). See also Walsh, "Cowardice Weakness or Infirmity."

112. *Hartford Daily Times,* Oct. 17, 1863. Scholars have begun to note the significant impact of homesickness on Civil War soldiers. See Frances Clarke, "So Lonesome I Could Die: Nostalgia and Debates Over Emotional Control in the Civil War North," *Journal of Social History* 41, no. 2 (Winter 2007): 253–82; and David Anderson, "Dying of Nostalgia: Homesickness in the Union Army during the Civil War," *Civil War History* 56, no. 3 (Sept. 2010): 247–82; also Ramold, *Across the Divide,* 45.

113. *Hartford Daily Courant,* Oct. 19, 1863.

114. John B. Cuzner to Ellen Van Dorn, Oct. 16, 1863, Cuzner Letters and Papers, CHS.

115. John B. Cuzner to Ellen Van Dorn, Nov. 19, 1863, Cuzner Letters and Papers, CHS. Cuzner expressed his impatience with the process in letters to Van Dorn on Oct. 29 and Nov. 19, 1863; see also his letter from Dec. 13. Soilders were then encouraged to reenlist with thirty-day furloughs and bounties, and Cuzner believed somehow that this was why the ten-day furlough was discontinued by December 1863.

116. George Robbins to "Friends," Oct. 29, 1863, Robbins Papers, CHS.

117. Sidney H. Hayden to "Uncle," July 27, 1863, Hayden Papers, EGPL.

118. Lewis M. Holcomb to Adelaide M. Holcomb, Sept. 2, 1863, Holcomb Family Papers, SBHS.

119. Wilmer H. Johnson to William A. Buckingham, Oct. 13, 1863, Governors' Correspondence, CSL. Relyea made reference to Musician Johnson helping to "furnish the needed supplies" on an expedition to the Dismal Swamp in mid-September. In the edited version of William Relyea's history of the unit, John Michael Priest and his fellow editors indicate that Johnson's "real name was Samuel Tudor," although there is no further explanation or reference for this. George Q. Whitney's list of members includes Samuel Tudor only with a note from Whitney that Wilmer H. Johnson was Tudor's "alias." It could be that Johnson was Tudor's pen name or that he wanted to downplay his prominent family name. Samuel Tudor's mother was the daughter of U.S. senator and ally to Thomas Jefferson, Stephen Rowe Bradley. See Relyea, *16th Connecticut Volunteer Infantry,* 101, and 204, note 2; AGO; and "Samuel Tudor," Whitney Collection, CSL. No Samuel Tudor is found on the Civil War Soldiers and Sailors System, www.itd.nps.gov/cwss/soldiers.cfm (accessed Apr. 27, 2008). In a November 1864 letter from comrade Cornelius Doty to the governor, seeking a furlough, Wilmer H. Johnson affirmed Doty's truthfulness and added after his signature, "Reporter for Hartford Courant & Conn War Record." See Cornelius Doty to William Buckingham, Nov. 8, 1864, Governors' Correspondence, CSL. In a letter from Portsmouth, Martin V. Culver informed his brother Jonathan, "if you can get the Hartford Post you will see a peace [*sic*] from the 16th every week." See Martin V. Culver to Jonathan Culver, Dec. 27, 1863, Culver Letters, private collection.

120. Peck served until mustered out in June 1865. See Franklin G. Peck to William A. Buckingham, Oct. 17, 1863, Governors' Correspondence, CSL; AGO 1869.

121. Austin D. Thompson to Electra Churchill, Aug. 17, 1863, Thompson Papers, CHS. Thompson also said he wondered if he would not be able to obtain a discharge if he "had friends that had influence."

122. Austin D. Thompson to Electra M. Churchill, Nov. 15, 1863, Thompson Papers, CHS. See also Belden Diary, Nov. 9, 1863, CHS.

123. The forty-five-year-old Irishman Gillen, married and a machinist by trade, was never seen again; it was rumored that he had fled to Canada. Gillen's age when he enlisted in July 1862 was forty-four. "Descriptive list of Deserters for the 16th C.V. for month ending August 31 1863," Muster Rolls, Returns, Regimental Papers, RG 94, Box 148 [unbound papers], NA.

124. "Descriptive list of Deserters for the 16th C.V. for month ending August 31 1863," Muster Rolls, Returns, Regimental Papers, RG 94, Box 148 [unbound papers], NA.

125. "Descriptive list of Deserters for the 16th C.V. for month ending September 30, 1863," Muster Rolls, Returns, Regimental Papers, RG 94, Box 148 [unbound papers] NA.

126. Sidney H. Hayden to Catherine Hayden, Aug. 3, 1863, Hayden Papers, EGPL.

127. Austin D. Thompson to Electra M. Churchill, July 17, 1863, Thompson Papers, CHS.

128. George Robbins to Jehiel and Dorothy Robbins, July 20, 1863, Robbins Papers, CHS.

129. Leland O. Barlow to Jane Barlow, July 24, 1863, Barlow Letters, CSL.

130. Leland O. Barlow to Jane Barlow, July 26, 1863, Barlow Letters, CSL.

131. Harrison Woodford to Harvey Woodford, July 20, 1864, Harrison Woodford Letters, private collection.

132. Leland O. Barlow to Harvey Barlow [Sept. 1863], Barlow Letters, CSL.

133. Sidney H. Hayden to Jane Hayden, Sept. 15, 1863, Hayden Papers, EGPL.

134. George Robbins to Jehiel and Dorothy Robbins, Oct. 27, 1863, Robbins Papers, CHS. A few weeks later, Robbins noted that two of the conscripts from the 8th C.V. were shot for desertion. See George Robbins to Dorothy Robbins, Nov. 17, 1863, Robbins Papers, CHS.

135. Sidney H. Hayden to Jane Hayden, Oct. 28, 1863, EGPL. This was a common sentiment among northern volunteers. See Ramold, *Across the Divide*, 111–12.

136. Robert H. Kellogg to Silas Kellogg, July 16, 1863, Kellogg Papers, CHS.

137. Robert H. Kellogg to Silas Kellogg, July 31, 1863, Kellogg Papers, CHS.

138. No one escaped. Robert H. Kellogg to Lucy C. Hale Kellogg, Aug. 10, 1863, Kellogg Papers, CHS.

139. Robert H. Kellogg to Silas Kellogg, July 31, 1863, Kellogg Papers, CHS. Kellogg was acting orderly sergeant.

140. Capt. Julian Pomeroy (Co. K), along with 1st Lt. William Miller (Co. G), Sgts. Samuel Fenn (Co. C), William Relyea (Co. D), Charles Roys (Co. G.), and Merritt Strong (Co. K), Cpl. John Gemmill (Co. A), and Pvts. William Case (Co. B), John H. Good (Co. E) and Samuel Wetmore (Co. H), were detailed on recruiting duty in Hartford. See Muster Rolls, Returns, Regimental Papers, RG 94, Box 147 [unbound papers], NA. Robbins explained to his parents in November that Sgt. Merritt S. Strong had returned to Connecticut "to enlist recruits for the Co. One man has gone from each Co. to get recruits for the regt. so that I don't think we shall even be troubled with conscripts at least I hope not." See George Robbins to Jehiel and Dorothy Robbins, Nov. 29, 1863, Robbins Papers, CHS. In January 1864, Lt. Col. John Burnham also returned to Hartford "to look after the interest of the regiment, in hopes of obtaining volunteers." See *Hartford Daily Times,* Jan. 18, 1864.

141. "An Appeal from the 16th Connecticut," Dec. 11, 1863, in the *Hartford Daily Courant*, Dec. 16, 1863. The author's initials are "N.C.S.," but these do not match with any obvious name in the regiment.

142. "Adelphi," Letter from Camp of the Sixteenth Connecticut Volunteers, Dec. 7, 1863, for *Connecticut War Record*, Jan. 1864.

143. Austin D. Thompson to Electra M. Churchill, Jan. 4, 1864, Thompson Papers, CHS. Fifteen recruits were en route to join the regiment the first week of Jan., all having mustered into the regiment between November 30 and December 28, 1863. See Muster Roll of Detachment of Recruits for 16th Conn. Nov & Dec 1863, Muster Rolls, Returns, Regimental Papers, RG 94, Box 147 [unbound papers], NA.

144. In an introduction written by Alice Collins, the grandniece of Pvt. Martin V. Culver, she states that the regiment had a total of seventy-five total recruits. See typescript, "The Letters of Private Martin Van Buren Culver, 16th Connecticut Volunteers 1862–1865," Culver Letters, private collection.

145. Culver, a house carpenter before the war, wrote his brother of "hewing timber for houses for the shoulder straps" while stationed at Portsmouth. When he built a house for "the lieutenant" in November, Culver ruefully declared, "if he does not let me come [home on furlough] he can go to Hell[;] I will get square with him sometime." See Martin V. Culver to Jonathan Culver, Nov. 23 and Oct. 18, 1863, Culver Letters, private collection. In January, Robert H. Kellogg described obtaining bricks for a fireplace and a supply of "good oak wood." See Kellogg Diary, Jan. 16, 1864, CHS. George Robbins remembered, "We spent the summer in building breastworks, slashing forests, building corduroy roads, digging rifle pits and doing picket duty." See Robbins, "Some Recollections," 24, CHS.

146. "Horse John" to Editors, Jan. 1 [1864], *Connecticut War Record*, Jan. 1864. It is not clear who "Horse John" was, but he was a soldier in the 16th C.V.

147. Austin D. Thompson to Electra M. Churchill, Dec. 6, 1863, Thompson Papers, CHS. More descriptions of the regiment's winter camp include "A Member of the 16th," letter dated Nov. 4, 1863, in *Hartford Daily Courant*, Nov. 11, 1863; "Horse John," Letter to the Editors, Nov. 5, 1863, *Connecticut War Record*, Nov. 1863; Sidney H. Hayden to Jane Hayden, Dec. 6, 1863, Hayden Papers, EGPL; J. Leander Chapin to Amelia Chapin, Dec. 13, 1863, Chapin Papers, CHS; Martin V. Culver to Jonathan Culver, Dec. 27, 1863, Culver Letters, private collection.

148. Sidney H. Hayden to Jane Hayden, Dec. 6, 1863, Hayden Papers, EGPL.

149. Lewis M. Holcomb to Adelaide R. Holcomb, Dec. 6, 1863, Holcomb Family Papers, SBHS.

150. Austin D. Thompson to Electra M. Churchill, Jan. 4, 1864, Thompson Papers, CHS.

151. The *Hartford Daily Courant* reported Beach "on detached service in command of a conscript camp located in Pittsburgh, PA" on October 5, 1863. In July, George Robbins noted that there were rumors of Beach's return: "The report is that Col. Beach is coming back. I hope that he is for we all like him." See George Robbins to Jehiel and Dorothy Robbins, July 20, 1863, Robbins Papers, CHS.

152. J. Leander Chapin to Amelia Chapin, Dec. 13, 1863, Chapin Papers, CHS.

153. Belden Diary, Dec. 7, 1863, CHS.

154. "Horse John," Letter to Editors, Jan. 1 [1864], *Connecticut War Record*, Jan. 1864. This soldier was also complimentary of Burnham: "For nobler and manlier officers than he, I know but two, and one of these is dead."

155. Champlin Diary, Jan. 17, 1864, CSL.

156. Champlin Diary, Jan. 18, 1864, CSL. Forbes Diary, Jan. 18, 1864, YU. Champlin further singled out Co. D: "Most of Co. D were drunk this afternoon and they had a big time." Samuel E. Derby recounted that as the regiment "were lying in wait for the boats" to leave Portsmouth, a group of men including Hiram Clark's brother-in-law Huber Bushnell, who was a "big fool" to sign the temperance pledge, "went around town and that day he drank some whiskey and helped to get one of the men in our company drunk." Derby thought the pledge was worthless and believed that his wife agreed: "you seem to think you dont want me to sign the pledge well my darling when your husband signs the pledge I will write and let you know all about it but I cant see the point." See Samuel E. Derby to Elizabeth Derby, Mar. 8, 1864, Derby Letters, CHS.

157. Austin D. Thompson to Electra M. Churchill, Jan. 18, 1864, Thompson Papers, CHS.

158. Champlin Diary, Jan. 20, 1864, CSL.

159. Forbes Diary, Jan. 20, 1864, YU.

160. Forbes Diary, Jan. 21, 1864, YU.

161. Champlin Diary, Jan. 21, 1864, CSL.

162. Henry E. Savage Diary, Jan. 21, 1864, CSL.

163. Samuel E. Derby to Elizabeth Derby, Jan. 26, 1864, Derby Letters, CHS.

164. Forbes Diary, Jan. 21, 1864, YU. Leland Barlow noted, "They had orders not to destroy anything, but they did not mind a thing about it; they burned everything except the Chapel, Hospital and two or three Officers houses." See Leland O. Barlow to Jane Barlow, Jan. 31, 1864, Barlow Letters, CSL.

165. Leander Chapin to Gilbert Chapin, Jan. 31, 1864, Chapin Papers, CHS.

166. Kellogg Diary, Jan. 21, 1864, CHS.

167. George Robbins to Jehiel and Dorothy Robbins, Jan. 26, 1864, Robbins Papers, CHS; "was mutiny but we were in an ugly mood." and "reason prevailed," from Robbins, "Some Recollections," 23–24, CHS. On February 14, 1864, Robbins told his parents, "Those men have arrived that were left in Portsmouth. The Noncommissioned Officers were reduced to the ranks, among them is Corpl. Robinson, Viberts another. it serves them just right I think they are kept at work every day. Jack Hill was among the number though he was reduced long before we left Portsmouth." Indeed, John Hill (Co. K) had been reduced to ranks in October 1863. See AGO 1889, 637. Neither Charles Robinson (Co. F) nor Henry Viberts (Co. F) had this reduction of ranks listed in the AGO (1869, 629–30). See George Robbins to Jehiel and Dorothy Robbins, Feb. 14, 1864, Robbins Papers, CHS. In his diary, Robbins wrote, "One Co. of the 13 N.H. have bought the line officers homes, but the boys will burn all that they can[.] Heckman ordered that nothing be destroyed[.] when Beach heard it he ordered the flag staff to be cut down." See Robbins Diary, Jan. 20, 1864, CHS. The next day, he wrote, "The camp was fired this morning at three o'clock after the tents had been taken down." He added, "some of the boys near being burned."

168. See Robbins Diary, Jan. 21, 1864, CHS. In his postwar memoirs, Robbins recalled orders being read at "dress parade for the regiment to be ready to vacate the camp at an early hour next morning, and to leave all buildings which had been erected with such care for a New Jersey regiment which had just arrived and were encamped nearby, member of which had already visited us and were gloating over their good fortune." Robbins was on guard that night and saw firsthand what happened: "A little after midnight the boys commenced to strike tents and drag them to a place of

safety. When this was done, in every company street fires broke out and soon the wooden structures were a mass of flames. The New Jersey men were a sadly disappointed lot seeing our fine camp go up in smoke. We had the highest flag staff in the Division and, determined that if we could not stay to enjoy the fruit of our labor no other regiment could, axes were procured from the Pioneer Corps and the pole came crashing to the ground and to complete the job it was cut into several pieces." See Robbins, "Some Recollections," 23–24, CHS.

169. Harrison Woodford, undated letter, PPM, copy also at SHS.

170. Richard Henry Lee to Adelaide R. Holcomb, Mar. 2, 1864, Holcomb Family Papers, SBHS.

171. Austin D. Thompson to Electra M. Churchill, Jan. 27, 1864, Thompson Papers, CHS.

172. John Burnham applied for a twenty-day leave of absence in order to attend a business meeting in Hartford. Deliberations were underway to consider ending the partnership he shared with his brothers and brother-in-law, and Burnham wanted to be there before any final decision was made. See John H. Burnham to John D. Wheeler, Jan. 9, 1864, John H. Burnham, CSR, NA. Burnham won approval for the furlough, with a ringing endorsement from the commanding general at Portsmouth, Brig. Gen. George Getty: "The Regt. is in a high state of discipline & sufficiency & under the circumstances I approve the application." See George W. Getty, Special Orders, No. 13, Jan. 10, 1864, in John H. Burnham, CSR, NA. Getty pointed out that Maj. Pasco was "on duty with the regiment," and Colonel Beach also approved Burnham's leave. Burnham was on furlough from January 15 to February 4, 1864. See John H. Burnham, CSR, NA.

173. Both officers would be restored to command after several weeks, although tragically Mix drowned en route to rejoin the regiment stationed at Plymouth. Ira E. Forbes, "Drowned While in Service," Forbes Collection, CSL.

174. Barnum Diary, Jan. 21, 1864, CHS; "Civil War Manuscripts Project," Joseph Hall Barnum, General Order No. 40, Mar. 19, 1864, located at www.chs.org/kcwmp/exams/BarnumJ.html, accessed June 20, 2008. Barnum's CSR lists him as "absent" and "In arrest" according to the Company Muster Roll for January and February 1864. See Joseph H. Barnum, CSR, NA. The Bound Regimental Papers further indicate that Barnum was "on arrest or confinement: Feb 1–29; Mar. 1–4; 7–31, 1864." See Bound Regimental Papers, RG 94, entries 112–15, Bound Records of the Union Volunteer Regiments, vol. 2, NA. According to the Records of the Bureau of Military Justice, Barnum had gone "awol at Portsmouth while embarking on the steamer 'Vidette' while Officer of the Day." During the trial, it was noted that he claimed to have had permission from the major "to leave and express home some money," but nothing was said about his newborn child. Barnum was found guilty and sentenced to a "reprimand." See Records of the Bureau of Military Justice, RG 153, NA.

175. Beach's CSR indicates that he was "absent" from the regiment, instead commanding Harland's Brigade in January and February 1864. See Frank Beach, CSR, NA.

176. *Hartford Daily Courant*, Feb. 8, 1864. This letter further described, "Major Pasco was put under arrest for disobedience of orders in allowing the camp to be burned; Capt. Mix for the same in allowing his house to be taken off the camp. Other officers are also under arrest, as follows. Capt. Barnum for leaving the regiment while officer of the day; and Capt. Morse and Lieut. Strong for absence without leave." This letter noted that the regiment was paid as they prepared to leave Portsmouth. Later, in an issue of the *Connecticut War Record*, "Little Mare," a member of the 16th C.V. wrote, "Lieut. Strong and Capt. Barnum have been relieved from arrest, the sentences of the

court martial in their case being promulgated. Lieut. Strong was found 'not guilty,' and honorably acquitted." Strong had been on furlough for ten days, but "his eyes being really in a bad state," he had "procured a certificate of disability" from a surgeon for five more days. This was the basis of the charges against him. He added, "Captain Barnum's sentence was to be reprimanded. The charge was 'neglect of duty,' I believe." See "Little Mare," letter to editor, Apr. 18, 1864, *Connecticut War Record*, May 1864. See also *Hartford Daily Courant*, Mar. 7, 1864.

177. "Horse John," Letter to Editor, Feb. 1, 1864, *Connecticut War Record*, Mar. 1864. He estimated that the men had spent "very near" $1500 on their "huts" and the officers "about as much more on their houses." In the April issue, "Horse John" claimed that Maj. Pasco became the "scapegoat for the sins charged to the regiment." "Horse John," Letter to Editor, Mar. 20, 1864, *Connecticut War Record*, Apr. 1864.

178. *New Haven Daily Palladium*, Feb. 9, 1864. The paper went on to note that the *Hartford Post* had recently published a letter from the regiment which made no mention of the incident, and thus, perhaps, all had been settled and the officers released. Still, the paper's location may have been circumstantial, as the *Connecticut War Record* originated from New Haven, although it published generally favorable stories about the regiment.

179. "Dixie," Letter to the Editors, Jan. 31, 1864, in *Hartford Daily Courant*, Feb. 13, 1864. On January 22, Samuel E. Grosvenor noted that the regiment left Fort Monroe at 4 a.m. See Grosvenor Diary, Jan. 22, 1864, CHS.

180. Forbes Diary, Jan. 21, 1864, YU.

181. J. Leander Chapin to Gilbert Chapin, Jan. 31, 1864, Chapin Papers, CHS. See also Champlin Diary, Jan. 22, 1864, CSL; Kellogg Diary, Jan. 22, 1864, CHS; Grosvenor Diary, Jan. 22, 1864, CHS.

CHAPTER SIX

1. J. Leander Chapin to Gilbert Chapin, Jan. 31, 1864, Chapin Papers, CHS. Ira Forbes estimated the time of arrival to be 11:30 p.m. on January 24. See Forbes Diary, Jan. 25, 1864, YU.

2. Warren Lee Goss, *The Soldier's Story of his Captivity at Andersonville, Belle Island and other Rebel Prisons* (Boston: Lee and Shepard Publisher, 1867), 54.

3. Relyea, "History of the 16th Connecticut," 160; also James G. Barrett, *The Civil War in North Carolina* (Chapel Hill: University of North Carolina Press, 1963), 213; Philip Katcher, *Lethal Glory: Dramatic Defeats of the Civil War* (London: Arms and Armour Press, 1995), 149–50.

4. Relyea further speculated that being sent to North Carolina was an "act of spite engendered by the sorely disappointed people who displaced us and who were special friends of the General commanding the department" (*16th Connecticut Volunteer Infantry*, 114).

5. Wayne K. Durrill, *War of Another Kind: A Southern Community in the Great Rebellion* (New York: Oxford University Press, 1990), 5–7, 138.

6. Champlin Diary, Jan. 25, 1864, CSL. See also J. Leander Chapin to Amelia Chapin, Feb. 14, 1864, Chapin Papers, CHS; Martin V. Culver to Jonathan Culver, Feb. 7, 1864, Culver Letters, private collection.

7. Grosvenor Diary, Jan. 23, 1864, CHS.

8. See "Horse John," Letter to Editor, Feb. 1, 1864, *Connecticut War Record*, Mar. 1864.

9. "Dixie," Letter to the Editors, Jan. 31, 1864, *Hartford Daily Courant*, Feb. 13, 1864.

10. J. Leander Chapin to Gilbert Chapin, Jan. 31, 1864, Chapin Papers, CHS.

11. J. Leander Chapin to Amelia Chapin, Feb. 14, 1864, Chapin Papers, CHS.

12. Champlin Diary, Jan. 25, 1864, CSL; "dull" from entry on Jan. 26, 1864.

13. George N. Champlin counted ninety refugees one day in mid-February, "about fifty were colored and a part of the other were rebel soldiers." He also claimed, "They report four hundred rebel deserters in the woods trying to get into and through our lines." See Champlin Diary, Feb. 19, 1864, CSL.

14. Kellogg Diary, Feb. 19, 1864, CHS. Emphasis in original.

15. Goss, *The Soldier's Story of His Captivity,* 55.

16. Harrison Woodford to Alma Woodford, Feb. 20, 1864, Harrison Woodford Letters, private collection.

17. J. Leander Chapin to Amelia Chapin, Feb. 2, 1864, Chapin Papers, CHS.

18. Leland O. Barlow to Jane E. Barlow, Apr. 17, 1864, Barlow Letters, CSL.

19. Forbes Diary, Apr. 16, 1864, YU.

20. Wiley, *Billy Yank,* 346–58; also Mitchell, *Vacant Chair,* 36–37; 92–93

21. Robert H. Kellogg to Silas Kellogg, Feb. 25, 1864, Kellogg Papers, CHS. For more on the local unionist population and African Americans residing in and around Plymouth, see Durrill, *War of Another Kind.*

22. Warren Goss described, "Schools had been established for the young and middle-aged colored population, under the able tuition of Mrs. and Miss Freeman, of Milford, Mass." Goss, *The Soldier's Story of his Captivity,* 55.

23. Forbes Diary, Jan. 26, 28, Feb. 1, 1864, YU.

24. See, e.g., Forbes Diary, Feb. 29, 1864, YU.

25. See Champlin Diary, Feb. 20, 21, 28, 1864, CSL.

26. Kellogg Diary, Feb. 21, 1864, CHS. Kellogg only makes mention again a month later. See Kellogg Diary, Mar. 28, 1864, CHS.

27. Grosvenor Diary, Feb. 28, 1864, CHS.

28. Robbins Diary, Mar. 6, 1864, CHS.

29. For examples of churchgoing and prayer groups, see Kellogg Diary, Jan. 30, 1864, CHS; Grosvenor Diary, Feb. 21, 1864, CHS; also Forbes Diary, Feb. 28, 1864, YU. For mention of the men playing "Base Ball," see Kellogg Diary, Feb. 22, 1864, CHS; also Robbins Diary, Feb. 27, 1864, CHS. In late March, George Robbins complained of not seeing a New York newspaper in nearly a month: "we don't know what the outside world is doing if we stay here any length of time." See Robbins Diary, Mar. 28, 1864, CHS.

30. Culver wrote, "Thare are several gals around hear [in] North Carolina clear to the handle rite smart I reckon." Martin V. Culver to Jonathan Culver, Apr. 15, 1864, Culver Letters, private collection.

31. Case, "Memoirs," SHS.

32. See Champlin Diary, Feb. 16, 1864, CSL; also Mar. 1, 1864.

33. Carpenter Martin Culver wrote of returning to his "trade" on April 15, 1864, at brigade headquarters, also commenting, "i have got a chimney and a fireplace so i live very well that is i

would if i had munny." See Martin V. Culver to Jonathan Culver, Apr. 15, 1864, Culver Letters, private collection.

34. Champlin Diary, Feb. 22, 1864, CSL; "splendid" and more details of the day's celebrations from Kellogg Diary, Feb. 22, 1864. Forbes wrote that a "large audience" attended Dixon's address at the church. Forbes Diary, Feb. 22, 1864, YU. Barlow described, "Celebration of Washington's birthday. Good time in the evening." See Barlow Diary, Feb. 22, 1864, CSL.

35. George Robbins to Jehiel and Dorothy Robbins, Mar. 8, 1864, Robbins Papers, CHS.

36. Case, "Memoirs," SHS.

37. See Leland O. Barlow to Jane Barlow, Feb. 28, 1864, Barlow Letters, CSL.

38. Grosvenor Diary, Jan. 27, 1864, CHS.

39. Sidney Hayden to Catherine Hayden, Jan. 25, 1864, Hayden Papers, EGPL.

40. Lewis M. Holcomb to "Aunt," Feb. 15, 1864, in "Lewis M. Holcomb," Whitney Collection, CSL.

41. J. Leander Chapin to Amelia Chapin, Feb. 2, 1864, Chapin Papers, CHS.

42. Martin V. Culver to Jonathan Culver, Feb. 7, 1864, Culver Letters, private collection; Austin M. Thompson to Electra M. Churchill, Feb. 6, 1864, Thompson Papers, CHS.

43. George Robbins to Jehiel and Dorothy Robbins, Feb. 7, 1864, Robbins Papers, CHS.

44. Leland O. Barlow to Jane Barlow, Feb. 28, 1864, Barlow Letters, CSL.

45. J. Leander Chapin to Gilbert Chapin, Jan. 31, 1864, Chapin Papers, CHS.

46. Lamphere, "Experiences and Observations of a Private Soldier," 18, MHS.

47. Robert H. Kellogg to Silas Kellogg, Feb. 25, 1864, Kellogg Papers, CHS. "Dixie" in a letter to the *Courant* described the raid under command of Lt. Col. Tolles of the 15th Connecticut "partly proceeded to Windsor, intending to capture three companies of rebel cavalry stationed there, but by some means their coming was announced, and then there was 'mounting in haste' among the gray uniforms, and there were no 'fleet steeds to follow,' the plunder amounted only to the appointment of three companies of cavalry, minus the horses, a valuable mail and complete set of brass instruments." See "Dixie," Letter to the Editor, Jan. 31, 1864, *Hartford Daily Courant,* Feb. 13, 1864. Both expeditions garnered appreciation from Gen. John J. Peck. In the second raid, Peck praised the soldiers "with satisfaction" for "breaking up the cantonment of a company of Georgia cavalry" on February 27, 1864. See *OR,* ser. 1, vol. 33, 106; also *OR,* ser. 1, vol. 33, 24.

48. See Forbes Diary, Feb. 29, 1864, YU. Forbes did not comment further on just who these men were (or were not). He was not one of the soldiers who volunteered or was chosen for this particular raid.

49. "Dixie" Letter to the Editor, "From the 16th Regiment," Feb. 9, 1864, *Hartford Daily Courant,* Feb. 17, 1864.

50. Benjamin B. Foster to Henry W. Wessell, Feb. 28, 1864, *OR,* ser. 1, vol. 33, 613. In this same correspondence, Foster directed, "The negroes on Roanoke Island should be prepared to resist a boat raid against the Island in case of attack."

51. Dixie," "From the 16th Connecticut," Mar. 2, 1864, *Hartford Daily Courant,* Mar. 17, 1864.

52. Robert H. Kellogg to Silas Kellogg, Mar. 4, 1864, Kellogg Papers, CHS.

53. Forbes Diary, Mar. 5, 1864, YU.

54. *Hartford Daily Courant,* Mar. 12, 1864.

55. "Dixie," Letter to the Editor, Mar. 12, 1864, *Hartford Daily Courant,* Mar. 22, 1864. See also Case, "Memoirs," SHS.

56. Forbes Diary, Mar. 7, 1864, YU.

57. Forbes Diary, Mar. 10, 1864, YU. While in New Bern, Forbes visited the "Colored" Day and Sabbath Schools, the Episcopal church, and the offices of the Christian Commission. See Forbes Diary, Mar. 13, 14, 18, 1864, YU.

58. Harrison Woodford to Harvey Woodford, Mar. 18, 1864, Harrison Woodford Letters, private collection.

59. Blakeslee, *History of the Sixteenth Connecticut Volunteers,* 52–53. George N. Champlin described, "A riot occurred in the Colored regiment over the [Trent] River and one hundred men of the 16th went over and brought in two or three hundred negro citizens." See Champlin Diary, Mar. 20, 1864, CSL; see also Barlow Diary, Mar. 20, 1864, CSL.

60. Robbins Diary, Mar. 20, 1864, CHS.

61. Kellogg Diary, Mar. 20, 1864, CHS.

62. Blakeslee, *History of the Sixteenth Connecticut Volunteers,* 52. See also "Horse John," Letter to the Editor, Mar. 20, 1864, *Connecticut War Record,* Apr. 1864; *Hartford Daily Courant,* Mar. 17, 1864. For reactions to Mix's death, see Forbes Diary, Mar. 11, 1864, YU; Harrison Woodford to Alma Woodford, Mar. 12, 1864, Harrison Woodford Letters, private collection; George Robbins to Jehiel and Dorothy Robbins, Mar. 13, 1864, Robbins Papers, CHS; Leland O. Barlow to Jane Barlow, Mar. 10, 1864, Barlow Letters, CSL.

63. This resolution was published in "each of the Hartford papers and the *Connecticut War Record.*" See *Hartford Daily Courant,* Mar. 21, 1864; *Hartford Daily Times,* Mar. 22, 1864; *Connecticut War Record,* May 1864. The officers also were to wear "the usual badge of mourning for thirty days." Some sources cite March 8 as Mix's death date. John B. Cuzner claimed that Mix had been absent from the regiment "since we left our camp at Portsmouth." He stated somewhat cryptically, "he was put under arrest for selling his house that he bought and paid for. An officer when under arrest is not allowed to leave camp usually but he was allowed to leave." Cuzner also described, "We had a meeting the other day and passed several resolutions concerning him which are to be printed in the *Hartford Post.*" Clearly, the men in the ranks participated in the resolution process. See John B. Cuzner to Ellen Van Dorn, May 15, 1864, Cuzner Letters and Papers, CHS.

64. "Drowned," by "Euclid," Terryville, *Hartford Daily Courant,* Apr. 21, 1864. The poem, rich in water and Christian imagery, also describes Mix's conveyance to a "blessed land" on "angels wings."

65. Relyea, *16th Connecticut Volunteer Infantry,* 118–19. Relyea added in retrospect, "Though fewer in line, its vigor, nonetheless waxed stronger everyday."

66. Forbes Diary, Mar. 21, 1864, YU.

67. Robert H. Kellogg to Silas Kellogg, Mar. 30, 1864, Kellogg Papers, CHS; see also Relyea, *16th Connecticut Volunteer Infantry,* 119.

68. Kellogg Diary, Mar. 21, 1864, CHS.

69. Kellogg Diary, Mar. 22, 1864, CHS. Emphasis in original.

70. Forbes Diary, Mar. 23, 1864, YU.

71. Champlin Diary, Mar. 24, 1864, CSL.

72. Champlin Diary, Mar. 25, 1864, CSL.

73. Champlin Diary, Apr. 6, 1864, CSL.

74. See Champlin Diary, Apr. 4, 1864. Champlin listed others from Co. I selected to go home to

vote: Sgt. Ezra T. Burgess; Cpls. Erastus Holmes, Harrison Woodford, George Faulkner, and Isaac Hamilton; Pvts. L. Oscar Lyon, George W. Maine, Orlando P. Smith, Edward Woodford, Samuel Nichols, and Amos Nichols. See Champlin Diary, Mar. 31, 1864, CSL.

75. Forbes Diary, Mar. 31, 1864, YU. The next day, April 1, he was unsure as they neared Roanoke, "Our destination still a mystery." See Forbes Diary, Apr. 1, 1864, YU. Forbes recorded that "it was decided to return to New Berne" and then they received orders to "return to Plymouth" on Monday, April 4. See Forbes Diary, Apr. 4, 1864, YU. Sgt. Henry E. Savage, also part of this select group, gave no indication in his diary of the reason either. See Savage Diary, Apr. 1, 1864, CSL.

76. Martin V. Culver to Jonathan Culver, Apr. 15, 1864, Culver Letters, private collection. Forbes estimated their return to be "about 11 o'clock" on Wednesday, April 6. See Forbes Diary, Apr. 7, 1864, YU.

77. Leland Barlow to Jane Barlow, April 11, 1864, Barlow Letters, CSL.

78. John B. Cuzner to Ellen Van Dorn, Apr. 3, 1864, Cuzner Letters and Papers, CHS. Cuzner gave no indications that he was a Democrat to this point, although he certainly showed no strong Republican tendencies. He seemed disinterested in politics, at least in his letters to Van Dorn.

79. Ezra Burgess to George Q. Whitney, Mar. 22, 1909, Whitney Collection, CSL. Emphasis in original.

80. Samuel E. Derby to Elizabeth Derby, Apr. 1, 1864, in James M. Kuras, ed., "Samuel Derby's War Letters," *New Hampshire College Journal* 10, no. 1 (Spring 1993): 8.

81. Kellogg Diary, Apr. 1, 1864, CHS.

82. Robert H. Kellogg to Silas Kellogg, [Apr. 1] 1864, Kellogg Papers, CHS. Emphasis in original.

83. Robert H. Kellogg to Silas Kellogg, [Apr. 1] 1864, Kellogg Papers, CHS. Emphasis in original.

84. George Robbins to Dorothy Robbins, Apr. 3, 1864, Robbins Papers, CHS. Emphasis in the original.

85. Robbins Diary, Apr. 1, 1864, CHS. It was not until August 1864 that Connecticut's General Assembly passed an amendment allowing soldiers to vote in the field. See Warshauer, *Connecticut in the American Civil War*, 107, also 144.

86. Sidney H. Hayden to Jane Hayden, Apr. 16, 1864, Hayden Papers, EGPL.

87. Leland O. Barlow to Jane E. Barlow, Apr. 11, 1864, Barlow Letters, CSL. There had been a handful of desertions while the regiment was in Plymouth and New Bern. Pvt. Edward Wilson, a recent recruit from Co. B, deserted on Mar. 13, 1864, while the unit was in New Bern. See "Descriptive List of Deserters form the 16th Regiment" for the month of March 1864, Muster Rolls, Returns, Regimental Papers, RG 94, Box 148 [unbound papers] NA. A note from the March 31, 1864, Muster Rolls Returns states, "Edward Wilson was a recruit just joined from our depot and a Sailor and may be in some Gov. transport under an assumed name."

88. Leland O. Barlow to Jane E. Barlow, Apr. 11, 1864, Barlow Letters, CSL. When Lt. Col. John Burnham returned to the unit in early February, George Robbins noted that he brought with him fifteen recruits. George Robbins to Jehiel and Dorothy Robbins, Feb. 14, 1864, Robbins Papers, CHS. Kellogg noted "twelve recruits" arriving in the regiment's camp on February 9, 1864. Kellogg Diary, Feb. 9, 1864, CHS. Jacob Bauer would reflect five decades later, "Towards the last of the war we received many recruits—a poor lot, who were induced through large bounties." Bauer, "Personal Experiences of the War," 5, PPM.

89. "Union" Letter to the Editors, Apr. 15, 1864, *Hartford Daily Courant*, Apr. 22, 1864.

90. Sidney H. Hayden to Jane Hayden, Feb. 23, 1864, Hayden Papers, EGPL.

91. Sidney H. Hayden to Catherine Hayden, Mar. 13, 1864, Hayden Papers, EGPL.

92. Lewis M. Holcomb to "Aunt," Feb. 15, 1864, in "Lewis M. Holcomb," Whitney Collection, CSL.

93. J. Leander Chapin to Gilbert Chapin, Mar. 19, 1864, Chapin Papers, CHS. Chapin's surviving letters do not show much consideration of the question of emancipation. In this letter, he repeats his reasons for fighting until "this rebellion is put down."

94. George Robbins to Jehiel and Dorothy Robbins, Mar. 8, 1864, Robbins Papers, CHS. Robbins joined his comrades at New Bern a few weeks later.

95. Samuel E. Grosvenor mentioned rumors of Confederate attacks; see Grosvenor Diary, Mar. 10, 13, 1864, CHS. Also, on March 24, 1864, Kellogg noted, "It is said that the 'rebs' are close at hand, their pickets having been seen & fired at today." But the next day, no attack came. Kellogg mused, though, that it "is confidently expected that they will tonight." Still, nothing occurred for nearly a month. See Kellogg Diary, Mar. 24, 25, 1864, CHS.

96. Robert H. Kellogg to Silas Kellogg [Apr. 1, 1864], Kellogg Papers, CHS. Other members of the regiment had a negative view of Gen. Peck. Ariel Case described him as overly excited and nervous. See Case, "Memoirs," SHS. Leland Barlow remarked of Peck, "They say he is not much of a fighting man, but first rate at fortifying a place; this place is very strongly fortified." See Leland O. Barlow to Jane Barlow, Mar. 27, 1863, Barlow Letters, CSL.

97. Robbins Diary, Apr. 11, 1864, CHS. See also Champlin Diary, Apr. 13, 14, 1864, CSL.

98. Robbins Diary, Apr. 15, 1864, CHS.

99. Harrison Woodford to Harvey Woodford, Apr. 16, 1864, Harrison Woodford Letters, private collection. George N. Lamphere later recalled that there was constant talk of the threat the *Albemarle* posed on Plymouth: "We heard a good deal about this monster, named the Albemarle and the rebel citizens said when she came down river show she would make kindling wood of our gunboats in the rivers and sounds." But Lamphere remembered dismissing such fears: "We did not seriously believe that the Albemarle could come down, and if she did we had no fear as she could not harm the land forces very much." See Lamphere, "Experiences and Observations," 18–19, MHS.

100. John J. Peck to Benjamin F. Butler, Apr. 14, 1864, *OR*, ser. 1, vol. 33, 280.

101. Henry W. Wessell to J. A. Judson, *OR*, ser. 1, vol. 33, 281. Peck and Butler squabbled over who was to send the reinforcements and when. See John J. Peck to Benjamin Butler, Apr. 19, 1864, *OR*, ser. 1, vol. 33, 282; also Peck to Butler, Apr. 21, 1864, *OR*, ser. 1, vol. 33, 284–85.

102. Peck even claimed, "In my judgment the non-arrival of the infantry at Plymouth is most fortunate, as they, together with the steamers, would beyond a doubt have fallen into the hands of the enemy." Peck further concluded, "General Wessell was supplied with provisions, forage, ammunition, and other requisites for a long siege. His casualties were small, notwithstanding some five successive assaults upon his lines." See John J. Peck to Benjamin Butler, Apr. 21, 1864, *OR*, ser. 1, vol. 33, 285. See also Peck to Butler, Apr. 25, 1864, OR, ser. 1, vol. 33, 287–88. Butler responded to Wessell's request for reinforcements: "You will have to defend the district with your present force, and you will make such dispositions of them as will in your judgment subserve this end." After the war, Ariel Case bitterly blamed Butler for not responding to Wessell's request for reinforcements and warnings about the Confederate ram. "Gen. Butler told him," Case alleged, "he had a ram on the brain, that there was no ram in the river nor no rebels in his immediate front and that he was as safe in Plymouth as he (Butler) was in Fortress Monroe." See Case, "Memoirs," SHS.

103. Robert J. Holmes, "Reminiscences of Plymouth," Apr. 14, 1903, Robert J. Holmes Papers,

AHS. For an overview of the ensuing Battle of Plymouth and its broader military significance, see Durrill, *War of Another Kind*, 188–210.

104. Oliver Gates Diary [May 1864], CHS.

105. Robert J. Holmes, "Reminiscences of Plymouth," Apr. 14, 1903, Holmes Papers, AHS.

106. Robbins Diary, Apr. 17, 1864, CHS. Also see Robbins, "Some Recollections," 25, CHS.

107. Lamphere, "Experiences and Observations," 20, MHS.

108. Hoke's numbers vary from ten thousand to fifteen thousand. See Barrett, *The Civil War in North Carolina*, 220. Barrett (213) gives the number of Union soldiers stationed at Plymouth to be 2,834, all under command of Brig. Gen. William H. Wessell. He lists four Union infantry regiments, the 101st and 103rd Pennsylvania Infantry, the 16th Connecticut, and the 85th Light Infantry New York; two companies of the 2nd North Carolina Union Volunteers; 12th New York Cavalry; six guns from the 24th New York Independent Battery; and two companies from the 2nd Massachusetts Heavy Artillery. In an earlier book, Barrett stated that Wessell had three thousand troops with four gunboats. See John G. Barrett, *North Carolina as a Civil War Battlefield, 1861–1865* (Raleigh, NC: State Department of Archives and History, 1960): 69. Estimates in the OR state that between ten to fifteen thousand troops under Hoke attacked on April 17. See OR, ser. 1, vol. 33, 305; also OR, ser. 1, vol. 33, 301. There are indications that black soldiers participating in the battle were part of the 10th USCT. See www.gowildnc.org/history (accessed Jan. 3, 2011). In materials located at the Port O'Plymouth Museum, estimates of Confederate strength are: 1,600 effectives vs. 10,000 or 12,000 Confederates, with the rebels outnumbering the federals eight to one. Robert J. Holmes biographical sheet, PPM. See also Wayne Mahood, *The Plymouth Pilgrims: A History of the Eighty-Fifth New York Infantry in the Civil War*, ed. David G. Martin, rev. ed. (Hightstown, NJ: Longstreet House, 1991), 168. Holmes estimated 2,400 Union troops facing 7,000 Confederates. See Robert J. Holmes, "Reminiscences of Plymouth," Apr. 14, 1903, Holmes Papers, AHS. The 2,834 number from Barrett matches the reported casualties (total killed, wounded, and missing) included in the "Return of Casualties in the Union forces commanded by Brig. Gen. Henry W. Wessells, at Plymouth, N.C., Apr. 17–20, 1864." But this number excludes, at minimum, the 16th's Co. H. See OR, ser. 1, vol. 33, 301. Blakeslee, referencing rebel newspapers, claims that the Confederate losses were 400–600 killed and 1,500–2,000 wounded. See Blakeslee, *History of the Sixteenth Connecticut Volunteers*, 61–62. Hoke initially reported three hundred casualties. See OR, ser. 1, vol. 51, pt. 2, 870. Also Juanita Patience Moss, *Battle of Plymouth, North Carolina (Apr. 17–20, 1864): The Last Confederate Victory* (Westminster, MD: Heritage Books, 2003), 149. Niven and Katcher both affirm Blakeslee's numbers. See Niven, *Connecticut for the Union*, 186; Katcher, *Lethal Fire*, 157.

109. Lamphere, "Experiences and Observations," 20, MHS.

110. Robbins, "Some Recollections," 25, CHS. Indeed, the weakest part of Plymouth's defenses were on the east side of the town. Wessell built no entrenchments there. See Durrill, *War of Another Kind*, 193–94.

111. Robert H. Kellogg to Silas Kellogg, Apr. 17, 1864, Kellogg Papers, CHS.

112. Leland O. Barlow to Jane E. Barlow, Apr. 17, 1864, Barlow Letters, CSL.

113. Lamphere, "Experiences and Observations," 20–21, MHS.

114. Forbes Diary, Apr. 17, 1864. Forbes also claimed that it was 9 p.m. rather than 11 p.m. See Ira E. Forbes, "The Fall of Plymouth 44 Years Ago To-Day," *Hartford Daily Times*, Apr. 20, 1908. But

another soldier gave the time as midnight. See "Little Mare" to Editor, June 1, 1864, *Connecticut War Record,* June 1864. See also Blakeslee, *History of the Sixteenth Connecticut Volunteers,* 55. A few members of Co. H or "Manchester Company," remained behind and ended up captured, including Pvt. Charles H. Golden. See "Charles H. Golden," Whitney Collection, CSL.

115. Kellogg Diary, Apr. 17, 1864, CHS.

116. Forbes Diary, Apr. 18, 1864, YU. See also Kellogg, "The Siege of Plymouth, N.C.," 4, Kellogg Papers, CHS.

117. Kellogg Diary, Apr. 18, 1864, CHS.

118. Grosvenor Diary, Apr. 18, 1864, CHS.

119. Kellogg Diary, Apr. 18, 1864, CHS. Emphasis in original.

120. Kellogg, *Life and Death in Rebel Prisons,* 29; a slightly different account of this is included in Relyea's "History of the 16th Connecticut," 172, CHS.

121. Kellogg Diary, Apr. 18, 1864, CHS. Emphasis in original.

122. Forbes, "The Fall of Plymouth." See also *OR,* ser. 1, vol. 33, 305.

123. Blakeslee, *History of the Sixteenth Connecticut Volunteers,* 55.

124. Robert H. Kellogg similarly wrote, "It mainly looks as if we would soon book our names at the 'Libby Hotel' Richmond, Va." See Kellogg Diary, Apr. 19, 1864, CHS.

125. Forbes Diary, Apr. 19, 1864, YU; see also "Little Mare," Letter to Editor, June 1, 1864, *Connecticut War Record,* June 1864. Decades after the war, George Robbins blamed the failure of the "water battery" in allowing the *Albemarle* to surprise the federal gunboats and attack the Union garrison. This "Water Battery," "so called, was an earth work on the bank of the river at the northern contest of the breastworks." Robbins alleged that a dark fog, combined with the inattention of the officers in command of the battery, allowed the Confederate ram to pass unharrassed. See Robbins, "Some Recollections," 26. Robbins claimed that he learned this from a wounded sentry after the siege.

126. Champlin Diary, Apr. 19, 1864, CSL.

127. Forbes Diary, Apr. 19, 1864, YU.

128. Case, "Memoirs," SHS.

129. Lamphere, "Experiences and Observations," 23, MHS.

130. Kellogg Diary, Apr. 19, 1864, CHS; also Robert H. Kellogg, "The Siege of Plymouth, N.C.," 5, Kellogg Papers, CHS. See also Forbes Diary, Apr. 19, 1864, YU.

131. Katcher, *Lethal Glory,* 10.

132. Grosvenor Diary, Apr. 19, 1864, CHS.

133. George H. Slaybaugh, "The Battle of Plymouth: The Gallant Defense of the North Carolina Town," *National Tribune,* Aug. 22, 1889.

134. Lamphere, "Experiences and Observations," 25–30, MHS.

135. Kellogg Diary, Apr. 20, 1864, CHS. See also *OR,* ser. 1, vol. 33, 305.

136. Grosvenor Diary, Apr. 20, 1864, CHS.

137. Blakeslee, *History of the Sixteenth Connecticut Volunteers,* 57.

138. Henry W. Wessell to John J. Peck, Aug. 18, 1864, *OR,* ser. 1, vol. 33, 299. In his report to Peck, who was no longer commander of the district, Wessell stated, "For some months previous to the date above mentioned [Apr. 20], I felt satisfied from information derived from various sources that a vigorous effort on the part of the enemy would be made to wrest the State of North Carolina from

our possession. The opinion was expressed to you in frequent communications, with the hope that the military force would be strengthened, and that at least one iron-clad gunboat would be added to the naval squadron for the protection of the sounds and rivers."

139. Quoted in Katcher, *Lethal Glory*, 157.

140. Bauer, "Personal Experiences of the War," 10–11, PPM. Bauer claimed "John McCardle" had the gun and "Jimmy Hayes" stopped McCardle from firing. But there was only a Patrick McCardle and Thomas Hayes in Co. G. See AGO 1889, 632.

141. Grosvenor Diary, Apr. 20, 1864, CHS.

142. See Robert H. Kellogg, "The Siege of Plymouth, N.C., 8, Kellogg Diary, CHS. Robbins, who was assigned to caring for the wounded, totaled "about 12" wounded and 1 killed. See Robbins Diary, Apr. 21, 1864, CHS. Scott Holmes, a direct descendent of Robert J. Holmes and modern regimental historian, counts 436 total men from the regiment engaged at Plymouth (23 officers and 413 enlisted men), with 3 killed and 12 wounded. Of those 12, Holmes finds 3 who died soon after the battle from their wounds. A total of 430 (23 officers and 407 enlisted men) went to prison. See Scott Holmes to Harry Thompson, Dec. 11, 1995, PPM. In an official report by Lt. Lucian A. Butts from the 85th NY, filed Apr. 5, 1865, Butts lists 463 total casualties from the regiment, with 23 officers and 440 men, a slightly higher number than Holmes.

143. See Robert H. Kellogg, "The Siege of Plymouth, N.C.," 9, Kellogg Papers, CHS.

144. John J. Peck to Benjamin F. Butler, Apr. 22, 1864, *OR*, ser. 1, vol. 33, 287.

145. See *Charleston Daily Courier* [May 1864], quoted in *Voice from Plymouth: Plymouth Pilgrims Descendent Society Newsletter* 1 (Winter 1996). Two scholars set out in 1995 to debunk the notion that there was a "massacre" of African Americans at Plymouth, and after sorting through numerous contemporary and postwar accounts, much of it contradictory, they rejected the claim that hundreds were wantonly killed in "cold blood." Weymouth T. Jordan, Jr., and Gerald W. Thomas, "Massacre at Plymouth: Apr. 20, 1864," *North Carolina Historical Review* 72, no. 2 (Apr. 1995): 125–97. George S. Burkhardt, *Yankee Wrath: No Quarter in the Civil War* (Carbondale: Southern Illinois University Press, 2007). Burkhardt more harshly judges what happened at Plymouth, calling it a "pogrom," and accepts the 300–400 death total. See also Durrill, *War of Another Kind*, 207–8.

146. Gates had earlier referred to the African Americans at Plymouth as "Negroes armed," implying that they were black troops, not contraband. See Gates Diary [May 1864], CHS.

147. Champlin Diary, Apr. 20, 1864, CSL.

148. Goss, *The Soldier's Story of His Captivity*, 61.

149. Robbins, "Some Recollections," 31, CHS.

150. Robbins Diary, Apr. 28, 1864, CHS. However, Dr. Mayer, using the alias "Little Mare," flatly denied any atrocity. Writing for the *Connecticut War Record*, "Little Mare" asserted that, because he personally witnessed Confederates "sending ten wounded negroes into my hospital to be attended to," he was convinced "that with the consent of the officers, no negroes were killed. "Little Mare," Letter to Editor, *Connecticut War Record*, June 1864. He insisted, "We were well treated in the main. Such things as forcing a number of sick men to exchange their boots and shoes for the broken shoeleather of the rebs, did occur; also, a thorough plundering was carried on. But cruelties were not perpetrated."

151. Butler explained to Halleck that Plymouth fell "because the theory of its defenses

presupposed an occupation of the river by our gun-boats, which would cover our flanks." See Butler to Halleck, Apr. 24, 1864, *OR*, ser. 1, vol. 33, 279–80. Peck faulted "open works" at Plymouth, which he thought were overly dependent on the gunboats, but he refused to take any blame: "Had all the works been inclosed," he wrote Butler, "the results would have been very different. When we were at Plymouth I called your attention to this feature of the system of defense." Peck to Butler, Apr. 25, 1864, *OR*, ser. 1, vol. 33, 293.

152. J. A. Judson to Lorenzo Thomas, Apr. 21, 1864, *OR*, ser. 1, vol. 33, 295.

153. Kellogg Diary, Apr. 20, 1864, CHS. Emphasis in original.

154. Kellogg, *Life and Death in Rebel Prisons*, 33. Kellogg implied elsewhere that Union commanders' failure to anticipate the Confederate ironclad attack led to their capture. See Robert H. Kellogg, "The Siege of Plymouth, N.C.," 9, Kellogg Papers, CHS.

155. Gates Diary [May 1864], CHS.

156. Champlin Diary, Apr. 20, 1864, CSL.

157. Forbes Diary, Apr. 20, 1864, YU. Norman L. Hope later emphasized that, even though they faced a foe with great advantages in numbers, it still "took the Confederates three days to get to us." See Norman L. Hope, "The Story of Andersonville," Norman L. Hope Collection, CSL. Karl Schubert simply explained, "We had to surrender." See Karl Schubert Diary, CSL.

158. After the war, Forbes listed the following soldiers as members of the color guard at Plymouth: Sgt. Francis Latimer (Co. C), who was the national color bearer; Sgt. William E. Bidwell (Co. G), the state color bearer; Cpls. Ira E. Forbes (Co. A), Charles G. Lee (Co. B), Lauren C. Mills (Co. E), Richard Powers (Co. F), Hiram D. Williams (Co. F), and John F. Bartholomew (Co. K), the color guards. He made no mention of anyone carrying the regimental flag. Mills was fatally wounded during the final charge by the Confederates at Plymouth and later died on April 28. See Forbes, "Color Guard, Sixteenth Regiment," Forbes Collection, CSL.

159. Mary Livermore, *My Story Of The War: A Woman's Narrative Of Four Years Personal Experience As Nurse In The Union Army, And In Relief Work At Home, In Hospitals, Camps, And At The Front During The War Of The Rebellion. With Anecdotes, Pathetic Incidents And Thrilling Reminiscences Portraying The Lights And Shadows Of Hospital Life And The Sanitary Service Of The War* (Hartford: A. D. Worthington and Co., 1888), 50. George N. Lamphere quoted Livermore in his own unpublished memoirs, written it seems in 1901, "I cannot from personal knowledge vouch for this story and never heard of it until I read it in this book, but that is not strange when it is considered that I, with a few other wounded men, was [sic] separated from the regiment just before the event occurred and I never saw the regiment afterward and have not to this day met to exceed three or four of its former members." Lamphere further called the story "beautiful and pathetic," "showing the bravery as well as the intense patriotism of the men of the 16th Conn. regiment." See Lamphere, "Experiences and Observations," 25, MHS.

160. See Forbes Diary, May 31, 1864, YU. Forbes wrote, "I have received a small piece of the 101st battle flag today. Given to me by Sergt. Boots, and [it] has been in several engagements—at Williamsburg, Fair Oaks, in the 'Seven Days,' fight before Richmond, on the Blackwater, at Kingston and finally at Plymouth, where it ended its career gloriously." Forbes's obituary included a version of the flag story similar to Livermore's. See *Hartford Daily Times*, Nov. 14, 1911.

161. Robert Kellogg Diary, Apr. 18, 1865, CHS. Kellogg wrote, "Going to the place where our

color staffs were buried we dug for a long while but without finding them. We were afterward told by a lady resident that the Rebels found them soon after taking possession of the town." In an unpublished postwar account, he further claimed that he gave the order to save the flags to Forbes and Latimer but that it was Burnham who ordered them torn into fragments. See Kellogg, "The Siege of Plymouth, N.C.," 7–8, Kellogg Papers, CHS. One of the few contemporary accounts omitted anything about recovering flag fragments. "Little Mare" (likely Dr. Mayer) stated, "One more fact, allow me to record: when the moment of surrender came, the color guard of the 16th C.V. aided by the Luiet. Col. commanding and the Adjutant burned the flag of the regiment, to keep it from falling into the rebel hands." See "Little Mare," Letter to the Editor, June 1, 1864, *Connecticut War Record*, June 1864. In a postwar story about Cpl. Leland Barlow (Co. E), the *Courant* quoted his diary the day of the capture and noted the brevity of his entries, stating, "he made no mention of the fact that the men of the Sixteenth Regiment, C.V., tore their flag from its staff, stripped it to tatters and concealed the precious fragments in their clothing." The paper added, "Very likely he would not have written it in any event." *Hartford Daily Courant*, Nov. 28 [1915]. The significance of the flag and the regiment's postwar image is further discussed in Chapter 9.

162. Letter excerpt published in the *Hartford Daily Times*, May 4, 1864; also see *Hartford Daily Times*, May 3, 1864; *Hartford Evening Press*, May 4, 1864. Beach was granted a twenty-day furlough and then ordered to report to Maj. Gen. Butler, commanding the Department of Virginia and North Carolina. He would eventually return to the Draft Rendezvous in Pittsburgh, where he had been on detached service previously; in July, he was transferred to Philadelphia to command the Draft Rendezvous there. He was not ordered to rejoin the remnants of the 16th Connecticut until October 1864. See Frank Beach, CSR, NA.

163. Gates recalled, "our little band had not slept since the attack commenced and no cooked rations for our camp was completely in range of their guns and was completely torn and riddled with Bullets shots and shells." See Gates Diary [May 1864], CHS. Samuel Grosvenor wrote the day after capture that he had "scarcely eaten anything the last three days." See Grosvenor Diary, Apr. 21, 1864, CHS.

164. Flower Diary, Apr. 21, 1864, CSL.

165. See Kellogg Diary, Apr. 22, 1864, CHS.

166. Bauer, "Personal Experiences of the War," 11, PPM.

167. Kellogg Diary, Apr. 21, 1864, CHS.

168. Gates Diary [May 1864], CHS.

169. Forbes Diary, Apr. 21, 1864, YU.

170. Champlin Diary, Apr. 26 and 27, 1864, CSL; Kellogg Diary, Apr. 22, 1864. Forbes wrote, "Our men trade knives, gloves, pens &c for cornbread and other articles of food." See Forbes Diary, Apr. 26, 1864, YU. Flower described drawing rations of bacon, meal, and beans on one day of the march southward. See Flower Diary, Apr. 25, 1864, CSL. Kellogg stated that they received "25 hard crackers and about 2 lbs of pork" on the first day of their captivity, marching seventeen miles and then sleeping in the open on the ground. See Kellogg Diary, Apr. 21, 1864, CHS; Forbes Diary, Apr. 21, 1864. Bauer recalled one of his comrades paying five dollars for a dozen eggs. See Bauer, "Personal Experiences of the War," 11, PPM.

171. See Bauer, "Personal Experiences of the War," 11, PPM.

172. "Miscellaneous Notes," Kellogg Papers, CHS. These appear to be spare notes Kellogg wrote en route to Andersonville rather than directly into his diary.

173. Gates Diary [May 1864], CHS. Gates estimated his "loss in clothes and Private Property about $100.00." Gates ended up buying a woolen blanket from one of his captors for a silver dollar and later reflected, "I felt bad to part with it not for its value but it was given to me by my wife last Oct. when I was home on furlough. The reb said that the Blanket was worth 60 sixty dollars in Weldon N.C. but the silver was too much of a temptation for him." See Gates Diary [May 1864], CHS.

174. Gates Diary [May 1864], CHS.

175. Grosvenor Diary, Apr. 27, 28, 1864, CHS. See also Forbes Diary, Apr. 26, 1864, YU.

176. Kellogg, *Life and Death in Rebel Prisons*, 34.

177. Robert H. Kellogg to Silas Kellogg, Apr. 20, 1864, Kellogg Papers, CHS; see also Kellogg, *Life And Death In Rebel Prisons*, 37. Kellogg, who just weeks before had been discussing hopes of an appointment to West Point, or an officer's commission, had no idea how dramatically his life was about to change. Kellogg had discussed West Point as late as March 31, although he had grown pessimistic about his chances for the appointment since he had not heard anything. See Robert H. Kellogg to Silas Kellogg, Mar. 31, 1864, Kellogg Papers, CHS. In his diary, he noted that Lt. Col. Burnham submitted his recommendation on Feb. 15. Kellogg Diary, Feb. 15, 1864, CHS.

178. George Robbins to Jehiel and Dorothy Robbins, Apr. 30, 1864, Robbins Papers, CHS.

179. *Hartford Evening Press*, Apr. 21, 1864. The first account was initially published in the *Springfield Republican*, the second in *the Philadelphia Inquirer*. See also *Hartford Daily Courant*, Apr. 22, 1864.

180. *Hartford Evening Press*, Apr. 24, 1864. On April 25, the *Press* stated that the garrison was "cut off from all communication" and that there was "considerable anxiety" in "this vicinity in regard to the unfavorable news from Plymouth, N.C."

181. *Hartford Evening Press*, Apr. 26, 1864. The paper reprinted Peck's official report of the battle, which further stressed the bravery of the troops. See also *Hartford Daily Courant*, Apr. 26, 1864. On April 27, the *Courant* reported that Company H had been spared capture.

182. Initially, it was incorrectly reported that the prisoners were headed to Richmond. See *Hartford Daily Courant*, Apr. 29, 1864; *Hartford Daily Times*, Apr. 27, 29, 1864. On May 3, the *Times* inaccurately reported that the 16th Connecticut was "said to be in Richmond."

183. Adelaide R. Holcomb Diary, Apr. 23, 1864, Holcomb Family Papers, SBHS. Lauren Mills's sister recorded in her diary, "Heard tonight that Lauren is probably taken prisoner or killed." See Ann Eliza Bancroft Diary, Apr. 23, 1864, Canton Historical Society, Canton, CT. Corporal Mills (Co. E) died due to battle wounds from the siege on April 28, 1864.

184. Adelaide R. Holcomb Diary, May 2, 1864, Holcomb Family Papers, SBHS.

185. Elizabeth F. Smith to George Q. Whitney, Dec. 28, 1905, Whitney Collection, CSL.

186. *Hartford Daily Courant*, May 5, 1864. Turner added that Capt. Burke had been wounded.

187. *Hartford Daily Courant*, May 6, 1864; Clapp's letter was dated April 25, 1864. See also *Hartford Daily Times*, May 7, 1864.

188. *Hartford Daily Times*, May 13, 1864; Bryant would die in prison in Charleston on September 27, 1864.

189. Mayer listed Pvt. Charles W. Squires (Co. B), "comminuted fracture of the thigh;

amputation in the lower third"; Col. Cpl. Lauren Mills (Co. E), "oblique fracture of the thigh in the middle third"; Pvt. Asahel Forbes (Co. B), "flesh wound of the thigh"; 1st Sgt. Silas Norton (Co. K), "comminuted fracture in the upper third of the radius and ulna; resection of both bones of the forearm"; Pvt. Henry Robinson (Co. K), "flesh-wound of the left side"; Pvt. Lawrence Shane (Co. K), "left shoulder, with fracture of the lower part of the shoulder blade"; Pvt. John Lawrence (Co. E), "flesh wound of the forearm"; Pvt. Asa Cook (Co. E), "flesh wound of scalp"; Pvt. Charles C. Drew (Co. C), "fracture of the skull, with wound of brain"; Capt. Burke (Co. A), "flesh-wound and contusion of shoulder"; Pvt. Ralph Allen (Co. F), "killed"; Pvt. James E. Martin (Co. F), "missing— probably killed." This totals one killed, ten wounded, and one missing. See *Hartford Daily Courant*, May 9, 1864. The *Courant* also reported Mayer's parole and subsequent arrival in Annapolis on May 2, 1864. See *Hartford Courant*, May 6, 1864. Pvts. Mills, Cook, and Shane would all die from their battlefield wounds: Mills on Apr. 28, 1864; Cook on May 9, 1864; Shane on June 3, 1864. Pvt. Martin was wounded and captured. He would perish in the Florence prison on January 28, 1865. See AGO 1889, 630.

190. *Hartford Daily Courant*, May 11, 1864. He singled out Adj. John Clapp for his "great bravery" in leading a drive against the attacking Confederates, shooting with his pistol and cutting down men with his saber. Andrew Johnson later appointed Clapp to brevet captain in 1868 for his "gallant and meritorious services in the battle of Plymouth, N.C., to date from March 13, 1865." In *Senate Executive Journal*, Tuesday, Apr. 17, 1868, 216, at http://memory.loc.gov, accessed Nov. 15, 2006.

191. *Hartford Evening Press*, Apr. 26, 1864. This same article reported on the fate of the captured officers, including Colonel Beach, Lt. Col. Burnham, Maj. Pasco, Quarter Master Robins, and Surg. Mayer, all going to Libby Prison in Richmond, where they "found one thousand Union officers, where food consisted solely of corn bread." *Hartford Daily Courant*, May 11, 1864. This clipping was also kept by Kellogg and found in his papers at the OHS. On May 10, 1864, Mayer's list of the wounded and killed from Plymouth appeared in the *Hartford Evening Press*.

192. Quoted in the *Hartford Daily Courant*, May 2, 1864.

193. *Hartford Daily Courant*, May 7, 1864.

194. *Hartford Daily Courant*, Apr. 26, 1864. The *Hartford Daily Press* on April 26, 1864, also stated, "The negroes found in the fort, government laborers, were shot in cold blood, after the surrender, it is reported."

195. *Hartford Daily Courant*, Apr. 27, 1864.

196. *Hartford Evening Press*, Apr. 28, 1864. This was again repeated the next day but with some indication of what might have happened to the captured soldiers: "the Richmond papers say the loyal North Carolinians were taken out and shot, and the rest of the prisoners taken to Richmond." *Hartford Evening Press*, Apr. 29, 1864. Hartford residents were also reading about the "Massacre at Fort Pillow" beginning in mid-April. See, e.g., *Hartford Daily Courant*, Apr. 16, 1864.

197. *Hartford Daily Courant*, May 2, 1864.

198. Cited in *Hartford Daily Courant*, May 7, 1864.

199. Bauer, "Personal Experiences of the War," 12, PPM. In Charleston, Kellogg learned that local newspapers had dubbed them the "Plymouth Pilgrims." See Kellogg Diary, May 1, 1864, CHS. In *Life and Death in Rebel Prisons*, Kellogg stated that the city papers named them this "sarcastically" (53). The name came from their appearance, notably their regulation-style hats, or "Hardee hats,"

which appeared to Confederates to closely resemble those worn by the Pilgrims. A member of the 85th New York remarked that the division had received these hats "much to our disgust." See Mahood, *The Plymouth Pilgrims*, 142.

CHAPTER SEVEN

1. Kellogg Diary, May 3, 1864, CHS. Emphasis in original. Most of the regiment entered the prison over two days, May 3 and 4; those who remained behind to care for the wounded did not enter the prison until June.

2. Grosvenor Diary, May 4, 1864, CHS.

3. Forbes Diary, May 3, 1864, YU.

4. Champlin Diary, May 3, 1864, CSL.

5. Gates Diary [May 1864], CHS.

6. Savage Diary, May 4, 1864, CSL.

7. William Marvel, *Andersonville, The Last Depot* (Chapel Hill: University of North Carolina Press, 1994), ix, 16–27, 56–57; Ovid L. Futch, *History of Andersonville Prison* (Gainesville: University of Florida Press, 1968), 17.

8. Some prisoners perished afterward in Charleston or Florence, or later as a result of their imprisonment. As with battlefield casualties, numbers vary widely regarding prisoner deaths. Kellogg states, "Our own regiment was over four hundred strong and the whole regiment captured at the surrender, 2,197, so that we were quite a company doomed to the miseries of *rebeldom*." See Kellogg, *Life and Death in Rebel Prisons*, 35. Emphasis in original. A note from the publisher of Kellogg's book states, "The author says nearly one-half of his regiment captured, died in about seven months" (19). In a letter after the war, Kellogg wrote, "Entering the Andersonville stockade as prisoners of war, some three hundred strong, early in May, 1864, the men of the 16th Connecticut regiment were young, strong, and in good condition, after nearly two years of active field service." See Robert Kellogg to Ira Forbes, July 18, 1907, Forbes Collection, CSL. Forbes, who carefully tracked the names of the dead, gave varying numbers. In 1907, he calculated that ninety-three members of the 16th died at Andersonville. See Ira Forbes, "A Southerner's View of Andersonville Prison," *Hartford Daily Times*, June 25, 1907. Another article by Forbes in the *Hartford Daily Courant* on Nov. 17, 1906, gave a total of 160 men dead from the regiment in the prison camps at Andersonville, Florence, and Charleston. And a 1906 article by Forbes in the *Connecticut Courant* listed eighty-six soldiers who died at Andersonville, forty at Florence, and thirteen at Charleston. Several more died from wounds sustained at Plymouth or soon after their release from prison. The total, then, would be 139. See "Sixteenth C. V. at Andersonville," *Connecticut Courant*, Mar. 15, 1906, newspaper clipping, Forbes Collection, CSL. In yet another place, however, he counted ninety-four total deaths from the regiment at Andersonville. See Ira E. Forbes, Andersonville, Forbes Collection, CSL. In a letter from Camp Parole, Kellogg listed the regiment's dead from all prisons and totaled them at 109. See *Hartford Daily Courant*, Dec. 9, 1864. In a final speech delivered to the regiment upon their return to Hartford in June 1865, Connecticut state senator Ezra Hall claimed that "more than two hundred of this regiment were starved and murdered in Southern prisons." Quoted in *Hartford Daily Courant*, June 30, 1865. Fox's *Regimental Losses* includes the 16th C.V. in his list of Union regiments

that "sustained unusually heavy losses by deaths in Confederate prisons." Fox counts 154 total prison deaths for the regiment. See Fox, *Regimental Losses in the American Civil War,* 524.

9. Costas and Kahn argue that northern soldiers who were captured with more of their comrades, or "friends," had an increased survival rate. (This is a variation of the "small unit cohesion" argument, usually applied to men in combat.) Yet, they also note that the single greatest determinant of survival was "the number of men in POW camps." See Costas and Kahn, *Heroes and Cowards,* 141–46. However, approximately 25 percent of the regiment imprisoned at Andersonville died there, a percentage not dramatically lower than the 29 percent overall mortality rate for all prisoners. Still, there was a perception among the men that their regimental affiliation saved lives. See also Benjamin Cloyd, *Haunted by Atrocity: Civil War Prisons in American Memory* (Baton Rouge: Louisiana State University Press, 2010), 164. For a useful discussion of regimental esprit de corps and "small unit cohesion," see Mark H. Dunkelman, *Brothers One and All: Esprit De Corps in a Civil War Regiment* (Baton Rouge: Louisiana State University Press, 2006), 9–11.

10. Kellogg described forming "a 'family' of 11" the first day in the prison. See Kellogg Diary, May 3, 1864, CHS; also Kellogg, *Life and Death in Rebel Prisons,* 58. Marvel explains that Wirz further broke down the "squads" of ninety prisoners into "five equal messes." Wirz relied on this system of organization to take roll every morning at 7 a.m., a process that could take, according to Marvel, "a couple of hours." See Marvel, *Andersonville,* 51.

11. See Gates Diary, June 19, 1864, CHS. Viberts and Gates had worked for the same builder before the war.

12. Gates Diary, July 25, 1864; Sept. 5, 1864, CHS.

13. When Grosvenor first visited the hospital he "came back feeling sad & disgusted." For examples of his "great exertions" to get men to the hospital, see Grosvenor Diary, May 12, July 10, 11, Aug. 15, 1864, CHS.

14. Bauer wrote, "When we were paid in Hartford he offered me a roll of bills for what I did for him, but I would not have it." See Bauer, "Personal Experiences of the War," 14, PPM.

15. Forbes Diary, May 24, 1864, YU. See, e.g., June 10, 1864. He did not indicate who the sick friend was, but he made frequent mention of "my friend Milton," who was ailing. There appears to have been no "Milton" among the captured soldiers from the 16th Connecticut. He also mentioned "Willie," whom he felt "as much attached to him as a brother." See Forbes Diary, June 28, 1864, YU. Karl Schubert, Elias Baldwin, and Thomas Crossley had additional stories of helping out one another while imprisoned. Schubert, however, perished in prison. Karl Schubert Diary, CSL; "Elias Henry Baldwin," Whitney Collection, CSL.

16. Gates Diary, Sept. 3, 1864, CHS. Gates observed in early September a higher casualty rate among those units captured with the 16th Connecticut. He thought it was because of the extra money and poor choices made by the men who had this cash to spend in the prison but also because these men had been stationed in North Carolina longer than the 16th Connecticut and had been already worn down by "fever and ague which left them less hardy than we were." These units were the 103rd and 101st Pennsylvania Infantry and the 24th New York Battery Co.

17. Ira Forbes, "Sixteenth C. V. at Andersonville," *Connecticut Courant,* Mar. 15, 1906, newspaper clippings, Forbes Collection, CSL.

18. See Champlin Diary, May 8, 10, 15, 28, 1864, CSL. Robert H. Kellogg similarly wrote on

May 9, 1864, upon hearing that the "war news today are good for us. The papers stating that Lee is defeated. In the evening quite a crowd of the 16th boys collected & feeling nicely over the reports we vented our enthusiasm in singing '*America*,' '*Star Spangled Banner*,' & '*Red, White & Blue*,' at the top [of] our voices, much to the edification of the Confederate Guards probably." Kellogg Diary, May 9, 1864, CHS. In his book, Kellogg added that the singing was done much "to the disgust of our guards on the stockade, though possibly not, for many of them were so ignorant it was doubtful if they knew one song from another." Kellogg, *Life and Death in Rebel Prisons*, 79. Ira Forbes references singing patriotic songs in June. See Forbes Diary, June 2, 7, 1864, YU.

19. Robert H. Kellogg to Silas Kellogg, May 25, 1864, Kellogg Papers, CHS.

20. Horace B. Steele to Julia M. Steele, May 25, 1864, Horace B. Steele Papers, CSL.

21. Robert H. Kellogg wrote, "Rumors of exchange are very prevalent but they may not be true." See Kellogg Diary, May 4, 1864, CHS.

22. John B. Cuzner, "Outside the Stockade," Cuzner Letters and Papers, CHS.

23. Grosvenor Diary, May 13, 1864, CHS.

24. Gates Diary [May 25, 1864], CHS.

25. Gates Diary, June 24, 1864, CHS. This story seems to have originated from an article in the *New York Herald* brought into the prison by a recently captured soldier.

26. Flower Diary, June 14, 1864, CSL. Even as late as August 1, when Flower was but five days away from death, he wrote, "More rumors about exchange and I hope and pray it may prove true."

27. Kellogg Diary, May 11, 1864, CHS. He was equally doubtful in August, affirming that "time will prove the truth or falsity" of such stories of pending paroles. See Kellogg Diary, Aug. 10, 1864, CHS.

28. Champlin Diary, June 11, 1864, CSL. See also Kellogg Diary, June 10, 1864, CHS; Gates Diary, July 6 and 20, 1864, CHS. Champlin recounted the false rumor that "the Plymouth troops are to be paroled prior to the sixth of June." Champlin Diary, May 26, June 5, 1864, CSL. For more on the persistence of exchange rumors, see Marvel, *Andersonville*, 92.

29. Gates Diary, June 21, 1864, CHS.

30. Champlin Diary, June 13, 1864, CSL.

31. Champlin Diary, June 22, 1864, CSL.

32. Gates Diary, July 20, 1864, CHS. One month later, Champlin tallied twenty-two more dead from the 16th. See Champlin Diary, Aug. 18, 1864, CSL.

33. Flower Diary, May 16, 1864, CSL. Flower began to suffer from severe diarrhea on June 15, 1864. Until his death on August 7, he complained of weakness, fever, having to "attend to his bowels" in the middle of the night, and loss of appetite, as well as severe pain in his kidneys. See entries for June 28, 29, July 1, 16, 1864. There were occasional days when Flower also thought that his health was improving. See, e.g., July 4 and 5, 1864. Forbes gives Flower's death date to be August 9. See "Joseph Flower, Jr.," Whitney Collection, CSL.

34. Grosvenor Diary, Aug. 17, 1864, CHS.

35. Savage Diary, Aug. 17, 1864, CSL.

36. Samuel Grosvenor wrote at one point, "I scarcely know what to write. All is monotonous. Our hopes for an exchange are not so bright as they may be sometimes." Grosvenor Diary, June 22, 1864, CHS.

37. Flower Diary, May 8, 1864, CSL. By the latter half of June, when Flower was stricken with dysentery, there were several days when all he recorded was the date of his captivity.

38. John B. Cuzner, "The Well," Cuzner Letters and Papers, CSL.

39. Robert H. Kellogg despaired over the prison existence one week into their incarceration: "Oh what a dull, tiresome life this is—nothing to read & nothing to do scarcely." See Kellogg Diary, May 12, 1864, CHS.

40. Champlin Diary, June 17, 1864, CSL.

41. Paul C. Helmreich, ed., "The Diary of Charles G. Lee in the Andersonville and Florence Prison Camps, 1864," *Connecticut Historical Society Bulletin* 41, no. 1 (Jan. 1976): 20.

42. Grosvenor Diary, July 4, 1864, CHS.

43. Forbes Diary, July 4, 1864, YU.

44. Kellogg Diary, Aug. 11, 1864, CHS; Kellogg, *Life and Death in Rebel Prisons*, 215.

45. Henry H. Adams Diary, Aug. 24, 1864, CHS.

46. Champlin Diary, Aug. 29, 1864, CSL.

47. Gates Diary, Aug. 17, 1864, CHS.

48. Gates Diary, May 31, 1864, CHS. He was further convinced that southerners were more committed to the war than northerners: "If only the north showed the same unity and resolve the war would be over in a month."

49. Gates Diary, Aug. 10, 1864, CHS.

50. Forbes Diary, May 14, 1864, YU.

51. Robbins Diary, Sept. 17, 1864, CHS. By this date, Robbins and other prisoners had been moved to Charleston. Henry E. Savage also made note of the day's significance in his diary: "Anniversary of the battle of Antietam and Sam Woodruffs death." See Savage Diary, Sept. 17, 1864, CSL. Pvt. Samuel Woodruff (Co. G) had died from diphtheria while the 16th C.V. was stationed at Portsmouth the year earlier.

52. Kellogg, *Life and Death in Rebel Prisons*, 76. Emphasis in original. Benjamin Cloyd discusses the "patient courage" prisoners sought to adopt in contrast to the active (and more manly) battlefield heroism Civil War soldiers and the northern public expected. See Cloyd, *Haunted by Atrocity*, 61–63. See Linderman, *Embattled Courage*, 257–61, for more on the perception that imprisonment was "harsher" than combat.

53. Forbes Diary, May 4, 1864, YU.

54. Forbes Diary, Aug. 20, 1864, YU.

55. Forbes Diary, Aug. 24, 1864, YU.

56. Forbes Diary, May 29, 1864, YU.

57. Forbes Diary, June 14, 1864, YU. Forbes admitted to occasional moments of doubt. On July 23, he wrote, "I do very much that is wrong and sinful. Oh! My coldness. I am far from loving Jesus as much as I ought to." See Forbes Diary, July 23, 1864, YU.

58. Champlin Diary, Aug. 1, 1864. When moved to Charleston, Champlin joined Cpl. William H. Jackson (Co. B) and Pvt. George T. Thompson (Co. I) in forming a prayer group as their incarceration continued. See Champlin Diary, Oct. 16, 1865, CSL.

59. Savage Diary, June 5, 1864, CSL. Leland Barlow described, "Religious meetings in camp." See Barlow Diary, July 19, 1864, CSL.

60. Flower Diary, July 28, 1864, CSL.

61. Flower Diary, Aug. 5, 1864, CSL. Flower is buried at Andersonville National Cemetery. See Nationwide Gravesite Locater, http://gravelocator.cem.va.gov/, accessed Nov. 17, 2008. The date of

his death written into his diary is August 9, 1864; the Nationwide Gravesite Locater cites Aug. 7, 1864, as does the AGO 1869, 648. However, Forbes listed August 9. See "Joseph Flower Jr.," Whitney Collection, CSL.

62. Kellogg Diary, Aug. 8, 1864, CHS. Kellogg recounted reading patients the "'Prodigal son' & the 'Sermon on the Mount'" on May 9; he had also read to them on May 8. See Kellogg Diary, May 8, 9, 1864, CHS. For more on the religious life of Andersonville inmates, see Futch, *History of Andersonville Prison*, 59–62; Marvel, *Andersonville*, 139–41.

63. Gates Diary, June 24, 1864, CHS.

64. Gates Diary, July 6, 1864, CHS.

65. Gates Diary, Sept. 5, 1864, CHS. Emphasis in original.

66. Grosvenor Diary, Sept. 6, 1864, CHS.

67. Grosvenor Diary, Sept. 8, 1864, CHS.

68. One day in August, Henry H. Adams recorded, "One man Died from Co. D." He rarely identified the soldiers. Others were more specific. Kellogg wrote on August 16, 1864: "Another of Co. 'C' has died this p.m. Ezariah Hale. His complaint was dropsy of the heart." See Kellogg Diary, CHS. Kellogg kept track of whether he knew the member personally: "Another member of our Regt has died today. Martin Hull of Co. 'E.' I don't remember him by name though I probably know him by sight." See Kellogg Diary, Aug. 26, 1864, CHS. According to Forbes and the AGO (1869, 653, and 1889, 628), Hull died on August 27, 1864. See Ira Forbes, "Martin Hull," Whitney Collection, CSL. Samuel Grosvenor wrote on August 11, "We learned of the death of Chas Wright of our own Company. Chas Degnan also died." See Grosvenor Diary, CHS. See also Henry H. Adams Diary, Aug. 20, 1864, CHS; Champlin Diary, Aug. 5, 19, 1864, CSL.

69. See Helmreich, "Diary of Charles G. Lee," 19. Oliver Gates also made special note of Bosworth's demise: "one of Company D. [in] our Regiment Died yesterday of chronic Diarrhea[.] he was a Corporal by the name of Bosworth [and] he was a good soldier and fine man[.] he was the first that have Died in our Regiment since we came into this Horrid place but there are quite a number of Sick[.] some I fear will not live long in here." Gates Diary, June 21, 1864, CHS. Bosworth is buried at Andersonville; see Nationwide Gravesite Locator at http://gravelocator.cem.va.gov/, accessed May 14, 2009. Whitney wrote that Bosworth "was born in Union Conn in 1844 and was 18 years old when enlisted, and proved a faithful soldier." See "Alonso N. Bosworth," Whitney Collection, CSL. His first name does appear to be spelled with a "z" rather than an "s." Barlow also recorded Bosworth's death on June 20; Barlow Diary, June 20, 1864, CSL. Ira Forbes wrote, "Corpl. Bosworth, Co. I our regiment died this morning. The first of our regiment that has died here." See Forbes Diary, June 20, 1864, YU. George Robbins, who had only entered the prison a few days earlier, wrote, "Bosworth of Co. D died today of the Diarrhea." Robbins Diary, June 20, 1864, CHS.

70. Examples of prisoners describing scriptures read, prayers offered, or some sort of makeshift service held for the dead include Barlow Diary, Aug. 13, 1864, CSL; Kellogg Diary, Aug. 23 and Sept. 6, 1864, CHS; and Forbes Diary, Aug. 23, 1864, YU.

71. Forbes Diary, Aug. 8, 1864, YU.

72. Gates Diary, June 24, 1864, CHS.

73. Gates Diary, June 26, 1864, CHS.

74. For example, see Gates Diary, July 19, 20, Aug. 14, 1864, CHS.

75. *Dedication of the Monument at Andersonville, Georgia, Oct. 23, 1907: In Memory of the Men of*

Connecticut Who Suffered in Southern Military Prisons, 1861–1865 (Hartford: State of Connecticut, 1908), 12.

76. "Sixteenth C. V. at Andersonville," *Connecticut Courant*, Mar. 15, 1906, newspaper clippings, Forbes Collection, CSL.

77. Kellogg, *Life and Death in Rebel Prisons*, 181–82. The AGO 1889 lists Damery's death as July 20, 1864, as does George Q. Whitney's postwar record. Damery, a native of Ireland, was a married farmer from Wethersfield with four children, all under the age of five. See 8th Census of the United States, 1860: Population Schedule, Wethersfield, Hartford, County, CT, at ancestry.com, accessed Jan. 31, 2009. George Q. Whitney wrote that Damery was "a native of Ireland, a Presbyterian and of Sterling and strong character, a very faithful and painstaking character." See "John Damery," Whitney Collection, CSL; AGO 1889, 621; also George Q. Whitney, "Prisons of the Confederacy," Whitney Collection, CSL. Forbes stated that Damery was the second member of the regiment to die at Andersonville. See Forbes, "Andersonville," Forbes Collection, CSL. But he was wrong: William Hitchcock (Co. C) died on July 10, followed by Henry Lindon (Co. D) on July 16, and Joseph Hoskins (Co. D) on July 18.

78. Gates Diary, July 19, 1864, CHS. These two were Patrick McCardle of Co. B and Albert Emmons of Co. K, who both died on July 16, 1864. Whitney erroneously stated that Damery "was the first member of the 16th Conn to die in the Prison Pens." He was one of the first, and perhaps the first in Co. A, but not the first in the regiment to perish in Andersonville. See "John Damery," Whitney Collection, CSL. Robbins noted that recruit Emmons "had been with the Co. but two weeks when we were captured." See Robbins Diary, July 19, 1864, CHS.

79. Forbes Diary, July 18, 1864, YU. Damery's name is mistyped as "Downey" in the transcribed copy. It seems pretty clear that it was Damery whom Forbes described; there was no "John Downey" in the regiment.

80. J. Leander Chapin to Amelia Chapin, May 29, 1864, quoted in "J. Leander Chapin Co. A 16th Regt. C. V.," Whitney Collection, CSL.

81. Forbes Diary, July 20, 1864, YU. Forbes later told a friend of Leander's mother that he died of typhoid fever. See Mary H. Williams to Amelia Chapin, Feb. 14, 1865, Chapin Family Papers, UGA. Whitney noted that Chapin died at 10 a.m. on July 20 and that he was "one of the first to succumb to prison life of the Regiment." See "Joel Leander Chapin," Whitney Collection, CSL. Gates also made note of Chapin's death. See Gates Diary, July 20, 1864, CHS. Champlin listed little more than Chapin's name and death date, as he would most other members of the regiment. See Champlin Diary, July 20, 1864; also Flower Diary, July 20, 1864, CSL. Kellogg referred to Chapin on August 5, when he described the loss of Pvt. David B. Carrie (Co. D.): "He was a very intimate friend of Chapin who died a few days ago & I trust their spirits are now united before God's throne." See Kellogg Diary, Aug. 5, 1864, CHS. On a loose scrap of paper tucked in his diary, he listed the date of Chapin's death and the time: "10 a.m." Sgt. Henry E. Savage noted, "Had funeral services for Chapin as he died inside the Prison." See Savage Diary, July 20, 1864, CSL. Chapin's body remained at Andersonville, and his brother Gilbert traveled there after the war to visit his grave. In his unpublished history of the prison, Forbes claimed that Chapin was just the third member from the regiment to perish in the prison. See Ira E. Forbes, "Andersonville," Forbes Collection, CSL.

82. Grosvenor Diary, May 8, 1864, CHS.

83. Kellogg Diary, May 22, 1864, CHS. Emphasis in original.

84. Kellogg, *Life and Death in Rebel Prisons*, 136, italics in original.

85. Kellogg, *Life and Death in Rebel Prisons*, 67, quote from 187–88.

86. Flower Diary, May 14, 1864, CSL.

87. Flower Diary, July 10, 1864, CSL.

88. Flower Diary, July 27, 1864, CSL.

89. Forbes Diary, July 3, 1864, YU.

90. Forbes Diary, June 2, 1864, YU.

91. Kellogg, *Life and Death in Rebel Prisons*, 240. Frances Clarke further discusses the debilitating effect homesickness or "nostalgia" could have on northern soldiers. See Frances Clarke, "So Lonesome I Could Die: Nostalgia and Debates over Emotional Control in the Civil War North," *Journal of Social History* 41 (Winter 2007): 253–82.

92. Cloyd, *Haunted by Atrocity*, 18–19.

93. Gates routinely used the word "brute" to describe the Confederate guards; "cowardly half civilized" from Gates Diary, June 22, 1864, CHS; "Slave driving Dupes," from July 6, 1864. For "crimes against all humanity," see entry for June 19.

94. Gates Diary, July 27, 1864, CHS. See also his entries from July 22 and 25.

95. Gates Diary, June 21, 1864, CHS. See also Charles W. Sanders, Jr., *While in the Hands of the Enemy: Military Prisons of the Civil War* (Baton Rouge: Louisiana State University Press, 2005).

96. Gates Diary, July 14, 1864, CHS. Emphasis in original.

97. Gates Diary, Aug. 23, 1864, CHS. On July 12, Gates complained about rumors that the "'nigger' question keeps us from being exchanged but I do not believe in any such story. I think when the [Grant's Virginia] Campaign is over we shall be exchanged." For more on the shifting racial attitudes of white Civil War soldiers, see Manning, *What This Cruel War Was Over*. The use of federal black troops did directly affect these prisoners because when the Confederacy refused to treat black soldiers as regular prisoners of war, the federal government halted all exchanges. It was a calculated move by Grant to break the Confederacy's fighting power because he predicted that exchanged southern soldiers would return to the ranks. William Marvel is critical of the federal policy and partly blames the Union for the awful conditions at Andersonville. See Marvel, *Andersonville*, x–xi, 25–26. More recently, Charles Sanders argues convincingly that both Confederate and federal authorities were to blame for failing to uphold the exchange system and ensure that prison conditions were humane. See Sanders, *While in the Hands of the Enemy*, 297–98. Also see Cloyd, *Haunted by Atrocity*, 19; and Glenn M. Robins, "Race, Repatriation, and Galvanized Rebels: Union Prisoners and the Exchange Question in Deep South Prison Camps," *Civil War History* 53, no. 2 (June 2007): 123–24.

98. Forbes Diary, July 12, 1864, YU. "Sgt. Lee" is Richard Henry Lee of Co. E.

99. Kellogg, *Life and Death in Rebel Prisons*, 75.

100. Forbes Diary, July 20, 1864, YU.

101. Forbes Diary, July 19, 1864, YU.

102. Forbes Diary, July 21, 1864, YU.

103. Forbes Diary, July 26, 1864, YU.

104. Kellogg, *Life and Death in Rebel Prisons*, 159, 182–83, 188–89. Robins discusses the negative attitudes Union POWs expressed toward Lincoln and the northern populace for not doing enough to ensure their release. See Robins, "Race, Repatriation, and Galvanized Rebels," 131.

105. Kellogg, *Life and Death in Rebel Prisons*, 188.

106. Kellogg, *Life and Death in Rebel Prisons*, 182. Warren Lee Goss, a member of the 2nd Massachusetts Artillery, imprisoned at Andersonville with the 16th C.V., recalled the petition circulating and acknowledged Kellogg for discouraging prisoners from signing it. See Goss, *The Soldier's Story of his Captivity*, 169–70. Goss published various versions of this book, the first appearing in 1867.

107. William C. Case, "Memorial Day Speech," Granby, CT, included in undated newspaper clipping, *Hartford Evening Post*, Holcomb Family Papers, SBHS. The story about Sergeant Lee became the stuff of legend. In his postwar Memorial Day speech, Case heralded Lee as the "brave spokesman of the day" and the 16th Connecticut prisoners as a "heroic band." Forbes provided varying versions of this story, including "Grant's Treatment of Colored Troops," *Hartford Courant*, Apr. 8, 1907, and his biography of Richard Henry Lee in the Whitney Collection, CSL. Forbes wrote, "Sergeant Lee was a noble example of manhood in civic no less than in military life." Also see Ira E. Forbes, "Exchange of Prisoners, An Incident in Connection with the History of the Andersonville Stockade," *Hartford Daily Times*, Oct. 15, 1907; and "Hartford in the Civil War," in Willis I. Twichell, ed., *Hartford in History: A Series of Papers by Resident Authors* (Hartford, CT: Press of the Plimpton Mfg Co., 1899), 229–30; also Richard Henry Lee Papers, SBHS.

108. Robbins Diary, July 22, 1864, CHS.

109. William B. Hessletine argues that these prisoner petitions, in addition to "stories of barbarities of Southerners led the officials responsible for the prisons to adopt a policy of retaliation while the people of the North clamored for exchange." See Hessletine, *Civil War Prisons: A Study of War Psychology* (New York: Frederick Unger, 1930), 223. Charles Sanders argues that the Andersonville petition was part of mounting pressure from soldiers and the public to change Union policy, but initially Lincoln and Stanton were unmoved. See Sanders, *While in the Hands of the Enemy*, 259–60. Forbes believed that a delegation of prisoners armed with the petition never made it to see the president due to the arrival of Sherman in central Georgia. See Ira Forbes, "Exchange of Prisoners, An Incident in Connection with the History of the Andersonville Stockade," *Hartford Daily Times*, Oct. 15, 1907. See also *OR*, ser. 2, vol. 7, 18–22.

110. *Connecticut War Record*, June 1864.

111. *Hartford Daily Courant*, July 11, 1864.

112. *Hartford Daily Courant*, May 6, 1864; Kellogg, *Life and Death in Rebel Prisons*, 188, 236.

113. Elizabeth F. Smith to George Q. Whitney, Dec. 28, 1905, Whitney Collection, CSL.

114. Nancy R. Phelps to Amelia Chapin, June 11, 1864, Chapin Family Papers, UGA. Leander had written his mother at least one letter on May 29, 1864, but she did not receive it until January 1865. See "J. Leander Chapin," Whitney Collection, CSL.

115. E. E. Strong letter, May 19, 1864, excerpted in *Hartford Daily Courant*, July 25, 1864.

116. E. E. Strong letter, June 6, excerpted in *Hartford Daily Courant*, July 25, 1864.

117. E. E. Strong to H. C. Strong, Aug. 14, 1864, in *Hartford Daily Courant*, Sept. 21, 1864. John Clapp's letters from Savannah were also making their way through the lines to Connecticut. See, e.g., *Hartford Daily Courant*, Oct. 1, 1864.

118. *Hartford Daily Courant*, July 22, 1864.

119. *Hartford Daily Courant*, July 22, 1864.

120. *Hartford Daily Times*, Oct. 1, 1864; AGO 1889, 619.

121. Mayer also indicated that Beach had gained release "through the special efforts of his friend

the Exchange officer." See Nathan Mayer to Sarah B. Mayer, May 1, 1864, Burnham Papers, CSL. Blakeslee writes that after Beach left Libby Prison in May, he "was assigned to various duties in Washington, only once rejoining what remained of the regiment. That was at New Berne, where he was taken sick, and soon departed on sick-leave." See Blakeslee, *History of the Sixteenth Connecticut Volunteers,* 101. Beach was home in Hartford by the first week of June. See *Hartford Evening Press,* June 6, 1864.

122. Day called Burnham a "brave officer" and "greatly esteemed as a man." See Calvin Day to William A. Buckingham, May 5, 1864, Governors' Correspondence, CSL; Nevin describes Day as the "richest" in *Connecticut for the Union,* 31. See also Talcott, "Prominent Business Men," in Trumbull, *The Memorial History of Hartford County,* 1:671.

123. "Verbum Sat," Letter to the Editor, May 3, 1864, *Charleston Daily Courier* [no date], quoted in *Voices from Plymouth: Plymouth Pilgrims Descendants Society Newsletter* 1 (Winter 1996).

124. This clipping was brought to the attention of both Army Chief of Staff Henry Halleck and Secretary of Navy Gideon Welles. See *OR,* ser. 1, vol. 35, pt. 2, 145, and *Official Records of the Union and Confederate Navies in the War of the Rebellion,* 30 vols. (Washington, DC: Government Printing Office, 1894–1922), ser. 1, 15:534. Original from *Charleston Tri-Weekly Mercury,* June 14, 1864.

125. Clapp gave his account in a sworn deposition in support of Burnham's attempt to gain a veteran's pension. See Affidavit of John B. Clapp, Mar. 16, 1881, John H. Burnham Pension File, NA. Clapp, among others, believed that Burnham's postwar "insanity" was "the result of his treatment in rebel prisons."

126. Affidavit of Henry W. Wessell, Apr. 20, 1881, John H. Burnham Pension File, NA. Burnham's mental illness and failed attempts to gain a veteran's pension are discussed below.

127. Testimony of Joseph D. Burnham, "Exhibit A," Feb. 1, 1882, John H. Burnham Pension File, NA. Ira Forbes recounted hearing of Burnham's imprisonment: "This evening we have heard from our officers in Macon. Lt. Col. Burnham, and Lieut. Langdon are very sick and in hospital. Lt. Miller has been quite sick, but is now recovering. The remainder of our officers are all well." See Forbes Diary, May 26, 1864, YU.

128. John H. Burnham, Letter to the Editor, Aug. 11, 1864, *Hartford Daily Courant,* Aug. 13, 1864.

129. John H. Burnham Letter to the Editor, Aug. 20, 1864, *Hartford Daily Courant,* Aug. 22, 1864.

130. Details of Burnham's second capture from Ariel J. Case to Sarah B. Burnham, Sept. 12, 1864, Burnham Papers, CSL; also Relyea, *16th Connecticut Volunteer Infantry,* 162; and *New York Times,* Sept. 17, 1864. The *Hartford Daily Times* reported on August 4 that Burnham had arrived home and on September 5, 1864, that he had just left for New Bern. See *Hartford Daily Times,* Aug. 4, Sept. 5, 1864. Official word of his exchange came on September 12, with orders to return to his regiment. See E. D. Townshend, "General Orders No. 255," Sept. 12, 1864, *OR,* ser. 2, vol. 7, 805–6; see also John H. Burnham, CSR, NA.

131. John H. Burnham to Sarah B. Burnham, Sept. 19, 1864, Burnham Papers, CSL.

132. John H. Burnham, CSR, NA. Champlin heard of Burnham's release from prison in August and his second capture while he remained incarcerated with the rest of the regiment. See Champlin Diary, Aug. 11 and Sept. 24, 1864, CSL.

133. *Hartford Daily Courant,* Sept. 14, 1864. Burnham left for Annapolis the first week of Dec. 1864. See *Hartford Daily Courant,* Dec. 10, 1864.

134. Undated newspaper clipping in Burnham Papers, CSL. The names and dates, again, do not

entirely match with the AGO. Just a few examples suffice. The paper lists "Joseph Haskins," dying on July 7, when "Joseph Hoskins" (Co. D) according to the AGO died on July 18; Noah Chapman's (Co. E) death is listed as Aug. 29, when the AGO lists it as Aug. 30; and Alonzo Hills (Co. B) is listed as dying on Sept. 20, when the AGO recorded his death as Oct. 6. See AGO 1889, 623, 626, 628. The *Hartford Daily Courant* published the list on Oct. 1, 1864, but referred to Dixon writing a letter including the list to the *Daily Press*.

135. John T. Porter to Amelia Chapin, Oct. 5, 1864, Chapin Family Papers, UGA. Porter was discharged with disability from the 16th on December 30, 1862, AGO. He reenlisted in the 1st Conn. Heavy Artillery in September 1864 but died on November 24. His grave states, "Died in Hospital, Broadway Landing, Va." He was in Connecticut on recruitment duty when he read about Chapin's death. See "John T. Porter," Whitney Collection, CSL; and findagrave.com, accessed Aug. 4, 2008.

136. Roselle Grover to Amelia Chapin, Oct. 14, 1864, Chapin Family Papers, UGA.

137. Joseph Doane's family also claimed that Buckingham had helped them with his exchange by writing directly to Gen. Foster. See J. Doane to John G. Foster, Oct. 17, 1864, Muster Rolls, Returns, Regimental Papers, RG 94, Box 147 [unbound paper], NA.

138. Caroline D. Hale to William A. Buckingham, Aug. 12, 1864, Governors' Correspondence, CSL. Kellogg's concerned parents, like most prisoner families, had heard little from their son since his capture, although they continued writing him. When Robert was exchanged in late November, he wrote his parents and said that at least two of their letters, from October 10 and 23, did reach him at Florence. See Robert H. Kellogg to Silas and Lucy C. Hale Kellogg, Dec. 4, 1864, Kellogg Papers, CHS.

139. Elizabeth Clapp to William A. Buckingham, Dec. 25, 1864, Governors' Correspondence, CSL; emphasis in original.

140. William A. Buckingham to Elizabeth Clapp, Dec. 27, 1864, Governors' Correspondence, CSL. It is unclear when Clapp was formally paroled, as the AGO lists the date as November 30, 1864, but he had not returned home by December 25, 1864. Whitney gives Clapp's date of parole as February 28, 1865. See "John Beadle Clapp," Whitney Collection, CSL; AGO 1889, 619. A letter to his mother dated February 4 was referred to in the *Hartford Daily Courant* on February 23, 1864. Clapp reportedly stated that he and the other officers with him from the 16th C.V. were in good health. Clapp survived the war to be discharged in May 1865.

141. Elizabeth Derby to William A. Buckingham, June 23, 1864, Governors' Correspondence, CSL; Pvt. Samuel E. Derby (Co. K) died at Charleston, South Carolina, on December 3, 1864. He is buried at the Beaufort National Cemetery, according to findagrave.com, accessed Jan. 25, 2008.

142. Mary E. Lee to William A. Buckingham, Oct 3, 1864, Governors' Correspondence, CSL.

143. Samuel Derby died in prison. Charles Lee died three months after his parole and is buried in the Wilmington National Cemetery in North Carolina. See AGO 1889, 622, 638. Also see Nationwide Grave Locator, http://gravelocator.cem.va.gov/j2ee/servlet/NGL_v1, accessed Jan. 31, 2008.

144. This soldier was not in the 16th Conn, but it is not clear in what unit he served. William A. Buckingham to Emily Ward, Feb. 4, 1864, Governors' Correspondence, CSL.

145. William A. Buckingham to Susan Greene, May 6, 1864, Governors' Correspondence, CSL. Deming would die in March 1865 soon after returning home to Rocky Hill. See "John E. Deming," Whitney Collection, CSL. The 1869 AGO, though, states that Deming died in Wilmington on March 10, 1865 (654).

146. William A. Buckingham to Benjamin Butler, May 5, 1864, Governors' Correspondence, CSL.

147. William A. Buckingham to J. G. Foster, Aug. 27, 1864, Governors' Correspondence, CSL. Joseph A. Doane, born in 1820, survived imprisonment, living until 1914. See findagrave.com, accessed Feb. 8, 2008. The town of Bristol also sent a petition urging an exchange, and the governor forwarded it to the War Department. Buckingham grew doubtful, however, that Lincoln, Stanton, or anyone in the administration could do anything to expedite the men's release. See Sidney Hayden to William A. Buckingham, Sept. 16, 1864 (emphasis in original), and Buckingham to Hayden, Governors' Correspondence, CSL. Hayden had to wait until December 16 to be exchanged. See AGO 1889, 622.

148. Kellogg Diary, Sept. 14, 1864, CHS. Kellogg made no mention of this fact in his public descriptions of his incarceration after the war, either in print or in speeches. While at Charleston, Champlin claimed, "Mike Gleason of Co. A 16th Conn has enlisted in the Rebel army with several other "Yankee" traitors." See Champlin Diary, Sept. 24, 1864, CSL. There is a Martin Gleason on the roster from Company A.

149. Norton Parker Chipman, *The Tragedy of Andersonville: Trial of Captain Henry Wirz The Prison Keeper* (Sacramento, CA: published by the author, 1911), 159. Moesner had also served for three years in the German army in the 1840s. He came to the United States, and when the war began, he enlisted in the 52nd New York Infantry. He was wounded at the Battle of Fredericksburg and discharged for disability. He found employment in a factory in Collinsville but struggled with the work, explaining, "I had never been used to manual labor." He rejoined the army after almost "every man in our factory enlisted." Moesner became part of the 16th Connecticut two months before the battle of Plymouth. See Augustus Moesner to George Q. Whitney, Mar. 17, 1903, Whitney Collection, CSL. Moesner's letter, written decades after the war, does not seem to be authored by someone struggling with the English language. Moesner reentered the military service after the Civil War and served in the U.S. cavalry for three years in the far west. Musician Karl Schubert (Co. K) noted the offer to work outside: "We were asked to enlarge the enclosure, but would not consent to it because it would help the Rebels." See Karl Schubert Diary, May 23, 1864, "translated from German for George Q. Whitney," Whitney Collection, CSL. Barlow also mentioned in his diary discussion of accepting paroles to work on expanding the stockade; see Barlow Diary, May 22, 1864, CSL.

150. Chipman, *The Tragedy of Andersonville*, 225; also 173. Kellogg Diary, Aug. 10, 1864, CHS. Buckingham was a steward in the hospital, and Spring worked in the cookhouse, where he was somewhat better informed than inmates inside the prison. He passed along to his comrades on "sick call" news of Lt. Col. Burnham's exchange and informed them (inaccurately) that an exchange was pending in mid-August. See Robert H. Kellogg, Aug. 10, 1864, CHS.

151. Sidney H. Hayden to William Hayden, Feb. 27, 1865, Hayden Papers, EGPL.

152. Kellogg Diary, May 23, 1864, CHS.

153. Champlin Diary, June 27, 1864, CSL. Robins describes the "unusual steps" some Union POWs took to "relieve their despair." See Robins, "Race, Reparation, and Galvanized Rebels," 135, 137–39.

154. Barlow mentions a "shoemaker" "working for the rebs," whom the men angrily lashed out at by shaving his head before allowing him to leave. See Barlow Diary, June 15, 16, 1864, CSL; also see Forbes Diary, June 15, 1864, YU. Henry Savage wrote in his diary that John Deming tried to obtain a parole to work as shoemaker for the Confederates. It is unclear if Deming was successful. See Savage Diary, July 30, 1864, CSL.

155. Bauer was part of the first group of prisoners removed from Andersonville and sent to Savannah. There he was given the job of overseeing the burial of the dead, which provided him extra rations. He used the food to trade outside the stockade. Bauer also befriended a German family residing near the stockade who gave him extra food and clothing, which was of enormous benefit to him. "I shall," Bauer wrote, "never forget their kindness." See Bauer, "Personal Experiences of the War," 16, PPM. Bauer's company mate Henry Savage seems to have noted this incident in his diary, although it is late July not August: "Jake was detailed to go out as clerk for head Surgeon but refused the situation." See Savage Diary, July 27, 1864, CSL. On August 23, Savage wrote, "Jacob Bauer went out on detail at headquarters this morning." See Savage Diary, Aug. 23, 1864, CSL.

156. Undated newspaper clipping, "Casper Young," Whitney Collection, CSL.

157. George Q. Whitney, "Prisons of the Confederacy," Whitney Collection, CSL.

158. Gates Diary, May 30, 1864, CHS.

159. Gates Diary, June 22, 1864, CHS.

160. Gates Diary, Sept. 26, 1864, CHS.

161. Gates also had a "General Pass," which he loaned to some of his comrades; this action nearly sent him back into the prison camp. He explained, "I shall be more careful in the future for my job is worth keeping and I may go home on it some day who knows." See Gates Diary, Oct. 25, 1864, CHS.

162. Gates Diary, Nov. 3, 1864, CHS. Emphasis in original.

163. Gates accepted the parole after the transfer to Florence. See Gates Diary, "an Explanation," written on the final pages of Diary III, CHS. He added, "Now we feel like taking Mr. Buckingham and others by the honest hand and making an apology for having written as we then felt. No truer man were or ever have been in my Regiment."

164. John B. Cuzner, "A Lively Buggy Story," and "Thanksgiving in Andersonville Prison," Cuzner Letters and Papers, CHS. Shields was identified by Cuzner's daughter Jennie Sperry. Sperry also identified comrades Cuzner listed only by initials: Musician Robert Holmes (Co. B), Pvt. Edmund Green (Co. B), Edmund "Lengthy" Root (Co. B), and 2nd Lt. Herbert Landon (Co. B). Cuzner describes them as enjoying the Thanksgiving meal that Shields obtained for them. Landon, however, was a commissioned officer, and not imprisoned at Andersonville, so "H.L." is another soldier, perhaps Henry Loomis from Co. B. It is not clear when Cuzner told his daughter these stories about Andersonville. Sperry related them in his voice without offering her own commentary, although she transcribed them in her own handwriting, planning to publish them alongside his wartime letters to her mother. Unaware of any hypocrisy, Cuzner mailed his sister Agnes a copy of the wartime poem "Dixie's Sunny Land" after his release from prison. It is a scathing account of the Confederates' cruel treatment of Union prisoners, and includes the lines: "We poor survivors oft were tried by many / a threat and bribe / To desert our glorious 'Union cause,' / and join the rebel tribe; / Though fain we were to leave the place we let them understand // 'We had rather die than thus disgrace / our flag' in Dixie's sunny land." See "The Song of Union Prisoners from Dixie's Sunnyland Air 'Twenty years Ago,'" in Cuzner Letters and Papers, CHS.

165. Kellogg Diary, June 9, 1864, CHS. The two men were "[Lucien] Case and Rufus Chamberlain of Co 'I.'"

166. Kellogg Diary, June 10, 1864, CHS.

167. Kellogg, *Life and Death in Rebel Prisons*, 133.

168. Kellogg Diary, July 30, 1864, CHS.

169. Forbes Diary, July 30, 1864, YU. There were four Woodfords from Co. I—Harrison, Edward, Sheldon, and Wallace—all cousins. It is not clear which one had the fight with Forbes.

170. Barlow Diary, June 10, 1864, CSL. See also Barlow Diary, May 10, 13, 15, 16, 1864, CSL.

171. Gates Diary, June 26, 1864, CHS. Forbes noted violence in camp, too. See Forbes Diary, May 19, June 10, Aug. 18, 1864, YU.

172. Glenn Robins writes that by late October, Andersonville counted only 4,208 prisoners; in November and December the prison turned more into a hospital, "tending to the captives too sick to travel. In early December there were less than 1,500 men in Andersonville prison by the months end the total was approaching 5,000." See Robins, *They Have Left Us Here to Die: The Civil War Prison Diary of Sgt. Lyle G. Adair, 111th U.S Colored Infantry* (Kent, OH: Kent State University Press, 2011), 61. See also Marvel, *Andersonville,* 225; and *OR,* ser. 2, vol. 7, 1082–83, for October numbers on Andersonville; by October 1, there were 8,218 prisoners.

173. Kellogg Diary, Sept. 1, 1864, CHS. Leland O. Barlow wrote, "A. J. Spring come in letting the boys have money. Got five dollars." See Barlow Diary, Sept. 1, 1864, CSL.

174. Andrew Spring, "Testimony," in Chipman, *The Tragedy of Andersonville,* 173.

175. Kellogg Diary, Sept. 2, 1864, CHS. Kellogg referred to "Thompson & the other boys who work outside." It is not clear which "Thompson" it was. Although it may have been Sgt. Austin Thompson. George Robbins, later credited Austin Thompson with keeping him alive by "securing permission" to work outside the prison at Florence and thus obtain extra rations. See Robbins, "Some Recollections," 45, CHS.

176. Champlin Diary, Sept. 6, 1864, CSL.

177. Forbes Diary, Sept. 7, 9, 1864, YU.

178. Grosvenor Diary, Sept. 10, 1864, CHS.

179. Kellogg Diary, Sept. 10, 1864, CHS.

180. Robert H. Kellogg to Ira Forbes, July 18, 1907, Forbes Collection, CSL. Forbes eventually left on September 15.

181. See Gates Diary, Sept. 11, 1864, CHS. During those five days, Gates sold his boots and pawned his haversack to obtain rations as more died around him. He was hesitant to sell his gold pen, which he used to write in his diary. He credited Hiram Williams's uncle, "Mr. Davis" for helping to keep him alive; Williams died on September 15. Gates also described a "whole detachment" volunteering to remain in the prison to take care of the sick and a "police force" organized to keep the peace. See Gates Diary, Sept. 13, 1864, CHS. See also Sept. 12.

182. Barlow Diary, Sept. 21, 22, 1864, CSL. A. S. Walker inscribed in Barlow's diary, "O. L. Barlow died on the evening of this day, Oct 9, 1864. His last words were: 'Tell my parents that I died happy and that I bid them all farewell and die trusting in the Lord." Barlow Diary, Oct. 9, 1864, CSL. The AGO records for 1869 and 1889 list Barlow's death date as October 11; in addition an article in the *Connecticut Courant,* probably by Ira Forbes, lists October 11. See "Sixteenth C. V. at Andersonville," *Connecticut Courant,* Mar. 15, 1906, newspaper clipping, Forbes Collection, CSL. Revelations 7:13–17 was inscribed on the next page. In the final pages of the diary was a careful listing of fifty-eight dead from the regiment, beginning on June 20 with Bosworth and ending on September 9 with Mathews. Barlow Diary, CSL; see also *Hartford Daily Courant,* Nov. 28, [1915].

183. Robbins, "Some Recollections," 43, CHS.

184. Savage Diary, Sept. 29, 1864, CSL.

185. Kellogg Diary, Sept. 13, 1864, CHS.

186. Gates Diary, Sept. 19, 1864, CHS.

187. Gates Diary, Sept. 22, 1864, CHS. Kellogg also described Strothers in a positive light in *Life and Death in Rebel Prisons*, 320, 323. Strothers was replaced by O'Brien, a surgeon described by Gates as being as "mean a white man as I ever met." See Gates Diary, Nov. 15, 1864, CHS.

188. Gates Diary, Oct. 20, 1864, CHS; also Nov. 20, 1864.

189. Champlin Diary, Oct. 1, 1864, CSL.

190. Gates Diary, Nov. 8, 1864, CHS. Ira Forbes also mentioned the arrival of goods from the Sanitary Commission in his diary. See Forbes Diary, Nov. 14, 15, 1864, YU.

191. Robbins, "Some Recollections," 44. In his diary, Robbins wrote, "About 1000 have gone out to try it," and "About 200 went out and took the Oath today." See Robbins Diary, Oct. 6, 17, 1864, CHS.

192. Savage Diary, Oct. 4, 1864, CSL. Among those Savage identified from the 16th C.V. were "Corp Done," "Nick Leonard" (Co. F), Nelson Rice (Co. A), and "Hdly" of (Co. G), all of whom he claimed "went out some time ago." Savage Diary, Nov. 6, 1864, CSL. There is no "Nick" Leonard, but Michael Leonard is listed as dying at Florence on November 23, 1864, according to the AGO; Nelson Rice (Co. A) has no known parole date. It is unclear who "Corp Done" or "Hdly" could have been. This is a typescript copy of the diary, and it could be that the transcriber misread the names. The George Champlin Diary, which is also a typescript from the original, has two entries that list specific members of the regiment who took the oath. On October 12, 1864, "Private Jones the smith of Co. I 16th Conn. Vo. Went out yesterday to take the oath of allegiance to the so-called Southern Confederacy." Most likely, the transcriber, Champlin's brother Oliver, misread this entry. It could be "Pvt. James M. Smith from Co. I." There was no soldier in the unit with the first or last name Jones in Co. I. However, Cpl. George Jones from Co. F., according to W. H. Jackson, on Nov. 6, 1864, took the oath of allegiance to the Southern Confederacy and went outside the stockade. See William H. Jackson Diary, Nov. 6, 1864, CSL; also "George Jones," Whitney Collection, CSL. Jones himself makes no mention of this in his own short postwar memoir, "My Prison Experience." Jones dwells on his starvation and scurvy and the fact that his only possession was a blanket when he was finally paroled. See George Jones, "My Prison Experience," Whitney Collection, CSL. Another entry in Jackson's diary on October 15 reads, "William Gaully, and wood of Co. D 16th Conn. Vol. Have gone out to the so-called Southern Confederacy." The punctuation and spelling is from the original transcription. There was a recruit in Co. D named William Woods, but no one who matches the name "William Gaully." Pvt. William Goarley from Co. D. is listed as dying at Andersonville, but no date is listed. This could, however, be the same man who took the oath and perhaps never returned to the ranks. Woods did and is listed as mustering out of service August 21, 1865. See AGO 1889, 625–27. See also Champlin Diary, Oct. 3, 4, 13, Nov. 17, 1864, CSL.

193. *Hartford Daily Times*, Aug. 15, 1864.

194. *Hartford Daily Times*, Oct. 5, 1864.

195. *Hartford Daily Courant*, Nov. 23, 1864. This account was given by Capt. J. L. Pastor of the 13th Tennessee Cavalry (Union); the paper says he escaped with Capts. Burke and Dickerson.

196. *Hartford Daily Courant*, Nov. 29, 1864.

197. See, e.g., *Hartford Daily Courant*, Dec. 30, 1864, and Jan. 4, 1865. The fate of the 16th C.V. was often highlighted, but prisoners from other Connecticut regiments were also mentioned.

198. *Hartford Daily Courant*, Feb. 9, 1865.

199. Alfred Dickinson, "Escape of Prisoners," *Connecticut War Record*, Dec. 1864.

200. *Hartford Daily Courant*, Nov. 19, 1864.

201. *Hartford Daily Times*, Mar. 16, 1865; AGO 1889, 619, 625, 627.

202. *Hartford Daily Courant*, Oct. 11, 1864.

203. *Hartford Daily Courant*, Oct. 12, 1864. See also *Hartford Daily Times*, Oct. 17, 1864.

204. Blakeslee, *History of the Sixteenth Connecticut Volunteers*, 99. See also Andrew J. Spring, CSR, NA. In a public speech criticizing the Confederates and Andersonville, Whitney referred to Spring accepting the Confederate parole "for some purpose outside the stockade." Whitney seemed to withhold judgment against Spring. See George Q. Whitney, "Prisons of the Confederacy," Whitney Collection, CSL.

205. *Hartford Daily Courant*, Oct. 12, 1864.

206. *Hartford Daily Times*, Oct. 17, 1864, emphasis in original. See also Sanders, *While in the Hands of the Enemy*, 75, 258–60, 314. There were many examples of the *Times*, in particular, blasting Lincoln for halting the prison exchange: "He sacrifices them to a lingering death of torture, for the sake of gratifying his fanatical notion of negro equality." See *Hartford Daily Times*, Oct. 20, 1864. Spring died in early 1866 from pneumonia, and his wife tried to argue that his death was due to his military service and imprisonment. However, her pension claim was denied. It may well have been because he accepted a Confederate parole while imprisoned. See Pension Record, Andrew J. Spring, NA.

207. James Whitney to William Buckingham, Dec. 27, 1864, Governors' Correspondence, CSL.

208. Champlin Diary, Dec. 17, 1864, CSL.

209. Forbes Diary, Nov. 30, 1864, YU.

210. Robert H. Kellogg to Silas and Lucy C. Hale Kellogg, Dec. 4, 1864, Kellogg Papers, CHS.

211. Gates Diary, no date, CHS. Gates specifically mentioned Pvt. Abijah Perkins in Co. F who died before reaching home. Perkins's death date according to the AGO is March 9, 1865, at Camp Parole. See AGO 1889, 630.

212. Bauer, "Personal Experiences of the War," 19, PPM.

CHAPTER EIGHT

1. Co. H included about thirty additional men and officers who had been on detached service when the regiment was captured. A complete list can be found in Bound Regimental Papers, RG 94, entries 112–15, Bound Records of the Union Volunteer Regiments, vol. 2, NA. OR, ser. 1, vol. 36, pt. 3, 432.

2. Blakeslee, *History of the Sixteenth Connecticut Volunteers*, 100.

3. Blakeslee, *History of the Sixteenth Connecticut Volunteers*, 100.

4. Ira Forbes, "Joseph Hall Barnum," Whitney Collection, CSL.

5. *Hartford Evening Press*, May 17, 1864; also *Hartford Daily Courant*, May 18, 1864. See also William A. Buckingham Letterbook, May 14, 1864, Apr.–Oct., 1864, Governors' Correspondence, CSL.

6. Joseph H. Barnum to J. A. Judson, June 6, 1864, Joseph H. Barnum, CSR, NA.

7. J. A. Judson to Joseph H. Barnum, June 9, 1864, Joseph H. Barnum, CSR, NA.

8. Joseph H. Barnum to Julian Pomeory, Aug. 21, 1864, Bound Regimental Papers, RG 94, entries 112–15, Bound Records of the Union Volunteers Regiments, vol. 1, NA.

9. Joseph H. Barnum to Ariel J. Case, Feb. 11, 1865, Bound Regimental Papers, RG 94, entries 112–15, Bound Records of the Union Volunteer Regiments, vol. 1, NA.

10. Joseph H. Barnum to Lorenzo Thomas, June 10, 1864, Ariel J. Case, CSR, NA.

11. Joseph H. Barnum to J. A. Judson, Apr. 3, 1865, Muster Rolls, Returns, Regimental Papers, RG 94, Box 147 [unbound papers], NA. Judson was Assistant Adjutant General, District of Beaufort.

12. *Hartford Daily Courant,* July 9, 1864.

13. *Hartford Daily Courant,* July 21, 1864. This letter was dated July 11 but not published until the 21st.

14. Blakeslee, *History of the Sixteenth Connecticut Volunteers,* 101.

15. Blakeslee, *History of the Sixteenth Connecticut Volunteers,* 100.

16. Blakeslee, *History of the Sixteenth Connecticut Volunteers,* 100.

17. *Hartford Daily Courant,* July 22, 1864. This letter was dated July 18, 1864.

18. "Roanoke," Letter to Editor, Sept. 19, 1864, *Connecticut War Record,* Oct. 1864.

19. Cornelius Doty to William A. Buckingham, Nov 8, 1864, Governors' Correspondence, CSL.

20. Forbes Diary, Mar. 2, 1864, YU.

21. *Hartford Daily Courant,* Mar. 22, 1864.

22. Bound Regimental Papers, RG 94, entries 112–15, Bound Records of the Union Volunteer Regiments, vol. 2, NA; AGO 1889, 621. In the Descriptive Roll for Co. I, it states that McSully had deserted from the Foster General Hospital on July 28, 1864.

23. Bound Regimental Papers, RG 94, entries 112, 115, Bound Records of the Union Volunteer Regiments, vol. 2, NA. The regiment's descriptive roll states that Pvt. Collins "deserted to the enemy at Hertford, NC on June 9, 1864." See also "Descriptive List of Deserters from 16th Regiment of Connecticut State Volunteers," Muster Rolls, Returns, Regimental Papers, RG 94, Box 148 [unbound papers], NA. "Roanoke" wrote, "the deserter was formerly in the rebel army belonging to a Texas regiment, and had but recently joined the Sixteenth"; see "Roanoke," Letter to Editor, June 22, 1864, *Connecticut War Record,* July 1864. It is not clear if this Collins is the same soldier that Jacob Bauer described in his recollections: "One old fellow (Collins) was very dirty and would not clean himself. So one fine day I detailed six men to take him down to the River and wash him. Well, they stripped him, put him in and straw scrubbed him until he was decently clean." But Collins "got disobedient" again, leaving camp without orders. Sgt. Bauer's punishment involved filling the soldier's knapsack with bricks, strapping it to him, and forcing him to stand atop a barrel in the sun. Then he "begged to be let down and promised to behave himself." Bauer had him strung up by the thumbs for another infraction but claimed that after all of this Collins became "a real good friend and soldier." See Bauer, "Personal Experiences of the War," 9, PPM. It is not clear when and where this occurred. The only other Pvt. Collins in the regiment was James Collins (Co. I), also a recruit, who served out the war, transferring to the 6th C.V. in June 1865. See AGO 1889, 635. Another recruit, Pvt. Orrin B. Hull (Co. E), a young farmer from Cornwall, Connecticut, deserted the regiment in March 1865, when he failed to return from a furlough after a stay in the hospital in New Bern. See "Descriptive List of Deserters from 16th Regiment of Connecticut State Volunteers," Mar. 1865, Muster Rolls, Returns, Regimental Papers, RG 94, Box 148 [unbound papers], NA.

24. See Bound Regimental Papers, RG 94, entries 112–115, Bound Records of the Union Volunteer Regiments, vol. 2, NA. The seven privates were James Anderson, Michael Redmond,

James Smith, Thomas Scanlon, Thomas Murry, George Ederson, and James Gallagher. On August 2, 1864, Ederson, Gallagher, and Anderson were sentenced to confinement at Fort Macon. Records indicate that Ederson and Gallagher were confined from August 16, 1864, until February 16, 1865, and then released "after serving out [their] sentence." See Muster Rolls, Returns, Regimental Papers, RG 94, Box 147 [unbound papers], NA. James Anderson was charged with "disrespect" after being found "drunk on guard at Roanoke Island" and yelling at a sergeant, "I won't obey you, you SOB." Anderson was sentenced to three months of hard labor and lost three months of his pay. "The Index Project," Civil War Data, from Records of the Bureau of Military Justice, RG 153, NA. Charged with "disobedience" for refusing to drill or put on their equipment, Ederson and Gallagher were sentenced to six months of hard labor and docked six months pay. See "The Index Project," Civil War Data, from Records of the Bureau of Military Justice, RG 153, NA.

25. *Hartford Daily Courant*, May 26, 1864; also *Hartford Daily Times*, June 4, 1864. Harris is buried in the New Bern National Cemetery. See findagrave.com, accessed May 31, 2009. At this meeting, the company appointed as president William H. Robinson, vice president Sidney S. Carter, Jr., and secretary Wilmer H. Johnson; Fred Ebell and William H. Allen were appointed to a "committee on resolutions."

26. "Roanoke," Letter to Editor, June 22, 1864, *Connecticut War Record*, July 1864.

27. "Muster Roll of the Field Staff of the Sixteenth Regiment of Conn Vols." Dec. 31, 1864, Muster Rolls, Returns, Regimental Papers, RG 94, Box 148 [unbound papers], NA.

28. *Connecticut War Record,* Dec. 1864.

29. Ira E. Forbes, "Company H in Service," Forbes Collection, CSL. "Veteran" wrote on Nov. 2 from Roanoke Island, that the 16th C.V., 85th New York, and 101st Pennsylvania now occupy the place [Plymouth]"; he added that "Lieut. Case is in command of the 16th, who are all well." See *"Hartford Daily Courant,* Nov. 10, 1864.

30. *Connecticut War Record,* Dec. 1864.

31. "Roanoke," Mar. 20, 1865, *Connecticut War Record,* Apr. 1865. See also Blakeslee, *History of the Sixteenth Connecticut Volunteers,* 101. Blakeslee stated that officers resided in private homes.

32. Joseph H. Barnum to G. W. Leonard, Mar. 20, 1865, Bound Regimental Papers, RG 94, entries 112–15, Bound Records of the Union Volunteer Regiments, vol. 1, NA. Barnum counted an "aggregate" of ninety-three men in the regiment.

33. For example, on December 15, Kellogg counted "thirty members of the 16th Connecticut & one officer, Luiet. Wm. Miller, arriving on steamers from Charleston." See Kellogg Diary, Dec. 15, 1864, CHS. Yet John Cuzner mentioned in February that Union prisoners were arriving from Richmond, but none from the 16th Connecticut since he had arrived in late January. See John B. Cuzner to Ellen Van Dorn, Feb. 19, 1864, Cuzner Letters and Papers, CHS.

34. Harrison Woodford to "Father, Mother, Sister & Brothers," Dec. 18, 1864, Harrison Woodford Letters, private collection.

35. "Our much loved," from Forbes Diary, Dec. 12, 1864, YU; see also Kellogg Diary, Dec. 12, 1864, CHS.

36. Martin V. Culver to Jonathan Culver, Mar. 16, 1865, Culver Letters, private collection.

37. John B. Cuzner to Ellen Van Dorn, Mar. 11, 1865, Cuzner Letters and Papers, CHS; Sidney Hayden to William Hayden, Feb. 27, 1865, Hayden Papers, EGPL.

38. See, e.g., Forbes Diary, Dec. 11, 13, 14, 17, 1864, YU. He mentions reading works of history, geography, religious books, and newspapers.

39. Kellogg Diary, Dec. 5, 1864, CHS. See also Robert H. Kellogg to George Q. Whitney, Oct. 15, 1909, Kellogg Papers, CHS.

40. Kellogg Diary, Dec. 6, 1864, CHS.

41. Kellogg Diary, Dec. 7, 1864, CHS.

42. John B. Cuzner to Ellen Van Dorn, Jan. 29, 1865, Cuzner Letters and Papers, CHS.

43. John B. Cuzner to Ellen Van Dorn, Feb. 9, 1864, Cuzner Letters and Papers, CHS.

44. Forbes Diary, Dec. 16, 1864, YU.

45. Kellogg Diary, Jan. 6, 1865, CHS. Kellogg's first furlough from Camp Parole was from Dec. 16, 1864, to Jan. 16, 1865. See Robert H. Kellogg to George Q. Whitney, Oct. 15, 1909, Kellogg Papers, CHS.

46. Kellogg Diary, Mar. 17, 1865, CHS. This was during Kellogg's second furlough. Kellogg references "Lena Norton," with whom he spent the evening, and a "Mrs. N." who actually gave the toast. They may have been two different women, perhaps a mother and daughter.

47. *Hartford Daily Courant*, Apr. 5, 1865. The *Courant's* editors, responding to this story, sought an establishment of a "Soldiers' Rest" to provide for returning prisoners of war. The paper stated, "There surely must be generous-hearted-citizens enough in this community to defray the expense, and if some one will take the matter in hand and solicit subscriptions, all the money needed can probably be raised without difficulty."

48. Robbins, "Some Recollections," 54, CHS.

49. Robbins, "Some Recollections," 56, CHS. Robbins further claims that a deliberate delay by a defiant young lieutenant who refused to sign his papers fortuitously prevented him from boarding the transport, which collided with the *Black Diamond*. See also George Robbins, CSR, NA.

50. The AGO lists Holcomb's parole date as February 28, 1865; however, "Memorandum from Prisoner of War Records," included in his CSR at the NA, states that his parole date was December 6, 1864, at Charleston. See AGO 1889, 628. There is also a letter from Colonel A. K. Root in the 94th N.Y., commander of Camp Parole, authorizing Holcomb to go on a thirty-day furlough beginning December 16, 1864, and ending January 15, 1865. Further certifications by a doctor and justice of the peace attest to Holcomb's "feeble health," also dated prior to February 1865, asking for an extension of his leave. See Lewis M. Holcomb, CSR, NA. His cousin Adelaide Holcomb noted in her diary, "Lewis is paroled," on December 17, 1864. See Adelaide R. Holcomb Diary, Holcomb Family Papers, SBHS.

51. "Wreck" from Florence J. Tryon to George Q. Whitney, Nov. 21, 1919; "so weak," from Frederick H. Williams to [George Q. Whitney], n.d., both in "Lewis M. Holcomb," Whitney Collection, CSL. Lewis M. Holcomb, CSR, NA. See also Laun, *The Holcomb Collection*, 92.

52. Adelaide R. Holcomb Diary, Dec. 23, 1864, Holcomb Family Papers, SBHS. See also Dec. 28, 1864.

53. Adelaide mentions Lewis's condition wavering through the several weeks he was home. Adelaide R. Holcomb Diary, Holcomb Family Papers, SBHS.

54. See George Q. Whitney, "Lewis M. Holcomb," Whitney Collection, CSL. Also Lewis M. Holcomb, CSR, NA. The surgeon listed his cause of death as "a Facial Erysipelas followed by Putrid sore throat." This is an acute, deadly form of strep throat. George Q. Whitney lists his death as due to diphtheria. His family finally learned of his death on June 19. When the 16th Connecticut mustered out on June 29, Addie wrote, "The sixteenth Regt. have arrived today. Lewis is dead. It seems hardly

possible." Adelaide R. Holcomb Diary, June 29, 1865, Holcomb Family Papers, SBHS. The Holcomb family had also heard that Richard Henry Lee was dead, but he survived, was paroled from prison, and formally discharged from the unit on June 15, 1865. See Adelaide R. Holcomb Diary, Mar. 13, 14, 29, 1865, Holcomb Family Papers, SBHS; AGO 1889, 627. See below for more on Holcomb's family seeking information on his death and burial.

55. *Hartford Daily Courant*, Jan. 12, 1865; also findagrave.com, accessed June 3, 2010.

56. Sidney H. Hayden to Oliver Hayden, Feb. 21, 1865, emphasis in original; for evidence of his unshaken Christian faith, see Sidney Hayden to Oliver Hayden, Mar. 3, 1865, Hayden Papers, EGPL.

57. Springman and Guinan, *East Granby*, 216.

58. Gates Diary, no date, CHS. Gates was furloughed on Dec. 16 for thirty days, but on Jan. 19, 1865, Connecticut physician F. Griffin described Gates's illness and requested a furlough extension. Gates returned on April 15, 1865, and mustered out with the regiment in June. Jacob Bauer recorded the return of "one of my old mates Orderly Gates of Co. F." See Bauer Diary, Apr. 15, 1865; AGO 1889, 629; Oliver W. Gates, CSR, NA; F. Griffin to A. R. Root, Jan. 19, 1865, Oliver W. Gates Pension File, NA.

59. "Feeling somewhat blue" from Jan. 3, 1865; "remain against my will" from Jan. 11, 1865, Jacob Bauer Diary, MHI. Bauer notes in his diary on April 2, 1865, that his daughter Allison was born April 2, 1861.

60. Jacob Bauer Diary, Jan. 16, 1865, MHI. It is noteworthy that Bauer's postwar recollections, which he wrote for his children and grandchildren in 1915, had a very different tone. He described Camp Parole as a "King's Palace," with delicious and plentiful food. See Bauer, "Personal Experiences of the War," 19-20, PPM.

61. John B. Cuzner to Ellen Van Dorn, Jan. 29, 1865, Cuzner Letters and Papers, CHS.

62. John B. Cuzner to Ellen Van Dorn, Feb. 9, 1865, Cuzner Letters and Papers, CHS.

63. John B. Cuzner to Ellen Van Dorn, Mar. 11, 1865, Cuzner Letters and Papers, CHS.

64. John B. Cuzner to Ellen Van Dorn, May 14, 1865, Cuzner Letters and Papers, CHS.

65. See John B. Cuzner to Ellen Van Dorn, June 15, 1865, Cuzner Letters and Papers, CHS.

66. Kellogg Diary, Jan. 1, 1865, CHS. Kellogg had been openly religious since his enlistment, but this was still a significant event for him. At least as evidenced by his diary entries, during those days following his release, Kellogg vowed a greater commitment to his faith than ever before. When he returned to Camp Parole, he sought new converts, attended prayer meetings, and joined a "Christian Association." He had done these things before his imprisonment, too. For example, on Sunday, January 29, he recorded trying to convince friend and comrade Norman Hope to become a Christian. Hope "admitted that he wanted to be a Christian but thought he could not live a Christian life in the Army, but would wait until he got home." Kellogg responded to Hope that "he might never live to see that time." See Robert H. Kellogg to Norman Hope, Jan. 29, 1865, CHS. In another entry, Kellogg mentioned attending a prayer meeting and joining the "'Christian Association'" See Kellogg Diary, Feb. 3, 1865, CHS.

67. Kellogg Diary, Jan. 9, 1865, CHS. It appears that Stebbins and Kellogg met on January 9, perhaps in Hartford, and a few days later Stebbins sent a letter to Kellogg to assure him that "the book is progressing well." It is significant, perhaps, that Kellogg remarked on how it "almost pays to be a prisoner of war," just three days before his visit from L. Stebbins. See also Robert H. Kellogg to George Q. Whitney, Oct. 15, 1909, Kellogg Papers, CHS; Kellogg Diary, Jan. 6, 12, 1865, CHS.

68. Kellogg Diary, Jan. 27, 1865, CHS. While at Andersonville, Kellogg suffered from an open,

festering scurvy sore on his right hand and feared he would lose the hand to gangrene. When the prisoners moved to Charleston, South Carolina, in September 1864, he was able to get help from a Confederate doctor and his hand healed, although he was left with a scar.

69. Kellogg Diary, Jan. 28, 1865, CHS.

70. Ira Forbes, "Robert Hale Kellogg," Whitney Collection, CSL.

71. Frontispiece, Kellogg, *Life and Death in Rebel Prisons.*

72. Kellogg Diary, Mar. 11, 1865, CHS. Kellogg obtained a second furlough home for two weeks, but his books kept selling in his absence. He recorded on March 23 upon his return to Annapolis, "I found to my gratification that Capt. Fox Post Adjt. had sold my books for me (200) & was keeping the money for me." See Kellogg Diary, Mar. 23, 1865. The next day he received another box of books and promptly sold them out that very day. See Kellogg Diary, Mar. 24, 1865, CHS.

73. Whitney did not arrive at Annapolis until late February, even though his parole date was November 30, 1864. See *Hartford Daily Courant,* Mar. 4, 1865. See also Bound Regimental Papers, RG 94, entries 112–15, Bound Records of the Union Volunteer Regiments, vol. 2, NA.

74. Bound Regimental Papers, RG 94, entries 112–15, Bound Records of the Union Volunteer Regiments, vol. 2, NA.

75. Bound Regimental Papers, RG 94, entries 112–115, Bound Records of the Union Volunteer Regiments, vol. 2, NA.

76. Blakeslee, e.g., received a leave of absence in mid-March for an additional thirty days. See Muster Rolls, Regimental Papers, RG 94, Box 147 [unbound papers], NA. According to the *Hartford Daily Courant* (Mar. 13, 1865), Blakeslee did not arrive at Camp Parole until early March anyway.

77. Jacob Bauer Diary, Jan. 18, 1865, MHI. Bauer received some sort of troubling news from his wife Emily, but he did not reveal the details in his diary. He wrote rather cryptically that the news from her would "probably [start] the new beginning of a new Era in my Life. God only knows what result it may have." See Jan. 22, 23 1865. On May 31 he implied that another man was involved: "I wonder what E means by answering that fool's letter, it makes me almost mad. I'll give him the correspondence he wants." Jacob Bauer Diary, MHI.

78. Jacob Bauer Diary, Mar. 9, 1865, MHI; "oh how dull," from Feb. 25, also "feeling low & blue," from Feb. 17. See Mar. 6: "Good many of our men are drunk and disorderly." Mar. 10: "two of our men [have] been put into cells for drunkenness[.]" Mar. 27: "A number of our men on guard [after having] stole whiskey and got drunk and a fighting [sic] resulting in their arrest and quarter[ed] in the guard house." Again, his postwar recollections paint a different picture. Of Roanoke, he wrote, "The soldiering here was an uninterrupted picnic. Very little duty, good quarters, good news from Grant and Sherman and our homes. We lived high on wild duck and goose and the best of army food." See Bauer, "Personal Experiences of the War," 20, PPM. Bauer also recollected sharing quarters with William Relyea, whom he said was a "fine cook."

79. The regiment received orders to move from Roanoke Island to New Bern in early March, arriving on the morning of March 5, 1865. See Bauer Diary, Mar. 5, 1865, MHI. John Burnham complained about Adj. John B. Clapp not returning to the regiment at New Bern, so Sgt. Bauer may have been filling in for him. Burnham wrote of Clapp, "He is needed more than any other officer in perfecting the records." John H. Burnham to Sarah B. Burnham, May 10, 1865, Burnham Papers, CSL.

80. For rumors of the regiment returning to active service, see Feb. 20, 1865; for mention of Sherman's visit, see Mar. 25, 1865, Jacob Bauer Diary, MHI.

81. Bauer describes Yellow Fever in camp in late April. Jacob Bauer Diary, Apr. 30, 1865, MHI.

82. Jacob Bauer Diary, Feb. 5, 1865, MHI.

83. Jacob Bauer Diary, Feb. 9, 1865, MHI.

84. Jacob Bauer Diary, Mar. 18, 1865, MHI; Bauer also counted the days of his enlistment on Mar. 23, Apr. 4, and May 13, 1865. Of the numerous examples of his worrying about his wife and family, one of the most poignant is, "I am thinking to[o] much of home and those at home worrying about me." May 17, 1865, MHI.

85. See Robert H. Kellogg to Silas Kellogg, Apr. 10, 1865, Kellogg Papers, CHS. Kellogg was en route to rejoin the regiment at New Bern. See also Kellogg Diary, Apr. 9, 10, 1865, CHS.

86. Robert H. Kellogg to Silas Kellogg, Apr. 10, 1865, Kellogg Papers, CHS.

87. Kellogg Diary, Apr. 17, 1865, CHS.

88. Kellogg Diary, Apr. 20, 21, 1865, CHS.

89. Robert H. Kellogg to Silas and Lucy C. Hale Kellogg, May 11, 1865, Kellogg Papers, CHS.

90. Kellogg was mustered out on June 1, 1865. He watched the remains of the 16th Connecticut return to Hartford on June 29: "Great day in Hartford on acct of the return of the 16th & 18th Conn. Vols. The 18th came first and rec'd a good welcome, then my old Reg., the veteran 16th came on a special train." Kellogg Diary, June 29, 1865, CHS; see also Robert H. Kellogg, CSR, NA. After witnessing the return of his regiment, Kellogg stopped writing in his diary for three months.

91. Robert H. Kellogg to Lucy C. Hale Kellogg, May 31, 1865, Kellogg Papers, CHS.

92. Kellogg Diary, June 10, 1865.

93. Ira E. Forbes, "Drowned While in Service," Forbes Collection, CSL.

94. George Hollands, "On the Massachusetts: The Midnight Collision on the Potomac Between the Massachusetts and the Black Diamond," *National Tribune,* May 14, 1914. Hollands complained that he never saw any press coverage, claiming that it "was not considered worth mentioning." The *New York Times* did publish an account of the collision on Apr. 27, 1865, reporting fifty dead from the crash. For local coverage, see *Hartford Daily Courant,* Apr. 28, 29, 1865.

95. The dead included Sgt. Samuel G. Grosvenor (Co. B), Henry S. Loomis (Co. B), Charles S. Robinson (Co. B), William T. Loomis (Co. D), Musician George W. Carter (Co. D), George N. Champlin (Co. I), and Edward Smith (Co. K). Among those who were "saved" and survived were Claudius C. Margerum, Henry B. Cook, Willard B. Sessions, and W. H. Knott. See "Collision of Black Diamond," Whitney Collection, CSL. Another survivor was Cpl. James B. Clancy (Co. A), who had suffered severely from scurvy during his imprisonment and almost lost his leg. He described himself as "one of the unfortunates to be on the transport *Massachusetts* which came in collision with the Black Diamond at the mouth of the Potomac River." He returned to Connecticut and lived until 1917, when he died at the age of seventy-one. See James B. Clancy to George Q. Whitney, Oct. 24, 1909, "James Bartholomew Clancy," Whitney Collection, CSL.

96. George N. Champlin to Oliver P. Champlin, Apr. 5, 1865, quoted in "Concluding Note," Champlin Diary, CSL.

97. See "George N. Champlin," Whitney Collection, CSL. Champlin's body was never recovered.

98. See Grosvenor Diary, Dec. 31, 1864, CHS; Daniel W. Grosvenor to Ira E. Forbes, Aug. 13, 1906, "Samuel E. and Joseph H. Grosvenor," Whitney Collection, CSL.

99. Martin V. Culver to Jonathan Culver, May 2, 1865, Culver Letters, private collection. See also Martin V. Culver, CSR, NA.

NOTES TO PAGES 186-187 • 333

100. Ira E. Forbes, "Drowned While in Service," Forbes Collection, CSL.

101. Jacob Bauer Diary, Apr. 12, 1865, MHI.

102. Jacob Bauer Diary, Apr. 17, 18, 22, 1865, MHI.

103. Jacob Bauer Diary, Apr. 24, 25, 1865, MHI.

104. Ira E. Forbes, "Company H in Service," Forbes Collection, CSL.

105. *Hartford Daily Courant*, Apr. 29, 1865.

106. Blakeslee states that Beach rejoined the regiment "only once" at New Bern but that his ill health caused him to take another leave of absence. See *History of the Sixteenth Connecticut Volunteers*, 101. Beach's CSR indicates that after Plymouth, he was on detached service in Pittsburgh and Philadelphia commanding the Draft Rendezvous stations in both cities. He had orders to return to the regiment on October 24, 1864, but it is not clear when he actually arrived to take command, nor when he left. On March 25, 1865, he was ordered to return to his prewar unit, the 4th U.S. Artillery, but four days later, this order was "suspended until further orders." See Frank Beach, CSR, NA. Robert Kellogg observed, "We saw little of him after the capture of the regiment at Plymouth, N.C. in April 1864." Robert H. Kellogg to Edward S. Holden, Dec. 13, 1909, Whitney Collection, CSL.

107. Blakeslee, *History of the Sixteenth Connecticut Volunteers*, 104–5. Those sickened by yellow fever included Pvt. Jasper A. Winslow (Co. H), who died on October 14, 1864, and Pvt. W. Chester Case (Co. H), who recovered but was discharged with disability in June 1865. See AGO 1889, 684.

108. Blakeslee, *History of the Sixteenth Connecticut Volunteers*, 105. Quote from *Hartford Daily Courant*, Dec. 17, 1864.

109. John H. Burnham, CSR, NA; see also John H. Burnham to Joseph H. Barnum, Mar. 31, 1865, John H. Burnham, CSR, NA. In a February letter, Burnham mentioned that he was "on duty" at New Bern and "living at present with Col. Upham at his camp." Upham commanded the 15th Connecticut. See John H. Burnham to Sarah B. Burnham, Feb. 14, 1865, Burnham Papers, CSL. Sheldon Thorpe confirms that Burnham was "Chief Provost Marshall at Newbern" until relieved in March 1865. See Thorpe, *History of the Fifteenth Connecticut Volunteers*, 341. It is not clear when Burnham was reunited with the 16th if at all before the unit mustered out in Hartford, as his Compiled Service Record does not indicate his presence with the regiment between December 30, 1864 (when he was "on the Records of Camp Parole, Maryland"), and February 22, 1865, when he became chief provost marshal. Also, according to his CSR, as late as May 1865, he was acting assistant inspector general "on Court Martial at New Berne, N. C." It is also true that the regimental records were incomplete during this time. See George D. Ruggles to the Commissioner of Pensions, June 29, 1881, John H. Burnham Pension Files, NA. Brig. Gen. Harland praised Burnham for his "invaluable" service; see Edward Harland to J. A. Judson, Mar. 14, 1865, OR, ser. 1, vol. 47, pt. 1, 984.

110. John H. Burnham to Sarah B. Burnham, Jan. 10, 1865, Burnham Papers, CSL. I initially misread Burnham's letter, believing that he was referring to the 16th. Unfortunately, this error made its way into a published article. See Lesley J. Gordon, "I Never Was a Coward: Questions of Bravery in a Civil War Regiment," in *More than a Contest of Armies: Essays on the Civil War Era*, ed. James Marten and A. Kristen Foster (Kent, OH: Kent State University Press, 2008), 144–74. However, on closer examination the date and context make it clear that Burnham was referring to the 11th C.V. and *not* the 16th C.V.

111. John H. Burnham to Sarah B. Burnham, Jan. 18, 186[5], Burnham Papers, CSL. Burnham dated this letter 1864, but based on its content and his location at New Bern, it must be from 1865.

112. *Hartford Daily Times,* Feb. 10, 1865. Robert H. Kellogg recorded reading this story: "The Hartford papers state that Lt. Col. B. has declined the Colonelcy of the 11th C. V. preferring to remain with the 'old Sixteenth.'" See Kellogg Diary, Feb. 10, 1865, CHS; see also William A. Buckingham to "Capt. Brown and other Line Officers of the 11th Conn. Vols," Sept. 24, 1864, Governors' Correspondence, CSL. Ironically, the 11th Connecticut would later be included in William Fox's top "Three Hundred Fighting Regiments," while the 16th Connecticut was not. See Fox, *Regimental Losses,* 181. The *Hartford Daily Times* (Dec. 20, 1864) falsely stated that Burnham had accepted the promotion. The *Hartford Daily Courant* (Dec. 20, 1864) stated, "Lieut. Col. John H. Burnham of the 16th C.V. to be colonel, vice Ward declined, with rank from Nov 17th."

113. John H. Burnham to Sarah B. Burnham, Mar. 9 [1865], Burnham Papers, CSL.

114. Colonel Upham reported 890 casualties, most of them captured, from the Kinston fight. See Charles L. Upham to H. H. Thomas, Mar. 11, 1865, *OR,* ser. 1, vol. 47, pt. 1, 998.

115. See "Report of Brigadier Edward Harland, U.S. Army Commanding, First Brigade, of Operations, Mar. 2–10," Edward Harland to J. A. Hudson, Mar. 14, 1865, *OR,* ser. 1, vol. 47, pt. 1, 986. See Thorpe, *History of the Fifteenth Connecticut Volunteers,* 87–92.

116. John H. Burnham to Sarah B. Burnham, Mar. 10, [1865], Burnham Papers, CSL. It is not clear exactly who any of these soldiers were to whom Burnham referred. The troops in Harland's First Brigade included the 9th New Jersey, 85th New York, 23rd Massachusetts, 2nd Massachusetts Heavy Artillery, and a battery from the 3rd New York Artillery. See *OR,* ser. 1, vol. 47, pt. 1, 984–86.

117. John H. Burnham to Sarah B. Burnham, May 10, 1865, Burnham Papers, CSL.

118. Jacob Bauer Diary, Apr. 28, 1865, MHI.

119. Jacob Bauer Diary, May 11, 1865, MHI.

120. Jacob Bauer Diary, May 12, 1865, MHI.

121. John H. Burnham to J. W. Atwell, June 6, 1865, John H. Burnham, CSR, NA.

122. *Hartford Daily Courant,* June 6, 1865.

123. Blakeslee, *History of the Sixteenth Connecticut Volunteers,* 106. Jacob Bauer seemed to think that the long delay in mustering out was due to the loss of papers when the unit was captured at Plymouth. See June 9, 1865, Jacob Bauer Diary, MHI. Bauer also stated, "The Recruit[s] will be transferred to the 6th and 7th Conn" (June 19, 1865). On June 22, Bauer noted that "3 of them run away." The *Courant* gave credence to Bauer's belief: "Major Pasco, of the 16th Connecticut arrived in this city yesterday, direct from Newbern, for the purpose of obtaining the necessary papers to enable the regiment to be mustered out of service. The regiment lost all of its papers at the time of its capture at Plymouth." See *Hartford Daily Courant,* June 14, 1865.

124. Jacob Bauer Diary, June 23, 1865, MHI.

125. Blakeslee, *History of the Sixteenth Connecticut Volunteers,* 106. See also *Hartford Daily Courant,* June 17, 1865.

126. *Hartford Daily Courant,* June 28, 1865.

127. S. M. Letcher to Gov. Buckingham, June 26, 1865, Muster Rolls Returns, Regimental Papers, RG 94, NA; the *Hartford Daily Courant,* June 28, 1865, confirmed these numbers.

128. *Hartford Daily Courant,* June 29, 1865. It is unclear why so few members of the regiment arrived at the depot in Hartford. The 1869 *Catalogue of Connecticut Volunteer Organizations* lists 707 total casualties from the unit, including 46 killed in action, 24 dead from battle wounds, 224 dead

from disease, 386 discharged prior to the muster-out, and 27 "missing at muster-out of regiment." This would make the 130 men present at the mustering out off by more than 150 men. See *Catalogue of Connecticut Volunteer Organizations*, 642. Former Pvt. Benjamin C. Ray (Co. F.) wrote in 1879, "The regiment went out 1000 strong, and returned home 135 officers and men, which we believe to be the smallest number of any regiment that returned to the State." Ray's casualty numbers differ only in killed in action and the number discharged. He estimated 46 killed in action, 24 died of wounds, 224 "died from disease," 336 "discharged prior to muster out of the regiment," and 27 "missing at muster out of the regiment." See Ray, *The Old Battle Flags*, 32. Quartermaster Sgt. Hiram Buckingham, who claimed to have participated in the parade down Main Street, remembered 150 men marching with him that day. See Hiram Buckingham to Ira Forbes, Mar. 3, 1907, "Hiram Buckingham," Whitney Collection, CSL. A 1931 newspaper clipping stated that the unit originally counted 1,348 men in its roster. See "Taps' Sounds for the 16th, Civil War Regiment [1931]," unnamed newspaper clipping, CHS. George Q. Whitney noted that 26 officers resigned from the unit and 2 were "dismissed," while 20 "served until mustered out." See Whitney Collection, CSL.

129. *Hartford Daily Courant*, June 14, 1865.

130. *Hartford Daily Courant*, June 29, 1865.

131. Blakeslee, *History of the Sixteenth Connecticut Volunteers*, 110.

132. Ezra Hall quoted in Blakeslee, *History of the Sixteenth Connecticut Volunteers*, 111–14. A native of Marlboro, Connecticut, Hall was a lawyer elected to the state senate in 1863 at the age of twenty-eight. See Ezra Hall, "Obituary Notice," *Memorials of Connecticut Judges and Attorneys As Printed in the Connecticut Reports*, vol. 44, 612–14. www.cslib.org/memorials/hallE.htm, accessed Feb. 8, 2008; see also Sherman Adams, "The Bench and the Bar," in Trumbull, *Memorial History of Hartford County*, 1:134. Hall further told the soldiers, "My blood chills when I remember that more than two hundred of this regiment were starved and murdered in Southern prisons—imaging more perfect the hell of secession and the barbarism of Southern institutions and chivalry, than any other page of the war." No mention was made of the men saving their colors at Plymouth, although this story may not yet have been widely known.

133. Details of the regiment's return from Blakeslee, *History of the Sixteenth Connecticut Volunteer*, 109–16; also *Hartford Daily Courant*, June 30, 1865. Burnham's farewell, issued as "Special Orders No. 10," reprinted in Blakeslee, *History of the Sixteenth Connecticut Volunteers*, 115.

134. "Heroes," "heroism," "self-sacrifice," and "gallant" were all words found throughout this long article. See *Hartford Daily Courant*, June 30, 1865.

135. *Hartford Daily Courant*, June 30, 1865.

136. *Hartford Daily Courant*, June 30, 1865. Some openly questioned the notion of "rebel cruelty." Just a few days before the 16th arrived home, the Democratic *Hartford Times* challenged the *Courant's* earlier statement that "thousands of Union soldiers died in Andersonville, Salisbury, and in other rebel prisons, simply from ill treatment and starvation." The *Times* insisted, "We don't know that. Nor do you know it. If you do please give us the names of a few of the 'thousands of soldiers' who have *starved* to death." This exchange was reprinted in the *Hartford Daily Courant* on June 27, 1865, with a long response by Dorence Atwater, who wrote in disbelief, "Can they make the public believe that the 65,000 that have perished in Southern prisons did not die for want of proper treatment?" See *Hartford Daily Courant*, June 27, 1865. With the regiment's arrival home, the *Courant* reacted:

"The 16th boys brought home with them bitter experiences in the Andersonville prison pens, and express great indignation at the *Hartford Times* on account of its attempted defense of the rebel authorities by claiming Union prisoners were not starved to death. We hope the *Times* will not delay in examining of these witnesses, and give its readers the testimony obtained in full." See *Hartford Daily Courant*, June 30, 1865. The issue flared up again in July, when a member of the 16th Connecticut responded to the *Times*' denial. According to the *Courant*, he was "a truthful young man, who shared in the horrors of the rebel prison pens at Andersonville and Florence for ten months." The soldier wrote: "I have heard my fellow comrades in their dying moments call upon their mothers and sisters to give them just one more piece of pie or cake, for they *were very hungry;* and others I have heard in their delirium call upon their Maker to send a just punishment upon their captors for the cruelties practiced upon them, and would then turn and say—'*I am starved, actually starved to death.*'" The former POW stated, "The sufferings undergone by us no pen can write, no pencil portray, and no tongue can tell; they were terrible." Quoted in the *Hartford Daily Courant*, July 17, 1865. Emphasis in original. The *Courant* commented that the fault lay with Jefferson Davis and Gen. Lee, who both "sanctioned the crime." For more on this topic of northern prisoner suffering, see Cloyd, *Haunted by Atrocity.*

137. Blakeslee, *History of the Sixteenth Connecticut Volunteers,* 106.

CHAPTER NINE

1. Chipman, *The Tragedy of Andersonville,* 164–66, 251–52, 327–31. The trial commenced on August 23 and ended on October 18, 1865. Wirz was charged with "combining, confederating, and conspiring, together with John H. Winder, Richard B. Winder, Joseph [Isaiah H.] White, W. S. Winder, R. R. Stevenson, and others unknown, to injure the health and destroy the lives of soldiers in the military service of the United States, then held and being prisoners of war within the lines of the so-called Confederate States, and in the military prisons thereof, to the end that the armies of the United States might be weakened and impaired, in violation of the laws and customs of war." He was also charged with "Murder in violation of the laws and customs of war." See Chipman, *The Tragedy of Andersonville,* 32, 35.

2. Robert H. Kellogg to Lucy C. Hale Kellogg, Aug. 16, 1865, Kellogg Papers, CHS. Kellogg also wrote about visiting Judge Advocate Chipman's house and hearing about the government's case against Wirz before he gave his testimony.

3. Robert H. Kellogg to Silas Kellogg, Aug. 21, 1865, Kellogg Papers, CHS.

4. Chipman, *The Tragedy of Andersonville,* 164.

5. Robert Kellogg, "Testimony," in Chipman, *The Tragedy of Andersonville,* 165.

6. Kellogg Diary, Oct. 4, 1865, CHS.

7. Robert Kellogg, "Testimony," in Chipman, *The Tragedy of Andersonville,* 223. However, in his book, Kellogg recounted Wirz's cruelties, including his banning rations when a tunnel was discovered and threatening to unleash a battery on the helpless prisoners upon learning of a new escape plot. See Kellogg, *Life and Death in Rebel Prisons,* 87, 105–6, 177–78. At one point, he accused Wirz of masterminding "cruel inventions to enhance our misery." And he referred to Wirz as "our inhuman prison commandant." See Kellogg, *Life and Death in Rebel Prisons,* 341, 228. In the 1867

edition, Kellogg added a separate appendix on the Wirz trial. Marvel is sharply critical of Kellogg and his testimony. See Marvel, *Andersonville*, 103–4, 244.

8. Andrew J. Spring "Testimony," in Chipman, *The Tragedy of Andersonville*, 173. Spring was asked whether he knew of any "particular and special acts of cruelty committed by Capt. Wirz personally." See "List of Questions sent to Andrew Spring to Answer in the Trial of Henry Wirz," Andrew J. Spring Papers, CSL.

9. Augustus Moesner, "Testimony," in Chipman, *The Tragedy of Andersonville*, 327–28.

10. Augustus Moesner, "Testimony," in Chipman, *The Tragedy of Andersonville*, 224–26. It is perhaps noteworthy that, years later, Moesner corresponded with Whitney and made no mention of his behavior at Andersonville. Moesner and Buckingham both received government pensions. Spring's widow Julia applied but was denied because there was not enough proof "to show incurrence of or treatment for any disability of the soldier" and because of her "manifest inability to show that his death from pneumonia on Jan. 4, 1866 was due to his military service." Andrew J. Spring Pension File, NA; see also Hiram Buckingham Pension File, Augustus Moesner Pension File, NA.

11. Cloyd, *Haunted by Atrocity*, 34.

12. Jacob Bauer Diary, June 30, 1865, MHI.

13. Recent historians who have explored the Gilded Age's changing value system, particularly its altered notions of individual "success" and hyper-masculine identity, include Scott Sandage, *Born Losers: A History of Failure in America* (Cambridge: Harvard University Press, 2005); James Marten, *Sing Not War: The Lives of Union and Confederate Veterans in Gilded Age America* (Chapel Hill: University of North Carolina Press, 2011); Richard Stott, *Jolly Fellows: Male Milieus in 19th Century America* (Baltimore: Johns Hopkins Press, 2009); and Greenberg, *Manifest Manhood*. For more on Civil War veterans and uneasy adjustment to postwar life, see Marten, *Sing Not War*; Dean, *Shook Over Hell*, 206–8; Stuart McConnell, *Glorious Contentment: The Grand Army of the Republic, 1865–1900* (Chapel Hill: University of North Carolina, 1992), 14–16; Linderman, *Embattled Courage*, 266–74. Linderman argues that "hardened" veterans came home with different values, while civilians clung to prewar ones. In the case of the 16th C.V., I argue that these men struggled to align their prewar (and early war) expectations of military service with their wartime and postwar realities.

14. Jacob Bauer Diary, July 5, 12, 1865, MHI.

15. See 10th Census of the United States, 1880: Population Schedule, Berlin, Hartford County, CT, at ancestry.com, accessed June 22, 2009.

16. Kellogg Diary, Oct. 2, 1865, CHS.

17. Kellogg Diary, Oct. 18, 1865, CHS.

18. Kellogg Diary, Oct. 26, 1865, CHS. Kellogg recounted that he had "sat up with Deacon Lee last night" on Oct. 17. Nine days later Lee died. See Kellogg Diary, Oct. 17, 1865, CHS.

19. Kellogg Diary, Oct. 25, 1865, CHS.

20. Kellogg Diary, Nov. 3, 1865, CHS.

21. Biographical information from Ira Forbes, "Robert Hale Kellogg," Whitney Collection, CSL. Amelia C. Gallup was fifteen years old and residing in Norwich with what appears to be her widowed mother Emily and four older siblings. See 8th Census of the United States, 1860: Population Schedule, Norwich, New London, CT, at ancestry.com, accessed Apr. 16, 2009. In 1870, the Kelloggs, then childless, were living in Concord, New Hampshire. See 9th Census of the

United States, 1870: Population Schedule, Concord, Merrimack, NH, at ancestry.com, accessed Apr. 16, 2009. When he was living in Manchester in 1879, Kellogg served in the Connecticut General Assembly and, according to Ira Forbes, "was the originator of the Tramp law which was passed by the Legislature in 1879 and served effectively in reducing the Tramp Evil in Connecticut." See Ira E. Forbes, "The Sixteenth in Public Affairs," Forbes Collection, CSL. The "Tramp Law" was meant to combat transient beggars, mainly men and often veterans, who in the aftermath of the Depression of 1873 were especially desperate. The Connecticut "Tramp Law," similar to one passed by New York, punished begging with imprisonment but notably did not apply to women or minors under the age of sixteen. Kellogg and Forbes seemed to lack sympathy for the fact that so many of these "tramps" were fellow veterans. The word *tramp* originated with marching and "tramping" in the Civil War. See Dan W. DeLuca, *The Old Leather Man: Historical Accounts of a Connecticut and New York Legend* (Middletown, CT: Wesleyan University Press, 2008), 17. In 1880, the Kelloggs were still in Manchester and had three daughters, Florence, Emilie, Annie, and a son, Rossiter. Robert's occupation was listed as "bookkeeper." Amelia's mother and two white female servants were also living with the Kelloggs. See 10th Census of the United States, 1880: Population Schedule, Manchester, Hartford, CT, at ancestry.com, accessed Apr. 16, 2009.

22. Ira Forbes, "Robert Hale Kellogg," Whitney Collection, CSL.

23. Emariah Gates died on December 4, 1874, in New London; she was thirty-five years old. See Oliver Gates Pension File, NA. See also 9th Census of the United States, 1870: Population Schedule, New London, CT, at ancestry.com, accessed May 13, 2009.

24. Gates described suffering from scurvy and rheumatism in his Andersonville diary, Aug. 7, 1864, CHS. According to the 1900 U.S. census, Oliver and Abbie Gates were residing with her mother, seventy-one-year-old Charlotte Fowler. See 9th Census of the United States, 1870: Population Schedule, New London, CT, at ancestry.com, accessed May 13, 2009.

25. Oliver Gates Pension File, NA.

26. Whitney claimed that Cuzner "married Ellen Van Dorn of Meriden, Conn July 8, 1865 that being the day the Regiment was discharged in Hartford, Conn." See "John B. Cuzner," Whitney Collection, CSL. July 8 was the day the regiment was "paid and discharge papers given." George Q. Whitney to Edward Burnham, July 25, 1908, "Edward Burnham," Whitney Collection, CSL.

27. By 1870, the Cuzners were living in Bridgeport. See 9th Census of the United States, Bridgeport, Fairfield, CT, at ancestry.com, accessed Sept. 13, 2008. The 1880 census listed the family in Bridgeport with their daughter Jennie, then five years old. See 10th Census of the United States, 1880: Population Schedule, Bridgeport, Fairfield, CT, at ancestry.com, accessed Sept. 13, 2008. See also "John B. Cuzner," Whitney Collection, CSL.

28. *Hartford Daily Times*, Nov. 14, 1911. Forbes wrote for the *Times* for several years. He also taught at a military academy in New Hampshire for a year before he began his journalism career in 1872.

29. A. Spalding, *Illustrated Popular Biography of Connecticut* (Hartford: Press of the Case, Lockwood, and Brainard Co., 1891), 187; also "Ira Emory Forbes," in *The Obituary Record of Graduates of Yale University Deceased from June, 1910, to July, 1915* (New Haven: Yale University, 1915), 233–35. Not much is known about Sarah Rhodes Short Forbes except that she was born in England in May 1848. She was a devout Christian like her husband. In 1894, she can be found serving as president of "King's Daughters," a women's prayer group that met regularly at the Fourth Congregational Church.

See *Geer's Hartford City Directory* (1894), 761. The Forbes had no children. See 10th Census of the United States, 1880: Population Schedule, Hartford, Hartford County, CT; 12th Census of the United States, 1900: Population Schedule, Hartford, Hartford County, at ancestry.com, Oct. 18, 2009. For more on Forbes and his efforts to tell his story of the regiment, see Lesley J. Gordon, "Ira Forbes's War," in Stephen Berry, ed., *Weirding the War: Stories from the Civil War's Ragged Edges* (Athens: University of Georgia Press, 2011), 340–66.

30. Mary E. Lee, General Affidavit, Sept. 17, 1877, in "Declaration for Widow's Pension and Increase," in Holcomb Family Papers, SBHS. See also Richard Henry Lee Papers, SBHS.

31. Laun, *The Holcomb Collection*, 83.

32. Deacon Asel H. Rice quoted in Laun, *The Holcomb Collection*, 84.

33. Robbins appears in the 1870 census residing with his parents in Plainville. See 9th Census of the United States, 1870: Population Schedule, Plainville, Hartford County, CT, at ancestry.com, accessed July 16, 2011; "clock shop" from 10th Census of the United States, 1880: Population Schedule, Waterbury, New Haven County, CT, at ancestry.com, accessed July 16, 2011. By 1880, the Robbins had two young children, Kate (6) and Arthur (6 months). The 1890 census notes the Robbinses married in 1868. See 11th Census of the United States, 1890: Population Schedule, Waterbury, New Haven County, CT, ancestry.com, accessed July 16, 2011.

34. "Frank Woodbridge Cheney," Whitney Collection, CSL.

35. Frank W. Cheney to Joseph R. Hawley, no date, in Learned, "The Letters of Mary Bushnell Cheney and Frank Woodbridge Cheney," SC, 208, 231. Ward did gain commission as a lieutenant but died in the Philippines on Jan. 6, 1900, while leading a frontal attack on a heavily outnumbered enemy position.

36. Learned, "The Letters of Mary Bushnell Cheney and Frank Woodbridge Cheney," SC, 253–54.

37. "Military History of Col. Francis Beach, U.S.A.," in Whitney Collection, CSL.

38. "Frank Beach," Whitney Collection, CSL.

39. Ira Forbes, "The Fall of Plymouth in North Carolina 44 Years ago," *Hartford Daily Times,* Apr. 20, 1908.

40. Ira Forbes, "Capture of Plymouth," 11, Forbes Collection, CSL. A 1908 biography of Beach praised his "reckless bravery" while trying to rally his men at Antietam. See Kinney, "The Memorial History of Hartford," in Trumbull, *The Memorial History of Hartford*, 1:98, note 1.

41. Joseph H. Barnum to William A. Barnum, Jan. 10, 1866, Governors' Correspondence, CSL.

42. Forbes was also complimentary of Barnum's journalism talents: "He made that paper a force in Hartford for many years. Captain Barnum handled a trenchant pen and was a man of more than common intellectual gifts." See Forbes, "Joseph Hall Barnum," Whitney Collection, CSL. Forbes later noted, "The order book and Company Rolls covering the period that Captain Barnum was in Command at Roanoke Island, the nucleus of the Regiment being present then, are in the possession of Charles H. Barnum, the only son of Captain Barnum." Forbes was hopeful that these papers would eventually be entrusted "with the Regiment some day." See Ira E. Forbes, "Company H in Service," Forbes Collection, CSL. There is no evidence that this ever happened.

43. Frank W. Cheney to George Q. Whitney, Aug. 20, 1902, Whitney Collection, CSL.

44. "Austin David Thompson," "Harrison Woodford," "William H. Relyea," Whitney Collection, CSL.

45. "Descriptive Report," Whitney Collection, CSL. George's older brother Amos is credited

with founding Pratt and Whitney. George Q. Whitney to Secretary of War, Sept. 1, 1904, Whitney Collection, CSL. These materials, totaling some five shelf feet of photographs, correspondence, newspaper clippings, and biographical sketches, make up the Whitney Collection at the Connecticut State Library and were donated in 1925. See Descriptive Report, Whitney Collection, CSL. Each biographical sheet has lines titled "Deserted," "Captured," "Escaped from Prison," and "Remarks," which often include additional biographical, especially genealogical, information.

46. Ira E. Forbes, "Sixteenth C.V. at Andersonville," *Connecticut Courant*, Mar. 15, 1906, clipping, Forbes Collection, CSL. Whitney and Forbes also sought to correct errors they found in the AGO reports. At one point, Whitney informed the Secretary of War that his own record was wrong: "Our state has made a Roster that has many errors in it, for instance my own is all right, except it says Paroled Nov 30th, 1864, when the fact is that I was transferred from Florence to Libby in Feb 1865 and released at the obstructions of the James river on Feb 24, 1865 and at our Adjutant Genl's Office I am informed they get that information from the War Dept." See George Q. Whitney to Secretary of War, Sept. 1, 1904, Whitney Collection, CSL.

47. Walter E. Smith to George Q. Whitney, Dec. 10, 1905, Whitney Collection, CSL. Whitney wrote of Smith that he was "a physical wreck when he reached home from the prison life in December." See "Walter E. Smith," Whitney Collection, CSL.

48. William Wakefield to George Q. Whitney, Feb. 26, 1911, Whitney Collection, CSL. Wakefield's age according to his enlistment was twenty-five; however, he gave the year of birth to be Apr. 29, 1835, which would have made him twenty-seven. It is not clear which date is correct. Wakefield asked Whitney to contact his congressman for assistance. Wakefield further explained to Whitney that his mother "always told me I was born in 1835" but that he had no way to prove it "unless the age could be found in some of the old school records." See William Wakefield to George Q. Whitney, Dec. 20, 1908, Whitney Collection, CSL.

49. In the case of Asbury Jobes (Co. D), Whitney called him a "good soldier and faithful, when there was no liquor in camp." But after the war, Whitney stated, "He has been a bum and at times a hard worker since his discharge, and had been of late years at Noroton a while and at Suffield off and on." Whitney explained that he attended the funeral more for the benefit of Asbury's brother, Richard, who had also served in the regiment. Nonetheless, Richard was touched by Whitney's attendance: "He expressed surprise at my being there, and tried to thank me. I told him no one need to be surprised at anything I did." See George Q. Whitney to Frank W. Cheney, Oct. 20, 1906, Whitney Collection, CSL.

50. Frank Cheney to George Q. Whitney, "about Dec. 1, 1900," Whitney Collection, CSL.

51. Frank Cheney to George Q. Whitney, Mar. 6, 1901, Whitney Collection, CSL.

52. Frank Cheney to George Q. Whitney, Feb. 1, 1902, Whitney Collection, CSL.

53. Mrs. Benjamin F. Costes[?] to George Q. Whitney, Feb. 20, 1905, Whitney Collection, CSL.

54. Mrs. E. J. Bannon to Mary Bushnell Cheney, Dec. 2, 1910, Whitney Collection, CSL.

55. Mary Bushnell Cheney to George Q. Whitney, Dec. 16, 1910, Whitney Collection, CSL.

56. George Q. Whitney to Frank Cheney, Sept. 20, 1906, Whitney Collection, CSL. Capt. Samuel Brown's sister thanked Whitney for sharing stories of her slain brother, explaining that although her family read all they could in the local newspapers during the war, "I know but little." See Fanny Brown to George Q. Whitney, Feb. 23, 1909, Whitney Collection, CSL. On Civil War veterans writing

their stories, reminiscing, and "yearning to be heard," see Blight, *Race and Reunion*, 158–70, 172–73, 179–92; quote from 179.

57. *Hartford Daily Courant*, Nov. 17, 1906. Samuel Griswold wrote, "I am sure none have done more for the records of our gallant 16th than George Q. Whitney." See Samuel J. Griswold to George Q. Whitney, Dec. 11, 1906, "Samuel Judson Griswold," Whitney Collection, CSL. See also Thomas Crossley to George Q. Whitney, Oct. 14, 1913, "Thomas Crossley," Whitney Collection, CSL.

58. "Alvin Porter Cole," Whitney Collection, CSL. Whitney wrote this after Cole's death in 1914. As stated above, Whitney was concerned with making corrections to the state's AGO records published in 1869 and 1889, which he deemed insufficient and filled with errors. Sometimes his changes were based on his own judgment; other times, on the aging memory of a soldier or other corroborating records. In one instance, the AGO records from 1869 and 1889 listed the date of Pvt. Thomas Lee Crownishield's discharge date as Dec. 18, 1862. But, Whitney wrote, "He was discharged at Falmouth Va Dec. 11, 1862 and received his pay in Washington D.C. Dec 17th so his Discharge reads by me." Whitney dated this statement "Jan 18, 1911," and signed his name with the title "Sec'y." See "Thomas Lee Crownishield," Whitney Collection, CSL.

59. After the war, Amadon served as a state legislator but spent most of his time raising a family and working as a machinist in his shop and foundry in Stafford. He died in 1904. See "William Perry Amadon," Whitney Collection, CSL. Also see 10th Census of the United States, 1860: Population Schedule, Stafford, Tolland County, CT, at ancestry.com, accessed June 17, 2009.

60. Alpheus A. Rockwell to George Q. Whitney, Oct. 11, 1904, Whitney Collection, CSL.

61. See "Alpheus A. Rockwell," Whitney Collection, CSL.

62. Hattie Skewes to George Q. Whitney, Nov. 16, 1910, Whitney Collection, CSL.

63. Alpheus A. Rockwell to George Q. Whitney, Dec. 9, 1905, Whitney Collection, CSL.

64. Undated newspaper clipping, "John L. Hart," Whitney Collection, CSL.

65. Mary Hart to George Q. Whitney, Jan. 23 [1916], Whitney Collection, CSL.

66. "John L. Hart," Whitney Collection, CSL.

67. Florence J. Tryon to George Q. Whitney, Dec. 11, 1919, "Lewis M. Holcomb," Whitney Collection, CSL. See also Florence J. Tryon to Charles H. Case, Nov. 25, 1919, in "Lewis M. Holcomb," Whitney Collection, CSL.

68. Tryon further mentioned reading Kellogg's memoirs, as well as John Ransom's. "It is hard to believe that such horrible things can be true," she wrote. "You must have an extraordinary constitution to withstand such an experience." Florence J. Tryon to George Q. Whitney, Nov. 26, 1919, in "Lewis M. Holcomb," Whitney Collection, CSL.

69. Florence J. Tryon to George Q. Whitney, Dec. 14, 1919, in "Lewis M. Holcomb," Whitney Collection, CSL.

70. Florence J. Tryon to George Q. Whitney, Feb. 7, 1920, in "Lewis M. Holcomb," Whitney Collection, CSL.

71. Florence J. Tryon to George Q. Whitney, Dec. 14, 1919, in "Lewis M. Holcomb," Whitney Collection, CSL.

72. "Jasper Hamilton Bidwell," Whitney Collection, CSL.

73. "James Richard Bradley," Whitney Collection, CSL. The AGO claims that Bradley was paroled on February 28, then discharged on June 28, 1865. See AGO 1889, 624.

74. Forbes estimated that he had completed "700 sketches of Sixteenth Regiment men" in July 1907. See Forbes Diary, July 23, 1907, CSL. The final number that he authored is unknown.

75. For example, Forbes wrote Webster E. Burbank, in Suffield, hoping to find out what happened to his comrade, Pvt. Leverett L. Burbank. But Webster could only respond, "He is not of my family only a distant cousin," and recommended that Forbes instead contact Benjamin Burbank, a brother. Forbes ended up writing, "He is supposed to have died some years ago in Pennsylvania. No definite record of that event has been obtainable." See "Leverett L. Burbank," Whitney Collection, CSL. The 1880 census shows an "L. Burbank" residing in Springfield, married with three children. He was employed as a farm laborer. See 10th Census of the United States, 1880: Population Schedule, Springfield, Bradford County, PA, at ancestry.com, accessed Aug. 5, 2009.

76. In the case of Pvt. Burton Hubbard, who perished in Andersonville, Forbes stated, "He was a faithful soldier to his regiment." See Ira Forbes, "Burton Hubbard," Whitney Collection, CSL.

77. According to the 1880 census, Horace Forbes was residing in Eureka, Furnas, Nebraska, with his wife and children. There is no record of him in subsequent census. See 10th Census of the United States, 1880: Population Schedule, Eureka, Furnas, NE, at ancestry.com, accessed June 9, 2009.

78. One day in 1906, he wrote in his diary, "On Saturday and Sunday I saw all of the Sixteenth men, who belong in New Haven, the visit being on behalf of the Whitney plan for statistics. While in New London two weeks ago last Sunday I saw Oliver W. Gates and obtained a good story from him. The same day, returning by way of New Haven, I visited Lieutenant Henry Bristol in Westville and was more than rewarded for the effort. Last Sunday afternoon after having found the members of the Regiment I attended __ service at the old Center Church on the green." Forbes Diary, Mar. 14, 1906, CSL. The next day, Forbes was thrilled to receive a letter from Dr. Edmund Pease, who had served as assistant surgeon in the regiment before being transferred to one of the USCT units. The men in the 16th had lost track of him for some thirty years. See Forbes Diary, Mar. 17, 1906, CSL. Many of the veterans contacted also expressed gratitude for Whitney and Forbes's efforts. See, e.g., Robert J. Holmes to Ira Forbes, Aug. 15, 1906, in "Robert J. Holmes," Whitney Collection, CSL.

79. Forbes Diary, June 26, 1906, CSL. Sometimes Forbes's biographies were only one page long; others ran several pages. Occasionally, Forbes and Whitney both contributed to a single soldier's entry. See, e.g., "Waldo James Gates," for which Forbes authored the narrative but Whitney corrected Gates's birth date and made other notes. In Whitney Collection, CSL.

80. Ira Forbes to Frank W. Cheney, June 21, 1906, Whitney Collection, CSL. Cheney responded by sending ten dollars to Forbes and forwarding the letter to Whitney.

81. Forbes Diary, July 8, 1906, CSL.

82. Forbes Diary, July 8, 1906, CSL.

83. Forbes Diary, July 16, 1906, CSL.

84. George Q. Whitney to Frank W. Cheney, Dec. 1, 1906, Georg Q. Whitney Collection, CSL. It is not clear specifically to what Whitney refers. He mentions setting Forbes on "C.A. Q. Norton's record day before yesterday and he has just sent me the results of his thorough investigation. I want some other facts to go with his and at a proper time I propose to spring the trap publicly and let him feel the pinch."

85. Samuel M. Fenn to Ira E. Forbes, Sept. 7, 1906, in "Samuel M. Fenn," Whitney Collection, CSL.

86. Linderman discusses how simple survival became "a source of pride" for veterans. See

Linderman, *Embattled Courage,* 272. Historians have paid increasing attention to the active role veterans played in changing the public memory of the war. Memory of prisoners has gotten less attention, except by scholars of Andersonville who dismiss many postwar accounts of the prison as exaggerated and overly politicized. See, e.g., Linderman, *Embattled Courage,* 275, 277; Hess, *The Union Soldier in Battle,* 187–88; Marvel, *Andersonville,* 323–24; and Blight, *Race and Reunion,* 152–54, 242–43. Two notable exceptions are Douglas Gardner, "Andersonville and American Memory: Civil War Prisoners and Narratives of Suffering and Redemption" (Ph.D. diss., Miami University, 1998), and, more recently, Cloyd, *Haunted by Atrocity.* Frances Clarke has stressed the virtuous suffering of northern veterans in *War Stories.* See also Janney, *Remembering the Civil War,* 107–8. Janney argues that Union veterans were unwilling to "forget" their animosity toward their former foes (5–6).

87. Blakeslee, *History of the Sixteenth Connecticut Volunteers,* 3.

88. Blakeslee, *History of the Sixteenth Connecticut Volunteers,* 5.

89. See AGO 1862.

90. Pvt. Charles L. Taylor kept his pieces of the flag, and they remained with his effects as late as 2000, when his descendants put them up for sale through J. C. Devine, Inc., Auctioneers and Appraisers. A flag fragment is also preserved in Robert H. Kellogg's Collection at the Connecticut State Library.

91. Kellogg described, "Color Sergeant Latimer first removing the silver inscription plate from that of the State flag. This he secreted on his person and carried through Andersonville, sewed into his lapel of his uniform coat. When finally exchanged about a year later, in the joy of getting clean clothes at Annapolis, he threw away his lousy old coat with the silver plate sewed up in it, and never saw it again, to his undying regret." See Robert H. Kellogg, "The Siege of Plymouth, N.C.," 7–8, Kellogg Papers, CHS. It does seem significant that, as in the story of the petition at Andersonville, Kellogg placed himself at the center of the narrative. For all his foibles and controversies with his comrades, Forbes did not do this in his own construction of regimental narratives.

92. Norman L. Hope, "The Story of Andersonville," Norman L. Hope Collection, CSL.

93. Robert H. Kellogg, "The Siege of Plymouth, N.C.," 7–8, Kellogg Papers, CHS.

94. *History of Battle-Flag Day, Sept. 17, 1879* (Hartford, CT: Lockwood and Merritt, 1880), 21.

95. *History of Battle-Flag Day,* 20, 21, 24, 32.

96. *Hartford Courant,* Sept. 18, 1879.

97. William G. Domonell, "The 16th Connecticut Regiment's Unique Flag," *My Country* 29, no. 3 (Summer 1995): 6. See also Samuel G. Buckingham, *The Life of William A. Buckingham* (Springfield, MA: W. F. Adams Publishers, 1894), 252; Guy Lemieux, "The Connecticut Hard Luck Regiment Lives Again," unpublished typescript in possession of the author.

98. Jacob Bauer, "Personal Experiences of the War," 11, PPM.

99. Ira E. Forbes, "Andersonville," Forbes Collection, CSL.

100. George Q. Whitney to Frank W. Cheney, Dec. 1, 1906, Whitney Collection, CSL.

101. See, e.g., "Address," Whitney Collection, CSL. More recent examples include the mayor of Sharpsburg, Maryland, reciting the flag story during a public ceremony in 1995 honoring a local church with a stained glass window depicting the famous "Prisoner of War flag." See Christopher Yeager, "Presentation," Sept. 17, 1995, copy in author's possession; Pat Holland, "Civil War Secrets Hidden in Stained Glass," unnamed newspaper clipping [1997], in author's possession. A regimental

history of the 85th New York claims that they, too, stripped their flag and tore it into shreds to be distributed among the men. See Mahood, *The Plymouth Pilgrims*, 185.

102. Livermore, *My Story*, 50–51.

103. Buckingham, *The Life of William Buckingham*, 252.

104. I have not been able to confirm the identity of Frank O'Brien and G. W. "Mortie," Williams. The Alabama artillery unit at Plymouth included the "Montgomery (Alabama) True Blues." Clearly, O'Brien and Burnham could not have met in New York in 1884, although perhaps they met years earlier. See Frank O'Brien, "The Story of a Flag and the Strange Bringing Together of Its Captors and Defenders, As Related by One of the Former," *Blue and Gray Magazine* 2, no. 2 (Aug. 1893): 143–45.

105. *New York Times*, Sept. 18, 1887.

106. This attitude fits with much of the postwar commemoration emphasis on celebrating common soldiers' courage and sacrifice, avoiding any specific discussion of the conflict's causes. The best exploration of these attitudes is Blight, *Race and Reunion*, 4–5, 189. Janney expands on Blight, arguing that reunion did not necessarily mean reconciliation, in *Remembering the Civil War*, 3–4; 160–96.

107. George Q. Whitney to Robert H. Kellogg, Sept. 12, 1906, Kellogg Papers, CHS. Forbes's nervousness, of course, may have been a clear sign of the trauma suffered from the war and the increasing mental debilitation that eventually led to his commitment. It is significant that Whitney found Forbes too nervous to talk about saving the flags at Plymouth. Relyea, however, seemed to accept Fowler's story. See Relyea, *16th Connecticut Volunteer Infantry*, 148–50. On July 8, 1865, the state flag "formerly belonging to the 16th Regt. Conn. Vols." was "received at Hartford, Conn, this 8th day of July 1865 of Bvt. Lt. Col. CC. Gilbert, USA, Act, Asst. Pro. Mar. Genl & Chief mustering officers, Conn." See Muster Rolls Returns, Regimental Papers, RG 94, Box 147 [unbound papers], NA. Another retelling of the flag story can be found in Steven W. Hill, *Connecticut Battle Flags: The Civil War* (Hamden: League of Women Voters of Connecticut Education Fund, 1986).

108. Ray, *The Old Battle Flags*, 31. Ray served as a private in Co. F and was wounded in the hip at Antietam. His occupation upon enlistment was "printer." According to the Whitney Collection, Ray suffered from the Antietam wound "all his life" and died from "cancer of the throat and starvation" in Jan. 1915. He also "learned his trade in Hartford at the *Hartford Times*." The AGO lists Ray as mustering out with the regiment on June 24, 1865; Whitney claimed that Ray was discharged for disability on December 10, 1862. See "Benjamin C. Ray," Whitney Collection, CSL; and AGO 1889, 630. Ray is buried in Spring Grove Cemetery. Findagrave.com lists Ray's date of death as Jan. 20, 1915 (accessed Dec. 10, 2008).

109. See "A Divine Hospital," *Save Historic Antietam Foundation Newsletter* (June 2007), http://shaf.org/2007/06/15/a-divine-hospital/, accessed Apr. 1, 2011. For a long time, Sharpsburg residents mistakenly believed that the church windows were created by Louis Comfort Tiffany. It was the redesigned flag, of course, that Tiffany of New York designed in 1879. Pat Holland, Sharpsburg's Town Clerk, discovered with the help of Scott Holmes, a direct descendent of Musician Robert Holmes, and Paul Parvis, formerly of the CHS, the Plymouth/Andersonville flag story behind the "The Connecticut Windows" in 1995 in time for the annual Heritage Festival. See "The Connecticut Windows," *Sharpsburg Heritage Festival '95* (Sharpsburg, MD: Sharpsburg Heritage Festival, 1995), 10; Pat Holland, "Background Information About the Stained-Glass 'Connecticut Windows' in the Christ Reformed Church," undated press release, in author's possession. The 11th Connecticut also has a smaller window signifying its participation in the battle.

110. *Catalogue of Connecticut Volunteer Organizations,* 641. Benjamin Ray used nearly the same wording in his 1879 description of the 16th at Antietam, *The Old Battle Flags,* 31.

111. Shafer was testifying in support of the service of Dudley Denison. See Testimony of W. J. Shafer, Dec. 4, 1900, in "Dudley A. Denison," Whitney Collection, CSL. This certification further stated, "These facts are recorded and preserved for the benefit of all who may cherish his memory." Again, it seems significant that Shaffer repeats with slightly different wording the description from the 1869 Connecticut Catalog and Ray's *The Old Battle Flags.*

112. Robbins, "Some Recollections," 14, CHS.

113. McGlone discusses divergent "constructed memories" and how individual memories, particularly of traumatic events, can be "rescripted" in "Deciphering Memories," 420–23, 438.

114. See, e.g., *Hartford Courant,* Feb. 16, 1910; *Hartford Times,* Aug. 1, 1908; Aug. 29, 1913; *Hartford Courant,* Sept. 17, 1907; *Hartford Post,* Aug. 29, 1912; Hartford newspaper clipping [1912], Kellogg Papers, CHS. In 1912, a Hartford paper stated that at Portsmouth the regiment "achieved a reputation for soldierly conduct and clean and orderly camp."

115. Newspaper clipping, 1908, Whitney Collection, CSL. There were a handful of veterans from other units in attendance, including Rev. Joseph Twitchell, formerly from the 71st NY. For more on veterans and their active role in commemoration, see Blight, *Race and Reunion;* Janney, *Remembering the Civil War.*

116. This paper further claimed that after the loss at Antietam, the regiment "never mustered 600 men." Unnamed newspaper clipping [1912], Whitney Collection, CSL.

117. Frank Cheney was credited with donating ten acres of land to the regiment for their Antietam monument. Unnamed newspaper clipping [1912], Whitney Collection, CSL. Charles Page from the 14th Connecticut explained that in 1894 the state assembly appropriated $1,000 to "any regiment or battery that desired to erect a monument on the battle-field of Antietam." See Page, *History of the Fourteenth Regiment,* 359.

118. "Invocation" by Rev. Charles Dixon, in Yates, *Souvenir of Excursion to Antietam,* 54. It is not clear why Peter Finch was not invited to give the invocation, for he was the regiment's original chaplain and still alive in 1901. However, Dixon had earned the affection of the soldiers, having a longer tenure with the unit and sharing the imprisonment experience, albeit not Andersonville.

119. Norman L. Hope, "The Story of Andersonville," Norman L. Hope Collection, CSL. The date of his remarks are unclear. Emphasis in original. He further insisted that only twenty-five inmates signed the petition requesting exchanges from the U.S. government.

120. Robbins, "Some Recollections," 36, CHS.

121. George Q. Whitney, "Prisons of the Confederacy," no date, Whitney Collection, CSL. It is not clear what the occasion was for this address, nor the audience, but Whitney began by acknowledging the "many favors done me by our good Mr. Twichell [Rev. Joseph Twichell]." For more on the outpouring of published descriptions of southern prisons' horrors (especially Andersonville), see Janney, *Remembering the Civil War,* 129. See also Marvel, *Andersonville,* 323.

122. "Address to Chairman and Gentlemen of Military Commission," Whitney Collection, CSL. Whitney was most likely the author of these statements. In this way, Whitney, Hope, Robbins, and Kellogg adhered to the main themes of postwar prisoner memoirs, as described by Cloyd—sacrifice, bravery, and northern virtue. See Cloyd, *Haunted by Atrocity,* 61.

123. Whitney, Hope, and Denison were all imprisoned at Andersonville; Cheney, the former

lieutenant colonel of the regiment, was shot in the arm at Antietam and discharged in December 1862. The final member, Theron Upson, was in a Connecticut artillery unit. See Frank Cheney, CSR, NA; *Dedication of the Monument at Andersonville*, 17.

124. Ira E. Forbes, "Sixteenth C. V. at Andersonville," *Connecticut Courant*, Mar. 15, 1906, clipping in Forbes Collection, CSL. Normal L. Hope, according to Forbes, was "one of the favorites in the Regiment" due to his "social attractions and capability." See Ira Forbes, "Norman L. Hope," Whitney Collection, CSL. Whitney described him as "cheery and jolly, a good singer and was always ready for genuine fun, and in so many ways a great help to the comrades, especially those in distress." See George Q. Whitney, "Norman Lambert Hope," Whitney Collection, CSL.

125. Mary Cheney to Lillian Hope, quoted in Lillian Hope, Address to the Women's Relief Corps, Hartford, May 12, 1906, Norman L. Hope Collection, CSL.

126. Lillian Hope, Address to the Robert O. Tyler Post, Women's Relief Corps, Hartford, May 12, 1906, Norman L. Hope Collection, CSL.

127. *Dedication of the Monument at Andersonville*, 23.

128. There was some debate among the commission members about the wording of the inscription before they reached agreement in July 1907. See Frank W. Cheney to George Q. Whitney, July 10, 1907, Whitney Collection, CSL.

129. Quoted in *Dedication of the Monument at Andersonville*, 71.

130. See David F. Ransom, "Connecticut's Monumental Epoch: A Survey of Civil War Memorials," *Connecticut Historical Society Bulletin* 58 (1993): 231.

131. Historian Richard H. Kohn notes the significant symbolism of the American soldier as a "political and cultural artifact for a nation diverse in culture, uncertain in unity and concerned through much of its history with proving its superiority to the rest of the world." Kirk Savage examines the universal American soldier as represented through the monument building at the turn of the century. See Richard Kohn, "The Social History of the American Soldier; A Review and Prospectus for Research," *American Historical Review* 86 (June 1981): 553–67; quote 555; Kirk Savage, *Standing Soldier, Kneeling Slave: Race, War and Monuments in Nineteenth Century America* (Princeton: Princeton University Press, 1997); "Primitive Manhood," from Greenberg, *Manifest Manhood*, 10.

132. Frank W. Cheney to George Q. Whitney, Mar. 25, 1907, Andersonville Monument Commission Papers, CSL.

133. Frank W. Cheney to George Q. Whitney, June 6, 1907, Andersonville Monument Commission Papers, CSL.

134. George Q. Whitney to Frank W. Cheney, Aug. 20, 1907, Andersonville Monument Commission Papers, CSL.

135. Frank W. Cheney to George Q. Whitney, Mar. 4, 1907, Andersonville Monument Commission Papers, CSL.

136. "Attendees at 1907 Monument Dedication," PPM. This list has seventy names but includes two "blank" entries and "Andersonville Soldier Boy." Jacob Bauer, John Cuzner, George Robbins, and Robert Holmes were among those who attended from the 16th C.V.

137. Bauer, "Personal Experiences of the War," 21, PPM.

138. Quoted in "Dedication of Connecticut Monument at Andersonville," *Hartford Daily Courant*, Oct. 24, 1907.

139. *Dedication of the Monument at Andersonville,* 27. Cheney also expressed his disappointment that the monument was unfinished because the pedestal had yet to arrive from the north. The ceremony went on as scheduled anyway.

140. Kellogg's address in *Dedication to the Monument at Andersonville,* 34–37, 23. He claimed, "Solicitations to enter the military service or civil employment of the Southern Confederacy were turned aside with scorn by them, though acceptance meant instant release from the fate that now so clearly stared them in the face." Luther Dickey, a member of the 103rd Pennsylvania who was captured at Plymouth with the 16th Connecticut and imprisoned at Andersonville, also noted that dying in battle had been well celebrated and recognized publicly, but suffering and dying in prison was little acknowledged. In 1910 he wrote, "In the judgment of the writer, the men who languished and died in the military prisons of the South, after enduring the horrors and miseries of these places for months were not surpassed in indomitable courage and heroic devotion to duty by any who fell in charging the ranks of the enemy, and that these men did fully as much as those who comprised the armies of Grant and Sherman." See Luther Dickey, *History of the 103rd Regiment of Pennsylvania Veteran Volunteer Infantry 1861–65* (Chicago: L.S. Dickey, 1910), 289.

141. "Address" by George Q. Whitney, Whitney Collection, CSL. See also Robert H. Kellogg to George Q. Whitney, May 25, 1907, Whitney Collection, CSL.

142. Robert H. Kellogg to George Q. Whitney, May 10, 1907, emphasis in original, Whitney Collection, CSL.

143. Robert H. Kellogg to George Q. Whitney, Mar. 17, 1909, Whitney Collection, CSL; Robert H. Kellogg to George Q. Whitney, Aug. 4, 1910, Whitney Collection, CSL. According to Norman L. Hope, it was "through the generosity of the late Col. Frank W. Cheney," that the replica was placed on the capitol grounds. See Norman L. Hope, "The Story of Andersonville," Norman L. Hope Collection, CSL. Warshauer notes, "Most of Connecticut's monuments focused on the idea of sacrifice, patriotism, and loyalty to the Union or the flag." See Warshauer, *Connecticut in the American Civil War,* 196.

144. Most of this manuscript did, it seems, appear in Hartford newspapers. Newspaper clippings of the history, as well as additions and corrections made by Forbes himself, can be found in the Forbes Collection, CSL.

145. Abbott had served as a lieutenant in the First New York Dragoons. Ira E. Forbes, "At Andersonville," in A. O. Abbott, *Prison Life in the South: At Richmond, Macon, Savannah, Charleston, Columbia, Charlotte, Raleigh, Goldsborough and Andersonville, During the Years 1864 and 1865* (New York: Harper and Brothers, 1865), 192–206.

146. Forbes, "On Andersonville," in Abbott, *Prison Life in the South,* 206.

147. Ira E. Forbes Diaries, 1904–1908, Forbes Collection, CSL.

148. Robert H. Kellogg to Frank W. Cheney, Aug. 22, 1907, Andersonville Monument Commission, CSL.

149. Robert H. Kellogg to Ira Forbes, May 24, 1907, Forbes Collection, CSL.

150. George Q. Whitney to Frank W. Cheney, Aug. 20, 1907, Andersonville Monument Commission Papers, CSL.

151. Frank Cheney to George Q. Whitney, Aug. 30, 1907, Andersonville Monument Commission Papers, CSL.

152. Martin V. Culver Pension Records, NA. For more on Civil War veterans' pensions, see

Theda Skocpol, *Protecting Soldiers and Mothers: The Political Origins of Social Policy in the United States* (Cambridge: Harvard University Press, 1992); Marten, *Sing Not War*, 16–17, 200–203.

153. According to "Fitch's Home for Soldiers," found at www.cslib.org/fitchres.asp (accessed June 4, 2005), forty-four members of the 16th Connecticut resided there. However, the death dates provided by this site do not always conform with other sources.

154. Burritt Goodrich's daughter, e.g., admitted her father to Noroton Heights on Jan. 23, 1911, according to George Q. Whitney, "being unable to give him proper care and being to[o] far from medical attention, but he survived but a week longer." Goodrich died on Jan. 30, 1911. See "Burritt Goodrich," Whitney Collection, CSL. For more on soldiers' homes, see Marten, *Sing Not War*, 5–6, 13–15, 173–98; Jeffrey W. McClurken, *Take Care of the Living: Reconstructing Confederate Veteran Families in Virginia* (Charlottesville: University of Virginia Press, 2009); R. B. Rosenberg, *Living Monuments: Confederate Soldiers Homes in the New South* (Chapel Hill: University of North Carolina Press, 1993); Patrick J. Kelly, *Creating a National Home: Building the Veterans' Welfare State, 1860–1900* (Cambridge, MA: Harvard University Press, 1997). See also McConnell, *Glorious Contentment*, 129–30.

155. Augustus Vanderman to Ira Forbes, Dec. 13, 1906, included with "Isaac C. Hamilton," Whitney Collection, CSL. Vanderman had served in the 1st Connecticut Heavy Artillery.

156. Obituary, *New York Times*, Aug. 17, 1904. It is unclear exactly how old Bingham was when he enlisted in August 1862. The 1900 U.S. census gives his birth month and year to be August 1847; however, his 1904 obituary claims that he was born in 1846. See 12th Census of the United States, 1900: Population Schedule, Bloomfield, Essex Co, NJ, at ancestry.com, accessed June 25, 2009; *New York Times*, Aug. 17, 1904. See also "Wells Anderson Bingham," Whitney Collection, CSL.

157. See Card Records of Headstones Provided for Deceased Union Civil War Veterans, ca. 1879–ca. 1903, National Archives Microfilm Publication M1845, 22 rolls; Records of the Office of the Quartermaster General, RG 92, NA, at ancestry.com, accessed June 25, 2009. See Sandage, *Born Losers,* for a broader discussion of personal economic failure and the nineteenth century.

158. *San Francisco (CA) Daily Evening Bulletin,* May 6, 1889.

159. See "Richard Hale Smith," Whitney Collection, CSL.

160. Ira Forbes, "George McNall," Whitney Collection, CSL. For more on suicide and Civil War soldiers, see Dean, *Shook Over Hell,* 156–60; Diane Miller Sommerville, "'A Burden Too Heavy to Bear': War Trauma, Suicide and Confederate Soldiers," *Civil War History* 59, no. 4 (Dec. 2013): 453–91; R. Gregory Lande, "Felo De Se: Soldier Suicides in America's Civil War," *Military Medicine* 176, no. 5 (May 2011): 531–36. Dean and Sommerville note that it is difficult to assess the overall rate of suicide among veterans.

161. I have identified sixteen members of the unit labeled as "insane." This total was tabulated from a variety of sources, including pension records, the Whitney Collection, obituaries, and the U.S. census.

162. Theodore R. Stearns Pension File, NA. Stearns had been residing in Illinois through much of the postwar era.

163. See "Austin Millen Tuller," Whitney Collection, CSL.

164. Edgar C. Tuller to George Q. Whitney, no date, Whitney Collection, CSL. Edgar became a Methodist minister in New Haven.

165. Bidwell died on Oct. 2, 1907. See "Thomas Bidwell," Whitney Collection, CSL. Bidwell enlisted in the 2nd Connecticut Heavy Artillery in April 1865, serving until mustered out in August 1865. See also AGO 1869, 208. According to the 1880 census, Bidwell was not listed as insane.

10th Census of the United States, 1880: Population Schedule, Spencer, Worcester County, MA, at ancestry.com, accessed June 24, 2009. There is no other corroborating evidence to support Whitney's claim.

166. See "Ithumar W. Butler," Whitney Collection, CSL. Whitney wrote of Butler that he "was of great service in the Regiment and liked by all." Of his mental illness, Whitney explained, "Insanity has been hereditary in the family, Butler's father having died of that malady." Whitney spelled Butler's first name with a *u*, but it appears that this is incorrect. Butler is last found in the 1870 census, employed as a druggist in New Britain. See 9th Census of the United States, 1870, New Britain, Hartford County, CT, ancestry.com, accessed May 12, 2011.

167. See "W. Chester Case," "Horace Smith," "Hiram Winchell Hart," "George Washington Hill," and "Joseph Irish," Whitney Collection, CSL; Hiram Buckingham Pension File, NA.

168. Ira E. Forbes, "The Sixteenth in Public Affairs," Forbes Collection, CSL. This company made stamped envelopes and wrappers for the government. Blakeslee was also appointed "Assistant Quartermaster General with the rank of Colonel under [Connecticut Gov] Henry B. Harrison."

169. Blakeslee never married. Many members of the regiment attended his funeral to pay their respects, and his pallbearers included William Lockwood, Norman L. Hope, John Gemmill, Jon B. Clapp, and George Q. Whitney. See Ira Forbes, "Bernard F. Blakeslee," Whitney Collection, CSL.

170. In wartime letters to his mother, Burnham frequently mentioned "Estelle," as she was called. See, e.g., John H. Burnham to Sarah B. Burnham, Sept. 19, 1864, Burnham Papers, CSL. See also Nathan Mayer to Sarah B. Mayer, May 1, 1864, Burnham Papers, CSL; where Mayer states: "Col. Burnham requests me to mention you, that you should inform Miss Ferry [sic] of his fate, and whereabouts; And that he is well; and full of hope."

171. 9th Census of the United States, 1870: Population Schedule, Hartford, Hartford County, CT, at ancestry.com, accessed Aug. 5, 2011.

172. See, e.g., Affidavit of Walter A. Loomis, Sept. 15, 1881, John H. Burnham Pension File, NA.

173. Affidavit of Dwight H. Buell, Sept. 14, 1881, John H. Burnham Pension File, NA.

174. Affidavit of Albert A. Burnham, Oct. 1, 1881, John H. Burnham Pension File, NA.

175. Affidavit of Edward D. Williams, Nov. 23, 1881, John H. Burnham Pension File, NA. Williams concluded that Burnham's condition was "the direct result of the hardships & exposure he suffered while in such service."

176. Testimony of H. P. Stearns, Feb. 3, 1882, John H. Burnham Pension File, NA.

177. John H. Burnham Pension File, NA. Joseph originally made the application on Apr. 27, 1881.

178. George C. Jarvis, C. W. Chamberlain and H. S. Fuller, "Examining Surgeon's Certificate," July 6, 1881; Affidavit of Charles W. Page, Nov. 17, 1881; Testimony of Charles W. Page, Feb. 3, 1882, John H. Burnham Pension File, NA. It is true that few doctors associated mental illness with military service at this time. See Dean, *Shook Over Hell*; also Lande, *Madness, Malingering and Malfeasance*, 157–92.

179. Nathan Mayer, "Physician's Affidavit," Mar. 15, 1881, John H. Burnham Pension File, NA.

180. In total, seven doctors gave their professional assessments, including the 16th Connecticut's first surgeon Abner S. Warner, who had resigned in January 1863. Dr. Warner was one of the doubters, pronouncing Burnham "capable of enduring exposure and fatigue without trouble or consequent sickness." See Abner S. Warner, "Physician's Affidavit," Mar. 14, 1881, John H. Burnham Pension File, NA.

181. Testimony of Joseph Burnham, Feb. 4, 1882, John H. Burnham Pension File, NA.

182. Homer Riggs to W. W. Dudley, Feb. 4, 1882, John H. Burnham Pension File, NA. Riggs also complained about the difficulties in obtaining the depositions, especially from the doctors at the Retreat, where there were numerous "interruptions by parties calling." Repeatedly, witnesses were asked if Burnham indulged in alcohol or visited "any place of amusement that would injure him mentally or physically," and most gave sworn testimony that he did not. Others noted that he occasionally acted as though he was "drunk," but insisted that he only occasionally drank, nor did he have other vices. Only one, Dr. W. H. Fremaine, asserted that Burnham's condition was due "entirely to the intemperate use of liquor & immoral use of women." See Affidavit of W. H. Fremaine, Feb. 2, 1882; see also Testimony of J. D. Burnham, Feb. 1, 1882, John H. Burnham Pension File, NA.

183. John H. Burnham, Pension Records, NA. Burnham's symptoms of extreme excitability, suicidal thoughts, and deep despondency appear to fit with modern-day diagnoses of Post-Traumatic Stress Syndrome, although most historians have been hesitant to apply this label to Civil War soldiers. Eric Dean tries in *Shook Over Hell.*

184. Obituaries from http://members.aol.com/SHolmes54/burnham.html, accessed July 5, 2008. See also 10th Census of the United States, 1860: Population Schedule, Hartford, Hartford County, CT, ancestry.com, accessed July 5, 2008. There appears to be a discrepancy over the year of his death, but his gravestone clearly reads, "Apr. 10, 1883," although it erroneously lists his age as "43." See www.findagrave.com, accessed Feb. 4, 2008.

185. "John Henry Burnham," Whitney Collection, CSL.

186. Forbes, "The Fall of Plymouth."

187. Undated newspapers articles at http://members.aol.com/sholmes54/burnham.html, accessed July 5, 2008.

188. Information on Forbes, including the actual application for his asylum committal can be found in the Forbes Collection, CSL.

189. *Hartford Daily Times,* Nov. 14, 1911. For more on Forbes's challenge to Blakeslee's account of Plymouth, see Gordon, "Ira Forbes's War," in Berry, *Weirding the War,* 347–52.

190. *Connecticut Courant,* Nov. 14, 1911. Psychologist Judith Anderson has noted, "What is clear from ancient and modern wars is that the combination of exhaustion, hunger, marching and fighting, all done at the mercy of the elements, is a recipe for psychiatric casualties." Men like Burnham and others from the 16th C.V. labeled as "insane" did not experience excessive combat but endured extended imprisonment and other afflictions of war. See Judith Anderson, "'Haunted Minds': The Impact of Combat Exposure on the Mental and Physical Health of Civil War Veterans," in *Years of Change and Suffering: Modern Perspectives on Civil War Medicine,* ed. James M Schmidt and Guy R. Hasegawa (Rosseville, MN: Edinborough Press, 2009), 146.

191. Robert H. Kellogg to George Q. Whitney, Dec. 28, 1907, Whitney Collection, CSL. Emphasis in original.

CONCLUSION

1. The five men were Frank W. Waterman, Walter E. Smith, Leopold Herlitschek, George C. Morris, and Charles E. Baker. Robert H. Kellogg was one of the twelve still alive, but he was unable

to return to Connecticut. Instead, he attended local Memorial Day commemorations near his home in Delaware, Ohio. See, e.g., newspaper clipping, *Delaware Daily Gazette,* May 30, 1931, Kellogg Papers, CHS. Bauer appears in the 1930 U.S. census; by then he was more than ninety years old. It is not clear when he died. See 15th Census of the United States, 1930: Population Schedule, Berlin, Hartford County, Hartford, CT, at ancestry.com, accessed June 22, 2009.

2. Newspaper clipping [1931], Kellogg Papers, CHS.

3. Ida Foster to Albert C. Bates, Jan. 17, 1907, CHS. Little additional information can be found on George Creighton. George Q. Whitney's short entry on him matches the basic information in the AGO. Creighton may have been an Irish immigrant. His granddaughter also donated a letter to the CHS that he wrote his wife from Portsmouth during the war.

4. Shirley McLellan, "Letters from a Survivor," undated newspaper clipping, *Royal Oak (MI) Daily Tribune,* in author's possession.

5. Jennie Cuzner Sperry, "Preface," Cuzner Letters and Papers, CHS. Sperry stated that her father, like "soldiers of all wars, do not care to repeat, or dwell on their war experiences." When her father did recount stories, she claimed, "he liked to tell the funny or pleasant incidents to amuse friends." See "Note," 70, Cuzner Letters and Papers, CHS. Sperry made deletions but seems to have retained most of the content of the letters. The originals have not surfaced.

6. Jennie Cuzner Sperry, "When the Sixteenth Marched Away," Cuzner Letters and Papers, CHS. A copy of this poem is included in Kellogg Papers, CHS.

7. Jennie Cuzner Sperry, Cuzner Letters and Papers, CHS.

8. Recently, a blogger has highlighted the unit and its members, among other Connecticut regiments. See John Banks Civil War Blog, http://john-banks.blogspot.com/.

9. The survivors' efforts contributed to and were influenced by the masculinized American culture of the late nineteenth century so aptly described by Alice Fahs, *The Imagined Civil War: Popular Literature of the North and South, 1861–1865* (Chapel Hill: University of North Carolina Press, 2001), 314–18, 288. Ann Fabian describes prisoners' memoirs as "monuments to suffering and sacrifice" in *The Unvarnished Truth: Personal Narratives in Nineteenth-Century America* (Berkley: University of California Press, 2000), 126, also 7.

10. Faust and Ayers, respectively, discuss the power of narrative and war in their essays, "'We Should Grow Too Fond of It'" and "Worrying about the Civil War."

APPENDIX

1. Leland O. Barlow to Harvey Barlow, Oct. 9, 1862, Barlow Letters, CSL.

2. Quote from George Q. Whitney to Secretary of War, Sept. 1, 1904, Whitney Collection, CSL.

3. Bernard Blakeslee, *History of the Sixteenth Connecticut Volunteers* (Hartford: Case, Lockwood and Brainard Co., Printers, 1875), 3.

4. Quoted in Blakeslee, *History of the Sixteenth Connecticut Volunteers,* 115.

5. Gates Diary, June 19, 1864, CHS.

6. Sidney H. Hayden to Jane Hayden, Aug. 22, 1863, EGPL.

7. Leland O. Barlow to Jane Barlow, Nov. 2, 1863, Barlow Letters, CSL.

8. Lewis M. Holcomb to Adelaide R. Holcomb, Nov. 1, 1862, Holcomb Family Papers, SBHS.

9. Douglas G. Gardner, e-mail to author, July 3, 2007.

10. Richard Henry Lee to Adelaide R. Holcomb, May 7, 1863, Holcomb Family Papers, May 7, 1863, SBHS.

11. See 8th Census of the United States, 1860, Population Schedule, Farmington, Hartford, Connecticut, at ancestry.com, accessed July 16, 2010. George Robbins, "Some Recollections of a Private in the War of the Rebellion, 1861–1865" [1918], typescript copy, George Robbins Papers, CHS.

12. Harrison Woodford to Mattie Woodford, Sept. 9, 1862, Harrison Woodford Letters, private collection.

13. "Harrison Woodford," Whitney Collection, CSL.

BIBLIOGRAPHY

MANUSCRIPT COLLECTIONS

Amherst, Massachusetts
    W. E. B. Dubois Library, University of Massachusetts
        William Smith Clark Papers
Athens, Georgia
    Hargrett Rare Book and Manuscript Library, University of Georgia
        Chapin Family Papers, 1862–1870
Avon, Connecticut
    Avon Historical Society
        Frank Hadsell Reminiscences
        Robert J. Holmes Papers
Canton, Connecticut
    Canton Historical Society
        Ann Eliza Bancroft Diaries, 1863–1875
Carlisle, Pennsylvania
    U.S. Army Military History Institute, Carlisle Barracks
        Jacob Bauer Diary
        Robert S. Brake Collection
        Civil War Times Illustrated Collection
        Civil War Miscellaneous Collection
        Lewis Leigh Collection
Columbus, Ohio
    Ohio Historical Society
        Robert H. Kellogg Papers
Durham, North Carolina
    Rare Book, Manuscript, and Special Collections Library, Duke University
        Henry C. Hall Papers
East Granby, Connecticut
    East Granby Public Library
        Sidney H. Hayden Papers

Fargo, North Dakota
 North Dakota State University
  George Lamphere Letters
Fredericksburg, Virginia
 Fredericksburg and Spotsylvania National Military Park
  Charles S. Granger Dairy
Granby, Connecticut
 Salmon Brooke Historical Society
  Holcomb Family Papers
   Adelaide R. Holcomb Diary
   Lewis M. Holcomb, Jr., Letters
   Richard Henry Lee Papers
Hartford, Connecticut
 Connecticut Historical Society
  Henry H. Adams Diary
  Samuel Bartlett Letters
  Joseph H. Barnum Diary and Papers
  Elizur D. Belden Diary
  J. Leander Chapin Papers
  John B. Cuzner Letters and Papers
  Samuel E. Derby Letters
  Joseph E. Flower, Jr., Diary
  Oliver W. Gates Diary
  Samuel E. Grosvenor Diary
  Robert H. Kellogg Diary and Papers
  Charles Gilbert Lee Diary
  William H. Relyea Papers
  George Robbins Diary and Papers
  Stearns Family Papers
  Electra Thompson Papers
 Connecticut State Library and Archives
  Andersonville Monument Commission Papers
  Leland O. Barlow Diary and Letters
  John H. Burnham Papers
  Connecticut Adjutant General's Office, Records of the Military Department
  Ira E. Forbes Collection
  Governors' Correspondence, 1811–1933
  Norman L. Hope Collection

William H. Jackson Diary

George Nelson Champlin Diary

Henry E. Savage Diary

Horace B. Steele Diary and Papers

Karl Schubert Diary

George Q. Whitney Civil War Collection, 1861–1925

New Haven, Connecticut

Sterling Memorial Library, Yale University

Ira Forbes Diary

Northampton, Massachusetts

William Allan Neilson Library, Smith College

Sophia Smith Collection

"Letters of Mary Bushnell Cheney and Frank Woodbridge Cheney," edited by Eileen R. Learned

Plymouth, North Carolina

Historical Society of Washington County, Port O'Plymouth Museum

Papers related to the 16th Regiment Connecticut Volunteers

Sharpsburg, Maryland

Antietam National Battlefield Park

16th Regiment Connecticut Volunteers Papers

Simsbury, Connecticut

Simsbury Historical Society

Alonzo Case Papers

Gavette B. Holcomb Papers

St. Paul, Minnesota

Minnesota Historical Society

George Nathan Lamphere Papers, 1891–1906

Washington, D.C.

National Archives

Record Group 94

Bound Regimental Records

Unbound Regimental Papers

Compiled Military Service Records of Union Soldiers, Records of the Adjutant General

Henry H. Adams

Joseph H. Barnum

Frank Beach

Bernard F. Blakeslee

        Hiram Buckingham
        John H. Burnham
        Ariel J. Case
        Frank Cheney
        Joel Leander Chapin
        Martin V. Culver
        John B. Cuzner
        Samuel E. Derby
        Ira E. Forbes
        Oliver W. Gates
        Lewis M. Holcomb, Jr.
        Robert H. Kellogg
        George Robbins
        Henry E. Savage
        Andrew J. Spring
        Theodore R. Stearns
    Record Group 15
        Pension Records
           John H. Burnham
           Hiram Buckingham
           Joel Leander Chapin
           Martin V. Culver
           Oliver W. Gates
           Robert H. Kellogg
           Augustus Moesner
           Henry E. Savage
           Andrew J. Spring
           Theodore R. Stearns
    Record Group 153
    Records of the Bureau of Military Justice

PRIVATE MANUSCRIPT COLLECTIONS

Martin V. Culver Letters, copies in author's possession. Used by permission.
Newton S. Manross Collection, copies in author's possession. Used by permission.
Harrison Woodford Letters

NEWSPAPERS AND NEWSLETTERS

Charleston Mercury
Connecticut War Record
(Hartford) Connecticut Courant
(Hartford) Daily Courant
(Hartford) Weekly Courant
Hartford Daily Times
Hartford Daily Post
Hartford Evening Press
National Tribune
New Haven Daily Palladium
New York Times
Royal Oak Daily Tribune
Save Historic Antietam Foundation Newsletter
Voices from Plymouth: Plymouth Pilgrims Descendants Society Newsletter

CITY DIRECTORIES

Geer's Hartford City Directory, 1861–1862
The City Directory of Hartford, CT, 1861–1862

GOVERNMENT DOCUMENTS AND PUBLICATIONS

Catalogue of Connecticut Volunteer Organizations (infantry, cavalry, and artillery,) in the Service of the United States, 1861–1865: with Additional Enlistments, Casualties, &c., &c., and Brief summaries, Showing the Operations and service of the Several Regiments and Batteries. Prepared from the Records of the Adjutant-General's Office. Hartford: Brown and Gross, 1869.
Catalogue of the 14th, 15th, 16th, 17th, 18th, 19th, 20th and 21st Regiments and the Second Light Battery Connecticut Volunteers; and the 22d, 23d, 24th, 25th, 26th, 27th and 28th Regiments Connecticut Volunteers for Nine Months. Compiled from Records in the Adjutant-Generals Office 1862. Hartford: Press of Case, Lockwood and Co., 1862.
Official Records of the Union and Confederate Navies in the War of the Rebellion. 30 vols. Washington, DC: Government Printing Office, 1894–1922.
Record of Service of Connecticut Men in the Army and Navy of the United States During the

War of the Rebellion, Compiled By Authority of the General Assembly Under Direction of the Adjutants-General. Hartford: Press of the Case, Lockwood and Brainard Co., 1889.

Report on the Treatment of Prisoners of War by the Rebel Authorities, During the War of the Rebellion. 40th Cong., 3d sess., 1869, House Rept. 45. Senate Executive Journal. 40th Cong., 2nd sess., 7 April 1868, 216.

War of the Rebellion: A Compilation of the Official Records of the Union and Confederate Armies. 128 vols. Washington DC: Government Printing Office, 1880–1901.

BOOKS

Abbott, A. O. *Prison Life in the South: At Richmond, Macon, Savannah, Charleston, Columbia, Charlotte, Raleigh, Goldsborough and Andersonville, During the Years 1864 and 1865.* New York: Harper and Brothers Publishers, 1865.

Adams, Kevin. *Class and Race in the Frontier Army: Military Life in the West, 1870–1890.* Norman: University of Oklahoma, 2009.

Allen, George H. *Forty-Six Months with the Fourth R.I. Volunteers in the War of 1861–1865, Comprising a History of Its Marches, Battles and Camp Life, Compiled from Journals Kept While on Duty in the Field and Camp.* Providence: J. A. and R. A. Reid Printers, 1887.

Alumni Record Wesleyan University, Middletown, Conn. 3rd ed., 1881–83. Hartford: Case, Lockwood & Brainard Co., 1883.

Anderson, Benedict. *Imagined Communities: Reflections on the Origin and Spread of Nationalism.* London: Verso, 1983.

Anderson, Fred. *A People's Army: A People's Army: Massachusetts Soldiers and Society in the Seven Years War.* Chapel Hill: University of North Carolina Press, 1984.

Anderson, Joseph, ed. *The Town and City of Waterbury, Connecticut, from the Aboriginal Period to the Year Eighteen Hundred and Ninety-Five.* 3 vols. New Haven: Price and Lee Company, 1896.

Ayers, Edward, ed. *What Caused the Civil War: Reflections on the South and Southern History.* New York: W. W. Norton, 2005.

Barker, Harold R. *History of the Rhode Island Combat Units in the Civil War, 1861–1865.* N.p., 1964.

Barrett, John G. *The Civil War in North Carolina.* Chapel Hill: University of North Carolina Press, 1963.

———. *North Carolina as a Civil War Battlefield, 1861–1865.* Raleigh, NC: State Department of Archives and History, 1960.

Bell, Andrew McIlwaine. *Mosquito Soldiers: Malaria, Yellow Fever, and the Course of the American Civil War.* Baton Rouge: Louisiana State University Press, 2010.

Benton, Josiah Henry. *Voting in the Field: A Forgotten Chapter of the Civil War*. Boston: n.p., 1915.

Berry, Stephen, ed. *Weirding the War: Stories from the Civil War's Ragged Edges*. Athens: University of Georgia Press, 2011.

Blakeslee, Bernard. *History of the Sixteenth Connecticut Volunteers*. Hartford: Case Lockwood and Brainard Co., 1875.

Blight, David W. *Race and Reunion: The Civil War and American Memory*. Cambridge, MA: Belknap Press of Harvard University Press, 2001.

Bruce, Susannah Ural. *The Harp and the Eagle: Irish-American Volunteers and the Union Army, 1861–1865*. New York: New York University Press, 2006.

Buckingham, Samuel G. *The Life of William A. Buckingham: The War Governor of Connecticut*. Springfield, MA: The W. F. Adams Company, Publishers, 1894.

Burpee, Charles W. *History of Hartford County*. 3 vols. Chicago: S. J. Clarke Publishing Co., 1928.

Burton, William. *Melting Pot Soldiers: The Union Ethnic Regiments*. New York: Fordham University Press, 1998.

Caldwell, James Fitz James. *The History of a Brigade of South Carolinians Known as "Greggs," and Subsequently as "McGowan's Brigade."* Philadelphia: King and Baird Printers, 1866.

Cashin, Joan, ed. *The War Was You and Me: Civilians in the American Civil War*. Princeton: Princeton University Press, 2002.

Castle, Henry Allen. *The History of Plainville, Connecticut, 1640–1918*. 1967. Reprint, Chester, CT: Pequot Press, 1972.

Chipman, Norton Parker. *The Tragedy of Andersonville: The Trial of Captain Henry Wirz, The Prison Keeper*. Sacramento, CA: published by the author, 1911.

Cimbala, Paul A., and Randall M. Miller, eds. *Union Soldiers and the Northern Homefront: Wartime Experiences, Postwar Adjustments*. Bronx, NY: Fordham University Press, 2002.

Clarke, Frances M. *War Stories: Suffering and Sacrifice in the Civil War North*. Chicago: University of Chicago Press, 2011.

Cloyd, Benjamin G. *Haunted by Atrocity: Civil War Prisons in American Memory*. Baton Rouge: Louisiana State University Press, 2010.

Coddington, Edwin. *The Gettysburg Campaign: A Study in Command*. New York: Scribner's, 1968.

Commemorative Biographical Record of Hartford County, Connecticut, Containing Biographical Sketches of Prominent and Representative Citizens and of Many of the Early Settled Families. Chicago: J. H. Beers and Co., 1901.

Connelly, Thomas L. *Army of the Heartland: The Army of Tennessee, 1861–1862*. Baton Rouge: Louisiana State University Press, 1967.

———. *Autumn of Glory: The Army of Tennessee, 1862–1865.* Baton Rouge, Louisiana State University Press, 1971.

Cormier, Steven A. *The Siege of Suffolk: The Forgotten Campaign, April 11–May 4, 1863.* Lynchburg, VA: H. E. Howard, Inc., 1989.

Costas, Dora L., and Matthew E. Kahn. *Heroes and Cowards: The Social Face of War.* Princeton, NJ: Princeton University Press, 2008.

Croffutt, William Augustus, and John M. Morris. *The Military and Civil History of Connecticut During the War of 1861–1865: Comprising A Detailed Account Of The Various Regiments And Batteries, Through March, Encampment, Bivouac, And Battle; Also Instances Of Distinguished Personal Gallantry, And Biographical Sketches Of Many Heroic Soldiers: Together With A Record Of The Patriotic Action Of Citizens At Home, And Of The Liberal Support Furnished By The State In Its Executive And Legislative Departments.* New York: Ledyard Bill, 1869.

Cunliffe, Marcus. *Soldiers and Civilians: The Martial Spirit in America, 1775–1865.* Boston: Little, Brown, 1968.

Davis, William C. *Battle at Bull Run: A History of the First Major Campaign of the Civil War.* Baton Rouge: Louisiana State University Press, 1981.

Dean, Eric T., Jr. *Post-Traumatic Stress, Vietnam, and the Civil War.* Cambridge, MA: Harvard University Press, 1997.

Dedication of the Monument at Andersonville, Georgia, October 23, 1907, In Memory of the Men of Connecticut Who Suffered in Southern Military Prisons, 1861–1865. Hartford: State of Connecticut, 1908.

Deluca, Dan W. *The Old Leather Man: Historical Accounts of a Connecticut and New York Legend.* Middletown, CT: Wesleyan University Press, 2008.

Dickey, Luther. *History of the 103d Regiment of Pennsylvania Veteran Volunteer Infantry, 1861–1865.* Chicago: L. S. Dickey, 1910.

Dickson, Paul. *War Slang: American Fighting Words and Phrases Since the Civil War.* New York: Pocket Books, 1994.

Downs, Jim. *Sick from Freedom: African American Illness and Suffering During the Civil War and Reconstruction.* New York: Oxford University Press, 2012.

Dunkelman, Mark H. *Brothers One and All: Esprit De Corps in a Civil War Regiment.* Baton Rouge: Louisiana State University Press, 2006.

Durrill, Wayne K. *War of Another Kind: A Southern Community in the Great Rebellion.* New York: Oxford University Press, 1990.

Dyer, Frederick. *A Compendium of the War of the Rebellion.* 1908. Reprint, Dayton, OH: Press of Morningside Bookshop, 1978.

Fabian, Ann. *The Unvarnished Truth: Personal Narratives in Nineteenth-Century America.* Berkley: University of California Press, 2000.

Fahs, Alice. *The Imagined Civil War: Popular Literature of the North and South, 1861–1865.* Chapel Hill: University of North Carolina Press, 2001.

Fahs, Alice, and Joan Waugh, eds. *The Memory of the Civil War in American Culture.* Chapel Hill: University of North Carolina Press, 2004.

Fantina, Robert. *Desertion and the American Soldier, 1776–2006.* New York: Algora, 2006.

Faust, Drew Gilpin. *Mothers of Invention: Women of the Slaveholding South in the American Civil War.* Chapel Hill: University of North Carolina Press, 1996.

———. *This Republic of Suffering: Death and the American Civil War.* New York: Knopf, 2008.

Fellman, Michael. *Inside War: The Guerrilla Conflict in Missouri during the Civil War.* New York: Oxford University Press, 1989.

Fiske, Samuel W. *Mr. Dunn Browne's Experiences in the Army.* Boston: Nichols and Noyes, 1866.

Foote, Lorien, *The Gentleman and the Roughs: Manhood, Honor, and Violence in the Union Army.* New York: New York University Press, 2010.

Fox, William F. *Regimental Losses in the American Civil War, 1861–1865: A Treatise On The Extent And Nature Of The Mortuary Losses In The Union Regiments, With Full And Exhaustive Statistics Compiled From The Official Records On File In The State Military Bureaus And At Washington.* Albany: Albany Publishing Co., 1889.

Frank, Joseph Allen. *With Ballot and Bayonets: The Political Socialization of American Civil War Soldiers.* Athens: University of Georgia Press, 1998.

Frank, Joseph Allen, and George A. Reaves. *Seeing the Elephant: Raw Recruits at the Battle of Shiloh.* Westport, CT: Greenwood Press, 1989.

Futch, Ovid L. *History of Andersonville Prison.* Gainesville: University of Florida Press, 1968.

Gallagher, Gary W. *The Union War.* Cambridge: Harvard University Press, 2011.

———, ed. *Antietam: Essays on the 1862 Maryland Campaign.* Kent, OH: Kent State University Press, 1989.

———, ed. *The Antietam Campaign.* Chapel Hill: University of North Carolina Press, 1999.

Gannon, Barbara. *The Won Cause: Black and White Comradeship in the Grand Army of the Republic.* Chapel Hill: University of North Carolina Press, 2011.

Giesberg, Judith. *Army at Home: Women and the Civil War on the Northern Home Front.* Chapel Hill: University of North Carolina Press, 2009.

Glatthaar, Joseph. *Forged in Battle: The Civil War Alliance of Black Soldiers and White Officers.* New York: Free Press, 1990.

———. *General Lee's Army: From Victory to Collapse.* New York: Free Press, 2008.

Gordon, Lesley J., and John C. Inscoe, eds. *Inside the Confederate Nation: Essays in Honor of Emory M. Thomas.* Baton Rouge: Louisiana State University Press, 2005.

Goss, Warren Lee. *The Soldier's Story of his Captivity at Andersonville, Belle Island and other Rebel Prisons.* Boston: Lee and Shepard Publisher, 1867.

Greenberg, Amy S. *Manifest Manhood and the Antebellum American Empire.* Cambridge: Cambridge University Press, 2005.

Hagerty, Edward J. *Collis' Zouaves: The 114th Pennsylvania Volunteers in the Civil War.* Baton Rouge: Louisiana State University Press, 1997.

Halbwachs, Maurice. *On Collective Memory.* Translated and edited by Lewis A. Coser. Chicago: University of Chicago Press, 1992.

Hess, Earl J. *Lee's Tar Heels: The Pettigrew-Kirkland-MacRae Brigade.* Chapel Hill: University of North Carolina Press, 2002.

———. *Liberty, Virtue, and Progress: Northerners and Their War for Union.* Brooklyn: Fordham University Press, 1997

———. *The Union Soldier in Battle: Enduring the Ordeal of Combat.* Lawrence: University of Kansas Press, 1997.

Hesseltine, William Best. *Civil War Prisons: A Study in War Psychology.* New York: Frederick Ungar, 1930.

Hill, Steven W. *Connecticut Battle Flags: The Civil War.* Hamden: League of Women Voters of Connecticut Education Fund, 1986.

Hines, Blaikie. *Civil War Volunteer Sons of Connecticut.* Thomaston, ME: American Patriotic Press, 2002.

History of Battle-Flag Day, September 17, 1879. Hartford, CT: Lockwood and Meritt, 1880.

Howard, Nora O. *Images of America: Avon.* Charleston, SC: Arcadia, 2000.

Hsieh, Wayne Wei-Siang. *West Pointers and the Civil War: The Old Army in War and Peace.* Chapel Hill: University of North Carolina Press, 2009.

Hurlburt, Mabel S. *Farmington Town Clerks and Their Times.* Hartford, CT: Press of Finlay Brothers, 1943.

Janney, Caroline E. *Remembering the Civil War: Reunion and the Limits of Reconciliation.* Chapel Hill: University of North Carolina, 2013.

Kammen, Michael. *Mystic Chords of Memory: The Transformation of Tradition in America Culture.* New York: Vintage, 1993.

Katcher, Philip. *Lethal Glory: Dramatic Defeats of the Civil War.* London: Cassell, 1999.

Keegan, John. *The Face of Battle.* New York: Viking, 1976.

Kellogg, Robert H. *Life and Death in Rebel Prisons: Giving a Complete History of the Inhuman and Barbarous Treatment of our Brave Soldiers by Rebel Authorities, Inflicting Terrible Suffering and Frightful Mortality, Principally at Andersonville, Ga., and Florence, S.C., Describing Plans of Escape, Arrival of Prisoners, with Numerous and Varied Incidents and Anecdotes of Prison Life.* Hartford: L. Stebbins, 1865.

Kelly, Patrick J. *Creating a National Home: Building the Veterans' Welfare State, 1860–1900.* Cambridge, MA: Harvard University Press, 1997.

Lande, R. Gregory. *Madness, Malingering, and Malfeasance: Transformation of Psychiatry and the Law in the Civil War Era.* Washington, DC: Brassey's, 2003.

Lane, Jarlath Robert. *A Political History of Connecticut During the Civil War.* Washington, DC: Catholic University Press, 1941.

Laun, Carol. *The Holcomb Collection.* Granby, CT: Salmon Brook Historical Society, 1998.

Lentz, Perry. *Private Fleming at Chancellorsville: The Red Badge of Courage and the Civil War.* Columbia: University of Missouri Press, 2006.

Leonard, Elizabeth. *Yankee Women: Gender Battles and the Civil War.* New York: W. W. Norton, 1995.

Linderman, Gerald F. *Embattled Courage: The Experience of Combat in the American Civil War.* New York: Free Press, 1987.

Linenthal, Edward. *Sacred Ground: Americans and Their Battlefields.* 2nd ed. Champaign: University of Illinois Press, 1993.

Livermore, Mary. *My Story Of The War: A Woman's Narrative Of Four Years Personal Experience As Nurse In The Union Army, And In Relief Work At Home, In Hospitals, Camps, And At The Front During The War Of The Rebellion. With Anecdotes, Pathetic Incidents And Thrilling Reminiscences Portraying The Lights And Shadows Of Hospital Life And The Sanitary Service Of The War.* Hartford: A. D. Worthington and Co., 1888.

Lonn, Ella. *Desertion During the Civil War.* 1928. Reprint, Lincoln: University of Nebraska Press, 1998.

Lynn, John W. *800 Paces to Hell: Andersonville, A Compilation of Known Facts and Persistent Rumors.* Fredericksburg, VA: Sergeant Kirkland's Museum and Historical Society, Inc., 1999.

Mahood, Wayne. *The Plymouth Pilgrims: A History of the Eight-Fifth New York Infantry in the Civil War,* edited by David G. Martin. Rev. ed. Hightstown, NJ: Longstreet House, 1991.

Manning, Chandra. *What this Cruel War Was Over: Soldiers, Slavery, and the Civil War.* New York: Alfred Knopf, 2007.

Marten, James. *Sing Not War: The Lives of Union and Confederate Veterans in Gilded Age America.* Chapel Hill: University of North Carolina Press, 2011.

Marten, James, and A. Kristen Foster, eds. *More than a Contest of Armies: Essays on the Civil War Era.* Kent, OH: Kent State University Press, 2008.

Marvel, William. *Andersonville: The Last Depot.* Chapel Hill: University of North Carolina Press, 1994.

McConnell, Stuart. *Glorious Contentment: The Grand Army of the Republic, 1865–1900.* Chapel Hill: University of North Carolina, 1992.

McCurry, Stephanie. *Confederate Reckoning: Power and Politics in the Civil War South.* Cambridge: Harvard University Press, 2010.

McPherson, James M. *Battle Cry of Freedom.* New York: Oxford, 1998.

———. *For Cause and Comrades: Why Men Fought in the Civil War.* New York: Oxford University Press, 1997.

―――. *Ordeal By Fire: The Civil War and Reconstruction.* New York: Oxford University Press, 1982.

Merrill, J. W. *Records of the 24th Independent Battery, N.Y. Light Artillery, U.S.V.* Perry: Ladies' Cemetery Association of Perry, NY, 1870.

Miller, Richard F. *Harvard's Civil War: The History of the Twentieth Massachusetts Volunteer Infantry.* Boston: University Press of New England, 2005.

Mitchell, Reid. *The Vacant Chair: The Northern Soldier Leaves Home.* New York: Oxford University Press, 1993.

Moss, Juanita Patience. *Battle of Plymouth, North Carolina (April 17–20, 1864): The Last Confederate Victory.* Westminster, MD: Heritage Books, 2003.

Mowris, J. A. *A History of the One Hundred and Seventeenth Regiment, N.Y. Volunteers, (Fourth Oneida,) From the Date of its Organization, August 1862, till that of its Muster Out, June 1865.* Hartford: Case, Lockwood and Co., Printers, 1866.

Murfin, James V. *The Gleam of Bayonets: The Battle of Antietam and the Maryland Campaign of 1862.* New York: Thomas Yoseloff, 1965.

Neff, John. *Honoring the Civil War Dead: Commemoration and the Problem of Reconstruction.* Lawrence: University Press of Kansas, 2005.

Nelson, Megan Kate. *Ruin Nation: Destruction and the American Civil War.* Athens, GA: University of Georgia Press, 2012.

Niven, John. *Connecticut for the Union: The Role of the State in the Civil War.* New Haven: Yale University Press, 1965.

Noe, Kenneth W. *Reluctant Confederates: The Confederates Who Joined the Army after 1861.* Chapel Hill: University of North Carolina Press, 2010.

Nolan, Alan T. *The Iron Brigade: A Military History.* 1961. Reprint, Bloomington: University of Indiana Press, 1994.

―――. *"Rally Once Again!": Selected Civil War Writings of Alan T. Nolan.* Madison, WI: Madison House Publishers, 2000.

Nudleman, Franny. *John Brown's Body: Slavery, Violence, and the Culture of War.* Chapel Hill: University of North Carolina Press, 2004.

The Obituary Record of Graduates of Yale University Deceased from June, 1910, to July, 1915. New Haven: Yale University, 1915.

Page, Charles D. *History of the Fourteenth Regiment, Connecticut Volunteer Infantry.* Meriden, CT: Horton Printing Co., 1906.

Prokopowicz, Gerald. *All for the Regiment: The Army of the Ohio, 1861–1862.* Chapel Hill: University of North Carolina Press, 2000.

Pullen, John J. *The Twentieth Maine: A Volunteer Regiment in the Civil War.* Philadelphia: Lippincott, 1957.

Rable, George. *Fredericksburg! Fredericksburg!* Chapel Hill: University of North Carolina Press, 2002.

———. *God's Almost Chosen People: A Religious History of the American Civil War.* Chapel Hill: University of North Carolina Press, 2010.

Ramold, Steven J. *Across the Divide: Union Soldiers View the Northern Home Front.* New York: New York University Press, 2013.

Ray, Benjamin C., comp. *The Old Battle Flags. Veteran Soldiers' Souvenir, Containing A Brief Historical Sketch Of Each Connecticut Regiment, The Various Engagements, Casualties, Etc., During The War Of The Rebellion.* Hartford, 1879.

Reardon, Carol. *Pickett's Charge in History and Memory.* Chapel Hill: University of North Carolina Press, 1997.

Relyea, William H. *16th Connecticut Volunteer Infantry: Sergeant William H. Relyea.* Edited by John Michael Priest. Shippensburg, PA: Burd Street Press, 2002.

Report of the 23rd Annual Reunion of Antietam Battlefield, September 17, 1889. Hartford: Press of the Case, Lockwood and Brainard Co., 1890.

Reunions of Connecticut Regiments for 1896. Compiled by B. B. Champlin. New Haven, CT, 1896.

Robbins, George, ed. *Diary of Rev. H. Clavreul.* Hartford: Connecticut Association of Ex Prisoners of War, 1910.

Robertson, James I. *Soldiers Blue and Gray.* Columbia: University of South Carolina Press, 1988.

———. *The Stonewall Brigade.* Baton Rouge: Louisiana State University Press, 1963.

Robins, Glenn M. *They Have Left Us Here to Die: The Civil War Prison Diary of Sgt. Lyle G. Adair, 111th U.S Colored Infantry.* Kent, OH: Kent State University Press, 2011.

Sandage, Scott. *Born Losers: A History of Failure in America.* Cambridge: Harvard University Press, 2005.

Sanders, Charles W. *While in the Hands of the Enemy: Military Prisons of the Civil War.* Baton Rouge: Louisiana State University Press, 2005.

Sandow, Robert. *Deserter Country: Civil War Opposition in the Pennsylvania Appalachians.* New York: Fordham University Press, 2009.

Savage, Kirk. *Standing Soldiers, Kneeling Slaves: Race, War, and Monuments in Nineteenth Century America.* Princeton: Princeton University Press, 1997.

Schildt, John W. *Connecticut at Antietam.* Chewsville, MD: Antietam Publications, 1998.

Schmidt, James M., and Guy R. Hasegawa, eds. *Years of Change and Suffering: Modern Perspectives on Civil War Medicine.* Roseville, MN: Edinborough Press, 2009.

Sears, Stephen W. *Landscape Turned Red: The Battle of Antietam.* New York: Houghton and Mifflin, 1983.

Sharpsburg Heritage Festival '95. Sharpsburg, MD: Sharpsburg Heritage Festival, 1995.

Sheehan-Dean, Aaron. *Why Confederates Fought: Family and Nation in Civil War Virginia.* Chapel Hill: University of North Carolina Press, 2007.

———, ed. *The View from the Ground: Experiences of Civil War Soldiers.* Lexington: University Press of Kentucky, 2006.

Silber, Nina. *Daughters of the Union: Northern Women Fight the Civil War.* Cambridge: Harvard University Press, 2005.

Sixteenth Regiment Connecticut Volunteers Excursion and Reunion at Antietam Battlefield, September 17, 1889. Hartford: Press of the Case, Lockwood and Brainard Co.,1889.

Skocpol, Theda. *Protecting Soldiers and Mothers: The Political Origins of Social Policy in the United States.* Cambridge: Harvard University Press, 1992.

Slap, Andrew L., and Michael Thomas Smith, eds. *This Distracted and Anarchical People: New Answers for Old Questions about the Civil War-Era North.* New York: Fordham University Press, 2013.

Smith, John David, ed. *Black Soldiers in Blue: African American Troops in the Civil War Era.* Chapel Hill: University of North Carolina Press, 2002.

Spalding, J. A., *Illustrated Popular Biography of Connecticut.* Hartford: Press of the Case, Lockwood, and Brainard Co., 1891.

Springman, Mary Jane, and Betty Finell Guinan. *East Granby: The Evolution of a Connecticut Town.* Canaan, NH: Phoenix, 1983.

The Story Of The Twenty-First Regiment, Connecticut Volunteer Infantry The Civil War. 1861–1865, By Members Of The Regiment. Middletown, CT: Press of the Stewart Printing Co., 1900.

Stott, Richard. *Jolly Fellows: Male Milieus in 19th Century America.* Baltimore: Johns Hopkins Press, 2009.

Stout, Harry S. *Upon the Altar of a Nation: A Moral History of the Civil War.* New York: Viking Press, 2006.

Sutherland, Daniel E. *Fredericksburg and Chancellorsville: The Dare Mark Campaign.* Lincoln: University of Nebraska Press, 1998.

———. *A Savage Conflict: The Decisive Role of Guerrillas in the Civil War.* Chapel Hill: University of North Carolina Press, 2009.

Thorpe, Sheldon B. *The History Of The Fifteenth Connecticut Volunteers In The War For The Defense Of The Union, 1861–1865.* New Haven, CT: The Price, Lee and Adkins Co., 1893.

Tourgée, Albion W. *The Story of a Thousand.* Edited by Peter Luebke. Kent, OH: Kent State University Press, 2011.

Trumbull, James Hammond, ed. *The Memorial History of Hartford County Connecticut, 1633–1884.* 2 vols. Boston: Edward L. Osgood, 1886.

Twichell, Willis I., ed. *Hartford in History: A Series of Papers by Resident Authors.* Hartford: Press of the Plimpton Mfg Co., 1899.

Ural, Susannah, ed. *Civil War Citizens: Race, Ethnicity, and Identity in America's Bloodiest Conflict.* New York: New York University Press, 2010.

Walker, William Carey. *History of the Eighteenth Regiment Connecticut Volunteers in the War for the Union.* Norwich: The Committee, 1885.

Warshauer, Matthew. *Connecticut in the American Civil War: Slavery, Sacrifice, and Survival.* Middletown, CT: Wesleyan University Press, 2011.

Weitz, Mark A. *More Damning than Slaughter: Desertion in the Confederate Army.* Lincoln: University of Nebraska Press, 2005.

Weld, Stanley B. *Connecticut Physicians in the Civil War.* Hartford: Connecticut Civil War Centennial Commission [1965?].

Wiley, Bell Irvin. *The Life of Billy Yank: The Common Soldier of the Union.* 1952. Reprint, Baton Rouge: Louisiana State University Press, 1971.

Wilkinson, Warren. *Mother, May You Never See the Sights I Have Seen: The Fifty-Seventh Massachusetts Veteran Volunteers in the Army of the Potomac, 1864–1865.* New York: Harper and Row, 1990.

Wright, Benjamin D. *History of the Descendants of Elder John Strong of Northampton, Mass.* 2 vols. Albany, NY: Joel Munsell, 1871.

Yates, Walter J., ed. *Souvenir of Excursion to Antietam and Dedication of Monuments of the 8th, 11th, 14th and 16th Regiments of Connecticut Volunteers.* New London, CT: 1894.

ARTICLES

Anderson, David. "Dying of Nostalgia: Homesickness in the Union Army during the Civil War," *Civil War History* 56, no. 3 (September 2010): 247–82.

Berry, Stephen. "When Metal Meets Mettle: The Hard Realities of Civil War Soldiering." *North & South* 9, no. 4 (August 2006): 12–21.

Brown, Richard. "Microhistory and the Post-Modern Challenge." *Journal of the Early Republic* 23, no. 1 (Spring 2003): 1–20.

Bussanich, Leonard. "'To Reach Sweet Home Again': The Impact of Soldiering on New Jersey's Troops during the Civil War." *New Jersey History* 125, no. 2 (2010): 37–60.

Cain, Marvin. "A Face of Battle Needed." *Civil War History* 28, no. 1 (March 1982): 5–27.

Clarke, Frances M. "So Lonesome I Could Die: Nostalgia and Debates over Emotional Control in the Civil War North." *Journal of Social History* 41 (Winter 2007): 253–82.

Domonell, William G. "The 16th Connecticut Regiment's Unique Flag." *My Country* 29, no. 3 (Summer 1995): 2–9.

Emmert, L. D. "Connecticut Men and the Battlefield of Antietam: Memorials Erected to the Sublime Courage of the Men Who Offered their Lives to their Country." *Connecticut Magazine* 11 (1907): 614–16.

Faust, Drew Gilpin. "'We Should Grow Too Fond of It': Why We Love the Civil War." *Civil War History* 50, no. 4 (December 2004): 368–83.

Grow, Matthew. "The Shadow of the Civil War: A Historiography of Civil War Memory." *American Nineteenth Century History* 4, no. 2 (Summer 2003): 77–103.

Helmreich, Paul C. "The Diary of Charles G. Lee in the Andersonville and Florence Prison Camps, 1864." *Connecticut Historical Society Bulletin* 41, no. 1 (January 1976): 12–28.

Holland, Pat. "Background Information About the Stained-Glass 'Connecticut Windows' in the Christ Reformed Church." Undated press release, in possession of author.

Jordan, Brian Matthew. "Living Monuments": Union Veteran Amputees and the Embodied Memory of the Civil War." *Civil War History* 57, no. 2 (June 2011): 121–52.

Jordan, Weymouth T., Jr., and Gerald W. Thomas. "Massacre at Plymouth: April 20, 1864." *North Carolina Historical Review* 72, no. 2 (April 1995): 125–97.

Kenyon, Ted. "Slain Suffield Man, Civil War Comrades Remembered." *Journal Inquirer*, May 23, 1998, 2.

Kohn, Richard. "The Social History of the American Soldier; A Review and Prospectus for Research." *American Historical Review* 86 (June 1981): 553–67.

Kuras, James M., ed. "Samuel Derby's War Letters." *New Hampshire College Journal* 10, no. 1 (Spring 1993): 5–9.

Lande, R. Gregory. "Felo De Se: Soldier Suicides in America's Civil War." *Military Medicine* 176, no. 5 (May 2011): 531–36.

Laun, Carol. "The Valiant Sons of Francis and Eliza Allen." *Southwoods*, May 1989, 4–5.

Lepore, Jill. "Historians Who Love Too Much: Reflections on MicroHistory and Biography." *Journal of American History* 88, no. 1 (June 2001): 129–44.

McGlone, Robert E. "Deciphering Memory: John Adams and the Authorship of the Declaration of Independence." *Journal of American History* 85, no. 2 (September 1998): 411–38.

Morrone, Peter J. "Disciplinary Conditioning and Self-Surveillance in Ambrose Bierce's War Fiction." *Midwest Quarterly* 54 (Spring 2013): 310–25.

Musick, Michael. "The Little Regiment: Civil War Units and Commands." *Prologue Magazine* 27, no. 2 (Summer 1995). www.archives.gov/publications/prologue/1995/summer/little-regiment-1.html.

Nord, David Paul. "The Uses of Memory: An Introduction." *Journal of American History* 85, no. 2 (September 1998): 409–10.

O'Brien, Frank P. "The Story of a Flag and the Strange Bringing Together of Its Captors and Defenders, as Related by One of the Former." *Blue and Gray* 2, no. 2 (August 1893): 143–45.

Phillips, Jason. "Battling Stereotypes: A Taxonomy of Common Soldiers in Civil War History." *History Compass* 6 (November 2008): 1407–25.

Ransom, David. "Connecticut Civil War Monuments." *Connecticut Society Bulletin* 58, nos. 1–4 (1993); 59, nos. 1–4 (1994).

Reardon, Carol. "Writing Battle History: The Challenge of Memory," *Civil War History* 53, no. 3 (September 2007): 252–63.

Reid, Brian Holden, and John White. "'A Mob of Stragglers and Cowards': Desertion from the Union and Confederate Armies, 1861–1865." *Journal of Strategic Studies* 8 (1985): 64–77.

Robins, Glenn M. "Race, Repatriation, and Galvanized Rebels: Union Prisoners and the

Exchange Question in Deep South Prison Camps." *Civil War History* 53, no. 2 (June 2007): 117–40.

Sommerville, Diane Miller. "'A Burden Too Heavy to Bear': War Trauma, Suicide and Confederate Soldiers." *Civil War History* 59, no. 4 (December 2013): 453–91.

Spear, Ellis. "The Story of the Raising and Organization of a Regiment of Volunteers in 1862." *Loyal Legion, District of Columbia Commanding, War Papers*. No. 46. Washington, DC, 1903.

Spooner, Henry J. "The Maryland Campaign with the Fourth Rhode Island." *Personal Narratives of Events in the War of the Rebellion: Being Papers Read before the Rhode Island Soldiers and Sailors Historical Society*, 6th series, no. 5. Providence: The [Rhode Island Soldiers and Sailors Historical] Society, 1903.

Walsh, Christopher. "'Cowardice Weakness or Infirmity, Whichever It May Be Termed': A Shadow History of the Civil War." *Civil War History* 59, no. 4 (December 2013): 492–526.

Weitz, Mark A. "Desertion, Cowardice, and Punishment." Essential Civil War Curriculum, April 2012. www.essential.civilwar.vt.edu/1079.html.

Weld, Stanley B., ed. "A Connecticut Surgeon in the Civil War: The Reminiscences of Dr. Nathan Mayer." *Journal of the History of Medicine and Allied Sciences* 19 (July 1964): 272–86.

MISCELLANEOUS

Burkhardt, A. W. "Forty Hours on the Battlefield of Antietam; or the Foeman Friend." N.p., n.d.

Gilbert, Rev. W. H. *Sermon Delivered in Granby, Conn., Jan. 4, 1863, at the Funeral of Roswell Morgan Allen, Private in Co. E., 16th Reg't. C.V. Who Died at the Hospital Near Washington, Sunday, Dec. 28, 1862.* Hartford: Charles Montague, 1863.

Ide, A. W. *Sermon Preached Oct. 8, 1862 at Stafford Springs, at the Funeral of Lieut. William Horton, of Co. I, 16th Conn. Regt. Volunteers, Who Was Killed at the Battle of Antietam, Sept. 17, 1862.* Holliston, MA: E. G. Plimpton, Printer, 1862.

Mayer, Nathan. "A Poem Read by Surgeon Nathan Mayer, October 11, 1894 at the Dedication of the Sixteenth Connecticut Where They Fought at Antietam, September 17, 1862." Hartford: Case, Lockwood and Brainard Co., 1894.

DISSERTATIONS, THESES, AND OTHER UNPUBLISHED SOURCES

Atkins, Jack Lawrence. "'It is Useless to Conceal the Truth Any Longer': Desertion of Confederate Soldiers from the Confederate Army." MA thesis, Virginia Polytechnic Institute and State University, 2007.

Bledsoe, Andrew Scott. "Citizen-Officers: The Union and Confederate Volunteer Junior Officer Corps in the American Civil War, 1861–1865." PhD diss., Rice University, 2012.

Gardner, Douglas Gibson. "Andersonville and American Memory: Civil War Prisoners and Narratives of Suffering and Redemption." PhD diss., Miami University, 1998.

Hamner, Christopher. "Enduring Danger, Surviving Fear: Combat Experience and American Infantrymen in the War for Independence, the Civil War and the Second World War." PhD diss., University of North Carolina, Chapel Hill, 2004.

Luebke, Peter. "Equal to Any Minstrel Concert I Attended at Home: Antebellum Popular Culture, White Northern Soldiers, and the Limits of the Civil War." Paper presented at the Society of Civil War Historians Annual Meeting, June 2010, Richmond, VA.

Vaughn, Walter Jeffers. "The Brand of Coward: Masculine and Patriotic Expectations in a Civil War Town." PhD diss., Case Western University, 1996.

ONLINE RESOURCES

Ancestry.com. http://home.ancestry.com/.

Chesson, F. W. "Connecticut 16th Regiment Graves." *http://pages.cthome.net/fwc/16-CT.HTM.*

Civil War Soldiers and Sailors Database. www.civilwar.nps.gov/cwss/soldiers.cfm.

Find A Grave. www.findagrave.com.

"Fitch's Home for Soldiers." www.cslib.org/fitchres.asp.

John Banks Civil War Blog. http://john-banks.blogspot.com/.

Nationwide Gravesite Locator. http://gravelocator.cem.va.gov/.

INDEX

16th C.V. (*continued*)

271n31, 271n33, 276–77n20, 278n46, 283nn110–11, 293n108, 294n111, 295n134, 303n87, 327nn22–23; disease and illness, 7, 15, 34, 39–40, 45, 48–50, 53–55, 57–58, 63, 65, 67, 72, 80, 86, 90, 92, 94–95, 99–101, 105, 107, 110, 112, 114, 119–20, 129, 132, 137, 146–47, 151–52, 154–55, 159, 164,166, 168–69, 174, 177–85, 187–88, 195–97, 200, 203–4, 214, 211, 222–25, 230, 232–33, 248, 268nn150–51, 268n153, 269n5, 270n11–12, 275n99, 275n103, 277n23, 279n62, 280n63, 282nn108–9, 291n77, 297n164, 307n150, 313n13, 313n15, 314n33, 320n121, 320n127, 321n135, 322n150, 324n172, 324n181, 327nn22–23, 329–330n54, 330–31n68, 333n106, 338n24, 340n47; draft: 110–12, 128, 288n27, 295n134, 295–96n140; drill/discipline, 5, 20–22, 23, 27, 37, 56–57, 58, 65–66, 71–72, 80, 81–82, 84, 94–95, 103, 106–8, 125, 136, 177–78, 187, 189, 224, 230, 288n27, 327–28n24; family ties within regiment, 13–15, 17–18, 289n50; flags, 23–24, 33, 140–41, 207–11, 225, 231, 308nn158–60, 309n161, 343nn90–91, 343–44n101, 344n104, 344n109; Fort Ward, 26–27; galvanized rebels, 164–66, 214, 322nn149–50, 322n154, 323n163, 324n175, 325nn191–92, 326n204, 326n206, 347n140; heroism/bravery, 2, 4, 9, 11, 14, 24, 37–38, 40–44, 46–48, 55, 58, 77–78, 83, 85, 101–4, 122, 126, 130–31, 135–36, 139–41, 143–44, 157, 172, 186, 187–88, 190–93, 206, 208–18, 224–25, 227–28, 230, 231, 233, 281n96, 287n17, 311n190, 315n52, 319n107, 320n122, 335n134, 341n57 (*see also* 16th CV: cowardice); home front, 6, 14–15, 23, 36–37, 47–48, 49–50, 54–55, 58, 66–67, 74–79, 85–87, 90, 97–100, 104–6, 109–10, 122, 127–29, 142–44, 154–59, 162–64, 169–72, 179–83, 189–92, 279n57, 279n59, 283n114, 283n121, 285n146, 294n112, 329n47; immigrants, 17, 24–25, 34, 38, 57, 87, 100–102, 164, 177, 230, 246n50, 252n112, 253n118, 258n65, 284n127, 351n3; identity as citizen-soldiers, 4–5, 18, 27,

34, 70, 80, 89–91, 95–96, 105–9, 113–18, 125, 277n38; lack of pay, 62, 66–67, 68, 73–75, 106–7, 285n144; marches, 27–30, 52–54; masculinity/manhood, 2, 3, 4, 23, 25, 42–43, 71, 78, 150, 188, 193, 213, 216–18, 228, 237n9, 264n110, 337n13, 351n9; mental illness, 50, 84, 151, 188, 209, 221–25, 230–32, 269n157, 320n125, 344n107, 348n161, 348n165, 349n166, 349n178, 350nn182–83, 350n190; morale, 28, 53–59, 62–69, 70, 71, 73, 76, 80–82, 85–91, 95–96, 103–6, 112–18, 128–31, 149, 156, 176, 183, 189; motivation, 12–19, 72, 73, 88–90, 103–6, 110, 112, 131, 149–50, 213, 218, 231, 282n109, 285n148, 292n95, 304n93; mustering out, 189–92; newspaper coverage of, 7, 11, 12–13, 24–25,36–39, 54–56, 61–62, 65, 74, 116–17, 130, 142–44, 158–60, 169–72, 191, 197, 212–13, 233, 302n63; numbers and strength, 51,54, 55, 56, 57, 58, 63, 68, 72–73, 86, 96, 110–12, 126, 174–76, 178, 184, 190, 334–35n128, 345n116 (*see also* casualties, conscription recruits); officers and leadership, 4, 5, 20–22, 24, 28–29, 50–51, 54–55, 56–57, 58, 62, 64–68, 71–73, 76–77, 80, 84, 85, 87, 90, 94–95, 97, 100–101, 106–8, 114–17, 126, 135–36, 158–61, 171, 174–75, 177–78, 186–89, 197–99, 213, 222–24, 281n94, 282n108, 284n128, 285m145, 291–92n78, 296n151, 297n167, 298–99nn174–75, 302n63; political attitudes, 16, 63, 65, 70, 77–78, 104, 108–9, 127–29, 169–70, 184–86, 196, 278nn46–49, 278–79nn51–54, 292n93; postwar, 192–226; postwar collective memory, 193, 206–28, 233–34, 344n106; racial attitudes, 4, 9, 11, 13, 16, 50, 60, 63, 65, 70, 87–89, 93–94, 100, 105, 122, 128, 156, 175–76, 206, 218, 232, 284n133, 307n146; raids, 93–95, 103, 105, 113, 123–124, 176, 287n17, 287n20; recruits, 111–12, 130, 177, 295–96n140, 301n47, 303n88, 334n123; religion, 16, 30,42, 46, 47–48, 60, 70, 76, 80, 84, 87, 94, 96–97, 131, 134–35, 136, 151–55, 162, 167, 175–76, 181–84, 209, 211, 219, 225, 231–32, 244n34, 288n23, 289n34,